W9-ANN-094

Empire State-Building

Eastern African Studies

Revealing Prophets
Edited by DAVID M. ANDERSON & DOUGLAS H. JOHNSON

Swahili Origins
JAMES DE VERE ALLEN

Being Maasai
Edited by THOMAS SPEAR & RICHARD WALLER

A History of Modern Ethiopia 1855–1991*
Second edition
BAHRU ZEWDE

Ethnicity & Conflict in the Horn of Africa
Edited by KATSUYOSHI FUKUI & JOHN MARKAKIS

Conflict, Age & Power in North East Africa
Edited by EISEI KURIMOTO & SIMON SIMONSE

Jua Kali Kenya
KENNETH KING

Control & Crisis in Colonial Kenya
BRUCE BERMAN

Unhappy Valley
Book One: State & Class
Book Two: Violence & Ethnicity
BRUCE BERMAN & JOHN LONSDALE

Mau Mau from Below
GREET KERSHAW

The Mau Mau War in Perspective
FRANK FUREDI

Squatters & the Roots of Mau Mau 1905–63
TABITHA KANOGO

Economic & Social Origins of Mau Mau 1945–53
DAVID W. THROUP

Multi-Party Politics in Kenya
DAVID W. THROUP & CHARLES HORNSBY

Decolonization & Independence in Kenya 1940–93
Edited by B.A. OGOT & WILLIAM R. OCHIENG'

Penetration & Protest in Tanzania
ISARIA N. KIMAMBO

Custodians of the Land
Edited by GREGORY MADDOX, JAMES L. GIBLIN & ISARIA N. KIMAMBO

Education in the Development of Tanzania 1919–1990
LENE BUCHERT

The Second Economy in Tanzania
T.L. MALIYAMKONO & M.S.D. BAGACHWA

Ecology Control & Economic Development in East African History
HELGE KJEKSHUS

Siaya
DAVID WILLIAM COHEN & E.S. ATIENO ODHIAMBO

Uganda Now
Changing Uganda
Developing Uganda
From Chaos to Order
Religion & Politics in East Africa
Edited by HOLGER BERNT HANSEN & MICHAEL TWADDLE

Kakungulu & the Creation of Uganda 1868–1928
MICHAEL TWADDLE

Controlling Anger
SUZETTE HEALD

Kampala Women Getting By
SANDRA WALLMAN

Slaves, Spices & Ivory in Zanzibar
ABDUL SHERIFF

Zanzibar Under Colonial Rule
Edited by ABDUL SHERIFF & ED FERGUSON

The History and Conservation of Zanzibar Stone Town
Edited by ABDUL SHERIFF

East African Expressions of Christianity
Edited by THOMAS SPEAR & ISARIA N. KIMAMBO

The Poor Are Not Us
Edited by DAVID M. ANDERSON & VIGDIS BROCH-DUE

Alice Lakwena & the Holy Spirits
HEIKE BEHREND

Property Rights & Political Development in Ethiopia & Eritrea
SANDRA FULLERTON JOIREMAN

Revolution & Religion in Ethiopia
ØYVIND M. EIDE

Brothers at War
TEKESTE NEGASH & KJETIL TRONVOLL

*From Guerrillas to Government**
DAVID POOL

Empire State-Building
JOANNA LEWIS

*Pioneers of Change in Ethiopia**
BAHRU ZEWDE

* forthcoming

Empire State-Building

War & Welfare in Kenya 1925–52

Joanna Lewis

Lecturer in History
University of Durham

James Currey
OXFORD

E.A.E.P
NAIROBI

Ohio University Press
ATHENS

James Currey Ltd
73 Botley Road
Oxford
OX2 0BS

Ohio University Press
Scott Quadrangle
Athens, Ohio 45701

First published 2000

1 2 3 4 5 04 03 02 01 00

British Library Cataloguing in Publication Data

Lewis, Joanna
Empire state-building: war and welfare in Kenya 1925-52 .-
(Eastern African studies)
1. Kenya - History, Military 2. Kenya - History - 1895-1963
3. Kenya - Social conditions
I. Title
967.6'2'03

ISBN 0-85255-790-6 (James Currey Cloth)
0-85255-785-X (James Currey Paper)

Library of Congress Cataloging-in-Publication Data is available from the Library of Congress

ISBN 0-8214-1398-8 (Ohio University Press Cloth)
0-8214-1399-6 (Ohio University Press Paper)

Typeset in 10/11pt Baskerville
by Long House Publishing Services, Cumbria, UK
Printed and bound in Great Britain
by Woolnough, Irthlingborough

Contents

Four

'Kingi Georgi, Mtukufu'

Five

'To Work Like a Nigger' or 'Shirk Like an African'

Six

The Imperial Politics of Inclusion

Abbreviations

KNA	*Kenya National Archive:*
AAAO	Assistant African Administrative Officer
ADC	African District Council
ag	acting
AG	Department of Agriculture
AO	Administrative Officer
ASCO	Assistant Soil Conservation Officer
ASWW	African Social Welfare Worker
CD	Community Development
CNC	Chief Native Commissioner
CRO	Civil Reabsorption Officer
CS	Chief Secretary
CV	Central Kavirondo
DARA	Development and Reconstruction Authority
DC	District Commissioner
DCS	Deputy Chief Secretary
DDWO	District Development Welfare Officer
DE	Director of Education
DEF	Ministry of Defence
DMS	Director of Medical Services
DO	District Officer
DO(CD)	District Officer (Community Development)
DWO	District Welfare Officer
EAC	Education Advisory Committee
FS	Financial Secretary
KAU	Kenya African Union
KCA	Kikuyu Central Association
KIO	Kenya Information Office
KSM	Kisumu
LNC	Local Native Council
MAA	Ministry of African Affairs
MNAO	Municipal Native Affairs Officer
MO	Medical Officer
NWC	Native Welfare Committee
NZA	Nyanza
o/c	Officer in charge
PC	Provincial Commissioner
PDWO	Provincial Development Welfare Officer
SEC	Chief Secretary's Office
SFC	Standing Financial Committee

Abbreviations

PRO	*Public Records Office:*
EAC	Education Advisory Committee
CSSRC	Colonial Social Science Research Council
CO	Colonial Office
DUSSC	Deputy Under Secretary of State for the Colonies
PAC	Penal Advisory Committee
SCWE	Sub-Committee on Women and Education
SSC	Secretary of State for the Colonies
SWAC	Colonial Social Welfare Advisory Committee (in official correspondence this is referred to as the CSWAC)
USSC	Under Secretary of State for the Colonies

Other abbreviations:

AGM	Annual General Meeting
Asst	Assistant
BBC	British Broadcasting Corporation
CCK	Christian Council of Kenya
CDW	Colonial Development and Welfare
CMS	Church Missionary Society
EAS	*East African Standard*
EAWL	East African Women's League
GNP	Gross National Product
HE	His Excellency
HMSO	Her Majesty's Stationery Office
HMG	His Majesty's Government
HW	His Worship
JAC	*Journal of African History*
JICH	*Journal of Imperial and Commonwealth History*
JMAS	*Journal of Modern African Studies*
KURH	Kenya Union of Railway and Harbours
KWEO	Kenya Women's Emergency Organisation
LegCo	Legislative Council
LSE	London School of Economics
MBE	Member of the British Empire
Min	Minute
MP	Member of Parliament
Mss	Manuscripts
NCO	Non Commissioned Officer
OBE	Order of the British Empire
PT	Physical Training
RAF	Royal Air Force
RH	Rhodes House
UN	United Nations
UNESCO	United Nations Economic Social and Cultural Organisation
WI	Women's Institute
YWCA	Young Women's Christian Association

Glossary

Note: words in this glossary, unless marked, are Swahili.

ahoi	tenants (Kikuyu)
anake	young men, warriors
askari	African soldier
banda	building
baraza	general meeting (newspaper title)
boma	building
dini	sect, religion
duka	small shop, trading post
fitina	trouble-making
fundi	labour gang
heshima	prestige
ithaka	land and freedom (Kikuyu)
kipande	registration certificate carried by African adult males
Maendeleo ya Wanawake	women working together for progress
maneno	words, news
manyatta	homestead dwellings arranged in circular enclosure (Masai)
mbari	sub-clan (Kikuyu)
mabati	corrugated-iron sheets
mtama	sorghum plant
muhirig'a	a Kikuyu clan organisation (Kikuyu)
mzungu	white man
ng'ambo	overseas/abroad
ngwatio	neighbourhood work party (Kikuyu)
najhi	pigeon pea
pamoja	broadcast
pise	rammed earth or clay used for building (French)
posho	maize meal
shamba	plot of cultivated land
shauris	meetings
toto	child
Uhuru	freedom/ independence
wimbe	finger millet

Maps, Diagrams & Photographs

Maps

Diagrams

Photographs (Rhodes House Collection)

Acknowledgements

I could not have written this book without the help of the following. First my friends and family. During my PhD and subsequently, support and solidarity came from so many. Nonica Dutta, Sophie Gilmartin, Dr Pat, Sue Bates, Movindri Reddi, Patsy Lewis-Meekes, the late Davidson Nicol, all my boyfriends who were sacrificed on the altar of my mission, Peggy Owens, Dido Davies, Mark Roberts and Phil Mulligan stand out in particular. In Kenya, I would like to thank Cecilia and Patrick Manyuira, Felix and Alan Carles, Regina Munene, Dave Anderson, Richard Ambani, Dorcus and Justus. Also, Olive Perriera, Betty Chappell and Roy Griffen.

During my time at Cambridge I enjoyed much encouragement and good times with a small but perfectly formed group of historians. I salute Tim Harper, Miles Taylor, Dave Jarvis and Jon Parry. Since being at Churchill I have benefited from the collegiality of many but in particular Neil Kenny, Andrew Webber, Jeyshri Dutta, Maria Tippett, Matthew Kramer, Martin Daunton, Paul Seabright and Lady Julia Boyd. At the African Studies Centre, Keith Hart and Peggy Owens were always there for me, as are now Casey Synge, Stephanie Newell, Ato Quayson and Sarah Irons. Peggy Owens and Shafuir Rahman bailed me out a million times with my computer problems. Indeed, without the patience and expertise of Alice 'Peg' this manuscript would never have reached the publishers. During the last stages of writing, my life was made easier by Louise Pirouet, Barbara Metzger, Chris, Delphini and the College porters, Carolyn Lye, Gary Locklea, Caroline Burt, Terry Barringer, Shey, and my hairdresser in Swansea, Scott Crawford Triggs, whose suggestion of highlights brought me back from the brink of the abyss that was Chapter 5. My subequent rehabilitation in Oxford was helped immeasurably by James Raven, Di and Ralph Thompson and Alex Craster.

Throughout this ridiculous process, above all and above and beyond the call of duty stand my mother and father, sister Sarah and brother-in-law Stephen, cousin Lisa and my Grandma. They fielded all my moaning, tears, and requests for money with their usual patience, Welsh wit and healthy scepticism. This is their book as much mine.

The institutions and foundations which have supported my research in various ways are numerous. The ESRC funded much of the research, also the Holland Rose trust at Christ's College. The African Studies Centre paid for the photographs to be reproduced. Churchill College financed short research trips and was extremely supportive in general. The staff at the Kenya National Archive, Rhodes House, the Public Records Office and the Churchill Archive were in all but a few unfortunate situations utterly wonderful. I thank my publishers heartily, the anonymous reader, and Margaret Driscoll.

The intellectual encouragement and support I have benefited from have been humbling. My undergraduate students rekindled my interest in the project; I would like to thank them all for giving me new purpose, secure in the knowledge that they will never know this. Colleagues I would wish to single out would be Miles Taylor, Tim Harper, Richard Rathbone, Saul Dubow and Barbara Metzger for commenting on drafts and ideas. You deserved better. Over the years, Ronald Hyam and John Iliffe have been generous with their vast knowledge. Keith Hart stands in a category of his own as he does in real life. One person suffered more than most and for that reason I dedicate this book to him in thanks and respect.

For John Lonsdale

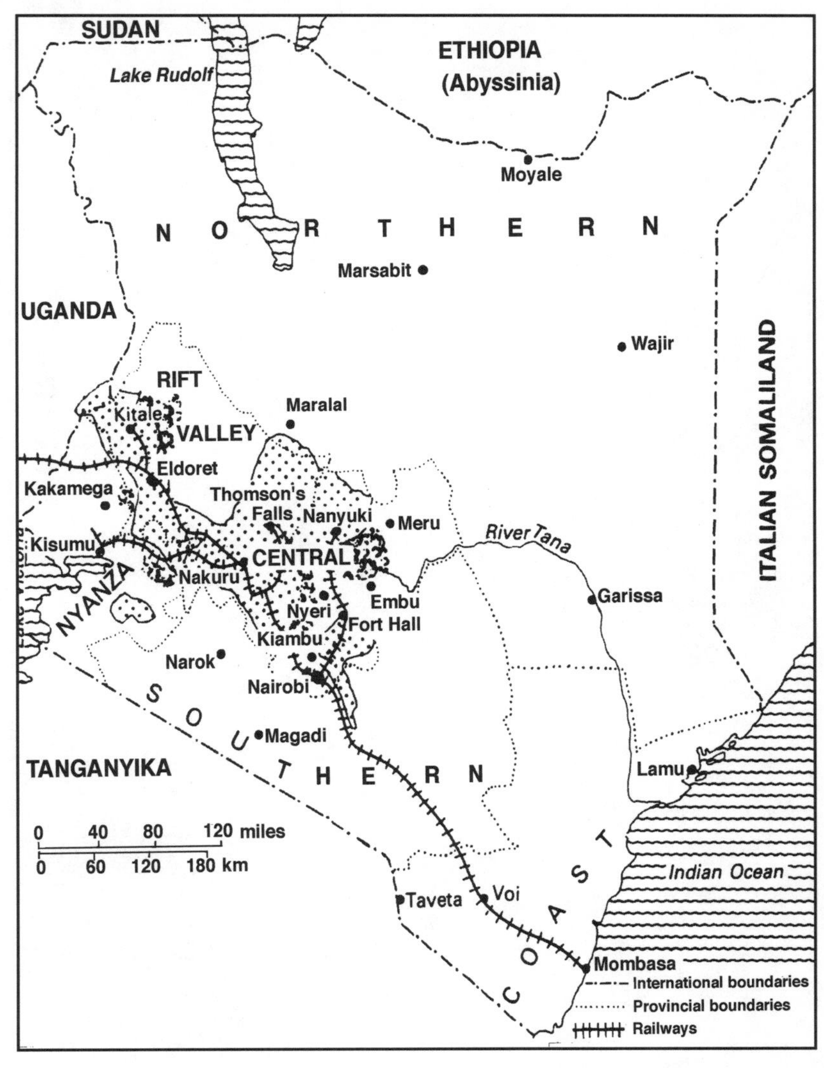

Map 1. General and administrative map of Kenya, showing the White Highlands

Source: Berman, *Control and Crisis in Colonial Kenya*, 1990

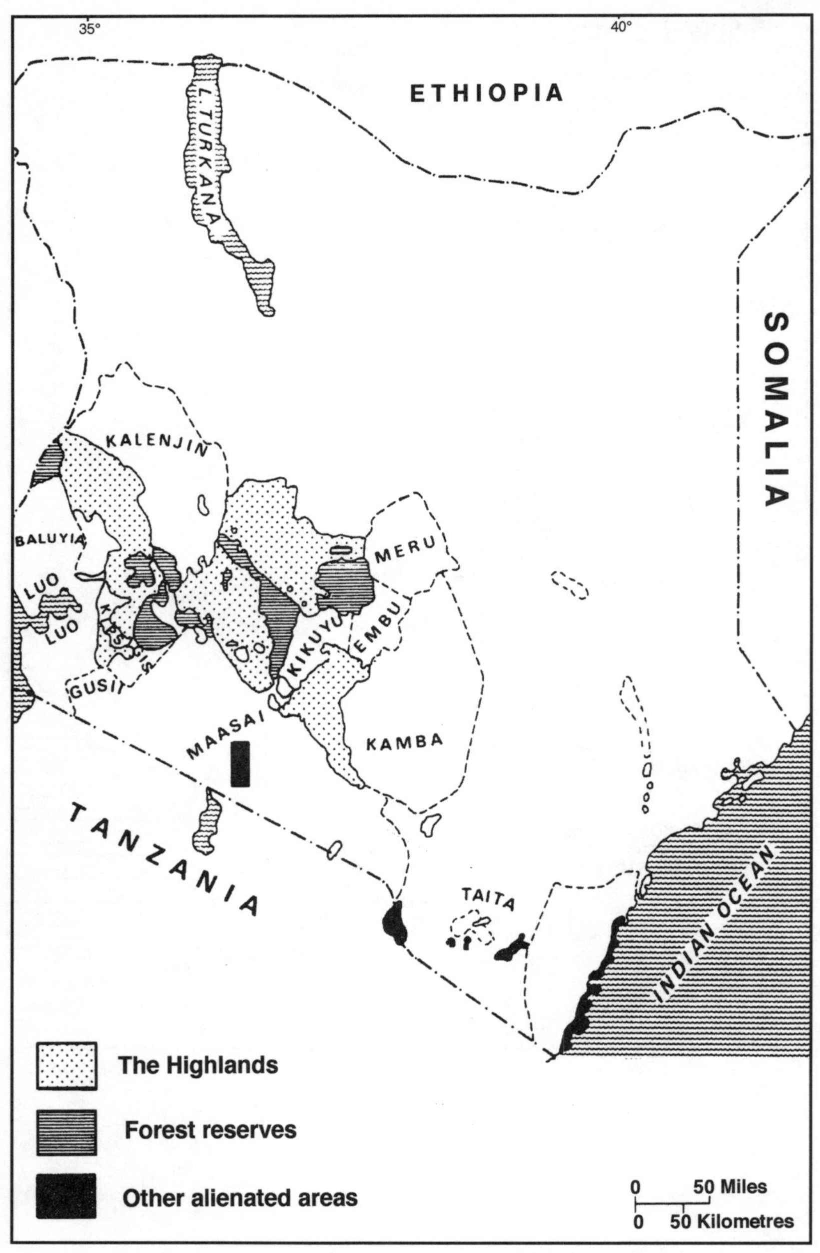

Map 2. Location of tribes and the White Highlands
Source: Throup, *Economic and Social Origins of Mau Mau,* 1987

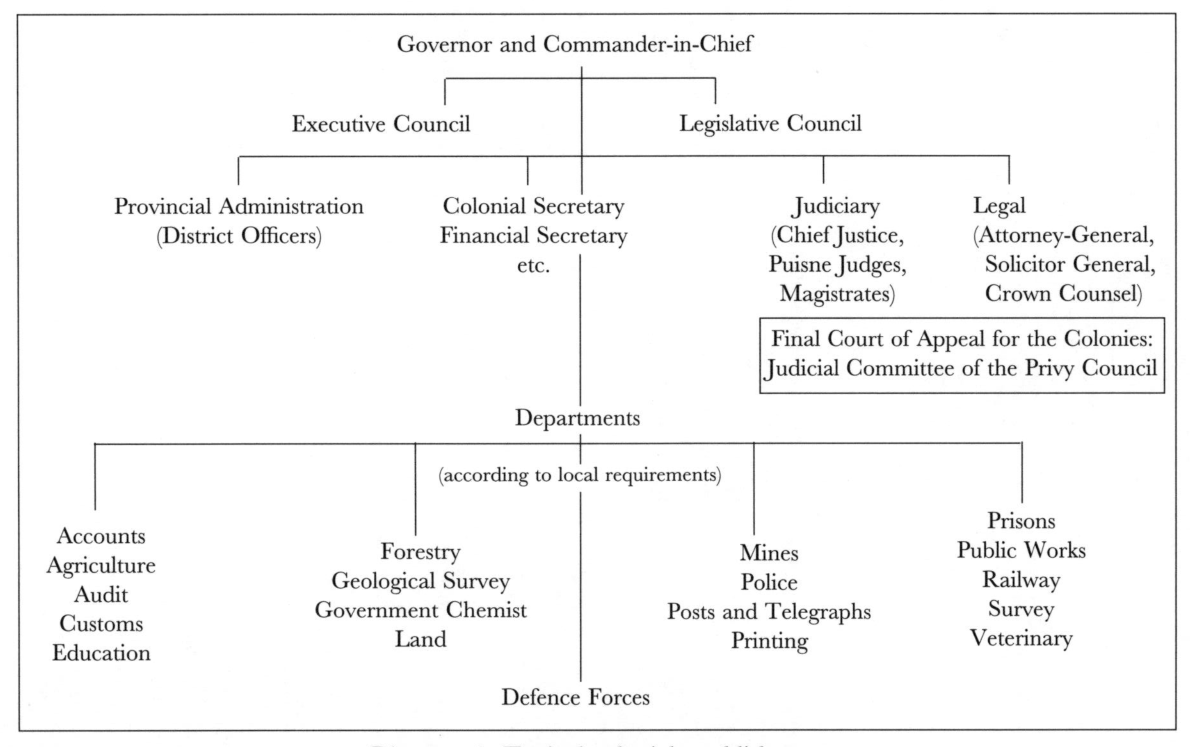

Diagram 1. Typical colonial establishment
Source: W. E. Simnett, *The British Colonial Empire*, 1942

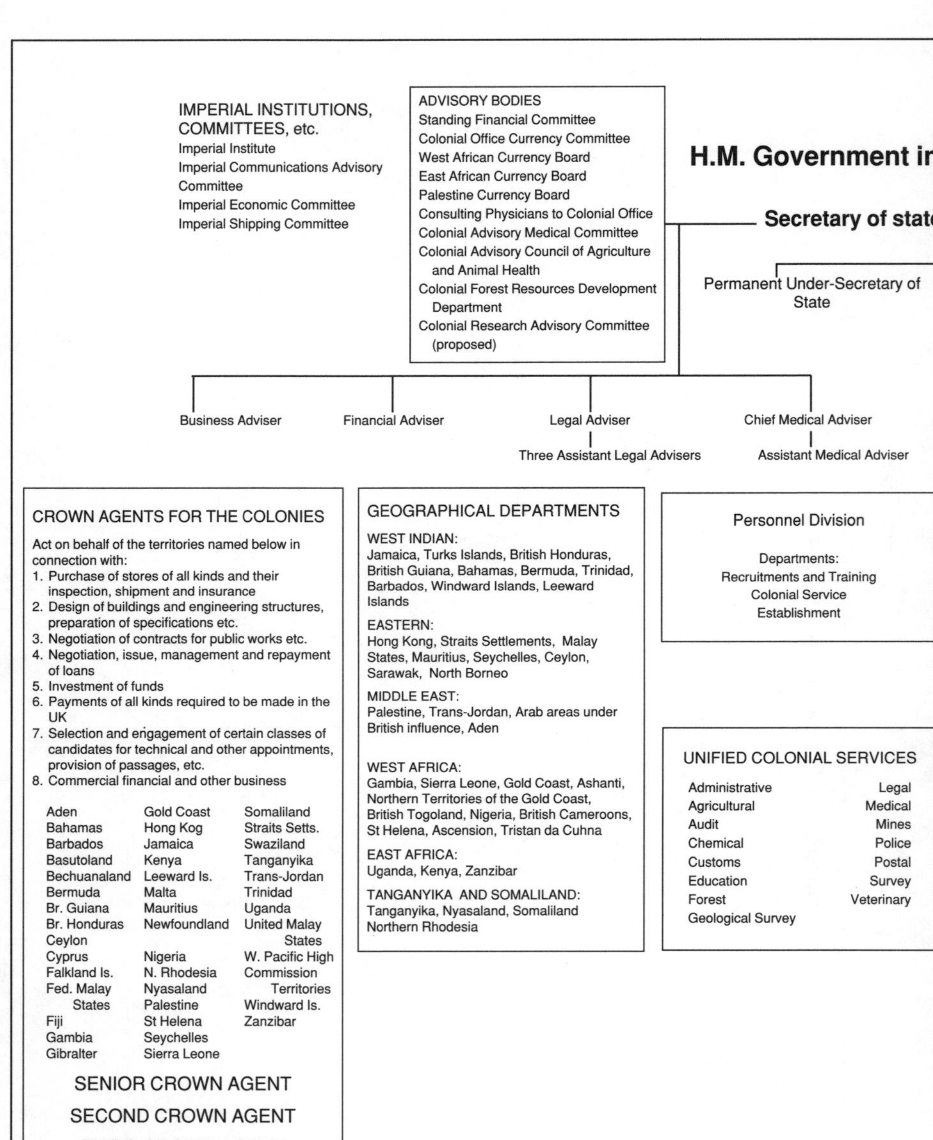

Diagram 2. British colonial empire administration and related organizations

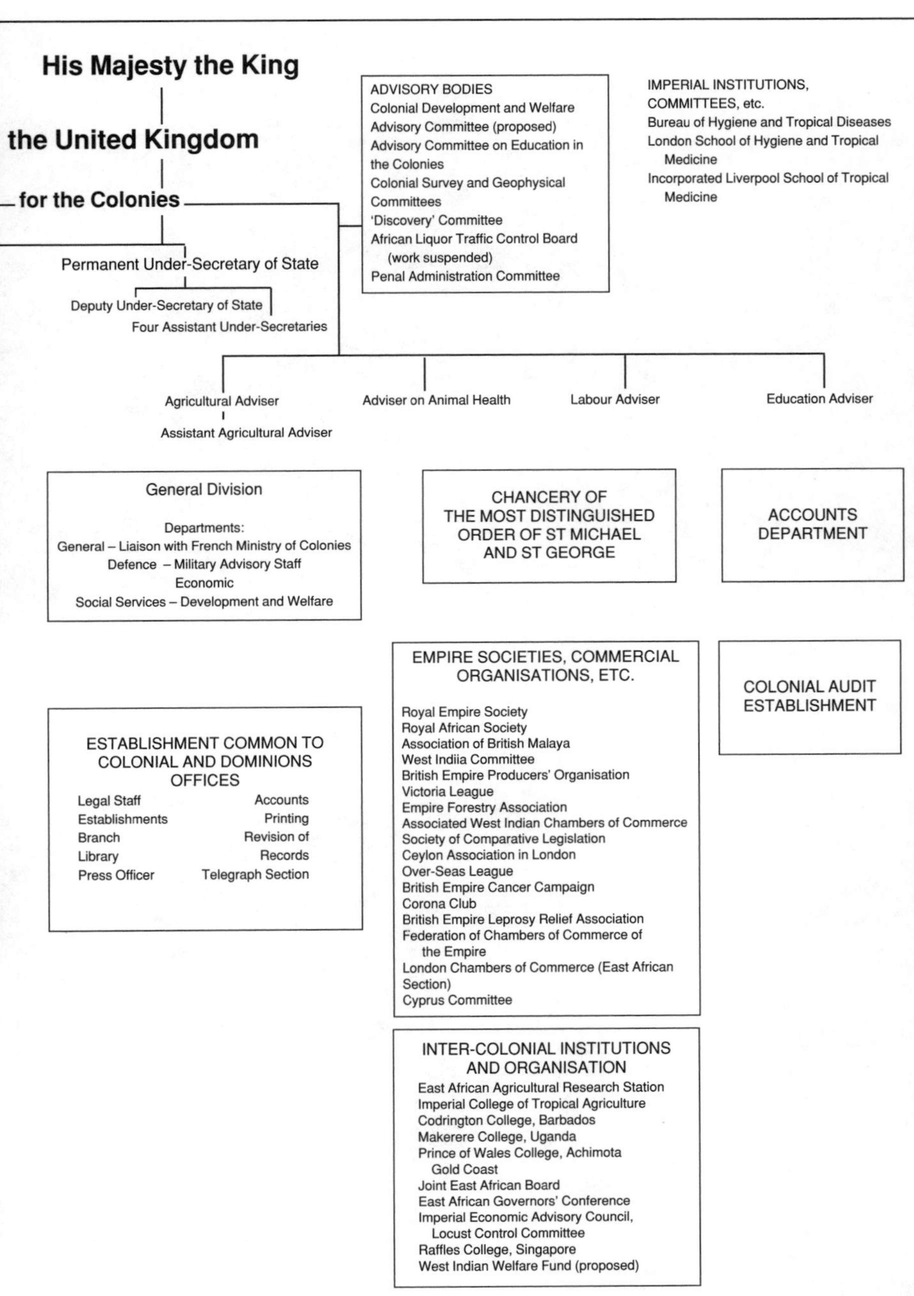

Source: W. E. Simnett, *The British Colonial Empire*, 1942

1. Farmers ploughing in Kenya Highlands (n.d.)

2. Hygiene demonstration, Nyeri Agricultural Show, 1931

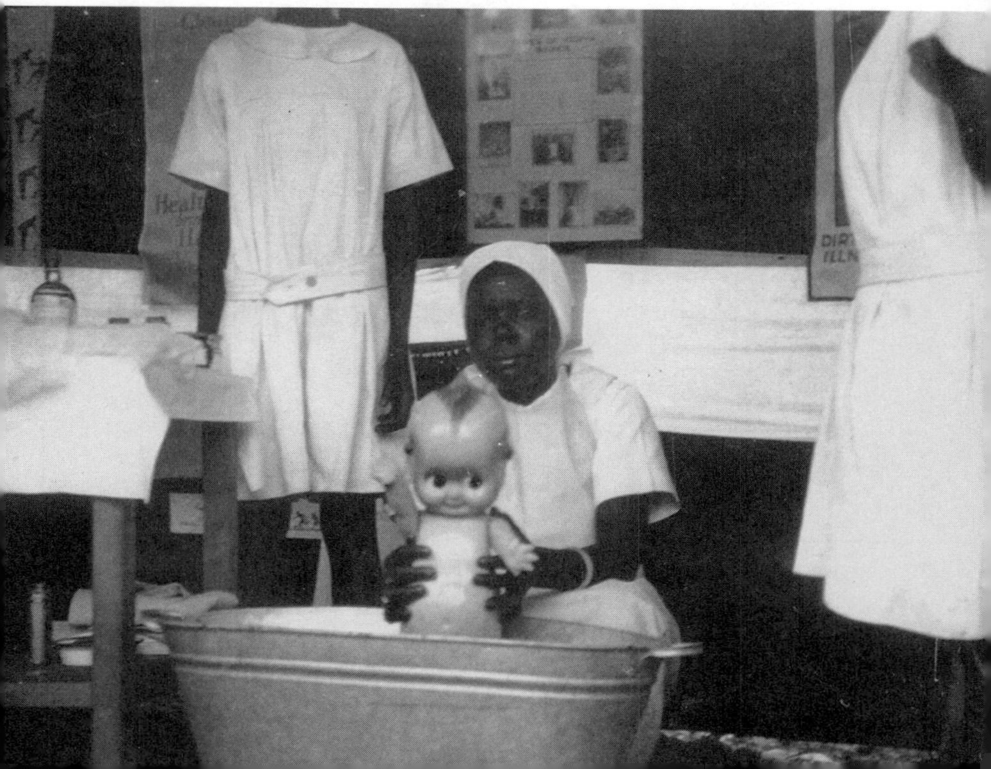

3. Women selling and buying, late 1920s

4. Work party in Central Nairobi preparing for the visit of the Prince of Wales to the colony, 1929

5. Kisumu main street, 1920s

6. KAR soldiers learning how to be teachers, c.1944

7. KAR teacher at Jeanes School, c. 1944

8. KAR soldiers being greeted by Ernest Vasey, Nairobi railway station, 1945

9. Prince of Wales at an agricultural show, 1929

10. Settler luncheon party (n.d.)

Introduction

'Pity for Poor Africans'[1]

This is a story about British imperial rule in Africa during the middle decades of the twentieth century. It turns on the way that development thought and practice became one of the most enduring legacies of colonial government. Encouraged to modernize trusteeship but enjoying little in the way of an extensive state structure or easy access to civil society, empire administrators looked to improve African welfare as metropolitan Britain launched its welfare state. Conditions overseas were very different, however. Colonies had fewer resources, no single moral authority and little in the form of a waged labour force that could afford to contribute to a national social welfare chest. Welfare and state-building were, therefore, inexorably intertwined in the colonies. Carving out loyal communities through material advance, forcing submission to authority, canalizing political opinions and insisting on communal self-help had to be central tenets of a welfare and development policy. In relation to this general pattern, Kenya was no deviant empire state.

It was, however, exceptional in that the patterns of welfare provision which followed British models and had Colonial Office approval were decidedly hamstrung by the colony's racial structure. As John Iliffe discovered in his history of *The African Poor*, Kenya's welfare operation was idiosyncratic and spartan, comparing unfavourably with that of other British colonies, and derided in 1951 by officials in London for being 'unprofessional and racialistic'. A switch from social welfare to community development produced a further neglect of the very poor. And there were no equivalents to the French tradition of community medicine with its female *assistantes sociales* (Iliffe, 1987: esp. pp. 193–213).

Yet it eventually became the rule. Many aspects of its official develop-

[1] Title of a poem by William Cowper written in 1798 reprinted in Chris Brooks and Peter Faulkner (eds), *The White Man's Burdens: An Anthology of British Poetry of the Empire* (Exeter, 1996).

ment practices which emerged by the 1950s survived throughout and beyond the colonial era and became common features of international development initiatives in the remainder of the twentieth century: the preference for producing or strengthening leadership; the focus on communities in the belief that they function for the good of everyone within them (i.e. the poor are by nature socialistic); the preference for a self-help approach to improving welfare; the neglect of women as key players in the social and economic sphere, particularly in post-war reconstruction programmes; the subordination of technical expertise, whether local or imported, to the needs of general administration; and finally, the side-lining of basic poverty eradication because of competing political or economic interests of the state.[2] It is a history of how contemporary development practice has its roots in the colonial period. As such, this is not a study of poverty but rather policy, especially since, in many instances, welfare policy was devoid of a great deal of recognition regarding the extent of poverty.

It rests on the following set of premises. There was always a transformatory element to colonial rule in that it sought to bring improvements in standards of living and quality of life according to the definitions of the day. The belief that intervention could achieve this had always underpinned the basic raison d'être of trusteeship and rested on notions of racial superiority. More and more colonial civil servants, like their metropolitan counterparts, believed in their ability to kick-start the engine of social improvement; they believed that they had strategies and wisdoms for creating progress which were superior either to abandoning Africans to teleology, or to pursuing radical or revolutionary change. Imperial prescriptions for social engineering increased in complexity and ambition during and after the Second World War. The influence of metropolitan practice was paramount: namely, the extension of the role of the state and the popularity among social welfare practitioners of the potential of community development through policy-making that had been subject to pragmatic reasoning analogous with scientific techniques. It became part of an imperial exercise in building up the social services of the state in order to modernize trusteeship according to new universal standards of government now expected of democratic powers. However, its effects barely matched its ambitions, due to a number of structural constraints Because of the racial, authoritarian,

[2] See Stan Burkey, *People First: a guide to self-reliant, particpatory rural development* (London, 1993). It is beyond the scope of this work to assess poverty and the many failed attemps to reduce poverty. My own understanding has been shaped by Claire C. Roberston and M. Klein (eds), *Women and Slavery in Africa* (1993); Iliffe, *The African Poor*, Robert Chambers, *Rural Development: Putting the Last First* (London, 1983) and Susan George, *A Fate Worse Than Debt* (Penguin, 1988). Two articles which assess the importance of self-help, the community and the role of the state which were key concepts during the time under consideration are Jennifer Widner with Alexander Mundt, 'Researching Social Capital in Africa', *Africa*, 68 (1) (1998): 1–24 and Hailu Abatena, 'The Significance of Community Self-Help Activities in Promoting Social Development', *J. of Social Development in Africa*, 10 (1) (1995): 5–24, both of which urge caution in relying on community.

compartmentalized and gendered nature of colonial rule, colonial practices in social welfare took a particular turn and set the pattern for much of twentieth-century development practice in clear-cut and often negative ways.

This book, then, offers a history of administrative thought and practice in colonial Kenya told through the ways in which Europeans tried to engineer social change in a white settlement colony riven by racial division. It builds on the rich and extensive work already carried out on the development and welfare aspects of the late colonial period by offering a localized case study of one strand in this dimension of imperial rule.[3] But it differs from past work by presenting a less reductive and homogenized view of colonial government through illustrating the divisions not simply between the CO and the administration, and Nairobi and the district offices but also the differences *within* departments and *across* generations, and by illuminating the alliances forged with external forces and actors. The major force driving events forward is the experience of the Second World War, flanked on either side by the tail-end of the Depression and the early violence of Mau Mau. The first of these auxiliary events fed into the war; the second was fed by it. However, it is the history of men and women at work whose labours reflected and affected their times which carries the story to its conclusion. The characters in the story were in the main English, white, middle-class (when not upper class) and more often male than female. They constituted an elitist mind-set engaged with the empire at various levels, made up mostly of colonial civil servants but also soldiers, farmers, academics, voluntary workers, politicians and clergy. They assumed that their actions were those of a minority which could transform the lives of an African majority, just as their ancestors had shoehorned a working class at home into universal respectability. They were comfortable with their mission to transform because they believed they were doing good. They were the compassionate ones. For many, Empire was a cause worthy enough to receive the war's domestic dream of a welfare state, ironically reversing the dwindling interest shown in empire and trusteeship in the 1930s (see Addison, 1982; Harris, 1992; Weight and Beach, 1998).

The subject of war and welfare in Kenya inevitably strays on to the terrain of the end of Empire. Kenya was the most high-profile and controversial of Britain's African colonies. With noisy white settlers, a capitalist system of production that was believed to be maturing nicely, the strategically important deep-water port of Mombasa and a fledgling but growing African political consciousness, it was the colony where imperial policies were often tested out first, where imperial relations were periodically strained to breaking point and where it mattered most if things

[3] For a general overview see M.P. Cowen and R.W. Shenton, *Doctrines of Development* (London, 1996) especially ch.1. 'The invention of development' pp. 3–59, and Michael Havinden and David Meredith, *Colonialism and Development: Britain and its tropical colonies, 1850–1960* (London, 1993).

went wrong. Kenya offers rich insights into colonial government during this period, despite not necessarily being typical. The Second World War had a gigantic impact on Empire and, unbeknown to those at the time, began the descent to the end of Empire. Most relevant here is the way it unleashed a new commitment to empire state-building, with a significant component to the new concept of the state being that of welfare. In Africa, this shift caused a major transition in the notion of trusteeship, already stirring in the frustrations of the Depression of the 1930s. The vagaries of indirect rule finally had to make way for the rhetoric of welfare and development in order to show that the imperial mission was neither finished nor a failure. How exactly this new mission worked in practice after the war tells us much about the inner workings of what were to be the last decades of British rule in Africa. Virtually no one during the time-frame of this study worked on the assumption that decolonization would be over and done with by the 1960s.

This particular tale of *Empire State-building* is told by means of the application and extension of four historiographies of Empire: the importance of war, metropolitan thought, the colonial state and gender. It runs through a quarter of a century on the basis that, to understand the effects of war, what happens before and after it must be included. It moves from London to Nairobi, up-country and back again. It involves lofty mandarins, clever women, isolated farmers and disgruntled Africans who were often in dispute over meanings of welfare as much as over actions. It explores meaning in the service of power through attention to official as well as unofficial texts. The basic argument is that the nature of the existing colonial state imposed limits on how far it could be changed. The precise reasons why the welfare organization was spartan and idiosyncratic, neglected the very poor, ignored women and failed to elevate departmental lore on to mainstream government and to address poverty, all have an explanatory significance for understanding the late colonial state in Kenya and state power in post-colonial Africa. Although the welfare organization remained a small one, it was proportionate to the shoe-string colonial government; though welfare staff were made painfully aware that size did matter, they compensated with the view that what you did with what you had mattered just as much. It received much in the way of backing from metropolitan experts, international organizations and the expertise of anthropology which had a significant impact on colonial social welfare policy. Although African voices were largely absent, representations of Africans were plentiful, since various individuals baited each other with critiques of rule in relation to welfare which purported to speak on behalf of African needs. So, by exploring this case study of empire state-building in relation to war and welfare, we can see more clearly how metropolitan, high imperial and local players interacted with one another and how the whole initiative quickly unravelled.

War and welfare

It is the paradox of war which sets the base-line rhythm of this narrative. Conflict is often contradictory in its effects, being simultaneously destructive and constructive. Wars are hugely disruptive, they cut through tradition and impose new rules. Yet they also consume continuity, invoke custom and strengthen old habits. They widen social spaces, throw up novel opportunities and unleash creative energies: they are especially keen to feed off the contributions of youth. Wars destroy people, ruin lives and damage relationships forever. Yet curiously they also give the gift of life. They demand that life is lived more intensely. People suddenly faced with imminent change or permanent threat have to move faster, to work harder and to search further afield to find solace. At the same time, all that is familiar, peaceful and unchanging can seem more intensely so, in the quiet of the home or in the shelter of a favourite landscape. Responsibility, work, travel, comradeship, sex and death all become much more available. Yet whilst basic and extraordinary human experiences multiply, in practice individual choice diminishes. The Second World War had just such a profound and ambivalent effect. It speeded up the application of established thought and allowed the emergence of new solutions to old problems. It gave the younger generation a louder voice. Yet it also confused, distracted and drained resources. It reprivileged certain forms of power and certain categories of people. Above all, for our story, it reimposed a masculine version of how African society functioned and how it might be changed.

The dialectical relationship between war and welfare in metropolitan Britain began a new phase in empire state-building in Africa. The relevant paradox of war here was its effect upon state-society relations. Sending men off to battle and making hefty claims on those who stayed at home partnered a more humane approach to managing people. This was the first war fought under the rubric of a universal franchise. The mass evacuation of key British cities in anticipation of an airborne German assault revealed unacceptable levels of deprivation. This gave added impetus. Meanwhile, the management of war was vastly increasing government's non-belligerent capabilities. Transportation, communications, medical treatment, food production and distribution were just some of the services which benefited from combat. Likewise, militarized bureaucrats and the full gamut of the professions became more efficient in their extraction of materials and manpower. Thus the war showed what the state could achieve when in interventionist mood; post-war expectations multiplied accordingly. Consequently a rapid 'nannification' of the state took place. William Beveridge's widely publicized welfare policy was, of course, at the centre of this new more intimate relationship. It was the point where the immediate self-interest of the state plus bureaucratic capability fused with a wartime need to maximize and reward collective effort. It had its roots in the dismal years of the Depression and was a synthesis of the various disjointed welfare and social insurance schemes set up in the inter-war period (see Jeffreys, 1987; Harris, 1975, especially pp. 252–3).

The present study takes the metropolitan historiography of the importance of the Second World War further into the colonial context. The impact of the Second World War in relation to colonial Africa has been well established. Most useful has been the concept of the war acting as midwife to a second colonial occupation – the 'thin white line' stood at 197 administrative officers in 1947 and at 350 ten years later. The numbers of men employed in the imperial professions – medicine, education, veterinary and agriculture – increased even more. War also speeded up the unfolding crisis within African society that ran parallel to this expansion but which colonial officials mostly ignored or at best misunderstood. Likewise, the negative impact of war in relation to enforcing systems of economic intervention and social control designed to benefit outsiders has been well documented.[4] Much of the details and significance of the ascendancy of colonial development and welfare can be taken for granted thanks to the considerable work on the subject. The way in which the war speeded up African social change has also been well documented (see Lonsdale, 1992; Iliffe, 1979). The present study extends our examination of the ways in which war had an effect on social policy in relation to empire, on the practice of colonial government more generally and on the further official marginalization of women. Soldiering had a particular impact on the direction of colonial social policy. The example of army 'habilitation' and the perceived effect of rounding up men and subjecting them to a tough regime in order to develop stoicism and discipline would feed into colonial social engineering tactics. Indeed, Mau Mau rehabilitation in the 1950s took a nostalgic but ultimately fateful sojourn back into army camp life, 'roughing up' becoming a central tenet of redemption.

Thus what is obvious – as the title of this study implies – is the strong connection between war and welfare in the twentieth century, manifested through the extension of the state; the sacrifice of life and the material cost of conflict have been reimbursed using the power of government to varying degrees. In the case of the colony of Kenya after the Second World War, such reimbursement is diluted and minimalist. However, there are less obvious connections which underpin the story. A central theme has to be the continuity in government practice between the time of war and a state of peace. This is certainly one of the enduring characteristics of the late colonial state in Africa. It has shaped the practice of post-colonial governance too. As this study shows, novel administration and new legislation after the war were flanked by the extension of controls of production and people designed for the war effort. The state remained 'at war',

[4] R. Rathbone and D. Killingray, 'Introduction' in Rathbone and Killingray, 1986: 1–19; J. D. Hargreaves, *Decolonization in Africa*, London, 1988; Low and Lonsdale, 1976; Kirk-Greene, 1980; and Berman 1990.

fighting African assertiveness, urban expansion and rural evasions. Indeed, the State of Emergency which hit Kenya in 1952 was little more than an intensive extension of principles of colonial government rather than a moment of aberration. Yet the pattern of continuity is even more universal. Post-war reconstruction in the recent past has reprivileged men over women and reoriented society back along more traditional lines of gender differences. Thus the universal quality of the rhetoric of war is far less inclusive in practice. Also, the way in which demobilized soldiers returned to civilian life and retired soldiers moved into civilian employment has affected the stereotypes of professional behaviour. Command and obey, authoritative leadership, control of information and observance of hierarchy remained far more intact as ways of bearing power in professional relationships in the twentieth century because of the incidence of war as well as the cult of soldier-worship in schoolboys and adult boys. The connection between war and the history of professional work culture has yet to be told.

Metropolitan politics and welfare

Recent work on imperial history has returned to the significance of metropolitan thought and action as the prime mover in the recent colonial and African past, although the key factor always remained the level of African collaboration officials could expect to put their plans into action. Things got done if 'Europeans invented' and 'Africans imagined' (Hyam, 1992, Part I; Darwin, 1988; Ranger and Vaughan, 1993). This study will argue that wartime Colonial Office officials and politicians were particularly inventive in that they applied more thoroughly to Africa what they knew about the working class in Britain and the experience of social engineering at home. Indeed, one insight into how metropolitan and African dynamics interacted after 1945, and the ease of handing over formal power, can be found in the history of class rule in Britain (see McKibbin, 1998; Clark, 1997). The creation of a universal electorate which grew in self-awareness throughout the twentieth century had major implications for party politics. Following the sweeping Labour victory of 1945 and the extension of the welfare state, Conservative party policy did not challenge the existence of such state provision. That the cost of administering empire could in no way compete with the resources needed to pay for social welfare in Britain, had become orthodoxy by the late 1950s.

Empire State-building highlights the way in which the new intimacy in state-society relations as a result of war was extended to parts of the empire such as Kenya. The fight against the Axis powers was a global effort, after all, and necessitated that demands were made upon its constituent parts. Colonies like Kenya were looked to for generous portions of men and materials. In such a time of direct rule from above, the boundaries and distinctions that separated those living below or overseas were suddenly, and conveniently, discarded. New needs ensured that what was hitherto unknown, hidden or distant, had to be, and could be, dealt with by the tentacular operational headquarters of a centralized state. Since the conflict inevitably required people to be prepared to make the ultimate sacrifice in a war which for many was not even theirs, so incentives and rewards had to be offered in exchange. And as chunks of the empire fell shockingly easily to foreign powers by 1942, so even racial rule began to irritate the imperial conscience since it bred such disloyalty. The political economy of the war in Britain is decisive here in relation to the improved entitlements for working people. As the British historian, Jay Winter, has remarked:

> During the two world wars, citizenship entailed the entitlement to command a bundle of commodities, including sufficient food, to enable each adult to contribute effectively to the war effort. (Winter, 1988)[5]

As a result, the 'habit of authority' with regard to empire changed decisively during the war, as welfare policy reveals.[6] First, colonial peoples were bathed in a new inclusivity by the imperial conscience at home. They were treated as extensions of British society. Their poverty was regarded as being universal and not exceptional, meriting the same kind of help as that given in Britain. 'Tropical East Ends' were registered by those who had gone into London's East Ends for the first time as a result of the evacuation programme. Race relations were castigated as a serious obstacle to the new intimacy required between state and society. Secondly, a growing consensus on imperial policy among the political Left in Britain ensured that an anti-traditional stance was strengthened. One MP destined to be the first post-war Secretary of State for the Colonies was keen to bypass traditional native institutions if they buttressed outworn custom, stopped initiative, upheld conservative chiefs, excluded the young and opposed democratic forces. This unprecedented rejection of indirect rule was given particular form partly as a consequence of an unfolding, one-sided love-affair with the modernizing potential of the socialist state, the third change in attitudes. State-centric and centralized sets of policies were more in vogue, again an extension of gathering thought within the Colonial Office during the 1930s. With admiring glances being cast at Russia by liberals and left-wing commentators alike, there was great optimism that state-sponsored scientific and technical projects, if planned carefully – planning became a fetish during the war because of the uncertain future – could lead

[5] See also Sen, 1981.

[6] See Thornton, (1966) for an explanation of why Englishmen and apparently non-Englishmen came to believe that 'Englishmen possess a political genius not readily granted to or at any rate found among others' (p. 13). Strong paternal rule was compatible with democracy, he argues, because after 1945 the middle-class Left in Britain learnt that men of other ranks simply wanted security.

to revolutions in agriculture, industry and population management. Colonies like Kenya soon felt the effects of these trends. A Colonial Development and Welfare Act was passed in 1940 and extended in 1945. The number of colonial civil servants was increased after the war – known as the 'Second Colonial Occupation'[7] – and guidelines were issued on the establishment of social welfare departments. Thus the metropolitan politics of war upheld by a generation scarred by the Depression and now frightened by war, produced not only a sentimental outpouring of emotion but also a copy-cat programme of slow-yielding reform for state-society relations to be applied in colonies like Kenya.

The importance of the input of metropolitan political economy in the history of empire in Africa is taken further in this story. It is brought closer to the history of the rise and fall of the late colonial state – the usual term for the period following the consolidation of formal rule after the First World War. That the preoccupations of metropolitan Britain and the political landscape at home were often refracted through imperial issues has been well established.[8] The concern with African welfare before and during the Second World War exposes this relationship in new ways. The mobilization of the home population required an extensive reorganization of health care, nutrition and housing. The adult population being fully enfranchised and fully engaged in fighting, was entitled to minimum standards of health and welfare from the government. William Beveridge symbolizes the belief in the power of the state to intervene to provide such a safety net for citizens unable because of their circumstances to provide this for themselves, so that they would then be less burdensome on the state. The Depression had scarred a generation already uneasy about the handling of the First World War. Meanwhile, the growing capacity of bureaucratic intervention in line with science and technology raised expectations.

Empire was not unaffected by the consequences of labour's new and hard-won entitlements. The period under consideration was believed by many politicians and do-gooders at home to offer the chance for a new constructive imperialism. Science and technology could be turned on Africa's perceived deficiencies in increasingly concentrated doses during the 1930s. The demands of war coupled with the Keynesian theory of economic management produced some money for a colonial state-managed welfare and development programme that mirrored developments at home. This experience and the ensuing ambitions were exported to the colonies, with Kenya being a crucial test-case. With the hopes and plans not realized by the 1950s and as the embarrassment of colonial race relations reduced Britain's prestige at the United Nations, it is not

[7] See Low and Lonsdale (1976) for the origins of this term.

[8] See for example, Miles Taylor, 'Imperium et Libertas? Rethinking the Radical Critique of Imperialsim during the Nineteenth Century', *J. of Imperial & Commonwealth History*, 19 (1) (1991): 1–23; Howe, 1993.

surprising that officials, politicians, trade unions and humanitarians accepted fairly easily that the age of Empire was over. The new more intimate entitlement relationship between state and labour in Britain also made a contribution to the end of Empire; the indebtedness resulting from the war ensured that there was not much money around either to fight against nationalist protest.

The metropolitan moral rearmament of Empire which took place during the war was to set the colonies an impossible mission. A major element of this was the imperial politics of inclusion. During the war the idea took hold in the imperial conscience that Africa and Africans were to be treated professionally as extensions of metropolitan Britain. This action represents the application of a learned experience borrowed from elite responses to the growing power of the working class at home, needs that quickly had to be met during the war. The middle classes were learning to act in this way in Britain, allowing others to imagine that they could become like them, believing it to be their moral and professional duty to canalize such a movement, and somehow in the process managing to maintain control of the major power bases in society. Many left-wing politicians and Colonial Office officials believed that Africa's problems could be best solved by metropolitan solutions. There was by no means consensus on this, just as during the war the Conservative Party was against any great extension of the state into people's lives.; they wanted a drop in levels of taxation and only reluctantly embraced the notion of national insurance. However, the political Left, who were to win the 1945 election with a landslide victory much to the Tories' amazement, regarded the state as being the vehicle that could deliver democracy, welfare and capitalist growth. What they failed to realize was that the state in Britain had been sensitized to universal need after extensive wealth creation through unfettered capital accumulation, the maturing of civil society, the establishment of a large tax base, and the creation of a single moral community. Not surprisingly, empire state-building was not very effective since these conditions did not exist in the colonial period of rule, nor have they existed in the post-colonial era. Beveridge was working with a self-perpetuating source of finance, had an eye on urban problems, could rely on the discipline of a single moral community and had been galvanized into tidying up a confused and partial system because of the state's ransom to the need for a healthy and compliant nation of fighters. He was also targeting women as the main bearers of the burdens of social welfare. The colonial state lost sight of this fact as well.

Gender bias and welfare

A third historiography essential to answering the question of why the project of empire state-building around welfare was so feeble, is that of the recent interest shown by academics in sex. It now goes without saying that the experience of being human is contoured by what gender signifies at a particular moment in time. For women this has generally been shown to be more negative, in that their life chances were prescribed by others, usually men, and were reduced to something less than their full social, economic, political and emotional capacity (less than the norm for men) simply by being female. The history of the colonial encounter has been enriched by much scholarship on African women, more recently on their relations with African men and with other women.[9] Empire was also a project that white women shaped in ways that made a difference because they were female, although the effect this had upon African women was by no means wholly positive. The previously homogenized presentation of colonial regimes has been well and truly outed. European women, whether as wives of administrators, as missionaries, as lobbyists at home, or working overseas as amateur do-gooders, nurses, teachers, welfare officers, are now seen as having played an important, if not at times contradictory, role in upholding the imperial project.[10] More recently too, we have been reminded that men are also bearers of gender; masculinity was not fixed or singular. Male competition, homosexual and heterosexual jealousies and public school childishness shaped their professional relationships as much as formal training.[11]

The application of gender as a historical dynamic has enabled this account to offer a more penetrating and variegated picture of imperial relations. Key players in the history of social welfare were white women, who were used by the state, often working either as professional spinsters or as married volunteers. They might have laboured away at the unglamorous end of municipal do-gooding or served on the new advisory bodies set up. Turning to the high politics of imperial rule, it was a woman – Margery Perham – who produced the most accurate and far-reaching critique of imperial rule during the Second World War: it was because she was a woman that she was able to do this. Also, a feminization of certain professions took place from the 1920s onwards which had an impact on the Colonial Office. Feminism and the extension of the franchise helped to politicize sections of European women after the First World War. Some began to campaign for changes in how the state behaved towards women.

[9] An inadequate survey of women and gender studies with special relevance, but not exclusive, to East Africa might begin with Boserup (1970), Obbo (1980), Robertson (1984) and Coquery-Vidrovitch (1997). For studies more focused on gender relations see Allman, (1996), Moore and Vaughan (1994), White (1990), Thomas (1996) and Geisler (1996).

[10] For example, Calloway (1993). This parallels the growing documentation of the profound ways in which the labour of African women sustained colonial states; for example, the labour of rural women in supporting the cotton industry in Mozambique during Portuguese rule in Isacman, 1996.

[11] On relations amongst the sexes see Hyam 1990, and more recently Rosamund O'Hanlon, 'Gender and Imperial History' in *New Oxford History of the British Empire* (forthcoming).

A key arena in this struggle was the League of Nations which – progressively for the time – included a high proportion of non-governmental representatives and women on its drafting committees. The Mandates Commission benefited from this. Having only one woman member nevertheless ensured that mandated territories had a policy on such issues as the need to educate women. London began to follow suit. Consequently during the 1930s, as enquiries into nutrition revealed the need to address women and a growing feminization of the welfare and health professions produced more information about women, so official thought at the Colonial Office began to link social welfare with them. Efforts were made to set up an enquiry in 1939, but the outbreak of war intervened. By 1945 its cumulative effect was to ensure that the new social welfare policy was based more upon metropolitan solutions and included African men. Women remained stuck on the merry-go-round of suggestion.

To an extent, the misapplication of metropolitan welfare state solutions was at the heart of the problem. Beveridge's aim was to rescue the community from without in order to bolster the family within. The maternity, child and family allowance system was a financial pact made between the state and its mothers. The Colonial Office embraced the concept of macro-state intervention, but missed the point that it was women in the domestic sphere who were being targeted to carry the burden of welfare. A gendered, minimalist, rural strategy was more appropriate and the colonial state already had one – on file, where it remained, or in the form of growing numbers of trained midwives, health visitors and agricultural advisers. The template opted for ensured a neglect of much needed structural reform, particularly, as we shall see, in the distribution of power and resources between the provincial administration and the technical departments.

The effect of war at the level of Colonial Office thought reinforced the same pattern in Kenya in the post-war period. By the late 1930s, evidence had come to light that more girls were attending school and that more women – African and European – were needed as health workers and teachers. This feminization of social engineering struggled in vain to gain a foothold. In the rush to demobilize, African soldiers took centre stage in social welfare models. Notions of masculinity were looked to after the war to solve issues of detribalization and the need to shore up the colonial state's hold on African society. Yet by the late 1940s, officials finally realized that the community centre initiative was succeeding because of the attention and support it was getting from women.

By tracking the story of welfare in post-war Kenya with attention to the treatment of women, the shortcomings of empire state-building can be fully appreciated. Not only were the implications of racial rule for welfare barely tackled head-on, but the masculinized agenda of welfare, which grew out of the war, further obscured its previous feminization as a profession. This was partly because of constantly having to deal with the administration's opposition to any new category of officer engaging with development. But the wartime rush towards metropolitan macro-state intervention hampered local endeavours and ran roughshod over Africa's particular set of circumstances. Although a more coherent colonial formula for African welfare and development was found by the early 1950s which included women, it was characterized by conservative notions of self-help and focused upon the community. As such it ignored structural factors and abandoned the care of the very poor. Overall, it did little to reverse the neglect of women as economic actors and state employees and of basic poverty eradication. Despite the increased capabilities of science and technology and the growth in knowledge about the contributions of women, the kind of professional specialist who could deal with gender differentials, social inequality and resource scarcity in a way that reduced poverty in Africa remained, and still remains, largely beyond the capabilities of elites to engineer through the state.[12] Colonial welfare strategies bequeathed a canon of thought and structure that was inappropriate to the social and economic agenda which the colonial state had set itself. More seriously it was inappropriate to Africa's needs and further marginalized women.

The late colonial state and welfare

This study builds on the historiography of viewing the late colonial state as central to understanding the fate of twentieth-century Africa (see Mamdani, 1996; Cooper, 1996: xi; Berman, 1990). Post-colonial theory has revived the old conundrum: how was so much ruled, so far away, for so long and with so little? Did size really not matter in this context? Through the development of more nuanced appreciation of the relationship between power and knowledge, historians of empire have moved beyond an essentialist concept of colonial thought and practice and the conventional locations of state power, and towards exploration of 'the mutual representation of the self and of the other' as well as returning to re-examine the relationship between government, bureaucratic practice and local society (see Kennedy, 1996; Thomas, 1994; Bayly, 1996). Finding new meanings in the service of power through old colonial texts and new archival sources owes much to post-colonial studies. The study of language, argument, metaphor and modes of representation has illuminated how the capacity to maintain colonialism was based less upon material power and why its confrontation was doubly difficult.[13] This book makes much use of

[12] This has not been fully addressed in recent works such as Mamdani, 1996.

[13] See Hunt, 1996: 324. For another useful commentary on the study of history see Greenstein, 1995, especially discussion of Carolyn A. Hamilton, 'Authoring Shaka: Models, Metaphors and Historiography' (unpublished PhD dissertation, Johns Hopkins University, 1993).

these techniques in order to re-examine the properties of late colonialism.

The effect of war on the colonial state was ambivalent, as already argued in relation to metropolitan impulses and the understanding of gender. Kenya, like other colonies, experienced the constraints that came with wartime imperial rule but also the impulse from a more humane element in colonial government. Empire had always been home to the extreme manifestations of such conflicting forces. Omnipresent were exploitation underpinned by compliance, obedience and submission, along with the reduction of African life to something much less than its full complexity. Yet traces of recognition of a common humanity had stubbornly gone to ground in the corners and crevices of the colonial encounter between black and white, especially between soldiers who had fought side by side in war. Material and emotional sacrifice, denial of self and a commitment to a universal notion of human experience supported islands of compassion. Undoubtedly much of this white do-gooding came from feelings of distress and pity for the suffering, misfortune or inferior status that was perceived to be intrinsic to having a black skin rather than a white one. And notions of doing something for 'poor Africa' could easily be adopted for reasons of self-promotion and personal salvation or simply to justify occupation. As an ideology it was very malleable, therefore highly durable and more than occasionally extremely dubious. Yet the genuine belief held by many was that life for the majority of Africans was unnecessarily nasty, brutish and short and they wanted to transform it otherwise. War gave new impetus to the humanist element of colonial rule.

Yet it was also a friend to repression and the application of force. War allowed colonial authorities to stamp out nationalist politics, to extend and control information gathering and the use of the press, and to commandeer labour and materials. As this study illustrates, the use of force to achieve social transformation was always an attractive option for many administrators, albeit often as a last resort. Soldiering and wartime demands gave the colonial state a militaristic edge as never before. Some officials dreamt of solving rural problems through mass compulsion; others believed that native deficiencies could only ever be remedied by the exercise or threat of force rather than through reason and free will. When the use of force was turned to in a systematic fashion during the Mau Mau uprising in the 1950s, this was merely a continuation of an established tradition of colonial practice but carried out on a larger scale. It reached back to the Second World War.

However, if wartime thoughts about African welfare pulled more on the strings of sentiment, the concept jarred much more with the colonial reality. During the war, welfare had become the new buzzword in Kenya. Yet little in the way of practical restructuring around this idea had emerged by 1944. The basic problem was that colonial government had been set up to fulfil tasks other than the delivery of a modern development and welfare programme; government was profoundly exclusionist, particularly of the young people, non-elites and women. So shaky were its foundations, that the preservation of the status quo was the most it could often hope to achieve in the absence of legitimacy and access to civil society. Also, because of the importance of these habits of colonial authority, the technical branches of government were subordinated to the administrative service in ways which the latter were less willing to tolerate. For in terms of the transformatory project being set out in London and the potential offered by science and technology, the specialist departments now had much more to offer than the district administration. As we shall see, they struggled in vain to gain a foothold in the mainstream of colonial government. Unlike the French system, political institution-building at the local level was much more central to the British district administration's sense of purpose. Similarly and not unrelated, their sense of embodying the monarchy and the law also ensured that the technical branches of government remained much more subordinate.

So, at the level of colonial government in Kenya, the period after hostilities ceased was shot through with a set of seemingly contradictory processes. On the one hand, a degree of self-reinforcement took place. The expansion in the role of the colonial state was proof of this. Numbers of administrators increased significantly; new departments were set up, welfare being one example; more attention was given to education, particularly higher education and so on. Cementing these efforts was a new sense of mission and optimism. A moral rearmament had taken place during the war built out of a belief in the potential of targeted technological wizardry and a concept of trusteeship that venerated the economic and social aspects of preparation for self-government.

On the other hand, trends were at work which sabotaged this project. With Britain reeling from the war, heavily in debt and having lost the status of major world power, empire was looked to as a means of plugging the gaps. Instead of mass injections of capital for state-building, the flow of resources went the other way. Sterling balances were spirited away for other purposes. Meanwhile, the hope that business would come on board and invest did not materialize in any significant way. In Africa itself, the effects of social change were moving at an ever quickening pace. Welfare and development seemed little more than white rhetoric as African nationalism struggled to have a voice. With no extensive state structure to work through and no easy state-society relations, efforts to achieve more direct rule had to turn back to indirect rule to do so; more social change seemed to produce more social unrest. The biggest problem facing the late colonial state's social transformation project was the way in which the push for more direct rule to achieve more welfare and development, required more indirect rule to take shape. The new concern with further modernizing trusteeship further exposed the colonial need for Africans with whom they could work and through whom they could reach African society. But white welfare remedies did not travel well across the racial divide after 1945. The ideology of racial paternalism became increasingly split between those who believed in autonomous, self-sufficient natives pulling themselves up by their own efforts in response to external dictates, and those who believed in citizenship and the possibility of a non-coercive relationship between the state and African society. In the preference for the term 'native' or 'African' at the time, we can often locate this conceptual difference.

Kenya's Welfare Organization illustrates these contradictory elements of the late colonial state only too well. The war allowed it to exist; the war, as well as London, shaped its focus. Maturing but meandering pre-war ideas about the betterment and control of Africans had found a new prototype solution. The demobilized African soldier aroused European hopes, fears and, occasionally, fantasies. Consequently in 1945 the colony found itself with a new administrative structure, the Welfare Organization. Its very existence was a triumph and it testified to the partial reinvigoration of the late colonial state. It became a vehicle for a set of practical handy hints and 'must-have' tips for the habilitation of Africans in rural areas. Fostering small-scale craft and trade enterprises, inculcating empire loyalty and reducing disease were just some of the principal goals, all to be achieved through village life, model families and the techniques of mass propaganda. The search for control was there too: in part due to the legacy of war, the organization was built around using the right kind of chap to discipline other chaps. Yet, by the end of the 1940s, the idea of including women was really taking hold for the first time.

This rag-bag outfit limped along and just made it to the end of the 1940s, thanks to the tenacity and self-confidence of officials who had been profoundly influenced by their wartime experiences, or who had been let in through the back door because of the conflict. Another mark of its success was the curious way in which it came to play a crucial role in the massive state-sponsored response to Mau Mau, with its features and philosophy being carried forward by African and Western governments, development agencies and charities long after the formal ending of colonial rule. The structure and substance of the post-war second colonial occupation thus endured – social welfare being one aspect of this. The ultimate coup of welfare and development was the way in which they concealed the fact that the empire continued to function as a financial support for a crippled Britain after the war.

The Second World War was a far more significant watershed in the history of twentieth-century government practice than the formal end of Empire ever was. The energy for the second colonial occupation came in part from officials who had begun to sign up to a more positive view of African capabilities and to a more professionally responsive type of colonial government. They sought to deal with difference coolly and calmly through the application of their particular expertise. Often marginal players within the least influential structures managed to act on their feelings, cut through the long-standing bureaucratic confusion, and slice up the rhetoric. Personal experience of inequality, memories of their wartime chums – a bone of contention with the establishment – or just plain war guilt were some of the reasons that could push individuals to operate on a wider notion of what it was to be African and to issue challenges to the more powerful. It often took them beyond the structures and systems that made them but clearly did not always control them. Moments of genuine compassion could never be ruled out completely.

What this history yields is a three-dimensional picture of the late colonial state. First, we take a slice out of colonial government via an intimate portrait of colonial administration in cross-section. Through debates about African welfare, we track the input from the Colonial Office, imperial pressure groups, the Kenyan government, local society, and the field administration and departments. Government was being changed by basic advances in communication and information control. Exchanges between London and Nairobi were notched up a number of gears. By the end of the 1940s it was much easier for marginal players to communicate with the Colonial Office and vice versa. Travel was easier. London put on conferences and dispatched circulars with much more regularity and better thought through.

Indeed, the war was midwife to a moral rearmament of imperial intentions towards Africa, as officials moved into the post-war period wielding a shopping list of economic and social wants from the state-building warehouse.[14] The centre gradually moved in on the periphery. Centralization and homogenization not only showed up the anomalies and inconsistencies in local practice; it also revived established conflicts. War speeded up this process. At another level it slowed the process down. The League of Nations and the creation of mandated territory had spelt more international and humanitarian scrutiny of colonial policy, provided that the colonial power saw itself as having prestige it did not want to lose. War interrupted this trend. Immediately after the end of the war, the United Nations focused its attention on reconstructing the economic, social and moral fabric of Europe. Among other consequences, this put a brake on attention devoted to social provision in Africa. War produced a commitment to a tentacular state structure for the empire; it also ensured that the feminization of the state taking place in the 1930s was lost sight of.

Secondly, we have new detail about individual actors as well as a new account of social welfare. The profile of the late colonial state is thus enriched. The role of Margery Perham is re-examined, the working lives of bottom-of-the-range welfare officers explored, and the new advisory committees, the contribution of *askari* and the role of public opinion are considered. The relationship between the administration and technical departments is touched upon. We find that the presumed division between

[14] Inclusion of the technical and state-building aspect of colonial government undermines the argument found in Robinson (1979).

frustrated but compassionate professionalism and die-hard racial paternalism was by no means clear-cut. Whether keen-to-modernize DCs, or urban administrators who saw Nairobi as humanly deplorable as well as politically dangerous, or agricultural and medical staff who were professionally frustrated, or progressive missionaries and settlers, each group contained conflicting elements. They all wanted change but disagreed among themselves as to how it could be achieved. Officials squabbled and competed for control over the state apparatus; new arrivals were regarded as a bunch of namby-pambies if they deviated from anything too far from a negative view of African capabilities. The social welfare department's history roams over all these terrains.

Thirdly, we see the late colonial state in motion. Social welfare experts in London failed to teach the colonial state the lessons of its own bureaucratic history. Meanwhile in Kenya, competition for resources, struggles over turf, class snobbery and male rivalry diminished the capacity of the new department to function more so than others. Nevertheless, its staff managed to cling on and to survive, finding a handle on African society which others missed. And when crisis erupted in 1952 – a major challenge to the colonial state – that handle was quickly grabbed and a pacific accommodation achieved remarkably swiftly. Yet its future was very much shaped by Africans themselves. This story turns out to parallel the whole drama of the late colonial state. Colonial governments found they could technically do more, but could actually achieve less. They tried harder, but, in the face of growing local opposition, their feelings were softer. Growing centralization only increased local rivalries and much of the key battles of the late colonial state were fought in relation to rural Africa and were not solely the preserve of labour departments in Mombasa or Nairobi.[15]

This tale of post-war government illustrates just how colonial power fragmented, whilst at the same time becoming more integrative and coherent. First, there was the way in which colonial officials became much more differentiated as bearers of power after the Second World War. A significant minority were changed by the war or found themselves in jobs which the war had created. Many technical staff became increasingly frustrated. District Officers in the most volatile districts could do little but keep the peace. Secondly, after 1939, a restrictive racial paternalism and its related philosophy of minimalist government became an ideology that fewer and fewer officials signed up to wholeheartedly. This was especially true of the war-baby administrators, urban-based officials and a younger generation of colonial civil servants. Most important, perhaps, was the lack of alternative trends towards a consolidation of power that could compensate for the above. The Colonial Office found itself unable to curb the excesses of the Kenya government. For them both, authority became more

[15] This view contradicts that put forward in Cooper (1996).

elusive. Meanwhile, African responses moved beyond the state's capacity to direct, let alone control. The second colonial occupation's empire state-building project was riven with a central contradiction. Some saw more state intervention as the vital mechanism needed to modernize colonies like Kenya and to overturn the failures of indirect rule; others saw it as a means of shoring up their own version of traditional African society, particularly the role of the chiefs and elders.

Yet the final outcome was in some sense a triumph. The structures that were in place and the ideologies they represented remained largely intact when formal Empire came to end. The colonial legacy of social engineering merely mutated as local elites wanted it to do. It deferred to metropolitan-type solutions. It was profoundly state-centric thanks to the Second World War, and as such was highly interventionist, censorial and controlling. It privileged men over women in terms of the assessment of their potential contribution to social, economic and political transformation. And, as in Britain, its greatest success was in maintaining elite access to power under the cover of a populist programme. Much more continuity runs through development practices in the twentieth century than was previously understood. The colonial welfare and development structures and ethos were largely kept intact at independence. Many of the officers involved in this area went on to work for international development and humanitarian agencies or their British and post-colonial equivalents, as did many of their offspring.

The rhetoric of welfare was probably influential outside the narrow professional focus but this is beyond the remit of this study. It might have criticized colonial policy in other spheres, influenced the claim to power or provided a cloak to obscure the form taken by colonial rule. Some, no doubt, used it to condone general indifference, neglect and racial intolerance. For others it became a conduit for their compassion that was contextualized within professional expertise and given practical expression. At times it was able to inspire individuals to tackle difference and inequality without despising the former or accepting the latter. However, it was usually dashed on the rocks of much harsher relations and the interests of others, suggesting that compassionate intervention rested upon an acceptance of inequality. Although a narrative of humanity ran through the imperial encounter, it was more often sidelined by authoritarianism, subjugation and neglect, setting the pattern for post-colonial states. This study explores how these conflicting forces were played out through war and welfare, and what were the constraints and options. Had technical and welfare specialists been able to assert their practical and occasionally gendered approaches to African poverty – the tension which runs through this story – this might have made some difference to the history of poverty in Africa. The reasons why they turned away from this and what they left in its place help us understand why government intervention has too often failed Africa's poor throughout the twentieth century.

This study has been based on research initially carried out in pursuit of a doctoral thesis. It has been converted into something that moves on to the scale of readability and up from the footnotes, specifically for undergraduate historians of Empire. However, the aim has also been to produce a more accessible account of the workings of the late colonial state in Kenya which might appeal to a wider audience including development practitioners and those without specialist knowledge of the country. Much attention is given to the deliberations and actions of individuals who had to communicate with each other across great distances, either from London, Nairobi or living in remote up-country towns and villages. Yet the amount of discussion and debate ought not to suggest that this was an easy or quick process, or that distance and separation were trivial matters, or that documents always speak the truth. The deference to hierarchy meant that field officers had to send communications via their immediate superiors. Only one particular branch of administrative thought and practice has been revived; as such, this is a partial account of colonial rule. It does not seek to represent the whole colonial administrative encounter but rather a set of events which have explanatory significance for enhancing our understanding of colonialism and the end of Empire in relation to the transformatory mission of British rule. If it conveys the essence of a fascination which, against all odds and after much provocation, still burns bright, this will suffice.

One

War, Welfare & Women at the Colonial Office

Empire State-Building, 1925–45

This chapter examines the outer arena of thought and practice found at the highest administrative level of empire, the Colonial Office. During the inter-war period and despite public indifference, officials made a strenuous bid to modernize the apparatus of colonial government, making it a time of radical internal reorganization and reorientation of policy. Indeed, many of the principles and structures put in place were to persist up to and beyond the end of empire in Africa, a moment barely imaginable at the time. A central component of this attention to trusteeship naturally consisted of devising ways to improve the lives of those over whom colonial governments ruled according to what was considered best at the time. Imperial attention to native welfare – the term of the day – increased in the 1930s, due to a number of mutually reinforcing processes. International organizations made the administration of empire a less exclusive province. More significant was Colonial Office anxiety about the effectiveness of indirect rule in Africa. Meanwhile the ability of modern bureaucracies to function as centralizing and standardizing systems of power was improving. As the Colonial Office found it could measure welfare and poverty better, a growing belief in state intervention pervaded the domestic climate. The Second World War ensured that these trends culminated in the politics of grand gesture – a Colonial Development and Welfare Act – reflecting a more intimate view of state–society relations. However, war also had the result of obscuring the effects of a previous trend towards a partial feminization within the welfare and health professions. Here welfare focused more on women, communities and micro-rural development strategies. A growing wartime obsession at home with urban disorder ensured that the new colonial social welfare advisory committee evinced little interest in such an approach. War ensured that metropolitan solutions and standards were applied more systematically to empire; it also prevented the Colonial Office from reading the lessons of its own administrative history. Modernization of colonial rule was as incoherent as it was incomplete.

Welfare at the Colonial Office in the 1930s

By the beginning of the twentieth century, the Colonial Office had swapped its damp and unstable building, dispensed with its office hours for juniors that ran from noon to 5.30 p.m. punctuated by lunch and games of darts or fives, and, instead, had become a serious institution (Hyam, 1979; Ashton and Stockwell, 1996: xxiii–cii). It was one of the smallest departments in Whitehall, although it continuously expanded up until the early 1950s. The Secretary of State for the Colonies – a political position – was flanked by a Permanent Under-Secretary (a civil servant) and a Parliamentary Under-Secretary (a politician). Below them were their deputy and assistant under-secretaries. Further down again were a range of permanent general civil servants increasingly augmented by specialist advisers, and underneath them were the clerks, typists and office boys. Apart from the General Department which dealt with protocol, these 'recording angels' worked mainly within a glittering array of geographical sections that were, for most of the Colonial Office's history, as remote from each other as the territories they administered. Initially, the Colonial Office was idiosyncratic, and a professional cul-de-sac which attracted – predictably – the more abstract and academic of Oxbridge graduates. A great deal of effort was put into patrolling receipt books and the ritual dismembering of ledgers in the noble pursuit of poor accounting and bad financial practice. Making personnel appointments also took up a lot of time. Much of the work was routine and consisted of the circulation of incoming information in strict order of hierarchy. Each officer would record his view. Such minuting tended to be excessive, patronizing but often extremely perceptive. From its inception the officials of the Colonial Office had a limited purpose – to give quick, expert advice and to record the reasoning behind the decisions taken by their political masters whom they were expected to serve loyally. As such, the office was historically restricted in its influence.

Initially the Colonial Office meekly absorbed the impact of an unstable environment in the first decades of the twentieth century. The British Empire was adapting to the shock waves generated by two events as profound and global as the century was ever to see. The First World War had torn the heart out of nineteenth-century imperial relations. After 1918, Britain, for example, was no longer able to supply huge amounts of credit to its junior trading partners. Nor was it able to resist the temptations of a more exploitative type of relationship with its colonies and dominions to ease the financial burden of the war. Simultaneously, such refinements were stimulating pockets of economic and political nationalism. When these later crystallized with local grievances, the result was a moment of political cohesion held together by a collective will to oust the 'imperial masters'.[1]

[1] See generally, Fieldhouse, 1981; Milward, 1972, esp. pp. 44–52; Anil Seal 'Imperialism and Nationalism' in Gallagher et al, 1973.

Meanwhile, disaster struck. In the late 1920s a world depression set in which was to last for nearly a decade in some places. Millions of people suffered, from Mancunians to Malagasies. At home, money was in short supply and unemployment plentiful. Colonial economies were badly hit. They had been re-fashioned for the purpose of integration into a world economic system. Consequently they tended to produce a narrow range of raw materials for sale in distant markets. Their choice was limited by local environmental conditions as much as by foreign demand. Suddenly planters and cultivators found that the prices they could command had plummeted. Loss of confidence, debt and overproduction had depressed demand in the power houses of early twentieth-century commerce and industrialization. When overseas producers increased output to make up for the fall in prices, prices fell even more. They had few resources to fall back on, could not easily diversify and so were tied more tightly into monocultivation. Meanwhile, the overall trend of prices for raw materials in relation to manufactured goods was moving downward. Switching to industrial production to compensate was simply not an option for the poorer colonial economies.[2] Thus the recuperation of revenue from imperial trade was declining on both sides.

Consequently the effects of international conflict plus global depression made up the wider context within which imperial powers like Britain operated. Since Europe's African empire had been hastily converted into administrative units at the beginning of the twentieth century, the world's balance of power had shifted decisively away from the position of domination enjoyed by the European imperial powers; however, few appreciated this at the time. Nevertheless, the home climate towards empire had turned a little chilly. The effects of the Depression made money for overseas palliatives more elusive. With poverty and social deprivation rising to appalling levels, particularly in towns and cities where it was more obvious, attention turned inward. Also a general uneasiness about the handling of British power overseas followed in the wake of the First World War and hovered over the successors to the far more confident Victorian ruling classes.

Yet, the 1930s proved to be a watershed for the Colonial Office. A more ameliorative attitude to welfare in the colonies took root well before the threat of another world war galvanized thought into action.[3] Indeed, the gradual abandonment of the principle of passive colonial trusteeship in favour of a more active one, grew out of a set of bureaucratic traditions which were peculiar to the Colonial Office and the inevitable consequences of the doctrine itself – stepping in to oversee the interests of non-national territory on the grounds that its people and institutions needed protection

[2] See Latham, 1981; P. Williamson, *National Crisis and National Government: British Politics, the Economy and Empire, 1926–1932* (Cambridge, 1992); Hopkins, 1973; Amin, 1988.

[3] See generally Pearce (1984). For a review of the negative effect of the war on established trends in colonial reform and reorganization see Lee, 1977, esp pp. 71–6.

and time to evolve to a state closer to that of the national territory. First, officials tended to identify themselves with ordinary native peoples. They regarded themselves as the true guardians of their humanitarian interests. Secondly, Colonial Office officials looked down on virtually every other type of person or group that came into contact with native peoples. Missionaries and non-governmental bodies were kept at arm's length or dismissed as being organizations which lacked their own capacity for impartiality and also their font of information. Many officials had indeed visited the territories they were responsible for at some point, although they worked for the most part behind desks in Whitehall. Hence they felt totally at ease in their sense of superiority.

Similarly, their affection for the colonies was matched by their contempt for colonials. The white community was seen as the most serious threat to the empire which they loved (Hyam, 1979: 39–48). Settlers, especially the British in South Africa, were regarded as self-centred, narrow-minded and dishonest. The business community fared hardly any better, and educated Africans even less so. Nor was the colonial service overseas spared. Governors were often considered to be idiots. District administrators were regarded as being of lower intelligence because they could not boast the same number of graduates with firsts and prizes (lots of twos with blues instead) – but were generally trusted to do the best they could, in view of the way they experienced conditions first-hand.

Thirdly, the Colonial Office did not believe that Parliament or the British public understood or appreciated the delicacies and contributions of Empire. This in part explains why they were against sending lower-class people overseas to build up artisan communities as a way of solving development problems, unlike Portugal which was only too happy to export its poor peasantry whenever possible. Although profoundly racist at heart, officials nevertheless balked at the idea of buttressing communities where one half could then put 'continuous and powerful pressure on us to repress the other half'. This was not considered a satisfactory system of rule (ibid.: 47). Ultimately the Colonial Office had to concede that even official interest in the empire outside of their department was at best fitful.

These bureaucratic traditions within the Colonial Office had to face up to a number of interlocking processes evolving throughout the inter-war period. One was taking place in the realm of international relations; another was firmly located in the colonies themselves; a third in the growing capability of administrative power, and a fourth in changing metropolitan attitudes to poverty and government by the end of the 1950s. The institution of the Colonial Office itself was already predisposed to respond to these crucial stimuli in the direction of substituting mild trusteeship from afar for one of more hands-on welfare and development directed from home.

From 1919 onwards, the world had a new international guardian of people who did not live in recognized states, and during the inter-war period a growing international conscience as to how such people ought to be treated began to touch upon the administration of empires. The Treaty of Versailles had ushered in a new era in inter-governmental relations, formally ending the First World War in 1919 and setting up the League of Nations. Turkey and Germany, as defeated powers, were not to have their empires returned, but what was to be done with them? Politicians on the Left were vociferously against annexation, so the solution adopted was a system of mandated territories. There were sixteen of them including territories in east, west and southern Africa and a Permanent Mandates Commission met twice a year to review their progress. This was one of the League's most politically sensitive and powerful permanent advisory committees. What it was policing was a new principle of trusteeship enshrined in Article 22 of the Covenant of the League, which stated that the well-being and development of people unable to stand by themselves 'under the strenuous conditions of the modern world' was a 'sacred trust of civilisation'.[4] Mandates were ranked on a scale of A, B or C according to their preparedness for becoming independent. When Iraq applied to become a member of the League in 1932, statehood was quantified as being able to provide government including a range of services and having financial resources and a legal system that was fair and protected minorities.

Mandated powers – of which Britain was one – found themselves subject to a new type of scrutiny relating to non-state peoples. The Mandates Commission required annual reports on how that trust was being catered for. It sent out questionnaires and asked representatives from the territories to come to Geneva. It built up an institutional memory which it used to assess progress and the mandated powers were aware of being monitored. They knew comparisons were being made and, not wanting to give away political points or be outdone by another power, it became increasingly important to show signs of good practice such as building schools, roads and hospitals. Indeed, Article 23 of the League's Covenant had addressed social issues, in part the consequence of having an unusually high ratio of women present when the Covenant was drawn up. Pressure from international women's organizations resulted in a woman being appointed as one of the nine members of the Mandates Commission. At its first meeting, the President welcomed the prospect of Ann Bugge-Wicksell's particular contribution to the 'study of those problems of *colonial administration* relating directly to the welfare of that half of the human race which both needs and deserves the special solicitude of those who are to govern' (emphasis added. See Miller, 1992, esp pp. 154–62). Consequently the mandated powers were pressed on issues of 'white slavery' – the buying and selling of women and children – infant mortality, domestic sanitation,

[4] I am grateful to Barbara Metzger for having shared her knowledge of the League with me. The Treaty of Versailles. Part I. The Covenant of the League of Nations (1919); see also Jones (1994).

the age of marriage and the training of midwives. Thus Versailles nudged forward another principle of international concern, that of how specific groups of human beings were treated regardless of the non-state status of the territory in which they lived. Colonial empires could not expect to remain immune.

The inter-war period also saw a related increase in the activities of welfare and humanitarian organizations; colonial empires would not be above their scrutiny either. Many took advantage of the new forums at Geneva and used the Covenant to bind their own causes to this institutionalized international conscience. British organizations, such as Save the Children British and the Society for the Protection of Aborigines were very much part of this dynamic (Miller, 1992: 1–6). The lobbying techniques of these organizations improved, as did their ability to network and give mutual support. This was particularly the case for the international women's organizations which the League had helped transform, giving them more opportunity to participate in official proceedings. With twelve countries conceding women the right to vote between 1918 and 1928, social issues moved higher up their agendas until a conservative and anti-feminist backlash during the Depression forced them back to narrower issues including the lot of professional women at work. Nevertheless, non-governmental organizations remained highly active. The carnage of the battlefields had deeply disturbed many Edwardians. Although a guilt clause had been inserted into the Treaty of Versailles making Germany and Austria virtually wholly responsible for the war, some religious figures and humanitarians in Britain felt differently. In the inter-war period they wrestled with the issue of how their Christian state ought to behave to serve the progress of humanity. The international conference became a popular format for this soul-searching. International conferences that debated issues such as world disarmament reflected this growing concern to improve the conduct of governments generally. The League of Nations provided a focus, a point of contact and a set of international standards which organizations tried to extend (see Kent, 1988: 30–1).

The colonial empires of the victorious powers were not to be immune from this new interest in how non-state people and vulnerable groups were treated by governments. In 1926, the League of Nations had passed a Slavery Convention and subsequently the International Labour Organization investigated the issue of using physical force to make people work, approving a Forced Labour Convention at its 1930 conference (Cooper, 1996: 25–56). Although not as flagrant as Portugal and Liberia in their use of coercion to make people work, by the 1930s Britain, and even more so France, failed to measure up to international requirements across their empires. In Kenya for example, officials knew they were banned from using force. They also knew that force was used by agents wandering around recruiting labour for farmers. Patience and charm were not prerequisites for such a job. One woman, known as the Asparagus Queen, would routinely lose her temper and had the habit of striking any African who irritated her. To be hit by a woman, black or white, was a matter of great insult.[5] In theory at least and in conference chambers in Europe, the principle of the universal, essentialist human being with standard rights shifted to include so-called native peoples, and the sanctity of colonial jurisdiction was never the same. Racial thought remained intact, of course, but Africa was no longer so remote as to be beyond the reach of international institutions that laid new stress on the protection of people and on the temporal nature of external control. The world was getting smaller.

Not surprisingly then, the newly empowered international conscience-keepers reinforced the efforts of metropolitan political organizations that were committed to changing aspects of empire, even to abolishing it altogether. In Britain, there were at least three strands to this tradition within minority political activism. Humanitarian groups such as the Quakers carried forward the anti-slavery banner and applied their morals to how native peoples were treated. A growing left-wing critique of colonialism on ethical and practical grounds was accompanied by a more radical position from Communist revolutionary groups. By the 1930s, the number of high-profile black people in Britain had increased and included more and more young intellectual nationalists fortified by the growing confidence of the Pan-African movement. Its supporters such as C.L.R. James, the Caribbean writer, found cells of educated middle-class white liberals willing to seek new associations that encompassed their goal of an end to racial rule. Added to the London Group on African Affairs was the 'Friends of Africa' as it became known by 1934, and the League of Colonial Peoples was set up in 1931. A defining moment for this burgeoning multicultural set was the Italian invasion of Ethiopia in 1935. For a while their unity was preserved in the International Friends of Abyssinia and members included a Kikuyu student at the London School of Economics, Johnston Kenyatta (see Bush, 1997; Howe, 1993).

Popular representations of Africa and Africans available in Britain were also slipping further out of the control of officials, with the expansion of cheap print, particularly the format of the novel. For example, in 1937 Ida Hurst published her account of travel in Africa, Abyssinia and the Gulf armed with only a hair pin and a pair of cheap glasses. *A Vagabond Typist* was advertised as 'an excessively frank book' presumably because she relayed her discussion on circumcision with a Kenyan when travelling on a *dhow*. However, there was no sensationalism of the 'black peril', no slippage into *Africana exotica*. Rather, she settled on a romanticized version of racial difference that required sympathy since 'black and white can never understand each other'. Africans were always smiling, she concluded, because they lived 'closer to Nature, as God intended' (Hurst, 1937, esp. Introduction and pp. 229–31). In the same series you could get

[5] M.W. Dobbs. RH Mss.504A162.

a first-person account of being black in *The Life Story of a Negro*. And whilst it was mostly a minority of white women such as Winifred Holtby or the aristocratic Nancy 'What is it now, drink, drugs or niggers?' Cunard who were prepared to violate the harsh taboos forbidding inter-racial intimacies and to pay the price, nevertheless more cautious white liberal males found themselves having to show enthusiasm for improving African welfare so as not to lose their footing on the moral highground.[6]

A second process well under way by the mid-1930s, which also had the effect of profiling the issue of native welfare, was a growing perception among officials at the Colonial Office that the general system for governing African colonies was proving less and less successful. A skeletal structure of administrative officers and technical experts in each colony set about dispensing their particular specialism through collaboration with local chiefs and elders, who, it was hoped, would discipline their locations accordingly, or enable European officers to do so. Popular discontent had erupted in south-east Nigeria in the late 1920s, again in 1930–1 and later in 1937. Northern Rhodesia flared up in 1935. Meanwhile, news of the Indian Civil Disobedience Movement spread further afield. Lord Lugard had established the basic principle of this system – indirect rule – in Africa following his dealings with the Sokoto Caliphate in what became Nigeria following the scramble for Africa in 1885. That the interests of the native population should not be subject to the will of local Europeans or Europeanized natives was among his basic concerns. Consequently, chiefs were made the agents of imperial rule in order that local institutions and customs could exist and adapt in some sort of syncretic rhythm with the development of resources. Chiefs were created where they did not exist, which was the case for much of eastern Africa, illustrating the inappropriateness of Lugard's prototype. Thus the Dual Mandate was born, a blend of two desires: to protect the vulnerable and to make the empire pay. It was also underpinned by racialist thinking, for it venerated the idea of racial segregation and the assumption that Africans would be incapable of self-rule for a long time (see Perham, 1960; Lugard, 1965; Bradlow, 1972).

By the early 1930s, the Colonial Office was holding to the increasingly gloomy view that native conditions in tropical Africa could not be expected to improve adequately under this set-up. The Colonial Development Act passed in 1929 had not helped. Its purpose was to alleviate economic stress in Britain, particularly the high levels of unemployment, a response that reflected the long-standing principle that the empire had to pay for itself as well as the financial pressures of the post-war period. Adding to the general unease by the later part of the decade, were reports of labour unrest. Particularly worrisome because of their scale, were the outbreaks of violence in the West Indies. These disturbances had caught

[6]Remark made by Margot Asquith provoked by Cunard's relationship with a black American composer, Henry Crowder, quoted in Bush, 1997: 217.

the attention of the Labour Party and trade unions who protested against the government's colonial policy. In 1936, the Colonial Office appointed a Labour Adviser and gave Lord Hailey the task of undertaking a survey of all African territories, one of a number of fact-finding missions inaugurated around this time.[7]

Kenya was usually somewhere on the cutting edge of controversy and conflict. Although not reflective of the experience and claims of all British African colonies, its affairs always commanded considerable attention in London, which makes it a particularly compelling and significant case-study. The Colonial Office had always considered this East African settler colony to be a hot-spot. The potential for friction was omnipresent, due to the range of incompatible forces present when the territory became more than a figment of the cartographer's imagination. But not much more, since Kenya was born out of the embellishment of a 600-mile footpath linking the coast to the shores of Lake Victoria. This area had acquired the title of the East African Protectorate in July 1895 and by the 1920s was commonly known as Kenya. A reluctant Foreign Office had been forced to act following a spate of lobbying in the wake of the British occupation of Egypt and Otto von Bismarck's temporary extension of domestic self-interest to piling up overseas possessions. London capitulated, throwing a strategic security blanket over the need to protect the head waters of the Nile. The British East Africa Company and the smattering of mission stations had to concede to a superior form of white power. Disease and famine eased formal occupation as much as quinine and rifles had made it conceivable. Swathes of land which seemed empty had often been temporarily abandoned in a time of hardship and dearth by the local population, particularly the Maasai and Kikuyu. Violence was the sharpest spur and a speedy process of violent conquest ensued in which African power was unceremoniously used to undermine itself.[8]

A railway came next, as it had always done, to shore up communications and defence. Amazingly, it transformed what had been a three-month journey into one that took three days. Less amazing was that it cost a lot of money. A source of revenue had to be quickly found to pay for the line, its upkeep and the fledgling colonial administration, for the Foreign Office had relinquished control to the Colonial Office in 1905. By this time, enthusiasm was growing for colonization. This was particularly encouraged by Sir Charles Elliot, the second governor, who helped promote the view that only large-scale cultivation could produce enough revenue to provide economic growth. When Hugh Cholmondely, third Baron Delamere, arrived in 1903 as a permanent settler, the cast was complete. Soon Kenya was one of a number of colonies in Africa which had a

[7] See Stephen Constantine, *The Making of British Colonial Development Policy, 1914–1940* (London, 1984) ch. VII, pp. 164-94; also Porter and Stockwell, 1987: 14–15.

[8] For the best account of the conquest of Kenya, see Lonsdale, 1989; also Berman, 1990, ch. 2, 'Contradictory Foundations', pp. 49–72.

population of white farmers. They set themselves the task of building up new farms borrowing from the South African system of *kaffir* farming, whereby Africans 'squatted' on the land in exchange for undertaking regular light cultivation duties as well as more sporadic but heavier work such as clearing virgin bush. Many of Kenya's early 'pioneers' were blood relatives or enjoyed close relations with certain influential members of the British aristocracy. It was fairly easy to establish a narrative of settler heroism which helped sustain the argument that white farming was the future, and that the native interest were best served by following this path. Indeed, it was partly through a readable biography of Lord Delamere, entitled *White Man's Country*, aided and abetted by Karen Blixen's popular novel *Out of Africa*, that the rhetorical conceit of settlers as romantic figures battling against the odds to spread hard work, decency and progress to a corner of darkest Africa reached its zenith by the late 1930s (see Tidrick, 1992: 130–71).

Thus, from the very beginning of settlement, white settlers were running in the opposite direction to the Lugardian nonsense of indirect rule. However, the Colonial Office remained committed to Britain's role of trusteeship, shored up by the knowledge of keener international scrutiny. The use, treatment and payment of African labour often brought settlers and government into conflict; suspicion of each other's motives was now becoming entrenched, although both groups shared a racially negative view of African capabilities. It was rather the case that their racial paternalism produced different solutions. The battle lines were soon drawn. The settlers had secured a strong position for themselves through unofficial membership of the colony's Legislative Council (LegCo) established in 1907. The colonial government meanwhile set up local native councils and a native affairs department. Trusteeship continuously battled with white paramountcy, and the Colonial Office lost ground in 1910 thanks to the mistaken appointment of Sir Percy Girouard as governor. Instead of standing up to the settlers, as it was hoped he would, he actively pressed for self-government. Events came to a head when, without prior consultation, he began to shove the Maasai people – the ultimate noble savage in the minds of many a sentimental official – into a single reserve on the grounds that they were unruly and had no commercial instinct. His efforts to make Kenya more settler accessible cost him his position but his dismissal was too late for the Maasai who were moved on (see Hyam, 1979: 47–8).

A government White Paper published in 1923 tried to settle the issue with a declaration that native interests were to be paramount, the hope being that the principle of trusteeship would be treated as inviolable (see Bradlow, 1972: 69–80 for a detailed account of this episode).[9] It was all a mess. A system of capitalist agricultural production was being built up, but

[9] *Memorandum relating to Indians in Kenya*, Cmd 1922 (London: HMSO, 1923).

it required sustenance from traditional forms of production. White settlers wanted self-government over a land that was not theirs. The Colonial Office wanted control over a system of government it had little power to command. The colonial government in Kenya was set on establishing authority through a set of people for whom it was not theirs to share: 'power over people was always slipping away from chiefs, just as power over capitalism escaped the state' (Lonsdale, 1989: 27). Meanwhile, chiefs and elders were interested in collaboration so that they could build up their autonomy.

It could thus hardly have come as a shock to Colonial Office officials in the early 1930s, when they discovered that, even after the 1923 declaration, acting on behalf of native interests produced little in the way of results. For example, Lord Walter Moyne was made Financial Commissioner in 1932 in order to make a report on Kenya colony.[10] The plan was that a fixed sum of revenue derived from direct native taxation be removed from Legislative Council control and earmarked for specific native services. The colonial government urged caution. Financial conditions were as difficult as the political ones. The problem was that Kenya's Europeans were to argue vociferously that the Fund would deprive them of their proper share of trusteeship for the native.[11] Powerful local white groups were resistant to Colonial Office-inspired change, wanting more autonomy rather than less. The Colonial Office soon had to face accusations of interfering in Kenyan affairs. Meanwhile, the colonial government preferred not to upset the fragile peace. District Officers were not so compliant. In some districts Africans had got to hear of the plans and used the local native councils to voice their support. In South Kavirondo District, the Kissi-Abakaria and Luo-Abasuba LNCs put together a petition asking for a proportion of their direct taxes to be paid into their local fund in part so that they would know what would be spent on 'betterment services'. Their local district officer E.V. Buxton was sympathetic, deciding that the document merited being made more coherent and then presented to the Provincial Commissioner. By January 1934 they had still not received a reply.[12]

The Colonial Office remained sympathetic to the suggestion and received little in the way of encouragement that they could afford to be complacent on this issue. Official administrative reports from the territory provided written proof of a growing problem. Reports tended to shy away from portraying anything unpleasant or negative, but Kenya's *Native Affairs Report* for 1933 confessed to a general lack of positive progress. There was no denying the fact that trusteeship and indirect rule were proving

[10] *Report by Financial Commissioner on Certain Questions in Kenya*, Cmd 4093 (London: HMSO, 1932). He went on to become Chairman of the Royal Commission of Enquiry into the West Indies rioting and later Secretary of State for the Colonies 1941–42.

[11] Correspondence located in PRO CO533/450/18 and PRO CO533/416.

[12] E.V. Buxton to PC (Kisumu), 2 January 1934. RH Mss.Afr.s.1103.

increasingly incompatible. The Depression was upsetting an already fragile local compromise. In Kenya, payment of taxes was becoming 'a matter of some difficulty to the native population'. This caused all sorts of problems for a colonial system of rule that to an extent relied upon collaboration and a degree of acquiescence. One of many examples was Aubrey 'Mug' Mullins's glum account in his handing over report in August 1935 of how the Galla had been 'very bad about paying tax lately in spite of the fact that they have sold a lot'.[13] In London senior officials debated the problem among themselves. Some argued that it was the fault of hut and poll tax no longer being paid communally due to the money shortage. Also to blame was the apparent trend of young men giving less help to their fathers and spending money instead on 'themselves and their girls'. As a result the hapless DCs had to spend more time on collection and less time on the 'advancement of the district'.[14] Kisii's DC was quoted as insisting that native authority was weak because chiefs and headmen were foreign to the Kikuyu. Elders moaned about the behaviour of the young 'but are indolent to take any steps to maintain any position of authority or power', he complained. Meanwhile Kamba opposition to government headmen was manifesting itself in 'a lack of public spirit in apprehending villains'.

Colonial Office mandarins earnestly minuted each other in an attempt to solve the conundrum of their generation. One official argued that switching to individual payment of taxes represented a departure from the first principles of indirect rule, carried out in the name of administrative convenience. Recognition of the individual as a unit independent of tribe or family was bound to break down parental or tribal control. But he also condemned the status quo most vehemently. Kenya's policy, he pronounced was 'one of expediency and improvisation … trial and error. I confess that I cannot see any conscious building for the future of 3,000,000 natives of Kenya and it is disturbing, having a regard to what Tanganyika territory is doing.'[15] Others were less worried, admitting that the situation left a good deal to be desired but content that it was 'probably as good as anything that can be devised with the resources available'. Assistant Under-Secretary of State Sir Cecil Bottomley's sympathy for DCs forced to spend time securing the last few halfpennies was unlikely to win him many friends. Kenya was indeed hampered by 'tribal constitutions that were not conducive to creating a link between the tribe and the European administration', he declared.[16] The situation appeared to be deteriorating further. Officials gloomily forecast that 'maintaining the authority of the older men' would be a problem since the warrior class, returning from work in a wider world, would be less willing to work for their fathers.

[13] Handing Over Report, Mullins to Windley, August 1935, p.2. RH Mss.Afr.s.760 (1).

[14] Native Affairs *Annual Report* 1933, ch.2. 'Political and General section', p.4, PRO CO5533/475/18.

[15] Garson, minute, 5 July 1935, ibid.

[16] Minutes dated 13 July 1935, ibid.

The significance of these discussions lies in this revelation of how the Colonial Office was beginning to comprehend that a new type of administration might be needed. Officials teetered on the brink of instigating a policy change. In a 'normal state of affairs', they agreed that they would not comment on or criticize the report, since local government was an internal matter. However, they now believed such non-interference could be 'taken too far'. Even sanitized annual reports that presented information already almost two years out of date were alerting the Colonial Office to the ways in which the dearth of revenue was producing 'a sketchy administration'. Also the shortage of resources had contrived 'a sort of underlying trend to bully the black man'. This was deemed to be something that might set back relations – a marvellous example of the bureaucratic euphemisms of the day – since reform of the native system would require officers to 'get in closer touch with the people' and strengthen 'native representation'.[17] London was now convinced that in future LNCs would have to receive a greater share of taxes for local investment; European opposition to such alterations in Kenya's revenue distribution would simply have to be circumvented.[18]

A third process unfolding simultaneously and having an impact upon the Colonial Office was the growing sophistication within administrative practice. Bureaucratic capabilities were continuing to expand at a smart pace. Partly the knock-on effect of running a modern war, technological advances in travel and communications were now being put to the use of government, its bureaucracy being paid out of the income generated from a large industry-based economy and tax base. The collection and dissemination of information increased in scope and speed. One immediate effect was to strengthen the hand of central government. The business of governing an empire was ripe to benefit from these changes and the Colonial Office made a concerted effort to run an empire state along metropolitan lines.[19] Although the first moves to consider problems of technical services in a general way had begun in 1909 with the creation of a Tropical Africa Medical and Sanitation Committee to advise the Secretary of State, followed by the Tropical Services Committee, the First World War then interrupted any further reorganization. The main wave of expansion in specialist services took place in the 1920s. In 1923 an advisory committee on Native Education was established for Africa. Between 1925 and 1930, advisers in agriculture, economics, finance and medicine were appointed for the whole empire. Leopold Amery (Secretary

[17] Ibid.

[18] Minutes, dated 3 March 1935, ibid. This policy has been criticized for systematically underdeveloping the African Reserves and creating a legacy of neglect; see Silberfein, 1989.

[19] This is based on a view of the four major dynamic influences in the development of modernity as being capitalism, industrialization, military power and – the most neglected one – administrative power: See Giddens, 1990, 20–22; Foucault, 1969.

of State for the Dominion and Colonial Office, 1924–9) had set up the Warren Fisher Committee to examine how the Colonial Office could become a more professional and efficient corps. Its report published in 1930 bore the signs of a new era in the institutional history of the Colonial Office. Measures were put in place to standardize head-office administration. Contact between the Colonial Office and colonial governments increased. Junior civil servants were required to serve for two years in a colony; the practice of appointing them to commissions of enquiry became more commonplace. More overseas travel was also expected of senior officials and specialist advisers. Similarly, more colonial civil servants were to be brought back home to work in the Colonial Office (Ashton and Stockwell, 1996: 'Introduction').

An important corollary of this reorganization was the way in which the centre was able to learn more about its constituent parts. Propelled by scientific and technological advance, knowledge gathering in London multiplied, producing a rash of surveys and enquiries, such as the extensive survey of nutrition carried out in the mid-1930s closely flanked by Lord Hailey's task of surveying all the African territories. Social mapping and scientific analysis thus yielded more information than ever before about the lives of the empire's indigenous subjects including women, as we shall see later. The creation of a new Social Services department at the Colonial Office was further proof of this push to produce a metropolitan-style empire state. A General Department had previously dealt with the subject, along with Defence, Aviation, and Communications. This move paralled the further professionalization of government in Britain which had widened the range of state activities in relation to looking after vulnerable citizens. The rise of the welfare state was well under way. Local government now incorporated much more variegated social welfare services.

A number of trends were converging at this point, greatly facilitated by the appointment of a new Secretary of State for the Colonies. Malcolm MacDonald held the post for a second time from May 1938 until May 1940. The son of Ramsay MacDonald, the first Labour Prime Minister, Malcolm was MP for Ross and Cromarty at the time but he had also cut his teeth on the London County Council. His description of the set-up he found when he first took on the post briefly in June 1935 suggested a man looking to update more than the decor, since he found 'a vast pompous Victorian style chamber where its occupant functioned as the Imperial overlord of more than 50 Colonial lands' (Sanger, 1995: 144). Unsurprisingly, he later condemned the Colonial Office administrative organization as unsatisfactory, particularly given 'the present importance of social services in the Colonies'. At his insistence, a new structure was to have responsibility for 'everything which is properly classed under the head of social services ... the improvement of labour conditions, nutrition, public health, education, housing and so forth'. Clearly MacDonald possessed a strong commitment to reform and had a personality that could inspire his staff to push for the same.[20] He had also worked with Lord Lugard as the British representative to the permanent Mandates Commission with regard to Palestine and Jewish immigration, and had developed a mistrust of the Colonial Office. However, he was also responding to events in the colonies. His first task in 1935 had been to deal with the labour riots in the West Indies, including sugar workers in St Kitts and Trinidad and coal-miners in St Lucia. These events played an important part in speeding up his moves to mop up the growing urban spillage of indirect rule, particularly since they had excited the interest of the Labour Party and trades unionists in Britain. He pushed through the appointment of a labour adviser at the same time as Lord Hailey was brought in to survey Africa and the enquiry into nutrition was begun.

These attempts to apply metropolitan standards of government to colonial bureaucratic practice were also attractive since they offered the potential for strengthening the Colonial Office's role in trusteeship. Setting standards for the modern management of social services in the colonies would necessitate a closer relationship. Hence civil servants were keen to put in a strong bid. It was 'a matter of the highest political importance', Sir Charles Jeffries (Under Secretary of State for the Colonies) announced to the Treasury, that the government should demonstrate 'unassailable justification for its claim that it acts as a beneficial trustee for its subject peoples'. And, as there was indisputably an urgent need 'for us to undertake an effective forward movement in developing the programme of social services':

> ... While the actual execution of developments in these matters must be carried out by the local staffs in the Colonies themselves, the initiative, inspiration and guidance must to a large extent be supplied from here, and the responsibility for seeing that these are properly done rests with the Secretary of State.[21]

The Treasury was convinced, at least for the time being, and agreed that a separate department was necessary 'in view of the greatly increased attention which seems likely to be given in the next few years to the social aspects of colonial administration', although it made clear that this would be subject to future developments and by no means permanent. Nevertheless, the often overlooked Colonial Office got its social service branch on April Fool's Day, 1939. Another new structure was in place to further the 'forward thinking'.[22]

[20] Sir Charles Jeffries (Asst. Under Secretary of State) to E. Hale (Treasury) 16 December 1938, requesting additional finance of £3,000 to cover the administrative costs of the new department, PRO CO822/33. It was followed up with a plea for an urgent reply on 1 January 1939: MacDonald was keenly interested and anxious to make early preparations, Tomlinson, Assistant Under-Secretary of State, to Sir James Rae, ibid.; see Porter and Stockwell, 1987: 16.

[21] Jeffries to Hale, p. 1, PRO CO822/33.

[22] Hale to Jeffries, 21 January 1939, ibid; Establishment Branch Notice no. 31, 7 March

Such a revolution in the art of colonial government unfortunately delivered a hollow victory. It enhanced in theory, but in practice it merely exposed the limits of central office power. By showing what needed to be done in the social services, the Colonial Office did win some ammunition in its battles with the Treasury and this would carry over into support for a large slice of taxpayers' money going toward colonial social services, as we shall see. However, the new empire state-building, founded as it was on the development of a closer relationship between the new professional branches at the Colonial Office and overseas administration, would have to overcome a number of obstacles if its goals were to be realized. Constitutionally, the colonial Secretary of State had powers of persuasion not command over colonial governments. This was a legacy of the principle of separate spheres which enshrined three long-established attitudes to empire. One was the nineteenth-century British Radical tradition of not allowing Parliament to be tainted by political practices that were considered anti-libertarian. A second was the principle of upholding the preparation of overseas territories for self-government. A third came from the accountants; colonies must not make claims on British taxpayers.

This preference for clear distinctions contrasted with the French attitude to its African Empire which was to solve the first two of these dilemmas by offering incorporation and the opportunity of becoming French. The Colonial Office thus found itself up against some of the unspoken rules of British colonial administration: defer to the man on the spot, and do not expect much in the way of resources so do only what is absolutely necessary. And, far from being eager for change and a modern-style government, many field administrators adhered to the view that native society was held together by customs that were best left alone. This was a position that sections of the left wing in British politics from the 1930s would now label as too conservative.[23] As we shall see as this story unfolds, efforts to establish a more metropolitan style of government faced numerous local obstacles. However, they did succeed in some areas. The empire state which developed as a result bequeathed an administrative structure which neither colonial nor subsequent African governments could afford and which endorsed the authoritarian tendencies of both.

Finally, a fourth trend working its way out in the 1930s and affecting Colonial Office attitudes to the provision of welfare, was the changing perceptions in Britain regarding the role of the state. The principle of non-interference in people's lives was losing ground in Britain, especially since

[22] (cont.) 1939, PRO CO822/33, J.E. Shuckburgh (Deputy Under Secretary of State) to Sir Cosmo Parkinson (Ag. Perm. USSC 1940–2 until he was seconded for special war duties in the colonies), 6 March 1939. Clauson was the first head of this branch but was succeeded by G.H. Creasy in November 1939.

[23] See Lee, 1967, ch.2 'The Structure of Empire', for a survey of the constitutional framework of operations, and ch.3. 'The Framework for Development', for a discussion of how this structure restricted the dynamism of the Colonial Office.

lives could be more easily measured and found wanting against average standards of living and Christian principles. After the right to vote was extended to all adult men and eventually all adult women, and in the wake of the carnage of the First World War, relations between government and people began to shift in more practical ways. The key area where this was played out was in relation to the role of state intervention in their lives. A conversion to state intervention amongst the official classes had its roots in the principle of a managed economy, established between 1931 and 1935 after the Gold Standard was abandoned.[24] Bureaucratic technology was now at the stage where the principle could be extended to the regulation of human beings before the point at which they needed remedial care and relief. By the 1930s, the lives of the poorer classes were well known to the social welfare professions and, since economic depression was endemic, were known not to be in great shape. Of concern was the degeneration in the towns and cities. With the speeding up of the drift of middle-class families into the suburbs and back to the rural areas, urban dwellers were poorer on average than they had been and more polarized. Anxiety grew that the practice of good citizenship and civic mindedness was floundering and that this would be detrimental to local government.

In the 1930s, various Royal Commissions of enquiry into local government were a precursor to the growing enthusiasm for more central planning and state provision so that people would have the means and incentives to participate as citizens. This was in the interests of the state. A work force that would put up with the demands of industrial production needed a domestic and social sphere that increased its incentives to work, and the state could supervise this. However, state intervention was also becoming the mantra of policy-makers within the Labour Party. Following the sting of defeat in 1931, intellectual socialism searched for a new set of formulas, particularly to deal with unemployment, and this, combined with concern to offer a bulwark against the threat of fascism in Europe, led many on the Left to embrace more state power as the progressive way forward (Riddell, 1995; Beach, 1998).

Another important section of society harbouring similar concerns consisted of various influential religious figures, who gave this debate a particular twist and added their weight to a growing consensus. Such contributions also helped English Protestantism maintain its loosening grip on keeping the middle class focused upon a particular project. Economic hardship was a great stimulant. A deep and penetrating agricultural depression in the last few decades of the nineteenth century – in part a result of the expanding trade links between Britain and the newly emerging large-scale wheat producers in North America, Argentina and Australia – had prompted the odd academic to find a solution to the social distress which accompanied rapid industrial growth and agricultural decline (Cain

[24] Ibid, p.44.

and Hopkins, 1993: 227–75). One of the most influential men reacting to these events was Thomas Hill Green, a philosopher and Oxford don. Green endeavoured to link his brand of Christianity to a practical formula for reducing poverty based on notions of citizenship. One of his most enduring legacies was to theorize a concept of progress and development based on a holy trinity of the community, the trade union and the voluntary association. Thus individuals, without coercion, could tame the negative tendencies of capitalism through collective and communal consciousness, and any divine intervention – in his secular world, the role of government – was only necessary to secure the conditions for these organizations to function. Indeed, the state was merely acting as the supreme community by promoting the habits of 'true citizenship'. So, although he venerated the role of civil society he acknowledged that without state control it could behave in very uncivil ways. Above all, he was able to offer a version of the state and a subject's relationship to it which was able to include the cherished notion of personal self-development.

Despite the typically inward focus of academia, T.H. Green's ideas made it to the outside world. His thought found practical expression thanks to the Oxford Settlement Movement which he inspired. This loose corpus encouraged young men of privilege to visit the back streets of large towns and cities – not an unusual event in itself, but this time the purpose was to live among the poor in order to help them find ways of becoming less poor by helping them create new social formations. Now it was possible to live the mission experience in your own city; there was no need to go overseas to find an escape from convention, some deserving poor people and a better prospect for salvation. Although Green died in 1882 at the age of 48, many generations of students had been touched by his thinking and were inspired to traverse, even for a short while, the barriers of class (Richter, 1964). Also he had bequeathed a social philosophy that seeped into many other institutions amenable to spreading the good news, from schools to churches and to life in the services. Green had helped to give Christian middle-class Britain a handbag philosophy for the new century: highly portable, it could be stuffed full of the basic cultural essentials of life. Not only had he helped provide strategies which encouraged and enabled the middle classes to adopt a more inclusive approach to their inferiors: they now had ways of making the lower classes more like them without altering their own institutions. He had enabled England to feel at ease with the scenario of more government.

Indeed, Green's thought provided an intellectual loop between arguments for the abolition of slavery and eventual disenchantment with racial rule among sections of the professional classes. Green endorsed the view that slaves had a right to citizenship because they shared a common human consciousness exemplified by the capacity of language and social relationships. His writings illustrate how the principle of the universality of human life was becoming more established. However, he also had to take great care to argue that a state was not justified in applying force to make its subjects live a better life since

> ... any direct enforcement of the outward conduct, which ought to flow from social interests ... does interfere with the spontaneous growth of those interests , and consequently checks the growth of the capacity which is the condition for the beneficial exercise of rights. (Green, 1941: 207)

This was the argument which he hoped would counter those in Britain who enshrined complete individual liberty as the best formula for social development. It would later have an impact on empire. By the 1940s African colonies still had state structures which were minimalist and relied upon indirect rule but they were trying more and more to mimic their metropolitan blueprint, obliged to keep the aim of universal standards of treatment of their subjects, if not citizens, in their sights. In the 1950s in Kenya, the state's recourse to the use of force, and the racial restrictions applied to native peoples, not only jarred with metropolitan standards and international laws, but could also be construed as blocking self-development, running counter to preparations for eventual independence and producing nasty abuses which undermined the conceit that, in comparison to 'Johnny foreigner', British rule was best. When by 1957 the argument that imperial possession provided economic advantage was stripped away, there was little left to rally the official mind.

Back in the late 1930s, then, Colonial Office officials were operating in an environment in which the relationship between the state and social welfare was blossoming. Again, leading religious figures had moved in step with the liberal left and centre in politics and made the partnership a close one. A generation that had escaped the trenches of the First World War focused their imaginations on combating unemployment and inequality. William Temple, who became Archbishop of York in 1929 and of Canterbury in 1942, did much to advance the consensus developing between social policy-makers and the more liberal wings of religious Britain. He wanted to make Britain more Christian, and so matched Anglican thought with a secular social programme. Temple popularized his ideas in *Christianity and the Social Order* published in 1942 which found a receptive audience (see also Kent, 1988: 24–9). In this book he laid out what a minimal Christian state ought to provide for its citizens; central to social regeneration was education. The onset of war had focused attention on planning for freedom; it made sentimental appeals to a British identity which included compassion and kindness more prevalent. Also a sense of urgency helped tease out more populist and compelling versions of past theory. Leading religious and social commentators spoke with one voice, pillorying poverty as the obstacle to family life and constructive citizenship, now billed as the crucial stalwarts in the fight against fascism. 'The meaning of rehabilitation', according to one observer, was that 'the individual must be set on his feet, enabled to function; and this can only be done as he becomes a member of a family and of society' (Lofthouse, 1944: 70. See also Lock, 1942; Mumford, 1943). Finally, there was Dunkirk with its accompanying fear of Nazi triumph, and the evacuation scandal that exposed urban squalor and the persistence of William Booth's late nineteenth-century 'submerged tenth'. Soon, all these trends would turn inward on the Colonial Office.

Highly significant for the attempt to create a new empire state, was the way in which the Second World War instigated an epic moment in the changing relations between state and society. In exchange for the demands made by war, an even closer intimacy between society and the state was offered to the working classes of Britain. As the war dragged on, the mood at home was increasingly one of planning for post-war social reconstruction and poverty alleviation. Winston Churchill told his War Cabinet in February 1943 that the approach to social security 'bringing the magic of averages' nearer to the masses was 'an essential part of any post-war scheme of national betterment'.[25] Such thinking was infectious. Consequently, metropolitan experiences and solutions would be re-applied to the empire in a much more systematic fashion. This would be particularly acute in the field of social welfare in the colonies, since the major component of the reward to the metropolitan home front was social welfare-orientated.

What were the main components of metropolitan social engineering on which the empire would draw? Best known at the time was the national insurance scheme of state benefits to individuals at their conjunctural times of need, which was largely a synthesis of a bundle of disjointed schemes already in existence before the war. The Report on the Social Insurance and Allied Services published in 1942, better known as the Beveridge Report, was an immediate best-seller. Beveridge was a good self-publicist and the government was keen to highlight its plans. Not all were in support. Conservatives privately remained sceptical, preferring not to have the state interfering and 'engineering' people's lives. They wanted taxation reduced and state involvement kept to a minimum (Jeffreys, 1987).

Yet the scheme was designed to be self-financing. It was based on a tentacular version of a centralizing state structure. Such sweeping intervention to increase universal welfare was radical in its application of entitlements that went beyond established levels. Yet it also enshrined conservative principles. The combination of both features ensured that the legislation went through and that it was dramatic. First, Beveridge reproduced a paternalism towards the poor that was patronizing and negative: the average working man was seen as pretty feeble.[26] Indeed, basic

[25] Note by Prime Minister, 15 February 1943. CHAR/23/11. Churchill Archives.

[26] *Report on the Social Insurance and Allied Services* (Beveridge Report), Cmnd. 6404 (London: HMSO 1942); Pinker, 1979: 21; Addison, 1982: 213. See also Mishra, 1989, who argues that social administration in Britain has always possessed a broad consensus and shared

characteristics of the poor, previously compiled by Edwardian female social philanthropists, were re-identified among the 'problem families' of wartime. Generic weakness included a mental horizon of about seven days, a view confined to the instant and the momentary. Prisoners to the need for immediate sensations, the poor were unable to be thrifty, loved gambling and preferred sugary substances to wholesome food. Such characteristics might also have been applied to Africans at the time.[27] Secondly, Beveridge placed women firmly back into the family. Motherhood and wifehood were the defining characteristics of being female, and welfare began with supporting women in the role of central linchpin to the family. This was a position that reflected the view of the majority at the time. However, efforts were made to curtail women's employment and educational opportunities to achieve this.[28]

Thirdly, the plan insisted on the principles of voluntary action and individual thrift. This went back to Samuel Smiles' masculine fundamentals of life:[29]

> The spirit of self-help is the root of all genuine growth in the individual... Help from without is often enfeebling in its effect, but help from within invariably invigorates. Whatever is done for men or classes, to a certain extent takes away the stimulus and necessity of doing for themselves; and where men are subjected to over-guidance and over-government, the inevitable tendency is to render them comparatively helpless ... the highest patriotism and philanthropy consist, not so much in altering laws and modifying institutions, as in helping and stimulating men to elevate and improve themselves by their own free and independent individual action.

For many settlers who had long been living in Kenya, this was part of the

26 (cont.) beliefs about the nature of 'social problems'; the 'nature of social welfare', its problems and resolutions 'were situated within a common-sense universe where everyone took for granted what was meant ... by poverty, homelessness or child neglect ...', p. 69.

27 McKibbin, 1990; ch.6 'Class and Poverty in Edwardian England', and ch.8 'The Social Psychology of the Unemployed in Inter-war Britain'. Mitzman (1985) would go further and argue that the suppression of popular culture is a basic feature of modern societies. Those in authority designate certain behaviour as immoral and use various means to discourage it, ranging from condemnation of witchcraft, homosexuality, masturbation and prostitution, although a major component of the 'civilizing offensive' has been 'efforts to reform what was viewed as the incurable licentiousness, vulgarity and lack of a work ethic of the lower classes'. For a discussion of popular myths about similar negative attributes among Kenyan Africans see Maugham-Brown, 1985, esp. ch.3 'Kenyan Colonial Settler Ideology'.

28 See Beveridge Report, pp. 53 and 135 for examples. At a national conference of representatives of leading women's organizations called by the government in 1943, the Minister for Health called for 'the speedy restoration of home life'; *Report of Proceedings, National Conference of Women called by H.M.G.*, London, 1943: p. 41; see also Wilson, 1977.

29 S. Smiles, 'Self Help', quoted in J. Stevenson, 'From Philanthropy to Fabianism', in Plimlott, 1984: 19.

staple diet of the English character. An interventionist state was its enemy, as it was for most Conservatives at home. Beveridge, the Labour Party and the new welfare state distanced white people in the empire from home. Yet, at the time, the architects of the welfare state did not want that structure to stifle initiative and responsibility but rather hoped that it would encourage voluntary action. Indeed, many social theorists of the day stressed the way in which the voluntary principle was linked with democracy and the exercise of civic responsibility. England's voluntary tradition, the experts insisted, differentiated it from continental Europe; it was a mechanism that would ensure that democracy survived the perils of totalitarianism.[30] Citizenship had become the new buzzword. It was easy to offer examples of this cherished principle in action which pulled the strings of national pride and sentiment, such as the sleepy village council, the bumbling parish committee or the invincible Women's Institute. National identity found a renaissance by enshrining rural England.

So towards the end of the 1930s, these four basic dynamics – a growth in international criticism, local disorder, expanding administrative capabilities and a greater role expected of the state in people's lives – were all having an effect upon the government of Empire. War procured a less than surprising but still dramatic climax when millions of pounds were pledged for welfare and social services in the colonies. Indeed, the Colonial Office had beaten metropolitan Britain to the political grand gesture. Centrally directed social welfare had long won over the hearts and minds of the Colonial Office; it became central to their new commitment to empire state-building.

The 1940 Colonial Development and Welfare Act

The imperial manifestation of the metropolitan welfare state era was, of course, the Colonial Development and Welfare Act of 1940. The synthesis of colonial and metropolitan social policy discussed above had reached its high water-mark. Without replicating the extensive scholarly literature on the subject, some aspects of this well-known event are relevant to this story and worthy of consideration.[31] Much of the credit for the Act belongs to Malcolm MacDonald: the right man, in the right place, at the right time but not for long enough. He had taken his seat as a Labour MP when the world Depression began to bite. Indeed, his maiden speech to the House

30 Beveridge Report, para.9, pp. 6–7. This was expounded by a number of writers in Bourdillion, 1945. A.F.C. Bourdillion, G.D.H. Cole and A.D. Lindsay linked the function of voluntary action with the protection of the basic elements of a democratic community, reflecting the dominant thinking of post-Webb Fabians at the time. See Wright, 1984.

31 It has has been described as 'the first systematic attempt to deal with general problems of growth in colonial territories'; Morgan, 1980: 2. Item 6A, PRO CO859/19/18. See also more generally, Ashton and Stockwell, 1996.

of Commons dealt with slum clearance and the neglect of the poorest working-class families. He delivered it alongside another new arrival, Megan Lloyd George, and other young newcomers included genuine working-class MPs such as Aneurin Bevan, the son of a Welsh coalminer, and Jenny Lee who came from a Scottish coalmining background. It was hardly astonishing, then, that, following the labour unrest that broke out in the West Indies in 1935, MacDonald would use his position as the new Secretary of State for the Colonies to look for social and economic solutions. The transition to macro state intervention colonial-style had really begun (Sanger, 1995: 61–206).

MacDonald's response was to set up an enquiry into the rioting, to bring in new advisers and to come up with a better version of the 1929 Development Act. Subsequently, the poor condition of Africa's native population was brought home by Lord Hailey's *African Survey* first published in 1938. He had provided officials with an expert's view of local conditions and proof that natives in Africa were held down by 'poverty, ignorance and tropical pestilence which is beyond their own capacity to alleviate'.[32] The big guns at the Colonial Office easily found consensus. Soon MacDonald and Hailey excitedly discussed ideas about how to mobilize technical development in the colonies. Hailey thought a fund would be 'a splendid move' and even suggested the territorial regrouping of colonies to facilitate development strategies, with individual technical departments being directed from one central colony. He wanted a new under-secretary who would visit the colonies and make contact with local organizations as a means of encouraging welfare projects. He urged that the work of the Indian Department of Commerce be applied to Africa, an indication of the unprecedented willingness to think big and to think comparatively. MacDonald was also thinking on lines of dramatic internal reorganization. He suggested that a mobile department be set up at the Colonial Office whereby a group of experts would visit one colony at a time and compile reports on development.[33] Elitist and paternalistic, they were both totally at ease in the role of a public spirited ruling class. They were happy to solve the problems of the masses whether at home or abroad, Hailey energized by the thought of bringing his Indian experience to Africa, MacDonald by trampling on the toes of past privilege.

However, they were also being influenced and encouraged to explore more radical approaches by a range of advisers and organizations. Professor W.M. Macmillan had written *Warning from the West Indies* and he, along with Margery Perham, an Oxford don, was brought in to advise the Colonial Office. Similarly, the Fabian Society, a progressive think-tank cum discussion circle which was growing in influence, was sharpening its

[32] Vincent Harlow to Sabine, 30 April 1943, PRO CO875/15/9/102/17 quoted in Smyth, 1985. For a discussion of the origins of the *Survey*, its ethos and relation to colonial development and welfare thinking, see Cell, 1989.

[33] Note of informal talk with Hailey (undated), Item 6A, PRO CO859/19/18.

ideas about how economic and administrative foundations should be laid in preparation for self-government in the distant future (see Porter, 1984). The Trades Union Congress had established a Colonial Advisory Committee in 1937 and was taking a special interest in the development of trades unions in the colonies as an important component of government policy. Meanwhile, the new Labour Adviser – the incongruous sounding Major Granville St John Orde Browne – had proposed the appointment of a development commissioner to oversee funds set aside for the West Indies' reparation programme. And since Colonial Office officials were arguing strongly for more control of colonial social and welfare policies, MacDonald was able to quash objections to a general fund for the whole empire on the grounds that it would represent 'the totalitarian efficiency from the centre at the expense of local liberties and individualism'.[34] With the Labour Party joining Churchill's coalition government in May 1940 and the inclusion of Labour Officers such as George Hall, a Welsh miner and now Under-Secretary of State for the Colonies, the pendulum swung further left and to the aid of MacDonald.

Lean, sinewy and with a set of sharp protruding upper teeth plus an 'eye for the ladies', MacDonald was willing and able to tough it out. Opposition from senior officials was hardly a shock to him. Sir Cosmo Parkinson, his Under Secretary of State, for example, was seventeen years his senior. The arrival of a fleet of new experts was bound to represent a threat to their own role. The answer was to make a few internal adjustments. Sir Cosmo was replaced by Sir George Gater who was known to have worked well with the Labour Party on social issues in the past, MacDonald having worked with him at the London County Council. He also brought in exceptionally able younger men, the most notable being Andrew Cohen, a move destined to make the 1940s a very dynamic period. Indeed, had the Colonial Office not been so stuffed with senior officials, the entry of a much younger cohort might have been delayed for another generation. All senior officials at the Colonial Office were now expected to make an overseas tour every ten years and, in a complete reversal of the rigid respect for seniority, discussions were to begin with comments from junior officials and then work up. MacDonald also went a few rounds with Kenya's white settlers which kept him on battle alert. Whilst the settlers were pressing for more control over the Legislative Council in 1938, thousands of Kamba people had trekked into Nairobi seeking an audience with the Governor. They were unhappy with the results of the Kenya Land Commission's report of 1934. The government had set in motion a destocking programme involving the culling of 100,000 of their cattle as an anti-soil erosion measure. MacDonald would not give settlers the assurance that majority rule would never come; nor

[34] Minute by Clauson, 11 August 1939, annotated by Sir Arthur Dawe who opposed the act, CO 825/250/10, quoted in Ashton and Stockwell, 1996, 'Introduction', Part 1, p. lxviii.

would he sanction the governor ignoring Kamba petitions. Rather, he used the occasion to suggest that they soon appoint African representatives to the LegCo. In 1944 this was duly carried out (Sanger, 1995: 149–54).

All this growing momentum of the late 1930s had to compete with the onset of the Second World War. The plans for a central fund had suffered a setback following the scramble to re-arm after the appeasement deal was struck between Neville Chamberlain and Adolf Hitler at Munich. Would they now be lost for good? It certainly made them less grand. Proposals for an £11 million fund were spliced in half. However, the war also brought with it a new sense of urgency and mission that revived flagging Colonial Office energies. The potential damage which disorder and bad publicity could create was now much greater. News had come through of a recent strike in Kenya. Officials feared that dissatisfaction would combine with living conditions rendered more unpalatable because of the War. A sense of betrayal over Abyssinia might be fuelled by enemy propaganda to alert 'the native to his comparatively low standard of life'.[35] The sight of British troops firing on unruly mobs would, as MacDonald pointed out, be a disastrous setback in the propaganda war. 'A growing consciousness' now existed amongst colonial peoples that 'the comparatively impecunious Colonial Governments have not been able to give them the standard of social services which are proper'. As we shall indeed see later, politicized Africans in Nairobi were quoting CO statements on their commitment to improving the social and economic conditions in the colonies. The economic demands of war could only exacerbate the situation and increase the capital to be made out of evidence of settler excesses at a time of rationing at home. So the Colonial Office attempted to put forward a new argument about the role of colonial government which tied it much closer to the task of addressing economic inequality. Officials now insisted that poor communities needed external help in order that they could then raise themselves out of their poverty:[36]

> On the strict merits of the case there is great need for the expenditure of more money on economic and social development in the colonies. These territories are mainly or wholly agricultural communities, they have not the wealth which accompanies the presence of secondary industries, and generally they cannot out of their own resources provide in any adequate degree the services which are now normally a part of civilized government...despite much constructive work during recent years, our medical, health, education and other social services are still not above what is really a low level.

That the situation for many native inhabitants in British colonies indeed stood below a very low level was hammered home at the beginning

[35] 'Colonial Development' Memo, paras 12 & 13, PRO CO859/19/18.

[36] Ibid., para. 10. See also Lee, 1977, p.70.

of the war thanks to some embarrassing evidence. Kenya was once again at the forefront of controversy, due to accusations of settler excess. Questions had been asked in the House of Commons about the amount of money spent on educating European children in Kenya in relation to the sums spent on African children. Critics were quick to come forward. Colonel Abbey wrote from Kenya of 'the outstanding inhumanity and selfishness of the settler community'.[37] He had just seen, he wrote, an orgy financed by the British Government 'whose anxiety to win the war had been taken advantage of by the settlers and business men in the Colony'. He painted a damning picture of African life in the Reserves. 'The condition of thousands of natives is worse than that of slaves of thirty-five years ago', he barked. 'Hospitals, medical services, more educational facilities, wells, water conservation, more land, fixed wages or trade unions, were all needed to enable the native to live better than a baboon.'

Convincing the Treasury that more British taxpayers' money had to be spent to deal with such situations was not going to be easy. The Colonial Office carefully put together what it regarded as an invincible case for setting up a fund. Cunningly, the announcement would be made on the day the enquiry into the West Indian riots was published. War had further clarified Colonial Office thinking and provided a new line of argument. First, if the colonies were to supply additional raw materials and manpower to the war effort, external investment was needed 'to maintain and extend certain services that ministered to the well-being and contentment of colonial populations which were currently inadequately developed'. Secondly, such a move would end British vulnerability to the Axis criticisms which were winning the propaganda war. 'The moral claim that we can make to be defenders of respect for the interests of small peoples against German intolerance of them', was being met with the German charge against Britain of mere hypocrisy on the part of a purely selfish imperialist power. Thirdly, 'colonial inadequacies' had unfortunately gone public.[38] The information gathering was now proving extremely valuable. The reports from the West Indian Royal Commission and also the Economic Advisory Committee on nutrition and Hailey's *African Survey* were held up as evidence of the problem. Heightened Colonial Office sensitivity to public opinion both at home and overseas resulted in the establishment of a public relations department at this time. This initiative was also fuelled by the perception, gathering force in the late 1930s, that official efforts were needed to counter the negative campaigning coming from outside organizations, the indifference to colonial issues shown in Parliament and

[37] Letter passed on to Secretary of State in January 1940, PRO CO533/522/15. This view reached the public domain living in war-time austerity, through the media sensationalism of the activities of the Happy Valley crowd brought to light during the trial of the Earl of Broughton for the murder of Lord Errol; Fox, 1982.

[38] Memorandum 'Colonial Development' enclosed in letter to Sir John Simon from MacDonald, 11October 1939, PRO CO859/19/18.

more generally popular ignorance about the British Empire aided and abetted by the national school syllabus (Smyth, 1985: 69; Ashton and Stockwell, 1996: Part I, xxviii–xxix, 1–10).

Although the onset of war had enabled the Treasury to reduce the initial amount requested, paradoxically, the war had also weakened the Treasury's position. The general demands of fighting a war in a democracy had reduced its power to say no. Popular broadcasters such as J.B. Priestley, using newspapers, magazines and the BBC, maintained the view that social improvement was an important war aim (Addison, 1982: Ch. 5; Hennessy, 1992). Cinema was also an important medium and official films were keen to support this position since it was valuable propaganda. Government films carefully presented images of a Britain and of being British that were underpinned by narratives of rejuvenation and reconstruction. During the war, the Ministry of Information (MOI) produced 624 films and the Colonial Film Unit 72. Issues such as poverty, housing and unemployment were surprisingly recurring themes woven into such films as *The New Britain* (1940), *Welfare of the Workers* (1940) and *Coalminer* (1940), the aim being to present a vision of a more egalitarian and kinder post-war era. To do this, film-makers had to use real people at work and for the first time clipped Oxbridge accents began to be replaced with regional accents or working-class voices. References to the pain of the Depression and the betrayal of 1918 were also used to draw attention to social issues in films such as *Wales, Green Mountain, Black Mountain* (1943); the images of Wales may have been stereotypical but it was a successful vehicle for the communication of the underlying message, that an economic agenda must and would dominate post-war reconstruction. The hypnotic lyricism of the script-writer, the poet Dylan Thomas, gave it added bite (Haggith, 1998):

> Remember the procession of the old-young men
> From dole to corner and back again,
> From the pinched, packed streets to the peak of the slag
> In the bite of the winters with shovel and bag,....

The Treasury did agree at first to a separate development fund for the colonies despite arguing that economic development was distinct from social service development: a country's welfare ought to be paid for by its own economic growth, following in the path of Western-styled modern development.[39] One Treasury official supported an advisory committee even if there were no fund, on the grounds that, although such committees were known to be a facade, they were useful facades, giving 'confidence in the Colonies and assisting with Parliament'. However, soon afterwards, the

[39] Note on Colonial Development and Welfare. Meeting between MacDonald, Sir Horace Wilson, Sir R. Wilson and Sir George Gater (Permanent Under-Secretary), 27 November 1939, PRO CO859/19/18. See also note to Sir C. Parkinson from C.G. Eastwood, 15 December 1939, ibid.

Treasury tried to drop the concept of welfare. Conceding that certain social services were necessary for 'the mise en valeur' of the colonies –

> H.M.G. has reached the conclusion that an additional effort must be made to develop the natural resources of the Colonial Empire, which are at present used inadequately and its industry, as well as take steps to improve the standards of life of its inhabitants to help to increase production … therefore for similar reasons health and education and other social services must be still further developed.

– Treasury officials feared that a welfare state approach would threaten the very core aim of British policy, which was to assist at least some of them towards self-government. Putting the colonies 'on the dole', they insisted, was anathema to this constitutional aim, since 'you cannot begin to have self-government unless you have financial responsibility ... a central fund ... did not provide the germ of constitutional government'.[40] The Colonial Office had an answer to this within easy reach. It thought the possibility of constitutional development too remote to justify such fears. Once again the officials reiterated the argument that imperial government needed to respond to changing conditions. Present grants-in-aid were designed only to help each colony achieve a minimum standard of administration, they opined, so a new grant system was needed to enable them to balance their budgets after 'an adequate standard' was achieved.[41]

The Treasury remained as unconvinced as the Colonial Office was unmoved. Self-belief and the moral high ground rallied the troops. MacDonald declared that he would make a statement on the basis that there would be a new welfare fund. Because these territories were poor now, this did not necessarily imply that they would always remain so, he insisted. United they stood; defiant they remained. Creasy, of the Social Service department, reiterated their aim of 'turning the African into a happier, healthier, and more prosperous individual, in which case all other subsidiary objects will automatically be obtained'.[42] Frank Stockdale, agricultural adviser, believed they had to protect the native from exploitation by big business; there was a danger that the new development and large-scale planning would cause the responsibility for African welfare to be handed over to companies and corporations. The Colonial Office, he believed, should have the same concern as Africans: that of increasing 'the margin in between the value of their produce and the taxes which have to be paid'.[43]

[40] Record of meeting with Hale (Treasury), 10 January 1940 and 6A C.O. draft Statement of Policy (undated), PRO CO859/19/18; minute by Hale, ibid. This issue is discussed in Chapter 2 in relation to Hailey's similar ambivalence towards the central provision of social services.

[41] Minutes of a discussion with Hale, 10 January 1940, PRO CO859/19/18.

[42] Minute by A. Creasy, 30 November 1940. Comments on Eastwood's Draft to Treasury. Letter from Creasy to Hale, 11 January 1940 summarizing their discussions with a restatement of the CO argument. Ibid.

[43] Minute from Sir Frank Stockdale, 4 December 1939, ibid. Former agricultural adviser to

Even Sir Cosmo Parkinson was exasperated with the Treasury's obstinacy. They must fight to keep welfare or social services in the act as a vital illustration of the new attitude that the colonies were 'to be provided with the services they ought to have and not only those which they can themselves afford', since the CO's credibility was at stake. The Treasury wanted to make as little of this as possible, he observed, but 'we want to make the most of it ... If we do not bring out a really satisfactory statement, the fault, as has happened before, will lie with the Treasury, but it is the Colonial Office which will be blamed in Parliament and the press, as has happened before, and will have to bear the odium.'[44] Finally, the Secretary of State was not for turning. 'My only comment', he told his advisers, 'is that if we are not now going to do something fairly good for the Colonial Empire, and something which helps them to get proper social services, we shall deserve to lose the colonies and it will only be a matter of time before we get what we deserve.'[45]

The Colonial Office, of course, won. It was a fight to stave off further diminution by the Foreign Office, always resentful of Colonial Office involvement in diplomatic issues. Also, the critical eye of the United States was beginning to penetrate the flimsy edifice of British trusteeship; with Lend-Lease imminent, American aversion to British imperialism would have to be softened. So, by the end of 1940, the Colonial Office could hold its head high and look any international organization in the eye, confident that it was learning from its enquiries and applying universally accepted standards of modern government. It had, on paper at least, a new commitment to improving the standard of living of those for whom it was the imperial trustee. A reconditioned philosophy of paternalist development represented a Colonial Office bid for importance and autonomy in a rapidly changing and critical diplomatic world. Colonial government would have to follow the principle that 'social reform in its widest sense was necessary for the political education of the people', and so doctors, health workers, sanitation inspectors, agricultural experts and social workers were all in theory being given a bigger part.[46] Many basked in a sense of achievement that the metropolitan rubric of good government now extended to the colonies. Hailey was as proud as punch. 'Our modern appreciation of the need for supplementing private initiative by state action', he observed, 'has been reinforced by the fuller recognition of the function of the state as an organization for promoting the economic welfare or safeguarding the standards of living of the population. That is a

43 (cont.) SSC, he became the first Comptroller of Development and Welfare in 1940 for the West Indies.

44 Minute by Parkinson, 12 January 1940, ibid.

45 Minute from MacDonald, 14 January 1940, ibid.

46 Lee, 1967: 4. The main political parties roughly shared this interpretation at the time. See 'Africa and the British Political Parties', *African Affairs,* 44 (176) (July 1945): 107–19 in which Lord Rennell (Liberal), A. Creech Jones (Labour) and Col.C.E. Ponsonby (Conservative) each gave a summary of their parties' colonial policy.

doctrine which has now been projected from domestic into colonial policy' (Hailey, 1943: 13; see also Simnett, 1942). MacDonald went on a public relations blitz under the banner of Britain helping the colonies. Britain was recognized by colonial peoples as 'the champion of the liberty of small peoples'; the newly established fund would allow the further spread of enlightened administration and freedom. And when he broadcast to the nation that 'Britain's Imperial genius is not spent; it is indeed at the zenith of its powers', he probably believed it.[47]

Would the hopes and dreams of the architects of the Act be realized? Malcolm MacDonald was moved on from the Colonial Office after two years in order to manage the air raid shelter programme. This may indeed have contributed to the slowing down in the pace of subsequent activities relating to the Act. Certainly a degree of passive resistance to the range of changes he had initiated was exhibited by some of the senior officials at the Colonial Office. But many others were avid supporters of the changes afoot. The establishment of a Colonial Economic Advisory Body in 1943 and a second approach to the Treasury for more funds for welfare and development were proof of the unease felt about the adequacy of the new arrangements and of the continued commitment to illustrating Britain's fitness to be an imperial power through state intervention (Ashton and Stockwell, 1996: Part I, lxxii–lxxvi and Part II, 174–219).

In any case, the political landscape altered in their favour in 1945. Labour came to power with a sweeping majority, in part the consequence of the longer process of maturing class politics and the ascendancy of the political philosophy of the Left combining with a great desire for a changed post-war settlement.[48] The prior groundwork at the Colonial Office would ensure that the arrival of the new Labour Secretary of State for the Colonies, Arthur Creech Jones – already an activist on colonial issues – meant less of a decisive break with tradition and rather more of a return to business as usual, quite a remarkable achievement considering the style and structure of the Office less than a decade before. It was the wider fall-out of the war upon an already teetering empire which would be the most significant constraint on the Act. There would simply have to be more money made available if the social projects were to be implemented. With the cost of the war escalating and the United States playing the role of hard-nosed moneylender to a hard-pressed Britain, the colonies were destined to pay more and receive less.

Yet a cruel irony which shot through the pinnacle of achievement

[47] 'Helping the Colonies', a broadcast talk by Malcolm MacDonald (undated). RH Mss. Perham. Box 705.1. Colonial Policy 23.

[48] For a review of MacDonald's two-year rule, see Pearce, 1984: 78–80. Although he tried to create a new generation at the highest level in the Colonial Office, he was not always clear in his own ideas, but by 1943 a revival in imperialism was under way and reform was about conserving imperial control. (p.80). The war was a drag on his efforts and the proposed land survey was abandoned (Addison, 1982).

within the empire state-building phase remained concealed. An animated Colonial Office, dazzled by Beveridge and worried by criticism, bequeathed a huge burden and further incoherence to the late colonial state. The war was to blame. It had placed a greater burden on the state, reflecting a sense of the enhanced capacity of bureaucracies to do things. Amery's emphasis on social services as the essential trappings of modern government, Hailey's local government cocktail of services and Beveridge's paternalist welfare state all celebrated a technically advanced and extensive state structure which was totally absent in colonies like Kenya. The Colonial Office rushed to apply this to the colonies, both as a measurement of the progress that critics of empire demanded and a vehicle for development itself. In so doing, officials lost sight of two important factors. First, Beveridge was working with a self-perpetuating source of finance, an established civil society and an eye on urban problems. Africa's endemic poverty was something different and required different remedies. Colonies like Kenya were also having to finance Britain's wartime debts in addition to relying on exporting only primary and not manufactured goods whose value in relation to primary products was steadily increasing. Although the prices for primary products sold on the world market increased markedly after the Second World War, this did not translate into any great increase in government revenue.

Table 1.1 Government revenue, 1939–49 (£)

1939	3,811,778
1940	4,811,412
1941	5,348,888
1942	5,595,025
1943	6,801,860
1944	7,734,333
1945	8,034,197
1946	9,057,390
1947	9,877,196
1948	11,411,664
1949	12,211,250

Source: Colonial Office Report, Kenya 1949 (Nairobi: HMSO, 1950)

With chronic balance of payments deficits, the colonies were restricted in their imports from dollar areas. Instead they had to build up reserves in London and were limited in their capacity to raise the level of expenditure in their own territories [49]

Secondly, Beveridge's grand design was to rescue the community from without in order to bolster the family within. His maternity, child and

[49] *Colonial Offfice Report, Kenya 1949* (HMSO, Nairobi, 1950); Michael Havinden and David Meredith, *Colonialism and Development: Britain and its Tropical Colonies, 1850–1960* (London, 1993) esp p. 275.

family allowance system was a financial pact made between the state and its mothers. The Colonial Office embraced the concept of macro-state intervention but missed the point that it was women in the domestic sphere who were being targeted to carry the burden of social welfare. A gendered, minimalist, rural strategy was more appropriate and remarkably they already had one – on file, where it remained.

Educating African women: the feminization of professional thought, 1925–40

Various constituencies within the Colonial Office had known since the 1920s that African women existed and that many of their professional experts regarded them as central to welfare and development. By 1940 they had forgotten they knew it. Not surprisingly, it was within the specialism of education that an abstraction of the African native as female first came to light. The African woman was to remain locked in the annals of the education department for over ten years. Education was one of the most established of the colonial professions. It was a highly mobile and easily transferable expertise, needing only a bible and a bicycle to get started. With missions, government and Africans all involved, the administrators of empire had had to move quickly to establish formal forms of association to oversee and direct efforts. There was an added impetus to develop official policy on education by the 1920s. The Permanent Mandates Commission was making noises about native education. And in 1923, the token woman on the Commission prepared a paper on the subject of the education and employment of women as indentured labourers in category B and C mandated territories (Miller, 1992: 156).

It was not therefore surprising that in 1923 an Advisory Committee on Native Education in Tropical Africa was set up. In 1925 it published a memorandum entitled *Education Policy in British Tropical Africa*, which contained specific recommendations about girls and women. In line with Colonial Office custom, colonies were urged to work out their own strategies for increasing educational opportunities for women and girls 'to soften the process of transition into modernity', and were told to treat the subject 'not as an isolated problem but an integrated part of this wider question'.[50] Paradox followed paradox. The transformatory potential expected of women – as both conservers and yet also modernizers – remained fundamental to Colonial Office thinking on African women for

[50] Extracts from Advisory Committee for Native Education in Tropical Africa: *Education Policy in British Tropical Africa*, Cmd. Parliamentary Paper No.2374, 1925, in SCWE 6/39 'Female Education in the Colonial Empire: Summary of Facts showing the Present Position', pp.3–5. See also more generally Ashton and Stockwell, 1996: Part II, ch.5 'Social Policies and Colonial Research'.

the next twenty years. It also remained marginal to actual practice. In rushing to adopt Beveridge, they lost sight of their own version of female-centred welfare. A commitment to pushing policies for women out into other structures and altering the state structure to this end also remained beyond their grasp. It set the pattern for most of the twentieth century.

In the 1920s, the men at the Colonial Office liked the idea of an educated African woman because of their views on African society. First, she would conserve tribal tradition. Even by 1925, experts predicted that African society faced the dangerous possibility of a breach between the generations; the fear was that old traditions were about to be lost forever because of the remoteness between elders and the young. Secondly – illustrating the almost impossible demands being set – educated African women were also to be the modernizers. This was in their role as wives. For as more men became educated, the memorandum stressed, so they should be able to marry 'educated mates', to ensure stable marital relations. Thirdly, some also had to become qualified women teachers giving instruction in hygiene, public health and care of the sick. Women trained in domestic and social hygiene were necessary if 'the high-rate of infant mortality and unhygienic conditions' were to be held in check.

African women were by no means the only women credited with such a range of skills and deficiencies. Rather, the views of the committee reflected established views among social welfare experts and educationalists in Britain, particularly their attitudes towards lower-class mothers. Towards the end of the nineteenth century, training in mothercraft had become fetishized by the state and voluntary organizations thanks to a coalition of anxious socialists, social imperialists, Fabians and eugenicists. A low opinion of the capabilities of mothers from poorer backgrounds was sustained up to the Second World War. In the 1930s, women were regularly criticized for their lack of concern with public issues and for being promiscuous and selfish. Women themselves did much of this criticizing. In 1939, the Hygiene Committee of the Women's Group on Public Welfare insisted that the drop in infant mortality was not due to girls having learnt cleanliness in the elementary schools, but rather to the effects of better ventilation, clothing and food. Indeed, 'the problem of teaching the principles of decent living to the future mothers of the race remained to be solved' (Davin, 1978; Holtby, 1934: 112; Hygiene Committee of Women's Group on Public Welfare, 1943: 3).

Within the Colonial Office of the 1920s, it was mostly men who addressed the subject of women's education and thus they tended to err on the side of caution. The only practical guidelines which the experts offered was a system of itinerant teachers who could visit schools, bringing new ideas and inspiration to local teachers. This was an elliptical reference to the Jeanes teacher system, adopted in Kenya in 1924 (see Chapters 3 and 4). It was a formula which grew out of white philanthropy towards black Americans – often referred to by whites at the time as negroes – in the rural southern part of the United States. In 1907, Miss Anne T. Jeanes, a Quaker from Philadelphia, had donated $1 million so that blacks could be educated in their rural schools according to their local needs. The cause was helped along by the Phelps-Stokes Fund. After the interruption of the First World War, American missions turned their attention to Africa. A joint American mission task force visited the continent in 1919, herded along by an outspoken Welshman, Dr Thomas Jesse Jones, who pushed the line that practical skills were more suitable to the needs of the American negro, a view increasingly disparaged by a new political force – educated black Americans and the Pan-Africanist movement – whose leading light was W.E.B. Dubois. In Africa, American missions faced less opposition and rather more in the way of support. The Secretary of the International Missionary Council, J.C. Oldham, was a convert to the Jeanes principle to such an extent that, by 1924, Kenya had a Jeanes School and money towards the salaries of six European teachers, paid for by the American Carnegie Corporation. African teachers would be trained in what was called rural uplift and then be expected to return to their villages to pass on what they had learnt to teachers, pupils and adults, moving from school to school (Sinnoven, 1995: 52–9; Lemielle and Kelley, 1994).

With the Jeanes experiment still in its infancy in East Africa and since it had as yet suggested no great emphasis on women, Colonial Office experts were left to grapple as best they could with the apparent 'delicacy and difficulties' involved in women's education. This was partly because it dealt with the realm of 'personal and domestic hygiene' which for officials was an awkward and quite possibly mysterious subject. Thus the 1925 memorandum concluded – using the language of eugenics – that only those with intimate knowledge of each colony's needs and the differences 'in breed and in tribal tradition' and aware of the social implications of education could judge what it was wise to attempt. The experts were scared of causing disruption. The great problem, they mused, was how to impart 'any kind of education which has not a disintegrative and unsettling effect', a fear perhaps magnified in this case because they feared their suggestions would be opposed by African men. In view of the pervasive chauvinism of the times, officials could not really have gone much further at this point, knowing so little about local conditions, African women and probably about women in general. At the time, the female of the species as a generic category was held to be intellectually inferior, emotionally immature and morally weak in relation to men. Attitudes to women had improved in many ways. A hundred years before, for example, women were publicly blamed for the number of black men living in England because of 'the strange partiality shewn for them by the lower orders of women ... they would connect themselves with horses and asses, if the laws permitted them' (Shyllon, 1977: 104; see also Harrison, 1984).[51] And

[51] Anti-suffragette arguments were based on the contrast between the sexes: women were less creative and lacked powers of logic and common sense, having instead an instability of

it was also the case that, on an individual or familial level, an important component of masculine behaviour was utter devotion to 'the fairer sex'. However, in the mid-1920s not all women in Britain were yet allowed to vote, whilst working-class women continued to be refracted through a masculine ideology of female inferiority that was more reductive, marginalizing and enduring than that applied to middle-class women.

Not surprisingly then, it was ten years before educational experts at the Colonial Office again found reason to consider the education of women. Typically, this cause was subordinated to a range of other needs; at this juncture, women were a means to meeting the needs of the community. A second Advisory Committee memorandum entitled *Education of African Communities* was published by the Colonial Office in 1935. It differed from its 1925 predecessor in some respects. Gone was the universal tribe or the amorphous native. The experts now referred to 'African communities' which had to be 'advanced', 'reformed' and 'educated'. This reflected metropolitan thought at the time. The need to resuscitate and support community life was a popular theme both within British social welfare circles and among experts working for the Mandates Commission at the League of Nations. Educationalists were generally much happier with the idea that adults could be educated as well as the young, and women as well as men, in the interest of what was termed 'rural betterment'. One crucial area of difference was the attention to the state in the 1935 report. The aim appeared to be more focused on the need to educate handmaidens of the state. For the hope was that 'agents' would be unleashed upon societies that were 'undergoing rapid change', who would be able to give instruction in farming, marketing of crops, health, hygiene and sanitation, thus rendering more permanent the work of the various departments. Radio and cinema could help in this, installed in village schools which functioned as centres of local betterment. It was here that women were inserted, as in the 1925 report, as means to a specific social outcome. 'The man alone can do little to teach the community as a whole without effective help from a married woman ... his work will always be crippled if his wife is entirely uneducated.'[52]

However, a degree of hesitation ran through the 1935 memorandum, a typical feature of Colonial Office reports in general at the time. Save for recommendations that women missionaries be incorporated into education

[51] (cont.) opinion and an excess of emotion. Some men saw this as positive; women lived in a separate moral sphere based on sympathy, emotion and understanding which gave them a greater influence than the franchise would ever allow (Harrison, 1984: 55–90). See also Smith (1987) for the argument that misogyny forms a concealed element in British culture, due to the social construction of gender needed to sustain masculine domination; see also Hoch (1979), ch.4. 'Masculinity as a Defence against Impotence'.

[52] *Memorandum on the Education of African Communities* (Colonial Parliamentary Paper No. 103, 1935); extracts contained in SCWE 6/39 'Female Education in the Colonial Empire: Summary of Facts showing the present position', PRO CO859/1/9.

councils and that new authorities be established, the report was thin on the specific ways in which women might be brought into community betterment. Far more collaboration between government departments was needed, the experts concurred, but the committee declared this to be beyond the scope of their enquiry, thus ensuring that the conundrum remained unsolved. Unfortunately, and no fault of the committee, a crucial piece of information was just about to break out of the margins and reach London. The Jeanes teacher system, in operation in Kenya now for a decade and constantly lauded by experts in London, had pushed the flimsy structure of collaboration between missions and government to breaking point. Indeed, closer examination of the Jeanes system revealed it to be failing miserably. Ironically, T.G. Benson, the Principal of the Jeanes School, was called to speak before the Education Advisory Committee, just as the report on community and education in Africa was being published. They heard that the one-year course for agricultural instructors had come to an end and that the two-year course in public health had been suspended. One in five of the teachers never returned to their districts, drifting instead into other jobs. Only 800 out of the 3,000 village schools were in touch with a Jeanes School teacher, who usually had no resources to carry out the work. Meanwhile, the missions found the teachers too secular and blamed them for a decline in spiritual growth. So, in the face of declining mission funds, the School shifted its focus towards the chiefs and elementary teacher training for government posts.[53]

The Colonial Office remained convinced that the Jeanes ideals, particularly in the realm of social services, were 'one of the most effective ways of educating the community'. A recent conference in Salisbury had reiterated what community development aimed to achieve: the pursuit of greater co-operation within villages, between communities and among specialist technical staff; the growth of cultural activities, sports, competitions and libraries; the promotion of co-operative marketing and savings guilds; and the organization of classes for women.[54] The Colonial Office was never more set on this path of development. How tragic, then, that the obstacles to this approach slipped from their view. Key issues were lost sight of, issues that would resurface in Kenya again and again unresolved. For this modest experiment was highly relevant: it exposed the lines of resistance to restructuring state–society relations so as to achieve their concept of rural betterment. Neither side was always playing the game, it seemed. The state lacked the resources and the will to make all its constituent parts co-operate. African society, on the other hand, had a range of agendas, not necessarily involving village development. Few educationalists in London could appreciate that young people often submitted to the discipline of the schoolroom because they wanted

53 Summary note of Jeanes School, 13 March 1935 by H.G. Hibbert; Minutes of 64th Meeting of the EAC, 19 December 1935. PRO CO533/461/19

54 Ibid.

modernization for themselves, hoping it would take them outside the restrictions of homestead, beyond the predictability of village life, and in the direction of the liberating, money-making town or city. The failure to develop a transformatory project that met the needs of the diversity of within African society would become more and more of a constraint upon official efforts after the Second World War came to an end.

Another problem set to resurface again and again was the lack of consensus between the experts and those on the ground. This is amply revealed by the testimony of one teacher trainer at the Jeanes School in the 1930s. Selwood Walford had a less state and community-orientated view of the transformatory role that Jeanes teachers could play. He claimed that at the time they were trying to discover

> ...acceptable ways and means to overcome basic poverty, and ill-health especially of the infants and mothers and to make the best use of what was available in the form of timber for building and furniture, clay for bricks and the land for produce to eat and sell, and to maintain soil fertility without frequently shifting to a new place. This kind of education was not always welcome by those who thought that the purpose of the school was to qualify the pupil for a white collar job.[55]

This is not to say that there was no heroism on the ground regarding the Jeanes School. The level of collaboration in such marginal activities was remarkable, and the achievements made with few resources ran little short of trapeze-like artistry. A typical school in rural Kenya was a simple oblong building made of mud and wattle. Logs were used as chairs. There might be one blackboard shared by four classes held in each corner of the room. Often reading material would be parts of the bible. Even the Jeanes School outside of Nairobi had no electricity or water and just one wood-fired stove. It seemed that the Selwood Walford approach found more converts when local elites were trained, perhaps because they had less need of an education for the purposes of achieving upward mobility. Also, by this time, discussion was encouraged in order to work out a curriculum that could help to produce 'better Africans rather than imitation Westerners'.[56]

Chief Jeremiah Segere from Kakamega went on the first chiefs' course in 1937 and was considered to be a model teacher. He worked out his own strategy, taking the best pupils from each school for training. He had to move slowly. Offence was easily caused by using African games and songs; the missions and government did not see eye to eye and different denominations did not mix easily. At Musingu, a demonstration unit for better living was set up. Here, for example, 'women were shown better methods of cooking; how to bath babies; how to keep cleaner homes ... then people could want to excel in having better homes, better cattle, etc'. Chief Jeremiah also found local support for his version of a scout

[55] A. Selwood Walford, Jeanes School Teacher, p. 3. RH Mss.Afr.s.1702.

[56] Ibid, p. 9.

movement. *Vagesi* were the boys who wore strips of Collobus monkey skin on their wrists and knees and had made a pledge to be kind and courteous at all times. All but the Catholics joined in.[57]

A phenomenon which the Jeanes teachers were helping to speed up by the mid-1930s was an increase in the number of girls attending school. Selwood Walford noticed this and suggested that the way in which the wives of Jeanes School teachers were being educated by the 1930s was making a difference. Chief Jeremiah's testimony provides further illustration of the tailoring of such education for a female constituency. Likewise, more missions began to offer rudimentary education for girls from the mid-1930s. The missions had been requested by men to provide them with educated mates. The problem was that, while the young men were at school, wives were secured for them and initiated so that the men were expected to be responsible for them. They wanted to buy time and according to the missionaries wanted to marry women who had knowledge of hygiene.[58] Increased attendance at school was quite an accomplishment. Previously mothers had been told that women could not learn to read. Girls were needed at home to help with chores much more than boys. Menstruation was also a constraint. Sensibly in view of their immediate prospects, many girls were keen to become initiated as soon as possible so that they could start setting up their own homes. This also constrained potential attendance. Yet the growth in the numbers of girls attending school was barely noticed in the 1930s. Indeed, with the intervention of the war, it would be a decade before this enthusiasm was officially recognized.

It was not just a cruel accident of fate that the Jeanes School's institutional history came too late for consideration in the 1935 memorandum on education for the community. It was always the case that centre-periphery dialogue slowed down when any kind of bad news was afoot. Even in the event of different timing, bureaucratic practice at the time was such that no kind of written report could present unsolved issues or problematics that required exploration. Instead, reports had to bristle with bold, strong, onward-Christian-soldiers-type recommendations, particularly since the Colonial Office used reports as a device to shore up its authority.

However, all was not lost by the late 1930s. Education was no longer the only expertise which tackled adult education and wanted women to pull the cart of social transformation, progress and tradition. As a consequence of the advances in scientific capabilities and bureaucratic management being applied in Britain by the 1930s, the Colonial Office was willing and able to make use of a much wider range of experts. Making reports and assessments was a central component of the empire state-building thrust examined earlier. One very active body was the Economic Advisory Council. Concerned to increase the productivity of labour and thus

[57] 'How I became a Jeanes Teacher' by Senior Chief Jeremiah Segere of Isukha, Kakamega. RH.Mss.Afr.s.1367(1).

[58] E. Mary Holding, 'The Education of Bantu Tribes', p. 49. RH.Mss.Afr.117.A580.

colonial revenues, information was needed about the lives of Africans so that planning and state intervention could proceed. As part of this ongoing quest, the council instigated a study of nutrition in the empire which was begun in 1936. Studies in nutrition had been pioneered by the Permanent Mandates Commission of the League of Nations as part of its effort to assess the development of the territories for self-government. It now made sense to assess the capacity of labour in the colonies by working out if dietary requirements were being met. Such thinking reflected the general optimism about the transformatory potential of metropolitan technology, its institutions and its scientific lore. Investigating nutrition, of course, meant that metropolitan experts found themselves having to pay closer attention to women.

The final report on nutrition published in 1939 included a number of tactics that linked the necessary improvements in health to state-sponsored policies designed for African women.[59] Indeed, the general recommendations included a more specifically gendered approach than ever before. First, better levels of education in agriculture, health and domestic science were needed overall, but the report stressed that girls had to be better educated, and so more women teachers were needed. This training in domestic science and health work ought to be organized by British experts. Secondly, the report wanted an adult welfare propaganda campaign to be set up. All components of this were made gender-sensitive. The radio, cinema and 'the magic lantern of the gramophone' were billed as also being valuable in the teaching of domestic science to women. Better departmental cooperation would result in demonstration sites being set up. Childcare instruction could be given at infant welfare centres, it was pointed out. And last, but by no means least, came the suggestion that officials set up a colonial version of a very British institution:

> a sort of women's club, meeting periodically partly for recreational purposes and partly for talks and demonstrations on such things as infant welfare and domestic science ... We suggest also that Colonial Governments should do their best to interest prominent local residents and, perhaps particularly, the wives of officials in local welfare work, especially among women. The wives of civil servants have often that rare commodity, leisure, at their disposal and they can do much to assist local populations.[60]

A clue to what else had helped orientate the Colonial Office in the direction of nutrition and women, lies in the report's reference to attempts in Palestine to train teachers in what were called environmental subjects. Two colleges – one urban and the other rural-orientated – had apparently

[59] *Nutrition in the Colonial Empire* (Cmd. 6050, 1939).

[60] Ibid, p. 7. J.A. Mangan argues (1990: 7) that many contributed to the maintenance of Empire by directing domestic orientated welfare policies, constituting an elite cadre of unofficial social workers 'which had won the good will of the subject races'.

made little progress in such training or with regard to the employment of women teachers. Palestine was one of the mandated territories established by the Treaty of Versailles. In the inter-war period concerns about the living standards and treatment of women in mandated territories received much more attention, particularly due to the efforts of women members who pressed for the provision of information and discussion of issues such as infant mortality, protection during child-birth and the traffic in women and children. Also more women representatives of non-governmental organizations travelled to Geneva to put their case to the various committees, to the extent that the women's international organizations and the League transformed each other during this period (Miller, 1992: esp. 134–6). This feminization of international concern regarding the mandates in particular began to waft through the corridors of the Colonial Office. New types of information were being collected and new procedures and standards of practice being set. In 1931, for example, a conference was held in Geneva on the subject of the African Child. The inquiries into nutrition firmly established the practice of sending out questionnaires to the governments of mandated territories. Whilst the Colonial Office was gently swayed by the new international standards in good parenting, it was also being prodded at home.

The existence of a League of Nations forum in which social issues and women's rights were being pushed forward, stimulated and shaped activism amongst sections of elite women in Britain. Liberally educated upper-middle-class women began to enjoy the thrill of taking up worthy and controversial political issues. Many joined the increasingly trendy socialist movements that were a welcome and rebellious alternative to the conservative chambers of debate which had tried to silence them (see Bush, 1997). The running of the empire was always a gift topic for the political Left in Britain in general and for feminists in particular. Not everyone was hung up about the empire, of course. Likewise, not all politically active feminists were interested in the welfare of native women and children. Even those who were interested in Africa after the First World War were more often captivated by race relations; Margery Perham and Winifred Holtby adopted various African causes following visits to South Africa.

However, a minority of women in the inter-war period did maintain a focus on the condition of native women under colonial rule. International organizations had been able to work with the League to include gender-specific issues relating to the mandated territories. This helped political and humanitarian activists in Britain to develop their specific complaints relating to the empire. They also learnt to be more outspoken and better organized in their lobbying tactics. A few began to criticize the government for not outlawing behaviour towards African women which in Britain would be illegal, another illustration of the universalizing tendencies unfolding. Forced marriage, bride-price, husbands beating their wives and polygamy were highlighted to expose government mendacity.[61] In 1936 Eleanor Rathbone – one of the few women MPs at the time and a regular at the League of Nations – asked the Secretary of State 'what action was being taken by colonial governments to prevent the forced marriage of African girls', following a letter on the subject from Kenya's Archdeacon Owen in the *Manchester Guardian.* Remarkably, two years later the Colonial Office found itself publishing an official document containing a mixture of unofficial and official action on the subject, in order to answer the criticism.[62]

This document illustrates the decline in the Colonial Office's exclusive control over expert opinion on colonial issues in Britain in the inter-war period. In November 1935, the British Commonwealth League had convened a conference on 'Marriage and Slavery', in response to Owen's accusations and the local Kavirondo council's call for the registration of marriages. Owen later praised the British Commonwealth League, and especially the efforts of Winifred Holtby before her untimely death in 1935, for their vigilance on this issue.[63] Kenya's leading anthropologist, Dr Louis Leakey, was present at the conference where he spoke in defence of native marriage. The Kavirondo LNC was, he insisted, dominated by 'a small detribalized, mission community', which, if allowed to impart its ideas, would be 'a burden of misery on the great mass of their own tribe'. He presented four points, appealing to a notion of cultural particularism. Each tribe had its own customs relating to sex, marriage and the position of women. What the women of one country regarded as ideal was not necessarily ideal for women of another country. Missionaries were primarily concerned with Natives who had broken away from tribal law and customs, and who were only a small percentage highly differentiated from the mass in Kenya. Finally – perhaps his most persuasive point as far as his audience was concerned – he doubted whether English matrimonial laws really made for equality and happiness in marriage.[64]

However, a retired academic put a different case. Professor Macmillan, formerly of Witwaterstrand University, South Africa, argued that they

[61] For an account of the controversy surrounding an earlier feminist discourse centred upon the 'liberation' of African women, at the Africa Inland Mission, Kijabe, Kenya, in the 1920s, see David Anderson, 'Maidens, Missions and Morality: The Kikuyu Female Circumcision Crisis', paper given at the East African Seminar Series, African Studies Centre, Cambridge University, 11 January 1992.

[62] *Correspondence relating to the Welfare of Women in Tropical Africa 1935–37* (Cmd. 5784, 1938); see Lonsdale, 1963.

[63] Letter to *The Manchester Guardian*, 16 June 1936; *Correspondence relating to the Welfare of Women*, pp. 6–8.

[64] Extract from *East Africa*, 14 November 1935, 'Happiness or Slavery? The Status of African Women', reprinted in *Correspondence Relating to the Welfare of Women in Tropical Africa*, pp. 1–6. For a discussion of *sati* and the Indian Social Reform Movement in nineteenth-century England as an illustration of how the Empire provided 'both a physical and an ideological space in which the different meanings of femininity could be explored or contested', see Ware, 1992, Part Three 'Britannia's Other Daughters'.

were neglecting the more pressing issue of the health of Africa's women: the prime cause of Africa's backwardness was the health problem. The Kikuyu had a bad habit of making 'beasts of burden of their women'. Indeed, he could vouch for the case of a woman who weighed only 90 lb. carrying a load of 120 lb. Speaking against this view was Johnston Kenyatta, then a student at the London School of Economics. During this time, he was moving toward closer political affiliation with the black nationalist cause, mingling with anti-imperialist activists through such organizations as the League of Coloured Peoples. The token black man on the panel spoke up for his sex. Women were burdened because of 'civilization', he argued, not 'tribal custom'. 'What the African needs is economic emancipation ... help us in the bigger things of life and the smaller social questions will solve themselves.' Even if these discussions did not produce a consensus, let alone a solution, they represented a departure in Colonial Office practice, since they showed an engagement with public opinion and an admission that the treatment of African women was an issue for government. However, they had to run to keep up with events.

Throughout the 1930s, these awkward questions from the hotchpotch of humanitarian and feminist activists were matched by a growing feminization within the higher levels of the health professions. The Colonial Office had come under increasing pressure from a number of women's organizations to consider women for administrative posts not so much on grounds of equal opportunity, but primarily for the interests affecting women in the colonies. Again, the League had established new precedents regarding the principle of equal employment opportunities for women where it was conceded that women possessed a sphere of expertise concerning issues affecting women and children. The irrepressible Eleanor Rathbone took a deputation of women into the inner sanctum of the Colonial Office in 1932. She argued that women advisers in the administration could improve general policy because they would consider women's and children's welfare from the women's point of view; they had lost out in improving the lot of women and children in India, and it would be a tragedy if the same thing were to happen for Africa. Officials remained adamant that the remoteness of the work among backward peoples made this impracticable; conditions in tropical countries were such that women could not be armed with 'executive and judicial functions'.[65] However, in the caring professions, they had to concede entry to more and more qualified women.

As a result, pressure on the Colonial Office to consider women's welfare was coming from new sources of insider expertise. For example, in 1936, a Dr Mary Blacklock wrote damningly on the 'Welfare of Women and Children in the Colonies'. She alleged that there had been a serious neglect of educational and medical aspects of women's welfare, 'in the

[65] Calloway, 1987; ch. 6 'Women as Colonial Administrators', PRO CO 850/14/2. Calloway PRO CO850/131/14/20508.

interest of corresponding services for men'.[66] This was a sufficient jolt to produce a response. The Colonial Office duly dispatched Blacklock's article to all departments in January 1937. They also sent out recommendations coming out of the Health and Education Advisory Committees calling for an increase both in the employment of women health workers in the colonies and in women's general education so that more would be capable of undertaking such work. The despatch stressed that the education of women was as important as that of men; governments were asked to equalize their expenditure on educational services between the sexes and to report on the development of women's education in their territories.[67] It was far more acceptable to officials to offer women more opportunities as teachers and health workers than to offer equal opportunities in the really powerful jobs such as administrators.

Moreover, there was a steady drip of evidence coming from the field that the practical benefits from employing women would help the ruling mission to bring betterment. Officials who had read the recent Annual Reports from Kenya on Native Affairs learned that certain departments acknowledged the female factor in educating other women and in securing long-term social progress. For example, in 1936 the Director of Medical Services had marvelled at the improvements female staff could make in child and maternity welfare.[68] The Education Department's conclusion in 1937 was that no real betterment could be achieved without improvements in women's education, for improvements in home life and standards of living, the basic ingredients for social advance, fell 'within the province of the women'. The Colonial Office was convinced. A circular was sent out giving details of domestic science teacher training in England and its relevance to colonial work. The author, Dr Philippa Esdaile, included a questionnaire – the League's favoured type of communiqué – about educational and training provisions for African girls. The replies revealed a pitiful situation. Kenya, by no means the worst, had 12 per cent of its girls of junior school age in school but not one girls' secondary school.[69]

It was in the intense atmosphere of 1939, with these recent damning reports in mind, that the Advisory Committee on Education decided to set up a special sub-committee with the purpose of reporting on 'the means of accelerating social progress in the Colonial Empire by increased education of women and girls and by welfare work among them'. Immediately their

[66] Blacklock, 1936, also quoted in 'Summary of Facts' SCWE6/39, CO859/1/9.

[67] 'Female Education in the Colonial Empire', p.1, contained in SCWE 6/39, PRO CO859/1/9.

[68] Extract from *Native Affairs, Annual Report, 1936*, p.85, PRO CO533/479/9; *Native Affairs, Annual Report, 1937*, p. 74, PRO CO533/491/5.

[69] EAC Memo despatched to colonies in April 1937 'Teaching of Domestic Science in England and its Application to work in the Colonies', PRO CO859/1/9. Gambia had 3% of its girls in school, Nigeria 5%, whilst Uganda had an impressive 33%. Statistics relating to the provision of domestic science and general education of African girls in African Colonies; SCWE 11/39 (undated), ibid.

focus fixed on Africa. At the first meeting the sub-committee adopted the suggestion that they concentrate on the backwardness of female education in Africa. Members was immediately showered with reports on education written or collected by women during the previous years. Membership was drawn from across the imperial ruling structure, and included the head of Social Services, representatives from the medical department, leading missionary figures and literacy campaigners and Margery Perham, the CO's senior University Aunt.[70] They learned that the subject had been tackled by an earlier sub-committee of the Education Advisory Committee but, 'for reasons which were not altogether clear', the whole subject was dropped after an interim report to the main Committee. By March 1940 they decided to re-group with the aim of producing a report that would seize the opportunity now created by the Welfare Act for at last securing some funds.[71]

It all boded extremely well. Established thought was within easy reach of the sub-committee. Indeed, the final report contained extensive quotations from the 1925 and 1935 policy statements, especially on community education as a precondition for social advance. So to a degree the committee members were simply jumping through the same hoops as their predecessors.[72] However, this time the focus was tighter and a clearer consensus shone through. Everyone agreed that Africa – a society in transition – was being pushed and pulled by the forces of modernity, which could be stabilized by educated African women working to maintain improved communities. African women were now firmly placed at the centre of society, with the affirmation that 'the two great tasks of rearing children and maintaining food production fall mainly upon them. In some areas they own and farm land and are the traders.' So, a new urgency was woven into their inherited narrative, as women's education was deemed to be of greater importance than that of men. Under modern conditions,

[70] Item 8, Minutes of the 97th Meeting of the Advisory Committee on Education (EAC) in the Colonies, 21 September 1939, PRO CO859/1/9. The members were to be Clauson (Head of Social Services) as Chairman, Keith and Mayhew (CO officials), Rev. J.W.C. Dougall (former headmaster of Jeanes School, Kenya), Bishop Myers or Father O'Callaghan (missionary educationalists), Miss Oakden, Miss Perham, Hans Vischer, and Miss Wright, Secretary from the Social Services Dept; Sir Edward Stubbs was to be invited to join later. The sub-committee was authorized to co-opt anyone they wished. Representatives of the Medical and Agricultural Advisory Committees were to be invited to help construct the Report.

[71] Minutes of first meeting, 17 November 1939, PRO CO/859/1/9.

[72] These included an article by Margaret Wrong written for the 1940 *Year Book of Education*; a Memorandum on Aspects of Welfare of Women and Children in the Colonies by Dr Blacklock (AEC 41/36) and an article by Dr Janet Welch, Medical Officer, Nyasaland at a Church of Scotland Mission Hospital. Also circulated were three government papers: 'European Women Employed by the Government in Colonial Territories'; 'Teaching of Domestic Science in England and its Application to work in the Colonies' and 'Colonial Office Notes on the recruitment of women for the Colonial Service 1931'; First meeting of SCWE 17 November 1939, PRO CO859/1/9.

rituals used to convey 'tribal and sex ethics' would decay, hence the urgent need to give women new moral sanctions.[73] According to this interpretation, newly empowered women were the obvious antidote to detribalization. It appeared that they were being set up as the answer to failures in patriarchy. Despite this great task of resuscitation, scant attention was paid by the experts to any structural constraints that might block this rescue remedy. Not surprisingly, then, despite the sense of epic struggle, the wide membership and the established thought, the initiative was doomed to remain a side-show. African women remained stuck on the merry-go-round of rural betterment, another illustration of the incoherence of imperial governance emanating from the centre that would return to haunt the post-war period.

Why was this the case despite the energy, insight and money floating around in 1939? One reason lies in the inclusion in the committee of so many women who had little influence within the Colonial Office itself. Their numerical presence did have the effect of substantially altering the official line on educating African women. They added texture to a previously one-dimensional construct of the young African girl in school. The final report not only addressed secondary and elementary educational needs in Africa. Certain women on the committee insisted that girls were not to be given second-rate vocational training. As in England, such schooling was to cover general character training, citizenship and responsibility, because they were being trained 'to positions of leadership',[74] although Margery Perham argued that African women had to be given an education that would help them in their traditional role of keeping the structure of society together. Others, on the other hand, wanted female education to be tailored to their changing environment. They ought to provide an education that the women wanted and not what African men seemed to want: 'suburban wives who could set a tray and pour tea'.

This latter view was supported by a committee of investigation at Achimota College in the Gold Coast, which reported in 1938 that it was a mistake 'to conceive of any education for Gold Coast women as adequate for their needs as members of the community, which was in any way dominated by domestic and maternal interests'. Due to the persistence of certain women on the 1939 sub-committee, the final report included the suggestion that further education for African women was not to pay any special attention to the needs of future wives and mothers, except as part of a good general education. However, those who argued this line were not likely to be influential enough to subsequently facilitate any great policy change along these lines. Nor did the female heavy-weights present like Margery Perham even take up the cause of women's education in general.

[73] SCWE, *Report on the Education and Welfare of Women and Girls*, 1940, p.16, ibid.

[74] Initially it was hoped that Margaret Wrong (involved with promoting Christian literature overseas), Miss Read, Mrs Johnston, Dr Blacklock and even certain African women in England could all be co-opted on to the sub-committee.

As we shall see, she had other agendas to clear. Whilst benefiting from the patronage of a man's world, there was less incentive to rail against it.

Another disabling element was the committee's approach to the 'general mass of rural women and girls', who were treated differently from those girl-pupils capable of responding to secondary education. Taking up the ideas of the 1935 memorandum, the sub-committee agreed that in relation to this category 'it was unnatural to educate the African woman or girl except as a part of her community', and the report concluded 'if therefore the education given is to meet the needs of the community, the remedy is ... to pay more attention to community education, of which the school is only one part'.[75] Adult education of African women could not therefore be the sole responsibility of education departments but required co-operation from agriculture, health and administrative staff. Libraries, newspapers and cinema could help and special adult education officers should be appointed to work among women, co-operating with all departments and extending 'the welfare propaganda work of these departments'. As to implementation, the report suggested that a new focal point be created for all these educational activities: 'an African adaptation of the community centre'. Metropolitan experience was being applied to the colonial situation. The theory that the community centre was a solution to rural decline and a flagging sense of civic responsibility was increasing in popularity during the Second World War. The report sold the idea as an attempt 'in highly individualistic countries to revive a flagging community sense', now believed to be fading also in parts of rural Africa and absent altogether from urban areas.

This was all well and good but it was not enough. The level of detail needed to back up the recommendations was missing. It need not have been so. What fundamentally weakened the effectiveness of the final report was its decision to exclude a detailed paper on community centres prepared by the Colonial Office Education Adviser, Christopher Cox. Malcolm MacDonald had made the appointment in 1936 along with the creation of a number of other specialist advisory posts. At the time Cox was a classics don at New College, Oxford. He had worked for a time in the Sudan, and he had a dream. A community hall, clinic and welfare centre would be run in co-operation with the local school, a mobile library and an audio-visual unit. Recently made feminine friendly, Cox staunchly argued that the most important aspect of the community centre model was that it would provide a much needed experimental forum for testing schemes for improving the education of women and girls – schemes that would equip them to function as 'mistress of the house and guardian of the young ... geared to providing a training for life in the Community, where women were likely to bear much greater responsibilities in the future than

[75] SCWE Report, ch.IV 'Development of Community Education', pp. 21–2, ibid. Perham and Oakden supported this view.

in the past'. He imagined how a woman sociologist at each pilot centre might gather data about women's activities inside and outside the home – their role in agriculture and commerce – so that education could be tailored to their real needs:

> Many of the ordinary subjects of the curriculum would have a new meaning, or at any rate, be subject to a different treatment. Hygiene ... and training for the home would be assimilated by practical experience in the Community and the school, to be supplemented later by more formal instruction. Girls and women would be assisted to become proficient in those aspects of agriculture and commerce which are essentially women's work.[76]

Cox knew, however, that for such a dream to become reality, a number of issues would have to be addressed – issues to do with the structures that were already in place. First, the community centre model would have to comply with local plans for indirect rule. It would need the support of the administration and would have to fit in with native councils 'which, in accordance with the British Government's policy on indirect rule, are gradually assuming greater responsibility in the sphere of local government'. Secondly, the centres would create the possibility of new types of officers entering established administrative terrain. Thirdly, community centres might be seen as threats to vested groups such as missionaries, and care would have to be taken to show there was no clash of loyalties, but rather 'a growing spirit of co-operation' which could strengthen congregations. However, committee members agreed that the whole subject of community centres fell outside their terms of reference, since they did not relate specifically to women. In practical terms women were still treated as a special subject even when they were being placed theoretically at the centre of society.

As mentioned, Cox's paper on community centres did not appear in the final report. This was unfortunate since Cox was outlining some of the major obstacles to state restructuring in Kenya that would re-emerge to haunt the post-war period. Neither he nor the sub-committee realized this – a damning indictment of the incoherence at the apex of empire. It seemed difficult to learn the lessons of their bureaucratic past, since the most accurate assessment of mainstream activites often came from attempts at the margins to break into that mainstream. Since these efforts were at the margins the mainstream took no interest.

Overall, the sub-committee failed to formulate a clear model that would ease the conversion of their recommendations into policy. Setting aside the community centre debate was a fatal error, for it encapsulated a basic

[76] 'The Community Centre'. Memo from C.W.M. Cox, 25 April 1940, SCWE 12/40, PRO CO859/1/9. As adviser, Cox replaced the two joint secretaries of the EAC, Mayhew and Vischer, when it was reorganized in 1939; 99th Meeting of the EAC 16 November 1939, PRO CO 859/2/43.

principle: if African society was to be restructured as they wanted, so too must the colonial state. To an extent they were constrained by factors they could do little about. They were just another panel making recommendations that colonies might or might not choose to adopt. They had no budget, nor any authority to monitor progress. Many of the recommendations were simply asking for the process of gathering sociological data to be set in motion.[77] Also, in the observation made in the report that community life could only be promoted by a new type of school and education according to 'the extent to which it is able to co-operate with the moral forces operative in native society', we can identify a typical example of the way in which professional expertise at the time failed to question whether such a unifying force could animate racially divided societies. By 1943 attention had shifted to higher education (see Ashton and Stockwell, 1996: Part I, lxxx–lxxxii and Part II, 338–54).

Another explanation lies within the wider bureaucratic culture. It was mediated by men who were not very interested in the role of African women in relation to welfare. Few men of influence took up the cause. Even Margery Perham failed to press her view that the educated African woman was the antidote to detribalization, so absorbed was she in the wider question of indirect rule. Male representatives on the committee had dampened the urge to make a bold statement on policy, preferring to 'trust the man on the spot' to plan improvements. Nevertheless, a report was produced and circulated widely. Yet surely in the reforming atmosphere of the war, the case for linking women and welfare would find a new niche?

Wartime initiatives in social welfare at the Colonial Office

Not so; it found the filing cabinet. This gendered concept of rural development disappeared from view. The nature of the report itself undoubtedly played a part in this. However, the war played a greater part. The timing of the report was disastrous for the chances of an established pre-war consensus on educated African women and girls moving into the mainstream of colonial government. War ensured that concerns about the damaging effects of detribalization and the need to implant social and economic improvements found other solutions. As we have seen already, a model of state-controlled development and welfare dazzled officials; planning for a world of macro-state intervention satisfied them as the best mechanism for raising standards of living in the long term. Micro-strategies directed at women and girls would find it difficult to compete with such a seductive alternative. However, wartime welfare initiatives did not come to a standstill after 1940. Less than two years later, the welfare merry-go-round was off again. Within the Colonial Office, there were

[77] SCWE Report (1940), pp. 31-2, PRO CO859/1/9.

signs of a new determination to make the empire state-building more responsive to social welfare needs in Africa. Yet women and welfare were still absent. What was it about this final wartime initiative which ensured that social welfare strategies for Africa – inclusive of women – whizzed past generations of officials?

The effect of war was to encourage officials to re-focus on men. African male social deviance and urban disorder came to dominate the Colonial Office's official line on social welfare as the war progressed. Metropolitan thought on social welfare was highly influential in this regard. Attitudes at home toward social welfare were being shaped by a number of processes. First, socialist argument had permeated government circles, bringing with it the implication that state intervention was necessary if society showed itself incapable of securing the welfare of all its members. Individual distress was no longer interpreted as 'a mark of social incapacity'.[78] This thinking was buoyed up by the demands of war, a second factor shaping metropolitan social welfare. As *The Times* proclaimed after Dunkirk in July 1940, 'democracy no longer meant the right to vote, but the right to work and the right to live'.[79] The rhetoric of power was not the only area that sharpened up its act. The experience of public administration during the war – food policy, rationing, clothes – naturally focused government attention on what was loosely termed social welfare. Thirdly, and flanking the fright of Dunkirk, came the revelations of urban squalor which accompanied the evacuation programme. Social workers found the lives of the urban poor to be still quite shocking. Lice, skin-disease, poor food, no proper washing and toilet facilities and inadequate clothing were commonplace. Now the 'submerged tenth' re-appeared as problem families:

> ... always on the edge of pauperism and crime, riddled with mental and physical defects, in and out of the Courts for child neglect, a menace to the community ... they are dirty and unwholesome in their habits through lack of personal discipline and social standard, often combined in the past or present with poverty and a discouraging environment. Most of them are capable of improvement in better circumstances and if educated in a wide sense. (Hygiene Committee of Women's Group on Public Welfare, 1943: xiii–xiv)

Consequently a great fear of anti-social behaviour permeated professional opinion on social welfare. The urban poor were found not to join trade unions, friendly societies or clubs and seldom attended church. They seemed always to slip through the helping hands of socializing agents. What particularly worried the experts were signs of growing instability in urban home life and that 'bad' mothers were rearing sick and unruly

[78] R. Titmuss, *Problems of Social Policy, U.K. (Cabinet Office) History of the Second World War,* (U.K. Civil Service Series, London: HMSO, 1950) pp. 505–6. Titmuss became a member of the Social Welfare Advisory Committee in 1953.

[79] Ibid., p. 508.

children. The war was blamed for placing more strain on families, especially since more mothers were now working. These factors began to be drawn together and woven into established theories explaining the growth of delinquency. Since the early 1920s British representatives at the League of Nations had always taken a particular interest in the Child Welfare Committee's deliberations on delinquency. Professional opinion once again pleaded that the conditions necessary for family life be supported so that the traditional nurturing of children into puberty could be maintained. Social welfare and delinquency experts argued that this was necessary to avoid the phenomenon of infantile dependence, a condition which led to the demand for maintenance without a corresponding sense of obligation and responsibility. Such dependence, they argued, explained the growth in totalitarian societies and backwardness in Africa.[80] It was an increase in juvenile delinquency that metropolitan social observers were most keen to nip in the bud, believing it was rare for a delinquent to come from 'a decent and affectionate family'. Religious and social commentators were arguing strongly at the time that poverty was the obstacle to family life, citizenship and Christian values. If a man was pauperized all these features would follow. So, unsurprisingly, they all converged on the argument that the state had to intervene to counter feebleness and thereby prevent delinquency.[81]

Whatever the home front could find, the colonies could find too. If the imperial equivalent to Dunkirk was the fall of Singapore in 1942, then the revelations at home following the evacuation scandal were mirrored at the Colonial Office. Anxieties about African urban degeneration multiplied. Troops arriving in West Africa had recently exposed the problem (Iliffe, 1987: 200). By early 1942 officials were concerned that juvenile delinquency was assuming 'rather alarming proportions', brought to light in evidence coming from a number of African cities such as Lagos and Freetown. Lagos's administrators had asked their Penal Committee to recruit a Welfare Officer to help and had seconded a member of the Prisons Department to undertake a survey. Colonial Office officials agreed that it was time to review the preventative aspects of delinquency which would include 'a miscellaneous variety of welfare work'. But they disagreed on whether a sub-committee of the Penal Advisory Committee (PAC) should undertake such an enquiry. Some argued it was not quite suitable for investigating such a topic, whilst traditionalists stuck to the view that delinquency in Africa was a local problem for those on the spot to solve.[82]

[80] Titmuss, *Problems of Social Policy*, pp. 404–23; Maberly, 1948: 163–5; Yellowby, 1980, ch.4 'The Growth of Psychoanalytic Influence'; R. Pinker, 1989: 84–7; Wilson, 1977, ch.5 'Welfare since the War'.

[81] Lofthouse, 1944: 89. See also C.W. Valentine, *The Psychology of Early Childhood* (London, 1942), Mullins, 1943; Bagot, 1940; Temple, 1942; Mumford, 1943.

[82] J.J. Paskin, 7 January 1942, Note entitled 'Juvenile Delinquency Juvenile Welfare', PRO CO859/73/11. Minute by Sir Kenneth Poyser, 9 February 1942, reply from Jeffries 9 February 1942, ibid.

However, old hands at the Colonial Office found it more difficult to have everything their own way. Penal experts were as enthusiastic for action as were younger newcomers into the colonial service. Alexander Paterson, from the Prison Commission, loudly supported such a sub-committee. Influenced by metropolitan developments, he had radical ideas about an expanded role for the colonial prison departments in the new sphere of welfare. He shared these with a newcomer to the Colonial Office, due to circumstances induced by the war. Dr Audrey Richards was a temporary principal in the Social Services department. Like a few other women, she had secured a junior position in the Colonial Office on the understanding that it was only temporary, as a result of the wartime man-power shortages.[83] Part of the English 'intellectual aristocracy' of the time, she was one of a number of women who had risen up the academic hierarchy in anthropology during the 1930s. She had worked in Northern Rhodesia under Malinowski; her study of the role of women and the family made her well-suited to the needs of the hour and she had also tutored students on the new LSE colonial training course. Since neither Paterson nor Richards were bureaucrats, they were less squeamish about instigating change. Paterson was clear in his mind; he wanted a permanent committee established to act as a Welfare Committee within the Colonial Office and as a parent body for all Welfare Committees in the colonies. This would make the fledgling structures now being established, particularly in West African towns, 'feel more firmly entrenched in colonial administration', he argued. And it would give London more say in the recruitment of probation officers, welfare officers and headmasters.[84]

A committee of enquiry was set up but Richards had to quell Paterson's expectations. She had found little enthusiasm amongst senior officials for more committees of enquiry. The Prime Minister had deprecated them, and she had experienced difficulty in even getting an ad hoc committee set up. It appeared that the optimism and energy at the beginning of the war had begun to fizzle out and the Colonial Office's established notion of trusting men on the spot regarding welfare in the colonies had resurfaced. Undeterred, the sub-committee got the bit between its teeth and charged headlong into considering 'the problem of young offenders in the Colonies and Dependencies' and advising measures 'to prevent children and

[83] Six other women were made assistant principals and as an experiment in 1944 women were sent out to the colonies as temporary junior administrators; Calloway, 1987: 139. Richards spent much of her time at the Colonial Office setting up with Lord Hailey the Colonial Social Science Research Council which was instrumental in planning the post-war programme of anthropological research, Blake and Nicholls, 1990: 336–7.

[84] As welfare was being extended in the colonies, he argued, more home recruitment of probation officers, welfare officers, headmasters would take place and such a committee could act as a Selection Board choosing staff for prisons, reformatory schools and probation services plus all welfare personnel; A. Paterson to A. Richards, 16 March 1942, PRO CO859/73/11. Paterson later became chairman of the resulting sub-committee, and Richards, its secretary.

adolescents from becoming delinquent'. Members were left to decide whether to include female juvenile delinquency. It seems they opted instead to invite Christopher Cox from the Education Advisory Committee to join them so that he could help formulate a policy for the after-care of delinquents.[85]

Their subsequent report illustrates just how much metropolitan thought was being extended to the colonies during the war. It was chequered by the home climate in a number of ways. First, we can see strong evidence of an urge to establish universal standards of bureaucratic practice within the empire. The report boldly stated that 'in a world that is now determining the basic principles that shall determine the way in which human beings shall handle other human beings, delay can no longer be suffered... It would be unfortunate if it were widely held that flagellation is the only instrument of justice that follows the British Flag.'[86] It was not just that in war an embryonic notion among the professions of a world society had edged further forward. The persistent offender, whether in London's East End or Nairobi's locations, was regarded by metropolitan experts as the victim of similar circumstances: a product of 'the tangled roots of social, economic or educational insufficiency, in hereditary tendency or family maladjustment'.

Secondly, we can identify a firm belief in the efficacy and moral duty of the state to intervene in order to socially engineer different circumstances. '[T]he problem of prevention awakens all the social and economic forces that surround the growing youth. It is a challenge to education, it questions the claims of labour.' Thirdly, the perception that juvenile delinquency was increasing dramatically in the colonies as it was at home, ensured that the emphasis on prevention was one of re-establishing authority, control and obedience.[87] Their evidence for this came from the apparent growth in

[85] Minute from Sir Cosmo Parkinson, January 1942; Richards to Paterson 18 March 1942, ibid Note on Juvenile Delinquency Sub-Committee (undated), ibid. Topics of relevance were wide ranging: Treatment of vagrants, destitute children, truancy, public assistance; Prevention through repatriation, hostels for young wage-earners, links between school, police and probation officers, school after-care, recreation; Personnel issues including the type of officers suitable for juvenile welfare, their functions, liaison with youth and labour organizations, and the division of departmental responsibilities between Prison, Education and Labour Departments; Training of specialized officers recruited in England and of local personnel such as probation officers, club leaders, hostel managers and youth leaders; Voluntary Groups and liaison with native authorities in Africa, women workers and missionary groups.

[86] PRO CO 859/73/11 paras 2 and 3. Flagellation was changed to whipping for the final draft.

[87] John Bowlby was beginning to popularize the link between childhood and recidivism. Family neglect and the emergence of isolated sub-groups were blamed and a premium put on the importance of boys' clubs; Bowlby, 1945; Yellowby, 1980: ch.6 'Social Work and Freudian Man'; Bagot, 1940; *Young Offenders*, Home Office Report, 1938. By 1949 metropolitan experts were arguing that 'one in every nine male persons becomes a delinquent,' Trenman and Emmett, 1949: 49.

colonial prison populations. Disorder, crimes such as theft and the paranoia of the authorities had further increased during the war. On the grounds of economic necessity governments had to explore ways of training 'the citizen from youth to obey the law'. In January 1943 the sub-committee found an agreed line on remedies. Trained welfare personnel could best be placed under local administration. A Director or Organizer of Social Welfare would work best if attached to the Secretariat as a special adviser (a conclusion reached by the Palestine Government in a recent dispatch). And a Social Welfare Advisory Committee ought now to be established at the Colonial Office.[88]

This was all too much for senior officials perhaps more comfortable with the use of the lash. A few officials felt the report should be made more suitable for the West Indies; it was too heavily Africa-orientated. Richards admitted it had been written mainly to suit the needs of African governments. It was decided on balance to stay with the original, in view of the 'urgent need in Africa'. Even so, Sir Charles Jeffries and Sir George Gater decided not to publish the report. Instead, they sent it unofficially to various colonies, asking for suggestions about what they considered to be far-reaching proposals, and not wanting to commit themselves to a document which might 'in certain respects not be altogether suitable'.[89] They took this line because the report exposed an extreme version of the new: London seemed to be telling colonial governments to set up new structures where they had none at all, and instructing administrators on how to deal with Africans.

Meanwhile, the report was discussed with great interest by various panels of expertise within the Colonial Office who did not find it all that radical. Some criticized it for not going further. Others wished it had not been written for colonial administrators alone, because a wider audience could benefit. Christopher Cox thought the report so important that he invited Alexander Paterson to elaborate upon its contents for the benefit of his Education Advisory Committee. This was partly instigated to deal with the allegation that the report was confusing with regard to which body was responsible for juvenile crime prevention. Richards wanted the British model followed, namely of regarding youth organizations as falling under the jurisdiction of education but that welfare officers would not be responsible to the education department.[90] Unfortunately, as we shall see later, post-war Kenya would take the confusion to a whole new dimension.

What is significant about the subsequent discussion is the way it reveals

[88] Draft Report, Part I, paras 1 and 2, PRO CO859/73/11; Minute from A. Richards, 18 January 1943, ibid.

[89] Note from A. Richards to Prof. Simey, 12 December 1942; Sir Charles Jeffries to Sir George Gater 19 January 1943, ibid.

[90] Extract from Draft Minutes of the 177th Meeting EAC, 15 October 1942, Paterson, p.3, ibid; Richards responding to criticism from Professor Simey about the confusion; minute from Richards, 12 December 1942, PRO CO859/73/11.

both the capacity for insight within the Colonial Office and its penchant for incompetence. For at this gathering, a gang of experts zoomed in on what was destined to remain an unresolved issue from the top to the bottom of colonial government. Yet at the same time they could do little with this information. What the educational experts wanted was a fundamental break with the established District Officer system. The big question many felt was whether, with the sudden expansion in social services, administrative officers or another cadre should assume responsibility. Could the administrative officer nurture such a constructive relationship (i.e. mediate between state and society), because he had to 'administer law, mete out punishment, collect taxes, etc.'? One member of the committee did go so far as to suggest that steps be taken to ensure that the administrative officer would recognize that his functions were changing: 'he would be in essence a welfare officer in the widest sense of the word and that the work of the various social services should be regarded as part of his work'.[91] They did not appear to know that this tied in with a deep anxiety among Colonial Office officials in the East African department, namely, that indirect rule was proving highly inefficient in terms of delivering services in colonies like Kenya.[92] Nor did they stop to question the barriers that racial rule might present in this, although few others would have done so at the time. With all the discussion about delinquency and more white officers, even a mind as astute as Cox's abandoned his community centre model and the role of women, strategies which he had so enthusiastically endorsed as being central to social welfare only two years before.

Nevertheless, this suggestion was tantamount to breaking a hallowed taboo of the gravest order. As such, it was well nigh impossible to orchestrate, as the rest of this book will show, and it goes to the heart of the weakness within the empire state-building project. With regard to the welfare and development agenda which the Colonial Office had set itself, the established administrative structure in the colonies would be quite unable to carry out the task. Technical experts working for departments had outstripped the general administrator – the District Officer – in terms of what their expertise could offer colonial peoples regarding their health and general welfare. However, since colonial rule was founded upon personal patronage, submission and racial domination, the District Officer could and would not yield any ground as a bearer of power. As a result colonial state intervention would remain focused more on discipline and on men, and far less on poverty eradication and on women.

[91] Ibid, p.3. Sir John Scott actually called for the number of District Officers to be reduced by half and their geographical areas widened. He supported the suggestion that administrative officers should receive prior welfare training in England; however, he wanted voluntary bodies to be encouraged to assist in remedial measures through detention homes and the provision of approved schools, to ensure a strong religious element which government schools would lack.

[92] Extract from 177th EAC meeting, p. 4., ibid. This was what Kenya's Information Officer argued when proposing that the colony employ a new cadre of welfare officer; see Chapter 3.

The 1942 report of the Juvenile Delinquency Committee did result in institutional reform. A Colonial Office Social Welfare Advisory Committee came into being despite the earlier lack of enthusiasm. Many colonial governments had asked for copies of the report, exposing the need for guidance.[93] But it was the rational argument put forward by Audrey Richards which beat down the in-house opposition to such a move. The Penal Advisory Committee was not equipped to deal with the big social problems that needed tackling, and there was an increased need for outside specialist advice on topics such as housing, town planning and rural organizations.[94] Her superiors generally came to agree with her.[95] Health and education had their own committees, so why not social welfare? Once the go-ahead was given, Audrey Richards might have thought her problems with social welfare were over. Rather, they had just begun. The amorphous nature of social welfare soon began to feel like a thick gluey substance from which it was impossible to escape. The effectiveness of such Colonial Office advisory committees was still open to doubt.

In emulating metropolitan social services and probation, the range of social welfare had been made absurdly wide. The new committee were to consider 'the training of Social Welfare Workers both European and Colonial; the Delinquency Services (prisons, probation, approved schools and borstals); Clubs and Settlements; Rural Welfare Associations (Rural Councils, Women's Institutes, Young Farmers Clubs, Co-operative and Thrift Societies), the relief of destitution (poor law, orphanages, etc)'. They had to advise the Secretary of State on matters he chose to refer to them regarding the social welfare of urban and rural communities in the colonies, the training of social welfare workers, and other related issues. Social welfare meant many things: implanting rural social betterment by animating civil society against social collapse; devising urban remedies for the incapacitated and the destitute; correcting the deviant; and training Africans to be their own social policemen. It was being built on two platforms: the modernized form of state intervention designed to regulate people's lives, and the traditional ways in which the labouring classes had collectively organized themselves since the 1890s to try to improve their

[93] A. Richards to K.W. Blaxter, 16 September 1942, PRO CO859/75/13. The Report had been promised to 4 African governments (Sierra Leone, Nigeria, Kenya, Nyasaland) who had immediate problems and had set up probation committees, whilst it was also needed by the Gold Coast, Tanganyika and Mauritius.

[94] Richards to Blaxter, 16 September 1942, ibid. She suggested experts on rural council work, Women's Institutes, Young Farmers Clubs, the new Ministry of Health scheme, and the National Councils of Social Service might be asked.

[95] One critic of the report was Professor Thomas Simey of the Social Science faculty at Liverpool University. Finding it unsuitable for West Indian conditions, he insisted that the youth organizations should be under the control of a Social Welfare Officer and generally found the suggestions for social welfare machinery confusing. Summary of criticism 14 November 1942 and reply from Richards 12 December 1942, CO859/73/11.

economic and political status through co-operative societies, social clubs and savings groups.[96]

Committee membership was also problematic. Officials agreed that a small panel of men and women able to liaise with experts in particular fields be assembled, rather than representatives of each aspect of welfare work. But there were other concerns regarding balance. Since the outbreak of war, great changes had taken place in the scope, and personnel of welfare work and the public attitude to it, which had produced 'a marked cleavage' between the older type of social welfare expert who had worked within one particular voluntary association all his/her life and younger ones, professionally trained and now in high administrative positions. Finally, in April 1943 an information circular was put together for distribution to all the colonies. The Committee's terms of reference were 'social welfare in urban and rural communities in the Colonies' and the training of social welfare workers, whilst its scope was listed as the relief of destitution, welfare services for the sick, clubs and associations for adolescents and adults, co-operative movements and thrift organizations.[97] Not everyone was happy. In 1944, Sir Charles Jeffries complained that the committee suffered from 'a preponderance of the female sex' and that, at the risk of making it larger, 'it would help to promote the effectiveness of the Committee if one or two men were added to it'. The problem was resolved by including two religious representatives. These had earlier been omitted for fear of arousing denominational jealousy. Officials preferred them to women, and so were now prepared to concede that the bulk of social welfare in many colonies was undertaken by missionaries.[98]

Like all new initiatives at the Colonial Office, remedying the absence of information took time. Details came in dribs and drabs. The Kenya

96 This was set out in a Draft Circular to the Colonies, 17 April 1943, CO859/73/11 informing them that the juvenile delinquency sub-committee had been dissolved and the Advisory Committee on Social Welfare appointed. See R.J. Morris, 'Clubs, societies and associations' in *Cambridge Social History of Britain, 1750-1950,* Vol. 3 (Cambridge, 1990) pp. 395–444 and Jose Harris, 'Society and the State in Twentieth Century Britain', in *Cambridge Social History of Britain, 1750–1950*, Vol. 2 (Cambridge, 1990) pp. 63–118.

97 Minutes of a meeting, 17 November 1942, PRO CO/859/73/11; Circular on the Social Welfare Advisory Committee (SWAC) 17 April 1943, PRO CO 859/75/13. Members were metropolitan experts drawn from the wide-ranging categories of social welfare: Carr-Saunders, Director of the London School of Economics., interest in social surveys, delinquency and co-operation; Margery Fry, penal reformer, Children's Magistrate; M.L. Harford, Chief Woman Officer of the National Council of Social Service, Sec. of the Woman's Group on Public Welfare, destitution expert; E.H. Lucette, Sec. to Managers, Dr Barnados; J.L. Longland, County Education Officer, Dorset, experienced in Rural Community Council work and clubs for the unemployed; M. Nixon, welfare worker in Palestine and Cyprus; Eileen Younghusband, tutor at LSE in social work, Principal Officer for Training and Employment, National Council of Girls' Clubs; Audrey Richards and Alexander Paterson. (Chairman was the Under-Secretary of State, Vice-Chairman, Sir Charles Jeffries, Assistant USSC).

98 Jeffries to Gater, 14 January 1944, PRO CO859/75/13, conveying the views of himself, Blaxter and apparently Mary Darlow also; minute by Jeffries 14 January 1944, ibid.

Government, for example, informed the committee of a youth council being set up; that Fortie Ross a development and welfare officer was undertaking a social survey in Nyanza; and that Nairobi Municipal Council had appointed Nicolina Deverell to work with African women. Indeed, the committee received a number of communications about urban African women's welfare and family life. Alexander Paterson turned his investigative skills from male delinquency to prostitution in Freetown. Accepting prostitution as inevitable, he argued that it should be controlled by public health and sanitary inspectors under the jurisdiction of the Medical Department, and not by the police, lest it threaten 'the tradition of family life in the country'. In 1944, D.E. Faulkner, a Social Welfare Officer in Lagos, sent the Committee a report about the large number of destitute children there. He found that these children did not usually have parents who lived together and he blamed their plight on single women.[99] Remarkably he had been able to discern an increase in promiscuity. Women were able to live as independent traders, suffering no financial embarrassment for lack of a husband. This produced 'the absence of family life' and, with the high cost of living, children were not welcome in towns.

This seemed to be a direct echo of the situation in Britain, where social welfare experts were castigating working mothers for producing 'latch-key' children. Indeed, Beveridge's welfare state was built on the premise that women would return to the home after the war: a wife would forfeit her right to a state allowance if her marriage ended due to her own doing. This produced a tendency to fall back on the old principles of mothercraft in both constituencies, thus stressing the domestic role of women. Indeed, the Committee learnt about plans to train prospective African mothers. It was considered newsworthy that a Miss McMath, Lady Education Officer, Sierra Leone, had co-operated with an African medical officer, Dr Margai, to produce a training course designed to teach prospective mothers what a woman 'ought to know': elementary anatomy, home management, how to avoid catching venereal diseases and the application of eugenics when choosing a husband – and all without offending tribal customs.[100]

This Committee and others were more successful than any before them in bringing more information more quickly to the attention of the Colonial Office, even if they seemed only to reflect back a mirror image of the East End. In the case of social welfare, the learning curve measured a state of local confusion. It was Audrey Richards' fingerprints that most marked proceedings. She was concerned to set up training for African welfare workers in East Africa and journeyed there to find out whether the Makerere Institute in Uganda could produce suitable officers. Her report was discussed in detail by the Committee in 1944. It was the first visit of its

[99] Various SWAC meetings 1944, PRO CO997/1.

[100] 'Training of Prospective Mothers in Sierra Leone', CSWAC 42/22, PRO CO997/1.

kind.[101] In Kenya she had found their welfare programme based upon incomplete development plans. Projects under discussion often overlapped with one another; there was confusion as to what European social welfare officers should do; and an urgent need for training demobilized African soldiers in rural welfare work. She wanted three types of rural training designed to improve social welfare. First, community training for village workers already trained as agricultural assistants, medical dressers and so on. Secondly, the training of rural village welfare workers in all-round village improvement, an extension of the system in Uganda. And thirdly, since community centres were favoured as the means for spreading welfare activities, community centre organizers were needed to act as instigators of various village societies and group activities. Urban areas would require similar community centre organizers, juvenile welfare officers and labour inspectors. All these were lower level welfare workers below the type of training given at Makerere. It was decided that the army school at Kabete in Kenya be used for this task after the war; the army school was the former Jeanes School.

However, the Committee's official response to such initial probing was predictable and somewhat inadequate. There seemed to be no discussion of the issues such recommendations threw up in relation to stepping on the toes of established institutions such as the District Officer, the mission station or the LNC. There was no revival of the debates which the Education Committee had been able to discern. There was no discussion of the Jeanes teacher system in Kenya which had tried and failed to do what Richards was proposing and which had been debated within various committees. The very newness of the Advisory Committee perhaps acted as a barrier to the institutional memory, but everything that it left out would return to haunt the post-war era. In the rush to replicate metropolitan solutions, the particularity of the African context seemed to matter less and less.

The Committee, like so many others, took refuge in the production of a circular stuffed full of guidelines and designed for distribution to all colonies in 1945. It was clearly designed first and foremost to pave the way for the introduction of white social welfare workers. It cited evidence that 'the community is an organic whole whose health and vitality depend upon the well-being of all its constituent members and on the good relations between them'. From this it was deduced that the state must be responsible for social welfare, in co-operation with voluntary effort. For the committee were equally certain that communal obligation in Africa was breaking down in the face of wage employment and urbanization.[102]

[101] 'Vocational Training for African Welfare Workers', CSWAC 54/44 by A.I. Richards, discussed by the SWAC 4 December 1944, ibid. This is returned to in Chapter 4.

[102] 'Social Welfare in the Colonies', April 1945, PRO CO859/519. This was in line with popular thinking on African societies; see L.P. Mair, *Welfare in the British Colonies* (London, 1944), the argument being that delinquency was not a problem in rural areas where the chief was respected and everyone could find employment on the land.

Consequently the social welfare worker had to wear quite a few hats. He would have to assist the administration and departments in aspects of their work which had a particular bearing on welfare and would encourage voluntary associations in social welfare activities. He would have direct responsibility for overlapping areas of activity not covered by existing departments: the promotion of community life through drama and music; activities auxiliary to the work of specialist departments, such as encouraging small stock-breeding, domestic management and youth groups; organizing the care of the aged, destitute, handicapped and mothers; and activities linked with court work, juvenile delinquents, ex-convicts and prostitutes.[103] The machinery suggested for these officers to work through was arbitrary and dependent upon what, if anything, was in place already. Admitting that their functions were 'part constructive and part ameliorative', priority was to be given to the former, not forgetting that colonial populations were predominantly rural. Readers were reminded that financial assistance for social service development was available under the Colonial Development and Welfare Act.

The Social Welfare Advisory Committee epitomized the shift that had taken place within the Colonial Office during the war. Metropolitan forms of social engineering and their corresponding bureaucratic manifestation were applied more vigorously to colonial issues. A new generation of professional expertise and more outside experts were incorporated. The centre was now prepared to become involved in how colonial administrators treated Africans. The committee also illustrates the way in which the feminization of the health and welfare professions was shadowed by the needs and the stress of war. The mission statement to governments contained no emphasis on women and welfare. Instead, the Committee issued the colonies with a muddled philosophy and an impossible multiplication of official tasks. Social welfare workers must do everything, it seemed. Finally, we can see how the Committee reflected the urge to universalize colonial problems and to standardize corresponding solutions. In doing so, the experts often lost sight of the particularity of Africa. The Committee had approached colonial problems with metropolitan social work models assuming an extensive state structure. For their plans to work and their hopes to be realized, the late colonial state would need to conjure up metropolitan circumstances: finance; co-operation between administration and departments; target groups in civil society to work through; and a single moral community. Had officials read the lessons of their own bureaucratic history more carefully without the distraction of war, they might have better understood that these simply did not exist.

[103] 'Social Welfare in the Colonies', pp. 2–3., PRO CO859/519.

Conclusion

War stirred up Colonial Office thought and practice in relation to African welfare and good government as never before. From the grand gesture of the Welfare and Development Act to the committees of enquiry and the creation of new advisory bodies, much institutional building clearly took place between 1939 and 1945. That it took place at all around the notion of bringing welfare to colonial peoples (and not natives) was in part the product of changes that had taken place in the two previous decades. The League of Nations, the evidence of the failures of indirect rule, the growth in administrative capabilities and the love affair with the potential of the state all made possible what was accomplished during the war. No more the 'mere recording angel' (see Hyam, 1979). It might have appeared to some that by the end of the war the Colonial Office had gone native in another sense. Sir Ralph Furse, director of Colonial Office recruitment, was set on recruiting fewer public school products and finding new types of officers. The Secretary of State for the Colonies could refuse to grant money for development projects if trade unions were not made legal. And following a race relations incident relating to the West Indian cricketer, Learie Constantine, officials even considered making it an offence to refuse hotel accommodation on the grounds of race (see Ashton and Stockwell, 1996: Part I, xxx and lxxxix–xci). Kenya's administrators, employers and settlers alike might well balk at these various developments. The post-war period was not going to deliver the kind of peace that could include everyone on their own terms.

However, war also distracted and as a result altered what was achieved in quite striking ways. One outcome was to perpetuate an institutional amnesia. A growing feminization within colonial professions had shown that attention to women might actually be central to their goal of social transformation as a means of bettering lives and thus fulfilling the requirements of trusteeship with regard to African colonies. This was displaced during the war by a return to a concept of social welfare that was administered by new white officials – men – and orientated towards shoring up men in the community and combating delinquency. In the rush to graft metropolitan-style solutions on to African society, the Colonial Office lost the plot. Even the Beveridge welfare state model had recognized that gender held the key to its plans.

Yet within lost paragraphs of Committee Minutes or among the discussion papers that were dropped, officials here and there had worked out what would be the major barriers to restructuring the colonial state in order that the agenda of welfare and progress could be realized. Minor officials recognized that indirect rule, the district administrator, the mission presence, and what Africans wanted needed to be addressed first. Welfare initiatives were fated to be stunted by structures of Empire that had developed to perform quite different tasks. Their superiors had other concerns, particularly to do with control. A tremendous sense of mission did screw their courage into place, as Malcolm MacDonald's huffing and puffing at the doors of an unsentimental Treasury well illustrates. A generation that had seen the human side of the Depression in the 1930s – in particular urban squalor and unemployment – were prepared to believe that state-centric solutions to alleviate such distress could and should be extended to embrace African poverty, particularly when colonial social problems were presented as being similar to those at home.[104] However, such compassion was also galvanized by a keenness to show the outside world that the colonial empire was still a worthy enterprise. Self-interest and job security were powerful motivations too. Technologized professions directed by the state seemed to offer the solution. A belief in the transformatory potential of the technological and scientific wisdoms of the day harnessed to new agents of the state loomed larger during the Second World War. This suggests that a deeper and less glamorous moral rearmament of empire had taken place, which provided the fuel to launch a second colonial occupation after 1945. In this regard a great deal was achieved, for the era of colonial development and welfare was able to mask a growing inequality in imperial relations.[105]

Would the lower levels of the colonial administrative structure find more coherence in the reforming atmosphere of war? The Colonial Office evidently could not teach them the lessons of their own pre-history, when it had forgotten them itself in the rush of war. However, before we look at what was happening in Kenya during the war, we need to examine another imperial arena of debate about welfare and colonial government which changed official policy both in London and Nairobi. The war had set in motion a number of shock waves which tested the capacity of Empire to respond effectively as never before. But respond it most certainly did.

[104] For a comparative case study see Harper, 1990: 90–91.

[105] Morgan (1980: 5) criticises the Act for being too small and cumbersome in its arrangements which made it biased against novelty. According to Fieldhouse, 'By means of a complex network of administrative controls ... these metropolitan states squeezed and exploited their colonies in Africa (and also in South East Asia) in ways never seen before ... between 1945 and 1957 Britain extracted some £140 million from its colonies, putting in only about £40 million under the Colonial Development and Welfare Acts', Fieldhouse, 1986: 6.

Two

'Tropical East Ends' in War

Four Witnesses to the Imperial Politics of African Welfare

Just as the Colonial Office was inching towards what it thought was a more secure footing, the ground beneath began to open up. This chapter presents four witnesses to the wider changes being wrought by the Second World War with regard to ideas about modernizing trusteeship in relation to Kenya. Together they illuminate a recurring narrative that would stalk the late colonial period in Kenya: the constant conflict between a barely yielding racial paternalism and the growing pressures for universal standards of government. The paradox of war at this level rests with the way in which the centre's needs and efforts to produce a single, clear line on empire, were met with greater diffusion and dissent on the periphery, for war made the distinction between the two far less perceptible. At the start of hostilities, the Colonial Office sent out its most prized trouble-shooter – Lord Hailey – to come up with the answers to the challenges of imperial rule, in the hope of stealing the thunder from the nationalist corner. The pace of events quickened, not least with the fall of Singapore to the Japanese in 1942. Significantly for this story, wartime debates about African welfare were to be tossed around by a much wider cast of players. A new, strident imperial conscience spoke up. Another imperial voice broke through and it was Margery Perham who drew up a sharper agenda for colonial government (coining the phrase 'Tropical East Ends' to refer to Africa's poverty). Similarly, African nationalism spoke up. The Kikuyu Central Association unwittingly offered penetrating reflections on the deepening fault lines running through the imperial project by 1945. Hard-pressed Africans who had read wartime propaganda – some because they were in prison – had replied. Local officials in Kenya were left reeling. Finally, the testimony of our fourth witness – the Kenya government's public relations adviser, who was a soldier on secondment – shows us that by the end of the war the colonial administration was uncomfortably caught between two paternalisms. Only the eventual end of Empire would offer a release.

Lord Hailey: the mandarin's guide to colonial rule

Lord Hailey leads as the first imperial witness, producing, as he did, the arch-mandarin's guide to post-war colonial administration in Africa. As we saw in Chapter 1, in 1936 the innovative Secretary of State, Malcolm MacDonald, wanted to luxuriate in a hot tub of new thinking. He looked among others to Lord Hailey – a proconsul with thirty-nine years experience in the Indian Civil Service – for a lead on Africa. Subsequently, Hailey published his impressive official survey of Africa in 1938. This established him as the leading policy adviser on Africa at the Colonial Office where he was considered 'head and shoulders above anyone else'.[1] William Malcolm Hailey was born in 1872 and gained a first in Classics at Oxford. He entered the Indian Civil Service in 1894, rose to became Governor of the United Provinces in 1929, and retired in 1934, one of only a handful to be rewarded with a peerage. He then began a second career in public service dedicating himself to issues relating to colonial rule in Africa, but applying his experience of the Raj and thus continuing a long-standing tradition of administrative cross-over.

Hailey was an intensely private man; his recent biographer, John Cell, could only briefly sketch the man who concealed himself in a public persona. In the official portraits of him which survive, we are shown a kindly Pilgrim Father sort of face with a large nose. He had a compulsive personality that drove him to dominate and control. The dread of being idle fused with a brilliant mind. This enabled him to digest massive amounts of detailed information, helped by having extremely competent and dedicated assistants. Throughout much of his working life he suffered from depression and kidney stones. Tragically, by the end of the Second World War, he had lost not only his wife but his two children. After his death in 1969, an obituary in *The Times* referred to him as the foremost British authority on African colonial administration after Lugard's death.

In September 1939, with the world now at war, Malcolm MacDonald turned to Hailey to make a report on local native rule in Africa. 'What exactly were we driving at in our policy of indirect rule?' he asked. 'What was the next step after we had set up sufficient local administrations?'[2] The war had intensified pressure to move in the big and controversial issues of colonial government. An earlier brainstorming session with a number of senior advisers including Margery Perham and Lord Lugard had helped establish Hailey's line of enquiry. Perham had warned the gathering that the 'intelligentsia' in Africa were rapidly acquiring political consciousness. They would now attempt to capture the state system which colonial rule

[1] Hailey, 1940–42; Kirk Greene, viii; for biographical survey, x.

[2] Meeting between MacDonald and Hailey quoted in Kirk-Greene, 'Introduction' to Hailey, 1940–42: xi; PRO CO847/15/47100/Pt.1 5 September 1939; see also Cell, 1992: ch.17, 'A Report and a Vision, 1941–1942'.

had imposed on them from above, so speeding up the political evolution of the native authorities was necessary 'to head them off' (Robinson, 1991: esp. p. 188; PRO CO 847/47135/39). She encouraged her peers to view Africa as being made up of two separate planes: the reality that was the tribe, and the state system artificially imposed from above. She suggested that the creation of large regional councils of native administration was needed to connect the two, an idea which Hailey was later to recommend. Hailey set to work, as he recalled, charged with considering how methods of representing African interests in colonial legislatures could be harmonized with local native authorities and how government institutions, both central and local, could be developed. Meanwhile, colonial governments were reassured that his labours were the product of his academic interest stimulated by the *Africa Survey* (Hailey, 1940–42: 1; Kirk-Greene, ibid.: xv).

The urgency that came with war, plus its practical effect of opening up travel lines and speeding up communications, seemed to give Hailey wings. He made an extensive tour of African territories where he met officials, settlers, chiefs, headmen, and even clerks, lawyers and mineworkers. He rejected the idea he should seek formal interviews with organized groups and political associations, but he insisted that he had continually tried to speak with all leading office-holders. He certainly met with some elements of an African Western-educated middle class, those who would have been put into the ubiquitous category of 'intelligentsia' (ibid.: vii). Remarkably, the report was finished and typed up by 1942. However, a series of delays held back publication until 1944 when 2,000 copies of *Native Administration and Political Development in British Tropical Africa* were circulated to colonial governments as a confidential document. It was not meant for widespread distribution. With little likelihood of its being a public relations exercise, we can take the text as representing a fairly accurate version of a senior adviser's position on imperial rule. Tucked into a short preface was the caveat that these were Hailey's own observations; they were not meant for publication, nor should they be read as reflecting the views of the British or any African (the term colonial was dropped) government (ibid.: xii, xxi–xxiv). It was, therefore, a typical Colonial Office half-way-house measure. It had to be packaged as a mere guide to administrative thought in order not to upset local sensibilities. Yet underneath, its design was that of a blueprint for change and a mechanism for debating general policy using specific examples. Indeed, it actually represented an official announcement that, from the Colonial Office's perspective, the past policy of indirect rule was at an end.

How did the report measure up to the challenge of producing a general mission statement of colonial rule that could function as a replacement to indirect rule? Detailed chapters on separate territories were prefaced by the General Review Chapter. Here Hailey with some gusto addressed an unprecedented array of imperial polemics including an attempt to pin down some 'Tendencies affecting colonial policy'. Other subjects he addressed ranged over 'The development of African racial consciousness', 'The present attitude of Africans to British rule', 'Means by which African opinion can express itself' and 'The growth of a middle class in Africa'. It was clear that Perham's evocation of a two-plane state-society scenario had sensitized the official mind to the relevance of what was happening to Africans, at the expense of attention to what colonial officials had on their minds. The final section of the crucial review chapter, 'The relative importance of political advance and economic and social development', was a précis of the conclusions and tenor of the whole report. It was tacked on to the end of the long introductory chapter and was one page in length, a somewhat excessively understated approach to the presentation of the report's overall position

The précis reveals much in spite of its flimsy appearance. Most importantly it highlights just how difficult it was, by the time of the Second World War, for even the most astute and experienced of imperial administrators to produce a coherent blueprint for colonial administration. It had always been so in practice, but when the empire state project needed one most, it still could not find one. In terms of producing a consistent line which complemented the welfare and development thinking at the Colonial Office and could be applied swiftly, the report fell somewhat short. Three weaknesses stand out in relation to social service provision. First, there was incompatibility between, on the one hand, a desire to encourage the state's capacity to intervene in order to uphold society's welfare, and on the other, the nurturing and extension of African structures of local government – in order to head off the 'intelligentsia' – since this involved buttressing the system of indirect rule (see Cell, 1992: 241–65). Secondly, the pursuit of social and economic amelioration was sacrificed to concerns with channelling political power. Finally and unsurprisingly, Hailey conceived of African betterment as municipal welfare based on a 1930s metropolitan model.

Yet – taking the first point above – the principles upon which he was balancing his ideas were radical and contentious for colonial administrators. Hailey had embraced the principle that state intervention was vital to making improvements in the material advance of society's most vulnerable members. In his summary of the tendencies affecting African colonial policy, he emphatically endorsed the new emphasis on government being 'an agency for the active promotion of social welfare'. He warned that, like the British Government, colonial governments would be judged according to whether they were able to function as 'agencies of social betterment', and by their capacity to 'assist in the expansion of social services'. Everyone now knew of the deplorably low standards of living in parts of Africa. Echoing the established thought of the League of Nations regarding the Mandated Territories, he was happy to insist that self-government would not be successful unless they could 'build up a social foundation adequate to bear the structure of the political institutions in which they will eventually find expression' (Hailey, 1940–42: 3–5, 62). This naturally made him effusive about an expanded role for central government, new social service committees and the application of metropolitan development and welfare funds. There was something of the structural materialist about his position. Absent were hints about racial deficiencies that made self-government an unobtainable goal for black people. Instead, there were references to widespread poverty. Also, Hailey insisted that 'the pursuit of political ideals' should not detract from 'the pre-eminent needs of social advance', and that the huge financial injection needed to meet the 'more elemental needs' of the African majority could well be used to maintain racial rule. However, this could easily be interpreted as a powerful argument for holding back from self-government for a very long time, that is, until the basic needs of the majority were met.

The problem was that the basic state structure in colonies like Kenya was too rudimentary to carry his expansive vision. For just as Hailey was advocating the application of more external resources, he was also favouring the revival of native treasures. He accepted that low standards of efficiency were a necessary short-term trade-off for the long-term education and incorporation of Africans into local government. Indeed, he conceded that where basic local government duties had already been handed over, little in the way of any comprehension of conventional accounting procedures had revealed themselves. Examples abounded of ledgers being dispensed with in favour of piles of stones (ibid.: 20–22). This was the stuff of District Officers' nightmares. Would metropolitan taxpayers, let alone District Officers, scared as they were by financial scarcity and rectitude – the bedrock of their institutional culture –, be as forgiving as Hailey? Would this be a solution to the 'lost administrative initiative and resolution' he was seeking to rectify? He was in effect asking the administration to set aside their deep-set prejudices against African politicians.

A second weakness lay in his pronouncements on social service provision. At first glance, this was being set out for administrators as being fundamental to restoring colonial state-society relations. Yet, on closer examination this was not the case. His message was that this area could indeed be neglected since it provided an important training ground for Africans in local government. Hailey had rightly taken the view that Kenya's local native councils were indeed the most developed local government network in Africa. By 1940 elected members sat on Kenyan LNCs and in some districts formed a majority. So he described them as progressive since they allowed 'native opinion' to be canalized and expressed. This was a good thing because it held out the prospect of soliciting African co-operation and an interest in further social and economic development. Indeed, it was via these institutions that Hailey had come into contact with a feature of African society hitherto unknown to him: African women. For example, he had learnt that women in Anlo had complained that additional levies designed to augment local revenue were falling upon what were mainly women's activities. Likewise, Kitwe's Native Advisory Council had suggested the inclusion of a female member, whilst women delegates had attended Kikuyu Provincial Association conferences.[3]

Naturally, then, Hailey was keen on paper to see these structures evolve at a smart pace. Regional councils might serve as intermediary bodies. Privately he did concede that these organizations were unpopular among the politically active. However, it would have been a very radical proposal indeed, and one beyond comprehension at the time, that would have stood as an alternative to the 'Lugardian dream' that more federal forms of native authorities could function and behave in style and power similarly to the established colonial structure (Kirk-Greene in Hailey, 1940–42: xix). Nevertheless he pressed on with suggesting that LNCs be given immediate responsibility for certain social services, admitting, as he freely did, that this was likely to reduce the standard set by central departments overseas of such services as sanitation, medical provision, dispensary services and market controls. As he lamented, this was 'part of the price to be paid', since it held out the opportunity for the 'political education of the African population' which the Colonial Office was, of course, under pressure to show that British rule was capable of pulling off. Hailey also tempted his readers with the caveat that, by encouraging local participation in welfare issues, this would be likely to diminish appetites for 'purely political discussions'. Likewise, the hope must have been that this would eventually reverse the decline in district taxation. If people were made more aware of social service issues and their provision, then they might be more inclined to pay up (see van Zwanenberg, 1975: 81; Hailey, 1940–42: 43, 223). So, whilst he lamented Africa's impoverishment and admitted that government would be judged on its capacity to deliver improvements, Hailey had reasons for being prepared to sacrifice the quality of social and economic state intervention on the altar of political considerations. In any case, his plans were designed for decades of gradual evolution.

Thirdly and finally, Hailey had little to say that would support the professionalization of the colonial state. If the welfare and development project was to be realized, technical and specialist staff would need to have a greater role in order to impart their specialisms. However, he suggested that departmental officers should hand over more of their work to the native authorities, rather than administrative officers – the colonial version of a Whitehall civil servant – handing over theirs. Indeed, he insisted that technical officers should not correspond on important matters with their departmental heads, without prior discussion with the local administration. Yet ironically, through his preference for the encouragement of LNCs, it was the duties and functions of the District Officer which these

[3] Ibid.: ch.6 'The African Background: Tribal Authority and Indirect Rule', and for Kenya in particular, see pp. 122–31, 212–21, also pp. 13–14. For an account of the development of local government in Africa see Hicks, 1961.

organizations were in fact making obsolete. Hailey preferred to carry on the tradition of the veneration of this administrative set-up, a tradition from which he himself, of course, came. Indeed, he was suggesting that departmental officers (veterinary, medical, agricultural, and so on) should be made more subordinate to the administration.[4] He did acknowledge that the relationship between different branches of colonial government and social service provision was confused. He suggested the appointment of more specialist officers in central government to work out the relationship between administrative officers and the LNCs. But he offered no precise details as to how such transfers should take place.

However, to expect anything else might be unreasonable, considering the wider context. It would have been virtually impossible for him to offer a neat set of instructions. In practice, the administrative system was built upon informal arrangements, conducted between men who had gone to similar schools, the same universities and married each other's sisters. Yet it was a system that privileged categories of men over others and there was a definite hierarchy, as we shall discover. So, unsurprisingly, Hailey's recommendations left the system of local compromise between like-minded European chaps largely intact, more concerned as he was to find mechanisms to fashion like-minded African chaps. This was after all the big administrative question of the moment from the Colonial Office perspective. Ultimately, he would naturally prefer ramshackle local arrangements rather than standardizing central agencies because he saw the local arena as a training ground in democracy and a place where elite aspirations could be satisfied. The evolving push and pull between central and local government was destined to place a particularly heavy strain on post-war welfare initiatives in Kenya since this was a novel area of activity which lacked the protective cloak of a tradition.

Hailey had been given a tremendous task and had risen to the challenge. Few if any could have completed such a survey of African colonies in the time he took, nor have produced out of this great diversity a single monograph which blended the general with the particular. He had grafted Colonial Office thinking – that the intelligentsia had to be stopped from having exclusive access to power and that social and economic issues had to have priority – on to a colonial reality that was hitherto opaque and out of London's reach. He had achieved much. He had identified some points of friction in colonial government, particularly where boundaries and relations were uncertain. He had pulled out the LNCs as being the best vehicle for moving state-society relations forward, which would have disturbed many officials on the ground since it represented an explicit

[4] Hailey, 1940–42: 14–18; ch.6 'Kenya' , esp. p. 223; ch.1, pp. 40–3. As Hicks observed in 1961 there were two contradictory tendencies at work in British government: a shift to the local level in some areas, as well as a move to the centre as co-ordinator and provider of certain functions. Partnership was the ideal formula to ease the inconsistencies. Hicks, 1961, ch.19.

acknowledgment of African political consciousness and the encouragement of local leaders.

However, the two aims he was being asked to weave into colonial government remained incompatible and Hailey did not bring them any closer together. He could not reconcile their strategy for political development with social and economic advance. This put him out of kilter with the Colonial Office he returned to in 1941, which was now engaged in lavish planning for post-war reconstruction with a greater emphasis on development and welfare rather than political reform. Indeed, Hailey wanted the technical branches of colonial rule to concede ground to the district administration; social services were to be the training ground for Africans in government. He saw no great problem with regard to injections of metropolitan capital to achieve a 1930s model of municipal local government. He did not recognize the absence of a variegated state structure and the racial paternalism of white District Officers as barriers to this plan. As we shall see later on, Hailey's bias gave the local administration in Kenya ammunition in its battles against the efforts of technical departments to gain a firmer foothold on mainstream administration. He helped buttress local distrust of central funding and disdain for allowing central bodies to direct what district officials and those with their background held to be better orchestrated from below. The provincial administration, therefore, had its own reasons for being very content with Hailey's study. The great paradox unfolding here, and to be carried on by the post-war 'Second Colonial Occupation', was that the more direct rule was sought, the more indirect rule needed to be invoked, in the absence of an extensive state structure. Yet even while he was working out policy in the early 1940s events were moving at such a pace that by 1942 the changes and challenges of the moment began to outrun even his astute calculations, and what was absent from them stands out even more: the racial factor in African and European interactions.

Margery Perham: The maiden-aunt

While Hailey was writing up his report which, by the standards of the 1930s, was impressive, the passage of the war ensured that the imperial agenda was subject to a dramatic re-write from without. By 1942, Margery Perham, godmother to the colonial service in the last thirty years of colonial rule, had assumed the role of the informed conscience of the English governing classes. She acts as a second witness to the ways in which war changed the tempo and content of discussions about colonial rule among an audience forced to think hard about Britain's world role and imperial obligations. As we saw in Chapter 1, Perham was already an adviser at the Colonial Office. She grew more adept at using media such as *The Times* and the BBC to publicize the challenges to colonial administration as she interpreted them. She also diffused her views at countless meetings of various non-governmental organizations, by writing letters to men of influence and, of course, through her academic writing and university lectures. It was partly through her tireless efforts that debates about Empire were placed on a hastily constructed metropolitan stock-taking agenda. She was able to take further the efforts begun in the 1930s to give 'the imperial mind a human dimension'. Highly patriotic, she 'demanded that her country attain the highest standards of government of the colonial peoples and she wanted the British public – or at least the policy formulating elite amongst them – to understand the nature and problems of colonial administration' (Smith and Bull, 1991: 1–20; Kirk-Greene, 1982).

Margery Perham was born in Bury, Lancashire in 1895, into a middle-class family. She read Modern History at St Hugh's College, Oxford where she obtained a first-class grade in her final examinations although women were not awarded degrees at the time. Her youngest brother was killed during the First World War and she grieved terribly over his death. Subsequently she became the first woman member of staff at Sheffield University, where she developed an interest in the colonial history of America and the anti-slavery movement. With a heavy workload, the strain on her health became too much and she suffered a breakdown. To recuperate she made what was to be the first of many visits to Africa in 1920. Indeed, it was the beginning of the most important relationship in her life. As she later admitted with a candour few could match at the time:

> I live on one plane – it is Africa always for me – I work, sleep, seek personal encounters, play games, enlarge my general knowledge, save my strength and money for Africa. Not – I do not pretend this – in some entire zeal for selfless service, but because I express myself in work for Africa.[5]

She returned to her *alma mater* in 1924 and was now in a position to benefit from the funds floating around Oxbridge. In 1929, a Rhodes travel grant enabled her to research into native administration which she then incorporated into her lectures. However, her sex, as well as the fact of studying what was at the time a marginal subject, conspired to make it difficult for her to secure a permanent post. An honorary fellowship brought in no money, so she began writing commercial articles and was commissioned by *The Times*. This need for self-sufficiency was crucial since it took her into the publishing world outside academia and helped her conceive of a society that was wider than that of the cloisters or the colonial service. The farm she had helped her sister to buy made her a neighbour of Lord Lugard. He, in turn, introduced her to his Africanist network. Illness again intervened but she was able to take a short course

[5] Comment made in November 1937, reproduced in Bull and Smith, 1991:6.

in anthropology at the London School of Economics where she was taught by Malinowski. By this time enthusiasm abounded in Oxford for the establishment of a course in colonial studies and in 1935 Perham became a university lecturer in colonial administration thanks to a bursary from the Institute of African Language and Culture. Colonial studies became a feature of Nuffield College, running parallel with the Social Reconstruction Survey directed by the Master of the college, G.D.H. Cole, left-wing activist and socialist theoretician. In 1939, Lugard proposed that Perham should replace Lord Hailey on the Permanent Mandates Commission. This was not followed up but she was brought in more closely to advise the Colonial Office, initially serving on the Advisory Committee for Education.[6]

What makes her a crucial witness in this story is the unique lever of entry she had into the colonial administration where she was able to publicize her concept of African rule. With her wide-ranging contacts at all levels of the administration, she was able to disseminate a credible summary of the challenges facing the government of Empire, particularly during the Second World War. Later on she helped innovate schemes such as the Devonshire training symposiums for fledging officers which were begun in the late 1940s. It was a remarkable achievement for a woman in a male-dominated world. Perham won the respect of the colonial service largely through her vast range of personal contacts. She moved effortlessly between district officers in their up-country *bomas*, governors in dusty colonial capitals and desk-bound Colonial Office mandarins. Her style, charm and energy exuded the impression that all 'knew her well, and ... that she at least, recognised the worth of what they were doing and the dedication with which they did it' (see Kirk-Greene, 1991; Robinson, 1991 especially for a review of key links with the Colonial Office).

Paradoxically, being female, which made her subordinate, was also a source of emancipation. Her sex gave her space in which to operate. Born of the same class parentage as the serving colonial officers, she shared a clear consciousness of race and was by no means a critic of chauvinism. Being a woman with a strong feminine presence helped her win over men, as she well knew. Yet her personal attractiveness partly came from the magnetism created by the interest and passion she always showed for her subject. Undoubtedly it helped that she was naturally handsome, amply proportioned, elegant and well-dressed. She could rake in the benefits from being an obvious and welcome contrast to the archetypal grey and crusty male academic. One admiring pupil recalled 'a quiet but confident and masterful speaker, she conveyed a splendid impression of controlled vitality, more like an eloquent athlete than a don...'[7] She was also happy to

[6] Information taken from the Margery Perham Archive, Rhodes House, Oxford.

[7] Robinson recollected that 'her exciting message was one at least of the reasons why I chose the Colonial Office when I joined the civil service...'; Robinson, 1991: 186.

submit to a romanticized view of colonial officers, personified by Dane, her 'man of action' in the novel she wrote set in Africa, *Major Dane's Garden* (1925). Indeed this *imaginaire* formed an ongoing relationship, possibly one variant of her many sublimated and unconsummated love affairs. Throughout her working life her fidelity to imperial masculinity as a worthwhile project remained unsullied (see Bush, 1997: 204).

Yet at the same time she was not one of them. As a woman, she was excluded from the inner circle, missed out on the late night bonding over port and cigars, and was not directly on the imperial pay-roll. Nor did she ever marry into the system. This mutual distancing from which she chose not to escape freed her to make critical judgments, so much so that she did not flinch from heightening the expectations placed on colonial government at a highly sensitive time. She was crucial in fashioning a critique that gently coaxed colonial administrations into rethinking their ruling strategies. In doing so her strength multiplied. She was able to pin down some of the profound problems of colonial rule in a way that those who were actually commissioned to grapple with them were subsequently quite unable to match.[8] The personal cost was huge. Falling in love and marrying might have threatened her professional role, particularly by eating into the close relations she had established right across society and over continents. Her sense of mission overruled her heart but it was not always a happy existence as a result. She knew she had paid a price.

However, her colonial suitors had metropolitan rivals and it was this group who actually helped her settle on a particular line during the 1930s and the Second World War. Perham moved among a range of interest groups and people which informed her views on Africa and vice versa. She had contacts with the ILO, the League of Colonial Peoples, the Anti-Slavery Society and the London Group on African Affairs. On her visits to South Africa in the 1920s she had been taken to the slums in Johannesburg which had deeply shocked her; subsequently the issue of race relations benefited much from her political activism in the 1930s. She also cultivated contacts with the political Left in Britain, helped by having Cole as a colleague. An important channel for this was the Fabian Colonial Bureau, set up by Rita Hinden to encourage research into colonial issues. It was through such an avenue that her friendship with Arthur Creech Jones blossomed in 1940. He was a rising star in the Labour Party, a champion of causes such as trade unionism and education and was destined to be Secretary of State for the Colonies.

Creech Jones and Perham were upwardly mobile provincials, from fairly well-heeled Northern families, and were both passionate about the political aspects of colonial issues and less interested in development. Close in age, it was not surprising that South Africa in the 1920s had brought

[8] Later Perham insisted 'It was of course easier for the travelling critic to recognise these forces than it was for a service scattered about Africa...' Perham, 1967: xix.

them both into the orbit of African affairs; in 1926, Creech Jones had instructed Clements Kadalie of the South African Industrial and Commercial Workers' Union on trade union organization. With his commitment to colonial affairs growing and now private secretary to Ernest Bevin, his mentor, Creech Jones was quickly involved by Perham in a joint Nuffield and Fabian Conference on 'The Future Status and Welfare of Colonial Peoples' held in July 1941. He would send her official documents as part of their developing correspondence. By the end of 1941, she was addressing him as 'Jon', soon as 'My dear Jon', and arranging times for them to 'walk and talk'. In 1946 she could invite him to spend a weekend on the Gower Peninsular with her and her sister, giving train times and detailed instructions for the guest house at Rhossili. It seems clear that he was a person she wanted to engage with and that, at the very least, a marrying of their minds unfolded regarding colonial policy during the dramatic opening years of the Second World War.[9]

Indeed, the Second World War was a traumatic time for Perham. Like many others, there were moments when she felt very restless. Highly significant was the way in which war took her into the East End of London for the first time. She became involved in the evacuation programme, a journey that was to have important repercussions for her views on Empire. Again conflict took away her closest kin, initiating a deep personal and spiritual crisis. Sorrow and anger eventually resolved themselves through a tighter embrace of Christianity. It was the fall of Singapore in 1942 that became the point of transition in her life; where the professional met the personal. It moved her to make a review of Empire that permeated a wide public constituency and split her career as champion of Africa into two phases.[10] Perham did not flinch from administering a strong dose of personal feeling and practical suggestion to a specifically colonial reading of the Singapore effect in two articles printed in *The Times*. Just days after the event, which Winston Churchill himself regarded as a disaster, her views were reiterated in a candid and fiery leading article which she had a hand in writing. These firmly established her as the authoritative voice of the Establishment on Empire.

A huge incentive to make a bold, radical statement on Britain and Empire came from the growing threat from American anti-imperialism. Britain's need for a massive injection of capital to help fund the war effort had made it vulnerable to American efforts to begin the melt-down of the

[9] Perham Collection. RH Mss.23/1.

[10] Perham to Creech Jones, 5 June 1940. Perham Collection. Mss.23/1. See Roland Oliver 'Prologue: The Two Miss Perhams', in Smith and Bull, 1991: 21–6. He argues that the effect was to bring her back into the realm of Christian orthodoxy which he claims caused her to rethink her views on what was best for Africa. See also A. Porter, 1991, who agrees that this was the pivotal point in her life. She interpreted Nazism as the antithesis of Christianity, the product of a failure to follow Christian values and by 1947 she had embraced Christianity as the vital humanizing element that would 'construct something on a deeper level than policy or even the existing imperial connection' (Porter, 1991: 93).

British Empire. Roosevelt had manoeuvred Churchill into signing the Atlantic Charter in 1941, Article III of which committed the signatories to the goal of self-determination and freedom. Although Churchill out-manoeuvred Roosevelt by insisting this related to the occupied territories of Nazi Germany, the animosity of middle America to the British Empire and the particular antipathy of American officials such as Sumner Welles (Under-secretary of State until 1943) ensured that pressure to extend the principles to the colonies reappeared in 1942.[11] Liberal and conservative thinkers on empire had resolutely opposed American interference and rallied round the pre-war concepts of international trusteeship. Perham certainly helped in this regard. By appropriating the language of self-determination and freedom through a vision of a reformed imperialism, she helped create a climate of self-confidence that stopped further American meddling in colonial issues, quite an achievement considering the unrest in India and the growing British indebtedness to various imperial outposts.

The fall of Singapore shattered the myth of white invulnerability. Military defeat could not be disguised as anything other than the result of a colonial people opting to withdraw allegiance from the British Empire in exchange for collusion with the dreaded forces of the Japanese. The shock of the 'Malayan disaster' was internalized and attention turned to the state of the empire as a whole, partly due to Perham's commentary, primed and well positioned as she was to work the spot-light.[12] 'The shock of defeat and loss in the Far East', she wrote, 'has shaken our minds open to the use of an opportunity for adjustment ... we must not seek relief from painful stocktaking.' At the time of her powerful articles and leaders in *The Times*, she was corresponding enthusiastically with Arthur Creech Jones. They both shared a deep irritation at the apparent lack of a policy toward colonial peoples. She agreed with him that the way colonial affairs were treated was disturbing. 'There are times when one despairs of one's country', she wrote early in 1942.

Already angry and aroused, Perham knew what she would say if called upon to sum up the dilemmas of imperial rule in the charged atmosphere following Singapore. Not surprisingly, then, *The Times* leader of 14 March 1942 soberly observed that the lessons of Malaya were many. The moment had come to make a dramatic break with an old type of colonial administration, ill-equipped to meet the demands of new government:

> ... the old order in colonial government has been exposed to a searching challenge ... the future lines of colonial policy are being struck out now, in the furnace of war; and the form which they will take will probably

[11] Wm. Roger Louis, 'India, Africa, and the Second World War', *Ethnic and Racial Studies* 9 (3) (1986) esp. pp. 306–12.

[12] Perham, 1967: 225–33. *The Times*, 'The Need for Stocktaking and Review' and 'Capital, Labour and the Colour Bar', 13 and 14 March 1942.

determine the future development of the colonial territories for many years to come.[13]

It seems she had tested out her position on Creech Jones earlier. Did he not think, she asked in January, that the old imperialism had been dealt a 'moral as well as a physical' blow, due to events in the Far East? 'There is something so utterly pathetic about a society like Malaya' she went on. 'It is like an antediluvian animal that cannot survive into...a new era.'[14]

As a result of these events Perham went public on a number of important criteria regarding the necessary reform of British imperial rule. One was the creation of a modern state structure in the colonies, and quickly. This desire to extend tentacular metropolitan state structures to the empire had grown out of the new inclusive view of colonial societies. Perham insisted that 'in their defects and in their virtues, they are extensions of our society'. Consequently her acceptance of sameness enabled her to embrace the idea of dramatic state reform. 'Modern inventions and administrative methods', she explained, 'have changed the whole tempo of human affairs...our new sense of the ramifying and remediable dangers of backwardness asks for new time-tables.' She compared the expansion in state activity of Italy and Germany. Their 'imperial dynamism', although repellent in its aims, offered useful lessons. The 'new techniques of the age' could be used by British hands for purposes of 'enlightenment and political education'. This would require a complete overhaul of administration, she argued; the modernization of the objectives of welfare and development made their realization incompatible with the 'old system and the old spirit, and the interests for which that system and spirit stood' (Perham, 1967; *Times* leaders, 13 and 14 March 1942).

Arthur Creech Jones was also a convert to the arguments for radical reform. 'We have held too narrow a conception of the purpose of colonial administration', he argued in a Fabian wartime pamphlet; the old-style liberal colonial doctrine had concentrated on political issues so that social welfare had been neglected. Generally, a more constructive imperialism was being championed by sections of the Left in British politics as the only way to bring democracy to Africa. Ironically, it was war which had raised the profile of empire to a home audience; in the inter-war period it had seemed to be slipping from view. Creech Jones was not at all squeamish with regard to abandoning indirect rule and local institutions. Rather, he was prepared to insist that 'native institutions must not buttress outworn custom, destroy initiative, solidify chiefly conservatism, exclude educated youth and oppose democratic forces'.[15] This generation of Labour activists

[13] Perham, 1967: 231–3. *The Times* leader, 'The Colonial Future', 14 March 1942.

[14] Perham to Creech Jones, 29 January 1942 and 10 February 1942, Perham Collection. RH Mss.23/1.

[15] Arthur Creech Jones writing in Peace Aims Pamphlet No.11, *Freedom For Colonial Peoples*, p. 24. Other contributors included Rita Hinden, Arthur Lewis and Lewis Namier. RH. Mss. Perham. Box 705. Colonial Policy – 23.

on Empire associated indirect rule with local elites and right-wing politicians and spokesmen at home, so more government and a larger state structure were seen as a way of subverting their hold on African society and bringing the kind of egalitarian social welfare which Labourites believed they had delivered to the lower classes in Britain.

Others went further in their vision of modernization. Sir Stafford Cripps (Lord Privy Seal) and Aneurin Bevan (Minister for Labour) had plans, big plans. They envisaged Britain applying its technical expertise in the post-war era and presiding over a world revolution to combat poverty, disease and illiteracy. Behind the scenes in 1942 they put together an elaborate plan for India designed to set in motion an industrial and agricultural revolution that could then be extended elsewhere. Both were inspired by the apparent success of the Soviet Union in engineering industrialization, and the standard of government being asked for by the International Labour Organization. The plans were dropped almost as soon as they had been aired. Not only did they require large amounts of finance from the British taxpayer. India had gone too far down the road towards national self-determination. The provincial governor of the Central Provinces and Berar would not be the last person to lament that much social progress could be achieved 'if we were allowed to be totalitarian and authoritarian'.[16] Margery Perham was certainly in their camp, if not quite sharing the same tent. In her public statements she put forward a number of areas where colonial intervention ought to be stepped up. First, a greater role for the Colonial Office; she wanted London to move away from 'first-aid and arbitration' to ensuring that remote colonial administrations did not relapse into stale routine. Secondly, she wanted governments to intervene to restrain the economic laissez-faire of the early pioneering days in order to safeguard economic welfare. Thirdly, she called for the harnessing of the potential of the people themselves, especially of women (Perham, 1967: 227–33 and various articles and leaders).

This last recommendation never received the treatment given to her other imperial babies. The Africa which enhanced her capacity for self-expression was very much a masculine world. This was partly the result of her policy always to seek out the person at the top. Consequently she was more likely to conceive of solutions in terms of adjustments in 'the male administrative structure and those who operated it'.[17] Perham seems to have been far more elitist in her attitudes towards African women. She held a more restricted view of the role of African women in colonial development and welfare than some of her female academic peers such as Audrey Richards and Lucy Mair. She saw them as repositories of the

[16] Louis, 'India, Africa and the Second World War', p. 317.

[17] Smith and Bull, 1991: 8–9. In 1950 she was scolded by Audrey Richards for her part in creating at Makerere College an 'elitist Christianity' that produced one or two Florence Wamalas at the expense of the wider community.

traditional ordering of community and 'less likely than their menfolk to be carried away by the heady gusts of nationalism': a force therefore of welcome conservatism. Despite her membership of the African Women's Education Sub-Committee, the topic seems not to have won much of her attention. Throughout her life, she only knew one African woman well, Florence Wamala. To a degree she had more in common with elite men than with ordinary women whether black or white. Perham preferred to apply herself to issues of race relations and political representation. She naturally viewed African development through a lens of gradually co-opting men into administrative structures – building a bridge between white power and African male civil jurisdiction. Like her peers it was the appeasement and incorporation of elites that commanded her ruling attentions.

Perham's wartime shopping list of reforms also included race relations. She explained to her audience how the 'brutal hammering of war' had put into sharp relief the weaknesses of plural societies such as Kenya and Malaya. A Japanese fleet sweeping into Mombasa harbour would be likely to receive a favourable response from the local dockworker, the Indian trader or the Kikuyu agriculturalist. Her choice of descriptors was significant. She had chosen to evoke Africans with separate identities and roles, and in so doing dispensed with the reductionist and racist label of the native. This humanizing device set the scene for her to question the very efficiency and morality of racially ordered societies. She warned against the assumption that a common citizenry was impossible (Perham, 1967: 266). Calling for a significant time-table revision in the preparations for self-government, she painted a damning portrait of how imperial rule was translated into schizoid social systems marked by division and separateness that were unnatural and unsociable:

> Relying upon its strength and in harmony with its main economic purpose, diverse groups, native or immigrant, pursue their material ends. Outside a few points of economic interaction they can minimise contacts with the other groups. Held secure and separate in the steel frame ... they need never find their true relative positions because the government will allocate powers and define relationships, sheltering this community and discouraging that, according to its own policy.

Perham was not one to alienate the man on the spot with whom she was familiar. Not surprisingly, then, she blamed personal humiliations and the gulf of ignorance on this 'enforced physical separateness'. She was careful to sympathise with the well-meaning DC, for 'many an officer works and overworks with the utmost devotion for the peasants in his charge, while in their clubs, and in European residential quarters, he and his wife may live almost wholly insulated from the aspiring educated minority of the country' (Perham, 1967; *Times* leader, 14 March 1942). It was clear that the war had moved forward her stance on race. On 6

March 1942, she told Creech Jones that 'if we conscript Africans for war or labour, this must be acknowledged by simultaneous measures for associating them closely with us through political and educational measures'.[18] More generally, during the war, the realization that there was a great similarity between the principles behind fascism and racial division began to grow. For example, Lord Moyne had pointed out that blaming Hitler for the Herrenvolk rendered Britain vulnerable to the accusation of denying equality in the Empire. Some officials feared a boomerang effect from African racial consciousness. Propaganda that highlighted German atrocities and contrasted with statements about democratic government was quickly withdrawn for fear that Africans, encouraged to hate one white race while gaining political consciousness, might easily transfer their animosity over issues of race to another set of whites. Likewise, Creech Jones warned that the hypocrisy of sheltering dubious practices behind high principles of trusteeship was being exposed by the war. The changes being wrought by the conflict in the colonies would help clarify what trusteeship now meant.[19]

Now, thanks to the war, what were termed plural systems were officially damned for being inefficient. The *Times* leaders in March in 1942 declared them to be 'embarrassing anomalies'. The condemnation went further. 'The defect of the British colonial system' was that 'it has been too long and too deeply rooted in the traditions of a bygone age, and that it has retained too much of that "stratified" spirit of inequality and discrimination, whose last strongholds are now being rapidly attacked and eliminated in our contemporary society'.[20] This was not simply insincere rhetoric. Perham, the likely author, confirmed her position in a letter to Creech Jones in the following June. If they were to avoid the fate of 'all that becomes atrophied', she warned him, they must adjust their minds. If they could not 'recognise coloured peoples as equal when they are such, and as potential equals when they are not, then I do not see how we can go on having an empire'.[21] This was Perham's warning to the Empire: adjust your attitudes on race; 'infuse a new energy' into your administration and strive to achieve 'a new and more intimate and generous relationship' with colonial peoples. This was placing a great deal of hopeful, if not naive, expectation upon white people who made a living from a political economy

[18] Perham to Creech Jones, 6 March 1942. RH Perham Mss.23/1.

[19] PRO CO875/9/6281/75A. CO Memo sent to African Governments, 15 December 1941. By 1941 colonial propaganda for African audiences concentrated on Britain's long-term economic objectives. When victory was more assured around 1943 the benefits of the British connection were stressed. See Smyth 1985; Peace Aims Pamphlet No. 11, *Freedom for Colonial Peoples*, p. 24. RH Mss. Perham. Box 705. Colonial Policy – 23.

[20] Perham, 1967: 232–3. See also discussion of Elspeth Huxley's comments in Chapter 3. Huxley echoed these sentiments in a warning issued to European society about the major social changes that the war had brought to Britain. Huxley and Perham were engaged in a heavy correspondence about racial rule in Kenya during the Second World War.

[21] Perham to Creech Jones, 21 June 1942. RH Perham. Mss.23/1.

of racial rule skewed in their favour and with a rigid belief system to match. Indeed, the suspicion of race increased in Kenya after the war. Perham could not see at the time that empire and racial equality were fundamentally incompatible.

What gave Perham's critique of pluralism added bite was her attention to the inadequacy of African living standards under colonial rule, a third strand in her wartime imperial reckoning. She challenged colonial governments with her revelations that something was wrong with the way colonial societies were functioning. Behind the impressive panoply of chiefs, courts and councils, she argued, 'the economic welfare of the people often springs helplessly up and down'. Ignorance about these 'tropical East Ends', as she described them, was hardly surprising. It was the need to evacuate families from metropolitan East Ends during the war which had reminded the national conscience that the poverty associated with the Depression had not receded (see Chapter 1). Perham herself had gone into the East End for the first time because of the evacuation programme, and this clearly fed into her commentary on Africa. It gave her a new vocabulary but also the sight, smell and feel of being poor. Only through knowing this at home could she, like many others, then apply the experience and condition to Africa. It was not knowing the African poor that moved her, but knowing it at home first.

Perham was not the only person experiencing this. In Kenya, a few Europeans began to raise the issue of the general ignorance about African living conditions and to suggest remedial action following the Mombasa scandal, Kenya's own Dunkirk.[22] In 1940 a maverick ex-administrative officer Shirley Cooke, an elected settler member of the Legislative Council (LegCo), had urged the government to organize sociological surveys in the large towns. His service on an Employment of Juveniles Committee and the Mombasa Strikes Committee had made him aware of the obstacles involved in obtaining accurate data, which he believed had severely hampered any capacity to make informed recommendations. 'It seemed to be no one's business', he insisted, 'apart from the amateur efforts of one or two enthusiastic missionaries, to study these vital problems. And these problems will become even more vital during the immediate post-war period.'[23] Clearly little was known about how Africans actually lived and the logic developing from this was that new forms of government were required to find out and to remedy the situation.

Nor was Perham a lone voice in Britain. Politicians and officials were presenting the empire and colonial policy to the British public in quite unprecedented ways. Malcolm MacDonald, for example, had given a

[22] Van Zwanenberg argues that a direct consequence of the 1939 Mombasa strike was a report made by Nairobi's MNAO on the employment and housing of servants in Nairobi, which provided a clear picture of urban poverty levels in relation to established benchmarks of living standards; van Zwanenberg, 1975: 39.

[23] S.V. Cooke to Governor, 21 June 1940, p.5, KNA MAA7/575.

broadcast talk which was also reproduced as a pamphlet, entitled 'Helping the Colonies'. Significantly, the cover had an abstract representation of a black person's face. It was part of the duty of trusteeship to help 'colonial peoples' – no sign of the native word any more – to move towards self-sufficiency; Perham had underlined this in her copy. MacDonald explained that British support was needed because the spread of enlightened administration and up-to-date health, medical and educational services was slow and costly. This was presented as part of the tradition of imperial policy, that of the transformation of colonies into nations and the Empire into a 'Commonwealth of Free Nations'. He preferred concepts such as the climaxing of British imperial achievements and devotion to well-being and happiness amongst the 'sixty million citizens of the colonial Empire'. Similarly, Arthur Creech Jones writing in a Peace Aims Pamphlet for the Fabians stressed the importance of belated attention to social welfare in the colonies. Having gone through aggressive imperialism and liberal imperialism, he argued that Britain needed to enter a new phase of constructive imperialism. Efforts to improve health, education, the economy and standards of living were part of the 'sacred trust' and needed to be as dynamic as possible 'so that colonial peoples may as early as possible take their place as free peoples in the commonwealth of free nations'.[24]

Perham presented the argument that poverty in Africa required immediate action. In developing her case she made the important contrast between the metropolitan situation and the colonial setting. The increase in the metropolitan focus on its own poor and the Beveridge settlement clearly opened up her analysis of the African context. As a result, she was able to point out how the colonial situation was fundamentally different from that in Britain:

> What are the social conditions, especially in the families and farms, of communities from which a large proportion of their young manhood is always absent? We do not know. As single, migrant labourers, these men are used in some areas during their best years as low-paid and, by reason of the colour-bar, permanently unskilled workers. Meanwhile the maintenance and care of the community, which provides them, and which in Britain, through wages, insurance, rates and taxation for social services, would be fully shared by industry with the state, is thrown upon distant and often impoverished tribal areas. (Perham, 1967: 229)

This was surely the crucial question which was never again articulated in such a clear manner. As knowledge spread that wages were inadequate to sustain families, it became clear that mechanisms to improve welfare had to be found. The tribe was being forced to carry the burden of social change and dislocation, exacerbated by racial rule. This was a radical explanation of Africa's poverty at a time when the absence of a state was

[24] 'Peace Aims Pamphlet No.11, *Freedom for Colonial Peoples*,. p. 27. RH Mss.Perham. Box 705. Colonial Policy.

seen as a big part of the problem. Her observation highlighted the danger of a state-centric approach when applied to Africa. How could metropolitan solutions solve Africa's poverty when few of the resources and none of the universal moral community existed on to which the state could be neatly grafted and nicely supported? But to meet the requirements of a metropolitan conscience and to secure international approval, the rapid deployment of the politics of inclusion meant unanimous approval of the application of metropolitan East End remedies to what were now deemed to be their tropical equivalent. It all translated into support for an expanded state-building project designed to be Africa's panacea and right.

The challenge Perham issued was unequivocal: to deliver more efficiently the reasonable components of modern administration. It was made all the more potent because of the way she held the attention of a generation of administrative officers who knew and admired her and believed she was on their side. Her prodding of the colonial system illustrated how everything had changed. There were new humanized categories of Africans, a shame of ignorance, new confidence that they understood where and how African society was in need. Also there was a willingness to hold up traditional institutions as elitist and anti-democratic. Consequently more was expected from colonial government. It demanded a tremendous upheaval: if society was to be restructured and reordered as it seemed to require for poverty eradication, then the colonial state would have to be restructured and reordered as well. Perham could not appreciate at the time that this would be too demanding on those living inside fragile systems of rule, to reform actively from the inside and to volunteer uncertain measures of self-liquidation. The future of state welfare and development was uncertain. Established systems of rule and racial paternalism would be more than a match, especially if metropolitan finance and manpower did not appear. Yet Perham managed to create a sense of urgency, a new pace and external pressure. If colonial governments could not provide from above the standard of social welfare now required of modern states, then racial rule would have to be loosened to allow the organization of welfare from below. This was Perham's contribution to the debates about how trusteeship was to be modernized.

The KCA: the African challenge from below

The imperial arena of debate during the war had an increasingly effective low political constituency which began to snap at the heels of its colonial rulers. As the effects of the Second World War began to bite, a politically active class of Africans in Kenya began to pick up the echoes of Perham's colonial reckoning in impressive and threatening ways. Because of the failures of indirect rule and the successes of African adaptation – the emergence of an indigenous aspirant property-owning class – the message of wartime imperial propaganda began to disintegrate. In the context of colonial repression and rural distress, both exacerbated by war, a maturing local ethnic and class-based nationalism found that it could harness London's message in order to advance its cause. In the texts these Africans read, they found a common language which enabled them to explain and further promote their concept of modern government, development and African welfare. What they most wanted was a loosening of colonial racial restrictions that allowed them to look after themselves as well as, more generally, freedom for all Africans. These men and women were part of a tightly knit political network which ensured that local, colonial and imperial politics were woven together through their written response sent back to London.[25] What happened in the war was that the compartmentalization between the metropolitan centre and the colonial peripheries was undone, partly because London had to make a bid to take the sting out of nationalistic protest.

Ironically this situation arose partly as a result of the success of the wartime propaganda campaign run by the Colonial Office's new publicity unit. For the first time the British Ministry of Information told administration officers to compile regular district reports for their perusal. The burden of war was harnessed on to the African population. As we shall see in the following chapters, they were encouraged, sometimes compelled, to join up, to work on war-time construction and production projects, enduring shortages and restrictions and seeing prices rise whilst wages did not. The colonial authorities were forced to pour propaganda into those localities which were hardest hit in order to diffuse resentment. A variety of technical media were used. These included the wireless, public address equipment and mobile cinema, as well as printed material: news-sheets, posters, pamphlets, leaflets, in schools, labour compounds, military establishments and at trading centres. Colonial propaganda had the potential to fire imaginations as well as quell frustrations. This was partly because it was written primarily with metropolitan audiences in mind, to show them why having an Empire should make them feel good about themselves. Thus the ideas and arguments it contained could well be something of a revelation when sent to Africa. Also, in the spirit of inclusion, colonial problems were often related to British problems and the solutions offered consisted of the same gradual expansion of the role of government. The state assumed centre stage. It was sold as 'a constructive agency responsible not only for law and order' but also for 'the welfare of its citizens'. Naturally, responsibility for this 'epoch-making conception' was attributed to the British people.[26]

[25] There is not space to do justice to the bulk of literature on the history of African political association in colonial Kenya. For work on the mobilization of a class-based politics see Furedi, 1989; Kanogo, 1987; and Spencer, 1985.

[26] See Smyth, 1985. For example, V. Harlow, 'The British Colonial Empire and the British Public', 30 April 1943, was published as a pamphlet in 1945, quoted in Smyth, ibid.

One group of Africans in Kenya who were exposed to the wartime metropolitan propaganda about the positive aspects of trusteeship were an aspirant upwardly mobile class that had been growing in political consciousness since the effects of the First World War were felt in the colony. Many worked for wages and they had bought property, but their ambitions and identity were restricted by the colonial political economy. Since African wages were appallingly low and living conditions usually deplorable in the towns, they lived as best they could, falling back on tribal ties to survive.[27] It was in these circumstances of material and social deprivation plus ethnic solidarity, that men formed themselves into new types of political associations and began to issue challenges to the colonial status quo. During the war, such organizations found themselves on the wrong side of the law and high-profile members were imprisoned. A list of complaints about living conditions in one internment camp was compiled by a trans-ethnic group of self-proclaimed political prisoners in 1941. The men were members of the Kikuyu, Kamba and Teita associations and were linked to the Kikuyu Central Association (KCA). The KCA had its origins in southern Kiambu where the Kikuyu Association was founded in 1919. Chiefs and alumni of the local mission schools helped swell the membership and the KCA spread to Fort Hall. Its popularity peaked during the female circumcision crisis but then declined throughout the 1930s (see Spencer, 1985, esp. ch. 3 and ch. 4).

Paralysis was to come. The KCA was banned by the authorities in May 1940. It had always been considered an irritant by the administration. Members of the KCA were usually dismissed as being juvenile, secretive and partisan when they criticized the government, or were pilloried for being reactionary and atavistic when they sided against the missions in the 1929–31 disputes over female circumcision. The level of disdain shown by many Europeans towards Africans who appeared to them to be masquerading as civilized Westerners increased in accordance with levels of anxiety in the colony; after the war it manifested itself in new support for a return to indirect rule so as to hold back their evolution and it was to peak during the Mau Mau rebellion in the 1950s. To calm nerves, the wartime petitioners went to great lengths to try to convince their detractors that they were members of organizations which were purely welfare orientated and not geared to espionage, the latest accusation they faced. Neither had they ever entered into communication with a foreign government. To

[27] For an interpretation of ethnic welfare associations as groups seeking to police male as well as female behaviour, making authoritarian bids to control the private lives of African men that were constructed from a different set of premises and obligations from that of the colonial state, see White, 1991: 'Welfare Associations and Prostitution, 1946–52' pp. 190–201, where it is argued that, while post-war colonial social engineering was an attempt to control African men's private lives by controlling their time and space, the welfare associations sought to control men's private lives by controlling their relationships and their mobility (p. 192).

prove their case, they recalled how in Nairobi sometime between 1939 and 1940 a member walking down Hardinge Street had found a cheque for sixty shillings made out to the Revenue Officer. He had taken the cheque to KCA headquarters, whereupon it was handed over to the government.[28]

What was particularly striking about this communication, which was forwarded to the Colonial Office, was the unprecedented use it made of statements and arguments put forward by colonial officials. Ingeniously the internees stated their corporate aims as being the social, economic and political development of the African. This replicated exactly the rhetoric used in a recent speech by the Colonial Secretary of State, reprinted in the *East African Standard.* As the prisoners explained, he had declared it to be 'an imperative duty to do all that is practicably possible to raise the standards of living of such people even during the War period alike for Humanitarian, Political, Economic and administrative reasons'.[29] They concluded therefore that the British Government's aims were theirs too, and they were united in the fight for a world where the common man had the opportunity to 'raise himself by his own efforts to the highest level of human achievement ... without the burden of poverty ...'. The rallying message of 'war for a fairer world for all' served to highlight their unfortunate plight and to sharpen their sense of unmerited wrong.

Colonial governments in practice did not appear to believe that Africans and welfare went together. They remained fundamentally suspicious of African associations formed for the alleged purpose of safeguarding members' welfare. Such associations inevitably called for sweeping adjustments in wages, labour regulations, and housing, plus major political reform, since for Africans living in Nairobi these were the areas where their welfare was being let down. Government intervention to meet the social costs of reproducing urban waged labour was virtually absent at this time. Conscious of an apparent increase in African associations, the government feared the potential impact this could have on collective politicization during the war. Consequently, officials began to keep a close watch on those they could now castigate as disloyal members of the British Empire, poised to agitate at a time of internal strain and vulnerability.[30]

Surveillance increased. A list of thirty-nine associations was compiled, each categorized in terms of tribe, whether political or welfare-orientated (more often both), geographical base, activities and leading members.[31] Most, such as the Ukamba Members Association, were described as

[28] Letter of complaint addressed to the Governor from political prisoners, West Suk Camp, Kapenguria, 15 December 1941, PRO CO533/543/2.

[29] Ibid., p. 2.

[30] For a comprehensive account of welfare associations and their relationship with the Malayan colonial state, see Harper, 1991, which shows how the Malayan state initially looked to new associational welfare networks for collaborative purposes in the early 1940s and then retreated into more traditional and 'safe' forms of co-operation.

[31] List of Associations 6 November 1945 sent to the CO, PRO CO533/543/2.

having a distinctly tribal appeal, dedicated to 'advancing their own'. A few were defined as purely welfare-orientated. The Luo Union based in Nairobi organized welfare and sport among the Luo. Even this, it was noted, required watching. Also purely welfare-orientated was Ramsi Scotch which organized welfare and dances (see Ranger, 1975), Similarly the Embu Friendly Society based in Embu was dedicated solely to securing the welfare of its members, as was the Buhaya Security and Unity Co-operation. Also in this category were the 'innocent' Kenyango Youths United Brothers Bookshop and Libraries Association and the Kikuyu Vehicle Owners Association based in Fort Hall. The latter was approved of because it encouraged co-operation in the purchasing of tyres and petrol in order to oust Indians from the transport business. Finally there was the Kikuyu General Union, whose aims were the prevention of prostitution and destitution in Nairobi. These were given official approval, but not its methods which included forceful repatriations with fines.

However, the majority were found guilty of blending welfare with political activity, and were, therefore, simply declared to be subversive. Some were found to combine a predominantly social welfare agenda with some political activity. The Afro-Asian Welfare League, for example, based in Nairobi, published a periodical that included political topics, whereas the Railway's African Staff Union was alleged to be an agency for agitation and unrest despite its declared aims being the welfare of its members. Similarly, the Young Basoga Association, based in Thika and Nairobi, was described as being dedicated to increasing wages and advancing Basoga by fomenting labour unrest. More troublesome still were the Kikuyu Associations such as the Kikuyu Barbers' Association which was described as a cover for the KCA and 'very political'; the Kikuyu Sports Club which attracted 'subversive types'; and the Watu Wa Mungu or Aroti, Arathiu, or Arawami organization, based in Central and Rift Valley Provinces, described as anti-European, anti-mission and prone to violence against authority. The Intelligence Department's definition of what was political and therefore subversive amounted to any evidence that Africans were discussing government policy and administration issues and were linked to the KCA in some way.

So, in practice, African mobilization even for self-help and welfare purposes could not be tolerated by the colonial state – a sign of its basic weakness. Focusing on the material aspects of trusteeship was attractive since it offered the possibility of a route away from protest politics, for, if the state could provide more, then, it was hoped, Africans would have less reason to move into political associations. Lacking access to massive material and manpower resources to provide welfare through an omni-present state superstructure, the government was trapped. It was unable to tolerate the development of an indigenous civil society in the new spaces where Africans had to live as best they could. Yet at the same time it desperately needed one to work through, in order to implant to any successful degree the expectations of trusteeship.[32] This meant it was limited to exercising power outside daily life rather than penetrating from the inside: 'dominating networks of ethnicity, they lacked the curb of civil society organized in political parties, trade unions, professional associations or churches. Without such political handles, white rulers were deprived of social purchase'.[33] Instead, force and repression were stepped up to prevent such organizations developing beyond the government's capacity to control them. A racially restricted colonial politics ensured that the control of information and the absence of freedom of speech became enshrined in the culture of the state.

However, African politics at this time was not confined to producing arguments that it was not subversive in war or troublesome in Nairobi. Its activists neatly expressed their class and racial predicament by means of making their own interpretations of the imperial project of colonial transformation. As such, they challenged Nairobi because they began to echo London. Disgruntled members of the KCA moved to register their understanding and approval of the development and welfare thesis coming from Britain, whilst at the same time indicting racial rule in Kenya.[34] This organization was more threatening than the fragmented welfare associations and it represented a powerful rural constituency that claimed the authority of the tribe. Its protest reached up to the highest level of the colonial authority. Lord Hailey, for example, received a long letter from the KCA, in which it chose to define itself in the language of reforming imperialism as an organization dedicated to the advancement of African people in East Africa in all matters social, economic and political'.[35] It complained that should an African express his thoughts or wishes, he was at once labelled an agitator and radical, his ideas branded as sedition. Yet it insisted that any investigation of colonial administration must be regarded as incomplete if its views were not taken into consideration.

[32] See Chapter 3 for discussion of this concept amongst the district administration.

[33] Lonsdale, 1992: 323; see also Jessop, 1990: 360–2. A modern state, he argues, as it seeks to become more involved in different spheres of society, appearing to grow in power, necessarily undergoes two types of change that ultimately decrease its strength: its own unity and identity diminish as internal structures and policy multiply; and as state intervention increases, so it depends more upon the co-operation of other social forces to secure its interventions. Paradoxically therefore a state can only be strong if it places limits on its own ambitions and power, and shares its power with forces to increase its infrastructural strength.

[34] For the origins of the KCA and its link with Kikuyu social collapse and concepts of political virtue, see Lonsdale, 1992: esp. 371–423. For two differing Marxist interpretations of the role of the KCA in Kenya's pre-independence political upheavals see Kanogo, 1987: ch. 4 and 5; Furedi, 1989: ch.3.

[35] Undated memorandum to Lord Hailey, PRO CO533/543/2. Their major complaint was that government policy as a whole was a conspiracy designed to pauperize the African by increasing dispossessions in order to step up detribalization thereby forcing more people to become tenants of cultivation to the Crown and a source of labour supply for the European settlers.

Conditions for many Africans had begun to deteriorate sharply. The KCA wrapped their complaints in a moral indignation produced by a collective assertion of 'unmerited wrong'. They asserted that white farmer-patrons had reneged on their obligations to their African labour. Now grown old and physically unable to give the same profitable work to their employers as in their youth, they were cast aside for having 'outlived their usefulness'. Settler paternalism had broken down in this particular setting, its welfare guarantees to African labour were being repudiated, illustrating a retreat from established arrangements of feudal-type reciprocity.[36] According to the KCA, tremendous hardship reigned in the absence of an agreement on wages, at a time when the cost of living had increased and production had been bedevilled by poor rainfall and locusts. The apparent outlawing of safety-nets such as the cultivation of riverbanks worried them, since it was a practice that had sustained many during the Depression. Also causing anxiety was the perceived shift in the process of selection in schools, causing an increase in the numbers of pupils between the ages of ten and thirteen being discharged from school. They also indicted the racial divide. Insisting that Africans were capable of representing their own interests, they insisted that they should not be barred from participating in self-help structures or education – processes they declared, echoing Perham's words, that were vital to the creation of 'modern machinery for modern man'.[37] They dismissed Hailey's precious LNCs as 'the mouth-piece of the District Officer'. And showing a clear awareness of administration arguments, the petitioners firmly stated that, as training grounds for African administrators, the LNCs lacked any credibility.

The end of the war merely strengthened the voices of protest. Having conceded the first African members of the Legislative Council – Eliud Mathu, a Kikuyu school teacher – the government was now faced with a new reconstituted KCA organization that had been founded to support him. The Kenya African Union consisted of a group of Africans from the major tribes in the colony. At the end of the war, this group sent a memorandum to Arthur Creech Jones, now Secretary of State for the Colonies, which contained much the same indignation and a sense of betrayal and an account of the deterioration in living conditions. 'In return to our Services', they bitterly complained, 'European Settlers have aided in changing of our normal life to the actual degrading status of slaves as squatters', a state of affairs far from the 'mutual cooperation and understanding as Africans

[36] KCA memo to Lord Hailey (undated), pp. 1–2, PRO CO533/543/2. See C. van Onselen 'The Social and Economic Underpinnings of Paternalism and Violence on the Maize Farms of the South-Western Transvaal, 1900-1950' (unpublished paper, March 1991) for a discussion of the structural conditions in which paternalistic relationships are most prone to erosion and from which side the rupture or alteration is most likely to emerge in relation to his case-study: Section 5. 'The Structural Erosion of Paternalistic Relationships', pp. 25–38.

[37] KCA memo to Lord Hailey, p. 3.

would have expected after living together'.[38] The KCA-KAU challenged the Labour Government to take action before 'the facts of the brutality' were shared with 'other audiences'.

Their testimony provides one of the earliest clues to the origins of what was to be known as the Mau Mau uprising, an event that would see the Kikuyu people ravaged by conflict and the armed response of an outraged state. A sense of the mounting insecurity generated by the disintegration of an economic and social system emerges from African descriptions of their predicament.[39] From this time on, the very moral economy of their way of life slowly receded into anarchy. Few officials at the time could discern the true extent of the unfolding drama. Like all moral economies, the Kikuyu's had been constructed from intricate social patterns woven together in this instance to ensure the well-being of a vulnerable and interdependent community living in a harsh and unstable natural environment. Power from wealth was all the more respected because of its purchase against such precariousness, so it was harnessed to civic virtue which was fixed. That is not to argue that it was egalitarian and always kind. The Kikuyu theory of labour served the partisan interests of powerful polygamous men, but care was taken to ensure that the authority of wealth was always questioned even in prosperous times, and especially by the poor. Thus the profits of power were always scrutinized because they demanded laborious social emulation and self-discipline. In this instance, we can see how a local political ideology attempted to critique the effects of the colonial period, according to its own standards of civilized behaviour.

The authors of the memorandum were able to convey to the highest colonial authority what the failures of indirect rule felt like: they bore witness to the pathology of their way of life. They portrayed African men as being increasingly forced to wander helplessly through the pages of the statute books, pushed into criminality by poverty. The education of their children was reduced to meeting the demands of settler labour and had become 'cultureless', imparting detrimental traits into the morality of the young. Everywhere there were signs of a degenerating social system that had once delivered order and continuity, allowing men to be fathers. The experience of living in Kiambu was increasingly the breakdown of patriarchy ending in paternal failure:

> The girls of the tribes who have had no prostitution, now lead prostitute life owing to such poverty. Man is compelled to sell his goats and sheep

[38] Memo on African Land Tenure, Social, Economic and Politics in Kenya, presented to Creech Jones, p. 6, PRO CO/533/544/2.

[39] See Lonsdale, 1992. Through an examination of the deep motivations of political action in the context of the moral economy of the Kikuyu people, Lonsdale has expertly shown that what was interpreted as an atavistic uprising of a tribe traumatized into violence by the experience of standing between the primitive and the modern, was in reality for the Kikuyu a complex and difficult struggle to fix civic virtue in response to the threats generated from massive socio-economic changes.

> to divorce his wives, and is forced in Olenguruone and Rift Valley Areas to denounce his fatherly right to his children in order to limit their family to the area of allotment given to these slave squatters.[40]

This struck a mortal blow at Kikuyu concepts of civic virtue. Men, particularly the poor, were being excluded from the means of production and so from the possibility of earning civic virtue. This was condemning the poor to being delinquent and feckless. Therefore, kindness to the poor was worthless, if not dangerous. Yet they wanted to work hard and show self-mastery, and indeed the squatters had done so but were being thrown off the land (Lonsdale, 1992: 338–40). The Kikuyu land-labour system, whose theory of labour taught that wealth and poverty were moral concepts, was disintegrating. Thus the continuity in the dualism of wealthy authority and feckless poverty was broken. This state of affairs began to create fear and insecurity. Not only were the young moving outside the control of elders but, as war demands increased and settlers were evicted, so it seemed that colonial and European power appeared to be changing. It was no longer vested in the same places, nor did it act in the same way. A creeping sense of terror invaded the household, since 'power which is not knowably social, must always be feared to be unknowably anti-social' (ibid.: 301).[41] After the Second World War and under the noses of the officers involved in the 'Second Colonial Occupation', the very components of, and right of access to, civic virtue – to act for the good of the community and to reap the rewards of responsibility – gradually turned into an issue that mobilized men and women to take arms with varying claims and objectives, through the fusion of 'an unrequited sense of merit' with 'a sense of unmerited loss'. Mau Mau became the violent manifestation of an internal sense of terror as the anarchic and broken state of the moral economy slowly revealed itself.

In an effort to find help, the petitioners turned to an outside model of virtue. They sought refuge in colonial politics. They called for the restoration of racial equality as a necessary precursor to African development. In doing so, they found use for the imperial wartime rhetoric they had read in the script of carefully targeted British wartime propaganda. They stressed how they did not possess any of the civil rights that were enjoyed by common people in democratic governments:

> In all social, economic and political activities for developing our country, we would highly appreciate practical encouragement based on mutual understanding and free from racial discrimination ... If their (sic) exist a real attempt to assist Africans to find a place in modern

[40] KCA Memo p.6., PRO CO533/544/2. This is discussed again in Chapter 6 in relation to the slide towards Mau Mau.

[41] See Lonsdale, 1992: 333–46. On indigenous systems of welfare see Iliffe, 1987 and Seeley 1985. Seeley shows (ch. 3) how, in Eldoret, the ebb and flow of different races, African, Indian and European, affected the pattern of welfare.

> world and to be participant and contributive men and women in a modern world, we request for those common rights of man freedom of speech, of press and of assembly without much delay.[42]

As these words testify, war enabled them to harness imperial rhetoric to their own interests, in this case a social crisis which threatened to undermine their authority. They used it to try to carve out a stronger place for themselves as contributive citizens, by means of the wartime politics of African development and welfare as the goals of trusteeship, and they were being heard by new audiences. Their ethnic nationalism grew faster as deteriorating local conditions jarred with their ambitions and with colonial propaganda. Their concept of welfare was about safeguarding their own systems of patriarchy, allowing African men to put their own house in order and own land they had laboured on. Restoration of their patriarchal dignity and self-help at the local level meant inclusion in the power structure of the colony.[43] The KCA-KAU was now able to measure its lot in relation to an imperial ideal of what it ought to have. Fighting for freedom against oppression and a world of free nations, as the speeches said, found extra meaning in the context of an internment camp or a fractured clan. African protestations complemented Perham's post-Singapore pleas for practical changes in colonial administration, and for 'a more thorough probing into colonial methods in "plural" societies to examine possible fissures that will prevent development into healthy communities', in a startlingly potent way. Criticism levied at colonial rule from both above and below was using strikingly similar language. The colonial government in Kenya found itself being squeezed on two fronts during the war. For the first time African elites and the metropolitan imperial conscience were suddenly speaking with a common voice.

The Kenya Government: a tale of two paternalisms

How did the colonial government in Kenya respond to the demands created by war? Perham had dramatized a real crisis in the imperial conscience. She had called for a new type of colonial government, using techniques of mass education to instil enlightenment and political education. She had exposed the immorality and inefficiency of plural systems. And depicting categories of Africans from her metropolitan experiences as well as knowledge of colonial social conditions, she exposed the impoverishment of the African tribe. African political elites echoed her with voices that

42 KCA Memo, p.9., PRO CO533/544/2.

43 See discussion in Chapter 4 on why the returning *askari*, in general less well educated than most politically active leaders, were not immediately the disruptive and radical influence they were feared to be. What little they had been given was enough to satisfy their needs within the local setting; see Killingray 1983.

spoke the metropolitan rhetoric of equality, self-determination and freedom from poverty. They discredited the LNCs and exposed colonial enquiries as shams. Hailey, just missing the Perham critique and deaf to the African protestations, had taken the 1930s as his point of reference and paid lip-service to the ideal of social advance as the priority of government. His welfare was about nurturing elite aspirations in order to unlock local financial resources and civic responsibility in the tradition of metropolitan local government.

Given that these three different witnesses testify to a fragmenting, unstable vision of how to proceed with the modernization of trusteeship, how did the senior officials in Nairobi perceive and respond to the challenges thrown up by the war? The most important members of the Secretariat in Nairobi were those officers who were members of an Executive Council. This consisted of the Governor, the Chief Secretary, the Attorney General, the Financial Secretary, the Chief Native Commissioner, and a growing number of representatives of technical branches including Education and Labour, Health and Local Government plus Commerce and Industry. Very quickly, the government – a loose term for such an entity, for, although made up of civil servants, it had to answer questions coming from the Legislative Council consisting of official and unofficial members – was placed on the defensive. It was asked to show how its structures functioned to secure the welfare of the African. A shift had taken place in official public language. African was increasingly substituted for Native. This was not trivial. It signified a concession to the metropolitan concept of state-society relations. The term native, as well as being derogatory, also implied self-sufficiency. The term African was less racially reductive but it was also suggestive of a legitimate constituency of demand upon government, like the label European or Asiatic. Natives were being given a modern identity in theory, but in practice there was little substantive alteration in state-society relations.

Awkward questions were being asked of the government before 1939: what exactly were African interests, how should these be protected and advanced; and who was best qualified to carry out this task? LNC members in Central Kavirondo had requested an increase in African political representation. They asked that the LegCo Member for Native Interests should attend the annual combined meeting of all provincial LNCs; that LNCs should have an opportunity to express their views; and that separate representation for Nyanza and Central Province should be introduced. When informed that the white representative of native interests on the LegCo hoped to attend one meeting of each LNC planned every year, the Council replied with a unanimous request that each of the four colonial provinces should nominate two representatives to look after their interests, one European and one African, to make eight seats in total on the LegCo. LNC spokesmen were again told to confine their attention to the immediate affairs of their district; the time had not yet arrived when 'natives' should be members of the LegCo. The timeframe for African transformation was a very wide one.

This prodding did produce an internal audit of the established patterns of co-operation with Africans in local government structures, the LNCs. Officials concluded that these were the proper breeding ground for African participants in a future executive structure. Privately they questioned whether the LNCs should be limited to local government in the English borough tradition, or whether modifications should take place giving them a greater share of the functions of central government. They also began to wonder whether this would give Africans enough responsibility of government, or if evolution along definite political lines would ever have to be taken.[44]

The war did not mean this issue was lost sight of; rather, the contrary. Liberal whites in the colony immediately tacked the imperial politics of welfare and development on to the long-standing local issue of the representation of African interests. As noted earlier, Shirley Cooke, a maverick ex-district officer, now LegCo member, submitted a paper on the subject to Lord Hailey, forwarding a copy to the Kenya government in June 1940.[45] The contents were also published in the *Kenya Weekly News* in March 1939. He pressed the Governor to give urgent attention to Native Affairs, warning that in the difficult months ahead the state of African opinion could well be the government's most serious problem. The only satisfactory way to address local agitation, he argued, was to remove its causes. 'The social, material and political welfare of Africans of this Country' had to improve, he insisted, and he offered practical suggestions. Cooke was convinced that African dissatisfaction grew from the arrangements for the representation of their interests in the LegCo in particular. Their two representatives had only recently retired from government service and were therefore regarded as members of the government. The potential for a clash in interests barely needed pointing out. A former CNC was now defending policies for which he had himself been responsible. Cooke also suggested that Africans should be selected as LNC chairmen.

In war, the Kenya government did modify its position, but only slightly. It certainly appeared to be able to reply more quickly to external criticism. The official line taken was that, in addition to the two unofficial LegCo members representing Africans – in 1941 both men were retired colonial officers – four Provincial Commissioners sat on the government benches as well as the CNC, and all were in close contact with African opinion.[46] It

[44] See discussions in KNA MAA7/575, esp. undated document passed on to the Governor from R.T.B. 12 April 1940; letter from LNC members, Central Kavirondo, to Governor 14 February 1940, ibid.

[45] PC (Central Province) to CS, 9 March 1940; S.V.Cooke to Governor 21 June 1940, KNA MAA7/575.

[46] 'The Voice of the African in Kenya Legislation', (undated) KNA MAA7/575:

was not difficult for officials to be satisfied that they were the true guardians of African interests, despite evidence that racial representation in the LegCo was in reverse ratio to actual numbers. However, a secret report at the beginning of the war admitted

> ...more contact is required between the members representing native interests and the natives they represent: they are apt, in spite of sound intentions to rely on their past experience rather than ascertain what the natives think is good for themselves, to stress what they think is good for natives; they are, in fact inadequately briefed with native opinion.[47]

This represented a modification in colonial government thinking. But just as the label 'native' and 'Kenyan Africans' mingled in the text direct, the negative position on racial capabilities remained. African representation was still easily dismissed as impossible in practice:

> They [Kenyan Africans] are united as yet by no common bond of language, creed or policy. They are divided even within the tribe, by local jealousies and ancestral enmities and it is only administrative control that keeps down inter-tribal raids and local 'incidents' ... There may be as many as four distinct languages spoken in the same district ... about 100 Africans pass out of secondary schools each year...the number of Africans who understand colloquial English and who could take part in a debate can be counted on the fingers and does not probably exceed six ... there are as yet no Africans who have a reputation which extends far beyond their own tribe and to appoint at the present stage of development even four natives to Legislative Council would be a mere temporary palliative which would soon become an acute irritant.[48]

The government could feel exonerated, for its plans were in line with Hailey's pronouncements.[49] It had a three-stage plan for the development

---

46 (cont.)

Race	*Population*	*Members in LegCo*
European	22,803	11
Indian	43,195	5
Goan	3,702	
Arab	15,481	2
Native	3,280,777	2

As proof of the greater interest and genuine sympathy for native development among non-officials, the report cited the vote of £50,000 for Makerere College.

47 'The Voice of the African in Kenyan Legislation', p. 3, KNA MAA7/575.

48 Ibid., pp. 2–3.

49 Lord Hailey, of course, was satisfied with this, but recommended that it would be advisable to introduce an additional stepping-stone between the Provincial Councils and direct African representation, in the form of a Native Affairs Council which would eventually elect members to the LegCo. See CO comment on discussion with Lord Hailey, 18 March 1942 PRO CO533/529/11.

of the native political system along the same lines as the English city burgesses. At the bottom the LNCs would provide opportunities for practical public service. Provincial Advisory Councils, drawn from the LNCs, would be purely advisory, helping to co-ordinate LNC policy 'as regards matters of communal interests, marketing, roads and the like', a bridge between native opinion and members who represented native interests on the LegCo. The third stage, described as being a long way forward, was to include a Native Assembly drawn from the Provincial Councils.[50]

However, maverick individuals like Shirley Cooke remained dissatisfied. In 1942 the Member for the Coast proposed that the LegCo should ask the government to follow without delay 'a progressive and far-seeing native production and welfare policy and that non-official Europeans be associated more closely in the formulation of that policy'.[51] Sensitive to this issue, at a time when the Singapore effect was still resounding through the Empire, a top-level meeting at Government House accordingly took place in September 1942. The Acting Governor, Sir Henry Moore, questioned each department head as to the state of particular schemes throughout the colony, looking for statistics that would indicate definite progress. Whilst the Director of Medical Services agreed that he could provide such figures for increased levels of expenditure, he was far from satisfied with the rate of progress. 'Insofar as the allocation of Government funds was concerned' he felt that 'Africans had not been neglected but general progress could not be made unless there was economic development and increased taxation'. Similarly the Deputy Director of Agriculture complained that whilst there had been improvements in production for which he could easily produce the necessary facts and figures, problems relating to land welfare and organization had been neglected, and the CNC commented that eradicating famine had been achieved only through a retrogressive policy that had led to land misuse.[52]

War let them off the hook just as it made them more vulnerable. Moore referred to the Secretary of State's recent comment that, while social services should be maintained throughout the Colonial Empire as far as was practicable, they could not be expanded in the present circumstances. The Governor also suggested that the planned provincial survey on the

[50] 'Voice of the African in Kenyan Legislation', p. 3, KNA MAA7/575. This was also conveyed in a meeting on LNC developments with Major Scupham from Tanganyika attended by the Deputy Chief Secretary and CNC. Scupham observed in no uncertain terms that, compared with Tanganyika, Kenya's difficulty rested on the absence of any real native authority to enforce LNC resolutions, due to the lack of hereditary Chieftainship among Kenyan tribes; their advantage lay in the way they provided an outlet for the views of the intelligentsia. This was a less optimistic view than Hailey's. Having the DC as LNC President was a drawback in Scupham's view, as in Tanganyika all execution of policy was left to the Native Authority, the Administrative Officer functioning as adviser and provider of services that the Native Authority was unable to carry out alone.

[51] Notes of meeting at the Secretariat (undated), discussed below, KNA MAA7/575.

[52] Ibid., p. 2. See Chapter 3 for an amplification of dissatisfaction in technical departments.

problem of land use and native land tenure could justifiably be postponed on the grounds that it would place too great a burden on the administration. Africans were being brought into closer association through Provincial Councils and the Standing Advisory Committees on LNC Estimates, and he suggested that Cooke be referred to a conference on social welfare held in Nairobi in 1941. The medical profession was not convinced – a precursor of what was to come. Its line was that much could have been achieved if the proposed research had been undertaken at Nyeri by a team of experts including a sociologist; the failure to circulate the prepared questionnaire and to appoint a Lands Secretary as proposed in 1940 was the real obstacle. The administration won the day; Hailey, after all, was praising the Kenya set-up and white settlers had to be considered. The colonial authorities in Kenya avoided accepting that the consolidation of local patronage networks was the only option they had for creating a 'responsible public opinion'. Their great fear was that LNCs would become mere channels for demands on central government which they could not meet. The limited nature of their response during the war ensured that the demands of the KCA were still ignored and it offered little in the way of immediate signs of welfare and development.

However, the issue of African welfare returned once post-war reconstruction dominated the horizon. The promises of finance under the new Colonial Welfare and Development Act stimulated colony-wide plans. Consequently questions were raised about African representation in the new plans. In 1945, Archdeacon Beecher (unofficial Member for African interests in the LegCo 1945–7) asked that LegCo be told about the steps being taken to consult with unofficial opinion in the process of compiling five-year district plans. Was the Government aware of the deep disappointment felt by responsible Africans at their exclusion from these discussions, he asked, and how would this be remedied?[53] The administration replied with authoritarian paternalism. Explaining why he refrained from allowing Africans to read his Development Report, Nyanza's PC Kenneth Hunter argued that Africans lacked the sophistication needed to comprehend the realities of government. Prone to the behavioural pattern of a disappointed child, 'the African is so apt to translate a proposal into a promise, and later to advance a plea of breach of faith if the proposal has not been effected'. The colonial relationship was evidently too tenuous in practice to allow mutual exchange at the local level, illustrating the deep obstacles to Hailey's other recommendations. Africans could not be taken into the government's confidence about provincial and colony-wide plans and policies. Such information was fiercely guarded.[54]

Instead, the government looked to improve its image. The atmosphere of greater attention to propaganda and getting the right message across had

[53] Circular sent to PCs from Acting Chief Secretary, 12 April 1945 for their responses, KNA PC NZA/3/570.

[54] PC(Nyanza) to Chief Secretary, 17 April 1945, ibid.

made an impact. The barrage of criticism from above and below required action. In order to improve its public relations, the government commissioned a specialist from the Army. Kenneth Gandar Dower had worked as a publicist for the East African Command. He produced four pieces of work under the general title of 'Methods and Aims of Native Administration in the Reserves'. They were later praised by the Colonial Office as being 'excellent' and 'a significantly new departure from the famous reticence of the colonial government', and were detailed as potential ammunition for East African public relations exercises.[55] These texts illustrate the Janus-nature of the colonial government. It sought to incorporate Perham's concept of an enlightened modern state turning away from pluralism but officials could not let go of authoritarian racial paternalism. The result was confusion. The administration was stuck between discourses, combining two languages of paternalism that were at odds with one another.

The language reflected this effort to combine local and external positions. The label 'Native' was in the title but also the term African appeared in the text; both were qualified occasionally with Kenyan. However, from the detailed description offered, the racial stereotype remained intact despite the new names, namely, that of a vulnerable child requiring the guiding hand of wise parents. Incapacitated by confusion, he was unable to understand his environment He needed his colonial rulers since they alone understood what he did not know and what he needed to learn:

> Whether he likes it or not he is involved in world economics. Whether he likes it or not he is involved in the clash of cultures... It is our responsibility that he is involved, it is therefore up to us to take something of the shock, to train the Kenya native to play his part in a strange and incomprehensible world, to adapt his social ideas and methods as far as is necessary, whilst retaining everything that we can.[56]

Here 'native' was happily used in relation to old notions of the omnicompetent colonial authority. General administrative objectives were set out in line with Hailey's vision of a slow evolution toward bringing 'to the native, mental, moral and material prosperity, to develop something of the British concept of political and legal responsibility as rapidly as is possible (but not more rapidly than is possible) and steadily improve his standard of life (within the limits of a balanced budget)'.

Yet Gandar Dower also tried to incorporate the challenge from Perham's prodding of the imperial conscience. The old language of colonial paternalism was supplemented with a new one that talked of government responsibility enshrined in the state. Dower used the new language of social services and development. The idea of the state and people having

[55] The four articles produced by K.Gandar Dower at the request of the Kenya Government were sent to the CO, PRO CO533/531/10

[56] 'Methods and Aims of Native Administration in the Reserves', article 1, p. 1., ibid.

entitlements from government, sat side by side with the concept of more feudal-type paternal relations. The two did not mix easily. Colonial government was now defined as African development, and as such used the metropolitan discourse of 'social service' provision. Gandar Dower told the history of administration as the introduction throughout the countryside of these services which had served as schools where 'Africans learnt that sickness could be prevented' and where 'ambition for better fields, better food and better children was stirred'.[57] This enlargement of the government agenda was clearly seen as a device that could be used to illustrate how much had to be done, thereby justifying continued trusteeship. However, the reality was different. For in the long term the government was also signing up to deliver a wider range of modern services alongside political exclusion on the grounds of race.

Gandar Dower, however, happily listed the 'milestones' already achieved under colonial tutelage, which included the 'first practical steps in democracy, the LNCs, the narrowing of differences between tribes and the importation of social services'. All these, he insisted, had won over the confidence of the natives to the extent that they would no doubt vote for keeping the 'White Man'. It seems an unfortunate choice of argument for European rule, since Africans could not, of course, vote at this time. Evidently this propaganda was aimed at a metropolitan audience. Yet it was to Africans that the authorities needed to speak, for the construction of an amenable and accessible African civil society was vital to their post-war plans.

Being forced to play the social service card did, however, bring with it a number of minor revolutions in government rhetoric. Gandar Dower's third publication entitled 'Physical and Mental Progress' divided the various areas of improvement that colonial government was busy working upon into medical, educational, agricultural and veterinary compartments.[58] In order to discuss health improvements wrought by colonial discipline Dower had to go beyond the African as an irreducible single category and talk about peasants and their families. It was explained that the systematic introduction of improvements in the health of the people had not begun twenty years earlier because at that time 'communications were too poor and people too shy'. Since then efforts had been made to learn what was happening among families. These had revealed the prevalence of preventable disease and ill-health, women often having seven or eight live births on average but a high incidence of infant mortality.[59] The new

[57] Ibid p. 2.

[58] 'Physical and Mental Progress' by K. Gandar Dower, PRO CO533/531/10. The article opened with a strong statement designed to establish without question the beneficial effects of colonial rule and to discredit critics: 'Whoever feels that the African was best left in his never-existent "happy savage" Utopia and is the worse for education and the European's economic influence ... will admit that he would probably rather be alive than dead.'

[59] Ibid., p.1.

emphasis on women points to the major revolution in official perceptions, at least on paper. Women had to be co-opted and trained for specific developmental reasons and the paper pledged government support in promoting the education of women:

> Yet only by educating the women of the tribe can that tribe be advanced in hygiene and sound veterinary and agricultural methods, and it is encouraging that within the last year or two there has been coming from educated Africans a sincere demand for the education of girls. This demand will be met.[60]

Dower even made a tacit acknowledgement of women having a no-nonsense political capability. He argued that the LNCs, as the first steps in British democracy since DCs, managed to get the names of the natural leaders of localities by having the confidence of the tribe. This avoided elections between nobodies 'which would carry little weight with the men and none at all among the important women of the tribe'.

However, by including attention to the 'mental' aspect, expectations were once again lowered and authoritarian paternalism reigned almost supreme. The overriding message was that a significant gap existed between current social service provision and what backward Africans were capable of understanding. Gandar Dower's readers were clearly expected to sympathize with the poor DC, since 'no D.C. would claim to understand the native way of thought'. He shocked European sensibilities with news that latrines when dug were not always used. (This was hardly surprising when the European 'comfort-station' gave natural cover to snakes, spiders and so on; a bush and a clump of leaves was, in practice, much safer). Enthusiasm for education was great, he conceded, but misplaced, since 'the motive is largely economic'.[61] LNCs had to be watched because of their lopsided expenditure; in 1934 they voted £22,728 for education but only £18,431 for agriculture and medical and veterinary services. Likewise, he dampened expectations of the numbers of educated African women increasing. Without career openings for African women, there was no immediate advantage in educating daughters when resources were scarce.

At the level of the colonial government, imperial arguments about the need for the state to tackle African welfare were ultimately dashed by racial thought. Dower explained ill-health and high mortality as the result of ill nourishment, a lack of knowledge about hygiene and an absence of purchasing power which denied ownership of the simplest means of cleanliness, soap and water. However, he stressed that in trying to spread

[60] Ibid, p.2. This echoed Perham's concern voiced in 1942 that 'Above all, we should start in real earnest to lift from the colonial peoples the vast dead-weight of female ignorance and backwardness', Article in the *Times*, 13 March 1942 reprinted in Perham, 1967: 227.

[61] Gandar Dower, 'Physical and Mental Progress', p. 2., PRO CO533/529/11.

the idea of a balanced agriculture that could provide a better diet and the money to purchase the essentials of hygienic living, the government had come up against a psychological barrier. The observation was casually made that 'the average African' still viewed health as a matter of luck and each new directive as something 'newfangled and suspect'. This mental aspect had to be broken, he argued; the missing ingredient had somehow to be found since

> ... revolutions in agriculture and hygiene could not be wrought without a change of heart and head and the African had to be inspired with ambition, to be given wishes and wants with regard to the things that are necessary for health ... that in order to get them he would work and adopt new methods.[62]

As the wriggling and writhing of the Kenya government illustrates, African purchase upon the colonial system had increased since the beginning of the war. The government was more vulnerable to a critique of good government that was inclusive of African welfare and the provision of modern social services. The reductive label of native, with its implication of self-sufficiency and a universal type, had rivals; official documents supplemented the term with Africans and Kenyan Africans. Out of this process of differentiation also emerged African women. This less crude configuration of African society automatically opened up the administration to wider demands. Not only did it suggest a more modern relationship with the state, but such intimacy would certainly require the state to behave differently. If society was to be reshaped along the lines of the new welfare and development variant of trusteeship, then the structures charged with this task would have to be reshaped accordingly. The way an army soldier with expertise in public relations was seconded to the administration illustrates a new willingness to be inclusive of outside expertise hitherto considered unnecessary. But in the slow pace of political incorporation, the rejection of African constituencies such as the KCA and the refuge taken in the mental aspect of African development, we can see that what triumphed was a refurbished racial paternalism. As Gandar Dower illustrates, a great deal of the Perham challenge had been digested, but if this was the best the colonial government could offer in return, and the Colonial Office was satisfied, then ultimately the rhetoric would be little more than that.[63] In the following chapters we shall see to what extent the

[62] Ibid., p. 1. Figures showing an increase in hospitals, in patients and out-patients treated at dispensaries and in expenditure since 1918 were tabulated as proof of the government's efforts, although, as the discussion of these figures revealed above, the Director of Medical Services was not totally convinced.

[63] For a comparison, see Duncan, 1992. He argues that, during the Second World War, the South African state appropriated the concepts of public health and social welfare to buttress its own power at a difficult time: its commitment to meaningful provisions was never more than lukewarm. He concludes that committees and commissions were used to give the appearance that the government was more committed to social welfare than it

colonial state went beyond offering good intentions and faced up to the challenge of improving African welfare according to the standards and goals it had set itself during the war, and, where it did not, the reasons why.

Conclusion

These four witnesses to wartime debates about African welfare and government have illustrated the contrast between the consolidation and growing coherence of an empire state-building project at the Colonial Office and the increasing fragmentation of imperial constituencies of opinion. Lord Hailey thought he was dealing with the prospect of financial resources and far-reaching timetables that could support the conversion of Africa into a laboratory of experimentation in social and political state engineering. Technical departments would have to lose out to the administration, economic development to political practice, central government to the LNCs. He wanted colonial governments to conceive of social welfare as municipal social services and a good place for Africans to learn civic mindedness. Less emphasis on the role of a white administrative cadre of scientific and technical specialists put him out of step with the architects of the Colonial and Development Welfare Act. Margery Perham pushed for more metropolitan solutions for metro-Africa problems. She damned race relations, wanted inclusiveness, and topped and tailed everyone's timetable for self-government. African nationalists, meanwhile, damned the LNCs as a sham, whilst portraying themselves as modern men who understood freedom, responsibility and development. They urgently wanted recognition as such, searching for a way to stop the moral fabric of their people being torn to shreds. Unable to tolerate the KCA or discern the growing crisis, the colonial government in Kenya accepted change in order to keep the status quo. Keen to acknowledge that social and economic improvements were their domain and the base-line for political freedom, they nevertheless insisted that the racial deficiency made this an uphill task and necessitated longer timetables plus local autonomy.

These conflicting views about African welfare and government reveal the way paternalisms of rule were in a state of flux and crisis. Paternal rule was being repudiated and redefined at both ends of the imperial axis.[64] At the metropolitan level, old ideas of mutual responsibility were found not to work; families were falling through the gaps. In response there was a redefinition of paternal tolerance articulated through the financial responsibility of the state to minister to those unable to cope at conjunctural

[63] (cont.) actually was. Fiscal demands could not be made upon white taxpayers nor the 'work ethic' be seen to be subverted.

[64] As Rousseau observed 'The strongest is never strong enough to be always master, unless he transforms strength into right, and obedience into duty', quoted in Van Onselen, 1991: 1.

moments of need. The new Beveridge paternalism was designed to paper over the cracks of capitalism, provided families were submissive; maternity, family and old age allowances insured against the collapse of the family at times of economic vulnerability, bringing the state closer to its needy. It demanded a much more intimate relationship between state and subject. The Colonial Office had no choice but to offer an imperial version of this shift in relations and enhancement of expectations. However, as Perham illustrated, old-style colonial rule would be an obstacle to achieving a 'new, more intimate and generous relationship' between government and society. It was not just the existence of racial rule that made such a transfer problematic. The absence of a single moral community, a self-perpetuating source of finance, an omnipresent state structure, muddied the waters.

Yet, ironically, at the time all sorts of colonial paternalisms were in crisis. Settler paternalism was breaking down as white farmers sought to capture the state as the sole provider of capital accumulation. Landowners attempted to control their squatter families, keeping wages down, releasing land and reducing feudal-type benefits. Employer paternalism had never really existed in practice; Africans were on average not receiving sufficient wages to support themselves. Most importantly, African rural paternalism was under pressure. The fine relationship woven between 'wealth, poverty and civic virtue' that had previously insured against insecurity and dearth was being repudiated, as the KCA-KAU had demonstrated. Rural capitalism especially threatened the poor (the majority), by increasing the risk of exclusion from land rights, thus imperilling their manhood. As Kikuyu colonial chiefs began to separate power from virtue, with local office bringing wealth, favour and access to visible benefits, so the Kikuyu moral economy was turned upside down. Public authority which came from the private achievement of 'saying and acting' that yielded wealth – God's reward for public virtue – was no longer constant (Lonsdale, 1992: 332–53). This group was hit especially hard. The largest tribe living most intimately with the European community and subject to changing class formation, the Kikuyu, who laboured in the towns, farmed in the Highlands and taught in the schools, was increasingly unable to function as it once had. Meanwhile, traditional DC paternalism in the Reserves was also under pressure. Forced to exact more than ever from African clients during the war and relying upon appointed chiefs to do so, the state imposed more farming restrictions and labour obligations than ever before. Africans found themselves subject to more *mzungu* madness than ever before.

Where metropolitan and colonial paternalism of rule met, supreme confusion reigned, which Gandar Dower threw into relief. In practice the metropolitan social welfare prescriptions were inappropriate to the colonial moment. As Margery Perham noted, rich industrialized countries allowed for taxation that was used in part to aid those whom capitalist relations of production and reproduction had failed. In Britain, community care was organized around the state's administration of social welfare to a minority, those who were pushed into conjunctural poverty at certain times. Thus the community was relieved of this burden and the majority were left able to take care of themselves, through self-help, responsible parentage, wise motherhood, voluntary organizations, all shaped in a particular direction by less obtrusive tentacles of the state.

In Africa there was no such single community, no voluntary organizations, no civic institutions, no easy way into the domestic arena of reproduction. In their place were increasingly uninviting and impoverished 'tribes', that government could not easily get inside and knew little about. Social welfare, the declared universal aim for all societies with responsible government, in the colonial case meant delivering social improvement for the majority. The metropolitan welfare discourse therefore gave the colonial agenda of government a confusing set of precedents because of at least five points of contrast: the smallness of the budget available for redirection; the communality rather than individuality of need; the lack of access to a civil society through which to work; the confinement to constitutional administrative mechanisms for talking about welfare; and the absence of a single political community that rendered African voluntary organizations unacceptable to the white community and Africans unwilling to submit to the same moral discipline as their European rulers. And in the confusion, the colonial state lost sight of the family, in particular women, as the central agent of community welfare.

Inevitably this confusion created a space for evasion. The old racial paternalism was left intact and poverty remained the collective inadequacy of communities. Gandar Dower pointed out that the problem was a total one; Africans were blighted by their concern with individual advance, lacking any propensity to see their interests as being best served by investing money and labour in communal betterment, in the schemes that the administration wanted. As Dower suggested, this was what district administration was all about: to 'improve the standards of living of the community as a whole', to goad whole tribes – a new expression of the old racial paternalism. As such, he made it a total administrative problem rather than a purely departmental one. New structural categories and alliances began to see ways in which Dower's prerequisite of 'a change of heart and head' could be wrought quickly and cheaply, so that '[The African] would work and adopt new methods because he was inspired with ambition and with want for the things necessary for health'. Kenya's racially skewed state-society relations would be likely to derail any universalizing tendency coming from outside.

Ultimately, however, no reforming force, transformatory model or racial theory would be any match for the dynamic of social change as exemplified by the warnings coming from the African nationalists. This, rather than any failure to adapt the colonial state to the wartime welfare and development agenda, curtailed the administration's plans much sooner than anyone could conceive at the time. As our four witnesses collectively illustrate, competing and contradictory elements within the imperial project of transformation were greatly exacerbated by the war. War stimulated debate about colonial transformation and encouraged debates about imperial rule.The Beveridge welfare package was the state's reward to society for enduring war. In the colonial context, this could not be replicated in practice in the absence of a political will, an adequate state structure and resources. In any case, African nationalists wanted freedom in return for loyalty, entering an era when the rule of a people by an alien force had become much more suspect and difficult to justify.

This chapter has been about defining the problems of imperial rule: how the late colonial state faced a crisis of paternalism and found a confusing array of prescriptions with which to read the problem and find a solution. Having moved from the metropolitan arena, then to the imperial audience, we now follow the players on the field during the war. How did a set of ideas generated in London measure up against the ways in which ordinary white officials and settlers thought about African welfare and good government; how were the issues debated in Kenya during the war?

Three

Village People, Family Men & Married Women

The Fantasies of Wartime Kenya

We now come up against what those in Kenya thought about African welfare and development: who was saying what to whom, where they briefly collided, only to move off again in different directions. For the Second World War also had a profound effect upon colonial thought and practice on the ground. In Kenya, one manifestation of this was an increase in general discussions about providing for the native population. The rhetorical statements and debates conducted in the high political arena and examined in the previous chapter, were made at a time when a much more wide-ranging set of local contributions were being generated by city dwellers, technical staff, district administrators and white settlers for each other's consumption. Welfare became the new buzzword. The onset of war had further upset the status quo in a colony already ill at ease following a spate of labour unrest. Some felt unsure as to what the future held but many were excited about what might be accomplished. Frustration, anxiety and exposure to external political currents prompted Europeans living in Kenya to debate how they ought to respond – and be seen to be responding – so that native welfare would be improved. It was a topic that proved to be highly seductive. A pressing subject on its own merits, particularly to people who considered themselves dutiful Christian men and women, it could also offer the means to shore up white moral authority over black or simply increase job security over a rival. All contributors shared a vision of orderly villages made up of families behaving in ways they believed would improve their welfare and bring control. However, the wartime consensus was short-lived. Not only did each group offer a different path toward this shared goal; there was little internal agreement either. Ultimately it was the paradox of war which shone through yet again. The energy and optimism that fizzed around the colony and stoked the engine of what was to become 'the second colonial occupation', also exposed the obstacles and constraints to real action. This chapter unearths the submerged boundaries which shaped colonial thought during this dramatic period. It is a story of confused minds, often unclear as to what the problems really were; at times too insecure to test out their theories, too isolated to find external sources of solidarity, or too blissfully unaware to care.

Introduction

Debates about empire state-building according to the prevailing fashion – the promotion of welfare and development of colonial peoples as an act of trusteeship – were not confined to the high politics of metropolitan discussions. During the Second World War, such a shift was mirrored at the local level but it took quite a different form, as we shall see in relation to Kenya, the settler colony with a reputation for failing to look after its African population. The news about funding for colonial development and welfare was no one-off event. As set out in the previous chapter, Margery Perham would soon give the imperial debate a strategic and moral direction that pointed toward better state provision; Lord Hailey had begun to explore the administrative and political implications of social development; Africans listened and the Kenyan government had to make a response. Simultaneously in Kenya, various white interest groups attempted to carve out a new role for themselves adapting their own vision of African welfare and development. Participants in this unprecedented exchange were drawn from those who had not left to fight. They carried on working much as they had always done and, for some, this provided a strong incentive to get busy.

Such a gear-change at this lower level was possible because the more alert members of white society had already begun to understand that African problems were increasingly social. Chiefs were finding it harder and harder to discipline the young people, to collect taxes and to extract labour. Life on the African reserves was increasingly congested and land disputes more frequent and fractious. The spread of agricultural production, orientated now more along capitalist lines, was highly uneven. Richer African farmers were able to take advantage of markets and labour but their existence by no means guaranteed a lifeline to their poorer cousins. Urban populations had expanded in a messy and uncontrolled fashion throughout the 1930s. The revelations that followed the Mombasa General Strike in 1939 became Kenya's very own evacuation scandal. Although female circumcision was less a contested issue than it had been among the Kikuyu – they agreed to disagree –, women's productive roles, particularly control over labour, were more in dispute. Indeed, African pressure at this time was generated by economic, social and demographic factors rather than political pressure.[1] Consequently concern with an apparent trend towards social breakdown had already manifested itself before 1939 in an obsession with detribalization. This was not perceived as simply an urban phenomenon, but was profoundly rural where many of the answers were thought to be found.[2] Many thought the damage and

[1] Lonsdale, 1968. See generally Iliffe, 1996, esp. ch.10 'Colonial change, 1918–1950'; Throup, 1987; and Thomas, 1998.

[2] See Cooper, 1996, for a full account of the colonial state's approach to issues relating to

disruption to African society, as they were manifesting themselves in Kikuyuland, came from exposure to the forces of modernization. Officials had long been encouraged by anthropological enquiry and the testimony of male elders to hold to the rather naive belief that pre-colonial peasant-farmer society was static, pleasantly communal and neighbourly. Consequently, there was a tendency among senior officials, including the Governor Sir Philip Mitchell, to take refuge in the view that the traditional pillars of rural living must not be undermined if further disorder was to be prevented.[3]

However, the war also threw up a range of new incentives and interest in more direct rule as the means to provide solutions to the above problems. As we have seen, the war had jarred into action a lethargic Colonial Office, aware of miserable living conditions, fearful of further unrest and mindful of the need for a propaganda victory. The announcement of generous external funds for colonial development and welfare was accompanied by requests to all colonies for information about their provisions for native welfare. In Kenya, such news and subsequent intrusions were flanked by the march of the extensive material and manpower demands of war, just at the time when strikes and unco-operative labour were having more and more impact.[4] The threat of violence ensured that after 1939 debates about African welfare found a new depth and reached a wider audience. Anxious to put their own house in order whilst others fought away from their farms and families, significant elements across the whole spectrum of European society made their own contribution to the welfare debate. Likewise, towards the end of the war, when prompted by the suggestions of post-war budgets and more funding, the debates about how to implant metropolitan-style social services and English village life enjoyed a renaissance. Technical staff, in particular, wanted to see more surgically-specific social engineering.

The eventual outcome was to be more direct rule but through indirect means: paradoxically, the government turned to elders and chiefs and away from the *nouveau riche* or upwardly mobile provincial farmers, so that the former would discipline the latter and all would look after those who had been left behind. They did not see that the very existence of the latter implied a degree of social differentiation and change which could not be reversed except at very great cost. By aligning authority figures with government policies, that very authority would be undermined.

[2] (cont.) labour. My own study differs from his view that the labour question was the key conundrum that shaped colonial thought and the end of empire. This view ignores rural Kenya which was where most administrators worked and where the source and cure for detribalization were believed to be located.

[3] For a thorough account of the problems of Kikuyu agriculture as seen from the perspectives of colonial officials during and after the war, see Throup, 1987, ch.4, 'The Problem of Kikuyu Agriculture'.

[4] This aspect will be discussed in more detail in the next chapter.

The nature of white rule in Kenya would also stand in the way of an easy translation of metropolitan solutions for social transformation, the subject of this chapter. Underlying structural constraints abounded. The strong racial flavour was a major drag. That is not to say that poverty was absent from the European community. The government was aware of a 'poor white' phenomenon as well as the existence of poor Asians, but the general preference for racial categorization meant that each group was considered in isolation from the others; they were viewed as constituting separate problems and requiring different solutions. In the case of the growing number of poor whites in the colony from the time of the Depression, the action taken to prevent 'degeneration' and maintain colonial racial boundaries ranged from re-migration, which was often tantamount to culling, to investment in boarding-school and compulsory education. In similar vein to Southern Rhodesia, whites regarded poverty among their own as a failure to maintain standards, but the Kenyan authorities were far less sympathetic than their southern counterparts since the settlers did not enjoy so much influence over the government. There was no land allocation scheme for poor whites and no protection from Asian competition for artisan and service-sector employment, whilst locals regarded going on the register of the Unemployment Committee as the route to deportation (Kennedy, 1987: 80, 91, 167–74).

Much more public and official thought was always given over to discussions about African betterment – the focus of this chapter. Trusteeship in practice meant that, relative to whites, Africans and also Indians endured a range of unequal access to the colonial state, to the land and to the law. Also, during imperial rule, their identities were ascribed with features beyond their capacity to control. The identity which white power ascribed to Africans reduced them to something less than Europeans. The presence of white settlers had magnified this imperial tendency to racism, a phenomenon older than colonial conquest but reinforced by the introduction of industrial technology, scientific practice and European cultural artifacts. Local peoples, in comparison, appeared more primitive and lacking in the inability to tame the natural world. £6 million had been spent on laying down the railway upon conquest, so the government had looked hopefully around for potential sources of export and income taxes. Kenya's settlers – 'the last eddy of the Victorian tide of British emigration' – were to fulfil that function and be the agents of large-scale agricultural modernization.[5] The great hope of large-scale capitalized agricultural production being the engine of modernization was still a flag which settlers waved to justify their economic privileges. So, rather than offering Africans the opportunity to grow lucrative cash crops as a solution to rural poverty, restrictions were kept in place and chiefs and elders looked to in order to

[5] Lonsdale, 1999: 534. See generally relevant sections in Kitching, 1980 and Mosley, 1983. Also, Lonsdale, 1986, and Bradlow, 1972.

discipline African society. The racially restricted view of the capabilities of African farmers, especially women farmers, took a long time to die, despite growing evidence by the 1930s of the contrary.

The scenario of settlers as the agents of wealth and prosperity never materialized. Settlement in Kenya was much more patchy than in other white settler colonies – covering about a fifth of all useable land, leaving in theory much of African agriculture in place. Undercapitalized, over-ambitious and unfamiliar with local conditions (and farming in some instances), the settlers quickly clung to the coat-tails of the more successful lowland company plantations of sisal or the upland coffee and tea estates. They constantly tempered the colonial government's pledge of trusteeship on behalf of the interests of the African population, in order to prevent the undoing of settler concessions. Fewer officials accepted this line by 1939, having seen the effects of the Depression on whites and the growth of output among African farmers. Fiscal rates, wages and land allocation still worked in favour of the settlers, who numbered approximately 30,000 in 1939, but only 20 per cent of this number actually lived off the land. Indians numbered around 80,000. The African population stood perhaps at nearly 4 million, of whom less than 5 per cent lived permanently in township areas.

The corollary of this unequal state of affairs was that white intentions towards Africans were subject to the suspicions and resentments generated by racial rule, easily symbolized by the exclusive White Highlands. For a growing number of literate, mobile and prosperous Africans, any welfare advice and development dictates smacked of the same racial contempt and unequal treatment. In any case, had they and their ancestors not survived and even prospered in the surrounding harsh terrain, with the help of strict obedience to certain rules and rituals? Encounters between black and white people were most commonly negotiated through an observance of racial difference, and the colonial state reinforced racial distinctions. The ultimate symbol of alien rule could be found in the pattern of representation in the colony's Legislative Council. Settler domination of this body through having a majority of elected white unofficial members would last until 1948, when it fell to a half (Africans had to wait until 1957 to get even a restricted franchise) (Lonsdale, 1999: 541). Little was understood by other than a tiny minority about how Africans lived. White paternalism, even at its most benign, was typically built on a negative view of African capabilities.

White rule was also hamstrung in other profound ways by the Second World War. Beyond the shared ideology of racial superiority, sharp differences ran through white society, although it was the violence which came in the wake of Mau Mau ten years later and the disputes over how to respond that irrevocably destroyed European unity in the colony. The European presence was made up of competing factions with different agendas, interests and lifestyles. Outside of Nairobi, the white population was scattered and isolated. Before 1940, farm families in Kenya numbered 2,000. Up-country dwellers were not just made up of owners of large estates who lived like aristocrats from a past epoch. Many farmers worked smaller acreages, or were employed as managers. Rural living might be a languid leisure experience for some – a more or less uninterrupted round of hunting, riding or sight-seeing safaris, whilst servants prepared silver-service meals, laundered one's clothes or tended one's extensive collection of semi-tamed pets. But for others it was a tough no-nonsense and no-hot-water existence, and it offered a simple life lived close to nature and for some, therefore, a life lived closer to God (see Kennedy, 1987; Fox, 1984; Huxley and Perham, 1944).

Certainly communication with the outside world was slow; telegraphic connections were a luxury, if an option at all. Making contact with a relative in Britain by letter often took less time than a similar gesture to a neighbour living in the next district. The telegraph was used but was an expensive alternative. News often travelled fastest via the colony's main newspaper, the *East African Standard.* Occasional provision-runs into Nairobi or holidays on the coast relieved the isolation. One of the few ways in which everyone came together was at a visit from a member of the Royal family, such as the Prince of Wales' visit in 1929 or at annual district or provincial shows (see photograph 9). From the late 1920s onwards these became regular events. Local regiments, government officers, settler farmers set up stands and all would mill around the various showgrounds, each with the standard podium and hoisted Union Jack. Whites were usually vastly outnumbered by African attendants who were not simply passive spectators. They were also involved in the official ceremonies as well as giving cultural displays of craftware, dance routines and ceremonial costumes. Normally settlers were not too fond of officials as a group. They regarded them as 'birds of passage; with no stake in the country'.[6] Social distance was easily assured through membership of separate clubs. Muthaiga was the Nairobi club for settlers; the Nairobi Club was the watering-hole for officials.

The war produced only a cursory alteration to this state of affairs. True, it did not respect exclusive zones of social separation, whether between Africans and Europeans, or settlers and officials. Army life made black and white live closer together; the war effort in general necessitated much more co-operation between farmer and official. However, wartime mingling could merely create more opportunities for the display of prejudice. One young soldier who arrived in Kenya soon after the outbreak of war described how he spent a 'hellish evening' at a settler dinner party in Nanyuki, because his neighbour was of superior rank and therefore chose to ignore him all evening.[7] Officials were by no means immune from such

[6] Various memoirs and official reports held in Rhodes House including Sydney T. Kelson. RH Mss.Afr. s.735.

[7] Memoirs of Willoughby Thompson. RH Mss.Afr.s.1534.

pedantic social ritual and petty codes of conduct. If hierarchy was not acknowledged through established procedure then officers were in hot water. Traditionally, no junior officer could correspond with a senior officer without going through his own equivalent senior officer. To end a letter sent to such a senior officer with 'yours faithfully' could provoke a severe reprimand. The correct form was 'I am, sir, your obedient servant'.[8]

The missions made up yet another constituency. They remained fairly aloof unless in trouble. They preferred to keep their hard-won congregations to themselves whilst providing their own medical and educational services in their own way (Hastings, 1994; Isichei, 1995; Iliffe, 1998). The potential for friction between government and missions was omnipresent. The administration set up chiefs as local clearing houses, demarcated government locations, kept a close eye on all headmen, village headmen, native tribunals and later Local Native Councils. The churches could easily interfere with the smooth running of this set-up, especially by having influence over those they had taught to read. Not all officials took such a negative view as the missions of practices such as female circumcision. Some strongly disapproved of missionary opposition to the less controversial of traditional African cultural practices such as all-night dancing, drumming and feasting. Missionary stations were the most problematic. They more than survived by offering refuge, religiosity in an uncertain world, medical treatment when in need, but most of all, literacy. Since each mission ran its own affairs, by the 1930s administrators often complained that they were usurping what they regarded as the only properly constituted authorities. They were also criticized by some administrators for their insanitary conditions, a result of preferring to have their adherents live in large settlements away from their *shambas*, and for their exclusivity.[9]

One of the most isolated groups of non-Africans in Kenya was the Indian population. They included those who could legitimately claim a share in the title of original pioneers. Originally, Indian labour had worked in gangs on the railways and then moved into workshops that serviced them or various public works departments. Others had became clerks in the civil service and many more set up in trade and commerce, growing in numbers as the townships expanded. Despite being the first and essential collaborators in the colonization of Kenya, they were the least loved by Europeans. White settlers resented their demands for inclusion in the voting franchise, especially when self-government in India became headline news. Officials often accused them of exploiting urban Africans by overcharging them for goods and essential foodstuffs. Since no white group took a great interest in their welfare – it was felt they looked after themselves, indeed often only too well – they are largely absent from the wartime discussions charted below (see Lonsdale, 1999: 534, 536, and more generally Gregory, 1993).

[8] T.R.L. Neston. RH Mss.Afr.s.1086.

[9] Handing Over Report, Mullins to Windley, August 1935, pp. 4–5. Aubrey Mullins collection. RH Mss. Afr.s.760 (1 & 2).

Added to these two weaknesses of minority rule – racial practice and divergent communities – was a third already hinted at, the precariousness of colonial authority. Resources for colonial government in general were sparse, so money pledged for welfare would inevitably have to compete with other claims; a little would have to go a long way. This latter point was the *Leitmotiv* of the history of colonial administration in Kenya as elsewhere in Africa. Extensive variation existed in the colony as regards climate, geography and peoples, so no two districts were quite the same. Remarkably, in 1939 the 'thin white line' in Kenya stood at around 200 men. Fort Hall was a district within the most populous areas of Kikuyuland. It was mapped out at 585 square miles, its westerly boundary consisting of the Aberdare Mountains, to the east the Tana River, to the north Nyeri District and to the south, Kiambu. A relatively small district, its population stood at around 300,000. It had 30-50 inches of rainfall per annum and the land consisted of steep ridges running into forest. The administrative headquarters was just outside the town centre. The DC's office had a tin roof painted red, and its walls were made of mud and wattle. Working in the district were the DC and the DO for the local area; an Agricultural Officer; a Soil Conservation Officer; a Medical Officer; a Nursing Sister and, last to be appointed, a Health Inspector. Assisting them were three African clerks who also worked as interpreters, a chief clerk, a district cashier and a court clerk. The rest of the *boma* consisted of a hospital with fifty beds; a small jail which functioned as a detention centre where prisoners could be detained for a maximum of three months; a larger prison filled mainly with convicted thieves and recidivists who were deliberately kept near their place of birth; a post and telegraph office, an office for the agricultural department and space for the Fort Hall LNC.[10]

Impressive as these buildings might have been in comparison with others in the town, they lacked running water and electricity. Lighting was supplied by paraffin lamp, either Aladdin or Tilley. All urgent communication would be tapped out by the Postmaster using his telegraph key. There were no telephones in any of the rooms. Everywhere the smell of singed or burning insects filled the air. The agricultural and health staff worked under enormous pressure. The big district plan was to move people away from their traditional agricultural practices. The land consisted mainly of steep rocky ridges. The effect of torrential rains, overgrazing and deforestation all pointed colonial minds towards pursuing a policy of contour terracing. It was known that women were responsible for most of the agricultural activities in the household; the men would only break up the virgin soil. Each man would have a number of wives who would be responsible for a garden. Yet no effort or even thought was given to targeting official policy towards women. Meanwhile, the health

[10] Memoirs of Willoughby Thompson. RH Mss.Afr.s.1534; Mss.Afr.s.839; Mss Afr.s.519(1).

department had the job of instilling improvements in the general hygiene and health of the whole population by getting people to build water supplies, construct pit latrines in homesteads and keep trading centres cleaner.

The district administrators at Fort Hall spent as much time in the field as the specialist staff and felt equally overstretched. Duties included supervising the payment of retainers and tribal police as well as tax gathering. Chiefs and headmen had to be listened to and their comments and complaints duly recorded. Central to the standard issue of equipment was the daily diary. Up until the war, much of the business of rule could take place sitting under a tree or whilst on a walk. A swift way of measuring the loyalty and effectiveness of the local chief or headman was whether he would muster a large *baraza*; whether he prevented people from sitting too close to the officer; if he kept the area for such meetings in the style and manner which the DO expected; and what sort of refreshments he gave him during the evening. New men on the job were told to smile and look wise; they were often told by their African interpreters when it might be to their advantage to smile. As Willoughby Thompson recalled, 'the main thing was to make people believe in you and what you said. Officers lacking a personality found it all very hard going.' *Barazas* were the occasion for answering questions about government policy and fielding queries about roads, hospitals and schools. Complaints were also lodged and discussions could continue into the darkness of the night around the camp fire. The other major activity was sitting in on African courts. A great deal of *fitina* had to be sorted out, generated by old family feuds, animosities and previous biases in legal judgments. Evidently, much of the capacity of colonial rule was generated through theatre: a power play was enacted through recognized ritual, the habits of command, clear signs of deference and the casual display of modern gadgetry.[11] Reliant on collaboration, any notion of a white-only and extensive colonial state structure cannot be sustained. Bearing power was an unstable process, constantly subject to renegotiation and requiring renewal. Being associated with others' technological prowess and the prestige projects of engineering triumphs was vital to the administrator's bid for obedience and respect.

In Fort Hall, as in other districts, there were missions. Officials were not the only white show in town. Officials tended to be critical of missionaries for their sectarianism and rush for converts at any cost. The religious pattern of each area could be a veritable mosaic. In Fort Hall, the CMS Anglican church vied with the Italian Roman Catholics, and both competed with an African Inland Mission presence. Also making their presence felt were the smaller Salvation Army, the Seventh Day Adventists and the Kikuyu Independent Schools Association. However, because of the variation in each locality and the remoteness of life, relations between

[11] For a general account of colonial service history see Kirk-Greene, 1999.

white residents varied enormously. A reason to get on, a mutual friendship or a shared activity could easily bridge the gap; often it was indeed bridge in the evenings, sport or safari in the daylight hours. Officials and their wives obeyed the social ritual of get-togethers on Saturday evening and Sundays for the usual card game, sundowners or perhaps a little dancing. The functioning of this system often depended on the commitment and social skills of the DC's wife in the role of '*boma* queen' and whether or not officers could keep their hands off each other's wives.

The particular conditions in which officials had to operate as best they could shaped bureaucratic practice quite considerably. In 1939, the effects of the Depression were still remembered, although there had been an upturn in recruitment between 1935 and 1938. Earlier in the decade, when Lord Moyne had arrived in the colony to find ways to cut costs, he asked the government to make savings of £200,000. This meant that leave was cut, travelling allowances cut and income tax introduced in 1937. Just as settlers went under, so some officers who were heavily mortgaged experienced the threat of, and actual, retrenchment which undermined morale. Personal servants such as cooks and houseboys were dispensed with, adding to the hardship among local people, now competing for work in towns with sacked African government staff.[12] Similarly, day after day of working alone with supporting African staff and servants, out in remote villages, giving orders, judging disputes, explaining a believed superior way of farming, of building a house or of tending a sick animal, were all experiences likely to make the prospect of procedural change, an adjustment of attitudes or greater centralization of policy less attractive. So, the implication for new initiatives in African welfare did not bode well. Not only was money in short supply. There were no-go areas like the White Highlands where settlers claimed jurisdiction over their labour. Nor was there a great political will at hand to help, nor a powerful central reorganizing agent, both necessary if the administration, especially the district staff, were to adjust their style.

However, these three constraints on the effectiveness of white rule – racism, divided communities and a precarious state structure – were less significant than the disruption from changes taking place within the African population. The greatest obstacle to intentions had nothing to do with intrinsic qualities of white power but rather the nature of what those intentions were directed towards. Colonial government could maintain the image of imperial control only if it could rely upon local stability and local collaboration. The appeal of European modernity was always strong and had long been adapted to local tradition. There is no more intriguing example of such elite action than the funeral of Chief Kinanjui, made Paramount Chief of the Kikuyu in 1908. He died of septic poisoning in 1929. Although he was buried in traditional Kikuyu style – in a sitting

[12] Neston, p.101.

position and wrapped in a goat skin – Canon Leakey said Christian prayers and a local bugler belonging to the King's African Rifles sounded the Last Post.[13] By 1939, the cumulative effects of access to a world outside of the traditional nexus of social, economic and cultural exchange was beginning to make it difficult for people to run their lives and those of others as they once had. The effects of having access to new markets, literacy and medicine were proving more disruptive, particularly among groups living in closest proximity to these opportunities. A more self-confident Christian literate elite, newly prosperous farmers, the tightening-up of group identities through the European label of tribe, and a dramatic fall in death rates, particularly in infant mortality, were just some of the deeper forces at work that would make colonial government much more complicated. Landless and poor Kikuyu, selfish landowners and a hyper-critical educated elite were the main administrative headaches of the day. These processes were unfolding at a time when the empire was being sucked into Britain's war effort, with the concomitant implication that recovery from war would make restorative investment at the periphery less and less likely an option. The colonial state was hardly master of its destiny or that of others at this point, as the incoming tide of African and global history slowly but surely submerged its shallow defences.

Nevertheless, from 1939 onwards, a growing number of Europeans, without any great sense of the structural implications involved, found themselves planning for how they would direct the state towards catering for the end of the tribe, the African social grouping of the inter-war period that had been shoe-horned into prominence by the colonial state. As we shall see, Kenya's confused and conflicting discussions about welfare during the Second World War roamed over all these dimensions.

Clever townsmen

Unsurprisingly white Kenyans living and working in or near towns were among the first to become embroiled in wartime discussions about African welfare. Nairobi, the colony's capital, had grown considerably in size, due to a synthesis between ambitious African and European needs. The trend towards urban living had been gathering pace. Population pressure was increasing, due mostly to a drop in the death rate of babies and young children. More Africans, needing money for taxes and school fees, moved or drifted into the town for the purpose of earning a wage. As labour presence increased, so did the opportunity to provide supporting services and so more workers decided to take their chances, even women, surviving as traders, *ayahs*, and – a minority – as prostitutes (Robertson, 1997: ch III, ch, 4; Hake, 1977; White, 1991). 'I never saw anything more degrading'

[13] 'Recollections of Kenya, 1906–3', M.W. Dobbs. RH Mss.Afr.s.504.A162.

was how Nairobi's longest-serving white police constable described the shanty town of Majengo at this time, and 'I was glad when they pulled the place down. Vice and drunkenness surrounded me on all sides, as did murder, suicide and rape.' Inevitably, a law enforcer, whose working experience of the city was through recurrent disorder, was perhaps alarmist and never saw the more tranquil and positive side of city life. Nevertheless, many other Europeans began to notice just how many young Africans were attracted by the prospect of town life. They flocked to the already congested locations looking for work when there was none, and they were often unskilled. Some became easy prey to unscrupulous landlords, who might be gun-barons or former prostitutes. But despite the conditions they usually never wanted to go home.

This phenomenon quickly became identified with what was referred to as the general problem of detribalization. Various European social commentators suggested that rural life was no longer what it used to be. Young men and women had lost their tribal identity. They were not obeying their elders and, to escape rural life, they were moving to the towns. Such an explanation was shot through with white guilt – regret and sorrow at the loss of stability and order which they felt European rule had played no small part in setting in motion. Typically, the problem was often refracted through the experience of the hurt and rejected father figure. The sad old man was how Constable Kelson evoked detribalization:

> Old men came to my station looking for lost sons. They were puzzled and bewildered. The young wanted to smoke, drink and drive motor cars. Their daughters painted their lips, smoked cigarettes and grew cheeky. They lived with other men and drank methylated spirits. They said 'Go home you old fool. Go and look after your goats'.[14]

Such an experience of alienation in parenthood was not unknown to fathers in Britain. The similarities were remarkable: replace goats with an allotment and the description could apply to a beleaguered sheep farmer looking for his daughter in the slums of Cardiff at the turn of the century. Likewise, in Britain, anxiety about 'spivs' was becoming pandemic. Living in large towns, these were young men from working-class backgrounds but not choosing to work as their fathers had, but instead evading rationing, supplying goods on the black market and identifiable by their vulgar suits and conceited demeanour.

Colonial officials responsible for urban areas were beginning to feel the heat of the rising temperature in townships. Closer to central government, Nairobi's senior officials were also aware of the Colonial Office's request in 1939 for details of native welfare mechanisms and the advice that governments should establish specific structures to this end. The government was still shaken by the Mombasa Docks Strike. It assembled a Native Welfare

[14] Sidney T. Kelson, p. 10. RH Mss.Afr.s.735.

Committee (NWC) in September 1939. Its terms of reference mimicked metropolitan government and included the co-ordination of departments concerned with the social services; advice on policy connected with the development of social services; and keeping the activities of private bodies in line with government policy. The spot-light was now falling on African welfare.[15] That it fell squarely on the issue and refused to budge, was the result of the persistence shown by the members of local unofficial organizations.

In April 1941, the Nairobi School Area Committee passed a resolution bringing the 'grave inadequacy' of African social welfare in Nairobi to the attention of their Director and the Governor. Serious overcrowding in the African locations, they argued, was causing a huge increase in prostitution (probably exacerbated by the presence of soldiers). Educational provision was declared to be useless, unless 'a wide scheme of social welfare, embracing programmes for housing, health and recreation, had been planned and funds provided to put it into operation'.[16] There was a sense of urgency and a keenness to look to other countries with more experience of the problems involved with having a large concentration of Africans in urban areas. Similarly in 1941, the Rotary Club of Nairobi raised the issue of urban African welfare, demanding that the NWC organize a conference on the subject. So pressing was the problem that the Rotarians had formed a Community Service committee to discuss how to improve African conditions in the capital. They identified low average wages as the major problem. But it was a polytechnic to train Africans for higher-paid positions that was put forward as an important part of the solution. Emotions ran high. The government was implored to harness the Club's desire to assist in what was deemed to be 'the tremendous problem of native welfare' and to use the large body of representative unofficial support 'to the fullest extent'.[17]

Officials were initially sceptical. Many argued that a conference would be unwieldy, rambling and inconclusive, unless directed to specific and well-defined objectives. However, the Director of Education took the initiative and departed from the previous amorphous approach to native welfare. He proposed a series of short conferences on separate areas of African welfare: housing and sanitation; education and recreation; maternity and infant welfare; and finally, wages and conditions of employment. This offered a clearer template for discussion.[18] Unable to stall any

[15] F.Cooper, 1987. He shows that c.1940 official attitudes changed: workers became 'social beings, whose culture, welfare, and relationships with each other and with employers were vital determinants of order and productivity.', p.2. See generally Mutiso, 1974: Appendix A, p.370.

[16] Surridge to Watherston 15 December 1943 in reply to letter sent from the CO, 3 November 1941, PRO CO859/75/10.

[17] F.T.Holden (Rotary Club President) to NWC Chairman, G.M. Rennie (Chief Secretary, known as 'Little Rennie' after the indigestion pill) 4 September 1941, KNA MAA7/574.

[18] DE to CS, 12 September 1941, ibid.

longer, the NWC agreed and an unprecedented conference on social welfare was held in Nairobi at the end of 1941. When, over a year later, the Colonial Office heard about it through a random newspaper clipping – indicating the paucity of information exchange – the Social Service Department excitedly asked for more details.

Their interest was justified, for the conference had unleashed a buoyant exchange of information and ideas. The openness and breadth of the debate were quite remarkable, suggesting the overdue nature of such a gathering. Officials were almost outnumbered by representatives of non-governmental organizations. The KURH sent a representative, as did the Salvation Army on the grounds that it took in wayward girls. Also represented was the Catholic Mission Training Centre, the Nairobi Chamber of Commerce which had two committees on welfare, the Toc H organization which ran an African soldiers' club and the CMS known to employ a trained sister who had studied social and domestic conditions. There were even two women at the conference, one specifically invited to speak on *ahayas*. With such a range of participants and a back-log of complaints, it was inevitable that the issue of improving African welfare quickly mushroomed into a huge and virtually impossible agenda. Yet, the conference was highly significant in that it provided a platform for the articulation of accumulated wisdoms. This represented a significant departure.

As was becoming more and more the case, the most perceptive contributions in the discussion on African welfare came from the medical profession. Doctors and their medical teams worked on the frontier between African distress and Western science. The profession's contact with the African population was often closer than most; likewise, their self-belief and enthusiasm for intervention were reinforced on a much more regular basis than in the case of many other officials. Setting a broken arm or stemming an infected wound won friends and fanned their sense of accomplishment , mutual good-will and possibility. African dressers spread the good news about modernization too. Modern medical practice had expanded in Kenya during the inter-war period to help justify increases in African taxation. By 1932, 17 permanent and 10 temporary hospitals were up and running, plus 77 permanent and 30 temporary dispensaries financed by LNCs. African dressers for the dispensaries were trained in the local hospitals. They might give out quinine, Epsom salts and administer injections, such as bismuth sodium tartrate for yaws, a relatively cheap remedy for a condition that could leave its victim with gaping flesh, a hole where the face had been or a leg hanging from the body by a piece of skin. Practitioners and patients were understandably impressed (Iliffe, 1998: esp. 38–41).

By the end of the 1930s, concern was growing among senior medical officers that prevention was falling behind the treatment of disease, thus hampering the work of the medical departments. It was no surprise that Dr Anderson, Chairman of the Municipal Council's Public Health

Committee, virtually set out the whole agenda of the subsequent debate on social welfare when his contribution to the 8 November 1941 conference called for:

> ... the reconstruction of the African family in Nairobi, and the acceptance of the fact that the urban type of native exists. It would also entail the development of his earning capacity by proper training, and his education in the rights and duties of citizenship... When other large amounts were made available, the development of the urban African must then include factors other than housing, such as administrative and public buildings (Halls, libraries, schools, training centres, hospitals and clinics) and all the usual amenities required in a modern town... The problem of the supply of African 'ayahs', the problem of undesirable women, and the problems associated with the delinquent and de-tribalised native would be automatically solved to a very large extent by the development of family life, and the sense of background and of responsibility that would grow with it.[19]

Here we find the basic tenets of the subsequent thinking on the need and possibilities for social engineering. First, family life was to be nurtured. Since urban Africans could no longer be ignored, they would have to be helped to better themselves as family men. This meant the state would have to intervene on two fronts; hospitals, houses, clinics and social halls would have to be provided to knit together the new self-discipline and identity that would come from family life. Likewise, Dr Martin, Nairobi's Senior Medical Officer, in a scathing attack on the lack of progress, called for a great expansion in social education since, without teaching Africans how to live in good houses, efforts would be wasted.[20] What they clearly wanted was a way to replace the discipline of the tribe with their brand of internal discipline. Their problem was that no obvious means existed for releasing 'social education' in Nairobi. Constructing it would be exceedingly costly.

However, theirs was not the only show in town. The full gamut of white opinion on what was best for urban Nairobi also made itself heard. The medical staff found a source of solidarity with Nairobi's new Municipal Native Affairs Officer (MNAO), Tom Askwith. He supported the idea that colonial administration in Nairobi should now incorporate African wives. More married women was his solution to Nairobi's welfare problems, a policy which first required more housing. However, he was keen that single women should be carefully controlled in the city; they were there by the grace of their menfolk. Askwith had quickly made extensive use of the Salvation Army and Missions when dealing with African girls 'in difficulty', and wanted an institution on the lines of a YWCA established.

[19] Minutes of Nairobi Social Welfare Conference November 1941. p.5, PRO CO859/75/10.

[20] Ibid.

Single women had long been considered unwelcome and a problem by colonial authority and African men alike. After the war efforts would be stepped up to control their presence and their trading activities.[21] Mrs Taylor (possibly invited on the committee to represent the EAWL) wanted provision for *ayahs* on the grounds of safeguarding the interests of European children under their care. The Director of Education was keen to appoint a woman superintendent of Female Education to deal with what was considered to be the problem of single women in Nairobi.

Others found neither married nor single women in towns appealing. Father Byrne, representing Catholic interests, wanted all African women in Nairobi returned to their districts, preferring to cling to the belief that tribal control still existed. The Chief Secretary did not disagree with the arguments for more state provision, but he pointed out that the cost would prohibit the problem from being tackled in any way other than gradually. It was cheaper and easier to assume that the tribe did still exist and that urban welfare could be solved by a return to rural life. An even more conservative view was to throw the burden on to African labour. One Municipal Councillor insisted that the African man had first to be goaded into becoming an efficient wage earner, so that he could pay for the necessary schemes. He blamed illiteracy for the persistence of low wage-earning power. According to this view, he would pay for the privilege of being detribalized by working more productively. A rather quaint suggestion came from the President of the Nairobi Rotary Club. He was certain that if Africans would only learn to use their hands, becoming 'general handy-men' – a popular concept particularly among former public school boys – their earning power would be increased and their welfare therefore self-financing.[22]

Nairobi's own DC could only patch up the existing muddle and blame a lack of resources for the slow progress, past and present. In this spirit, he suggested a further conference to discuss the issues raised, along with plans for a canteen selling cheap and nutritious lunch-time meals, paid for by the Native Trust Fund. He argued that everything that had been discussed was already established municipal policy: the future appointment of a social welfare officer, possibly a woman, to deal with domestic hygiene; a tightening of the Vagrancy Law in its powers over Undesirables; a £30,000 Housing Loan Scheme for married couples; and hostels for *ayahs*. But there was little finance available and employers were not forced to provide more housing and welfare facilities for their labour. Only a recommendation was ever issued.

A similar spurt of activity burst out in smaller townships up-country, with a similar absence of any significant outcome. The debate in Nyanza Province was presided over by one of Kenya's most astute administrators,

[21] Ibid, p. 4; see Roberston, 1997: 132–3.
[22] Minutes of Nairobi Social Welfare Conference, pp. 6–7.

Sidney Fazan. In February 1940, Fazan approved the creation of a council to advise on township native problems and a Native Affairs Sub-Committee, both proposed by Kisumu's DC.[23] Kisumu was a port-town that had grown up on the shores of a lake (see photograph 6). Its main street included some of the town's better shops or *mabati* which had corrugated roofs, the occasional petrol pump and a number of bars. It was lined with open storm drains. The sub-committee relied on a 1927 circular for its basic thinking. 'Natives in Urban Areas' had been published as part of a Local Government Commission Report which had sought to 'investigate and make recommendations for the betterment and control' of the urban population.[24] This illustrates how little the Kenya administration had previously been required to think about towns. Yet directly fresh thought was applied to urban welfare, proposals multiplied whilst budgets did not. A legacy of neglect and an absence of precedents increased the difficulties of the tasks to hand. Items considered pressing were African housing, health services and medical facilities (now separated), education, social amenities, recreation, standard of living in relation to wages, labour, juvenile employment and prostitution. Kisumu's agenda was suddenly more replete than any metropolitan social service portfolio: a broad mixture of social, medical and educational provision and policing aimed at the whole community.

Even with such new enthusiasm, by 1939 it was difficult to get to grips with the legacy of urban neglect. One issue could dominate a whole meeting and, even then, the magnitude of the task could become overwhelming. Housing, fundamental to any urban programme, took over one single meeting. Medical representatives stressed the need for long-term solutions, more familiar perhaps than others with the physical consequences of urban squalor. A Health Department report on housing conditions in Kaloleni, the Kisumu African township, had revealed 'a state of affairs that would be a disgrace to any township', but conditions in other areas of the town were held to be even worse. Medical staff deemed it useless to address the problem in piecemeal fashion, providing accommodation for a limited number of residents, since any partial scheme 'must defeat its own ends'.[25] Agreement was reached that any scheme would have to be designed for the whole African population, the African family model taking centre stage. The problem was that those deserving state provision were all poor in the colonial context, in contrast to the conjunctural poor – those thrown into poverty due to a change in their normal circumstances – whom Beveridge faced in metropolitan Britain. Kisumu township planning came from the minds of technical officers who dreamed of large budgets.

[23] ADM.14/9/4 Fazan, PC (Nyanza) to DC Kisumu 21 January 1940 Native Welfare Committee, KNA PC/NZA/3/1/572.

[24] Minutes of Kisumu Township, Native Affairs sub-committee, 27 February 1940, ibid.

[25] Ibid, p. 2. The Committee agreed to refer to a minute of the Townships Board, Nairobi 23 July 1927 in connection with the Native Location at Eldoret.

Welfare at this local level quickly became costly because it started from almost nothing and had to include almost everything. In the apparent absence of any recognized civil society in places like Kisumu which lacked the familiar cohesive discipline of church, family, business associations and clubs, colonial solutions to African welfare had to incorporate bringing Africans under the same moral discipline as that of the DC. This inner instinct for betterment would then bring willingness to take up regular employment and to build clean square houses, a sense of civic duty and pride. Instead of living on their wits, unable to cope with the lack of tribe, Africans, living as families, would carry new ambitions, new community responsibilities and new guilts. Ultimately African self-control would, it was hoped, demand less from the government. The paradox for the local administration was that colonial betterment had so far produced indiscipline and ingratitude and political agitation. Apart from funds, the crucial difference was that the metropolitan example of state provision could rely on social obedience, since there was some moral cohesion derived from the universal franchise.

There were yet more immediate obstacles. Kisumu's administration soon discovered that they knew absolutely nothing about these town dwellers. A proper housing plan required a census: how many Africans needed housing, their marital, occupational and general economic status, all had to be found out.[26] There appeared to be no established policy, not even communication with other Councils – such as Nairobi – for advice. A request, therefore, had to be made to the proper authority so that information could be gathered. Such a lengthy process was brought to a standstill by a different perspective, that of an older generation of district administrators. Two years later Sidney Fazan asked the Chief Secretary to withdraw his approval of the provincial land and population survey requested by his township team at Kisumu.[27] Scarred by financial uncertainty exacerbated by slump conditions, and always fearful of a breakdown of order, old hands like Fazan saw such surveys and welfare as an indulgence. Betterment had to come after control. The survey would be useless, he explained. Economic conditions were exceedingly abnormal, and so were family budgets: 39,000 more men than usual were away from home in civil or military employment. More land was under cultivation than usual due to the war effort; more cattle were being sold and prices were abnormally high.

Typical of the administration's wartime perspective, Fazan wanted resources to go towards extra administrative staff to buttress control through more white contact. Staff shortages were especially acute in Nyanza, he claimed, where half the colony's manpower and productive output was produced with one-eleventh of the administrative staff. This

[26] Ibid, pp. 1–2. An application was made under the Statistics Ordinance.

[27] Fazan to CS, Adm/3/18/4 6 March 1942, KNA PC/NZA/3/1/572.

was preventing officers, including senior staff, from getting out among the African people as much as they should:

> Contact is apt to be confined to barazas at which, on the whole, more time is given to explaining to the natives what the Government wants than in finding out what they think. The natives on the whole have behaved magnificently but we must remember that, in many ways, their loyalty is personal to their officers, past and present, and is in danger of fading when contact is removed.[28]

His solution was a more intimate type of administration, offering to listen and then explain. It rested on the Administration's confidence in personal rule and its adherence to the principles of paternalistic authoritarianism. Any sign of new types of officials doing old jobs in new ways, such as the collection of information by others for others, represented a threat to their hold on what was viewed as a finite amount of white authority. Without easy money for urban programmes, new welfare initiatives were quickly smothered by established thought. It was cheaper and made more sense to insist first on the moral uplift of the rural majority before building infrastructures for African families. Poverty thus reverted to being more to do with moral deficiencies rather than a material condition solved by providing houses, hospitals and community centres.

Old paternalisms of rule therefore became still more attractive at the local level: it was the DCs' special contribution through personal example and authority that would eventually open the gates to a moral transformation and long-standing and meaningful betterment and control. In the initial atmosphere of wartime optimism, where almost everything seemed possible, the ideal African urban family was an expensive but worthy solution. But welfare easily slipped back to being a moral problem for many administrators who vetoed the urban initiatives which often foundered in the absence of resources. They remembered the post-1918 slump and were dismayed by the metropolitan state welfare solutions proposed for township problems.

Tentacular technicians

Devising methods of African transformation using the tools of family-orientated men and married women was by no means an exclusively urban preoccupation. Indeed, it formed the backbone of much administrative wrangling in rural Kenya at the same time. Well before 1939, technical officers, high and low, were already fighting their own war on a number of fronts. One effect of the Second World War was the creation of a climate of discussion and new structures of government that provided a much needed opportunity for disgruntled and marginalized technical

[28] Ibid.

administrators to speak out in favour of a reorientation of district administration towards the wisdoms of the specialist officer. They used the argument of improving welfare to sustain their case.

Colonial administration had always included specialist departmental branches. By the 1930s, colonies usually had, at a minimum, technical departments that dealt with agriculture, medicine, veterinary matters, education and labour (see Diagram 2). Each had a director and a hierarchy of field staff, ranging from provincial heads, to officers responsible for districts, down to their assistant staff. In many areas, assistant staff were African and, in rarer cases, women. Unlike administrative officers, having a technical job often signified a non-Oxbridge education. Both the administration and the departments saw themselves as bearers of the most important aspect of the colonial mission, of good government, and if possible, of transformation. Administrators brought judicial wisdoms, supervised tax collection and sat with the chiefs. Technical staff believed they helped feed people, stopped disease and could change the face of a hostile terrain. Often both shared mutual disregard for the other's competence. Public school 'house' competitiveness and the clash of male egos could breed petty jealousies and compound professional demarcations, leading to terse and prickly working relations. Yet there were far more cases of strong and productive working relationships developing, especially where a district posed a particular challenge and provided the conditions for solidarity. Much of the rivalry was friendly and there were many reasons to co-operate, loneliness being one of them. Technical staff were well used to working in remote conditions, often in the face of opposition, and they grew tough. They were occasionally uncompromising and idiosyncratic and were often loners. To survive, their self-belief had to be extremely robust. Although some preferred to stay within the realm of practical no-nonsense work in the field, others wanted to engage with the politics of colonial government to improve the standing of their own specialism, and so tacked this on to their sense of mission.

It was the new Native Welfare Committee, set up in Nairobi, that initially made department staff jump for joy. At this gathering, the Directors of the Agriculture, Education, Medical and Veterinary Departments (not the Labour Commissioner) were at last eyeball to eyeball with Provincial Commissioners. With welfare the defining aim, they could now set to work to make the claim that their technical expertise was the most vital link in the chain of native betterment. The CNC was made chairman and the first meeting of the NWC took place in November 1939. Issues relating to nutrition, native systems of land tenure and agricultural practice dominated early meetings and special meetings were arranged to consider specific related issues. Agriculture and health were particularly fertile breeding grounds for officers keen to link welfare with a more intimate type of technical administration. For example, Denzil Blunt, Kenya's Director of Agriculture, used the forum to protest against the proposed cuts in agricultural training at government schools.[29] He argued on behalf of his colleagues that the administration should begin from the fundamental truth that agriculture was 'essential for African welfare'; moreover, neglecting agricultural training would weaken rural life, which in turn would 'increase the dangers likely to arise as a race begins to obtain some rudiments of education'. And he even went so far as to call for the replacement of European with African staff, on the grounds that real progress would only be made this way because of the comparative cost of European staff. A pragmatist, Blunt saw that, in the long-term likelihood of insufficient white hands, ways had quickly to be found to transmit technical skills to African ones.

Both the Departments of Agriculture and Health had a strong tradition of non-conformity and innovation to defend as well as being bearers of a sense of crisis. Just as thinking on urban families had been prompted by the 1939 dock strike, so the earlier agrarian crisis of soil erosion had prompted thoughts of encouraging enlightened peasant self-interest in improved husbandry, as opposed to coercing tribesmen in soil conservation work.[30] Agricultural Officers launched their wartime proposals on a platform of failed attempts during the previous decade to successfully coax others to implement new departures in African husbandry (see Anderson, 1982: esp. ch. 4 and 5). The experience of Baringo District illustrates this well. Depression had hit this district badly. Declining settler agriculture depressed the demand for African labour, pushing men back into the already overcrowded Reserves. Hut and poll tax payments were dependent upon migrant and labour wages, and 50 per cent of all African tax revenue was used to subsidize the settler economy. There was little investment in the region and one junior Agricultural Officer, Colin Maher, after a fact-finding tour through the Reserves in the mid-1930s, wrote of the 'almost complete lack of economic and social progress during the last forty years of British rule'. Attempts to improve the situation had produced little in the way of a result. The post of Reconditioning Officer came into being in 1930 but lacked a coherent policy and support at the provincial level: the use of force to gather communal labour was quickly withdrawn due to external criticism; the self-help nature of the work was difficult to sustain since schemes were unevenly distributed and disrupted traditional grazing patterns. LNCs were reluctant to collect the annual one shilling cess, whilst the Secretariat severely pruned any plans for further schemes

[29] Education Department Circular No.37 of 1940. 'Agriculture in Elementary and Sub-Elementary Schools', 20 September 1940, KNA MAA7/574. Complaints were made at a NWC meeting by Blunt, the Director of Agriculture, and the Senior Agricultural Officer (Coast Province), Norman Humphrey; Humphrey to Blunt, 14 March 1941, ibid.; D.L. Blunt to CS, 26 July 1941, KNA PC/NZA/3/1/572.

[30] For example, see D.L. Blunt to CS. 'Development of Native Reserves' 3 March 1944, KNA MAA7/574. For an analysis of the political economy of the Kenya land and agricultural settlement up to the Second World War see Anderson, 1984; Anderson and Throup, 1985.

(ibid., esp. 228–38). Maher was also partial to a bit of social engineering. He routinely recommended that the government concentrate on creating a more settled type of agriculture and animal husbandry. This was the route towards a relatively prosperous peasantry. Only then could stone masons and carpenters develop as a viable class of artisans.[31]

The medical profession was doing the same. An earlier generation of Medical Officers had doggedly tried to spread their public health wisdoms. Margery Perham, travelling in Africa in 1929, reported favourably on the pioneering work of Dr Paterson, then Kenya's Chief Medical Officer. Paterson was 'a fastidious bachelor, rather affected in manner, with an enthusiasm, bordering on obsession, for latrines' (Perham, 1976: 188–9). He had an obsession with grandiose schemes such that the whole Department became subordinated to his predilection of the moment. Paterson once instructed all Medical Officers to plant fruit trees around dispensaries. His attempt to irrigate the Tana River area foundered when he discovered water could not run uphill. He gave a junior MO, Dr Philip, the task of getting Masai to rear chickens from maggots found in the dung on *manyatta* floors, but the breed he chose, Rhode Island Reds, were totally unsuited to hot conditions and perished (Carman, 1976). He personified the approach of the Medical Department: a penchant for eccentricity, a belief in the efficacy of adult education, and a concern to enliven the appeal of rural life.

In an attempt to demystify the public health wisdoms of his day, Paterson had built a large demonstration unit at the annual Nyeri show (see photograph 2) on the theme of disease, health and cleanliness. This was exactly what Whitehall's experts wanted to see on a large scale in Africa, and Perham was impressed. She described in detail the model dirty *duka* that was complete with 'an aged, filthy native ... spitting and scratching in realistic fashion'; warriors had gazed in horror 'at a huge model of a tape worm which the demonstrator was waving in front of their faces...' (Perham, 1976: 189) This was the best type of education for Africa she had ever seen, worthy of investment. But it was still an approach to colonial government which had remained elusive.

The new welfare committee was not poised to bring in a revolution in administrative techniques and priorities where others had failed. By March 1941 it asked the Governor to reconstruct the Native Welfare Committee by making the Chief Secretary chairman of an identical line-up in an attempt to achieve better fulfilment of the functions for which it had been set up. All was not going well. As a forum that could effectively critique colonial administration in the forceful way that technical staff would have liked, the NWC was fatally flawed. First, its agenda was swamped by an enormous range of issues. For example, the agenda at one special meeting

[31] 'Partial Survey of Agricultural Resources and Potential of the West Suk Reserve' by Colin Maher. February 1935. RH Mss.Afr.s.740.

on medical matters ranged from the training of African women for nursing, anti-malarial measures at Mombasa, yellow fever prevention at Kisumu and extra beds and housing for African staff at government hospitals. Native welfare covered all aspects of government and there was much that needed attention.[32] Secondly, there was no one with the authority to untangle long-standing bureaucratic anomalies. The CNC was not a powerful enough figure to do so; the Chief Secretary had more power, but even he lacked the authority for reform. Thirdly, the view of the administration still held sway, as illustrated by the slanging match that erupted between the provincial administration and the technical departments during a special NWC meeting to settle planning procedures.[33] To appease Nyanza's PC, the agreement reached was still 'suggestive rather than mandatory'.

As if to illustrate how little effective thought there had been in the past decade or more, the outcome was again, as we saw at Kisumu, based on a 1927 Secretariat circular, which had already suggested the monthly meeting system between technical and administrative staff, now favoured by the former. Left to preference and personal rapport at the local level, the administrative learning curve and restructuring process was clearly moving onward but ever sideways. This did not bode well for the likelihood of technical gurus being able to use the NWC to make a clean assault on the agenda of mainstream administration in order to re-fashion it according to their own established wisdoms.

Nevertheless, the NWC did help their cause, particularly through facilitating joint action by senior medical and agricultural staff that was unprecedented and would not have taken place without this wartime reform. This is illustrated by an important circular entitled 'Marketing of Native Produce' widely circulated by the NWC in 1943.[34] It contained extracts from two statements made by the Directors of the Agricultural and Medical Departments. What may seem a vague statement of policy nevertheless signified a bid to orientate government towards engineering market-orientated African families, presented as the base-line of rural welfare. Both were taking an essentially assimilationist line, believing that Africans could and should become economic individualists, and that they would understand development, and would know how to consult technical advisers, a move away from the coercive ordering of DCs and chiefs. Blunt believed that adult education could give Africans a sense of 'commercialism ... integrity and business acumen'. He wanted existing marketing centres developed into social centres with dispensaries, schools, agricultural

32 Memo on Proposals put forward by the Director of Medical Services at a special meeting of NWC 10 June 1941, KNA MAA7/574.

33 Record of Joint Meeting 20 November 1941 between the CNC (Chairman), the CS, four PCs and o/c Masai District, plus the Directors of Medical Services, Education, Agriculture and Veterinary Services, pp. 2–5, KNA PC/NZA/3/1/572.

34 'Marketing of Native Produce', Circular from CS, 5 October 1943, KNA MAA7/574.

demonstrations, etc. Such a move would, he argued, make it possible to give wide publicity by practical demonstration to improvements in housing conditions, diet and so on, and also facilitate the development of village or home handicrafts. Central to his vision was a restructured rural order where self-help mechanisms could be fostered, giving African families the incentive to solve their own welfare problems.

Lockhart, Director of Medical Services, took the same sort of view, but focused more on the cultivation of a material basis for welfare. He attached his inherited departmental lore to the new wartime spirit of reform and advocated a more tentacular government to regulate households. He regretted that

> ... little attention has so far been given to ... ensuring the correct and economical distribution of locally available food supplies, or of making supplies of those essentials of domestic life which must be imported from overseas, available at prices which the masses of the people can pay ... little skilled technical attention has yet been given to the matter while the education of the potential consumer has been left almost entirely to the health worker and the entrepreneur.[35]

The metropolitan experience of wartime mobilization and increased state intervention gave weak colonial governments new – if impossible – standards of interventionism. Lockhart argued that such basic commodities constituted the bed-rock of African welfare, viewing Africans in families of 'potential consumers'. The experience of wartime regulations had drawn his attention to the minutiae of basic material welfare, showing how improvements could easily be made in the supply and distribution of 'all the ordinary essentials of sanitary life: soap, water, fuel, blankets, cloth, shoes, enamelled ware, lamps and oil, building materials, mosquito nets as well as foodstuffs', if governments had a mind to do so.[36]

Lockhart advocated radical reform. He backed the recent efforts by the Agricultural Department to improve marketing for export purposes, but regretted the absence of a public health commercial service, and the lack of specialist government guidance to promote private commercial services and African trading. He wanted a Department of Trade and Industry and Supply created and a social economist employed to ensure that the supply of the 'essential consumer goods' to the masses was the first priority of trade. Lockhart's tentacular government for Blunt's villages not only needed the reform of local administration but also demanded a less racially restrictive view of Africans. It required Africans who would demand the variegated support services for a new type of domesticity that enlightened African families would need when they were no longer benighted native tribesmen. Just as Paterson had believed that, if people could be relieved of their parasites, their lethargy would vanish and they could then be induced to

[35] Ibid., p. 2.
[36] Ibid., p. 1.

grow cash crops which would improve their standard of living, in the same way, if the disorder of tribe could be removed, order and welfare could spring from the new restructured family communities that were the new 'social centres'. Technical staff were evidently seizing the moment to put across their strongly held views.

Despite the consensus developing around a clearer vision at the top of the departmental pyramid, and facilitated by the NWC, this appeared to produce little in the way of immediate positive results during the war years. An important setback was a lack of solidarity inside each department. Those staff who chose to engage with the debate were not always supportive. Indeed, some held virtually opposing views. There was much confusion especially in relation to areas such as Central Province as to whether supporting the creation of an affluent peasantry, with some able to pay wages for labour, was the way to proceed. As has been well documented, the myth of 'merrie Africa' attracted much support. Officials such as Sir Philip Mitchell heeded Lord Hailey's warnings relating to India, namely that their mistake had been not to halt the development of individual land tenure and the growth of 'large bodies of rackrented tenants'.[37]

One such doubting Thomas was Colin Maher of the Agricultural Department. He had long believed that economic individualism was the cause of all the present ills and not their solution. He was moved to put pen to paper. The onset of war, and particularly evidence of some support in Britain for self-determination among 'the so called "intellectuals" in and out of Parliament', had given him the incentive to seek out a wider audience for his particular planning prescriptions. He circulated a detailed piece on 'Planning for Africa and the African' in 1941 which he sent to the Fabian Colonial Bureau, happy to acknowledge in his covering letter that this organization would be helping Britain to shape its policy in the future. It was widely discussed. As Rita Hinden of the Fabian Bureau explained to Arthur Creech Jones, its President and soon to be Secretary of State for the Colonies, Maher shared their ideals but claimed that his wide experience made him approach matters in a different way.[38]

What had irked Maher were the 'sentimental vapourings' in Britain that portrayed Africans as underprivileged Europeans. In other words, he was against the universalizing tendencies in the rhetoric of high colonial policy. Adopting this position – building a policy around reversing this and seeing the situation as one of black versus white – would, he lamented, reproduce in East Africa all the evils which socialism claimed to be against. For him Kenya was already a corrupted place. The profit motive had become king; the native law and tax justice system was corrupt as was the government in general. Workmen and traders were dishonest in their

[37] There is an extensive literature on this. See for example, Throup, 1987: 72–7; Berman, 1990: 300–46.

[38] 'Planning for Africa and the Africa' by Colin Maher; letter from Rita Hinden to Arthur Creech Jones, 24 December 1941, RH ACJ/7/3/17.

dealings and landowners were becoming more selfish. Only education in honesty, reliability and social responsibility plus massive efforts to raise standards of nutrition and adjust land tenure could stop the rot. So, in quite dramatic and emotive ways, some of Kenya's technical footsoldiers were aware of wider political currents and making a bid to get socialism to adopt their particular viewpoint. It might have been a smaller world in 1945, but it was not necessarily a more comprehensible one, the likes of Maher having lost confidence in the mission of transformation. Yet for the Fabian Colonial Bureau, how could it be otherwise than that wage-earning larger farmers would alleviate rural poverty and bring lasting prosperity? And from their perspective, could Britain stand the charge of abandoning Africans to live as they had always done?

The use of force was also problematic. Some officers looked to it as the only solution, especially when full of Doomsday scenarios. The gloom which dominated the thoughts of many in the Agricultural Department was relieved by a random call to arms. M.D. Graham, an Agricultural Officer in Kakamega district shared Margery Perham's wartime enthusiasm for state intervention to safeguard the community and he was prepared to take it to an absolute dimension. Like her, he looked enviously at China, India and Russia with their land policy based on state control.[39] War had provoked in him a sense of wanting to seize the moment. Failure to act now would amount to 'a betrayal of trust ... immaturity, irresponsibility and an absence of duty'. Or was it not the case, he challenged his peers, that they lacked 'the guts to risk their comparatively secure position'? From his perspective, the situation was grave. According to his calculations – published in the *East African Agricultural Journal* in October 1941 – 10–12 acres was probably adequate for a family of five in a two-season area, yet in parts of North and Central Kavirondo families were subsisting on 2 acres. Graham argued that only compulsion was up to the challenge facing the Reserves. A landless class would have to be created and organized and trained to live in villages, where people acquired 'a settled outlook and a philosophy that fits a fixed Agricultural system'. The sense of impending disaster felt by hard-nosed environmentalists in the early 1940s, who saw ecological disaster all around, meant that they put their faith in mass compulsion rather than peasant self-interest.

Graham also went further than his superiors in his prescriptions for government reform, going to the heart of the relationship between technical staff and the district administration, which his superiors had side-stepped. His mass compulsion solution also demanded significant adjustments in government, in favour of the technical departments. For what was Hailey's quaint local compromise, was Graham's barrier to effective

[39] Abridged version of a report dated 15 February 1944, by M.D. Graham, Dept. of Agriculture, Bukura, Kakamega addressed to ag. Senior AO, Kisumu, KNA MAA7/602. It was then sent to the Secretariat and forwarded to Dr Isaac Shapera in preparation for his visit to discuss anthropological research in Kenya in relation to land tenure.

administration because of 'touchy, dogmatic representatives' of different departments capable only of 'sporadic efforts' and as such

> It is ... absolutely essential to kill 'Colonel Blimp' in Kenya if anything worthwhile is to be accomplished ... Interdepartmental cooperation in the past has been largely the result of individuals having the same ideas, meeting and working together by chance, not design.[40]

Echoing the post-Singapore editorial in *The Times*, Graham insisted 'It is for us to be the leaders, not the humble servants of an old-fashioned, imperial administration'. Local laws and regulations were largely ineffectual because of the lack of empowerment of technical officers, being advisers by statute. 'We have been the mere tools of the Administration, for whatever our advice may be, it is left to us to carry out ... to use our small force of instructors to do the policing and the teaching', he lamented. Indicating the depth of estrangement that could exist, he asked rhetorically whether there was 'a single administrative officer who polices his District and tries to prevent such laws from being broken', adding that departments were also to blame for accepting the situation.

Only technical experts, Graham opined, could see the real problems and stem their effect by 'getting the right message across to the people'. His corresponding solution was to radically reorganize local administration around new centres.[41] Each administrative centre would have an officer from the Agricultural, Veterinary, Educational and Forest Departments backed by specialist researchers in central laboratories, so that teamwork would 'cut out the existing inter-Departmental antagonisms which the African finds so confusing'. However, it was white officers who were the key to his vision. He did not share Blunt's belief in educated Africans. It was still too much, he insisted, to expect an African to teach another African how to farm, 'for he is not a farmer and to ask him to train others in this art is quite absurd'. So agricultural staff were profoundly divided as to African capabilities. Judged against this deeply felt set of wrongs, Margery Perham's critique of what needed righting in colonial rule seems less watertight. Perham had correctly noticed the disabling effect of racial prejudice with regard to colonial government; she had sounded the last post for colonial labour relations based on the South African kaffir model. Yet she had failed to highlight the marginalization of technical expertise within bureaucratic practice as a comparable drag on efficient rule.

A similar divergence in the views held within departments was being played out between senior members of the medical establishment. On the surface, Lockhart found support for a health and welfare-orientated village administration. A Senior Medical Officer in Nyanza, Harden-Smith, was also thinking about ways to organize public health around a social centre.

40 Ibid.: pp. 1–2 and 7.

41 Ibid.: pp. 3–4 and 6–7.

He set out his ideas in a paper entitled 'Preventive Medicine and Welfare in Native Reserves' which was circulated among senior medical officers.[42] A common concern among doctors was the dearth of preventive health work, and he had turned to Nairobi's municipal welfare structure to find a blueprint for the rural setting. He planned that every LNC President should have on his staff at least one of the following: a Welfare Officer, a Lady Welfare Officer and a Development Officer, who would work from a social centre. Each would initially be European, fluent in the vernacular and with their own staff. They would lecture at *barazas* with the help of other departments, and, unsurprisingly, the Lady Welfare Officer would encourage women and girls at *barazas*, in their homes, and in schools.

This new administrative category would be responsible for the general 'pioneering work' carried out by Health Officers, that was prevention-orientated. These Health Officers, he insisted, were the unsung heroes of African rural administration, since 'no one else in the District – and this includes Missionaries – took any but a very mild interest in what they were doing and such interest as was taken was not always favourable ... for the most part they worked alone'. He praised them for courageously abandoning their technical confines and setting about improving general standards of living in the circumstances they found: 'They trained carpenters, masons and brick makers, experimented with local building materials, held meetings and *barazas*...'. Here then was an attempt to tackle the lack of support for an unglamorous, but probably the most effective, form of communication between African households and European technical wisdoms of the day. The problem had been that public health work lacked status and credibility because it fell between a number of departments.[43]

Again, Lockhart seized this opportunity to extend the debate and in doing so drew out the difference in his perspective and that of his subordinate officer. Lockhart now ran with the gendered approach which Harden-Smith had introduced. Keeping his sights focused on the 'lower levels of the sanitary hierarchy', he produced another paper on rural welfare. His more detailed vision of a new technicalized rural landscape, rather than containing white welfare workers, was peppered with health centres employing African women under Medical Department jurisdiction. He described his ideal African woman. She would be:

> ... respectable, anchored, local, intelligent and accustomed to a fairly high standard of living. In fact the educated wives of our own and other departments' more educated officers. It seems to me that if such women were given quite a short course of instruction, they would be able to

[42] Harden-Smith, December 1944, KNA PC/NZA/3/1/570.

[43] Ibid. Vaughan argues that from the 1930s preventative public health was not a fashionable area for medics to be in, with the elevation of cultural difference and the increasingly technical appearance of biomedicine; (Vaughan, 1991: 46–7).

> effect considerable improvement in these matters among their more backward sisters. They would be likely to set about the problems with more comprehension of the difficulties than any welfare officer and the effect of their work would be at the lowest and therefore the most important level.[44]

Confident that the Army and a planned Sanitary Inspectors School in Nairobi would provide male sanitary workers, he was anxious about training women health workers. Certainly both government and missions neglected the education of girls in favour of education for men. In Mere District for example, separate schools for girls were first started in 1933. As already noted in Chapter 1, Mary Holding, a missionary teacher, recollected that tentative steps towards providing education for women were largely a response to such a request from young African men who had received missionary education, and who felt constrained because young wives had been secured for them, taken through initiation and thus had become their responsibility, a little too soon for their own ambitions. Also, according to Holding, they had begun to ask for wives who had some knowledge of hygiene.[45]

The slow increase in numbers of female pupils was – perhaps unsurprisingly – blamed on local constraints. Initiation interrupted attendance. Girls were often keener to become homeowners – setting up their own cooking pots, as it was called at the time. They were also too useful at home. Their mothers were often the greatest obstacles to girls attending school, many of whom had been told that women could not read. The situation apparently began to improve when literacy campaigns were targeted at younger women, with numbers increasing significantly after the war.[46] It was little wonder then that Lockhart desperately sought support for a pilot scheme at Siaya in Nyanza where a nucleus for a health centre existed and 'the urge of uplift is most marked'. It would provide vital ammunition in the battle to convince sceptics and produce a formula. It was a vision of husband-and-wife teams busy replicating themselves in enlightened detribalized family units. To Lockhart the key welfare problem was access to the domestic household arena, which neither the DC nor the Medical Officer, both white men, could enter, but which trained African women could: exactly what the CO's education advisory committees had argued in the previous decade.

However, Lockhart received a swift rejection and in the process was given a patronizing lecture on the essence of African thought. Again there was little intra-departmental consensus. Harden-Smith rejected the potential role to be played by African women and placed himself behind the authority of the DC. He insisted that since so much primary social and

[44] DMS to Ag. Senior MO, Nyanza, Kisumu 20 December 1944, KNA PC/NZA/3/1/570.
[45] E. Mary Holding, 'The Education of the Bantu Tribe', RH Mss.Afr.117.A580.
[46] Ibid.: 49–51. Also see discussion in Chapters 1, 5 and 6.

economic development was needed in rural areas, the majority of preventive work should be orchestrated by the district administration as part of a general and basic welfare programme since

> For many years – perhaps generations – Africans would, I think, regard the combination of preventive and curative services as merely quaint (see 'Characteristics of African Thought' by J.W.C. Dougall, price sh.1/50 at the C.M.S. Bookshop), and, since preventive work consists mostly of telling people what they should do – many of the things that they do not like doing – there should be the greatest possible authority behind the advice or instructions given. In Native Reserves that authority belongs only to the District Commissioner who seems to be regarded not only as having material power but also a sort of divine right accorded to no other being (see Chapter on Archaic Man in Jung's 'Modern Man in search of a Soul').[47]

According to this view, betterment could only come from obeying orders out of respect for authority, since Africans could never understand betterment, nor carry it out of their own free will. This closed his mind to the possibility of African women as health workers: they would have no better understanding of the difficulties of 'domestic uplift' than European women and missionaries, he insisted. His crucial litmus test was a sense of duty, as explained by the Principal of Makerere in a recent address: 'Africans, whose tradition is one of very narrow clan loyalty and discipline, very seldom, if ever, show the sense of vocation which is often taken for granted by people whose ancestors have lived for centuries in the Christian tradition.' The experiments with Jeanes School teachers, which had been conspicuously absent from welfare debates up to this point, were Harden-Smith's evidence. The teachers, he insisted, were agreed to have been a failure for three reasons: first, a lack of adequate supervision; secondly, a lack of vocation; and thirdly, a lack of authority 'which might have been derived from association with the District Administration'.[48]

Here then was a racially restrictive spin on the assimilationist approach to African development, with betterment achievable only through submission to the same moral authority as the DC: a welfare officer could only succeed by hanging on to the DC's coat-tails. There might also have been an issue of job security. Junior officers like Harden-Smith had more to lose if their posts were opened up to Africans. More importantly, such a view fitted into the gathering momentum against economic individualism. Medical experts too could find reason to back indirect rule and the will of

[47] Harden Smith to Lockhart 15 January 1945, copy to PC (Nyanza), KNA NZA/3/1/572. Kenneth Hunter to Rennie 13 January 1945; KNA PC/NZA/3/1/572. For a detailed examination of the Secretariat's plans see next chapter. After leaving the South African Army in German East Africa, Hunter served in Kenya from 1919 to 1954. He began as DO in Eldoret, administered the Nandi in the 1920s and was o/c Turkana; Chenevix Trench, 1993.

[48] Ibid.: p.1.

the chiefs. With evidence growing that the intake of animal protein among the Kikuyu was declining, blame was foisted upon African farmers choosing cash crops such as maize and wattle rather than sticking to communal food growing practices and the cultivation of traditional calcium-rich crops such as *wimbe* and *njahi* (see Throup, 1987: 67).

So, throughout the war, technical staff made concerted efforts to bring about a change in administration by means of debates about African welfare. Illustrative of the new channels of communication and debate being opened up was an unprecedented attempt at alliance building in 1945 with the next Secretary of State for the Colonies by the one and only Alexander Paterson. Congratulating Arthur Creech Jones on the humane quality of the Colonial Office's memorandum on Mass Education, Paterson nevertheless challenged him as to whether their socio-economic policy was sufficiently dynamic. Evidently seeing himself as a fellow socialist, Paterson felt that he was able to spell out the challenge of colonial rule according to the standards the Colonial Office had set themselves, in the hope of a sympathetic response. In Central Province alone, 80,000 people had to be removed from the land, and this could only be done by providing well-paid full employment 'in the Sir William Beveridge sense of the term', he explained.[49] All our modern science and imaginative political and managerial skills would have to be called upon, he urged, asking the Secretary of State to visit the colony with an economist and a scientist in tow. In addition to proof of the strong support for the Labour Party's position among certain colonial officials, this also highlights the firm belief in what could be achieved among even battle-weary professionals on the ground. Even without the cost of the Second World War, such a huge social engineering project would hardly have been feasible in view of the extensive reliance upon indirect rule and the need to avoid local opposition, as well as the internal opposition to an elevation of technical criteria within colonial government. As the post-war period would illustrate, Paterson's demands would be beyond the capacity of the late colonial state to deliver. It did try intervention once more through chiefs and elders; it did carry on bench-terracing and reducing death rates and so forth; but when the Blunts of the colonial administration realized that this came with complications, frustrations and racial restriction, many would be resigned to calling it a day for their mission. However, this was not before many others had turned to their old resource to get their orders carried out: the use of force to achieve their notion of transformation. Mau Mau would be the final administrative crisis which merged these two perpetually conflicting but increasingly estranged versions of colonial paternalism, with disastrous results.

Unfortunately, by the end of the war, departmental heads had not been able to command a consensus around their vision for the future of the

[49] A.R. Paterson to A.Creech Jones, 11 August 1945, RH ACJ/7/3/17.

administration. They had made strenuous attempts to seize the welfare debate to advance their interests and, they believed, those of rural Africans. The major bureaucratic vehicle they had for this was a weak one. More seriously, they were divided internally as to the capabilities of Africans and the role of women, therefore their solutions were profoundly different beneath the consensus over villages governed by technical specialists. This was a blow which doomed their ideas to a further round of frustration, since the district administration was even more threatened by the new categories of administrators being put forward, whether European or African. The model of small-scale projects aimed at poverty eradication through basic medical and agricultural support was once again lost. The promise of more staff after the war in what became the second colonial occupation held out some grounds for hope, but it would remain difficult to break up the relationship between generalist district officers and their system of control through equally generalist chiefs: technical expertise never broke free of this subordination which set the pattern for the rest of century. As the next section will illustrate, the administration had their own ideas about improving welfare.

District plans about plans

Initially, the administration were less interested in the widening debates about welfare. Many were running districts that had to shoulder the many demands of war and were feeling the strain. However, when the need to plan for the peace arose, they joined in the fetishization of post-war development plans. The district administration also took up the idea of reorganized village life as the route to welfare and development. This too was attractive to them, since in their version, like everyone else's, they were the central players. Their version was constructed around white teams which they controlled. Imbued with a bureaucratic tradition of stringent efficiency, financial accountability and local autonomy, the administration were much more glued to the concept of sharing power only when assured that the right sort of chap had evolved. Therefore they tended to be more conservative: the search for their own mirror image was a continual thread in their reasoning. Until then Africans could not be given more power than they were thought capable of handling, and would thus require the living example of the DC at all times.

It is easy to comprehend why Kenya's up-country district administrators were less impervious to passing trends and less interested in drastic reforms. As the supreme bearers of colonial power – however partial and illusory this may have been in reality – they were comfortable in that position. Indeed, some had lived like medieval barons, dispensing meagre patronage, literally laying down the law, brokering disputes and sleeping with their choice of local talent. Their self-justification usually lay in the belief that they represented the British Crown but also lived closer to native peoples than other whites, knew their ways better and could therefore best govern them. Conscientious officers were as much amateur enthnographers, botanists or anthropologists. For example, on taking up the post of DC in Moyale in 1932, Aubrey 'Mug' Mullins took possession of notes compiled by his predecessor, detailing local personalities, all common trees and plants used locally, words found in local place names and a list of diseases routinely found in local animals.[50] Mullins kept up the tradition and made copious notes in a diary format – a habit which many had been inducted into in boarding school – detailing virtually every experience and acquaintance thought to be of relevance.

Strict adherence to notions of duty and loyalty, keeping to regular personal habits such as not drinking before sunset, writing long letters home and maintaining a diary were some of the most important elements of a junior district officer's daily routine which he turned to in order to survive the isolation, bouts of illness and weight of responsibilty from being charged with overseeing territory that might extend for a hundred square miles. Some grew into such responsibility with humility and respect for local custom and people. Others became conceited and despotic. Colonial service was not always viewed by contemporaries as a glamorous career or an admired choice of profession. A popular jibe was that if a young educated man was not particularly outstanding at any one thing, he ought to find a career in the colonial service. Many actively sought out the career, propelled by a variety of impulses including a desire to be of public service, to live an athletic life (particularly if they had excelled at sport), to be obeyed, to meet the challenge of transforming an exotic or forbidding land, to 'help the poor black man', or to run from romantic failure. George Orwell's alter ego in his novel *Burmese Days* was happy to hide his disfigured face and pock-marked skin in the remoteness of his post. Flory's emotional life was tormented by his feelings of loathing and admiration for everyone and everything around him that was a product of 'imperialism', whether black or white, and he despised himself all the more for his situation. Characteristically he showed little sentimentality when describing the district officer equivalent in the empire of the Far East around the 1930s:

> There is a prevalent idea that the men at the 'outposts of Empire' are at least able and hardworking. It is a delusion. Outside the scientific services – the Forest Department, the Public Works Department and the like – there is no particular need for a British official in India to do his job competently. Few of them work as hard or as intelligently as the postmaster of a provincial town in England... And most of them are fools. A dull, decent people, cherishing and fortifying their dullness behind a quarter of a million bayonets. (Orwell, 1950: 60)

[50] Aubrey Mullins, RH.Mss.s.760 (1&2).

Back in Kenya, towards the beginning of the war, the district administration participated in the new debates about welfare largely in defence of their position. At the NWC for example, DCs counter-attacked against the departmental technocrats to ensure that they remained the conduit of government welfare services. When township welfare came on the agenda, administrators reacted by putting themselves in pole position. In 1940, Nyanza's PC, Sidney Fazan, had recommended that the DC be Chairman of a new all-African advisory council on township welfare to the LNC. He also suggested that he be invested with authority to invite non-Africans to attend meetings as he wished and that all recommendations should be referred to the Township Native Affairs sub-committee for advice 'before any action is taken on them'.[51] The welfare arena might offer an opportunity to satisfy select Africans with participation in local government, but their activities still had to be shadowed by the DC. As Fazan had reminded his superiors, the district administration had its task cut out more than most. The extra demands placed on Africans during the war years were administered via their relations with local chiefs and elders. In some districts the burden was great. And there were growing disparities between provinces. Central Province was becoming more and more congested and tense, whilst Nyanza Province faced the dilemma of how to manage agricultural change and soil erosion.

It was not until the end of the war when plans had to be made for the post-war period, that the district administration became constructively engaged with debates about welfare. In 1944, Fazan's old-style view was challenged by a younger generation from below. District officers were encouraged to put up their own ideas of how Colonial Development and Welfare money should be spent.[52] A mood of optimism, a desire for action and a belief in the potential of planning for a second colonial occupation abounded. LegCo was credited with creating 'the first Government structure expressly designed for functional development'. Memoranda hurtled back and forth between the layers of government. In a whirlwind of suggestion, bursting with colony-wide profiles, projections and plans, the land in relation to its people was scrutinized and subjected to a set of more determined and intent administrative principles.[53]

The prospect of new funding was the stuff of heady district daydreams. One young officer, Paul Kelly, produced a memorandum which was widely circulated amongst the administration.[54] It was written in response to the

[51] Fazan to DC (Kisumu) 21 January 1940, KNA PC/NZA/3/1/522.

[52] Rennie (CS and Member for Development and Reconstruction) 22 September 1945 Circular Letter No.190, KNA PC/NZA/3/1/570. A questionnaire was attached to serve as a basis of comparison for proposals and as a yardstick for development schemes.

[53] 'Reorganization in Kenya', Quarterly Notes, *African Affairs*, 44 (177), (Oct.1945): 141–2; Low and Lonsdale, 1976. For an explanation of the ultimate failure of the planning initiative, see Berman, 1990, ch.6 'The Colonial State & the Political Economy of Growth 1940–1952', esp. pp.281–9.

[54] 'A Note on Post-War Planning for Kenya Africans', circulated by ag.CS to all PCs and o/c

CD for Nyeri P. Wyn Harris's own written plan which was based on a division of Kenya by its people according to their agricultural progress. One of Wyn Harris's previous posts had been that of Settlement Officer for Kikuyu Land Claims, so unsurprisingly perhaps he viewed the colony as over-populated and desperately needing urbanization, birth control and secondary industries.[55] Kelly took a different view regarding the country as under-populated. His background is important because it contained all the ingredients of what was to enthuse those who became part of a younger generation of officers enchanted with the idea of post-war second colonial occupation. He seems to have blended traditional aspects of colonial administration with a more modern approach which marked himself and others out from the Wyn Harris generation. First, Kelly had been well-groomed by his superior Jack Clive, who had instilled in him a strict code of conduct: cheerfulness; courtesy to all, whatever their class or race; and a commitment to giving Africans their money's worth. All important were tangible signs of progress; this meant dispensaries, health centres, tribunal offices, and particularly permanent stores and shops. Secondly, the war had given Kelly a new set of wheels. He already knew the colony's new Information Officer, Eric Reginald St Aubyn Davies, from their stint together in Turkana;[56] Davies had persuaded him to run a mobile cinema which he did from the end of 1943 until April 1945. The deciding factors were twofold. Gilbert Rennie would be treating his reports as intelligence, so the post had an air of greater significance. The appointment was also a way of appeasing his conscience for not being directly involved in the war. Thus Kelly drove around showing films on a twenty-foot screen held up by tent poles, the transmission wires usually suspended through the middle of the audience who sat in the nearest site resembling a natural amphitheatre. Kelly learnt how to splice, mend the strips and even to make his own films.[57]

Such endeavours testify to the ethos of perseverance and the learnt experience of triumph in adversity and with faulty equipment. A sample

[54] (cont.) Masai District, Ngong, Northern Frontier District, Isiolo and D.C Turkana District, Lodwar. 30/11/1944, KNA PC/NZA/3/1/570. Copy also sent to Kenya Information Officer. Kelly was a raw district officer at this time. He was to become very involved in the agricultural programmes during Mau Mau and was passed over for PC promotion, ending his career as DC, Kilfi. He took Holy Orders on retirement. (From correspondence with Thomas Colchester, 9 August 1989.) Kelly was praised for his work in promoting communal projects when he was DC at Kitui, 1948–52, in Hill, 1991: 27–8. He retrospectively described the memorandum as an 'effusion'; Kelly to Lonsdale, 29 June 1993.

[55] Percy Wyn Harris became a district officer in Kenya in 1926; Settlement Officer for Kikuyu Land Claims, 1939–40; DC (Nyeri) 1941–3; Labour Liaison Officer, 1943–44; Labour Commissioner, 1944–45; PC (Central Province) 1946–47; and his last post in Kenya was as CNC 1947–49 after which he became Governor of Gambia.

[56] Davies was a Cadet in Kenya in 1928; DC (Nairobi) in 1940; Information Officer, 1943–45; deputy PC 1946; PC (Coast Province) 1947–49; and Chief Native Commissioner, 1949–53.

[57] Paul Kelly, RH. Mss. Afr.s.2229/1.

diary entry recording a viewing at Kimilili, North Kavriondo in 1944, is shot through with a sense of precariousness:

> *January 6th Thursday*
> Crowd of about 5,000 twice started to move off. National Anthem recorded too soft. Volt metre failed. Soil erosion film refused to run, query bad disc. Showed 1. Raising Soldiers. 2. Kenya Police. 3. Welfare. 4. Snake Charmer. 5. Manhunt. 6. British Empire at War No. 10 ... only two Kangas to manage crowd of this size ... Headman Nyaranga promised but failed to produce men to clear the site.[58]

Misadventure due to over-enthusiasm set in motion a chain of events that would lead to the chance reading of Wyn Harris's planning document. Thrashing around the countryside, vehicle maintenance left much to be desired. Following an accident when the brakes failed on the way to Marakwet, Kelly was forced to stay a while with his old chum Jack Clive at Eldoret. Here he read the latest circulars, and fired up by his own recent experiences, he set to work writing one of his own. It found favour as he recalled, and it was copied to all districts. Typical of the turf war, he was reprimanded for not liaising more with the Information Department.

Kelly's memorandum was the product of the times, written by someone shaped by the times. The war had enabled such an energetic administrative fledgling to experiment, to chug around the countryside and to marry technology with public relations. As a result, his perspective and sense of the possible were different. 'Post-War Planning for Kenya Africans' contained a startlingly new vocabulary, as the title showed: natives were Kenya Africans. Kelly had dispensed with the traditional categories of race and tribe that had always contoured administrative practice. Instead, he divided the country into three production zones. Each was to have a vigorous development plan based on his optimistic premise that the colony was under-populated and could support 20 million Africans if the correct development plan was put into practice.[59]

Kelly excitedly anticipated the development potential of a more penetrative type of white team rule – a youthful optimism in a revamped British rule. Once again, it was the image of village life as the replacement to the tribe which was central to visions of development and welfare. This had a structural and a cultural aspect. So that a campaign of mass ruralization would help the British 'atone for decades of meanness', villages would be moulded, he envisaged, from established trading centres, and would consist of schools, public houses, churches, cinemas, chiefs' units and cottage hospitals. It was hardly radical, for here was the most recognizable and romanticized benchmark of English civilization being paraded in response to the promise of metropolitan funding and the tightening net of external accountability this would bring. Aware of the Perham critique

[58] Ibid., Ch. V, p. 6.
[59] Kelly, 'Note on Post-War Planning', p. 1, KNA PC/NZA/3/1/570.

perhaps, he argued that the British taxpayer was now likely to demand something more for his money than 'indefinable things like indirect rule, political development, tribal loyalties. He will expect the tangible signs of civilisation, schools, hospitals, houses, fertile and productive soil.'[60]

Kelly was able to believe that a more vigorous white administration would fashion Africans into respectable peasants not tribesmen, not simply because his views on racial difference were more flexible. Attitudes to his own culture were now more buoyant. He was certain that the lack of confidence in British institutions which was characteristic of the 1920s and 1930s was disappearing. 'We are beginning to feel', he insisted, 'that the British way of life is not inferior to other systems, may even be better, and that we could do worse than give the African our culture.' This new self-belief was a consequence of the experience of war, and of winning it in particular. In any case, there was evidence that they could not stop Africans adopting a European way of life.[61] This realization had clearly encouraged Kelly to explore the cultural aspect of colonial rule. He went to great lengths to present an administrative formula that would direct the inevitable process of Africans becoming more like Europeans. So he was more enthusiastic about the potential of an active anglicizing process. His African villages were to be held together by what he had experienced: the vigorous English methods of character training, including scouting, boarding schools, religious education, games and even the country-badge system. The aim was to mould citizens capable of sustaining their own welfare through self-betterment and self-control:

> Good citizenship must be taught, and conventional behavior must become a habit by the rigorous enforcement of law and order. Associations and clubs must be encouraged, and the fullest possible use must be made of demobilized N.C.O.s. Christianity should be actively taught in Government African schools ... Councils and Central Government should give more for funds for the promotion of games, and experts should be employed to teach them ... women and girls should have their own pitches at the village schools.

This was a fundamentally conservative concept of welfare that elevated the role of a civic-minded male head of the household. Completely or semi-detribalized Africans might well possess European externalities, but, he warned, their 'Africanness' was retained at the core. Within the argument of the time that sought to justify racial rule, was a growing school of thought which insisted that European civilization had been taken in second- or third-hand, transplanted by half-educated Africans, few of them

[60] Ibid., p. 4.

[61] Ibid. See Vaughan, 1991, for an account of the reification of cultural difference at the expense of racial and environmentalist theories, especially ch.2, 'Rats' Tails and Trypanosomes: Nature and Culture in Early Colonial Medicine', and ch.5, 'The Madman and the Medicine Man: Colonial Psychiatry and the Theory of Deculturation'.

having much contact with the more 'European' and 'only those who have talked with them a good deal ... realise how little they *understand*'.[62] So, although he acknowledged greater capacity for change, Kelly's re-defined trusteeship was found to be even more replete with white responsibilities. Thus, for the district administration, change was a way of making things stay the same.

However, Kelly's balm of social welfare designed to soothe the sores of detribalization, although somewhat muddled, was radical in other respects. He was keen for alternative government to be applied. Grappling with urban welfare problems forced him to accept roles for a welfare professional and anthropological researcher, as necessary components of effective post-war administration. There was a dearth of information about the effects of urbanization, he argued, particularly in relation to the Kikuyu youth who lived near Nairobi. Tribal discipline lacked its controlling element, he warned, so

> Figures showing, for example, what proportion of urban and rural youth now pass through initiation will be of immense assistance to social welfare workers ... the solution of 'detribalisation' lies in the encouragement by appointment of European and African welfare workers, youth leaders, games masters and mistresses, and by actual grants to clubs of money and playing fields, of every kind of social activity, from debating societies to swimming pools.[63]

It was open-minded for the time to suggest that two anthropologists should work in Nyanza and Central Province advising the government on 'how to harness what remained of tribal institutions and loyalties to the advantage of social welfare', although since the Nandi and Meru retained the bulk of their institutions, he conceded that their initiation rites as pubescent discipline were best not substituted with games, fagging, scouting and confirmation ceremonies. And Kelly argued in detail that welfare officers had a crucial role to play, a departure that many in the administration could not welcome in the same way. In his world, they would run mobile cinemas – 'the most effective instrument of mass education', he declared, believing the Information Officer's calculation that 8 mobile vans and 6 stationary projectors could reach an annual audience of 6 million.[64] Nevertheless he urged caution. 'There is a danger after the war', he noted, 'of unleashing too many Europeans on the African all holding their *barazas* and sickening the native with "maneno".' But, in the absence of clear knowledge and because he saw a solution to detribalization in yet more detribalization, in theory he heartily approved of new officers

[62] See Leith Ross, 1944, who wrote from the perspective of a Nigerian memsahib and was given an enthusiastic review by Elspeth Huxley, one of Kenya's most famous spokeswomen, in *African Affairs* 43 (172) (July 1945): 142–3.

[63] Kelly, 'Note on Post-War Planning...' p. 5, KNA PC/NZA/3/570

[64] Ibid., p. 3.

sharing in these tasks. It was a formula that was being applied not just to urban areas but also to many rural ones.[65]

As an appetizer to the increase in the colonial presence that would take place after the war, welfare officers were fast moving beyond the realm of fantasy. Due to the recruitment of African soldiers (discussed in detail in the next chapter), the district administration began to face the prospect of a new cadre of officers. In 1944, Fortie Ross was released from military service to take up the trial post of Nyanza's Provincial Development and Welfare Officer.[66] A circular gently broke the news that Ross would be on tour with the Family Remittance Officer, providing a link between *askari* and their homes, monitoring a recently introduced army form used for correspondence relating to 'Domestic Affairs'. The district administration would be hard pressed to object, since funding was not an issue and the post was billed as nourishing ties that were crucial for the morale of the troops. Support for welfare officers also came from the colony's new Information Officer, Eric St A. Davies. He had been a DC but had temporarily taken up this post created by the needs of war. His tours had revealed an increasingly differentiated African rural society, not so much 'tribal' as 'agrarian' or 'village', he argued, which could greatly benefit from having social centres run by welfare officers.

In a paper widely circulated among the administration and LegCo members, entitled 'Welfare, Mass Education and Information', Davies maintained that such an officer, who was European (and not linked to health, as Lockhart wanted), could end the deadlock among development initiatives at the district level, particularly the current stalemate, blamed on African apathy and indolence, in the face of insufficient European staff to enforce local projects.[67] At his command would be the new techniques of propaganda: mobile cinemas, film strip lectures, the distribution of pamphlets and still pictures, adult literacy classes, broadcasts, talks at the *baraza*. Equally important were to be the Welfare Officer's conversations with 'the man in the coffee house or in the field', and – such was the degree of Davies's open-mindedness for the time – 'with the woman grinding corn in the village or bargaining in the market place'.

Davies was very clear as to what the duties of such an officer would be and he listed them with the greatest precision to date. He would work in a location designated by the DC, supporting general development plans with house and dam building, grazing and grass planting, soil management,

[65] As Frederick Cooper observed in post-war Mombasa, 'productivity and urban order appeared to demand that the African worker cease to be African at all. His nutrition, his family life and his attitudes toward labour, career, property and achievement had to become those of the modern working man' (Cooper, 1987: 9).

[66] Adm.20/2/1/28, Circular sent to all DCs, Nyanza 15th May 1944, KNA PC/NZA/3/1/572.

[67] Letter to CS from Information Officer E.R. St A.Davies 13 July 1945 accompanying 'Some Notes on Welfare, Mass Education and Information', KNA PC/NZA/3/1/572.

and lectures on the use of money, the 'real' value of stock, health and hygiene, civics and general knowledge. He would undertake more general development work in the district, supervising 'social centres and wireless reception posts, organizing football teams and scout troops, encouraging arts and crafts, fostering co-operative activities, arranging for the supply of building materials'. The officer should be young, keen, hard-working and 'with a real liking for Africans'; he should keep a comprehensive diary of his work and have an African clerk. With European assistants in the larger districts in addition to African helpers, Davies also mapped out one male and one female European officer each for the townships of Eldoret, Kisumu, Kitale and Nakuru to work as probation officers responsible for the welfare of all races. Like the departmental heads, Blunt and Lockhart, he also possessed a more positive assessment of African capabilities and inter-race relations. He believed that such a cadre of officers could stimulate Africans 'not only to take part in what Government is doing for them, but to do something for themselves'. Davies's job description matched perfectly the conclusions of the various Colonial Office committees of enquiry of the 1930s, but the incoherence of imperial rule had prevented officers on the ground using their arguments to badger the unenthusiastic.

Despite a growing consensus that the solution to African welfare lay with social centres manned by development generalists, the district administration had two trump cards to play in their fight back. One was the way in which such plans demanded a drastic change in the status quo of the White Highlands. In admitting that welfare in the settled areas presented the greatest problem, Davies was giving tacit reference to the difficulty in getting his energized village model into the sullen zones of the White Highlands. Moralizing about welfare required a dismantling of settler domination, and this dragged down any initiatives. A second was the fact that senior government officials in the colony were usually former DCs and not sympathetic to moves that might threaten their terrain.

The extent of solidarity, especially from on high, is illustrated by Gilbert Rennie's response as Chief Secretary to Davies's paper. Where Davies had listed the functions of welfare officers, Rennie had crossed this out and written 'DC is a welfare officer'.[68] Davies's hero signified someone sharing in the DCs' special relationship. Nor was his argument for division of duties taken well. Davies had argued that the welfare officer

> ... must be completely divorced from any type of duties smacking of 'authority' which tend to widen the gulf between the D.O. and the common African – tax collection, court work and the like. He must spend most of his time on safari, much of it on foot. It would help

[68] 'Some Notes on Welfare, etc', KNA PC/NZA/3/1/572. Gilbert McCall Rennie held the position of Chief Secretary from 1939 to 1948. From 1945 he was also Chairman of the Development and Reconstruction Authority.

greatly if a welfare officer were married and his wife travelled with him and worked amongst the women.

In the margin Rennie's 'No' underlined three times appeared at this suggestion of a two-for-the-price-of-one option, on the grounds that a huge gulf existed between the DC and the common African. Protecting the system he had come from, Rennie and other senior officers like him would fight not to have the DC dumped with all the unpopular jobs like law enforcement and tax collection, whilst welfare officers became the benign force of local administration and the friendly face of colonial rule, on the flimsy ground that they were mobile, chatty, and able to persuade by showing pictures of why policy from above should be followed from below. Kelly's and Davies's acceptance that such an officer could be the broker between the villagers and technical wisdoms would be opposed by many more. Towards the end of the war, their plans for a small army of welfare officers in a local administrative landscape re-orientated around social centres, appeared to be no more than empire state-building in the air.

However, it was soon clear that the district administration was keen to have new social centres, but would rather manage the welfare effort itself. Towards the end of the war, discussions were taking place throughout the colony about development planning in the post-war period. The district administration was naturally at the centre of these plans about plans. By 1945 the district administration and its advisers had found an acceptable form of reformed administration around welfare and development. The division of districts into agricultural zones 'for administrative convenience' facilitated their decision that 'a most important post-war aim should be the development of Social Centres'. One centre per year was to be built as soon as materials were available after the war and a hydrographic survey of each area carried out to ensure adequate water supplies.'[69] A social centre was usually defined as a place with a cottage hospital, a store and produce market, a dairy, a hide *banda* and store, an information and reading room with bookshop attached and equipped with wireless and strip film projector, and arena for mobile cinema show, a sub-post office, a beer hall, a police post, shops for cycle repairs, shoe repairs, a blacksmith, butchers, tailors, and a place for spinning and weaving, should the demand be high enough.

Such tighter administration at the local level was to be built on the premise of new developmental budgets. For example, the administration in Central Kavirondo was keen to make a census of the native population

[69] Notes from a meeting at the DC's office Kericho, 17 September 1944 to discuss post-war development in Kericho, KNA PC/NZA/3/1/570. It was attended by the Economic Secretary, Troughton, PC (Nyanza), DC (Kericho), Col. Matheson, Major Dawson-Curry, H.Coxon, Dr. Wilkinson, the Ag.Senior AO (J.T.Moon), Provincial Development Officer (F.E.V.Ross),Veterinary Officer, Asst AO (G.Gamble), Asst Supt Police (Capt.Gribble), E. Anderson, and the DO as Secretary.

after the war, plus a nutritional survey to establish what deficiencies existed in diets and how these could be countered with locally produced foodstuffs. Plans included the treatment of venereal disease with penicillin at cottage hospitals where sufferers would be controlled as in-patients, the construction of a central leprosarium on a lake island for complete segregation, and a blitz on bilharzia in addition to tsetse control experiments. New road construction was to improve crop distribution. And, importantly for making administration more thorough, telephonic communication between Kisumu and Maseno and to all police posts and social centres was included.[70]

Unsurprisingly, central to the post-war plans for new administrative social centres was the appointment of more district officers. The final plans contained requests for an additional DC and four DOs. The argument used was that the DC, relieved of all routine office work, could then behave like 'the Commander of a battlecruiser', responsible for the normal routine work of the district and able 'to perform effectively his function of integrating the work of all Departmental Officers as a single team'. Unsurprisingly therefore, in the post-war planning discussions in Nyanza, the PDWO was not to enjoy an established position. Although Fortie Ross, in this role, was present at the discussions, his administrative post was missing from future plans. An earlier district planning meeting held in September 1944 had decided that the planned social centres required a District Welfare Officer to visit and supervise them, who must be regarded as 'an integral part of the scheme'.[71] But this recommendation did not make it as far as the main report signed by the District Commissioner for Central Kavirondo.

In line with Lord Hailey's thinking on technical staff, such officers were to be stationed at or near each centre, but were to be a temporary feature, being replaced as soon as African personnel became available; one European, preferably a Health Officer selected from among this temporary staff, would ultimately supervise each zone or division, 'keeping the Makerere-trained workers up to the mark'. Instead, the DC would delegate duties to junior administrators and to the chiefs: 14 chiefs' houses and offices were to be built plus locational camps consisting of a small officer's house, boy's quarters, and interpreters' quarters at 12 sites in the district. The social centre model had become the major site of administrative competition. The district administration tried to carve up development between themselves and Africans, just as the heads of the technical departments were also trying to do. Medical officers tried to reprioritize health and link it to returning soldiers in the plans for zonal development around villages. Dr Bullen, a local Medical Officer, commented that 'very

[70] 'Post War Development Planning ... 5 Years, Central Kavirondo', signed by DC (CV) undated but file position would denote October 1944, pp.10–11, KNA PC/NZA/3/570.
[71] Ibid., p. 7.

little could be done in the matter of village water supplies, sanitation and health services so long as natives were permitted to live in unhygienic hovels scattered throughout the Reserve. Thirteen thousand African soldiers would be returning to the district after the war and this scheme offers a ready-made means of absorbing a large proportion of them in useful employment and in settling them with their families in improved conditions, which life in the army had led them to expect'.[72]

Even in 1945 such plans could really be little more than this, when faced with the reality of imperial crisis and African social change. Although the new model village scenario found favour among district officers – as they agreed, from the point of view of controlling people 'the advantages of having the whole population concentrated at certain accessible centres would be manifold' – in practice such a development programme proved elusive, even for this dominant branch of the administration.[73] (A subsequent attempt at such a policy for the same reasons was tried out by Julius Nyerere in his *ujamaa* village policy for rural Tanzania). First, the expected financial package did not materialize. For example, at a meeting in Kericho held towards the end of 1944 to discuss post-war development, Troughton, the Economic Secretary, warned that plans should be restricted to genuine development projects, 'those calculated to increase the taxable capacity of the people – as opposed to mere amenities', and kept to projects that might reasonably be accomplished within a five-year period.[74]

Secondly, there was the ever present danger that family-targeted welfare would be overwhelmed by social crisis because of the compulsion element in their plans. A preliminary planning meeting in Nyanza had agreed that an anthropological survey to investigate land tenure was necessary since zonal development meant that deteriorated land should be closed off, with the 'compulsory transfer of populations for limited periods of uncertain duration'. A tendency to procrastinate and buy time from surveys pervaded such meetings. Troughton had declared that only when this information was available would it be possible to consider how best 'to mould and change these customs in conformity with correct farming practice while retaining the good will and co-operation of the people themselves'. Although the distinguished anthropologist Evans Pritchard was to be approached, Archdeacon Owen had, in fact, already spent two

[72] 'Post War Development Planning ... Central Kavirondo', [undated] p.9, KNA PC/NZA/3/1/570. See next chapter for detailed discussion of the role of the *askari* in welfare development.

[73] Part of extract from Minute 2/iii of minutes of meeting at Kisumu early September 1944 signed by the D.O., ibid p.9. F.E.V. Ross attended, as did Walter Odede (Assistant Vetinary Officer at Maseno and temporary member of the LegCo in the absence of Archbishop Beecher) another African John Paul Olola and Archdeacon Owen, plus representatives from all departments and the Administration.

[74] Meeting held at the DC's Office 17 September 1944 to discuss post-war development in Kericho. J.F.G.Troughton, Economic Secretary, p.1, KNA PC/NZA/3/1/570.

months carrying out anthropological investigations in the district and he found the Luo in possession of a flexible system of tenure and, therefore, saw no need for the plans to be delayed.[75] Such tentativeness was the product of fear. Nyanza was Kenya's largest and most populous province with a huge agriculture-based population. The plans threw into sharp and awkward relief the need for, but lack of, real authority and technical capability.

In an over-crowded Central Province, the Kikuyu heartland, a similar discrepancy existed between administrative thought and actual capabilities, as policy about land use, the base-line of a development strategy, always quickly revealed. Immediately preliminary surveys and propaganda attempts were inaugurated, Africans asked questions about government policy. The immediate and unintended effect was to 'arouse African opinion' to dangerous levels.[76] For example, a planned 'medico-agricultural survey' in South Nyeri – a vital part of the development plans – in order to investigate land boundaries, *shamba* ownership, trends in agriculture and related customs, had quickly produced a sharp reaction from local people. The administrative hierarchy was asked to stem the distrust with a 'definite statement of policy'. The problem was that any such statement, if honest, would have to include three points: that the average family was barely subsisting on agriculture alone at the expense of the soil's fertility; that populations were increasing at a rate of 1.8 to 2 per cent; and – political dynamite – that 10,000 families had to come off the land in South Nyeri. Tomkinson, Central Province's PC, feared an early revival of agitation, if the Kikuyu realized that more and more people would have to come off their Land Unit since

> ... present wage levels do not make that prospect tolerable to them nor do they give any sense of security to their thoughts. They will want to know what employment is likely to have to offer them and their families ... and what is to become of them when they are no longer able to work.[77]

A third and final obstacle was an absence of general agreement among the district administration as to the way forward regarding new families living in modern villages. All branches of the administration, it seemed, were unable to reach agreement through their debates about welfare. Tomlinson was in charge of a province further down the path of social differentiation and he was not convinced. Consequently he perceived African class formation to be the new social bogey that added to the threat of social collapse. What made him regard talk of new family-targeted welfare as naive, was evidence that enlightened families were rich and

[75] Minute 2(ii) of the first meeting of the Planning Committee reprinted, KNA PC/NZA/3/1/570 p.11.

[76] PC (Central Province) to CS, 14 May 1945, KNA PC/NZA/3/570. Copies to other PCs.

[77] Ibid., p.2.

selfish. Rural change was producing new landowners from the more educated sections of the population: 'Antagonistic to tribal institutions' and with as yet 'no consciousness of civic responsibility', these groups were charged with stirring up 'distrust and discontent among the more backward and ignorant men and women'.[78]

Rather than encourage the development of the big landowner and employer of labour, the administration saw its job as to make such men 're-orientate themselves on clan lines sufficiently to ensure their conformation to sound land usage', which, of course, demanded firm action by the ever necessary DC. Changes in general land distribution and practice had to be enforced. This meant dealing strictly with those Kikuyu who, whilst possessing *shambas* in their own *Ithaka*, were also *Ahoi* in order to gain other benefits from the use of neighbours' land, and with those *Ahoi* who had been left with no land to cultivate. It was a view of welfare administration that went back to the basic model of the clan and the chief, and, in order that services were to be spread equally, unsurprisingly it also led neatly back to the DC. The administration found other evidence to support their view. For example, in North Kavirondo, the Kano plains had been taken over for rice growing during the war. A post-war development plan to plant gum trees to dry up the swamps and provide fuel was agreed by the administration and then put to the LNC, who rejected it on the grounds that, had the local officers been confident of the scheme, they would have done it anyway. It was therefore dismissed as a trap.[79] Years of top-down racial rule was clearly preventing an easy and quick transition to development and welfare by mutual consent.

This suspicion of local capabilities was the logical rationale of an administration which grappled with land reform, local control and social collapse. Understandably, they believed that only the traditional concept of local rule by divine right could hold the rural order together and, according to the particular local circumstances, deliver betterment and control. Theirs was an unavoidable perspective. Years of picking and choosing headmen, sitting under trees in full view of large crowds of locals, of documenting and recording plants, places and personalities, all combined to suggest a special relationship that was the best kind of white and black relationship. It was also easy to be nostalgic, along with the older men of the villages. Did they not tell them over and over again that law and order was never so good as it used to be? Perhaps officials could not help but envy the simple but effective old African approach to punishment: if a man stole, beat him up; if he stole again put his left hand into the fire, then his right; and if he stole once more, roll him down a hill wrapped in banana leaves that had been set on fire.[80] No wonder crime

[78] Ibid.
[79] K.L. Hunter, 1929–50, RH Mss.Afr.s.1942.
[80] Willougby Thompson, RH Mss.Afr.s.519 (1).

was remembered as being much less. It probably was. Inevitably, the end of the war heralded a renaissance in the practice of indirect rule by the administration through chiefs and elders considered loyal and modernizing.

As the contributions of the district administration to the wartime debates about African welfare reveal, their vision was also built on a new re-ordered village life, but one specifically including old ways and customs. They too were divided as to how to proceed. But perhaps they knew better than most that the greatest obstacle to action lay in the immediate opposition from Africans with whom they would have to negotiate in order to avoid conflict and disorder. The problem was that the very precariousness of a prosperous life and the corresponding need for a complex range of alternatives, which had previously enabled the administration to make the most of their toeholds, were already working against officials. By the end of the war, there were whispers moving around with the men who had spent time living in townships. 'The white man grows fat on your toil; he cuts open your bellies and sprays poison on your crops; he causes locusts to fall from the sky. Before he came there was rain.'[81] With settlers battening down the hatches in the exclusive White Highlands and doing well out of the war, African farmers might well say that the city spiv had a point.

Settlers and the new racial maternalism

Wartime debates about African welfare went beyond administrative circles. The European community also took up the challenge to redefine the aim of white rule in the context of growing local tensions and a closer metropolitan audit. While the Colonial Office prodded the Kenya government by resorting to circulars, reports and a visit by its chief anthropological adviser, Audrey Richards, unofficial groups and individuals outside of government took to romanticizing about African welfare. Settlers sensed that they might well be left out of the debates about how tribes could be transformed into an agrarian peasant society and self-respecting town-dwellers. It was an issue that required them to make a stand. For the new standards expected of modern states not only challenged the DC's feudalism. They also struck at the very heart of the settlers' paternalism.

Stimulated by the atmosphere and possibilities of war, settlers made nostalgic sojourns into a fantasy world of Merrie England. Political groupings talked of white welfare responsibilities. Non-governmental organizations provided new forums for discussion, especially for women settlers. Only church organizations seemed to be absent, focused more on their own communities; not party to government discussions and not so drawn into the politics of white rule, they had less interest in joining in the

[81] Sydney T. Kelson, p.9, RH Mss.Afr.s.735.

debates. Generally, settlers looked to re-ordered villages as their ideal solution. They put less emphasis on the state taking the lead and more upon individual actions. They shared profoundly racist views. And, as this group illustrates most sharply, all their attempts to give Africans an improved, more European-like community were crafted by minds naive to the practical limitations of their suggestions when inserted inside a racially divided society lacking a single moral community. These good intentions were essentially viewed by Africans and a growing body of critics in Britain as 'white' intentions. However, settler contributions did contain a variety of formulas which reflected their different agendas.

The settlers who had made Kenya their home and a place to bring up their families were not a homogenous group. They were most often English but there were many other nationalities including South African, German, Italian and Scottish. Not all farmed huge estates in relative prosperity or at least nominal security. For the smaller-scale pioneer type of farmer, life was shot through with a multi-faceted precariousness. Debt, labour problems, sick cattle, failed crops were universal topics of conversation. Surviving the natural environment commanded much energy and concentration. Domestic life could consist of a daily exposure to potential hazard. Without warning, the skies could suddenly darken. Instead of this heralding a dramatic storm to clear the air, a plague of locusts would descend. Crops, kitchen gardens and lines of washing could disappear in a matter of minutes. Take a walk next day to survey the damage and one single flying red ant might hurtle into your eye, nip your eyeball and leave you blinded for days with the inflamed 'Nairobi Eye'. In the time it took to drive across the valley, now recovered, to stay with friends, a battalion of safari ants might have marched across your lawn and decided to munch their way through the main wooden foundations of your house. Unaware, and in holiday mode, one carefree act of barefoot verandah charades might allow just enough time for a jigger flea to burrow fast and deep into your heel to make a quick nursery for its maggot-like larvae. However hung-over its owner, a shoe left carelessly on the guest room floor overnight required rigorous morning inspection lest a scorpion had found it first. And as you leave to drive back, stopping to admire the rose buds just coming to bloom in the oh so English rose garden in readiness for the Nairobi Flower Show, step back on to an African puff adder and you could find your itinerary somewhat rescheduled.

More seriously, relations with the surrounding African population could be tense. Many settlers lived in constant antagonism with their neighbours. From the time he worked as a government surveyor in the 1920s before trying his hand at farming, T.R.L. Neston felt the resentment, even if he did not appreciate its reasons. When locals realized he was allocating their *shamba* land for soldier settlement schemes after the First World War, they cut through his survey lines, pulled up a survey beacon and stole his theodolite. His second farm – his first at Kipkarren having failed – was subject to an arson attack by a group of local Nandi, which they blamed on the innocent actions of young *toto*. Living through the Second World War was making him even more uneasy. He believed that Italian POWs who were fraternizing with African labour were combining forces to belittle the British. It was a well articulated fear. Outsiders who did not obey the rules of racial separation had undermined their cultivated prestige. This was a device designed to keep the lid on local animosities and it required keeping a distance from locals, not getting involved in their lives to suggest superiority and maintaining a sense of mystery and the possession of god-like qualities and skills. For Neston and for others, these were unsettling times.[82]

For other settlers, however, the war was a time of excitement and possibility. Powys Cobb was a settler who had first bought 30,000 acres near Molo at the beginning of the century only to have it repossessed due to the First World War, a failed experiment in cotton and the change in currency rates from one rupee commanding one shilling and fourpence to a florin. His second venture at Mau Narok in the Rift Valley had picked up, thanks to the Second World War. His cattle and sheep had developed nicely. He had 2,000 acres under cultivation. Average yields were 7 200lb bags of wheat per acre, or 15 and a half 180lb bags of barley per acre.[83] Providing labour was cheap and willing, this yield which was by no means outstanding could be maintained. Mechanization held out the possibility of greater returns and less hassle. Prosperity thus boded ill for the squatter farm labourer doing most of the work. Sons of settler farmers and a younger generation of farmers had left to join the King's African Rifles, travelling outside of Kenya and some going to the Far East. They mixed more with other whites and also worked more closely with Africans. Some took up desk jobs in Nairobi. Women settlers also found themselves running the farms on their own, working for the war effort in special wartime posts in Nairobi or joining voluntary groups to care for a range of casualties. When hostilities looked to be ending, the issue of what form post-war Kenya would take began to vex many settlers. By 1944, they joined vigorously in the debates about African welfare.

The idea of reorientating Africans around a model of English village life had a strong appeal. Those who felt less threatened by not being perched in the White Highlands embraced the detribalization-to-village-life model. One man who tried to publicize his views was Malcolm Mason, a farmer from Mombasa, with '18 years of knowledge of the Colony and the heart of a countryman'. He also advertized himself as a close personal friend of the governor. Mason envisaged African life being achieved through rural villagization with African trading villages. 'In almost every area there is a suitable spot', he insisted, 'for making a village properly laid out for the

[82] T.R.L. Neston, RH Mss.Afr.s.1086.
[83] E. Powys Cobb – daughter's reminiscences, RH. Mss.Afr.s.2058.

occupation of Africans, who want to carry on the village trades, as we used to know them in England.' His blueprint came directly from his understanding of English history, from the apparently 'very primitive times' when the village craftsman was the mainstay of the village and agriculture was dependent upon various tradesmen and craftsmen.[84] Planning, he believed, could prevent 'anything shoddy from creeping in' and secure 'the right atmosphere', where the 'right man' could build up 'the right ideas'. H. I. Lakhani, an Indian from Kisumu, also lobbied the government on this matter. He too believed that trading centres should be turned into social centres, as soon as funds were available, for the manufacture of 'better citizens'.[85]

Yet ironically, Mason wanted villages that would be Indian-free zones. 'The more intelligent African who has learnt a trade', he opined, was continually pushed out of the skilled market by the small Indian *fundi,* 'known for employing his own people'; he had found Africans generally more thorough than the Indian, who 'generally skimps his work'. Mason, like many other settlers, could display strong sympathy towards Africans when they were represented as lovers of the country life and close to nature, akin to the trusty yeomen of old, and in contrast to the stereotype they held of the Indian, an urban dweller who, it was believed, 'has fleeced the African in the Reserves and Towns'.[86] With such an extreme form of social engineering being a key factor, the element of discipline and control was central to Mason's plan. Village advisers were to be installed who would function as the 'English schoolmaster' and, paid for by the Development Fund, help the African 'to make his start on the same lines that the greatness of England has been built upon'. Each District Council would establish village bye-laws; every village would appoint its own headman and village bobby (a retired soldier, paid for by the government).[87]

Part of the enthusiasm for such a solution came from similar ideas being generated in Britain at the time. Discussions of post-war reconstruction often paid homage to the myth of the countryside as the repository of the English character, a place where life was untainted and everyone was cheerful and honest. The *Times Weekly Edition* (Export Section) had popularized the revival of rural industry and crafts in a series of articles. The Rural Industries Bureau and the Women's Institutes, featured in Lord Justice Scott's report on the post-war planning of the English countryside, were lauded as the leaders of a rural revival which was moulding old traditions to suit modern conditions. The Rural Industries Bureau trained men in various crafts and industries and taught business methods and marketing using established craftsmen; the Women's Institutes were

84 Mason to Lieut.Col.W.S. Marchant. 2 June 1944, KNA MAA7/859.

85 H.I. Lakhani, Kisumu 16 December 1944 to PC, KNA PC/NZA/3/1/570.

86 Mason to Marchant 2 June 1944, KNA MAA7/859.

87 Ibid, p.3. Enclosure, p.1.

credited with a similar function but on a smaller scale, holding craft classes all over England and even producing articles for overseas export.[88] Mason believed that this kind of revolution would be almost universally welcomed: a number of intelligent Kikuyu had been consulted and were in favour of villages; the majority of settlers would be eager for the introduction of African village life – their wives would be willing to help in spinning and weaving – apart from a few of the diehard settlers who 'did not really count today anyway'.[89]

This was highly optimistic. For many other settlers African villages were the ultimate nightmare. Mason, living in the Coast Province, unlike many other settlers had land he was willing to spare for such an initiative. In the White Highlands a similar scenario would be unthinkable. Eric Davies, the Colony's Information Officer, was one of the few people at the time who recognized that welfare in the settled areas constituted a major problem. Only a fragile consensus existed that any new villages should not become 'dormitory areas' for labourers on the nearby farms, but should include a social hall, post-office, beer shop, bookshop, craftsmen's shop and police post, and have 'positive supervision' to prevent the emergence of 'little Kiberas'.[90] Davies wanted Welfare Officers to visit farms to work among the women and children, giving advice to employers and labourers about building their own information rooms or social halls. But, as he candidly noted, the welfare worker could only be put to use in centres where each householder lived off sufficient land to cultivate a small garden, which had the advantage of keeping his wife fully occupied and providing an income that was not based on illicit brewing or prostitution, 'often the only means of subsistence in some of the less fortunate ngambos in this country'.[91] By implication he was linking African family welfare to land redistribution. All this demanded that settlers should treat their squatter labour as permanent residents with permanent land rights on the White Highlands. This they were clearly unwilling to do – a law passed in 1938 excluded all Africans from holding permanent rights – and now their hope was that mechanization might reduce the need for labour in any case. In the post-war reality Mason's dream of the settled-area trading village peopled with African family units became a nightmare for the majority of settlers. After the war attitudes would only harden towards even the more modest plans for welfare in the Reserves.

The village was not the only suggestion being put forward. Some settlers worked in pairs to get a different solution supported by the government.

[88] See 'The Revival of Rural Crafts' subtitled 'Importance in Post-War Planning' by Norman Wymer. 1 November 1944, KNA/DEF/10/68.

[89] Mason to Marchant, 2 June 1944, p.2, KNA MAA7/859.

[90] Kibera was a slum area in Nairobi regarded as notorious; 'Some Notes on Welfare, Mass Education and Information', Eric Davies, 13 July 1945, p.5. KNA/PC/NZA/3/1/572.

[91] For discussion of the settler view in the 1940s see Throup, 1987, ch.5, 'The Kikuyu Squatter Problem'.

Such was the case of Patrick Williams and Olga Watkins. Both had convoluted links with the administration and moved more freely within unofficial circles. Williams was a settler who had taken the wartime post of Director of Training. Watkins was the wife of an official and had a high-profile public life independent of this role. Both were captivated by the idea that a colony-wide African youth programme could tackle the problem of African welfare.[92]

Again, colonial initiatives were feeding off movements in Britain geared to inculcating popular loyalties in the face of external threats. By the end of the 1930s, notions of citizenship, as we have seen, found keen supporters in Britain in the face of the growth of fascism abroad and urban degeneration at home. Citizenship offered a way of forging a more intimate relationship between state and society. Williams had received literature from an organization dedicated to a refined concept of Imperial Youth citizenship: the Empire Youth Movement,[93] which advertised Imperial Citizenship as 'the ready acceptance of discipline and the efficient and happy discharge of duties whatever their nature'. Begun in 1937 with offices throughout the Commonwealth, its London co-ordinator was Major Nee based at the Royal Empire Society. According to the organization's own propaganda, it aimed to stimulate a spiritual crusade using the youth of Empire. Its founders were fearful that democracy – defined as Christianity in the form of government – was receding, whilst, in contrast, Russian youth had been mobilized by a new religion: a rebellion against discipline, moral standards, elected government and the very spirit of man. So they wanted to match faith with faith, their central aim being to revive patriotic principle focused on the monarchy in order to recreate 'a vibrant love of country and a faith in its mission'; their working definition of a patriot was someone who did not demand 'material incentive to do his utmost service to his country'. Metropolitan lack of interest in the empire also fuelled their anxieties. Their plan was to develop the patriot as an antidote to the 'apathy and uncertainty with which the British Empire is generally regarded to-day, particularly in Great Britain'.[94]

Such a formula based on youth organizations and special events stressing God and the King and directed primarily at British youth, had an instant appeal in the colonies too. An emphasis on individual status and creating a sense of effective action through local participation in group activities might offer a solution to detribalization. Pat Williams believed so; Olga Watkins agreed and they began canvassing support for a Kenyan version. The war was throwing up all sorts of opportunities and Williams' wartime work experience undoubtedly put him at ease with planning

92 For an account of her husband life's see Watkins, 1995 and the forthcoming biography of his wife by the same author.

93 'Some Further Notes on the Empire Youth Movement', KNA PC/NZA/4/5/12. Williams appears again in the next chapter on demobilization.

94 Ibid., p. 7.

large-scale projects for the whole colony. He produced a fourteen-page paper on youth camps which the CNC encouraged him to publicize and which was eventually printed as a formal document. It was designed for all eighteen-year-old African males and would absorb surplus manpower and materials released when hostilities ceased. Williams presented an overview of the prevailing views on youth, insisting that there was

> ... a realization among tribal elders, missionaries and Government officials and others that something is wrong with the outlook of the young African towards life. That money and the obtaining of money is the be-all and end-all, that authority, whether it be Government or tribal, need not be treated with respect, and that the rural life, the soil and work in connection with it are to be despised.[95]

Their plan was to set up a youth camp in each district that would house 500 youths for five months twice a year. This would, it was argued, ensure the compulsory attendance of all youths at some point during the year preceding their registration as taxpayers. Camp life would consist of physical training followed by work on local development projects such as house building, *shamba* cultivating, soil conservation, and road and dam construction. And it would be a stipulation that, within three months of leaving the camp, the young men should teach their sisters or girl-friends to read. Women would thus benefit indirectly, since they would then find husbands of 'better character and more hard working'. It was an attempt to enable the state to reach Africans without relying on the DC-tribal chief relationship. Traditional native authority figures and age-grade organizations would be substituted by a European camp commandant – the ubiquitous imperial handy-man – 'the ideal scoutmaster' who was believed to carry around with him an abundance of 'energy, patience, an appreciation of discipline, an ability to improvise and personality', precluding the need for any sort of training. Although even he would have to be assisted by forty trained African instructors, but they too would be of 'the right type'. Thus the colony-wide youth scheme Williams and Watkins put forward appeared to be a cheap and cheerful proposal, a form of pre-familial discipline that was a substitute for tribal control. It was an attempt, delivered in rallying wartime tones, to put into practice Perham's call for the application of new types of government. As such, it combined a feature of rural English life with the scale and deliberation of communist techniques. They were confident that such a plan would find cross-racial support.

However, such an apparently modest proposal was fraught with difficulties. Williams did at least understand that it would require administrative reorganization. Co-operation between missions, agricultural, educational, veterinary and welfare officers would be needed – a scenario which greater minds had been unable to produce. Local knowledge had to be amassed and enshrined in new officers, European and African. This was

95 Williams, 'Youth Camps: A Proposal' and Appendix.

not something the district administration would welcome, as we have already seen. Williams also realized that the approval of the people would have to be won. This he felt could be achieved through a large-scale propaganda campaign by the district administration. These two goals would be difficult enough to achieve, but there were other more abstract problems to getting such a scheme started. The plan required that white welfare intentions should be separated from racial rule. Most significantly Africans would have to accept that they were genuine and development-orientated. Meanwhile, white settlers would have to be converted to the view that African youths were like English youth and that small-scale projects teaching basic lessons in development could produce citizens at the service of the community. It was a tall order.

The youth camp proposal initially found a sympathetic ear within government circles. PCs liked the idea but felt African approval might not be forthcoming, especially from the older generation; tribal land shortage might also be an obstacle. If preliminary enquiries revealed a semblance of support, they suggested that one camp might be tried out at Kericho for all sixteen-year-olds, after an intensive propaganda campaign explaining the scheme to people in the area.[96] Olga Watkins set to work and wrote to a number of leading figures in the colony who they believed could speak for African opinion. Eliud Mathu was high on the list being Kenya's leading African politician. A year later his reply was received. Mathu did subscribe to the same post-tribal doom and gloom scenario as Pat Williams, agreeing that African parental and tribal control had weakened. He conceded that a mass education campaign using the normal mechanism of schools and voluntary organizations 'must deal with adults and children of both sexes. This is essential. That the African should more and more resuscitate the sense of voluntary service is indisputable.'

However, after careful consideration, Mathu believed the proposals would not receive the general support of the African people. In a sorrowful tone he wrote

> I do not see how you can convince the African that youth camps are not forms of military service or labour conscription. The attendance is compulsory by legislation... The Camps are to be run by military Officers. The majority of the youths are to go out to work for the local population without payment... All these are difficult to interpret in any other but terms such as conscription and militarism.[97]

Since the camps would require a large acreage, tribes such as the Kikuyu and Baluhya could not provide land for social services 'without

96 P.E. Williams to E. Mathu, 16 May 1945, including a summary of a recent discussion of Provincial Commissioners, KNA CD5/309.

97 E. Mathu to Williams, 6 June 1946 p. 2, KNA CD5/309. Mathu was Kenya's leading African politician from 1944 to 1957, becoming increasingly critical of the government during the late 1940s; see Roelker, 1976.

enduring great hardship'. Indeed Mathu's own solution and base-line of improved African welfare as an alternative to tribe began from the opposite perspective to compulsory heartiness. He defined African welfare as compulsory education, technical training and higher wages. Five months of 'military discipline' for sixteen-year-olds was woefully inadequate and inappropriate, he maintained; compulsory education for their children was the only way to deal with the youth problem. And to prove his point he calculated that the recurrent annual expenditure of twenty camps could cover the cost of compulsory education in Nairobi.[98] The moderate voice of African opinion testified to the reality of welfare within racial rule – whites helping blacks to cope with a fundamentally rotten system.

Even whites were sceptical. Olga Watkins consulted Carey Francis, Headmaster of the Alliance High School for Boys.[99] He also took a year to respond. Francis offers an insight into the gloomy European construction of Africans at this time; his reaction raised the barrier of race, but from a white perspective. He was in sympathy with the suggestions but feared that the 'dreadful leaders' of Africans would create insurmountable obstacles to such a programme. Francis believed that the leadership problems were rooted in the way most educated Africans blamed their troubles on the Europeans who took their lands, paid low wages and kept the best jobs. He admitted that there was a core of legitimate grievances, which, if he was an 'emerging African', he would find difficult to bear, such as being snubbed and despised by quite inferior Europeans as well as the glaring contrast in living standards which 'cannot ultimately be right'. Yet he insisted that most of the African case was complete rubbish. African educational attainment was appalling low; corruption and bribery were rife among chiefs, tribunal members, clerks, dressers and headmen; and success in entrepreneurial activity was minimal.[100]

Francis's opinion was significant. He was well respected and also influential. Writing to a like-minded and feminine soul, he perhaps felt free to give rein to his paternal views on Africans. In a tragic tone he lamented that Africans were unable to see that they were only beginning, wrongly believing that they had arrived:

> If they would recognize the failure and the need for improvement we could help ... we know well that we have many failures too...Africans cannot progress until they see their faults and their limitations and today they see none of these... They are, I believe, children, children

[98] Ibid., pp.1–2. An apposite remark was made by Kenyatta at a KAU meeting; Lonsdale, 1992: 327.

[99] C. Francis to P.E. Williams, 4 May 1946, KNA CD5/309. Serving with the Church Missionary Society in Kenya from 1928 to 1962, Francis was Headmaster of Alliance High School from 1940 to 1962, where he quarrelled with three African masters, one of whom was Eliud Mathu, who left the staff. See Kipkorir, 1969.

[100] Francis to Olga Watkins, 4 May 1946, KNA CD5/309.

who could grow up, and quite soon into fine men but if only they know that they are now children....

Fearful of copy-cat rioting following the students of Egypt, India and Indonesia, Francis was sceptical about what could actually be done: the possibilities for 'growing up quietly' were receding. Settlers were being accused of wickedness; all missionaries, himself in particular, were considered suspect. Offering no constructive ideas himself but wanting the camps tried out, he still concluded that the project was a non-starter; they would be opposed by the present African leaders on the grounds of being derogatory. Secondly, he asked, 'are they not really trying to do, in essence, what two generations of missionaries and schoolmasters have tried to, with greater opportunities but with little success?'. Securing Eliud Mathu's support would make or break such a project, and the Governor would be instrumental since Francis believed he was 'probably the only European who still counts to Africans here'.

As this episode illustrates, the morality of social welfare in the colonial context was more or less hopeless. Francis recognized this, but not for the right reasons. European elites did not appreciate the problem their racial paternalism unleashed, and African elites saw racial exclusion everywhere. Even when Europeans agreed on a plan for African welfare, whether village or camp life, all these good intentions were ultimately white intentions, which did not incorporate African concepts of moral community. As such, they were building skyscrapers in the air. In Britain, the Beveridge settlement – underpinned by a social welfare ideology that attached similar solutions to its feckless residuum, those deemed culturally unable to cope with life – was imposed within a single moral community and the communality of a universal franchise. Trying to impose betterment within a system of racial exclusion and mutual suspicion was too demanding an endeavour. One of the many negative aspects of racial rule was the brake it put on social development at the village level. Unsurprisingly Williams' and Watkins' efforts were not to be rewarded even with a pilot scheme. At a meeting between Williams, the Chief Secretary and the Chief Native Commissioner in late 1945 Williams was told that it was impossible at the present time to start definite arrangements for youth camps. The plans had served a short-term purpose by getting the Colonial Office off their backs but were then quietly abandoned.[101]

However, other areas of white civil society had also been activated. European political organizations could not afford to be so cynical; they needed to show their commitment to African betterment. The Electors' Union, a loose grouping of white settler voters, illustrates just how many sections of white society contributed to the wartime debates on welfare.

[101] Record of a meeting held in the Office of the CNC, 5 November (no year given but file position of document would suggest 1946), KNA CD5/309.

The rhetoric of white settler politics had changed by the end of the war, in step with the times. In public statements the term 'African' was used instead of 'native'. Pledges were made that 'continued [white] leadership must also be combined with a greater measure of service'. Whites were on the defensive, following the demands of war and the Perham critique of Empire. They had to acknowledge that Africans were now seeing the outside world for themselves and demanding increases in political representation and 'a higher rate of development in educational and other social services'.[102] Less willing to oblige on the first, whites found that the new social service benchmark of government for development did open up lots of palatable avenues for action. Thus the Electors' Union stressed the important role of the European community working with the government, as individuals and corporate bodies, to encourage 'the medical, educational, agricultural and industrial welfare of the African people'.

Indeed, they used the history of Kenya to argue that they had always been at the forefront of development in any case, describing the White Highlands as virgin land and their role as teaching the African 'by precept and demonstration all that he knows of Western civilization'. They were keen to insist on the concepts of community, civic responsibility and responsible citizenship, a device which would shore up their moral claim to racial rule. 'The unofficial European community', they argued, 'and especially the farmers have risked more and played by far a greater part in the actual development of the country than any other community. It is for this reason that we consider that it is our duty to plan for the development of the African towards our objective of a contented and prosperous community.' In addition to the 'natural sympathy' which Europeans held for Africans which had been strengthened by the comradeship of the two World Wars, efforts had been made, they claimed, to forge closer personal contact with some of 'the more balanced Africans'.

So important was this topic that the European Electors' Union produced a pamphlet on African Development at the end of 1945 which included a detailed chart prepared by their African Affairs Sub-Committee. This gives an insight into the internal landscape of white thought on racial rule. Their detailed pyramid model of African development had three converging strands: material, which included a minimum wage, industrial policy, pensions, social security, maternity and health centres; mental, involving character building, community centres, radio and cinema, craft training and a universal language; and moral, including racial understanding and co-operation, Young Farmers Clubs, the creation of responsible leadership, youth and adult associations, churches, Boy Scouts and indigenous planned development institutions. They regretted the need to highlight a

[102] 'The Electors' Union – African Development Plan – Introductory Memoranda', based on the conclusion of the Electors' Union of Kenya Conference, January 1946, KNA CD5/309.

'lack of balance and civic responsibility' in some African leaders, but, due to a current absence of 'a sense of integrity', continued European leadership was vital for the sake of the backward masses, so frequently victimized.[103] At this level, it was so-called character building which was billed as the key to better welfare, and planned a pathway to 'a happy, honest, self-reliant and progressive African, his career being entirely dependent on his own efforts, ability, intelligence and character'. They gave little attention to programmes designed for women in particular, for example, not even the Girl Guides or homecrafts, let alone agricultural training. Welfare meant measures to secure self-betterment and self-advancement which was largely a masculine project at this level, perhaps because most of the leading lights in the Electors' Union were men. The self-belief and the sense of mission surrounding European rhetoric on African development jarred with the jaded views of Carey Francis and the racially sensitive Eliud Mathu. They would carry on ignoring African feelings about racial issues at their peril.

European women were by no means silent nor just mouthpieces for their husbands. They had their own forms of association and they too made contributions to the welfare debates. During the war, some non-governmental organizations had increased their activities in relation to relieving social distress and discomfort in Nairobi. Charity-orientated organizations thus found it natural and within their ambit to contribute to debates about African welfare. Settler wives were one such group. The amount of work undertaken by women both privately on farms and in the public arena had increased during the war. So extensive was the latter, that the wartime welfare activities of the European-wife set had to be co-ordinated by a Kenya Women's Emergency Organization established in 1938. Its President was Lady Moore, wife of the Governor, and one of the leading lights was Mrs Eyleen Harrold, a Quaker, who later was instrumental in inaugurating Kenya's Federation of Social Services in 1953. She was extremely efficient at publicizing European women's voluntary work in the colony. In Nairobi this included running a hostel for women workers in the city, a canteen for convalescing African soldiers, the East African Military Nursing Service, the Women's section of Services' Clubs, the organizing and teaching of spinning and weaving, the training of Army cooks, a network of recreation and lecture services at hospitals, as well as working in waste-depots and workshops. The work of what was described as the Empire's Women's Institutes was a subject of much congratulation at the Colonial Office. Officials greedily converted their efforts into tasty morsels of wartime propaganda for general consumption.[104]

The East African Women's League, in particular, had expanded its

[103] Ibid., pp. 1–2.

[104] Ibid. 'The K.W.E.O' by Eyleen Harrold; PRO CO875/16/12 Public Relations, Press: Women's periodicals contain numerous articles on the wartime voluntary work of women in Kenya.

activities and subsequently its organizational network. Two new committees were added in 1945: a General Social Welfare sub-committee and a Standing Health Committee.[105] The League was fast becoming one of the most powerful non-governmental organizations in Kenya. It was able to bring together concerned minds from the white settler community, government and voluntary organizations, and made representations to the Colonial Office. Its members were less focused upon overtly political issues and were concerned with the domestic lives of women. By 1945 it was well able to give those with a line on African welfare a louder voice. Indeed, the organization was scolded in the press for behaving like an alternative parliament.

One example of its growing success regarding its public profile that contributed to such accusations, was the way in which the League was able to give Elspeth Huxley an outlet for her views on African welfare, whilst tacking on its own message. Huxley had the credentials of a respected settler spokeswoman. She was the biographer of the settlers' founding father, Lord Delamere. She was well known for her amusing and somewhat flattering stories about white life in Kenya. Huxley gave an address to the annual meeting of the Mau Summit-Londiani Lumbwa branch towards the end of 1945, held in a Mrs Pickford's house in Londiani, which was reported at length in the *East African Standard* in 1945.[106] The talk illustrates the attempts at reappraisal taking place in some European minds at the end of the war as well as their limitations. Huxley, like her great friend and confidante, Margery Perham, with whom she had debated many of the issues of colonial government, was in a position, when given a public platform, to speak with a degree of candour and perceptiveness that was beyond the grasp of many officials and politicians of the time. Huxley was an expert in observation and in self-expression, and her contacts with the imperial conscience-keepers in London gave her great insight into metropolitan thinking. She was credited by the League's President, Lady Sidney Farrar, with being able to deal 'so openly and ably with many vital and controversial questions of the day'.

Huxley was able to warn the settler-improvement coalition of two changes that would affect their lives dramatically. The first, coming from outside, was a new social philosophy which underpinned a world revolution that would tear apart their pluralism. She argued that

> the feudal way of life where every individual's place in society was laid down for him by arbitrary class and colour distinctions was passing in

[105] Minutes of the first Social Welfare Sub-Committee, May 1945 and third meeting of the Standing Health Committee, May 1946, KNA CD5/301.

[106] Annual meeting of the Mau Summit-Londiani Lumbwa branch of the EAWL at Mrs Pickford's house Londiani; Extract from *EAS* (date and author missing c.1995) p. 3; 'Housing and Training of New Settlers' Wives and Families', sub-heading 'Of Supreme Importance and Vital to Future of Kenya' – Mrs Huxley, KNA CD5/301.

Africa as it had done in Europe. The objective to which all were now moving, willingly or unwillingly, was a world in which everyone was judged entirely by his achievements and capabilities. An outstanding example of this was the fact that, for the first time in the history of the British Isles, commissioned rank in the armed services had been awarded on a basis of ability rather than on social position.

The second change came from within. The educated African was now a force to be reckoned with. The mission-trained literate had less than 'attractive qualities', whilst commanding an unhealthy excessive respect from illiterates:

> For good or evil the African had been encouraged to discard his old ideas, and if the better educated ones appeared to have lost much of their former cheerfulness and attraction, Europeans had themselves to thank.

Traditional education had not equipped the African to move forward into greater civilization, and Huxley called for a more practical and universal type of curriculum.[107]

Certainly the language used by whites when talking about blacks had changed. 'African welfare' rather than the old concept of 'native well-being' was now the acceptable vocabulary. But beneath this little else had changed. Africans were categorized by notions of educated or not educated, troublemakers or dupes.[108] And as these racially paternalistic comments testify, Huxley also failed to give her audience any sense of an African perspective and point of view; she was blind to the needs, ambitions and fears of those reduced to literates or non-literates. European perspectives, even when well-meaning and well thought out, were always shaped by the tremendous degree of social separation that existed and that they upheld. And as Huxley's representation of Africans illustrates, European portrayal of difference was a total act of diminution:

> Black in complexion, woolly haired, sturdily built, cheerful yet superstitious, brave yet indolent, shrewd yet ignorant, prolific yet disease-ridden, pliable in nature yet with deep-rooted obstinacies – they, it is scarcely possible to doubt, are the inheritors of Africa's future. And just as their past is a puzzle to all observers – why, alone among the great races of mankind, did they stand still in the race of progress, building no permanent houses, finding no means to improve their soil, learning no science, evolving no industries, above all inventing no forms of written word and creating no worthy form of art – so is their future at whose solution no wise man would care to guess. (Huxley, 1941: 16)

107 For a discussion of apartheid South Africa and the white strategy of elite-pacting – the notion that elites can be brought together in negotiations to cut a more or less private deal above the heads of the populace – see Sau, 1991: 18. In South Africa, the Afrikaner fixation with social engineering was begun systematically by Verwoerd and his Bantustan scheme.

108 Extract from *East African Standard* (date and author missing, c. 1945) p.3, KNA CD5/301.

One crucial way in which the League made a unique contribution to debates about welfare was through the inclusion of women – white and black. Taking the first, this was in part related to the wider agenda of maintaining settler authority. The role of the settler wife in setting the right example to African women was highlighted. The League announced a plan to build a residential club near the Edgerton School of Agriculture, where new families would be housed and wives trained.[109] Settlers were to exhibit positive examples of responsible citizenship to new arrivals. This was partly to stave off 'a land hungry population'; as Lady Farrar was keen to stress, 'if the country were to flourish economically and support the social services for all races which it needed' then the highlands must be developed to the highest pitch of productivity by settlers and not given over to peasant agriculture. Settler wives had an important role to play by setting high standards in the domestic sphere; sensitive to external accusations of decadence in an age of austerity, Huxley called for a move away from the practice of 'one boy, one job'. Also, the League announced plans for its 'pet project': a training centre for African domestics. And the range of contributions settler wives could make was extended. Huxley herself was making a tour of East Africa to investigate the reading requirements of literate Africans, since literature was the most important vehicle for ideas which in turn influenced behaviour. Invoking racial stereotypes, she described how Africans 'devoured' any book, however dull; their reading appetites were 'insatiable'. She suggested that League Branches therefore got involved in building up better libraries outside of Nairobi.

The League also tied in the role of European women with a need to educate African women. This was linked into an argument that African standards of living had to be raised in order to free more land for large-scale cultivation: 'the prevailing custom', Huxley observed, 'whereby the African husband worked on European farms for part of the year while the wife clung to and cultivated the family plot in the Reserve' had to be eliminated. In this context greater emphasis was given to 'African Women's Education',[109] as a way to curb the alarming African birth rate that was increasing by 2 per cent per annum. Huxley blamed this on the spread of Christianity and monogamy. She forecast somewhat accurately that the African population would double in thirty years, bringing Indian-style poverty and malnutrition. In addition, this would increase pressure on the land. Therefore, crusading European women, who would educate African women in their ways, would encourage birth control now prevalent in Western Europe. And hey presto, this would mean less pressure on European-held land.

Huxley had borrowed arguments from academia to arrive at this position. These enabled her to put forward a cultural variant to the argu-

[109] Ibid. This was a sub-title in the *EAS* article.

ment of racial difference which targeted women. Huxley had read a publication entitled *The African as Suckling and as Adult*, which she believed illuminated 'many hitherto obscure patches in the African brand of human nature' (Huxley, 1945; Ritchie, 1943). The key argument was that, unlike white babies who were weaned between six and eight months which gave a clear sense of time and of the mother's independence, the African baby, in contrast, was not weaned until two or three years of age. 'An illusion of omnipotence' developed, which was dealt a severe blow at weaning when the mother returned to the father, producing a fatal ambivalence of emotions and generally a state of mental confusion. The long-term consequence was held to be an incapacity to integrate which curtailed the development of self-reliance, mental clarity, initiative, self-discipline and balance. Thus, 'he can scarcely fail to disappoint his friends'. Huxley used this to argue that infant welfare was the logical foundation for African education and training, and that 'in neglecting women's education as it has been, a cardinal (if partly unavoidable) mistake in policy has been made.'[110] The fundamental role of women in African betterment was given a new urgency in the nurture argument by settler-women maternalists who saw a future for themselves, and the Kenya they knew, in the concept of settled African families. But would such a brand of feminization of the professions remain on the social policy-making agenda when the war ended? As the next chapter shows, soldiers and war dimmed the prospect even more.

As all the examples have illustrated, the world outside Kenya had touched many settlers during the war in new ways. At least some sensed that their racial paternalism had to pay more attention to welfare. As we see from their contributions, although their responses varied, their underlying position remained unchanged. Some chose to speak directly to the source of their anxiety. Illustrative of this was the decision taken by a settler woman, Mrs Francis Wilson, to write to the Labour MP, Arthur Creech Jones, a trades union man and a stern critic of African exploitation, who was now Secretary of State for the Colonies. Her attempt to counter his criticism of colour prejudice rested on a two-fold strategy that was very much of the settler-feminine variety and contoured by the effect of war. One line was to try to persuade Creech Jones that colour consciousness in Kenya was based on different customs. It was a matter of fact, she argued, that African men used a food bag not washed since their wife had woven it; that Africans sat on their heels to eat and so were vulnerable to parasitic infections. It was perhaps an unfortunate choice of example that

[110] Huxley, 1945. Similarly a high profile had been given earlier to a review of S. Biesheuvel, *African Intelligence*, South African Institute of Race Relations, in *African Affairs* 43 (173) (October 1944): 174–7. The subject was declared to be so important to the future of Africa that all the main chapters were summarized. These included the role of the cultural milieu and the home environment of the urban African. The conclusion was that bad conditions stunted intelligence.

she further illustrated her point with an attack on table manners. Accounts of difference using the example of Africans eating food with loud sucking movements and rolling the food around in a wide open mouth might not have struck a chord with Creech Jones, since it was an accusation often levelled against the working classes whom he represented. Secondly, she tried to convince him that there was little difference in social relations in Britain and Kenya. *Askari* had guarded settler women during the war; Kenya's towns were a disgrace but so were towns in Britain. Aware of his indignation at the idea of injustice toward Africans, she accused him of the same toward his own kith and kin. Ultimately she tried to reach him via the suggestion that their whiteness created a special loyalty, for she ended her emotional plea with Kipling's 'We are of one blood ye and I'.[111] But as the post-war period would show all too soon, such pleas would not cut much ice with the outside world if African welfare did not show signs of improving. The new universality meant that the settlers looked more and more like the odd ones out. Their solutions were more vulnerable than most to being viewed as rhetorical, self-serving and racial. Again, it seemed the welfare debate would as likely as not come to naught.

Conclusion

According to the imperial agenda set out in the previous chapter, had those who actually had the job of carrying it out found any answers? In contrast to the imperial audience, in the colonial setting there was, for a fleeting moment, a universal agreement around the benefits of village life, disciplined husbands and domesticated wives. The solution, which emerged during the war out of administrative squabbling and racial paternalisms, was the ideal of the African family as a substitute for tribal control. Inevitably debates about problems and solutions had serious implications for the structure of colonial government and the input of whites, which were hard to tackle. The essential issue should have been how to remodel colonial government to respond to new African needs: how villages could be politically represented other than as chiefs' subjects. Debates usually got little further than trying to drum up support for welfare as the submission to European cultural practice, material goals and scientific lore, all to be foisted on complex, resource-scarce and highly specific social systems. Nevertheless, a new faith in the possibility of Africans living bettered lives – with less disease, less drudgery, more discipline and more modern ways – contained a glimmer of a new colonial humanity, that poverty and racial difference were not synonymous.

The problem was that everyone had different and opposing ideas about how this could be achieved: urbanization with women or without them;

[111] Mrs Francis Wilson to Arthur Creech Jones, 1 March 1944, RH ACJ7/4.

white district teams run by the administration; white district teams run by medics, by agricultural staff or by special welfare officers; or more settler paternalism through sleepy villages, with scrubbed up youth and women less inclined towards breast feeding. Consequently, there was no lasting re-moralization of Empire as called for by Perham. Administrators had not begun to do more than argue ill-temperedly about the reforms which Hailey had dimly sensed were necessary. And KCA demands that they should be taken seriously were, as Mathu illustrates, continuing to fall on deaf ears. An inconsistent and incomplete welfare discourse swiftly came up against the rocks of colonial practice. The debates about welfare expose the fatal flaws running through the late colonial period, not least the growing estrangement within administrative paternalism. Debates became increasingly bitter between those who argued that the use of force was the best tool of African transformation and those who believed that manufacturing an African will to transform was possible and preferable.

However, a different model for African betterment and control was poised to break momentarily through the local constraints, able to convert a babble of suggestion into a single discernible policy. As the administration dragged its heels and the welfare debate began to wane, post-war development was picked up and transformed into a single programme with a budget by the returning African soldier. And administrative calculation changed from heady speculation about what niceties could be achieved with the right circumstances, the right budget and the right official, to panic about what nastiness might erupt if they did nothing.

Four

'Kingi Georgi Mtukufu'[1]
African Soldiers & the Second World War

This chapter exposes the wartime consensus which emerged out of white opinion on the peacetime potential of African soldiers. From the outset of the European conflict, Kenya made a significant contribution to the British war effort. Part of this contribution came from soldiers who fought in the King's African Rifles. As the threat of military defeat diminished, thoughts turned to the issue of demobilization. In discussions both inside and outside the colony, the thought of African soldiers returning to their homes en masse became an object of fear and then a focus of hope. Army education and the new technologies surrounding propaganda appeared to offer an exciting path forward that led back to the rural setting. As emotions ran high and optimism even higher, an image of a trained and disciplined askari *became the sought after embodiment of the good detribalized African living in clean and orderly villages. The previous meandering and inconclusive debates about welfare presented in the previous chapter suddenly found a new focus – even – a small budget helped along by advice from the expertise of anthropology. Plans for post-war development and welfare soon included a role for demobilized soldiers within a new branch of state practice, namely social welfare. The* askari *stepped in as the intellectual link between the metropolitan solution to welfare based on macro state intervention and self-help coping strategies within the colonial reality. The colonial project of transformation fixed upon a new prototype. What emerged was unprecedented in the administrative history of Kenya. It further illustrates the dynamic effect of the Second World War with regard to shaping bureaucratic practice in the twentieth century. However, the outcome pleased no one, being so partial and underfunded. The initiative also resulted in the reprivileging of men over women.*

[1] I am grateful to John Lonsdale for reminding me that *Kingi* was pronounced kinky. This was the first line of a World War II battalion song sung by Tanganyikan soldiers to the tune of 'Clementine': '*Kingi Georgi, Kingi Georgi, Kingi Georgi mtukufu*'; in English 'King George His Majesty'. Reproduced in Clayton, 1978: 44.

Introduction

The material and manpower requirements of world war in the mid-twentieth century created a new dynamic of historical change in Kenya. For Britain, as for other colonial powers, the Empire would be instrumental in the Second World War. In essence, this repeated the pattern of the First World War. Colonies like Kenya were drawn into the conflict in a number of ways. They were required to supply cheap raw materials, in some instances completely changing their patterns of production to suit wartime requirements. They found themselves shouldering shortages of imported goods now needed at home. Levels of state intervention increased in line with the degree of super-exploitation being demanded in the name of war. There was a ruthless edge to the commandeering of unskilled labour. A Production Board controlled the distribution of machinery, stock feed and fertilizers with grim determination. Elaborate attempts were made to pool production. Sometimes the more imaginative projects came to a sticky end, as with the huge rice fields planted in the south east of the colony following the loss of Burma. Just before harvesting the whole lot was whitewashed overnight by a flock of migratory birds (see Rathbone and Killingray, 1986: esp. introduction and chs 1–5; Lipscomb, 1956: 75–89). And, once again, the colonies helped to sustain the formal military superstructures required for actual battle.

The demands of war were not made equally on all colonies; their effects were not experienced uniformly by all peoples within all colonies. In Kenya for example, it was European farmers who mostly found opportunity to produce prodigiously for high profit. Where the effects of war were negative, such as the reappearance of famine following food shortages, this was overwhelmingly the experience of African populations (Keylor, 1992; Iliffe, 1979; Spencer, 1984). Although both Europeans and Africans took up arms, the far larger number of *askari* – a term which signified a black soldier, never a white one – were fighting for a King and a country they had never seen and against 'monsters' which were not their own. Although the war did change people's thinking and attitudes, the perception among officials that it had done so, and therefore ought to be factored into post-war plans, may have had the greatest impact. Soldiers and ideas about soldiers shaped the peace in quite dramatic ways. The further professionalization of the armed forces through the disciplined and concentrated application of resources and technology enhanced expectations of social engineering in general. As we shall see, one aspect of this dynamic would be the curious change in the formal structure of welfare provision inside the colony.

Men in uniform: the KAR in the Second World War

The experience of supplying soldiers for the war effort inevitably made an impact in colonies like Kenya. Most African colonial territories within the British Empire always had their own military capabilities throughout the imperial occupation. In normal times, these overseas forces were expected to be financed by the colonies themselves, which was not unsurprising in view of their relatively low comparative strategic and economic advantage to Britain plus the absence of external threat. Britain's African colonial armies were organized on a regional basis. The Royal West Africa Frontier Force covered West Africa; Southern Rhodesia had a separate armed force, as did South Africa. However, the set-up for East Africa was a little more complex. Here the magisterial King's African Rifles (KAR) came into being in 1902 when the Foreign Office ordered the amalgamation of a rag-bag collection of irregular companies to ensure a greater degree of control and efficiency (see Moyse-Bartlett, 1956; and the extremely useful Parsons, 1996; also Clayton and Killingray, 1989; Clayton, 1988). The KAR consisted of military forces drawn from Kenya, Uganda, Tanganyika and – for military purposes, since it was outside of Eastern Africa – from Nyasaland. When strategy dictated it, the region's military command also took charge of the Somali Camel Corps, the Rhodesian African Rifles (RAR) and the Northern Rhodesian Regiment (NRR).

Throughout its history, officers of the KAR were mainly British, although some white settlers enlisted as officers and ordinary soldiers (NCOs). Africans formed the bulk of NCOs and made up the labour gangs, or specialist units as they later became known, needed to sustain the battalions in times of military action. According to official statistics, over 31,000 Africans were enlisted into the KAR during the First World War and an estimated 120,000 worked as porters and general labourers in the East African Military Labour Service, many of them dying from malnutrition and disease. During the 1914–18 war, the troops had initially successfully defended the Ugandan Railway from German threats before being drawn into the invasion of German East Africa under the command of General J. C. Smuts. Smuts believed the KAR could survive the terrain and task as well as minimizing the political cost of South African losses, and he used East African soldiers to pursue a smaller German force led by General Paul von Lettow-Vorbeck up, down and across a good part of the continent. The number of soldiers and supporting labour then dropped dramatically in peacetime to rise again even more dramatically following the outbreak of the Second World War, reaching an estimated total of 320,000 *askari* and non-combatant conscripts.

During the Second World War the established reputation of colonial forces such as the KAR grew and reached wider audiences. Although only the French showed willingness to bring African soldiers into the European theatre of war, there was much opportunity for valour on African soil. Military 'high-ups' had ensured that the subsequent routine tasks of defending positions in remote and difficult areas were made more endurable by upgrading battalions charged with such duties into full combat status. KAR muscle and ingenuity had its first test in the British Somaliland campaign of 1940. After triumphing over intense heat and having to operate from defensive positions when they were used to mobile offensive bush operations, they then advanced into southern Ethiopia. After eleven months of fighting, white Italian troops were driven out largely by the fighting skills of the *askari*. Then, in 1942, the KAR played a crucial part in the invasion and capture of Madagascar. According to the official correspondent of the East Africa Command, K. C. Gandar Dower (later lost at sea), in the first eight weeks of their advance from Majungo to Ambalavo the KAR were engaged in much heavier combat than British or South African troops, finally pursuing an army of 6,000 men for 650 miles over 56 days and across 3,000 road blocks before 'liquidating' it with the loss of only 120 men. Once Japan entered the conflict, the KAR moved towards the eye of the storm in the Far East. Madagascar was invaded and successfully occupied in May 1942. The efforts of the KAR in Burma were crucial in the Allied recapture of Rangoon and Mandalay. The changes in technology and the further professionalization of army life had ensured more jobs as basic engineers, gunners, sappers, drivers, educational instructors and medical auxiliary staff (Smallwood, 1945; Moyse-Bartlett, 1956; Allen, 1984; Killingray, 1989; 1979).

However, the action of the military was not always uppermost in the minds of the Kenya homefront. In January 1941, the invasion of Somaliland was easily eclipsed by the fate of a Happy Valley settler recently turned soldier with a reputation for married women and for wearing tight and skimpy black velvet shorts. The murder of Lord Errol captured all the newspaper headlines along with the subsequent trial of Sir Henry Delves Broughton, since his 'most treasured possession' – how he described his wife – had been having a very public love affair with the penniless but devastatingly handsome Earl. Similarly, the significance of soldiering in the history of Empire, particularly the role of local militias in colonies like Kenya, ought not to be overstated. The number of soldiers in relation to the whole population was small; their capacity for active intervention was limited. Undoubtedly official violence – meted out through real as well as symbolic displays of military force – was an essential element in the establishment of formal systems of colonial rule in eastern Africa as elsewhere, and in the subsequent functioning of low maintenance imperial control (Ranger 1993a; 1993b). Yet overall, so-called 'pacification' was more an internal process of accommodation through collaboration and mutual self-interest than of forceful submission and the annihilation of opposition (see, for example, Lonsdale, 1985).

Nevertheless, colonial armed forces did contribute to conditions which allowed for the display and abuse of authority by the military and by other bearers of European power. One of the early tasks of the KAR was to deal punitively with gangs of raiding nomadic peoples from Somalia, Ethiopia and Sudan. Those who had to carry out much of the dangerous and bloody hand-to-hand combat were Africans; some were enslaved into the colonial forces where such a system already existed as in southern Sudan (Johnson, 1989: 79–82; Parsons, 1996: 8–9). But this pattern and the experience of recruitment were not the only features of the whole period. By 1939 African soldiers were not simply tragic, press-ganged victims. The appeal of military service was multifarious. Young African men were mostly socialized through single sex–age grade systems that were strong on machismo, quasi-militaristic in nature and imbued with strict notions of honour. The status of warrior commanded great respect in many communities; it was a necessary part of the passage of an adolescent to the stage of being a credible elder within the clan or community. Adolescent energies spent on the thrills of raiding, settling group disputes and male rivalry made premeditated violence, physical prowess and sexual conquest inextricably bound together. Part of the propulsion to join up came from all the usual dreams of adventure and opportunities to exhibit valour and to win respect.

Colonial officials did consciously exploit this macho factor in order to increase African recruitment where it was not popular. When recruiting soldiers in Nyanza at the beginning of the war, a senior local administrator, K. L. Hunter, evolved a strategy for dealing with the lack of enthusiasm after an incident at a *baraza* when one man publicly announced his refusal to join up.[2] Hunter questioned him as to his sex and accused him of behaving like a girl, then took a garment from a girl in the crowd and gave it to him. By this time the man was asking if he could join up, but amidst roars of laughter from the crowd Hunter made him sit among the women. It proved quite effective. It was an ancient and universal strategy that was well used by men as well as women. At its most extreme it was tantamount to bullying and to recruitment by emotional blackmail.

However, the main factor in recruitment was the economic benefits it could offer. Many joined up to escape the confining congestion of the African Reserves, and recruiting officers had to make sure they did not interfere with the need for local labour for wartime production. At this time, African farm labourers might earn 14 shillings a month. Once they entered the training depot this would rise to 20 shillings, and 28 shillings when posted to a battalion with the prospect of earning up to £4.10 shillings per month plus food and clothing (Smallwood, 1945:216). An overriding concern with domestic issues and local life remained constant both before and during the war. Home life, farming and local ribaldry featured among the self-sustaining narratives which appear in many of the marching songs

[2] K.L. Hunter. p.10. RH Mss.Afr.s.1942.

sung by *askari* and porters on active service. One of the many versions of 'John Brown's body' sung by Kamba soldiers and porters illustrates this, the Swahili in perfect rhythmic timing to the original melody (the awkward sounding English translation follows) (Clayton, 1978: 50):

Solo: *Watu wa Nairobi wanaishi na raha,*
Watu wa Kisumu wanakufa na njaa,
Watu wa mashamba wanapenda kushiba,
Ila watu wakamba!
Chorus: *Simelini tunakuja!* (repeated three times)
Wanafunzi Wakamba!

(The people of Nairobi live in comfort,
The people of Kisumu are dying of hunger,
The people on the farms like to eat too much,
Except the Wakamba!
Out of the way, we are coming!
The Kamba boys!)

Here we find evidence of the way the war contributed to the consolidation of local identities around the notion of tribes, which had been taking place since the colonial authorities began imposing stricter notions of peoples: where they belonged and to whom they belonged. Recreational activities played an important role in this. When 'Fluffy' Fowkes, a Divisional Commander, visited his men in Ceylon on New Year's Day in 1944, he was entertained by distinctly tribal football competitions and displays of Akamba dancing. Perhaps the most important figure in recruitment was the local tribal elder or chief. The participation of chiefs in the recruitment of soldiers could have an overtly self-interested aspect. Some used the moment to try to settle local homo-social struggles, particularly over younger age grades and errant youths. Their participation could also include a deliberate political calculation designed to help secure a particular end. Yet pure sentiment and reciprocating generosity might also have played a part. Many chiefs, tribal elders and ordinary Africans were simply told that the English needed their help and they responded. Duty, compassion and the opportunity to bond were still sentiments which shaped African responses to the red strangers now among them. In Fort Hall for example, many of the younger men enlisted in the East African Labour Supply force, and the local Spitfire fund could command long queues of men and women wanting to help.[3]

The number and activites of KAR African soldiers in the Second World War came to the attention of civilians in the colony. Over forty new battalions were created during the war and half as many new support units, although after 1945 nearly all of these were disbanded. Each battal-

[3] Blundell, 1994: 78; Jackson, 1997; Willoughby Thompson. RH Mss.Afr.s.519(1).

ion was assigned a number with its territorial identity, such as Nyasaland 1/1 KAR. This system upheld the established army practice of allowing for an easy temporary amalgamation of forces should the military need arise. A battalion usually consisted of approximately 600 men and the average ratio of black to white soldiers was sixteen to one. The KAR was categorized in military terms as a light infantry force. Guns ranged from the hand-held to heavier artillery pieces that had to be mechanically transported and assembled *in situ*. Tanks were also used. *Askari* quickly acquired a reputation for having a gift for mechanics and being quite capable of using range finders and slide rules.

The way the KAR remained an extremely heterogeneous force which saw action far beyond the colonial boundary was impressive. It was possibly the most truly imperial of colonial armies in terms of its cosmopolitan flavour. Among the first generation of light infantrymen in the KAR were veteran soldiers from the Sudanese Army – notorious for using soldier slaves – who had been separated from their command during the Mahdist revolt in the 1880s and were summoned by Lord Lugard into Uganda to quell a local uprising. Likewise, many of the first KAR officers were either veterans of the Egyptian Army or were seconded from the Indian Army (Parsons, 1996: 8). Soon, soldiers drawn together from the whole of East Africa were to find themselves posted to Italian Somaliland, Abyssinia, Madagascar, the Middle East, Ceylon, Burma and India. The peculiar features of imperial rule shaped the experience of soldiering in the empire in very distinct ways.

However, during the Second World War, established practices were beginning to break down or at least to be questioned by a younger cohort of recruits. Although the mind-set of the commissioned officer class reflected the pervasive racial nature of imperial rule, racial paternalism produced a strong tendency for upper-class officers in particular to take personal responsibility for the welfare of their soldiers. The growing number of middle-class officers were not always at ease with this relationship and some obsessively enforced rules and regulations, demanding tedious and masochistic signs of spit and polish. The military fetishized hierarchy of all types. Soon after young Willoughby Thompson arrived in Athi River Artillery Camp, he was thrown out of a local restaurant by a colonel. This was because Thompson, an officer, was dining with a sergeant, his friend Jack Knight. Such ritualized snobbery was resented and left a bitter taste.[4] Young British officers also began to feel the unfairness of differential rates of pay. What irked them was not so much the 1940 ratio of £41.15 per month for a European, £12.17 for an Asian and £1.10 for an African until they had direct experience of the downside of preferential treatment; settler soldiers were made sergeants and paid £25.00 per month with no income tax while an English sergeant was paid

[4] See Englander and Mason, 1994; Willoughby Thompson, p. 31.

£16.10 and had to pay income tax. To young British officers who had made a career decision to move to the KAR in order to take advantage of the higher pay and better conditions as well as the landscape and its many attractions, the lesson that inequality could bite was not lost.[5]

Also the practice of recruitment according to strict notions of racial typing loosened. Certain tribes had long been identified as natural fighting peoples, the so-called martial races such the Nubians. In Kenya for example, the Kamba were considered by many European officers to be desirable soldiers because of their reliability. Some distrusted the Kikuyu. For example, Colonel Thomas Leahy was told they were not reliable in combat; a company had mutinied in the First World War and they were despised by other tribes (Parsons, 1996:293–7; Johnson, 1989; Hansen, 1991). However, the Kikuyu worked as redoubtable 'penpushers' during the Second World War, their distrusted mission education suddenly transforming them into a valuable cog in the military machine, although they also joined up in their thousands as army drivers, medical orderlies, artisans and batmen. Tribal complexions might have diversified but the cleavage between black and white remained. For example, only African soldiers had to have their heads shaved. Their uniform was different too. Khaki drill bush shorts were the staple outfit with a pillbox hat and a red tarbush for ceremonies. Usually barefoot, their sandals for the field were made out of old machine tyres. They carried a rifle, bayonet and *panga*.

Thus the Second World War gave the KAR its greatest opportunity to expand and, as a result, to show what black and white could achieve together. It was not to be a smooth transition. In peacetime, colonial military forces were controlled by their respective colonial governments. In wartime, the War Office swiftly took command in order to integrate the forces into wider military offensives and army groupings. In 1939, the KAR found itself under a new East Africa Command and soldiers were recruited in large numbers. This caused some initial friction. Army regulars resented the new officers who they felt could not match their own knowledge of the native and the bush. However, the distinction between Colonial Office and military authority was always somewhat arbitrary. In times of peace, the colonial forces were under the jurisdiction of the Colonial Office in London through a General of Colonial Forces who was seconded from the British Army. Likewise, British officers and NCOs were often seconded from the home forces and endured local and thus lower rates of pay.

The contribution of Africans to the Second World War changed and grew as the events of war impacted upon the British Empire. The military high command initially conceived of the KAR as being part of a defence force for the hinterland of the Suez Canal. By 1941 some of the supporting specialist units were required to leave the KAR battalions and head for the

[5] J.E. Moore. RH Mss.Afr.s.1715(191).

Middle East. As a result many African Pioneers initially saw more action than the KAR battalions, such as the men involved in keeping open the port of Tobruk in Libya. When Tobruk finally fell to the Germans in May 1942 many were killed or taken prisoner. Following the entry of Japan into the war and the fall of Singapore in March 1942, eighteen KAR and NRR battalions plus supporting units were dispatched to the Far East on the understanding that they would not simply release other troops for more active duty. African soldiers found themselves negotiating the notorious Kabaw Valley in Burma with its dense jungle, difficult terrain and virulent diseases. *Askari* morale and discipline was never more tested than in this particular campaign. Troops from East Africa were engaged in active combat right up to the end of the war. One East African brigade helped to recapture the Arakan region; another distracted enemy forces whilst Britain and India moved against the Japanese in Mandalay which provoked a defiant Japanese response at the Irrawaddy River in February 1945. Thus by the end of the Second World War the KAR had impressively built upon its established reputation on active duty. It could hardly do otherwise since it was on the winning side.[6]

Thus the wartime expansion of the KAR was not without its stresses and strains. The potential for friction was omnipresent for at least three reasons. First, the military and the Colonial Office did not always see eye to eye. The colonial authorities preferred a minimalist force that was strong on deterrence but low on cost. When external military authorities took over, their preference was to upgrade, train and expand the local forces, which could put them beyond the government's peacetime budget. Secondly, differing standards of treatment for colonial and home armies provoked public and professional criticism. For example, the practice of flogging African soldiers at a time when it was forbidden for British soldiers came under intense scrutiny during the Second World War and was eventually suspended (Killingray, 1994). Army law forbade corporal punishment but it was a legal form of punishment under local colonial ordinances.

Different treatment according to race became an increasing irritant for some *askari*. African soldiers who were aware of the glaring disparities had to be sporadically placated. Rates of pay, living conditions, remuneration and leave of absence were periodic points of contention between the ranks. Although *askari* were subordinate and indoctrinated into a culture of obedience, they too had bargaining powers. Superior in number, they could withhold co-operation, spread dissent, exploit rivalries and animosities between officers or even desert the company. Outbreaks of individual as well as group forms of retaliation and protest were not common but did take place. Fragging – the slang for murdering a soldier in combat – was not unknown. Officers were murdered in Ceylon and

[6] Parsons, 1996: 41–5; Moyse-Bartlett, 1956: 614–71; Colonel Thomas Leahy, RH Mss. Afr.s.1715 (163).

Burma where the 11th Division had to be taken out of action because of discipline problems.[7] Senior officers would often blame insubordination on an absence of moral fibre or the effects of alcohol or cannabis. However, grievances over living conditions, leave and unfair treatment according to race were more likely causes.

The experience of being an *askari* was always an ambiguous one. On the one hand, they generally commanded more status, a better rate of pay and superior living conditions than their civilian counterparts. On the other hand, their working lives could potentially be stamped by racial discrimination that was experienced in a more concentrated and tangible form. Physical separation and differing treatment according to racial type were features of mess life. Yet the most committed African soldiers showed themselves to be as brave and as skilled on the battlefront as their European counterparts, sometimes much more so. However, counterparts were not always to hand. Although the number of white NCOs did increase during the Second World War with the recruitment of local white Kenyans and Southern Rhodesians, Africans continued to swell the ranks of NCOs in massively disproportionate numbers and to work as conscript labourers. Of course, this reflected patterns of recruitment in the British army at home, and the way three-quarters of men in the US and British armies were not in combat. Ordinary rank and file soldiers were drawn disproportionately from poorer, lower-class English backgrounds and included large Welsh, Irish and Scottish contingents. A popular 1930s English music hall song recounted thoughts of a working-class 'cockney' soldier sent overseas and began as follows:

> I am baked and I am thirsty, in this blasted burnin' sun,
> For the sand's got in my system, and it's damned near spoilt my gun,
> But our blue-eyed baby captain, who is learnin' 'ard to swear,
> Say we're 'oldin' up the Empire, though we're far from Leicester Square.[8]

Nevertheless, during the Second World War, attitudes amongst black and white soldiers became less fixed. Officers from more elitist British backgrounds believed themselves not to have been overtly racist. In retrospect, many insist that those soldiers who had been brought up in the colonies were much more likely to be offensive and openly hostile to African troops. Certainly it was not unnoticed at the time that South Africa did not allow black men to participate in conflict; Southern Rhodesia showed reluctance and many African soldiers from Bechuanaland, Swaziland and Bastololand were never trained. However, the

[7] Parsons, 1996: 45–8; 225–8; letter from George Shepperson to Parsons, 23 July 1996.

[8] 'Tommy out East' by Alan Sanders, reproduced in Brooks and Faulkner (eds) 1996, 361–2. Rudyard Kipling also wrote a number of poems using the persona of the lower-class soldier in the empire, such as 'Tommy', 'Private Ortheris's Song', 'Gunga Din', 'The British Soldier' and 'The "Eathen"', reproduced in Keating, 1993.

tendency was to defer to such racial prejudice and not confound it, and although the French army was reputed to have black officers unlike the British, they could not rise through the ranks and were mostly Indo-Chinese and from the West Indies (Headrick, 1978).

Geography and the experience of combat affected attitudes, especially when an element of vulnerability appeared. Describing his time in Burma, John Cowan wrote about how his attitudes underwent a transformation. 'We were interdependent, I more on the men than they on me and I came to trust and admire them. They could cope better with the monsoon conditions, were exceptionally skillful with *pangas* and were diplomats.' Once an African sergeant temporarily took over the patrol when they became lost at night. Yet Sergeant Johana 'not only had the ability, but the decency and tact to save me from humiliation, and he never referred to the matter afterwards'.[9]

Time and time again, in the words and world of Lieutenant Donald Bowie, 'the African's intelligence was proved despite illiteracy'. Serving overseas had changed attitudes. Many believed them to have excellent memories since they did not commit anything to paper, which was very handy in the steamy jungles of Burma; likewise, their superior skill with the panga was a godsend. Perhaps above all, in the universally hostile and unfamiliar terrain, African soldiers died in the same pain or heroism as any others. Their place at the final Victory Parade in London was assured and the photographs recording their contribution reached across the Empire. By the end of the war, it is likely that more European soldiers held a positive view of African capabilities than ever before. Although many still belonged to the 'banana-eating buggers' school of army race relations, some could believe in the equality of outstanding individuals. Cowan could never forget the poignancy of seeing his Ugandan battalion for the last time:

> They were fine soldiers, resolute, resourceful.... I stood among them for the last time. We had been together for two years and it was hard to say goodbye. I lit a cigarette for Sergeant Johana and gave him my lighter which I knew he had always admired. It had been made by an Italian prisoner of war and I had had it inscribed with the Swahili word 'kumbuka' – remember. A quick hug and he was gone but I have not forgotten and I like to think neither has he.[10]

The experience of being a soldier among African troops during the Second World War was profound and had a lasting effect on those directly

[9] Correspondence with John Cowan – a Kenyan settler who joined the KAR shortly after his eighteenth birthday – 4 February, 1998.

[10] 'Random Recollections' by John Cowan (unpublished); Lt. Donald Bowie, RH Mss.Afr. 1715 (241A); correspondence from Sir Roger Swynnerton (a colonial agricultural officer before entering 1/6 KAR 1939–42) and Brigadier M. W. Biggs (subaltern in the KAR) seen thanks to the generosity of Tim Parsons and John Lonsdale, and which contains very positive memories of their African counterparts.

involved, many of whom set to work after the war putting into practice their wartime experiences. In Kenya, the KAR was seen to have played an important role in the war, and this would have implications for what demobilized KAR might be thought capable of contributing to the peace.

The demobilized soldier

As the Second World War showed signs of being resolved, a view began to emerge among observers of British affairs and the empire that African soldiers might well be doing much more than quietly eating bananas when peace returned. Anxiety about returning soldiers was not new nor confined to *askari*. In Britain thoughts had also turned to the demobilized 'Tommy' (see, for example, Summerfield, 1981). What would he do? How would he behave? As the threat from Nazi Germany eased off by 1944, those watching events at a safe and possibly unreliable distance found their local anxieties easily transformed into imperial ones. In June 1944, readers of *The Times* were warned that, upon the defeat of Japan, 'the flow of *Askari* out of the army will be a torrent, and … the challenge will test our statesmanship' (Easterbrook, 1975a: 33). The subsequent raft of expectations and tasks laid out for returning *askari* was indicative of a growing consensus among empire watchers, military men and government officials. Separately, they began to argue that *askari* could carry forward their hopes and standards for a better post-war world back into the African interior. It might seem remarkable that, despite only a few years or even months of training and experience of army life, so much was expected of the *askari* by so many outside the territory and not an inconsiderable number within. As the huge range of post-war planning taking place in Britain illustrates, war had to be seen to have a wider purpose that just defeating the opposing side. Post-war agendas were being set out by the men and women who, in 1945, preferred to vote in a new government rather than return the heroic war horse, Winston Churchill. They were a generation inspired by a tremendous self-belief and optimism, having risen collectively triumphant from the brink of defeat. Just as Margery Perham had offered the reading public a more inclusive version of Empire and government in 1942, so it became more natural within professional circles at the end of the war to apply what was expected of British soldiers to African ones (Lonsdale, 1975b: xiv).

From 1944 onwards, a number of individuals – ranging from interested amateurs, active soldiers or professional do-gooders – took it upon themselves to publicize their views on the effect of war upon 'the African'. They published articles in specialist journals, in periodicals that had an imperial audience and in broadsheeet newspapers. One of the first empire activists to draw attention to the imminent danger of the sudden exposure of Africans to the modern world thanks to the war, was the educationalist and professional Christian, Margaret Wrong. At that time she was Secretary to the International Committee on Christian Literature for Africa and was working on the publication of the 1944 Colonial Office report on Mass Education in Africa produced for the Education Advisory Committee of which she was a member.[11] She had travelled through parts of Africa during the war years. Her writings testify to the alarm she experienced following a number of chance discoveries. Top of the list was undoubtedly stumbling across a group of Nuer tribesmen, who, as they languidly leant on their spears, had calmly enquired of her as to the latest prices of European plane fares. Coming a close second was quite probably the sight of the Paramount Chief of the Yoruba reading an English translation of Adolf Hitler's *Mein Kampf* (Wrong, 1944).

It was widely reported that the Second World War had changed Africans. For Margaret Wrong, as for others, evidence abounded that Africans who had 'travelled far' were changing the mind-set of others in profound ways. The production and circulation of printed material had increased everywhere; Wrong had evidence that in the new camps of the East African Command, the sale of literature was quite impressive. Yet her great fear – shared with others – grew from a certain belief that this material was not necessarily of 'the right type' and was producing 'destablised minds'. Of course, at this time many feared the appeal fascism might have; this was the great bogey – justifiably perhaps – of the moment. Its appeal was believed to be greater among uneducated people, those who could not read. However, Wrong's implicit warning that colonial subjects were not going to be so easily ruled after the war was also accompanied by a strong belief in the great potential of the right type of controlled literacy training in the colonies.

Wartime soldiering gave educationalists a new lease of life. During the Second World War, adult education as a post-war project floated around the consciousness of a public interested in the overseas mission. This was due to the popularization of a notion that classes held for African soldiers had been extremely effective. One Army chaplain had described the system as 'the finest extra-mural university' he had ever seen in Africa; soldiers writing home had the effect of encouraging their wives to learn to read so that they and their children could keep up with their husbands. Missionaries were more inclined to focus on literacy and Christian teaching rather than a more specific curriculum geared toward a particular practical aim. However, Margaret Wrong used this scenario to argue that, if African economic and social development was to take off, 'the spread of literacy to whole populations' was the first step in raising standards of living. She took a pot shot at the new developments in

[11] For an account of Margaret Wrong's distinguished career see Brouwer, 1995 and Sinnoven, 1995: 216–24 on the growing perception of the importance of adult education toward the end of the war.

communication technology, in her insistence that, whilst broadcasting and films were useful, only the written word could 'drive home teaching given by other means' (Wrong, 1944:108–10). Literacy campaigns targeted at particular 'growing points' of individuals in relation to their needs and interests were crucial, she argued: a Soil Conservation Officer in Kenya could not combat the view that working on the land was for 'the fool of the family' nor an African dispenser install 'habits of cleanliness' in African mothers unless people were already literate.

The Colonial Office was also working itself up into a fit of mild enthusiasm for some new iniative. Wrong had suggested that mass education officers ought to work with District Officers. East African colonial governments were lagging behind those in West Africa which were giving selected Africans advanced training in mass education techniques. At that time, the Colonial Office Memorandum on Mass Education in Africa was published – in 1944. It had been prepared by the Education Advisory Committee and was wholly supportive of the primacy of literacy education, centring on the argument that literacy was the vital ingredient for good state-society relations. Literacy made people co-operate more readily with welfare agencies; literate people were more able to understand and control the rapid changes taking place in family and village life. Literacy training would produce subjects who could understand local and international issues: 'democratic local government could not nowadays be in the hands of a mass of ignorant and illiterate people', the report had warned (Wrong, 1944:109). Thus we have here an attempt to put literacy at the heart of social engineering.

However, not everyone was happy with this emphasis. Others evidently felt it was too parochial and quaint and they needed to think bigger. Arthur Creech Jones, about to become Secretary of State for the Colonies and a member of the Education Advisory Committee, found the report lacking in specifics. He criticized it for paying little attention to the problem of poverty; for showing no regard for the kind of mass projects under way in Russia or China that were comparable to the African context; and for having a religious focus which would dissipate energies because of denominational competition.[12] In general, he was critical of the report for ignoring the wider context. In line with his fierce communist ideals of the time was his assertion that adult education would founder without broader changes in wage levels, race restrictions and property distribution.

Women as a specific target group were an issue limited to questions about further educational provision. In 1945, the journal *Oversea Education* published an editorial criticizing the Commission on Higher Education in the Colonies for its policy towards women. The Commission was charged with ignoring the needs of women, the issue of curriculum differentiation

[12] Sinnoven, 1995: 220–1; Note of 4 March 1944, Box 34, Creech Jones Papers, Rhodes House Library, Oxford.

according to sex and the pioneering work carried out in women's higher education by women like Miss Buss and Miss Beale.[13] What was needed, according to the editorial, was 'a corps of wise and enthusiastic English women, supported by African women, trained in England, to get the good work started'; there were many such women already employed in the colonial service and by Christian Missions. There seems to have been little corresponding warning about the short-sightedness of not making special provision for the mass education of women in the interest of raising standards of living and no banner waving for the sort of experimental projects in lower-level education that had been suggested earlier by Lockhart, Kenya's Medical Department Director, discussed in the previous chapter. Nor would the situation change when the idea of the educated African soldier captured the imperial imagination. However, Christian missionary views on post-war social reconstruction in colonies like Kenya increasingly had to compete with secular views.

During 1944, debates about demobilization and post-war reconstruction took on a new urgency in relation to Empire, as they did in relation to the British Isles. Commentators with experience of Kenya and knowledge of army life found a platform for their views in respected journals and periodicals such as *African Affairs* and the *Quarterly Review*. These were read carefully by a discerning public with an interest in Britain's imperial obligations and by professionals who actually carried out those obligations. Reflecting the general shift towards planning and state intervention, observers who now wrote about the colonies wanted plans to be made for post-war reconstruction. The image of the returning soldier was thus naturally seductive. Commentators believed demobilized soldiers would be returning in vast numbers to colonies like Kenya. Secondly, they shared the view that *askari* could make a significant impact upon their return. However, they were divided as to whether that impact would be destructive or constructive.

The fear that returning African soldiers would run amok drew on a number of preconceptions about army life. It was readily assumed that conditions in the army would have been much more favourable than living conditions in the Reserves; an appreciation of this contrast could, it was argued, create a great deal of anger. A Mrs Fane, writing in *African Affairs* in 1944, feared mass discontent would erupt among soldiers when army life put into 'shocking relief' their normal living conditions (Fane, 1944). The East African soldiers had, she believed, 'slept in something better than the malodorous, dark and smokey hut of their childhood; they have used the furniture of house and table: they have known the comfort of clean body and laundered clothes'.

[13] Notes 'The Higher Education of Women in the Colonies', *Oversea Education*, 17, 1 (1945) p.216. The editorial argued that in the case of British Malaya there was a special need to recognize the paramount importance of well-educated women in the growth of community life.

Another common perception, shared by Margaret Wrong, was that army life and travel would have destabilized 'their simple minds'. This was one of the allegations put forward in an article on returning soldiers published in the *Quarterly Review* in 1947. Its author, A. J. Knott, who seems likely to have had direct experience of army life, warned his audience that, since *askari* had experienced 'things, places and people formerly beyond their ken', they would be less willing to resubmit themselves to the discipline of traditional tribal authority. He went so far as to suggest that they would be 'sufficiently strong in numbers to constitute a section of the community fully capable of upsetting the whole basis of tribal life on which the peace and harmony of village and reserves is built'.[14] The idea that soldiers had become so very different following their experience of army life had its origins in the assumption that so profound and different was this moment in relation to their former lives that their personalities and behavioural practices would crumble.

Some commentators prophesized possible violence. Knott forecast a period of considerable strain as *askari* would be undaunted by 'tribal authority, old fashioned elders or even D.C.s'. Literacy was partly blamed for this likely scenario, since *askari* would, it was believed, be better equipped to articulate their grievances. Knott knew of the officially sanctioned censorship of letters written home by African soldiers. This was normal practice in war. Soldiers were spied upon when on leave and a corps of Voluntary Native Intelligence Agents had been set up under the command of the anthropologist, Louis Leakey.[15] The censorship of letters, which soldiers knew was being done, had uncovered their concerns about demobilization plans, gratuities, and resettlement schemes. Perhaps some might even have embellished their concerns for the benefit of all their readers. If the *askari* was not heard sympathetically, Knott warned, he might well resort to 'something stronger than mere words'.

Yet in the short term, the actual destabilizing impact of the returning *askari* proved to be negligible in the post-war era. At the end of 1946, for example, Eric St A. Davies had found that, in South Kavirondo District at least, returning soldiers appeared 'more anxious to lie back than to do anything else'. Official efforts to encourage them to save were floundering because savings were immediately withdrawn. Some soldiers did apply for trading licences; most wanted to be labour overseers or prison warders. Very few appeared to be taking an immediate and leading part in the internal affairs of their districts; few had been selected by local people as members of the locational councils. Yet many *askari* objected to the way

[14] Knott, 1947. For a later version of this argument in the 1950s see J.C. Carrothers, *The Psychology of Mau Mau* (1954, Government Printer, Nairobi). He argued that the problems of adjustment to rapid social change had traumatized primitive African minds, producing schizoid individuals forced to seek refuge in old habits of atavistic barbarism, so terrifying was the sense of confusion.

[15] See Leakey, 1974 and on Leakey more generally, see Berman and Lonsdale, forthcoming.

they had to pay the arrears in their LNC rates that had accumulated while they were away.[16] Not all ex-*askari* became politically active immediately on their return, the war having in some instances provided a point of contact between government officials and returning soldiers. *Askari* were concerned with other more everyday issues which kept their focus home-based initially, plus the fact that the experience of being in military service and combat can often have a conservative effect on individuals.[17] Soon, however, the increase in unemployed men included returnees who did not want to work on agricultural estates. In addition, the gangs who opposed terracing and later formed the basis of Mau Mau armed units in the forest included ex-*askari*. The underlying labour and land issues in the colony inevitably failed to deliver in many instances the kind of lives soldiers wanted to come home to.

What is significant, however, is that fears about the negative impact of the returning soldiers were a reality at the time in Britain and in the Empire. Stories circulated about returning *askari* who were showing themselves eager to use their whips for other than decorative purposes, and were refusing to walk anywhere. Also, Medical Officers had let it be known that many *askari* carried or had suffered from venereal disease. Official statistics were patchy but, from the most complete records that were compiled for 1944, evidence pointed to a much higher rate of venereal disease amongst East African soldiers. Half of all reported medical conditions consisted of sexually transmitted diseases in 1944.[18] The access of troops to brothels when on active duty was the reason for these apparently high levels. Whether campaigns were mundane or difficult, sex was often a welcome and obvious form of recreational pursuit that was universal among rank, class or colour. Prevention was difficult when the desire for abstention withered, especially when soldiers were as much sought out by local prostitutes as they actively sought sex for payment.[19] Army film strips told stories of *askari* returning home sick and infertile after catching venereal disease from brothels that had not been certified as 'safe houses'.

Part of the explanation for the discrepancy between the belief in the potential for disruption and the actual disruption which occurred, lies in the way that, for some commentators, the *askari* were a mechanism for expressing long-standing anxieties and political agendas regarding settler

[16] Eric St A. Davies, 'Annual Report 1946 – South Kavirondo', p. 5. RH Mss.Afr.s.513.

[17] Knott, 1947: 107. In West Africa the effect was more marked; see Killingray, 1983. For a different view see Shiroya, 1992. See also Parsons, 1996: 287–92 and Crowder, 1987. There is evidence that the military rituals adopted by some Mau Mau freedom fighters were a legacy of being in the British army, but few Kikuyu had been front-line soldiers.

[18] W.F. Mellor, *Casualties and Medical Statistics: Official Medical History of World War Two* (London, 1972).

[19] For a seminal discussion of the whole subject see Hyam, 1990: esp. ch.6 'Prostitution and Purity'.

society in the post-war era. As Knott argued, the returning soldier might be 'more insistent on the rights and privileges of a citizen of his own country', an acknowledgement perhaps of the effects of British wartime propaganda which emphasized freedom from alien occupation (Knott, 1947: 103). Geoffrey Hunter, former manager with Dalgety and Company (a well-known farmers' agent) and member of a string of East African war committees, believed that soldiers would have false expectations, which he blamed on Labour Party rhetoric. In one of his articles published in *African Affairs* his settler mentality came to the fore through his use of the term native and a subtext which suggested the limitations for change in colonies like Kenya (Hunter, 1944). With a worried glance at the metropolitan political settlement, he warned that 'unrealistic expectations and comparisons' might give people the idea that East Africa could support some type of massive state project geared towards social service provision. 'Many natives', he argued, 'have led an Army life – they have been overseas ... and living in a standard they never thought of. All this, just like the Beveridge Plan in Britain, can only be maintained if there is some wealth to pay for it' (ibid.:131).

Settler interest came to the fore here since the real post-war problem was held to be the 'condition of the native'. The interest in the *askari* could be used to bolster racial rule, since it could be argued that a little soldiering would not make much difference to the post-war colonial economy. Hunter, for example, put forward two solutions: end the policy of attempting to stop detribalization via the system of casual labour, and make Africans work much harder. The working man in England possessed an efficiency handed down from generation to generation, learned the hard way, he explained. In contrast, 'the average native at the prime of life develops in character and in intelligence only about to the extent of an English school boy. Consequently, he needs a great deal of guidance.' He believed that there was little experience of slumps or competition, but he also put forward another popular belief, that the African was held back by the Indian population. And his final advice to development planners was not to let 'sentiment' prevail over 'common sense'. Native labour had to become more efficient:

> if his standard of living and education is to be altered ... a few thousand Europeans, even if taxed to the limit of endurance, can never provide the wherewithal to educate and to doctor some 12 million natives. (ibid.)

In complete contrast, many experts chose to give testimony to the constructive potential of *askari* in the immediate post-war period which transcended Hunter's racially restricted one. The trained soldier came to represent an acceptable version of the type of African whom many believed colonial rule had unwittingly unleashed: the detribalized native. The detribalized African had already considerably troubled the minds of missionaries. Their once sure-fire congregations were no longer as unquestioning and accepting as of old. Some wrestled with the creeping sense of having unleashed disobedient men and women who no longer fitted easily into rural life, a fear that was to return ten years later when Mau Mau had to be explained.[20] Africans also participated in the debate. S. I Kale, a local CMS teacher in Lagos, suggested to readers of *Oversea Education* that they might better understand detribalization if they conceived of it as *déraciné*, caused by the drift to towns and cities which produced a resulting loss of sympathy with the world in general (Kale, 1941).

Any evidence that detribalization – a major pre-war concern – was not wholly disastrous would probably be seized upon. The *askari* provided this reassurance, since educationalists and army officials alike were fired by the belief that the army's education programme had created a new type of African man. The work of the East African Army Education Corps was becoming well known. For example, when writing about the achievements of the KAR, Captain Smallwood had insisted that in East Africa and under military discipline 'large scale native education can be practised for the first time'. Soldiers learned to read, discussed wartime affairs and received instruction on army rules and regulations. Any old room could be transformed into a classroom. Permanent information or reading rooms were set up; libraries were established; broadsheets and newsletters were specially prepared. Between 1941 and 1943 the Jeanes School turned out over 600 African unit education instructors, and two were posted to each infantry battalion; by 1945, over 800 Africans and Somalis had been trained as unit teachers, information officers, propagandists, welfare workers, interpreters and Swahili teachers (see photograph 6). According to Smallwood, they spent between three and four months at the School studying subjects such as Land and Home Betterment and Methods of Saving.[21] Their motto was 'first a man, second a soldier, third a teacher'.

It was believed at the time that the army had given its soldiers the chance to learn 'a little more than was needed for the immediate performance of their military duty' because it had looked to the future (Knott, 1947:104). Undoubtedly, the prospect of being able to instil military discipline and the correct attitude if soldiers were literate was appealing to the military authorities. Yet, as in the British war effort, army educationalists were committed to informing and teaching a wide curriculum. With bureaucracy and surveillance going into overdrive, mass observation

[20] Lewis, 2000; E. Hitchens, 'Mau Mau and the press in Kenya, 1950–54' (unpublished undergraduate dissertation, Faculty of History, Cambridge University, 1998).

[21] Smallwood, 1945: 217–18; see Parsons, 1996: 213–14 for a dicussion on the double-edged sword effect of army education which was appreciated at the time by commanding officers and Easterbrook, 1975: 42–4; Hawkins and Brimble, 1947.

helped create a strong interest in levels of morale, and resources were set aside for an Army Bureau of Current Affairs that would instil servicemen and women with a sense of mission. Likewise, *askari* were given access to populist African newspapers such as *Baraza* and soldiers welcomed the news that came 'from our behind' (Englander and Mason, 1994: 3–8; Parsons, 1996:211). Each regional grouping of battalions also had a military broadsheet. *Askari* and *Jambo* were tailored for East African troops as well as *Kwetu Kenya* (our home), again illustrating the importance given to encouraging loyalty. Past misgivings gave way to general hope that the educated *askari* would return home and, through example, pass on what he had learnt to those who had stayed in the Reserves. Such a wartime pill of army education seemed to offer a solution to the disaffection of rural life. The post-war challenge – how to make rural life capable of satisfying the ambitions of the younger generation – was now subject to military notions of habilitation, both pre-habilitation and re-habilitation. It was a line on social engineering that would be returned to.

The *Askari* began to be more sharply represented as the embodiment of the good citizen for many metropolitan observers of Empire. Experts argued that if civilian back-up and training were offered to soldiers, they would behave as responsive and responsible citizens. This rested on the assumption that *askari* could put into practice the same techniques they had learnt in war and would thus enable communities to sustain their own welfare. According to Mrs Fane the *askari* possessed an enriched morality as a result of exposure to improved physical comforts; they would want 'a new and better way of life for themselves and their fellows', she insisted (Fane, 1944:56). Knott also drew comfort from the apparent popularity of the uniform, badge and rank. The *askari* had good reason to consider himself a cut above those who had not worn the King's uniform, Knott assured his audience, 'for he has a wider outlook and has been trained to discipline and regular habits of mind and body which improve his intellect, his health and his usefulness to the state, as well as his influence among his less fortunate fellows' (Knott, 1947:99).

Improved inter-racial co-operation was another possibility which the *askari* appeared to offer. The official line being put across to the reading public was that a range of British ranks had 'learnt to work with Africans gaining each other's trust and confidence'. The language used was suggestive of a mental leap away from the derogatory label of native. Talk was not of the 'East African native', but the 'East African soldier' and the African man', a vocabulary with which men with experience of soldiering were more at ease. A practical illustration of this was Kenya's Director of Training, Patrick Williams, whose proposals for a colony-wide system of youth camps were floated on the understanding that partnership between European and African men of the 'right type' was now possible. 'The human material' now existed, he claimed, 'for carrying out much of the works side of Colonial Development Programmes, with results that may be as great economically as socially'.[22] Here then was a potential answer to Margery Perham's earlier call for a new more intimate type of relationship with colonial peoples. It seemed they now had the technology to believe it to be so.

'Flagships of hope': propaganda, manliness and an army for peace

The answer coming publicly from the Army itself was an emphatic 'Yes'. This fed into the general outpouring of emotion and optimism stimulated by being at war. Support for the view that African soldiers were a dynamic force for good came from the top of the East African military hierarchy. General Sir William Platt of the East African Command publicly stated that the army had deliberately provided a great educative opportunity for its African soldiers. Education had turned men into better soldiers, he insisted. He had good reason to hope so, for the apparent shortage of skilled white labour made the scenario whereby African soldiers could replace British ones rather attractive. As Sir William delicately explained, trained native troops could 'relieve our island here of a burden which the modern manner of warfare makes her too small to bear'. Yet he seemed genuinely confident that the technical skills which the *askari* had learnt were the stuff of exciting new class formation, creating superior employees. However, he added a note of caution which belied his racial thinking. Training and guidance would have to be provided, he warned, if these skills were to be put into practice without the 'conditioning or habilitation' provided by the army, to correct what he described as 'The African tendency (it is a habit) to forget quickly during any period of leave or absence from work...' (Platt, 1946: 34). Yet typically of many European officers, Sir William mixed pride with paternal affection when reminiscing about African soldiers. He described to readers of *African Affairs* how 'the body of the *Askari* has been developed till he resembles a well trained racehorse with a bloom on his skin like a ripe black grape'. The obvious pleasure some European soldiers took from observing the growing physical prowess of young African men was not necessarily a sign of rampant homosexual desire. Here it was partly a consequence of the particular – the incidence of under-nourishment and disease among new recruits – and the usual – professional pride and the projection of the self-belief in the essential goodness of barrack life for a man. Platt described how the Army's efforts in 'habilitation' had arrested the physical manifestations of disease and hunger.

Drawing pleasure from a voyeuristic worship of soldiering was as popular

[22] Patrick Williams, Youth Camp Proposals, pp. 13–14, KNA CD5/309, discussed in Chapter 3. For an affectionate account of life in the forces, see Hanley, 1946.

a pastime as ever during the Second World War. The *Army Quarterly*, for example, contained a series of short articles entitled 'Epic Fights' which included maps and battle plans. Soldiers and military personnel were invited to write in with accounts of their wartime voyages and expeditions. Such admiration could include a shared appreciation of hyper-masculine physicality and touched on nostalgia for the innocent enjoyment of single-sex life. Empire was a fertile terrain for such fantasies and Africa had always produced more than its fair share of military figures whose alleged heroics helped to transform them into popular icons of a hyper-masculinity. Lawrence of Arabia had had a hand in his own myth-making, helped by the natural advantage of range of local props, from marauding Arabs, galloping camels, superhuman desert crossings and dressing up in what looked at first glance like women's clothes (see Dawson, 1994; Asher, 1998). More modestly but within the same tradition nevertheless, Patrick Williams wrote enthusiastically about his plans for post-war youth camps which were modelled on army life because they promised to deliver key features of received notions of masculinity: the camps would, he was sure, 'toughen the individual ... pay honour to manliness ... [and] encourage stoicism'.[23] That is not to imply homosexuality was absent. Army life as well as the empire in general created places and situations where British homosexuals could find relief from the repressive laws at home, and pursue a 'queer' life under the cover of homo-sociability within exclusively male domains. Situational homosexuality was also prevalent, encouraged by the intense levels of isolation, loneliness and uninhibited freedom which life in the army, when combined with empire, could often enforce. Combat and the threat of death had the effect of increasing libidinous desire and the need for affection which might not have easy heterosexual outlets.[24] When there were such easy outlets, they were usually embraced. A local brothel in Addis Ababa once became an unofficial officers' mess. *Potto di Notchi Pendulante* gave much opportunity for tales of heroic prowess and a prize was awarded for the most outstanding sexual athleticism. It was often the captured Italian POW doctors who were given the job of clearing up the venereal diseases.

Homosexual acts which took place because of an aggressive exploitation of the differential power relations between officers and African soldiers were a minor hidden feature of colonial army life. Physical punishments were meted out by some white officers who were able to indulge their propensity for sado-masochism. This was also a learned experience of public schools where repressed and sadistic masters or senior boys could and often did sexually abuse younger boys. Most acts of physical punishment were carried out by African NCOs under orders. There was much

[23] Williams, Youth Camp Proposals, p. 8, KNA CD5/309.

[24] See Aldrich, 1996; Costello, 1985: esp 155–73; Lt. Donald Bowie, p. 6. RH Mss.Afr.1715 (241A). Also more generally see Lane, 1995; Nandy, 1983.

unofficial 'roughing-up' that went unreported. However, there were some consensual sexual liaisons between ranks. Occasionally officers who made unwelcome demands or advances were reported by *askari*; cowardly or brutal superior officers were often curbed by retaliatory and unexpected behaviour from the lower ranks. There was much more to army life, however.

During the Second World, a more fraternal bond flourished between white and black soldiers serving together. In most wars, violence bonds and creates new forms of association. For the majority of officers, their unequivocal fondness of army life and for their *askari* was an innocent extension of their 'boy-man' existence. The empire facilitated this perpetual public school nirvana whereby emotionally stunted men could relive the more pleasant aspect of public school adolescence: the single-sex camaraderie, love of childish humour (including making up nicknames), and the absence of forbidding nannies. The irony was that, whilst African men were urged on to manliness, many Europeans revelled more in boyishness. The opportunity to be a man's man in the army was not the same experience for all British soldiers. For the more upper-class officer, single-sex life unleashed the 'passion of friendship', the chance to make sentimental attachments and to play lots of bridge. For the lower ranks, their manliness could be endorsed by displaying their physical strength, toughness and sporting achievements. African soldiers were exposed to this regime of hyper-masculine behaviour plus a moral manliness that had been crafted in the late Victorian era. This was a brand of evolutionary development theory. Implicit was a strict moral code based on the Christian doctrine of transcending 'juvenile limitation' and the 'sublimation of the animal instinct' through reason.[25]

These principles were easily applied to Africans as they had been to working-class men, both viewed as childlike and much more at the mercy of their uncivilized urges. The shared aim was to transfer the unspoken qualities of the 'right chap' or the 'right type'. This was a man who could naturally make a system work properly and who could be relied upon to carry out the necessities of any particular task, whether routine, new or unpleasant; for example, army corporal punishment was justified providing it was meted out by 'the right type'. In this way, if there was excess or abuse, the person could be blamed rather than the system. This type was considered the right stuff because he judged by experience, not by the book; had a character built upon a notion of the common good; and was as much in control of his sentiments as he was of his aggression. The key litmus test was sport. If a chap could be relied upon in games to play by the rules and to put his team, not himself, first, then he was considered like-minded and the right type and welcomed to the club (Mangan, 1986).

[25] For the best scholarly account on this subject see Hyam, 1990: esp. 'Empire and Concepts of Manliness' pp. 71–9; Green, 1995; Roper and Tosh, 1991; Vance, 1985: esp. 195–201.

Meanwhile metropolitan minds were increasingly impressed with the idea that the homo-social nature of army life and its disciplined environment could return better citizens back to society. Well aware of the successes of wartime posters, leaflets and radio broadcasts, many were readily seduced by evidence that wartime army publicity campaigns had achieved a great deal.[26] This not only massaged away their worries about African soldiers but also tempted them with a formula for post-war reconstruction. Consequently, metropolitan expectations for demobilization and post-war reconstruction in the colonies ran high by the end of the war. The professionalization of the art of conducting a war campaign, and the new technologies available for this, fed imaginations, greedy for fast results.

Captain Dickson was the officer in charge of the mobile propaganda unit of the East African Command. He exemplified the new professionalization taking place. Between 1944 and 1945 various articles appeared in those same specialist metropolitan journals which had an empire-focused audience. True to his occupation, Dickson was an able and willing promoter of his own work. He described the unit as 'a potted, mobile edition of the Aldershot Tattoo'. This, he claimed, had reached an audience of over one million people. The unit included 28 *askari* drawn from twenty different tribes. It had worked its way through a number of colonies and protectorates and invoked considerable popular acclaim. Dickson evocatively described how they formed a single corps of African 'missionaries'.[27] Throughout his text, religious metaphors abound. For example, one of his concepts of development, 'living life more abundantly', was taken from the Anglican Book of Prayer. Films, talks and side-shows, where *askari* explained a branch of army work or an aspect of the war, were accompanied by gymnastics displays. The unit also indulged in a little pageantry to display changes in warfare.

Although Dickson admitted weapon firing was the biggest attraction – elders usually asked to be issued with guns – he was adamant that his men convincingly proved that similar techniques

> ... will help arouse the rural African from his primeval torpor: in this manner it is even now paving the way for post-war progress. It is seldom that the arts of war and the arts of peace can have a proper aim, but the Propaganda Unit has shown how a spear for freedom may easily be beaten into a ploughshare ... Its emphasis, now on the destruction of the Axis, may later be on the reconstruction of the African. (Dickson, 1944: 13)

Again this was something the Colonial Office was interested in backing. The Colonial Office's Education Adviser apparently had urged the post-

[26] For metropolitan Britain see Grant, 1994; McLaine, 1979: and Nicholas, 1996.

[27] Dickson, 1944; they had been successful in the 1941 recruitment drive among the Batswana in Bechuanaland, Jackson, 1997: 408.

war employment of *askari* as general 'vermin destroyers' (ibid.: 18). So efforts had to be got under way to publicize the positive aspects of the trained *askari*, which was, of course, what wartime propagandists were trained to do. Dickson produced all the necessary evidence that, 'with guidance, training and technical support, all things were possible. The healthy *askari* looked good; their athleticism and self-discipline would be copied. Numerous letters full of gushing admiration for the men's physical abilities were mentioned. The star of the show was their twelve-year-old bugler, Jowana, from the Western Nile. His fan-mail was usually addressed to The Dwarf or The Pygmy from the Congo as few could believe he was still a child.

The big attraction was that Africans themselves apparently envisaged the *askari* as a prototype for the 'modern detribalized African man'; the founders of the next generation of 'real Africans' and not tribesmen. 'The lesson for post-war administrators', Dickson confidently asserted, was that an 'appeal to the African sense of manliness far outweighed any appeal to his instinct for money'. And Dickson confirmed the glowing prospect for improved race relations. Many Europeans were for the first time seeing Africans perform tasks which they themselves could not do, producing genuine feelings of admiration which in turn were appreciated by his men. Part of the attraction of military service for Africans was the close and sympathetic contact it offered with Europeans. Some evidence suggests that the subsequent fondness felt by ex-*askari* towards the army sprang from their sense of racial equality. Formerly barred from the same shops or bars, it mattered that they now drank from the same cup, ate the same food and pissed down the same holes. Obviously, Africans were making their own input into the process of crafting a new masculine identity, enjoying the physicality of army life and the opportunities to show off their prowess.[28] They gave Dickson the evidence which he presented to a receptive audience that here was the 'ideal African man', who put racial distrust to one side, seemed to appreciate European progress and obeyed orders.

In Britain, war had dramatically shored up the sense that information, when harnessed to modern technology, was a supremely powerful force. Posters and film supplemented pamphlets and magazines as popular forms of cheap mass communication. Such a testimony was particularly appealing to already receptive metropolitan audiences, since it offered solutions to the perceived crisis of imminent mass detribalization. *Askari* promised to deliver orderly and responsible citizens, capable of sustaining their own welfare and who were not concerned with tribal difference. However, Captain Dickson offered a rationale and a blueprint not just for *askari*. He also presented a general strategy for civilian 'habilitation' imbued with an almost missionary fervour:

[28] See for example, Waruhiu, 1975. I am also grateful to Mr Ziphamndla Zondi (Magdalene College, Cambridge) for his useful comments on masculinities and gender.

> Our one endeavour must be to raise the standard of living for Africans in the sense that 'they may have life more abundantly'. Life means doing. That lesson is being learnt to-day by *askari* and it is a lesson that can be passed on after the war ... There will ... be many Africans who have undergone over four years of military discipline, with all the experience it implies... Cannot something of this be carried on into civil life, to bring about a group loyalty in the village? (Dickson, 1944: 17–18)

What we see here is one example of the cross-over of military concepts of turning civilians into soldiers and then wounded soldiers back into civilians, being offered up to the state for general application. For example, towards the end of the war, Brigadier Crew elaborated upon the latest techniques in 'pre-habilitation, re-habilitation and revocation' in the *Army Quarterly* journal. Recruitment had revealed what were termed physical and mental imperfections. These men were not weaklings, he explained, but had been the 'victims of poverty, malnutrition, faulty hygiene and education', having missed out on the opportunities that could provide for 'normal growth and development of mind and body' (Crew, 1944). So, once basics were identified, habilitation and then repair, or at worse convalescence, could all be applied in various doses, the latter including more rest, games and sports. It would be during the war against the Mau Mau in Kenya, that the concept of rehabilitation would be turned to again.

The idea of a peacetime campaign of mass education using the techniques of adult education extended by the army during the Second World War appealed particularly to metropolitan audiences, because it answered the 1942 post-Singapore call for a more intimate and modernized style of imperial rule. In her articles for *The Times* Margery Perham had drawn attention to the apparent success of mass education campaigns and rural development in Turkey, China and Russia, in spite of their limited resources. Dickson, like many others who worked in the field of propaganda and information dissemination, possessed an almost self-righteous belief in his work. With typical gusto, he put forward a number of guidelines for such a campaign in Africa. First, Africans needed to become more involved in campaigns of betterment in order to fire their 'enthusiasms' and 'sympathy' for it. The vehicles for this included inter-village choirs, the Country badge system, sports and athletics, the English Scout movement, and an official 'school on wheels' employing 'trained and disciplined Africans in a carefully thought out plan of propaganda' that used the Jeanes School and the Pathfinder Movement, as well as the Missions and Education Officers. Secondly, propaganda itself ought to be more exciting and sensitized to its audience. He pointed out how some newsreels had backfired. British politicians walking off planes and inspecting munitions factories, followed by shots of African soldiers wading neck-high through torrential rivers, whilst balancing enormous gun wheels on their heads, had provoked more questions than they had answered (Dickson, 1944: 13).

The lesson was that colonial government in general ought to take note. Dickson suggested the glamour of the poster and the spectacle of pageantry to replace the 'perambulating collection of Medical Department bilharzia-specimens'. Unsurprisingly, Kenya's Information Officer had been pressing for exactly the same sort of campaigns (see Chapter 3). More and more people were arguing for a special European officer who was to be put in charge of such a programme. Some were even articulating the major obstacle to the realization of its potential. In a rare public acknowledgment of the tensions between colonial administrators, Dickson confirmed the kind of strain which a handful of advisers at the Colonial Office had also identified (see Chapter 1). He warned that the 'destructive class snobbery' shown by district administrators to officers working in new branches of government would have to end. 'Common, undignified ... not in keeping with the best tradition of the service ... self-advertising hustlers ... the unhappy reporter, almost a gentleman in his drab Burberry' was Dickson's version of how information officers were viewed by District Officers. Colonial governments in general had a 'dangerous and grotesque attitude' to propaganda; Africa was suffering as a result because men qualified in these techniques were not given a chance to put their expertise to work (Dickson, 1944: 17). Simple class differentiation was not the only reason for their unpopularity. Edwardian notions of manliness, reproduced more faithfully in the Empire, were being transgressed. Good Christian gentlemen were modest, self-effacing and disdainful of parading prowess.

Women had virtually disappeared from the scene. Dickson might have been despised by administrators for being effete or a 'dandy', but this was certainly not as a result of being too friendly with the girls. These accounts of post-war education campaigns had few specific strategies for women or indeed an awareness of the need to focus upon women at all. An awareness of the gendered nature of agricultural activity, for example, was lacking. Since imaginations were fired by soldiers writing about soldiers, the plans naturally contained a strong male bias. However, the potent images, fiery language and messianic fervour of Dickson's testimony made a significant impact at the time. In 1945, Dickson's work was enthusiastically reported upon with the aid of photographs in *Oversea Education*.[29] Official photographs were more abundant, due to the wider use of photography during the war. The visual image transformed the potential of the *askari* into a much more tangible product.

Among the images reproduced to illustrate Dickson's work were two juxtaposed group scenes. One depicted young warriors either squatting or standing around. Their expressions were sullen, their dress traditional.

[29] 'Army Education in and for Africa', *Oversea Education*, 17 (1) (1945): 230.

Accessories included spears, shields, face and body paint and ostrich feather necklaces. Serving as a poignant contrast, was a completely different set of African men described as 'Trained P.T. Demonstrators attached to the Unit'. This photograph consisted of a closer shot of six happy smiling faces. Their regulation hair cuts and army shorts made them easily differentiated. The men stood in a line each with their left arm cradling the same heavy timber. According to the caption, each member of the team came from a different tribe and was taught a different trade. Here was visual proof of the transformative power of adult education and European training.

The editorial verdict accompanying the photographs and the account of propaganda work was unequivocal. Demobilized soldiers, trained in the Army School of Education at Kenya's Jeanes School, should continue in peacetime the educational team methods practised by the army's Mobile Unit. The Advisory Committee on Education in the Colonies had apparently received a similar suggestion from Colonel Sellwood, officer in command of the Jeanes School Centre in Nairobi where soldiers were trained as instructors. Education experts in London were impressed by new evidence that Africans had become educators, not only in the Mobile Unit but also as troop instructors serving in Burma.[30] The journal was keen to support a special course for Sergeant Instructors in Basutoland planned for 1945. The way it concentrated on what was billed as education for the good of the community, was impressive. Handicrafts, music, dancing and drama, the construction of model villages, problems of land settlement, the work of experimental farms, and a study of local machinery for development planning featured on the proposed curriculum.

Ideas about demobilized soldiers cross-fertilized with the growing interest in the role of community centres. This suggestion was finding much support at the time in Britain within discussions about post-war reconstruction at home. So what was good for Britain was good for the Empire. Metropolitan visions for demobilization were further sharpened when the concept of the community centre taking off in rural Africa was aired. The possibilities in post-war propaganda disseminated from a village centre were immense; one editorial explained how the war had unleashed such a possibility. News centres or information offices had been hastily constructed to 'counter rumour and foster a sense of urgency', often through haphazard but enthusiastic efforts on the part of members of the public.[31] Their evolution into a sort of 'club-house' had then turned into a 'community centre movement' which, according to the editorial, was developing into something more elaborate in a number of colonial territories. Cadbury's had recently donated £4,000 for two centres in the Gold Coast in Ashanti and Eastern Provinces; Tanganyika had appointed

[30] Ibid. See discussion below.

[31] Quarterly Notes, 'Community Centres', *African Affairs* 44 (176) (1945) 95–6.

an officer to assist in the building of centres after receiving £50,000 from the Development and Welfare funds for club-rooms, lecture halls and reading rooms. In Kenya, it was known that district conferences were full of the same ideas, although only two information rooms were in operation. Reports had also come through that Lagos and Ibadan in Nigeria had recently acquired African Women's Social Welfare Committees. These activities were seen as exciting solutions to a problem which concerned socially-conscious observers at home: the tedium of rural life. '[T]hey may have become a panacea for officials, faced with demobilisation problems', metropolitan minds agreed, but also 'they fulfill a real need ... This incipient movement is part of a world-wide attempt to combat what Marx termed the idiocy of village life.'[32]

An interest in demobilization was not confined to the metropolitan arena of professional discussions. In Kenya, concern with demobilized soldiers had taken a slightly different path. As early as 1942, soldiers were linked to general plans for the development of individual districts, an indication of the sense of an underlying need for action. However, by 1944 there was little to show for all the plans and good intentions, despite the fact that the vision emanating from District Officers mirrored that of Captain Dickson's suggestions for transforming swords into ploughshares. Initially, senior colonial officials were anxious to find ways to ensure that the skills of European men and women serving in the British Forces would be put to use in the colony when the war was over.[33] In May 1941, the government appointed a committee for this purpose, chaired by Charles Mortimer, Commissioner for Local Government, Lands and Settlement from 1939 to 1946.

A year later the issue of African military reabsorption came on to their agenda. The committee asked the Director of Education to chair a special sub-committee to make recommendations. Both committees produced reports – the Mortimer Report (Main Section) and the Mortimer Report (African Section) – in May 1943, calling for immediate action and the creation of an interim organization. Consequently, in August 1943 the government set up a Civil Reabsorption Board, headed by Ernest Meredyth Hyde-Clarke, then Assistant Secretary responsible for defence and soon to gain a liberal reputation as Labour Commissioner.[34] Both reports explicitly linked 'the reabsorption of the ex-soldier of all races' with

[32] Ibid., p. 96.

[33] 'Demobilization and Military Training', (undated), KNA/DEF/10/85. Concern persisted about the shortage of woman-power in the colony, especially teachers, nurses and stenographers; KNA/DEF/10/88 and 89.

[34] The Board was divided into three: Administration and Welfare, chaired by C. T. Davenport; Vocational Training, chaired by P. E. Williams; and the Employment group; see KNA/DEF/10/66. A Women's Section emerged as a result of Mortimer's recommendation. Run by Mrs Catherine Griffiths, it was responsible for organizing the reabsorption of European women after release from national service and the post-war training of women; Annual Report (Women's Section) 1945, KNA/DEF/10/67.

improving welfare and development in the colony. Also, both clearly reflected the metropolitan belief in the power of central planning; the main report declared that `the process of adjustment from a war-time to a peace-time economy will have to be directed by deliberate national planning, which must include relatively large schemes'.

Illustrating the way in which colonial policy was subject to a wide critique from outside opinion even in wartime, the report was praised in *African Affairs*. It was a welcome recognition, one commentator argued, that the employment of ex-soldiers was part of wider post-war employment issues, which the state could and should intervene to regulate.[35] However, a qualification was quickly added. Readers were reminded that 'the African himself' would determine whether the plans would work; he would first have to learn 'the value of money, integrity, honesty and the concept that work produced the things worth having'. This report explicitly linked demobilization to the long-standing assumption that more and more Africans were becoming completely detribalized.

An example of military logic, soldiers were divided up according to the apparent extent of their detribalization, as tribal natives, the partly urbanized or the permanently urbanized. The last two categories were not to be discharged until they could be 'beneficially absorbed into acceptable forms of wage-earning'. In the minds of the Mortimer Committee, as in the imaginations of metropolitan experts, the *askari* could become a task-force that would carry the rest of Africa forward into a modern cash-based economy.[36] This was illustrated by a further list of recommendations: training centres overseen by a Director; new employment openings in the Reserves; more employment in the Settled areas; an increase in secondary industries and a Civilian Labour Corps that would mount a 'total war' against soil erosion and deforestation (Mortimer (African) Report quoted in Fane, 1944: 58). Measures to stop the drift away from the land were also suggested. Agricultural Training Schools, better marketing and land tenure investigations were to accompany the expansion of villages as vital centres of community life. Also central to the Mortimer vision was a corps of married welfare officers – civilian sergeant majors – who would oversee rural life, ensuring that villages were 'orderly, beautiful and clean'. Their duties were to include 'simple sanitation and hygiene, house building, well and dam making, tree planting, bridge building'. The report gave assurances that Africans would welcome this sort of guidance and that the Colonial Development and Welfare fund plus increased rates levied by LNCs would foot the bill. It was to be a popular idea in principle, but the constraints outlined in Chapter 3 would once again cast their shadow.

At this time, a consensus was developing around the potential of the soldier. The district administration also linked *askari* demobilization to

[35] 'Progress Report on Demobilization, 1944', 10 February 1944 p. 12. KNA/DEF/10/68.

[36] Taken from a section in the Mortimer African Report entitled 'Emergence of a Cash Economy', ibid.

plans for improving post-war levels of development and welfare but with local variations. In areas where the number of soldiers was relatively high, fears about their disruptive effects featured in wartime district plans. Machakos District had been a major recruiting ground for Kamba soldiers. By the end of 1940, 4,400 men had joined up to escape the poverty and drought of an over-populated Reserve, with a further 2,000 Akamba signing up at recruiting centres outside the district. In 1942 5,545 were recruited (Easterbrook, 1975: 30). The two overriding concerns of administrators were land shortages and the returning *askari*.[37] Sights were set on making better use of the land and on building up a farming community which was 'sufficiently prosperous to maintain by its earnings a class of professional men, craftsmen, traders and general wage earners'. The *askari* was viewed as a temporary problem but, if handled carefully, one that could bring benefits.

Machakos's DC admitted that the economic conditions in the Reserves might provoke unrest. The general economic situation was acknowledged to be worse than in 1938. The war had depleted land resources, caused food prices to rise because of famine and masked their effects due to the short-term prosperity that had come in its wake. However, Machakos planners hoped that the *askari* could become useful under certain circumstances. Though they were initially disinclined towards manual agricultural work and expecting higher pay and better conditions, it was believed by the administration that a welfare officer could induce them to work in labour corps. The view was also seemingly shared that army life had given the *askari* an 'enlarged vision of life' and made them 'promising subjects for social improvement'.[38] Also, the district planners hoped that ex-*askari* with good records could be made supernumerary headmen attached to chiefs on Grade 'A' African Civil Service. They would make other ex-*askari* feel represented, reduce the potential for discord, and start organizing soil conservation.

In Nyanza Province, administrators were able to keep a cooler head, being much less close to rural disaster than Central Province. They were able to keep hold of the family unit ideal as a solution to detribalization, and linked the *askari* into this formula in their post-war plans. Hunter had recently replaced Fazan as PC and both were relatively progressive in their attitudes. Both administrative and technical staff believed that zonal development around villages would have a greater chance of success if returning *askari* and their families could live there, because they would be used to the improved conditions found in army life.[39] They endorsed the

[37] 'Machakos District – Post-War Development Plan', KNA MAA7/602, submitted by the DC (undated but most likely written sometime in 1944). The report was forwarded by the Secretariat to Dr Issac Shapera who was making an anthropological survey of Kenya.

[38] Ibid p. 9.

[39] 'Post War Development Planning ... Central Kavirondo', (undated), KNA PC/NZA/3/570. Previously discussed in Chapter 3.

proposal – borrowed from the Associated Chambers of Commerce in South Africa – outlined in the Mortimer Report, 'though somewhat vaguely', that a peacetime army of construction should be assembled. Central Kavirondo planners were confident that such a plan could be 'the master key to the dual problems of absorption and of demobilised soldiers, and large scale and rapid constructional development after the war, both in Native Reserves and settled areas'.[40]

However, by the end of the war, the widespread district and provincial plans that linked soldiers in with zonal development as well as retraining programmes had not materialized. Nevertheless, hopes were still high. Imperial observers and military public relations men had invested a great deal in promoting the wartime achievements of education when applied to *askari*. Optimism also abounded in the potential of technology. Surely all this could not come to naught.

Swords to ploughshares and war to welfare

African soldiers returning home to rural areas did provide the necessary stimulus to combating bureaucratic inertia and structural constraint. However, the outcome was to prove less than satisfactory. In late 1944, the Civil Reabsorption Board in Kenya appointed a Director of Training, Patrick Williams. He immediately produced a report on the training of African ex-servicemen, forwarded to the Colonial Office in March 1945. Williams had been influenced by the further education and training plans circulating in Britain, which had reached the Ministry of Defence in Kenya.[41] He forecast a huge problem that required an Executive Demobilization Authority and a Civil Directorate of Demobilization. He calculated that 95 per cent of service men would be sent home to the Reserves, only 5 per cent being completely detribalized; 4,000 would seek immediate work; unrest would develop three to six months later when their savings would be exhausted and home life would begin to pall; and 40 per cent would seek supplementary income to their *shambas*. Steps had to be taken to 'protect the African from his unthrifty ways'.[42]

Unsurprisingly, certain missionaries and white settlers began to register unease at the prospect of large numbers of returning soldiers. This moment of panic did focus attention first on the need for European welfare officers to help *askari* find work and to stem the inevitable drift into the towns. This new category of officer was to point the disgruntled *askari* towards the planned training courses designed 'to catch the Army artisan before he

[40] Ibid., p. 5.

[41] 'Proposals for the Training of African Ex-servicemen' with covering letter, PRO CO822/118/5, 1945. For example, Ministry of Labour and National Service Pamphlet 'Further Education and Training Scheme', KNA DEF10/68. Easterbrook, 1975:. 53–7.

[42] Williams, covering letter, p.9, PRO CP822/118/5.

was discharged' in order to prevent the emergence of 'a real grouse'. It was a preventive move to socially engineer the pacified *askari.*

In April 1944, plans were afoot in Nyanza to put in place a Provincial Development and Welfare Officer (PDWO). The job of paying family remittances in Nyanza and Central Provinces, undertaken by army demobilization officers, was making up less than one-third of the total work generated from soldiers serving in the Forces. Consequently, a new post to encourage 'free letter' forms for correspondence and to arrange broadcasts in local vernaculars to coincide with *barazas* held by Family Remittance Officers seemed logical.[43] The PDWO was to assist the PC in all matters relating to the African soldier, since these additional duties were agreed to be a civil and not a military responsibility. The post was advertised as the first of a number of Provincial (and perhaps District) Development and Welfare Officers, as suggested – although 'on a more limited scale' – by the Mortimer Report.

Such an officer represented the ubiquitous 'handyman' of public school and Oxbridge days whose wife could also prove useful, and so the request was made that

> We should therefore like to see attached to the Provinces married welfare officers of the handyman type... We need hardly say that such men and women should be most carefully selected. Example is better than precept, and consequently their manner of living and the way they run their own homes would have great effect, good or bad, on the Africans they influence... Africans will live in well-built cottages, with better water supplies, a balanced diet, adequate clothing, and a measure of simple sanitation, together with the means for the encouragement of cultural activities at village centres, such as meeting halls, cinemas, libraries, and sports grounds as well as the normal amenities of commerce, such as the post office, tea houses, shops, craftsmen's workshops, etc.[44]

Thus the favoured formula for rural development through a particular type of family life was now to be executed by army personnel. This new officer was the link of wartime demobilization with post-war development.

The idea of the family was not forgotten, within which a role for women was envisaged. Evidently the hope was that such handymen with their valuable experience of working with Africans in battle would be willing to dirty their hands like the Sanitary Inspectors praised by Lockhart in the previous chapter. In addition, such officers were to pick out ex-*askari* 'of the right type' for the various planned educational training schemes to be run by the Director. Under sustained pressure to think about demobilization, the Secretariat in Nairobi accepted that 'special staff' were needed to help with certain activities that were part of 'the normal

[43] Precis for Standing Finance Committee (SFC), 22 April 1944, KNA PC/NZA/3/1/572.
[44] Para 73 of the Mortimer Report (Africa Section), pp. 1–2.

progressive development' of African areas and still considered to be 'the responsibility of the Provincial Administration'.

Eight officers were engaged as Civil Reabsorption Officers (CROs), with duties restricted to the welfare of returning *askari*. They would then become Development and Welfare Officers 'extending their work to cover all types of community development within their districts'. Placed under the direction of the PC, they would be members of the planned Provincial Development teams, co-ordinating 'the welfare side of native development and betterment schemes', in addition to 'maintaining close contact with discharged soldiers, especially the disabled'.[45] The salary scale for PDWOs and DDWOs was to be commensurate with that of a Senior Agricultural Officer and Agricultural Officer respectively. However, installing such an officer was not so straightforward.

The obstacles to such officers being able to carry out their work, which the educational experts at the Colonial Office had raised in 1939, immediately surfaced. The most serious handicap was the lack of authority given to the PDWO. This was apparent from the instructions given to one of the earliest officers. In May 1944, Nyanza's DCs received official word that Fortie Ross, released from military service – he had experience of welfare duties during his time serving with troops in the Middle East – was ready to take up the post of PDWO.[46] His salary was covered by the demobilization vote. He was to go on tour with the Family Remittance Officer, providing a link between *askari* and their homes and monitoring the recently introduced `Domestic Affairs' forms used for correspondence, which were deemed to be of the utmost importance since they affected the morale of the troops. The district administration were assured that Ross had been 'impressed with the importance of keeping in the closest touch with the D.C.s ... he should take every opportunity of discussing his subjects with them'. Ross's duties were wide-ranging; 'further ventures' were listed as the development of information rooms, village centres and a mobile Post Office Savings Bank, whilst he would have full-time use of a mobile cinema.

The Secretariat was clear as to what he would not being doing. He was to have no executive authority, although on his tours of the Province he would contact both District Commissioners and the officers of the Medical, Agricultural and Veterinary Departments and glean ideas from them as to 'village Betterment' and 'Post-War Development'. Nor was he to attempt to hear any local *shauris*. These were restated as being the responsibility of the District Commissioner and his District Officers. He was free to find out what his local Africans thought about such subjects as the return of the *askari* and the catch-phrase '*msaada ya vita*', translated as 'reward for help'.[47] Ross would have to rely on the goodwill and co-

[45] Ibid.

[46] Circular sent to DCs (Nyanza) 15 May 1944, Adm 20/2/1/28 KNA PC/NZA/3/1/572.

[47] Ibid.

operation of the district administration to make his job work. This was exactly in line with what Lord Hailey had put forward in his recommendations regarding the position of technical staff. Would it be a repeat of the fate that befell the Reconditioning Officer in the 1930s?

However, support for a post-war welfare officer with a wider remit came from a number of sources. First, from the Colonial Office itself. In August 1944, Audrey Richards, African anthropologist and member of the Colonial Office's Social Welfare Advisory Committee at this point, visited Kenya to help formulate the colony's future social research and training plans. A special meeting of the Native Welfare Committee was called to meet her.[48] Ever persistent, the Director of Agriculture had submitted another memorandum on agricultural training in government schools.[49] The CNC asked Dr Richards how other territories co-ordinated the various branches of education, pointing out that in Kenya veterinary, agricultural and medical training had hitherto been separated in watertight compartments, and 'the pupil was therefore at a loss to understand how one man could combine all three and be for example an efficient mixed farmer'. Richards was able to report that this had been successfully achieved in Uganda and the Gold Coast. The lesson seemed to be that '[w]ith regard to co-ordinating the different messages of education...the ultimate solution lay in the adoption of the CO's view that Administrative Officers should in the future be trained also as welfare officers'. Quick to reply, the Governor retorted that 'welfare work in native areas must come under the Administration'. Here was the fundamental difference.

From the Governor's perspective, the managerial duty of the administration was already welfare; any subsidiary activities had to fall in line with existing local set-ups, that is, under the jurisdiction of the DC, the 'man-on-the-spot'. You had to have people in obvious command, as African responses would only come forth when faced with authority. However, the view from the Colonial Office was different. The administration must be energizers capable of teaching Africans the things they needed to know in order to make them healthier and better farmers; training not governing, with the DC as chief clerk to the LNC. In the minds of the Whitehall mandarins – if Audrey Richard's interpretation was correct – was a much more democratic vision of what welfare entailed. It focused upon improvements in grassroot standards of living, as this was conceived of at the time. It implied that a shared view of development was possible, reflecting a shift in attitude towards racial difference. Communities

[48] Notes of a meeting of the NWC to meet Dr Richards, 6 September 1944, KNA MAA7/592. Present were the Acting Governor, Sir Henry Moore, the CNC, and all heads of technical departments. Present by invitation were the Economic and Development Secretary, A.M. Champion, the Director of Training, the ag.Information Officer, Wyn Harris (Labour Liaison Officer) and Miss Janisch (Superintendent of Female Education).

[49] Item IV 'Agricultural training in Government African Schools', p.3, ibid. For an account of earlier efforts by the Director of Agriculture on this matter, see discussions on the efforts of the technical staff in Chapter 3.

could become self-sustaining if only the local officer could achieve local participation and get the whole imperial enterprise moving. To do that, he had to become a trainer of people. This difference in interpretation was never to be resolved.

Articulating the way in which white officers were bearers of a power which – to Africans – was representative of an arbitrary and racist system, was beyond the consideration of even the most progressive adviser at the time to consider. Even Dr Richard's answer – coming out of anthropological thinking of the time – to the question of what development and welfare plans should look like, which Kenya's senior administrators faced up to in a moment of self-analysis, remained beyond the capacity of the late colonial state to put into practice. She was searching for a way in which rural people living in Africa could be vested with the wisdoms of more than one branch of technical expertise – the kind of scientific knowledge believed to be the vital missing ingredient in African development – but she herself had no idea of the organizational implications of such restructuring. She told the Committee how, in Uganda and the Dutch West Indies, co-ordination had been achieved by training 'in schools where agricultural, veterinary, and hygiene were taught side by side; the pupils were turned out as jacks-of-all trades'. Evidently, she shared their belief in the transformatory potential of the colonial mission.

In October 1944, the potential duties of a welfare officer were again discussed by the Secretariat. Audrey Richards had given them a new comparative perspective to think about. Ceylon had Rural Development Officers who were responsible for cultural and practical aspects of what was described as 'social advancement'; Uganda employed an Information Officer who dealt with culture, as well as specially trained assistants involved with house-building and water supplies. Kenya's Chief Secretary was moved to suggest that their own soil conservation staff might in future be given broader training, as suggested by the Director of Agriculture. This would increase the usefulness of their work in the seasons when they were not actively engaged on soil conservation. He also suggested that after the war discharged Engineer and Medical Corps personnel might be employed, presumably as development officers. However, there were no plans and no resolve to take the matter further. Likewise, strong support for welfare officers seemed only to come from relatively marginal figures at the time. For example, Eric St A. Davies, the colony's Information Officer, put on record his support for a new development and welfare organization 'in view of the rapidly increasing number of *askari* returning to civil life'.[50] Carrying forward the vision of a soldier-to-citizen formula in peacetime, so clearly envisaged by so many in and out of government, was no straightforward matter.

[50] Davies, 'Some Notes on Welfare', KNA PC/NZA/3/1/572.

The key problem was the lack of enthusiasm for welfare officers among senior officials in Kenya. The colonial government had come under pressure from the Colonial Office, particularly via the Social Welfare Advisory Committee which was now reasonably well established. As a result two officers had been sent on a social science course held in Witwatersrand University, South Africa. One was Dr Philip, former member of the Medical Department; the other Fortie Ross. Referring to Dr Philip, Sir Charles Mortimer gloomily noted in April 1945 that the Secretariat was virtually committed to the position that 'on his return, for the time being at any rate, we will regard him as the Government adviser on social welfare'.[51] This was formally agreed in November 1945. The Colonial Office had suggested that Nairobi appoint a female welfare officer, a relatively junior officer to assist in the planning of social welfare work in the city, and that they accept a visit from a metropolitan expert in the training of welfare officers. None of these suggestions were welcomed. Here was a classic example of bureaucratic delaying techniques. A decision on the first was requested from the Standing Finance Committee, but no particular recommendation for the appointment was given. The appointment of a junior social welfare officer was referred to a sub-committee of the Development Committee recently set up under the chairmanship of Dr Paterson to consider social welfare generally. The gestured preference for waiting for advice from the Colonial Social Welfare Advisory Committee put the matter on extra hold.

No sooner was this agreed than government officials talked themselves out of any such commitment. Senior officials agreed there was 'a distinct danger of confusion if we get too many so-called experts on social welfare problems at the same time'. Instead, the CO was informed that since a report on social welfare was being prepared, any person coming from the UK could not be 'in on the floor in so far as the planning of welfare policy is concerned'. The CO queried this decision. So did the government in Uganda. They both wanted an expert to make a prolonged visit to assist in welfare training.[52] Nairobi refused to budge. The appointment of an expert would be inadvisable at this stage, they insisted; no commitments could be made until the middle of 1946 when they would have a clearer idea of future policy, and 'more information regarding the funds likely to be available to finance welfare services generally'.[53]

[51] Ag. CS to DMS and DC (Kisumu), 30 March 1945, KNA PC/NZA/3/1/572. 'Note to CS, FS, and CNC from Sir Charles Mortimer', 27 April 1945, KNA MAA7/528; see also R. Mutiso, 'The Evolution of Social Welfare and Community Development in Kenya', Appendix A, p.371.

[52] Draft letter to Cohen from Surridge (undated). Dr Philip would be asked to comment on the proposals and the CSWAC would later be approached for advice, KNA MAA7/528. According to Iliffe, with regard to the provision of welfare, '[w]hat Kenya and Tanganyika stumbled towards, Uganda did coolly and deliberately'. Uganda being relatively richer found its way towards progressive policies more easily. Iliffe, 1987: 204.

[53] Draft reply to CO (undated) pp. 1–2., KNA MAA7/528.

Fears about returning *askari* plus external pressure had ensured that a new organization called Welfare was established at the end of the war, but the government showed little sign of widespread enthusiasm.[54] Support was grudging and the structure kept as minimal as possible. The Director of Education, C.E. Donovan, and Dr Philip, who was put in charge of the Welfare Organization, had to fight to have Mary Kenny – a social worker dealing with Europeans and Asians in Nairobi – transferred to the organization. They argued that her work fell outside the usual jurisdiction of the Education Department; her appointment had been temporary pending the establishment of a welfare organization and both now wanted her to begin learning about African welfare work. However, the Director of Education stressed that, even with the establishment of a proper Welfare Organization, his Education Officers would still be the 'authorized persons' for checking undesirables in the town.[55] The Deputy Chief Secretary and the CNC remained unconvinced that Dr Philip's organization was sufficiently advanced for him to accept Mrs Kenny. Nor did they warm to the idea of an organization having any great dynamic role in the field. 'The new organization for Social Welfare', they agreed, 'was merely an extension of the existing welfare work performed by the D.C.s in districts and by the local authorities in the townships.' After yet more wrangling, Kenny was eventually transferred to the Welfare Organization to work in conjunction with the Municipal Welfare Workers who were to be paid that year from Education Department funds.[56] This proved to be somewhat of a small victory. Dr Philip might have thought he had won the battle, but he was not about to win the war.

By the end of 1945, a more restricted version of welfare officers was put in place. With Dr Philip away in South Africa, the district administration had made sure they kept the activities of any welfare officer to a minimum. Whilst Dr Philip and Fortie Ross were away undergoing training in South Africa, officials in Kenya carefully prescribed their future activities, as the next chapter will show. A meeting of DCs agreed to re-establish their control by reiterating first that such officers had to be 'of the right type'.[57] Secondly, their duties were to be more focused upon modest social welfare

[54] In November 1945 it was formally agreed that Dr Philip should be appointed Social Welfare Adviser to the Governor as Head of a new Social Welfare Organization.

[55] Notes of a meeting held at Secretariat, (undated), KNA MAA7/528.

[56] Ibid pp. 1–2.

[57] PC (Central Province) to CS, 22 November 1945, KNA PC/NZA/3/1/570, quoting Min.19/45 from DCs' meeting, 13 September 1945, p. 1. Copies were sent to other PCs and officers in charge, plus the Information Officer but not to Dr Philip who was away. Ten areas were proposed: 1. Youth Movements, 2. Recreation, including football, cinemas and plays, 3. Handicrafts and arts (both occupational and commercial), competitions and displays of arts and crafts, 4. Rural Industries (Tanning, weaving, basket-making etc. including buying raw materials and assisting in marketing), 5. Domestic Science, 6. Social supervision of beer houses, 7. Encouragement of savings, 8. British Legion, 9. Information Rooms, 10. Liaison with Co-operative Societies.

projects. There was no space allowed for an officer with a much wider role, as envisaged by Eric Davies, Patrick Williams and Audrey Richards, who would be 'development'-centred, co-ordinating more technical-based development projects and establishing links between departments via a new central organization.

The Central Province model quickly became a blueprint for others, as the district administration toyed with the question of demobilization. As a result, when Dr Philip returned in 1946 as Social Welfare Adviser, he faced an established district version, restricted in scope and responsibility. Welfare Officers, Hunter observed, 'should be directly responsible to D.C.s and not be members of a separate Department'.[58] All PCs, he claimed, were in general agreement and had decided to discuss the matter further. Since little could be done until welfare officers were appointed, he suggested that, for the time being, welfare should be dealt with through a sub-committee of Local Native Councils, where Departmental Officers could attend: it would not be 'sound policy' to set up an extraneous committee, but far more sensible to combine it with a committee of the LNC, which might meet every three months with the Information Officer allowed to attend. In line with Lord Hailey's view, welfare as the DCs conceived of it was seen as best left in the hands of locally accountable and controllable LNCs which could learn slowly how to organize it, once they had sure ways of paying for it. The handful of new welfare officers would have to blend into the post-war scenery as best they could. For some, the situation quickly became desperate. However, the *askari* as a peacetime good citizen was to have a post-war incarnation

African social welfare workers

Once welfare officers were in position, the issue of how to bring in trained *askari* was easier to solve. Patrick Williams, the Director of Training, set about mustering support for a retraining programme. He used the findings of the 1943 Mortimer Report to argue his case. The major obstacle to harnessing *askari* potential was the usual one of attitude, he argued. Once discharged, he feared that the *askari* would not be prepared to strive for the standard of living he had enjoyed in the army when he discovered the proportionate amount of hard work involved in civilian employment.[59] He did not explain this in racial terms but rather as being the result of having access to land, so that paid work was not essential. Many did not possess any great technical knowledge of immediate usefulness, or were illiterate, whilst those who had mastered some training would quickly forget it. The main obstacle to these good intentions was finance. The colonial

[58] Ibid.

[59] 'Proposals for the Training of African Ex-Servicemen'. Covering letter from Williams (undated) pp. 5–6, PRO CO822/118/5.

government largely saw it as the duty of the British exchequer to provide resources for soldier reintegration. Britain was, of course, bankrupt and scraping around to reward its own citizens through the welfare state. In Kenya, the training schemes and reabsorption programmes which eventually materialized were paltry in comparison with the avowed intentions and perceived needs.[60]

Yet, remarkably, a training scheme for African *askari* which was designed to turn these men into social welfare workers was up and running by 1946. Part of the explanation for this lies in the way the Colonial Office initiated discussions with the Kenya government about specialist training schemes. Generally, CO policy was to encourage local initiatives in Africa itself, rather than taking people overseas. Training was high on the agendas of the social welfare and education committees towards the end of the war. Makerere College in Uganda was envisaged by London as the ideal place for Africans who wanted access to higher education. The Kenyan Government found itself under pressure to establish local programmes of social research and training in line with the allocation of funds set aside in the Colonial Development and Welfare Act.

At an East African conference in May 1944, the Secretary of State for the Colonies told the Governors present that he wanted a start made in 'planning the part which Makerere should play in training social welfare workers in African surroundings and also in providing a research centre for East Africa in social studies'.[61] Richards, representing the SWAC, was dispatched to East Africa to help draw up vocational training for social welfare officers and to advise on a more general type of educational course. The time was ripe, she declared, for such a programme, especially since problems ranging from land tenure in Kenya and the progress of education for women and girls needed attention. Anthropological expertise was ever more tightly entwined around the colonial social transformation project.

During her visit to Kenya, the issue of training social welfare workers came up at a special meeting with an impressive line up of old hands; William Marchant was present as was H.E. Lambert, Arthur Philips and Percy Wyn Harris.[62] Dr Richards intimated that metropolitan opinion

[60] For a comprehensive treatment of this see Parsons, discussion of 'Job Placement and Vocational Training', pp. 264–9.

[61] Telegram sent to Governors' Conference received 12 May, 1944, KNA MAA7/592. Also, in a letter to Sir Charles Dundas, Governor of Uganda, Oliver Stanley (Colonial Office) admitted that the 'arguments in favour of training social workers in African surroundings rather than European are of considerable weight'. He promised a sympathetic response to any proposals from the Colonial Research Committee, 15 May, 1944, ibid.

[62] A.I. Richards to Cox, Educational Adviser (Colonial Office) 23 April 1944, ibid. Marchant was the CNC; Lambert – a retired DC – was the Government Land Tenure Adviser; Percy Wyn Harris was the Labour Liaison Officer who then became Labour Commissioner late 1944–6, then PC (Central Province) 1946–7, rising to the post of CNC in 1947. Arthur Philips was a member of the Colonial Service, a trained lawyer and later Professor of Law at Southampton University.

favoured schemes that would train African social welfare workers on African soil.[63] Those who subsequently worked for five years in the field might then be sent to the London School of Economics or to the Jan Hofmeyer School of Social Work in Johannesburg. Dr Richards offered Uganda as a useful model. She reported that rural assistants were attending two-year courses run in Serere and Bukalasa. Also, the Secretary of the Development and Welfare Committee was considering plans for a six-month course for 200 demobilized soldiers who would then be employed as 'rural social workers'.

She believed that similar special training at Makerere was not the answer. Rather, colonies would have to make their own plans for two compelling reasons. Firstly, such a course could not cater for the large number of the more general rural type of welfare worker which was, she believed, now needed. Secondly, there were simply insufficient numbers of potential entrants with adequate secondary education to qualify for specialized training at the level Makerere could offer. In the face of this pressure, senior officials conceded. They pledged a commitment to African welfare training. They assured her that the government was hoping to appoint a welfare officer to each of the larger districts after the war. Marchant insisted that they all recognized the need for African staff trained in social welfare. They would look favourably on social welfare courses at Makerere.

The welfare workers to whom Audrey Richards had given her support became part of Patrick Williams' beleaguered post-war training package. He wanted three new types of training centres as part of an African employment strategy. In addition to the inter-territorial training Centre 'A', a Centre 'B' in Kenya was to train a maximum of 630 ex-service men at any one time, either to find waged employment under rural conditions or to establish themselves in a selected trade. When district development plans earmarked suitable sites, Centres 'D' would form pools of skilled men, partly made up of those trained at Centre 'B' to give them three months of practical instruction with supervision, all of whom would work on government and LNC projects or as contracted labour.[64]

The Jeanes School at Kabete, already taken over by the Army for teacher training, was to be the third type, or Centre 'C'. Here, a maximum of 360 men at any one time would attend one of a number of training courses offered to ex-*askari* with above-average educational qualifications. The Jeanes School was to pioneer a number of new courses in addition to training African clerks for the government or the private sector, and lower primary and primary teachers for the Education Department and Missions. Simple book-keeping and how to run a shop were the

[63] Minutes of a meeting held in the Secretariat 30 August 1944, KNA MAA7/592.

[64] 'Post-War Development, Employment and Training of African Ex-Servicemen', published by the East African Command for the Kenya Central Employment Bureau, 1 October 1945, PRO CO822/118/6.

basis of a three- to six-month trading course. Courses in agriculture, survey techniques, medical and probation work were also suggested. Williams' most novel proposal was courses in Social Welfare and British Legion club management.[65] The Social Welfare course would last a year and was designed for ex-*askari* educated up to Primary VI level. The successful candidate needed a recommendation and a guarantee of employment by their DC, and had to be 'a man of some standing in his community'.[66] Interestingly, married quarters were to be made available only for this category of trainee, evidence that wives were seen as an important asset. Rates of pay were to be from 60 to 90 shillings per month; since they were to be paid by LNCs, rates would vary.

Williams' plans for the Jeanes School as his Centre 'C' did materialize but unfortunately little else did. The eventual record for retraining and re-employment overall was not great. By mid-1946 the African Central Employment Bureau jointly inaugurated by the Civil Reabsorption Board and the Labour Department in 1945 had placed 900 of its 3,500 registrants; the single Native Industrial Training Depot planned for artisan training was only able to take trainees from 1946. Only 2 per cent of demobilized *askari* were either placed by the special labour bureau or completed Jeanes School training (Easterbrook, 1975: 53–7). Centre C or the Jeanes School had the distinct advantage of already functioning as an army education centre which had long enjoyed much support, as we have already seen. A course in social welfare work also materialized.

The prior acceptance of the European Provincial Welfare Officer helped, plus the fact that pressure from Dr Richards forced the Secretariat to consider ways in which certain African men might undertake 'social welfare work' in the Reserves under guidance. In October 1944, the Secretariat agreed that a start should be made 'in a small way by giving African welfare workers training in practical subjects on the Uganda lines'.[67] Libraries were to form part of the Information Rooms which already existed in many Districts, according to officials. These were to be run by the Information Room clerks until trained librarians from Makerere could be obtained. The Demobilization Vote was to cover the cost of African staff: a full-time clerk and a part-time PT Instructor who would be shared with other courses. Fortie Ross was to run the course, assisted by the Adviser on social welfare, Dr Philip, who would arrange lectures by outside technical experts.

It was to be for *askari* primarily and married men were to have

[65] Ibid. For the British Legion course, ex-*askari* had to be selected by the British Legion and appointed to posts before commencing the course; attendance at selected areas of the social welfare course was to be part of their training. See MAA7/859 report of a district meeting of the British Legion, Laikipia Branch 12 December 1945.

[66] 'Post-War Development, Employment and Training'. This is discussed below.

[67] Minutes of a meeting held at the Secretariat, 5 October 1944, chaired by Rennie, Minute 43/44 'Social Welfare', KNA PC/NZA/3/1/570.

preference. The lowest qualification accepted was to be a pass in the Primary School examination and a further educational course in the Army – preferably the Army Education Instructors' Course – or army experience in educational or welfare work.[68] Applications were to be made through the DC who was instructed to select as far as possible men who were married and held some standing in their community. If insufficient suitable ex-servicemen applied for the places, the DC was permitted to allow civilians to take the course with a maximum of 8 civilians being allowed to attend in 1946. Rather meanly, the 50 cents a day allowance for food was not granted to civilians.

The first course for social welfare workers which began in 1946 taught 40 men. The Director of Training's statement of welcome in Swahili tells us a great deal about the conceptual level of communication between a white officer and a black audience. It was felt of sufficient interest to be circulated to all DCs. As the script reveals, the central message put across was that 'time was money'. Williams told the ex-*askari* how their cash allowance was a preparation for life, not a wage: 'It is part of your training to learn how to use it and we will teach you.' The government, he declared, wanted hardworking and honest men of good character to receive this money, who wanted to help themselves. Poor performance and misbehaviour would be met with immediate dismissal. In true Captain Dickson style he challenged them: they had it in their power to bring to themselves and to Africa, the rewards of prosperity – if they followed the school motto – 'Twice as much work in half the time – and first class work'.[69]

There was an important practical element to the course. This was mostly provided by a model information room and house at Wangige's, a market centre in the Kiambu Reserve, selected as a divisional centre. A planned expansion of clinic facilities was to enable health care to be taught at the site. Situated four miles from the Jeanes School, Wangige's was included specifically to give trainees experience in gaining the confidence of ordinary people. The district had an established and active co-operative African Agricultural and General Purposes Committee which offered a focal point for local activity. Hence the centre was considered an excellent model for training in welfare, especially since 'the people are at the present moment more than generally responsive to new ideas for Village Betterment'.[70] It looked like a perfect formula for success. Had no one tried this before?

68 C.R. Philip to CS, 4 December 1945, KNA MAA7/495. He found actual standards to be much higher, some applicants already having taken a course in teacher training.

69 Williams sent a copy to the Social Welfare Adviser, 18 February 1946, KNA MAA7/495.

70 KNA MAA7/495. 'Note on African Social Welfare – Kenya' (undated and unsigned). The successful candidates arrived at Jeanes School on 22 March 1946 where they were to stay until 14 December with a three-week break in August.

The forgotten Jeanes teacher experiment

Adult training for participation in community betterment was not without precedent in Kenya. The Jeanes School teacher of the inter-war era was in fact a preview of what Williams and his supporters were trying to achieve. The school had also taken seriously the provision of some educational expertise for women – as wives of school teachers. Yet when the Colonial Office took up the issue of welfare and women's education in 1939, this seems not to have formed part of their discussions (see Chapter 1). Undoubtedly, the work of the school was further obscured by the war and the interest in women as wives could not compete with the African *askari* as the new man. This illustrates the institutional incoherence of the late colonial state: ill-equipped to comprehend the lessons of the past and unable to make strategic policy decisions based on a reading of its own history. Past lessons were not learnt at this level and the war worsened an already imperfect situation. Ironically, the Jeanes School had been taken over by the army because of the declining success rate in adult education.

Had they looked closely, Williams and Philip would have found a number of crucial problems inherent in the Jeanes School teacher experiment which had important lessons for their own plans. The emergency discussions about the school which took place in the latter part of the 1930s touched upon a number of issues that ought to have been uppermost in the minds of the architects of the ex-*askari* to social-welfare worker formula. First, too much had been expected of the teachers who lacked adequate back-up services. In 1935, the school's principal, T. G. Benson, had told the Colonial Office's Education Advisory Committee just how difficult it was for one Jeanes School teacher to supervise all schools in their vicinity, eight being the average number. Secondly, once released into the field, problems of control quickly surfaced. Basic development work always required co-operation from technical officers, chiefs and the administration, which was difficult for European officers to secure, let alone individual mission-trained African teachers.[71]

In 1935 the fundamental problem inherent in organizing a new structure of trained men to go out into the African villages to instil the acquired wisdoms of agricultural and medical development was obvious. As Benson observed, 'at present the Missionaries, District Officer and other Government officers are concerned in the development of the African; the D.C. has the co-ordinating authority in each area'. His agents were the chiefs' headmen whom he felt bound to support. He had little time for other agents especially if they were not bound to take orders direct from him – the first indication of how inflexible the hierarchy could be. Some felt that Jeanes School teachers were disruptive 'because of their

[71] Minutes of the 64th Meeting of the EAC, 19 December 1935, PRO CO533/461/19.

missionary background'. Benson believed that the majority of rural teachers in elementary village schools 'should be trained for rural community work by courses at the Jeanes School centre together with their wives'. He wanted the Kenyan government to examine the future of the school especially since expenditure had to be reduced to £40 per head, making economies of scale more attractive. They had to have '120 men of first-rate intellectual and moral calibre' to make the system work.

As to salaries, Benson could only offer a messy compromise, reflecting the situation in the field. He suggested that the government should pay the Jeanes teachers, whilst recognizing that this would ensure that the District Education Boards would demand control over them. Benson insisted that supervision should be left in the hands of the missionaries, since the teachers did not feel loyal to the District Officer. There was much for the Advisory Committee to grapple with. It remained divided as to which was more influential: the example of the model community school strategically positioned or the mobile supervisory teachers. One member, Dr Maclean, insisted that the real problem was how the teachers actually functioned after training: their relations with junior department officers, sanitation and agricultural officers, and how they could best work with them. The very progressive nature of their work meant that they did not fall neatly under one administrative branch. They were not simply a branch of the Education Department. Ideally they assisted the administration as a whole and contributed to the general effectiveness of various departments. Dr Maclean could cite a number of success stories in this regard including cases of successful co-operation in Southern Rhodesia, Nyasaland, and the South of the United States.

The Committee's final recommendation, reflecting its overall belief in the Jeanes School teacher programme and ideals, was that, 'for the sake of the community', elementary education might be less important than education directed to 'social welfare' and that efforts towards the latter 'should not be subjected to a less effective type of education'.[72] They all failed to see that the problem to address lay not in the Jeanes School philosophy, but in the way African society and colonial agents interacted and the racial divide which ensured that compassionate motives were translated as overbearing dictates. The decade ended with recourse to using traditional nodes of local authority with the decision to include a course for chiefs, they had the advantage of being less liminal in relation to administrative patronage and promotion, and had more reason to be loyal (King, 1971: 175).

Thus, at a time when its future had never looked more shaky, the Jeanes School was taken over by the army and used as a training centre. The school then slipped into the plans for post-war training and demobilization and ex-*askari* were looked to instead of chiefs as a new variant of the Jeanes

[72] Ibid.

teacher. Instead of being responsible to mission authority, these teachers would be answerable to the administration. The whole process was ambiguous. Debates about how to transmit technical wisdoms for the betterment of the African rural community, and a recognition of the prominence of women in such schemes, were unfortunately lost. The basic forms of betterment were not questioned. Was there any debate about the Jeans school teacher failures in relation to the African social welfare workers? The likes of Captain Dickson of the East African Command had cited the 'idealism' of the Jeanes School method of teacher training; it was what was needed, in order to reach the villages and not just chiefs and headmen via a team of experts versed in mass propaganda techniques. So, here possibly was an attempt to revert to the principles of the early 1920s, using ex-soldiers instead of trained civilians, plus the latest techniques in mass communication.

Part of the explanation of this apparent failure to engage seriously with the lessons of the past lies not just with the interruption of war but also in the struggle to keep the training scheme on the road. Patrick Williams and the new social welfare staff were quickly embroiled in desk-top skirmishes to defend the training schemes they had so lovingly crafted. This made dwelling on past glitches less attractive and less likely. Not everyone shared their vision of ASWWs. Dr Philip's confident assertion that the training of African social welfare workers 'was to receive first and urgent consideration' did not seem to extend very far.[73] The social welfare fraternity first had to try to guarantee that ASWWs would have salaries higher than those for elementary teachers. Philip insisted that the standard required for the trained *askari* was far ahead of the qualifications needed for the latter, which was completion of Standard IV, so that candidates were frequently rejects from primary schools. Unfortunately, the issue of who should actually pay the salaries remained unresolved for it was tied to an important disagreement over who should pay for welfare schemes in general.[74] Funds were needed to pay 40 men for half the month of December 1946, totalling 1500 shillings.

Community centres

Community centres were at the heart of the thinking behind the transformatory role of the trained *askari*, yet Dr Philip had to seek assurance from the CNC that the government would pay for welfare centres,

[73] Record of a conversation between Philip and CNC 23 November 1945, Philip having just returned from completing his social science course. KNA MAA7/495.

[74] Philip to CNC 9 December 1945, KNA MAA7/495 and Note issued entitled 'African Social Welfare, Kenya. 1.Training of African Social Welfare Workers'. (Undated and unsigned but typeset would suggest the Social Welfare Adviser and file position would suggest early 1946), ibid.

information rooms, and European staff housing in Central and Nyanza provinces and some settled areas. 'The question of funds', he insisted, 'for the building of Social Halls, Information Rooms, etc., and particularly whether they should be part L.N.C. and part Government is one for you to decide'.[75] The CNC, however, pushed the responsibility back to the district. This was in line with Lord Hailey's recommendations on social service provision, which undercut the more radical initiatives of the welfare and propaganda wartime enthusiasts. The CNC was adamant that social welfare was 'primarily a matter for local government bodies, and if this is accepted, responsibility for paying these men will fall on the L.N.Cs'.[76] Government would contribute by means of a grant system 'when the relationship between Government and L.N.C. has been finally resolved – at such a rate as to include provision where necessary for these services'. The CNC's reply fudged the issue. The details of paying the salaries would not be finalized until 1946 when he proposed to consult all provincial commissioners about LNC provisions nearer the time the welfare workers were due to complete their course. Dr Philip was left without the assurance he desperately needed to inspire trainees and to attract the 'right men' with firm terms of employment. Men applying for training, he protested, were already concerned about their future prospects.[77] Of course, the decision to consult the PCs held out little hope for the kind of guarantees that Williams believed the trainees ought to be given.

The training package for ex-*askari* also created further disagreements. Trainees were provided with food and accommodation (not clothing) and received a 60 shilling allowance a month, of which 24 shillings was given as a cash payment broken down into 6 shillings per week. Ten shillings was kept aside for the man's family and twenty-six shillings was to cover blankets, clothing and necessary equipment such as books, tools and a bicycle on leaving, payable subject to completion of the course.[78] This had all been carefully worked out by the Director of Training. Yet the scheme had a highly controversial element: a daily cash allowance of 2 shillings. Williams appeared fixated on the idea of teaching the principle of self-sufficiency and responsibility, believing that the army fashion of supplying everything 'has led to young Africans being completely improvident'.[79]

The men who held on to the colony's purse strings were quite appalled. Troughton 'nearly hit the roof' when he learned that the Kenya trainees were receiving such a daily allowance which, at 2 shillings, he considered far too high. This had the unfortunate knock-on effect of putting the Secretary for Finance on full alert lest 'the demobilization and training

[75] Philip to CNC, 9 December 1945, KNA MAA7/495.
[76] CNC to FS, 24 November 1945, ibid.
[77] Williams to FS, 27 November 1945, ibid.
[78] Mundy (ag.FS) to Potter (FS Uganda) 26 March 1946, ibid.
[79] Williams to Philip, 18 February 1946, KNA MAA7/495.

organization might be letting the Kenya Government in for large sums in other directions'. Even Uganda's Financial Secretary was upset enough to take the matter up with the Kenya Government, protesting that the more generous Kenyan allowance was causing difficulties in his colony'.[80] Williams was bitterly disappointed. He insisted that the allowance proposal had been submitted by the Governors in Conference in June 1945 to the Secretariats and the Civil Reabsorption Board. He was adamant that the proposals had been discussed with all Members of the LegCo, the Secretary of State and the men of finance, Surridge and Troughton. In any case they had been published in a pamphlet. Ultimately, all he could do was to criticize the government for changing its mind. As he pointed out 'it was hoped to get a free grant from H.M.G. to cover training on an East African basis and perhaps now that ... the cost of training is to be borne by each Government, people are getting "cold feet"!' Men applying for training, he protested, were already concerned about their future prospects. At the end of the war, it seems that no one wanted to pay for the conversion of the African soldier back into a peacetime army of good citizens despite the clear vision and purpose displayed in the earlier local and metropolitan debates.

However, as the war came to an end, the social welfare training scheme was kept alive by a combination of public fear and insider optimism. Concerns about demobilization ensured that training schemes were not sacrificed to administrative meanness. Throughout 1945, the colony's newspapers reported complaints regarding the government's preparations for the demobilization of ex-*askari*. For example, Eliud Mathu, recently appointed as African member of the LegCo, accused the government of dragging its feet; *askari* believed that information was not reaching them because the authorities knew they would not be able to keep their word; no meeting to discuss African reabsorption had been called. Shirley Cooke had also publicly criticized the `lack of co-ordinated plans' for demobilization. These and other voices raised in complaint nudged the CNC into announcing that the matter of training welfare workers – with which he claimed to be personally very deeply concerned – was in hand. He assured LegCo that a training course would start in April 1946.[81]

By early 1946 plans for the posting of the ASWWs were taking definite shape. Those districts that were to receive European Welfare Officers to help with the demobilization process were to be allocated the first ASWWs. The Governor stressed that funds had to be found for this work to proceed first in Machakos and Kiambu, where the problems of returning *askari* were believed to be most severe. Thirty-four would be available for posting to districts at the beginning of 1947.[82]

[80] Potter to Mundy 20 February 1946 and Mundy to Potter 26 March 1946, ibid.

[81] Note dated 4 March 1946, ibid; Easterbrook, 1975: 38–41.

[82] Williams to Social Welfare Adviser 18 February 1946, KNA MAA7/495; Decisions made at PCs' Meeting, January 1946, KNA MAA7/588.

The scheme also had the support of a handful of district administrators, such as the relatively progressive PC for Nyanza. The problem, however, was that, even in those districts where such support was evident, a lack of local resources held back initial efforts. The kind of commitment pledged by the Governor was clearly not enough. The absence of a helping hand from a central fund was deeply felt. Hunter had registered his personal commitment to the social centre scheme in February 1945 and called for the recruitment of African welfare workers.[83] Significantly it was married ex-*askari* he had in mind, who resembled the trusty yeoman of old: 'such men', he suggested, 'should be the English peasant farmer type, accompanied by their wives if possible ... as he will be practical in his ideas, and more important his standards will be as close to the African standards as possible and thus far more likely to be imitated, than if we recruit Europeans of higher standards, when the gap would be too great'.

In Nyanza, where the colonial mind had not yet broken down under the weight of seemingly intractable problems brought about by the effects of social and economic change, a space was held open for the potential contribution the model African family could make. Hunter had endeavoured to get local construction started in advance, so that facilities and materials would be ready for the returning soldier. But even PC enthusiasm was not enough. In an effort to produce locally the materials needed for the new buildings, Hunter had started up a brick-making scheme with the Divisional Engineer at the Public Works Department. Initial results were not good. The bricks were found to be of poor quality and there appeared to be a general lack of effort, blamed on an excess of cash in the Reserves. A welfare worker, he doggedly believed, could help by stimulating such local schemes in future. He asked for help in the immediate construction of centres. The Divisional Engineer was also supportive. He proposed that, if his Department built the centres, brick-fields or stone quarries could be established at each centre. He would also train local labour in order to leave an established industry for instructors to then supervise.

Nyanza's PC was under pressure from African men to show preparations for demobilization. Africans were impatient, he warned, to learn what form the much talked about post-war plans would take. He had managed to refrain from publicizing plans, fearful that, if they did not materialize, he would have to deal with accusations of a breach of faith; Africans had 'taken part in discussion on these plans and are anxious to know something about them'.[84]

Although the scheme to retrain *askari* for a developmental and good citizenship role in rural areas did get off the ground, it soon emerged as a fairly skeletal set-up which was too dependent not only upon local goodwill

[83] Hunter to CS 28 February 1945, KNA MAA7/588.

[84] Ibid., pp. 1–2.

but also on a hotch-potch of financial sources. The obvious tension in areas like Nyanza was not to be relieved via central funding for social centres, so local energies and enterprise were constrained. Responsibility for building the social centres and living quarters was to remain with the PCs. Mortimer (Member for Health and Local Government) informed the administration that information rooms should be urgently built during 1946. LNCs were 'invited to construct' 34 rooms at a cost of £300 each inclusive of a house for the ASWW, and individual proposals were to be submitted to the Social Welfare Adviser for approval.[85] Each LNC was instructed to include in its 1947 draft Estimates necessary provision for the salaries of all Welfare Workers falling within their jurisdiction. Half the capital cost was to be borne by the LNC and a sum not exceeding £150 was to be reimbursed from Central Government funds, which in turn came from the Development and Reconstruction Authority 1946 Estimates. The 34 information rooms were to be installed as follows:

Central Province:	Machakos	4	*Nyanza Province:*	North Kavirondo	6
	Kiambu	4		South Kavirondo	6
	Fort Hall	2		Central Kavirondo	4
	Embu	2			16
	Nyeri	1			
	Meru	1			
		14			
Rift Valley Province:	Nandi	1	*Coast Province:*	Digo	1
	Elgeyo-Marakwet	1		Teita	1
		2			2
	Total	**34**			

Senior officials, it seems, were happy with the set-up and also hopeful that this was the way forward. Mortimer reported with optimism that the municipal authorities and District Councils were in the main keen to proceed with the construction of social centres for Africans; subject to local variation, they included information rooms, libraries, recreation rooms, public assembly rooms and a canteen for the sale of liquor. He could confidently cite a number of projects that were already under way and supported by various joint funding schemes. Nakuru District Council had granted £250 for a centre to get started at Dundori. In addition, £250 had come from the Central Native Trust Fund and £200 from the local Farmers' Association. Meanwhile Mombasa Municipal Board were

[85] Circular Letter No.102 3 July 1946 from the Member for Health and Local Government (Mortimer) to all PCs, officers in charge, and extra provincial districts, with sufficient copies for DCs, KNA MAA7/588.

building a social centre at a cost of £17,000, an amount which Mortimer suggested was more than the beer profits could support, thus indicating the level of municipal support.[86]

Tentative agreements appeared to emerge about social centres for Africans in the Settled Areas. Capital costs of construction were to be shared equally between government and the District Council which would actually build them. The deal was that the government would advance the District Council's share of the capital cost as an interest-bearing loan, with profits or losses on recurrent expenses to be shared equally between them. Mortimer was convinced that, in view of the sums of money required, a request could justifiably be made to the Secretary of State for a package of loans and grants from the Colonial Development and Welfare Vote. He believed he had reason to be optimistic since £50,000 had been granted to the Tanganyika Government for Social Centres at district headquarters and in selected rural areas. LNCs were to be given assistance in similar schemes, whilst the construction of social centres within urban African Housing Schemes could be funded by grants and loans from the Housing Fund created by the 1943 Housing Ordinance. For example, the Social Centre at the Makongeni Housing Scheme in Nairobi was to be financed by the Housing Fund, consisting of a loan and grant from the Colonial Development and Welfare Vote, and half by the Municipal Beer Profits Fund. The Colonial Office were pushing for such centres to be provided since a 'scheme' deemed eligible for funding as defined by the Ordinance included a recreation centre, an addition which the Secretary of State had emphasized should be included.[87] In practice the social welfare centre was not going to be so easily inserted into the Settled Areas.

Events in Kericho township illustrate the weakness in the colonial welfare project as it was applied, watered down and restrained by racially divided communities. In June 1945, the District Committee in Kericho agreed, in principle, that, provided sufficient land remained for normal township development and the Township Committees were consulted, land for social centres in Kericho and Chemagel could be allocated. The PC had agreed that 50 acres might suffice rather than the 200-acre site first suggested. But Kericho's DC objected. He insisted that, in future, others should bear this responsibility, as 'any further development on these lines might well be undertaken by the tea companies themselves who will be the biggest users of such amenities'.[88]

Even more ominous was Mortimer's verdict. He did not see the necessity for a centre in Kericho, refusing to treat its inhabitants as settled. The bulk of the population, he argued, was either in the Native Land Unit 'which should have its own provision without attracting natives unnecessarily into the Township', or lived on the tea estates. The latter

[86] Mortimer to Chairman of DARA 8 February 1946, KNA MAA7/859.
[87] Ibid., pp. 1–2.
[88] DC (Kericho) to PC (Nyanza) 25 June 1945, KNA MAA7/528.

should provide their own Welfare Centres, which he said they mostly did.[89] In addition, he felt that Chemagel Township was too small to provide 50 acres. Despite the divergence of opinion as to what welfare should consist of and who should pay, his Council was of the opinion that any social welfare activities, financed from public funds, should be administered and controlled by the established local authorities and no one else. Clearly, in this situation, the notion of social welfare was going to be yet more difficult to insert without a rural African context to fall back upon. As J.B. Thomson, Clerk to the Trans Nzoia Council, noted, there was 'a considerable difference between providing welfare services in towns and in rural areas'.[90] Municipal welfare in large towns was largely financed by beer shops. In rural areas where the labouring poor lived and worked on European estates, social centres for African farm workers could only be opened at week-ends and would have to compete with home-brewed *tembo*. In the absence of a high proportion of rate-payers, support for welfare was lukewarm. Opponents also argued that making such a financial commitment was a gamble: it could not be expected that 'rural centres will provide the financial means for their own growth, nor with their profits cover to any extent the maintenance costs'.[91] Would workers walk the long distances to make use of halls?

The attitude of the Secretariat was becoming distinctly lukewarm in private as the Second World War drew to a close. The enthusiasm in London for centres and the hopes for the retrained *askari* were cut down to size by local constraints. In September 1945, Marchant, the CNC, confided to the Chief Secretary, Rennie, that the community centre model being peddled by the Colonial Office was not generally suitable for colonial conditions except possibly in Nairobi, and that such social services were properly the function of local government bodies.[92] Charity organizations were looked to instead. He suggested that the CO papers should be sent to Mrs Rennie, Chairman of the Youth Council.

However, the issue did begin to draw in other members of the administration for guidance. Marchant thought it was time to get information about welfare from the Municipal Native Affairs Officer, Thomas Askwith. He was later found to be in support of community centres and pointed out that this was on the lines of what was already being done in Nairobi. However, senior government ministers considered that they were doing rather well and had gone quite far, possibly far enough. The Colonial Office was to be told that there had been much discussion on welfare subjects generally. Although they conceded that little had actually been done beyond the formation of the Youth Council and the establishment of

89 Mortimer to CS, 14 July 1945, ibid.

90 Note on 'African Welfare as a District Council Activity', J.B. Thomson, 27 June 1945, sent to all other councils in the province, p. 1., KNA MAA7/859.

91 Ibid., p. 2.

92 CNC to CS, September 1945, KNA MAA7/494.

the Pumwani Centre for Africans, the foundations were being laid, they insisted, for welfare work in the future. Just how insecure these foundations were in the immediate post-war period will be the subject of the next chapter.

Conclusion

Thus, whereas the welfare discussions about villages and African families set out in the previous chapter failed to produce much in the way of action, the *askari* did. The modest and incomplete Welfare Organization is proof of this. As we have seen, the *askari* factor in wartime planning gave Kenya a Welfare Organization and enabled the colony to fall into line with the Colonial Office's earlier recommendations. Suppport from a wide range of metropolitan interest groups had helped, notably from welfare experts and the discipline of anthropology. Social welfare appeared as an individual item under the General Staff section of the Administration budget in official estimates of revenue spending planned for 1947, and had a total budget of £5,021.[93] The European staff for social welfare consisted of one adviser, one officer and four female officers in Nairobi. Significantly for the future, the CROs who were engaged in welfare work were funded by the £186,960 allocation for Demobilization, Reabsorption and Training.[94]

Retrained soldiers playing a part in the 'second colonial occupation' was a likely scenario for a number of reasons. *Askari* were the heroes of metropolitan post-war imaginings. That Africans were increasingly unable to look after themselves and migration to towns was creating unsavoury environments, now floated around the imperial consciousness. The duty to bring scientific and technological wisdoms to bear upon African rural poverty was the unifying thread running through variations on a similar theme. The shared base-line of development centred upon how to reorganize agriculture and stop soil erosion; how to make families healthier, and make them live in villages and be less poor; and how to reorientate self-discipline along these lines. For metropolitan experts who criss-crossed the boundaries of Empire, the *askari* encapsulated the dream of a post-war army of energizers carrying out a colonial translation of metropolitan self-financing welfare and development, circumventing the scenario of financial liability. He was the link between the Beveridge model of welfare based on individuals contributing to their own coping strategies and state interventionism through levers of control.

[93] 5. Administration – General Staff, p. 45 in 'Estimates of Revenue and Expenditure of the Colony and Protectorate of Kenya and of the Development and Reconstruction Authority for the Year 1947' (Colony and Protectorate, Nairobi), passed by the Legislative Council, 5 February 1947.

[94] Ibid., War Expenditure – Civil, p. 72.

Secondly, putting former soldiers into government appealed to the local modernizers in Kenya. Since the majority of Africans were believed to be poor and so was the state, the burden of lifting them out of their poverty had to be shoved back on to the LNCs and on to themselves: the only way to enhance social conditions was to find ways to improve the ability of their own communities to look after themselves in rural areas and to stop the drift to the towns. Experts in propaganda techniques, educationalists and departmental staff increasingly believed that the DC and chief arrangement was no longer adequate to stem the perceived malaise of African society: the crisis of imperial administration was also a crisis in African society. They had found little joy in breaking the stranglehold of the administration. The *askari* was potentially one of the more radical aspects of the 'second colonial occupation' since he circumvented the indirect rule approach which was back in favour among those who preferred a revival of traditional patterns of rule.

Yet the retrained *askari* could also appeal to conservative minds. Not only had he been trained and disciplined, but he also fitted into a rural-centric solution. Senior administrators expected another post-war slump. Nairobi and urbanization now offered no solutions to rural problems: they were the embodiment of rural failure. Although less enthusiastic, many district administrators were keen that disciplined *askari* should return home to help raise standards of living, working either as labourers on development schemes, as civilian sergeant-majors or as traders and craftsmen. Patriarchy had a new champion. Well fed and nicely toned, the *askari* were an obvious and the only clear target group for reintegration as a rural task force.

Askari certainly seemed to have behaved in the hoped-for fashion on their immediate return. Homecoming absorbed attention. As the KCA petitioners had hinted at, what African men wanted was the restoration of their patriarchal position at the local level. Immediate inducements given to the ex-*askari*, especially where they were drawn from poorer families, shored up their fragile domestic base which was enough to satisfy them in the short term. In this way, they were like their British counterparts: 'interested in improved opportunities in their home society; and that was still largely encapsulated by the local level... And at this level there appears to have been a remarkable revival in the integrative power of the colonial system.' It was a sign of the success still to come from a re-working of the administrative relationship between European and African men when they each appeared to be offering what the other wanted.[95] However, as local conditions deteriorated, the debates about the right to freedom from a foreign power – so prevalent in war propaganda – would make former *askari* active nationalists.

95 See Lonsdale, 1975b: xv. However, according to Easterbrook, the view that demobilization was 'remarkably smooth' failed to take into account the impact ex-*askari* had upon the African community which by the 1950s was to promote significant change (Easterbrook, 1975: 57).

Finally, finding jobs for *askari* was a worthy project in the eyes of many of their fellow white soldiers. European men caught up in the administration of war, such as Patrick Williams and Captain Dickson, felt they had dealt with Africans in new ways. Homo-socialization through combat could have positive effects on race relations. According to former soldiers, men serving with the Forces came to regard their *askari* not as natives, but as African men, who had matured under their paternal guidance; no longer men-in-waiting but able to rise to the challenges given them. In their writings they dropped terms like 'colonial' and 'native' for European and African, and Kenya as nation. They confidently believed that, if *askari* were given examples and aims, they would understand, which would make others obey. They had submitted to the same discipline, had become more 'like us', and could be dispatched to make others the same without supervision. However, this was an area where self-congratulation, wishful thinking and retrospective sentimentality could get to work. The view that 'we, who had been in the war saw the African as an individual with whom we had shared much hardship, and above all, much comradeship. The colonial relationship of governing and subject races had been eroded' was perhaps not a view that all African soldiers might have agreed with, let alone all whites.[96]

The *askari* factor helped the Welfare Organization come into being with a distinct African element. The price was that welfare as a means of energizing African communities became more of a masculine idea of good citizenship, sportsmanship and being an honest chap. The warning given by the Superintendent of Dagoretti Approved School, D.C. Cameron, slipped into the background. Responding in 1945 to Pat Williams' proposals for a network of camps for male African adolescents as a substitute for the discipline of tribe, Cameron insisted that:

> To endeavour to teach a better standard of living for the African man without including any propaganda or training for the African woman would seem to me to be a short-sighted policy, for not until the women are included can any form of training have a widespread effect. We surely want to improve the home standard. Most of the juvenile delinquency of today is caused through bad homes and lack of parental control.[97]

This was not to say that the education of women and their role as home-makers were absent. For example, publications from the Associated Country Women of the World based in London penetrated the Defence Ministry about the benefits of Home Demonstration Agents for the rural community who ran clubs which arranged lectures by outside specialists, as pioneered in the USA.[98] Such a notion was clearly present in plans to extend female education.

[96] Blundell, 1994: 85. Blundell was involved in the demobilization process.
[97] Cameron to Chief Secretary, 5 June 1945, KNA/PC/NZA/4/5/12.
[98] *The Country Woman – Home Demonstration*, July 1944, KNA/DEF/10/68.

Official wartime proposals did paid homage to the view that 'the social implications of allowing too great a time lag between the education of boys and girls are serious'.[99] In a tone and style that now sounds irritatingly patronizing, supporters of advancing provisions for women put forward the view that 'in parts of the Empire more educationally advanced, the best native leaders have been considerably aided by the fine types of women whom many of them have married'. Officially, the training of African girls was to 'give the majority preparation for marriage and skill in home crafts' – as it was in Britain at the time – although a 'small but increasing number should be equipped for careers'. Post-war plans included three provincial training centres for African women, a Froebel Training College and Hostel for European Women in Nairobi, a hostel for European Women at the Egerton School, and a training college for Indian women. From this emerged a scheme to create three interdenominational centres to train African women as elementary school teachers so that they could then educate the women and children. Nyanza, Rift Valley and Central Provinces were earmarked for training centres staffed by specialists in domestic science, physical training and health work.[100] Realizing that traditional communities did not exist in towns and that educated men required matching companionship, African women were seen as a stabilizing agent in the context of change: since 'women are of social and economic importance ... the individual woman, in order to live fully, must see herself not only as an acquisitive individual but as a contributing member of a group. Women's and girls' work must therefore be planned on a community basis.'

However, the overall trend was profoundly negative. Unlike the *askari* who offered the possibility of immediate action, women were less accessible to the state and became less so in relation to men. Disadvantaged by acknowledged past neglect, 'the lag in African female education' was explained by the 'fact that so small a number of European women were able to participate in African affairs in early days'. Hence the new concern to first provide training for European women in 'home and health-craft' and modern secondary courses. The training of African women was left to the Education Department's more traditional curriculum, to missionaries and to the ad hoc efforts of individual women. Although it was a vision of African women that reduced them to a collective mass more thoroughly than African men, wartime plans for African men also sprang from efforts in social engineering. The main difference was that plans for educating and using African women were not woven into wartime strategies for betterment to the same degree as they were for men.

Returning *askari* had other issues to grapple with on their return. They

[99] 'Application for Assistance from the Colonial Development Fund – Education of Women and Girls in Kenya Colony', ibid.

[100] Education of Women and Girls in Kenya' (C.& P. Kenya) undated, 'Elementary Teacher Training and Village Education', pp. 3–4, KNA/DEF/10/68.

had fought hard, had lived cheek by jowl with Europeans and had been given new dreams and old promises. Would the rhetoric of war hold up to the reality of peace? At the end of 1945, *askari* coming home by train stepped down on to the platform at Nairobi station to find a surprise reception for returning soldiers. They could see bunting, cups of hot tea and a table of cakes. To their dismay, it was for Europeans only.[101]

[101] Conversation with John Nottingham (ex district administrator, Kenya), Cambridge, 12 April 1998.

Five

To 'Work Like a Nigger' or 'Shirk Like an African'

White Opposition to Social Welfare 1946–8

This chapter looks at the initial outcome of attempts at state-building in Kenya in relation to providing a government welfare service for Africans. As the previous chapter illustrated, the new Welfare Organization was by no means in a secure position after the end of the Second World War. In 1946, the Colonial Office appeared to offer a lifeline in the form of a clear endorsement of social welfare. Yet London and Nairobi diverged in their visions, illustrating the poor structure of communication as well as the lack of agreement within even a single and by no means extensive area of government. The local view was forged from a particular blend of wartime and rural experience: a belief in the transformatory power of propaganda and the debilitating effects of rural poverty. Unfortunately, the decision to concentrate on adult education did not yield any great or immediate success. Resources were scarce, post-war issues far more controversial. African journalists refused to take the bait and the kind of interdepartmental co-operation needed to circumvent these constraints could not be conjured up by such a marginal outfit as social welfare. Then adding to the gloom, white opinion turned vehemently against both the theory and the practice of the organization. The colony's most influential European newspaper, followed by angry settler farmers, the local head of state – the Governor, Sir Philip Mitchell – and missionaries, all volunteered a set of damning criticisms. Welfare challenged their labour relations and smacked too much of socialist Britain. The organization appeared to be collapsing under the strain of settler rancour but also administrative failure, both combining to ensure that Kenya lagged further behind its East African neighbours and that its welfare organization faced a slow, painful destruction.

Introduction

By the end of the 1945, the time for talk and planning was over. Peace had arrived and with it the beginning of a new epoch. Carrying forward clear expectations and obvious relief was a generation settling back into normal working and living conditions, alongside those barely touched by five years of turmoil. For both these camps in Kenya, that normality was underpinned by a racially skewed social, political and economic system which overwhelmingly privileged whites over blacks. Yet, if the superstructure had survived virtually intact, its internal dimensions had been transformed: the immediate effect of the war was to complicate group identities. European settlers, African peoples and colonial officials were each increasingly made up of divergent factions. Most white males of middle age and above had been asked to stay in Kenya and manage agricultural production for the war effort. Farmers who had done well out of the material demands of war were joined by demobilized younger officers returning from billet rooms and battle fronts and a different generation of men and women less parochial in outlook and in search of fulfilling employment.

As always, new arrivals came and stayed in 1945. Some came to work and profit, some to escape socialist Britain, lured by the promise of access to cheap domestic help. Some still came to shoot, fish and sleep around. Others yielded to the standard imperial role-playing fantasy centred upon leaving home to live as pioneering saviours of a land where time had begun but then forgot. Some wanted to start a new life to escape the memories of war. Some had simply fallen in love with the landscape, finding themselves seduced by the fecundity of nature or the magic of the mountains. Among the passengers on the same troop ship sailing to Mombasa in February 1947 was a young woman wanting work and to live with her family. Cloda Alison had spent four demanding years in the WAAF. When she arrived she found 'a man's country' that was harsh and she took a while to find her place. She also found love and a husband but any romance with life in the colony was destined to be shortlived. Five years later, her mother would be found in a pool of blood, slashed to death in the family's house, whilst her step-father was buried alive facing the magic mountain, Mount Kenya. A former soldier James Stapleton was also on board ship with his family. Like many others, the war had left him unsettled. He had raised the £1,500 to satisfy the board of selection for the colony's settlement scheme. White hopes were high that 500 British ex-servicemen of the right type could be enticed to make Kenya their home.[1] One high-profile new arrival was the Duke of Manchester who embodied the new wave of pioneer spirit in post-war Kenya.

The end of the war and the new arrivals produced a surge of energy and optimism among the white population. The relief of simply 'coming home' and the assurance that Kenya's destiny was now on track following the dark days of the Depression were a legacy of the war. Had the colony not shown that it was a pivotal part of the Empire and that East African agricultural output more than justified whites in Africa? And the labour of Italian prisoners of war had produced a new tarmac road between Nairobi

[1] Interview with Cloda Alison, Cork, Ireland, 21–22 May 1996. Their cook also lost his life in this notorious Mau Mau attack; Stapleton, 1956: 13; Lipscomb, 1956: ch.VII 'Post War Settlement'.

and Naivasha that followed the same route across the Rift Valley floor which fifty years before had been an elephant trail followed by Captain Macdonald. But the war effort also left scars, a residual uneasiness and feelings of resentment. Harold Macmillan had ensured that London had rebuffed a white settler wartime initiative to secure support for the self-government of the White Highlands. Their new Governor, Sir Philip Mitchell, had been appointed to the post in 1944 in order to re-assert metropolitan authority over settler politicians in particular. Yet had they not fed hundreds of prisoners of war and Ethiopian evacuees? This had generated the sense of being a dumping ground for a huge problem not of their making. The shortage of protein in the colony had resulted in the systematic slaughter of game. The Laikipia plains around Rumuruti and towards Nanyuki had allegedly lost much of their wildlife, particularly zebra, kongoni, Grant's gazelle and topi. The massive effort involved in reorienting production for the war, such as harvesting sisal and pyrethrum for the Americans, again showed settlers how diminutive they could be to outside forces. The feeling of emasculation brought about by a peace that was lost because 'the spiv was king' would grow in the post-war years (Best, 1979: chs 9 and 10; Lipscomb, 1956: ch. VI).

The same range of experiences also existed for Africans, with the added gradation of tribal complexion; there were more returning Kamba soldiers and prospering Kikuyu farmers. African families found themselves with more taxes to pay, more mouths to fill, more boys to educate. Confidence might well have been high among Europeans – they had after all shown their collaborative value – but it was hardly so among Africans. Rising populations, congested reserves and low incomes were not easily offset, even for those able to test out the opportunities to be had from the town or the comfort of the Christian gospel. The countryside was not immune from the negative effects of inflation and a shortage of goods.[2] Yet, for the first time in the colony's short history, Nairobi markets were places where African women could now be found trading in ever increasing numbers. Poverty and racial discrimination weighed heavily upon urban Africa. Muga Gicaru, for example, went to Nairobi to escape the restrictions of the Reserves. He found he could barely exist on his weekly wage and could eat only one meal a day usually in 'Burma' market:

> This was situated on a piece of waste land, where a number of Africans, mostly ex-soldiers, had set up stalls. I have seen people eat food in dirty places but I hope never to see anyone eat in such a filthy place. The place had no sanitation at all, and all water had to be fetched in a bucket from a quarter of a mile away... The settlers did not at all like the idea of Africans supporting themselves by trade at a time when the farms wanted labour. One night the market was burned down and the

[2] For the best summary of the effects of the Second World War on Africa, see Rathbone and Killingray, 1986, esp. 'Introduction'.

stall-holders had all their goods destroyed. No one could understand how the fire had started, for we knew that the 'Burma' market was one of the most orderly places in the city. (Gicaru, 1958: 145)

Another son intent on coming home after the war was Jomo Kenyatta, destined to be the leading spokesman for the Kikuyu. He left Britain to return to Kenya at the end of 1946. He too had done his bit for the war, working as a farm labourer in Storrington in England. A regular at the White Horse public house, he was nicknamed Jumbo. This, even more than his involvement with the Pan-African movement, may have shaped his thinking. He had helped Kwame Nkrumah organize a Pan-African Congress meeting in Manchester, but, more offensive perhaps to white Kenyans, was his marriage in 1942 to an English governess, Edna Clarke. His decision to leave her and their son for Kenya, although their reunion was always understood as a future reality between the couple, would be manipulated as further evidence of his untrustworthy and dastardly character. His Pan-Africanist involvement enabled him to make discursive connections between nationalism in exile and home-grown Kikuyu politics; in 1945, the International African Service Bureau published his pamphlet, *Kenya: Land of Conflict.*

The stay in Britain had probably saved Kenyatta from arrest, for the time being. The Kikuyu Central Association was outlawed at the beginning of the war and its leadership arrested until their release in 1943; there was no hard evidence to suggest that they were in touch with Italian Fascist groups, it was just one of the allegations they faced. The KCA, once easily pigeonholed by colonial officials as the colony's only powerful African political organization made up of reactionary Kikuyu elite, was to share the political stage with another organization following the war. The Kenya Africa Union was founded in 1944 to give form to a more pan-tribal movement for freedom, known to be achieving more success in West African colonies such as the Gold Coast. It was Kenya's first nationalist party. Ambition, experience and a sense of mission combined to push Kenyatta to become President of the KAU in 1947, ensuring that it became a Kikuyu-dominated organization committed to African freedom. Now the colony had an organizational superstructure in which the imported rhetoric of nationalism combined with a local grievance and agenda: whites off the best land. The call for freedom from colonial rule among young nationalists would not be silenced easily (see Berman and Lonsdale, forthcoming; Best, 1979: 158).

Yet, as Keyatta found on his return, the African and Kikuyu political landscape had become much more complex. With population levels increasing and demobilized soldiers returning home looking for work, many moderately resourced and poor men found their expected lifestyle of rearing goats, growing maize, supporting a family and upholding their communities thwarted. Richer farmers were not helping them out. It became more obvious that the loss of land and traditional rights to Europeans was the cause of their plight. Meanwhile, a growing rump of successful Kikuyu farmers now challenged the settler line that they were bad farmers because goats ring-barked trees and pulled grass out at the roots and they wasted the land on growing maize. They could argue that bench terracing was being carried out; racial restrictions prevented them from growing certain cash crops, and it was simply the shortage of arable land that was holding them back. They resented the way in which the colonial state had abandoned them in favour of an alliance with settlers and elders which squeezed them out. Kenyatta's conservative and elitist views were grounded in solutions that drew on an elder's view of what was best for Kikuyuland and sat uneasily with many of the Kikuyu supporters whose life experience was very diffierent. Over half of all Africans living in Nairobi were Kikuyu, as were two-thirds of the squatter communities on white settler land.

Officials too were not the same as their pre-war counterparts. There were more of them; some had fought alongside Africans as well as other Europeans; many brought in new specialisms as well as keen enthusiasm, such as the demobilization officers discussed in the previous chapter. One new arrival was George Hampson who had joined the Colonial Service in 1946. He was known as one of Ralph Furse's men (see Kirk-Greene, 1999: ch. 3). Sir Ralph Furse had initiated a new attitude toward training and recruitment for the Colonial Office during the war. He speeded up the recruitment of officers from outside public schools and, with admiring glances at French achievements, set up training that paid more attention to practical skills, public relations and the 'artistic and spiritual background of the people'.[3] Indeed, Hampson attended the first ever systematic Training Course for colonial officials on leave, held at Cambridge University. Hampson had already been to East Africa as a result of his wartime army service. When the war ended, he had resumed his university education at St Catherine's College, Cambridge where his tutors generally encouraged entry into the overseas civil service. They had an easy task with Hampson. He already had a keenness for adventure and for life, traits instilled in him by his sober and conscientious grammar school masters, the generation that had escaped the 1914–18 slaughter and who were thus especially mindful of repaying a debt to society. His first posting was to be to Northern Frontier Province. Kenya was not a popular posting at the time because of the presence of settlers. Although glad to return to the colony having felt its charm during the war, Hampson was not only of lower middle-class stock but he was of a generation that did not go to Kenya to fight another war.[4]

[3] 'An inquiry into the system of training the Colonial Service with suggestions for its reform to meet post-war conditions': memorandum by Sir R. Furse, 27 February 1943. PRO CO877/22/16. Extract reprinted in Ashton and Stockwell, 1996: 27–39.

[4] Interview with George Hampson, Tunbridge Wells, 20 June 1996.

More surface cohesion came from the imperial will to power in the form of an ideology and state structure that underpinned the 'second colonial occupation' (Low and Lonsdale, 1976: 12–16). Numbers of administrative officers increased from 117 to 213 between 1945 and 1957. State intervention had a strong local as well as a metropolitan appeal. From the vantage point of the Colonial Office, as we have already seen, war brought a new commitment to state intervention both as a sound principle of modern government over which they had more control, and as an economic necessity now that Africa looked like assuming the main mantle of formal empire, following the loosening of ties in the Far East and India. From the perspective of the field administration, more officers meant more opportunity for controlling the trend towards the erosion of authority held by chiefs and elders, and for holding back selfish entrepreneurs and disruptive politicians. Consequently, there was little incentive to remove the whole range of wartime controls, production boards and pricing mechanisms. The increased levels of economic intervention ushered in by the war were set to continue. Officials were keen to impose what they regarded as better crops, better cattle and better farming practices in order to raise productivity and standards of living. As a result chiefs, headmen and District Officers found themselves under pressure to impose these dictates which in turn increased local resentment and protest against them. By the end of the 1940s, as a result of official intervention and goading 'Africans were now finding themselves governed as never before' (ibid.).

No money, no staff, no consensus

Highly symbolic of the administrative changes wrought by the war was the addition of a small department dealing with welfare to the central government of the colony. Immediately it came into being in 1946, the fledging Welfare Organization was dogged by a number of barriers to effecting its mission, barriers which suggest that the pathology of the late colonial state in Kenya was deepening. First and foremost, the forces which backed social welfare both in Nairobi and at the Colonial Office did not speak with one voice against the forces which opposed it. All too soon this state of affairs was to prove farcical, if not disastrous. Dr Philip, the colony's social welfare adviser, immediately found himself contemplating a future in which only uncertainty could be guaranteed. Most serious by any standards was the absence of funding earmarked for a corpus of European welfare staff stationed in each district, within the financial estimates for the following year. This omission was flanked by other gestures suggesting that nothing less than a wall of scepticism garrisoned the government. The Secretariat swiftly rejected Philip's proposal that they should install an officer who would organize scouting, guiding and similar youth movements in the colony. Such an officer was considered unnecessary.

This decision contrasted with the response in Uganda to a similar request. Kampala's officials had agreed to appoint such an officer whilst Nairobi's top brass remained steadfastly opposed, even refusing to accommodate the ardent pleas from a number of well-known local figures. The Bishop of Mombasa had written to the government in the strongest terms, stressing the value of scouting for promoting 'good citizenship, self-discipline, self-reliance and the recognition and inculcation of high moral and spiritual values'. Likewise, Grace Wilkinson, Commissioner of the Girl Guides Association in Kenya, argued the same but for girls. Guiding, she insisted, could make a very real contribution to 'the advancement of African womanhood', but only if carefully supervised. Without strict control over the training of teachers, she warned, African guide companies might well become 'a source of actual danger and embarrassment'.[5] These protestations were to no avail, for no such officer was appointed. Kenya's tendency for conservatism and sensitivity to settler criticism shone through.

That such a gloomy scenario from the Welfare Organization's perspective had developed so soon after the duties of the then fictitious Social Welfare officer had been severely pruned by the district administration (moreover, whilst Dr Philip was away in South Africa) might well have sunk morale beyond easy retrieval. However, Philip was a man of reputation and no stranger to grappling with seemingly overwhelming tasks. His apprenticeship with the former Director of the Medical Services, the eccentric Dr Paterson, a keen Labour supporter, had prepared him well. One of Paterson's pet projects had been to eradicate parasitic infestations in Africans, which he blamed for their alleged bouts of lethargy. He chose Dr Philip to travel throughout the colony to make a preliminary survey so that an anti-hook worm campaign could be mounted. It was a wise choice according to a contemporary, for Philip then toured the country 'for all the world like an evangelist preaching elementary sanitation', being 'an exceptional man with a gift for oratory and wide knowledge of Swahili'. For his herculean labours he was awarded an MBE (Carman, 1976: 128–30). With the arrival in the colony in 1946 of a Colonial Office circular from the Social Welfare Advisory Committee setting out a rationale and guidelines on social welfare, Dr Philip began once more to beat a forward path through lonely and unfamiliar terrain.

It was lonely because the Colonial Office's advisory committee in London failed to come to his rescue. After almost three years of deliberation, the social welfare experts serving on the advisory panel had felt they were ready to circulate a general set of guidelines for colonial governments to put into practice, illustrating the slow pace of bureaucratic ritual which was particularly pronounced within a new structure.[6] It was first published

[5] CS to Philip, 17 June 1946, KNA CD5/269.

[6] Colonial Office Memo No.11 'Social Welfare in the Colonies'. Dispatched 22 September 1945, covering letter from G.H. Hall, KNA MAA7/585. See discussion in Chapter 1 for CO origins of this CSWAC publication.

in September 1945 and later reissued in 1946. It was strikingly based on metropolitan solutions, and was more than ever before inclusive in its approach to African society, following Margery Perham's conscience-steering after the fall of Singapore. The experts on the committee had been sensitive enough to the terrain they were entering to see the necessity for a restatement of the basic rationale for social welfare, as being part of the mainstream duties of colonial government. They established the course of recent developments at home as offering a viable and appropriate model of government for the colonies. Social services in Britain had expanded in the previous forty years, they explained; the government had recognized the importance of the well-being of the community as an 'organic whole', and had encouraged the interaction of voluntary effort with public administration.[7] This required a statement about the role of a colonial government. Indeed, government as a concept was defined as 'the organ of the community' and, illustrating the influence of ideas about universal state provision, that government must accept responsibility for education including adult education.

The importance of building up the community began to be given prominence. Experts argued that intervention to save the community was sorely needed because traditional communal obligation in Africa was now in decay. This was similar to anxieties about the erosion of community in Britain. Indeed, the Labour Party had built its post-war reconstruction plan around the idealistic view that a more responsible society could be achieved through state support of, even the creation of, community. What had troubled the likes of Sir Stafford Cripps and Aneurin Bevan in particular were the city slums which war had brought into prominence. Poverty, poor houses and a policy of deliberate segregation had resulted in 'castrated communities', according to Bevan (Fielding et al., 1995; esp. ch. 5).

The view of African society metropolitan experts on social welfare now offered was not that different. The memorandum contained an abstract analysis punctuated with references to turbulent change and dangerous voids, since the 'supernatural sanctions' which enforced traditional moral codes within small kinship units had ceased to operate in rural areas most affected by waged labour, and where large mixed communities had developed in towns. Perceiving a state of rapid detribalization, Colonial Office advisers feared that rampant individualism would replace the practice of social obligation believed to underpin traditional rural life. The immediate task for the colonies was thus deemed to be to try to re-cast 'a self-conscious and self-respecting community'. Hence social welfare was defined as 'a community effort [which] must be developed within the community'. What this philosophy illustrates is the way in which it was predicated upon a view of Merrie Africa that lived in the imagination – a

[7] CO Memo 'Social Welfare in the Colonies', p. 1, ibid.

benign, caring and sharing place which corresponded to similar myths about olde England. Welfare as a metropolitan concept of engineering communities and propping up systems at their point of breakdown left little space for a discussion on the barriers of racial suspicion and African poverty. The Colonial Office's plan rested on the assumption that colonial states could enlist the co-operation of the people themselves, partly because social welfare services were to be staffed by 'members of the community they serve': the emphasis was on the givers, on rational governmental solutions, rather than on the receivers.

Unsurprisingly then, the recommendations made about practical institution-building mirrored metropolitan solutions. Experts wanted a specialist social welfare machine to be put in place now in each colony. A central organization with an adviser in each colony was to employ specialist social welfare officers to bring other countries' technical experience to bear on 'similar [problems] in the colonial sphere'. Services to correct or support needy minorities replicated services offered at home. A subsequent SWAC memo sent to all colonies in February 1946 on recruitment and training of welfare workers also reflected this tendency. Family casework, the care of the sick, treating delinquency, and the 'special moral supervision' of women and girls indicated the kind of areas which welfare workers were supposed to focus upon.

The range of functions expected of specialist social welfare officers was remarkable. They must promote community life and culture. They must help the administration and technical departments in aspects of their work with a bearing on welfare, and promote specialist activities not covered by existing departments. These were listed as the promotion of cottage industries, horticulture, small stock breeding and domestic management through Scouts, Boys' Brigades, Youth Councils, Mothers' Unions, and Women's Institutes. They were to organize care for the especially needy such as the destitute, aged, and physically and mentally handicapped. Finally, they must help rehabilitate delinquent adolescents, ex-convicts and prostitutes. But, overall, they were to give priority to 'constructive' work rather than this 'remedial' help. Despite being largely based on metropolitan problems and solutions, this almost perversely long shopping list of service wants did nevertheless offer a clearer model of social welfare than had previously been possible, and it came with an explicit argument for government with social welfare. However, a strong consensus around this version of social welfare did not subsequently materialize in Kenya.

The metropolitan vision of social welfare proved not to hold the answer to Dr Philip's immediate post-war problems. Indeed, what quickly emerged were two different visions of social welfare illustrating the incoherence of the imperial structure at this juncture. Although Philip was happy to play down the 'remedial' aspect of social welfare work to a degree not too far removed from Colonial Office expectations, his own blend of constructive action was fundamentally different. With his assistant, Fortie Ross, Dr Philip produced his own version of the London memorandum. Mass adult education – the very subject the Colonial Office had extracted from the purview of welfare – was to be the basis of social welfare work, the Education Department in Kenya having disclaimed responsibility for mass adult education.[8]

The Philip and Ross memorandum instead highlighted two fundamental premises. One was the need to establish a peacetime propaganda movement similar to the war effort and to the kind of work Philip had been involved with when working in the Medical Department. His memorandum stressed the need to feed Africans with certain 'information and knowledge', on the grounds that this was now vital in order to stave off unrest. His vision of social engineering was anchored to preventing the further breakdown of law and order. The colony's Interim Report on Development was cited to remind readers of the universal agreement that 'unless the African population can be taught to appreciate what is happening, there is a real danger of social upheaval', whilst successful development and rehabilitation measures had to carry with them 'the full understanding and co-operation of the people as a whole'. In addition, the memorandum quoted the findings of the Mass Education Report from the Colonial Office which had urged colonies to quickly find ways to help Africans 'as a community' to understand and appreciate the forces which had radically changed their lives. These kinds of arguments already put forward in Kenya by the Information Department and Nyanza's Provincial Commissioner, were perhaps clung to more dearly in the hope of appealing to a more conservative mindset within the administration.

The second organizing principle within the local social welfare formula was the need to tackle poverty. This was set out very clearly – much more explicitly than London's vision – in what began to sound like a strong mission statement. In strident terms, Dr Philip insisted that the most pressing problem facing the colony was the way in which

> ... the great majority of the non-European population of the Colony are underfed, badly housed and poorly educated and can consequently never play a proper role in the development of the Colony nor achieve that degree of well-being which a well organized society should aim to provide for its members.[9]

The experience of war combined with local conditions as experienced by a medical officer to produce this stress on organization and attention to basic human need. Professional duty was linked with the provision of basic standards of living, so that Africans could behave as good citizens for their own good and for the good of the colony. Such a view rested upon a

[8] 'Memorandum on Social Welfare', by C.R. Philip and F.E.V. Ross, dated January 1946. 'Appendix A', p.3. KNA DC/KSM/1/1/194.

[9] Ibid., p.1. This extract was taken from the recommendations contained in a recent report of the Sub-Committee on Social Welfare, Information and Mass Education.

theory of inequality that was not premised on racial disability but rather on human capabilities that were conditioned by environmental factors. This thinking was a product of the wartime belief in the role of the state, similar to that being advanced in the Britain of the Left. Just as the architects of the Colonial Development and Welfare Act had presented their case at the beginning of the war, poverty was being used to explain why Africans were not active in their own development. This was different from the more racially dismissive view that the irrevocable condition of the native was to blame. But it was a theory which could still encompass notions of inferiority, cultural backwardness, and bad habits coming out of the experience of slavery or poverty.[10]

Thus, for the social welfare experts in Kenya, their version of social welfare was primarily an exercise in mass education because it tackled both of these problems simultaneously: dissipating unrest, whilst at the same time disseminating handy hints for material improvement. Philip and Ross desperately urged that a new cadre of European and African welfare workers be appointed. Much more central to their vision were African staff, since they were to be the vital link between European welfare administrators and African communities. They were cast in the role of the benign spy, running information rooms and collecting local news about progressive Africans. Such 'mass observation' – a phrase reminiscent of the information gathering which took place during the Second World War in order to learn about the lives of ordinary people – would uncover 'local gossip, prejudice, superstition, rumour, suspicion and misunderstanding'.[11] They were expected to involve themselves in handicrafts and arts, social surveys, organize 4-H clubs, encourage the use of facilities and services offered by other departments and – indicating the link with ex-*askari* – liaise with the British Legion. After dealing with adult literacy, libraries, sport and cinema, then came the subject of domestic science which raised the issue of women welfare workers. The danger of neglecting to train African women was acknowledged, but at this stage Philip and Ross were satisfied to leave local councils to decide whether European wives with 'a bent for social welfare work' would receive an honorarium, remain voluntary or become salaried. Unfortunately not only was theirs a local vision of social welfare which was not strongly reinforced by Colonial Office specialist advisers at the time, vital in the face of local opposition. It also faced the additional problem of being eclipsed by more pressing concerns which precipitated the publication of not one but two further memoranda to add to the confusion.

The fragile nature of the restructuring capacity of the Second Colonial Occupation at this level soon became apparent. In January 1946 the

[10] See previous discussion in Chapter 2. Hailey declared it to be a universal truth that 'the heritage of slave labour is irresponsibility and lack of forethought'; see Hailey, 1945: 636.
[11] 'Memorandum on Social Welfare', pp. 6–14. KNA DC/KSM/1/1/194.

government appointed 20 additional administrative officers but not one single welfare administrator. The recommendations made in the social welfare memorandum had been shot to pieces. District Commissioners were adamant that only when extra staff were available could specialist welfare work be undertaken. After a meeting with the Acting Governor, Henry Moore, and William Marchant, then the CNC, the social welfare duo were forced to amend their official line on social welfare, the official explanation being that Provincial Commissioners had not yet had an opportunity to 'give detailed consideration to the matter'.[12] Philip's priorities were swept aside and the administration's views triumphed. Faced with this decision, he found himself having to make concessions to the view that the District Officer was a welfare worker.

Illustrating the desperateness of the situation, a second Philip and Ross memorandum endeavoured to emphasize that the additional administrative officers should be allocated to districts where social centres were most advanced so that they might undertake the duties of a Social Welfare Officer and supervise the initial activities of the African staff. The 40 ex-*askari* in training were to be allocated in relation to the information rooms planned. Philip and Ross asked that European welfare officers be called Social Welfare Administrative Officers and that Social Welfare Workers would be the title given to the Africans being trained, whilst social welfare centres would in future be called community centres. Their weakened position forced them to adjust to the line of the administration; their case for a separate field structure had suffered a setback. They agreed that administrative officers or district commissioners could attend courses on social welfare either at the Jeanes School or when at home on leave. In the interim, they asked for the administration's co-operation to 'pave the way and get the masses receptive' for later welfare work. 'African Social Welfare Committees of the L.N.C.s with advice from Departmental Officers could do much ground-work in 1946', they agreed. Finally, they conceded that 'the customary meetings of D.C.s and their Departmental Officers...taking place regularly in connection with all the rehabilitation and development plans in the various districts [would] in fact be social welfare meetings'.[13] They had little choice in the short term but to allow the administration to absorb much of social welfare. The district administration had to be appeased, since they strongly believed they, and they alone, ought to do this work. It seemed a humiliating start for the Welfare Organization.

However, all was not lost. In an effort to retain the distinctiveness of social welfare from the activities of the administration, the principle of targeted Africanization of local government was turned to in desperation. This was what Lord Hailey had recommended in his survey of native

[12] Ibid., 'Appendix B', January 1946; ibid.
[13] Ibid., p.4.

administration published in 1943, discussed in Chapter 2. Progressive Colonial Office thought was looked to for support. Dr Philip returned to the notion of social welfare as the mechanism needed to release the civic and development potential of Africans themselves. Unbelievably, a third memorandum on social welfare was written, this time to refute points raised by Charles Tomkinson, Central Province's Provincial Commissioner, in November 1945.[14] Understandably, Tomkinson believed that Welfare Officers should be directly responsible to the District Commissioner and not members of a separate department. For him and for many others this was the only way of actually achieving anything. They were desperate to have more staff in order to carry out their ideal relationship between white power and African subjects. Dr Philip tried to argue that all the 20 additional administrative officers allocated for 1947 should have social welfare training, on the grounds that they could then 'form the nucleus of the Welfare Officers of the Administration if it is accepted that Welfare Officers should be directly responsible to District Commissioners'.

This concession raised the worrying prospect of the basic philosophy of social welfare as set out in the first memorandum being completely set aside. So Philip, prepared to stand his ground, raised the crucial issue of involving Africans in welfare discussion and devolving responsibility to lower levels. He argued against the view of the administration that extraneous welfare committees would have to wait until welfare officers were appointed. Rather, he urged that Welfare Committees 'should be sub-committees of the Local Native Councils, with certain other Africans including women ... and possibly certain other members co-opted from local traditional councils'. He had in mind the type of initiatives taking shape in Nyeri at the time. These sub-committees were vital to his plan to implement the principle of community self-help without coercion from above. As he explained, after the 'right kind of propaganda'

> these African Welfare Committees would themselves put forward proposals as to Welfare activities which would be coming from the African masses more or less on their own volition, and if thought feasible and approved, would be far more likely, when put into operation, to meet with success than any proposals which might be suggested by departmental Officers and so have the appearance of being as it were imposed by government.[15]

His suggestions were moving too fast even for those in the administration who in theory backed LNC development along the lines recommended by Lord Hailey. The gap between London and the administration was widening, for greater inclusion was a principle which the Secretary of State for the Colonies was fundamentally committed to as a strategy for main-

[14] 'Appendix C'. 'Notes on a letter of 22nd Nov 1945 on District Welfare Committees to the Chief Sec. from the P.C.(Central Province)', C.R. Philip, January 1946, p. 1. Ibid.
[15] Ibid., p. 2.

taining empire in a post-war world, as we shall see in the final chapter. For frustrated marginals such as Philip and Ross, bringing in Africans had the advantage of loosening the grip of their rivals. In the meantime, however, the Welfare Organization faced an impasse in its efforts to establish a corps of specialist field officers, whilst even concentrating energies upon adult mass education was to yield little joy. Disseminating propaganda in peacetime became more difficult for the late colonial state.

'Philanthropy plus 10%': the perils of post-war propaganda

The new Welfare Organization might well have hoped to achieve more by busying itself with adult education using techniques of mass information. The apparently successful record of adult education in the army plus the application of new techniques of mass communication both seemed to hold out infinite possibilities of transforming swords into ploughshares, as the previous chapter illustrated. This had been a learnt feature of government during the Second World War in Britain as well as in the colonies. In June 1946, the colony's new Advisory Committee on African Publicity and Information met for the first time, inspired by what was remembered as its predecessor's wartime successes.[16] Dr Philip was well and truly on board. This advisory body was – not surprisingly for the time – an all-male affair. It was not without some surprises, however, with a European and African membership. In addition to Dr Philip, other members included H.E. Lambert (retired senior official), Wyn Harris (when he became CNC), Ernest Hyde-Clarke (Labour Commissioner), Norman Humphrey (senior agricultural officer), F.J. Khamisi, and Henry Mworia. Khamasi was at that time General Secretary of the Kenya African Union. Mworia was Jomo Kenyatta's Press Secretary, which makes his co-optation all the more remarkable. By this time he was already saddled with a reputation as a leading spokesman for educated, Bible-reading and dissatisfied Kikuyu opinion. In 1945, he founded the first and most influential Kikuyu newspaper, *Mumenyereri,* meaning the guardian (see Lonsdale, 1992).

Sub-committees mushroomed to tackle specific areas but no one suggested a separate campaign designed for African women. Dr Philip became chairman of two sub-committees; Mass Education and Welfare, and the Finance sub-committee. He also served on a number of other sub-committees: Labour, Agrarian Policy, Visual Propaganda and Entertainment but not , rather bizarrely, on the Civil Reabsorption sub-committee. His attendance rate was only exceeded by that of the colony's Information Officer, who was a member of all the sub-committees. Yet, despite the blanket coverage of the Advisory Committee's possible activities and the number of willing hands, turning good intentions into a workable system

[16] Minutes of first meeting, 19 June 1946. KNA MAA8/15.

was not so easy. By February 1947, Wyn Harris, the new CNC, was exasperated by confusion in the dissemination of information with 'too many people trying to do the same thing in slightly different ways'. He called for immediate suggestions as to how they could be tied up into one working whole under a co-ordinating centre, with a clear chain of command.[17] Why such disorganization so soon after a successful rural wartime propaganda campaign and with the social welfare staff and information officer in place?

The explanation reveals some of the congenital weaknesses of post-war colonial government. 'Getting the right message across', as the official mind viewed the task, was hampered by a number of serious problems. The fundamental issue was that African elites saw it in reverse, finding it difficult to see information deemed to be for their own benefit as anything other than an effort to give legitimacy to a racial and profoundly arbitrary system of rule, merely sly propaganda. The attempt to disseminate welfare propaganda after the Second World War illustrates the paradox of the Second Colonial Occupation. It provided a theory and a moral rearmament of government which would be enduring; yet it also signalled the end of empire, for it could not find adequate practical means to achieve its remit.

As administrators like Dr Philip soon discovered in their new post-war roles, the combined task of combating poverty and spreading Empire loyalism soon became overwhelming. Four sets of obstacles stood in his way. One was the crucial difference between wartime propaganda and post-1945 needs. Much of the efforts undertaken by wartime information departments and army public relations exercises centred upon explaining the war; pulling people together to fight an evil enemy; and encouraging poor sons to leave congested and boring Reserves. Peacetime information campaigns had to address much more profound and controversial problems of colonial rule. Initial stabs at the most pressing post-war issues proved fruitless as a small operational team attempted to wrestle with mountainous questions. The main committee on African Publicity and Information quickly abandoned their plans to popularize co-operative farming as a solution to the 'big problems of land utilization and settlement'. This decision was taken when the two African members on the committee stressed the need for caution on land issues. Mworia warned that Africans were so sensitive that they would immediately equate discussion about land with its impending loss. Panic and unrest would break out, the exact opposite of the intended effect. The main committee quickly agreed not to run a general publicity campaign and opted instead for 'an oblique approach'.[18] It was agreed that Mworia would write an article for the

[17] Minute 1., Minutes of 3rd Meeting of Advisory Committee, 17 February 1947, KNA MAA8/15.

[18] Minutes of 1st Meeting, 19 June 1946, pp.3–4, KNA MAA8/15.

vernacular press, introducing the idea that clan farming was a traditional Bantu idea. This rapid retreat from undertaking surgical strikes at key issues hampered the generation of quantifiable results that could yield proof of their success. Without a round of quick-fire examples, the procurement of further funds to match would be yet more difficult.

A second obstacle lay with the shortage of materials. Securing resources was difficult from the outset. An inadequate budget to match the task severely restricted the potential impact of mass adult education. Despite the pledges made during the war, in peacetime the money was simply not made available so that the wartime vision could be realized. The general committee on African Information and Publicity was realistic, acknowledging early on that they could only make a start in a small way.[19] As they quietly lamented, although departments, the administration and organizations like the African Settlement Board would benefit from their work, they would not be contributing money for publicity purposes. Just how small the start would be soon became apparent. It was a ludicrous situation. Only one mobile information unit was in operation until September 1946, when, thanks to Chaundy at the Education Department, they inherited a second 'travelling information room'. This resulted in a grand total of two mobile units for the whole colony. It was hardly the incarnation of a welfare propaganda campaign that was to take the districts by storm, as recommended, for example, by the Colonial Office's Economic Advisory Council in its report on nutrition and labour output in the colonies, discussed in Chapter 1. The report had called for a massive campaign to educate adults as well as school-children: to be successful, it would require a colony-wide initiative embracing the use of leaflets, lending libraries, cinema, the magic lantern and loudspeakers, whilst all local officials would have to become agents in 'getting across welfare work' with their homes and gardens serving as 'models of virtue'.[20]

The situation in post-war Kenya bore little resemblance to this vision. At the most basic level there was a practical problem in getting anything printed at all. The Government Printer was already burdened by a shortage of staff, machinery and paper. Eventually the Army's printing machinery was purchased to try to circumvent some of the obstacles.[21] Even when material was printed, points of dispersal remained elusive. The information rooms-cum-social centres were barely established. The plan was that 857 information centres would be phased in from 1946 to 1950, concentrated initially in Kiambu and Machakos Districts. Progress would inevitably be slow with such a timetable. Alternative suggestions included enlisting the CMS African booksellers as distributors of information sheets,

[19] Minutes of 1st Finance Sub-Committee Meeting, 3 September 1946. Ibid.

[20] *Nutrition in the Colonial Empire*, Cmd.6050 (1939) esp. pp. 107–16. See earlier discussion in Chapter 1.

[21] Minutes of 2nd Meeting of the Advisory Committee on African Publicity and Information, 17 July 1946, KNA MAA8/15.

and remarkably, as an interim measure, setting up hundreds of kiosks on roadsides similar to telephone booths where people could fish out a handful of leaflets. It must have been with a sinking feeling that the committee privately agreed at their very first meeting that 'inadequate publicity would be got over in the critical period of the next five years'.[22] They were right. The competition for resources and a government that was at best ambivalent towards mass adult education meant that long-term and slow yielding projects like publicity and welfare remained neglected. Yet this was not by any means the most serious barrier to effective action.

A third obstacle was Africans, the targets of the printed material. In addition to the internal constraints operating upon the enthusiasms and plans of Dr Philip and his fellow publicity gurus, they came up against an increasingly potent external one. In post-war Kenya would Africans take the bait? What the Advisory Committee on African Publicity and Information regarded as vital information, imparting technical wisdoms that would secure African development, literate Africans increasingly regarded as propaganda efforts to bolster white rule. The message of betterment did not travel well across the racial divide. Early efforts to counter this growing perception among a growing African readership seem to have done little to diminish the trend. The Mass Education and Welfare sub-committee spent much time trying to reorganize *Pamoja* (meaning together), the official broadsheet put together for Africans. Perhaps it was the name that was at fault, they mused. The East African Women's League's social welfare committee submitted a couple of suggestions and possible new titles considered were *maendeleo* (progress), *tangazo* (bulletin), *leo na kesho* (today and tomorrow) and *mbele* (forward).[23]

Ultimately it was not the packaging but the content which made the paper non-essential reading. The sub-committee felt it wise not to cover local or world news, nor to publish letters sent to the editor, so it was hardly a newspaper. These restrictions, felt necessary in view of the perception that Africans were likely to be destabilized and distracted by controversial issues and the reality of an outside world which included self-governing nations, inevitably reduced the chances of *Pamoja* securing a significant growth of readership that believed what it was being told. An additional factor in the declining appeal of the official vernacular press was the spread of newspapers produced by Africans after the Second World War. They increasingly offered an alternative and a blueprint for what newspapers ought to contain (see Gadsden, 1980).

As African channels of communication increased with the spread of vernacular broadsheets, so official frustration mounted. *Baraza*, a popular African newspaper, took the decision to stop publishing material produced

[22] Comment attributed to H.E. Lambert. Minutes of 1st Meeting of the Advisory Committee, 19 June 1946, ibid.

[23] Minutes of 1st, 2nd and 3rd meetings of Mass Education and Welfare Sub-Committee, ibid.

by the Kenya Information Office. This was explained by the editors as a response to accusations coming from its readers that it was spreading European propaganda.[24] Nothing was going to be published in future which might be interpreted as government propaganda.[25] Officials quickly noticed that these media were proving to be more and more uninterested in reporting news from the government. They also found the commentaries increasingly libellous. The Governor had publicly criticized an edition of *Baraza* for carrying no items on farming, hygiene in the home, the village or general improvement, whilst its leading article focused on Bulgaria's wish to dispense with its Royal Family. Consequently, the editor of the *East African Standard* was ushered in to talk to editors of African newspapers about newspaper ethics. The Kenya Information Office became increasingly anxious as to whether their message was reaching its target audience. They seemed to have less and less of an entry point into African society.

By the end of 1946, announcements about important meetings and *barazas* designed to encourage reporters from African newspapers to attend, gave way to attempts to organize informal press conferences with African journalists.[25] For example, in November 1946 the Registrar of Natives addressed representatives from *Mutai*, *Coast African Express*, *Gikuyu*, *Habari*, *Mwalimu*, *Ramogi*, *Baraza* and the Kenya Information Office. So serious was the situtation that, earlier in the same month, a candid exchange had taken place at a meeting arranged between more senior figures from both sides. Ernest Hyde-Clarke, the Labour Commissioner, met with a selection of African newspaper editors. Present were Musa Amalemba and Joseph Ruo from *Baraza*, Joseph Katuri from *Mutai*, Victor Wokabi from *Gikuyu*, plus John Kipsugut from the Information Office. This meeting offers a unique insight into contemporary debates about colonial rule. Ideas about welfare were the means by which the political economy of the colony was contested.

At this interface of black and white power, two differing concepts of African welfare fought for the moral high ground. Hyde-Clarke found himself having to plead for a recognition of mutual interest: Europeans and Africans were in the 'same economic boat', he insisted.[26] The white colonial mind clung to a concept of the mutual obligations of employer and employee and the mutual responsibilities of citizens. Hyde-Clarke reminded his audience of the welfare element in British rule. The colonizing motive was 'philanthropy plus 5%'. British people came to Kenya, he argued,

[24] Minutes of 2nd meeting of Mass Education and Welfare Sub-Committee Meeting, 9 August 1946, Minute 5, pp. 2-3. KNA MAA8/15.

[25] Notes of an informal press meeting held in the KIO, 20 November 1946, ibid.

[26] Notes of an Informal Meeting held in the Labour Office, 1 November 1946, ibid. Starting out as a coffee grower in Kenya, Hyde-Clarke joined the administration in 1927. He worked as Civil Reabsorption Officer during the war and was Labour Commissioner and Legislative Councillor betwween 1946 and 1951.

'because they are able to make small profits and at the same time to look after the education and betterment of the people'. Likewise, settlers still gave out rations as payment for agricultural labour, not to save money but because Africans must eat a balanced diet. Workers would not spend higher wages on better food. Hyde-Clarke then explained the long-term development goal for Kenya: 'What we want to see in the future is native villages both in the Reserves and in the settled areas where the workers are able to live with their families.' Africans must learn to build better houses and have fewer children; their wives must cease to subsidize African agriculture with their labour.

Hyde-Clarke clearly wanted a gendered approach to development to include domesticating African women on the lines of an old-fashioned view of Western women's role in industrial societies: remove women from production together, or if in production subordinate them to men, and encourage them to be housewives. Such a view of how women could be discriminated against was now out of step with progressive thought on equal pay and rights at work, at least for professional women, which the feminist movement had campaigned for during the lifetime of the League of Nations, as we saw in Chapter 1. Likewise, the contribution of women to the war effort, in terms of food production, factory work and professional expertise, was also shoring up the position of women as equal contributors to society in Britain. However, establishment opinion generally expected them to hand back their jobs to men after the war and slip quietly back into the home. Hyde-Clarke's view, which was quite prevalent at the time in Kenya, was premised on the view that the potential workforce could be reduced if women were removed: men would have to work harder; the state would not have to look after them; and more land would be released for large-scale production which alone could increase the country's GNP. At this point, women and the family as means of economic as well as social engineering had re-surfaced with a new pragmatism born of urgency. Some officials at least began to understand that their efforts to build a mutual alliance was being undermined because their prospective partners realized they were regarded as racially inferior according to the legislation on the colony's statute books and rejected this verdict. By 1946 such a quest was already proving elusive for this reason.

What little evidence of the African response survives in the official record of the meeting, indicates that this enunciation of colonial development and welfare was contested. They and their audience had a different concept of welfare. From the perspective of Western educated Africans living in Nairobi under colonial rule, welfare improvements required European employers to increase wages and the government to provide better living conditions in general. Hyde-Clarke, in turn, rejected this alternative. Harder work had to precede better wages, he insisted, and he delicately explained racial difference in terms of cultural practice. Africans needed European guidance because they did not attach any stigma to idleness, he explained: they did not have 'to work hard in order to keep alive'.[27] Several Africans again queried this. Colonial rule could teach them little while it entailed exclusion from the White Highlands, unfair racial legislation and Nairobi's slums. Responding to criticism about European land, Hyde-Clarke insisted that the average European could get more out of the land than the African, and also preserved the land better. It was the business of government 'to try to get you people up to that standard. Until you can farm well, and care for and preserve your soil, you are in no position to demand more land.' Official attempts to impart colonial wisdom had to seek refuge ultimately in racially paternalistic scolding. Getting the right message across from the European point of view became fraught with more and more obstacles. The difficulties in securing access to African civil society through its burgeoning urban newspaper culture and readership were destined to grow.

If social welfare was to have any success over controversial issues, in the absence of resources and a docile audience, then departmental co-operation was its only hope. Unfortunately, pulling off a co-ordinated adult education campaign was equally problematic. The inherited structure of the colonial state once again showed how difficult it was to execute the kind of restructuring that Margery Perham had called for so that it could function as a modern government. This is illustrated by the tragic fate of the rural mobile information van. Dr Philip understood that administering African betterment through publicity campaigns required all departments to work together. As Chairman of the Finance sub-Committee, he called a meeting of departmental directors, representatives from the Finance Department, African Settlement Board and the Labour Commissioner.[28] He did not invite representatives from the administration, perhaps keen they should not try to take over or scupper his initiative. He explained that the skeleton mobile information unit working in Kiambu was too small to be effective and called for departmental co-operation to increase its scope. As the discussions of the earlier Welfare Committee had illustrated, whilst everyone wanted co-ordination in theory, especially if they could control it from their particular district foothold, it was not so easy to orchestrate in practice and descended into a local tug-of-war.[29]

Realistically, the co-operation needed for the mobile information unit to realize its potential was unlikely to be forthcoming, in light of all the past failures from the top to formulate interdepartmental co-operation outside of ad hoc personal relations. In retrospect, the mobile van lumbering across the plains represented the last mechanism through which colonial power could work in order to better African communities via

[27] Ibid., p. 3.

[28] Meeting of Finance Sub-Committee, 20 September 1946. Minute 1 'Co-operation of Departments in the Mobile Information Unit'. KNA MAA8/15.

[29] See discussion in Chapter 3 of the Native Welfare Committee.

adult education, before the problems generated by colonial rule got out of hand. Even with better co-operation, would the one or two vans have anywhere to go where they could find an audience? The cumulative effect of the constraints already listed was to deny an easy focal point for information and propaganda: a handle on African society remained as evasive as ever. This issue was appreciated at the time. At the meeting of the Finance sub-committee referred to above, Hyde-Clarke wanted each department to have its own 'foci' in the form of information rooms, health centres, agricultural and veterinary schools, which could then be stimulated by mobile units.[30] He understood well that Africans had to be brought together and a point of official contact established which would form a permanent channel for adult education and propaganda covering many subjects. He suggested a survey be undertaken to find out what focal points already existed so that planned centres would enable as much of the territory as possible to be covered as quickly as possible. Surveys required money and took time.

The learning curve was destined to be a gradual one, made more so by financial stringency. As we have already seen, information rooms were going to be established in rural areas according to a slow timetable because of the paucity of funds from central government. Likewise, manpower within departments was in short supply. Dr Martin from the Medical Department reported that he could not promise trained personnel to run the planned health centres 'for a long while'. He told his audience of his hope that 'a team, representative of all departments' would 'eventually be established at each social centre'.[31]

Dr Philip's model of social welfare seemed further from being realized. The system of colonial rule had not prevented his emergence as the welfare adviser but it was unwilling or unable to accept the advice. His plans would, if realized, make the administration redundant as its organizers, and so it was strongly opposed, as were other state-building initiatives which involved deference to technical staff. Even in the comparatively less controversial area of adult propaganda there was little joy. With many issues considered too controversial to be tackled, a shortage of resources, an increasingly sceptical African audience and a lack of co-ordination and co-operation at the district level, the enthusiasm and planning sparked off during the war fell on much stonier ground in post-war Kenya. But worse was soon to come. European public opinion in the colony began to turn against any sign of pandering to African demands and metropolitan socialism. Social welfare was vulnerable to both these accusations.

[30] Meeting of Finance Sub-Committee, 20 September 1946. KNA MAA8/15.
[31] Ibid., p. 2.

A public outcry

White opinion was about to provide little in the way of external support that might have mitigated some of the internal difficulties. As Dr Philip was struggling to have his plans for adult mass education assume a semblance of reality, European public opinion moved decisively against state intervention and vented its frustration against the already beleaguered Welfare Organization. The general climate inside the colony was fuelling a mood of retrenchment. The first eighteen months after the war were remembered by settlers as being difficult, although the colony subsequently experienced boom conditions (Lipscomb, 1956: ch. viii). With the end of hostilities came austerity and financial shortages. The pressure to reorganize for the reabsorption of ex-soldiers had eased as *askari* appeared to slip back into rural life without the expected furor. Instead, crime and urban disorder were on the agenda, partly due to the way events in Nairobi often dominated the headlines in the white settler press. Undoubtedly, Nairobi began to look and feel very different from a European perspective. The city's African population trebled between 1939 and 1952.

From an African perspective, the inequalities of racial rule were ever sharp. African wages continued to trail behind inflation. The majority of workers in the city lived in squalid slum conditions. By 1947, the police and the administration had lost effective control over these areas (see Throup, 1987: ch. 8). Little was done to reverse what Margery Perham derided as the artificial separation of races who lived side by side. Europeans had little idea of actual living conditions or their demoralizing effects upon Africans. It was easier not to know. 'Islands of white' were artificially maintained by means of a collective obsession with borders, fences, carefully laid out white-washed stones that marked out territory as well as functioning as necessary symbols of a superior technical know-how, racial separation and the taming of nature. Most settlers kept large dogs and opted for the fortified ranch-type entrance. Although the post-war years turned into a boom time for many, the underlying trend for many settler farmers was negative: profit margins dwindled whilst their African labour proved less willing to work under the same regime without long-term security. For remote white estate workers, life continued much the same and it took little to wear down their patience or sap their goodwill in the battle to survive a hostile environment. One of a number of former soldiers who chose to make a living by writing popular fiction based on their wartime experience in Africa and India, was Gerald Hanley. He had worked in the Press Department of the Army. He described the fictitious Mambango estate where

> It was always too hot, even during the rains when the jungle steamed in the sun like drying washing, when cigarettes swelled with damp and green mould formed on a leather hat-band in an hour. People were

> there because they had to be there; they found no pleasure there, no sense of victory over the jungle, no pleasure in feeling as pioneers. Mambango was a kind of lonely hell, lonelier because there were fourteen people who had slowly drained each other night after night for years.[32]

The underlying fault lines within the political economy of the colony soon eclipsed the fin de guerre optimism. Those white settlers who regularly read the *East African Standard* now shared a creeping sense that their Second World War had not solved anything in terms of their futures. The scene was set for the outpourings and predictions of the planning enthusiasts, mass educationalists and rustic environmentalists who had leapt up to nourish discussion on African welfare and development during the Second World War, to be replaced by the views of unsentimental hard-liners and sceptics.

In March 1946, the most influential settler newspaper made a bid to turn public opinion decisively against the government's welfare organization, with the unwitting help of the East African Women's League. *The Standard* sent a reporter to cover an address to the League at its AGM held in Nairobi Town Hall on behalf on the Welfare Organization. *The Standard* was the most popular daily newspaper read for local and overseas news. The League – known sometimes unaffectionately as the colony's alternative parliament – had become more active in welfare issues, able as it was to boast 45 branches, 2,500 members and with £10,000 at its disposal. The League and the Welfare Organization were natural bedfellows. The League already functioned as an unofficial welfare department: its constitution pledged members to be active in 'instruction to promote the welfare of women and children of all races'. It had a standing committee on social welfare and a health and hygiene committee. During 1946 the League sent a deputation to the Chief Secretary to secure an extension in the provisions made for suspected lunatics in Nairobi Prison. It also wrote to the Secretary of State calling his attention to a number of welfare issues including the need for a comprehensive Children's Act in the colony, a new Lunacy Bill, better hospital accommodation especially for Asians and African women, improved African education and greater efforts to restore the fertility of the soil.[33]

It was natural, therefore, that Fortie Ross, the government's new social welfare assistant, should agree to talk informally on his organization's plans. He had recently read two books sent out by the British Government, one on social welfare and the other on adult education. His talk was enthusiastically received. He had been inundated with questions.[34] Many

[32] Part of a description of a fictious plantation estate set in East Africa in the late 1930s; Hanley, 1955: 20–21.

[33] Report on Year of Progress in the *East African Standard* (EAS), 26 March 1947. KNA CD5/301.

[34] Correspondence from Fortie Ross, 9 January 1995.

raised issues about the welfare of women. Since health and agriculture were subjects which concerned women more, surely then, one woman asked, 'better results might be obtained by having trained women, European and African, to teach these subjects to women in the reserves'? This went much further than the male-focused agenda of the welfare fraternity, but Ross showed inclusive properties. The only women-centred plans were for European women to teach African women how to prepare more nutritious meals at canteens that would be attached to the community centres, but Ross did later ask for details from the League's President, Lady Eleanor Cole, about the training of women agricultural leaders and the other 'valuable suggestions made about mobile propaganda, cooking demonstrations and so on'.[35] He was eager to accept the League's guidance. There were few alternatives. Previously the government had had little official contact with African women. Offering a candid insight into the realities of male–female relations, Audrey Richards later observed that her anthropological research conducted in Africa in the 1930s and 1940s was greatly helped by the fact that she was female, for if a European man talked to an African woman it was assumed that he wanted to sleep with her.[36] Any woman with any experience of interacting with African women could become an instant expert. Ross's talk and the discussion seemed to have been a great publicity success that had yielded practical results. Two days later the picture had completely reversed.

A report and editorial on the talk soon appeared in *The Standard.* Its contents prompted Ross to make a telephone call to the CNC to beg clemency for not submitting his talk for official approval beforehand.[37] Ross had fallen easy victim to the *Standard*'s decision to discredit official plans for social welfare. The paper presented welfare for Africans as pandering to the idle with elaborate recreation schemes; his talk was billed as 'Banishing Boredom in the Reserves', with the provocative sub-title, 'EAWL hears about state welfare scheme'.[38] The *Standard* portrayed 'an embryo Government organization' obsessed with recreation schemes for Africans. Scant attention was given to Ross's insistence that the inculcation of self-help was the most important aim of African adult education. Instead, it was 'bands for boredom' that made the headlines. Ross had presented ideas that had filtered through the pages of metropolitan specialist journals during the war, that army initiatives like information rooms ought to be transferred to the African villages to counteract what the Russians called 'the idiocy of the villager's life' and what Americans derided as 'dull uneventful communities'. A similar disease infected Kenya, he argued, in

[35] Mrs Armstrong for F.E.V. Ross to Lady Eleanor, Cole 23 March 1946. KNA CD5/301.

[36] Recollection of a conversation with Dr Richards by Dr Ray Abrahams, Department of Anthropology, Cambridge University.

[37] Ross to Lady Eleanor Cole 26 March 1946, KNA CD5/301.

[38] 'Banishing Boredom in the Reserves', *EAS,* 23 March 1946, p.3; Ross's notes made during the talk, KnA CD5/301.

the form of a drift to the towns and rising alcoholism. He had also wanted to convey to his audience how Captain Dickson's experience with his wartime mobile propaganda van had convinced him that 'recreation should be the most important part of social welfare. Vital to build up the community spirit, recreation was less likely to become political than the indoor club or debating society.' Ross's enthusiasm in his own private life for sport and fitness led him to suggest to his audience that 'football, for example, was a small beginning in the field of self-government'.[39]

The Standard's editorial on this vision – described later by Ross as 'venomous' – ensured that the reading public would be less than impressed. The powerful image of a row of healthy, smiling Africans grasping a tree trunk that had captured the imagination of metropolitan audiences now stalked the nightmares of the reading public in Kenya. No moral or political pressure existed to offer welfare concessions to an enfranchised mobilized labour force such as the pressure there had been in Britain during the early years of the war. Instead, a hard-nosed Kenyan colonial public, living with post-war austerity and insecurity, demanded work and obedience from their labour before reward. The editorial entitled 'Banishing Boredom' had a tone of patronizing amusement: 'Much could be said which might hurt the good and earnest people concerned', but readers were advised to make allowances for enthusiasts, however disturbing and irritating they might be.[40]

Yet the newspaper went to considerable trouble to rubbish the plans on the grounds that they were built upon an unrealistic model of African life. It was the stuff of picture-books to talk of Africans living 'a regenerated and happy rural life', playing in bands and concerts at village centres, innocently discussing current affairs and digesting innocuous literature at information rooms, abstaining from excessive drinking when rounding off the day in the new coffee houses and canteens.[41] Kenyans were warned to be on their guard against the modern jargon of the new specialist:

> ... unless we watch the word 'social Welfare' particularly closely the whole thing will run away with us. Properly planned African villages are an absolute necessity if there is to be ordered progress. In them there should be a place for the African trader and artisan, the African school-master, the church, the village policeman and all the best elements of ordered rural family life as we know it in Britain. There should also be a village hall, or 'social centre' as the modern jargon has it. But the development must rest on something solid and we must

[39] He later wrote a book on this passion which easily found a commercial publisher because of the central importance of games in the overseas education mission: Ross, 1961. This was one in a series of books on physical education which included a set of three by R. J. Picton-Hughes called *Physical Education for Boys* which was advertised as 'A complete programme of physical training mainly for teachers in schools in Africa'.

[40] 'Banishing Boredom', editorial in *EAS*, 23 March 1946, para.1, KNA CD5/301.

[41] Ibid., para.2.

constantly beware of the facile and fascinating but somewhat fantastic conceptions which find expression in such phrases as that football is a beginning in self-government and the referee is a Governor in embryo! It is easy to be carried away by all this enthusiasm and sail dreamily around among fleecy clouds enjoying luminous visions of thousands of earnest welfare workers teaching the blessings of civilization through chess or ludo and a can of beer in the village hall, and no less earnest Africans brought up to be good citizens on a diet of the right kind of pamphlets and lectures.

The view generally held by white settlers about the capabilities of Africans and the role of the state was now very much at odds with those of the Colonial Office specialist advisory committees and many senior Whitehall officials. Their differing pronouncements on the welfare officer illustrate the growing impasse. The SWAC's view of such an officer was of a dedicated plucky specialist tackling problems which could not be solved by sitting behind a desk or using conventional methods. Such men would stand out because of their 'enterprise, enthusiasm and originality'. They were vital to tackle 'human problems ... by human contact ... with all the flexibility and variety of approach on which the variety of human nature depends'.[42] What this signifies is the chasm that now existed between the political programme of post-war reconstruction emerging out of the British Labour Party and that of the white settlers. Socialist ideology during the war had stressed the need to break down barriers between communities that formerly lived separately; to find common humanity and to ensure that private interest pursued a deeper social purpose. Indeed, an important component of the plans for building up a responsible society was to make the pursuit of leisure activities more populist (Fielding et al., 1995: esp. ch. 6).

Finally, in order to discredit the initiative completely, the editorial poured scorn on the organization itself. *The Standard* decisively opposed the idea that new forms of government required new types of officers. This line would appeal to its readership. Settlers generally considered officials to be feeble and naive; there was still not a lot of easy movement between the two groups.[43] Social Welfare and Mass Education might be the 'new magical terms of the day', the newspaper counselled, but, as with propaganda, they tended to gobble up huge sums of money and employ vast numbers of people, without yielding much in return; welfare workers would be the type of specialist who would become 'difficult to control in terms of public policy'. Any future advancement in government welfare provision should be cautious and slow: social welfare was a luxury that could not be afforded for a long time.[44] The message was clear. Further

[42] CO Memo on Social Welfare, 1945, p.7, KNA DC/KSM/1/1/194.

[43] Interview with Sir Derek Oulton, Magdalene College, Cambridge, 18 November 1997.

[44] 'Banishing Boredom' editorial, *EAS*, 23 March 1946, KNA CD5/301.

involvement by metropolitan Britain was not wanted and settlers were entitled to remain steadfast in their self-belief as the people who knew what was best for Africa. Although sharing the same ideal of neat and orderly villages, the most influential settler newspaper evidently backed the view that control through the discipline of labour was the mechanism that would yield funds and the right to have planned recreation time: only after a 'day's honest toil' would the African be entitled to his leisure.

Such detailed and pugnacious treatment could only have negative repercussions. Sensing this – though never wavering from his views – Ross privately berated himself for what he had not said. 'I should have made it clearer I was talking ... about spare-time activities ... that the African man should relieve the woman of her heavy loads before thinking of recreation... And it would have been good for the *Standard* to have heard from Mrs Kenny of the poor white problem looming up', he confided to Lady Eleanor. 'Little did I know', he wrote to Dr Philip, 'that my innocent chat about our plans, to what I'd expected to be a fairly informal meeting, was going to be so reported on or I'd have refused to go near the EAWL.'[45] The Colonial Office Memorandum on Social Welfare had noted that the vulnerability of such schemes lay in the way the social welfare services would pay 'handsome, imponderable future dividends in increased well-being and prosperity, but they were immediately a cause of expenditure and not of revenue'.[46] It contained no advice on how to deal with such criticism.

Naturally, many settlers in the colony found this profoundly unsettling. *The Standard's* article had been like a red rag to a bull. One group of farmers wrote to the newspaper agreeing that the best prevention of boredom was 'good hard honest work', as the Governor had told the Kikuyu at Nyeri in 1945.[47] If plans to replicate the pleasures of army life were being followed, then, they inquired with sarcasm, was the government going to include a brothel in the planned villages. These anxious White Highlanders exposed their fear of African labour moving beyond their paternal control, and in doing so restated the 'lazy native' thesis. 'People capable of sitting for hours chattering about women, food and money' were unlikely to be easily bored, they cautioned. What they needed was 'to be forced to work'; Africans were so well off, they claimed, that labourers were 'reluctant, inefficient, and almost impossible to obtain'. And venting venomous aggression, they concluded, 'Someone once upon a time used the phrase "to work like a nigger". The popular version nowadays is "To shirk like an African", whatever the last word may mean.' The wider usage of the concept 'African' symbolized the threat to the Kenya they knew vis-à-vis the rights of labour; they preferred the South African terminology, for it reflected South African labour relations.

45 Ross to Lady Cole, 26 March 1946, KNA CD5/301.
46 CO Memo 'Social Welfare for the Colonies', 1945, para 19.
47 Extract from the *Sunday Post*, 14 April 1946, KNA CD5/301.

Others were less blatantly racist, but felt that their paternal commitment to African welfare was working but being ignored. Charles Platt, Chairman of the Dundori Farmers' Association, drew attention to the contributions of settlers to African welfare.[48] They had voted for an African Community Centre, donated £200 and then built a dispensary, with no more than the promise of government assistance to date. He claimed that in time local Africans would run the Centre themselves and for their own benefit. His message was that African welfare was alive and well in the capable hands of a conscientious European voluntary sector, and was well used to coping with government neglect.

The social welfare cause did have some sympathisers but they were few. One was the aristocratic Lady Eleanor Cole, who privately consoled Ross in a four-page letter.[49] He must understand, she said, that white settler opinion was divided over social welfare. Anyone working seriously for the African knew the danger of boredom and the need to counter it wisely; 'not letting him drift into immoral or political organizations which will do him nothing but harm'. From this white perspective, welfare was attractive because it was seen as a mechanism for staving off an interest in politics, since a recurring paternal worry was that the ordinary African would be vulnerable to being duped and confused. Lady Eleanor suggested that, since Kenya did not have enough like-minded souls to go round, a 'travelling circus' of experts ought to be assembled who would re-visit locations every six months. She had an example to hand in Miss Dodds who was travelling around schools of all races. Lady Eleanor suggested that she should be accompanied by a doctor and dietician who could give talks and demonstrations. This formula was a recurring fantasy across the Empire, echoing the recommendation for visiting teachers made twenty years earlier in the Colonial Office's 1925 paper on Educational Policy in Africa and the 1939 Nutritional Survey.[50] It remained beyond the capacity of the late colonial British state to realize.

Some settler women had a greater stake in seeing the government restructure itself if they were keen that African women should be catered for. Lady Eleanor also took up the question of the education of African women, so far absent from the Publicity Advisory Committee's agenda and pretty low down on that of the Welfare Organization. African women could be reached better through women instructors in subjects such as child welfare, health and hygiene, cooking, dietary instruction and agriculture. If it were made known that such positions were open to women, she insisted there would be no shortage of willing candidates from their own

[48] Letter from Charles F. Platt, *East African Standard,* 16 April 1946, KNA CD5/301.

[49] Lady Cole to Ross, 31 May 1946.

[50] See discussion in Chapter 1 of *Education Policy in British Tropical Africa* (Cmd. 2374, 1925), esp. pp. 6–7 and *Nutrition in the Colonial Empire* (Cmd. 6050, 1939) which suggested that specially trained local women should work as health visitors and that travelling propaganda units include 'health vans with cinema apparatus', pp. 118–19.

'Kenya European youth' and from overseas.[51] Although hers was a gender-aware enthusiasm born of a desire to make African women more like herself, it was not solely the product of a strong notion of cultural superiority but also a belief that this transformation would make them less poor. A younger generation of settler wives and aristocrats might well rally round but voices in opposition spoke more loudly. Nor was the League in a particularly belligerent mood. In her 1947 annual review of the League's work, Lady Eleanor mourned the way they had apparently failed to enlist the co-operation of the press.[52] Many believed the League had gone too far and become 'meddlesome'. Criticism had exploded in the settler press after the League debated the conscription of women. Enraged settler women told members to express their opinions as individuals to the LegCo, and to admit to being either 'a self-elected political party, a secret association which extracts subscriptions for secret purposes' or a 'social society'.[53] Also, the League's suggestion that a new identity card be carried by all races was far too radical for most settlers to contemplate at the time, at least not without a large brandy. The League could not offer the Welfare Organization a great deal in the form of support and counter claim at the time, having to face up to public criticism itself and to make the decision to pull back from contentious issues. In any event, little could have been achieved in the face of what soon followed.

Another unequivocal endorsement of the general opposition to welfare came from the very apex of the government. The Governor – Sir Philip Mitchell – used an after-dinner speech delivered to an influential and select white settler audience in March 1946 – a meeting of the Royal Society of St George – to make it clear that he did not believe that the majority of Africans could be goaded into an enlightened state of modernized behaviour through welfare.[54] Settlers need not have feared his reputation of being anti-white, it seems. His dogged preference for indirect rule, distrust of African politicians and die-hard racial paternalism meant that they found much common ground. Mitchell's main tactical device used to discredit state welfare was to revive the older discourse on the fundamental characteristics of 'the African', offering a quick recap of racial differences. His speech was widely reported in the settler press. It was replete with much of the classic symbolism that characterized the rhetoric of intrepid white heroism. Mitchell used the metaphor of St George and the dragon to argue his case. Europeans facing the African dragon of 'primitive ignorance and indolence' was his flattering opening. No one, he assured his audience, could expect to transform the African into a strenuous European. To avoid future disappointment, he urged recognition of the natural limits

[51] Lady Cole to Ross, 31 May 1946, pp. 2–3, KNA CD5/301.

[52] Article in the *EAS*, 'EAWL Conference: No new schemes until earlier ones are implemented'. 26 March 1947, ibid.

[53] Extracts from a collection of letters printed in the *EAS*, April–May 1947. ibid.

[54] Article in the *Sunday Post*, 20 April 1946, 'The Postman's Knock'. KNA CD5/301.

of their material, which he defined as 'the intrinsic poverty of Africa itself and the psychology of the native'. But being English, he told a receptive audience, they would not give up. It was

> ... part of our sublime cussedness to persevere in the face of incredible odds. We have proved that both in war and in peace. And so we shall continue in our endeavour to make Jerogi an industrious peasant and to inculcate habits of hard work and thrift which he himself regards merely as *mzungu* foibles.[55]

Mitchell used the classic imperial notion of the white man's burden, the myth of heroism and the self-belief of being the chosen ones. He summarized the English condition; always 'measuring ourselves against self-assumed responsibilities'; always finding a dragon in the way needing to be slain because 'we choose the paths where dragons lurk'. It was part of that valiant spirit of adventure that had made Britain much more than a 'damp little island in a grey northern sea' (see Dawson, 1994: esp. ch. 3; Philips, 1997; Mackenzie, 1988).

Sir Philip was deliberately mining a rich seam which had served the white settler well. Africa had long been fictionalized as the destiny of white heroes who grappled with the threat of the natural world and native inhabitants. Adventure novels, travelogues, diaries and biographies had enjoyed a wide audience from the Victorian era onwards. In the twentieth century, the genre expanded with the increased availability of cheap print as well as the cinema, the most notable example being the novels of Edgar Rice Burroughs. Tarzan, King of the Jungle, usually found himself buried up to his perfect pectorals in the blood and gore created by hordes of frenzied and cannibalistic locals, provoked by game-hungry French aristocrats or scheming profiteering Germans. The hero was inspired by Rudyard Kipling's *Jungle Book* adventures and bore all the marks of being the insider as well as an outsider in a land he had tamed with the aid of his hyper-masculine heroics, love of animals, and a British umpire's command of fair play. Another revival of the African adventure genre was set to take place in the 1950s in the wake of Mau Mau. Cheaper and easier photographic reproduction and the widespread reports in the press of barbaric atrocities, acted as spur to established and would-be authors of 'Boy's Own-for-adults' accounts of hunting game and journeys made through perilous terrain. Privately, settlers found such romanticism tiresome, but the image had its uses, particularly when they were put on the defensive in relation to Africans; white heroism was then a handy benchmark of civilization in contrast to black deficiencies of character.[56] This kind of adventure

[55] Mitchell, *The Sunday Post*, 20 April 1946, ibid.

[56] Typical were Stoneham, 1954 with an early chapter called 'Knight of the Muzzle-loader' and Merfield, 1956); Burroughs, 1916; Joseph Bristow, *Empire Boys: Adventures in a Man's World* (London, 1991) esp ch. 5; Sandison, 1967; see also Lewis, 2000; Ruark, 1954. It was a revival not confined to British writers, see Sommer, 1953, nor to Africa, see Shilling, 1957.

story was most often told either through the first person of a man or the central character was a male hero. His triumph over man and beast tended to exemplify the value of English stoicism and rugged individualism, the need for a firm command of the natives and the trouble women could cause men if left unattended. It was usually only women writers who concentrated on fictionalizing women as brave heroines and plucky pioneers who were making a distinct moral contribution to empire and/or bravely flying in the face of convention.[57]

Mitchell's slaying of Jerogi speech with its invocation of settler heroism was part of a wider stratagem to wriggle out of the tightening grip of metropolitan government. It represented a local attempt to stop the conversion of trusteeship from indirect rule and into welfare and development. The Second Colonial Occupation threatened the status quo of local autonomy, so it was not surprising that the Governor would choose to throw cold water on the welfare and development consensus coming from the Colonial Office. He at once stated that external injections of millions of pounds into the Reserves could produce great results:

> I am not one of those who glow with pride at the thought of millions of pounds (not my pounds) being handed out by the English parliament as grants in aid of black folk six thousand miles away. Except, on one condition: that this incredible concern for alien people brings back some solid return in the way of better trade and larger markets for British goods ... it is the only condition on which a nation of colonialists can remain solvent ... we have of course built on these solid foundations of hard common sense. What we have to see to is that our old plain sense, with its slight varnish of hypocrisy, is not submerged in the modern waves of sentimentalism.[58]

The bulk of the population had to live on the land by agriculture or animal husbandry, he argued, whether we like it or not; Kenyans could teach Africans to do so 'at a higher level'.

Mitchell also used the topic and the occasion to reject political advance on the grounds that, as guardians, the British had to 'resist the temptation of giving to an immature ward an excessive degree of freedom from control, before he is ready for freedom'. His formula was simple and long-term, as he had recently explained to officials in the East Africa Department: slowly raise productivity and stop environmental destruction.[59] This alone would yield the British tax payer-investor some return for his money. Mitchell also gave full rein to his profoundly negative view of the African

[57] Webster 1997; in the Indian context see, for example, Grewa, 1996, and Ricciardi, 1981.

[58] For a discussion on the pervasiveness of settler ideology as a product of the general ideology elaborated to protect the economic interests of the metropolitan ruling class, see Maughan Brown, 1985, esp. pp. 74–7.

[59] See Frost, 1992, esp. ch.16. Mitchell to Creasey, 28 August 1945. See also discussion on agricultural productivity in Chapter 6.

peasant's capacity for self-improvement. Poor in soil, deficient in rainfall, lacking minerals and rivers, Africa was also handicapped by the human element, he explained. Being 'bottom dogs', the majority did not fall in with modern concepts of development.[60] Jack 'Kikono' (one-armed) Clive, in charge of African co-operatives, gave new proof of this; Mitchell related how Clive's experience had illustrated the shallowness of African business interests, concerned only with immediate profits and easy dividends.

Racial paternalism abounded. The generic lazy native was brought to the forefront of the anti-welfare discourse. 'The African wants an easy life', Mitchell reminded his audience; he 'can't be bothered with progress. We must not invest millions in a society that can give results only on thousands.' Nor did Mitchell endorse a significant role in constructive government for an emerging Western-educated and professional class of Africans (in contrast to the Welfare fraternity, for example). He was committed to keeping the category of 'educated African' at a distance from any effective power, preferring to shore up the position of traditional figures of authority. So instead he opted to articulate his fears about their influence over the uneducated and argued against treating them as a separate class – on the extraordinary grounds, considering the privileges accorded to Kenya's whites, that this would give the impression that government approved 'class regulations and legislation which are opposed to the democratic'.[61] It would be an uphill task 'to interest literate Africans, already white-collar conscious, in mere handicraft and farming' was his honest appraisal. Even the most imaginative rural self-improvement schemes would not satisfy their naturally political ambitions.

From Mitchell's perspective, the Colonial Office had set the Empire an impossible task in view of the range of natural constraints he believed were operating in colonies like Kenya. In his view, all Africans were feckless and poor, partly a product of the environment in which they eked out a precarious existence. Consequently, the application of modern philosophies of welfare and social interventionism of the type Perham had called for after the fall of Singapore would be cosmetic, counter-productive and largely ineffective. He was far more conservative in outlook than Hailey and the architects of the colonial development and welfare formula: he took refuge in a return to indirect rule in order to maintain the status quo. He might have backed gradual assimilation but he could not dismantle any of his racial beliefs. His words of comfort reiterated long-standing settler myths and bolstered their self-image. It was not a message of collaboration and concession but rather of going it alone. It was delivered to an influential gathering and reported widely in the press. It was designed to rescue

60 Frost admits that Mitchell did not appreciate the mood of frustration and expectancy amongst the vastly increased number of young educated African men after the war. Consequently he mistakenly failed to give such men responsible posts in local government; Frost, 1992: 182.

61 Mitchell article in the *Sunday Post*, 20 June 1946, KNA CD5/301.

white Kenyans from the expectations of the metropolitan vision that jarred with their colonial reality.

In this frank talk, he showed how at home he was with a racial paternalism that envisaged only gradual change if economic conditions allowed it. His apparent reluctance to take up the appointment of Governor, fearing settler opposition to his view that race relations had to be approved, has fuelled speculation that he was simply another disciple of gradual trusteeship and no different from Hailey or mainstream thinkers on Empire within the Conservative and Labour Parties in Britain: he was committed to African advance and to reorganizing Makerere as a college of higher education; and he appointed seven new African Administrative Assistants in 1946.[62] Yet even if the rhetorical nature of his St George and the dragon speech is taken into account, his reputation as being anti-settler seems the greater myth, and his strong personalized politics became increasingly dominated by racial paternalism towards African peasants and a growing dislike of African political leaders. And for the likes of Fortie Ross, his views held out little comfort.

Nor was there a sudden respite for the Welfare Organization. All too soon yet another influential sector of European opinion also made clear its opposition. Certain missionaries were more than alarmed at the role that alcohol would play in government plans for African welfare. This was seen by officials as a necessary self-financing component of welfare. However, it alienated a hitherto naturally sympathetic constituency of support. In April 1946, the Secretary of the Christian Council of Kenya, Capon, informed the Chief Native Commissioner that his organization viewed the proposals to fund social centres with the profits of brewing with 'a grave disquietude'. He had sent copies of his letter of complaint to the *East African Standard*, *Kenya Weekly News* and *Baraza*, explaining his decision on the grounds that this was a matter of considerable interest to the public at large.[63] Such plans, he argued, gave official sanction to African drinking; few European landowners were keen to hand over land for social centres because of 'the inevitable consequence of African liquor consumption'. The view he elaborated reflected an enduring theme of racial stereotyping that was also applied to the lower classes at home: Africans, like children, were not capable of drinking alcohol; they soon became addicted; and they were highly unpredictable and violent when drunk. They knew no moderation and always gravitated towards excess. In addition, Capon accused the government of going against native custom. It was a misconception that young African men drank beer, he insisted. He offered an alternative: tea sold at 10 cents a mug.

Welfare clearly touched upon many of the big sensitive issues, such as

[62] For a view of Mitchell as benign governor see Frost, 1992: esp. ch.13 'If I Cannot Retire', pp. 174-85. For evidence that he sustained a distance between himself and settlers on a social level more rather than a political one see Throup, esp. ch.3.

[63] Capon to CNC, 5 April 1946, KNA MAA7/859.

the treatment of labour and the responsibility of government. Vulnerable to attack from such a respected body of opinion, the government responded. It denied that African social welfare would be funded solely from native beer sales; direct assistance was available and LNCs were encouraged to contribute funds; and local authorities would decide if the canteen at the social centre was to serve alcohol or not.[64] Dr Philip's point that canteens selling native beer already existed in social welfare centres in municipalities and townships, one being included in the plans at Dundori, was no comfort to those who were happy with the previous distinction between life in towns and rural areas.[65] They did not want to see the degenerative habits of bachelor migrants to the towns seep into rural life.

The accusation of African drunkenness at social centres continued to be levelled by settlers throughout the 1940s in an attempt to close them down. For example, the Dundori social welfare centre drew much criticism in the press from local farmers. The Dundori Welfare Association passed a motion declaring the centre to be a growing menace to law and order and demanding swift government action. Drunkenness and general misbehaviour apparently abounded and it was alleged that some Africans were afraid to go near the centre, fearful of having their throats cut.[66] Villages and social centres were a difficult political proposition for settlers. African drunkenness at Dundori was seized upon because it represented independence – African labourers outside their control. Here was one more illustration of the crisis of paternalism, as settlers fought to retain their right to dominate their labour at a time of mounting suspicion.

As Philip and Ross struggled to get their welfare philosophy adopted by the administration, so European opinion offered little in the way of support for their cause. Kenya was always a settler colony and white racial prejudice, when activated, could act as a brake on government policy in ways that were absent in other East African colonies. Indeed, settlers' complaints, provoked by welfare projects, served to unify opposition to such initiatives and drew out general anxiety about London's post-war agenda. Metropolitan posturing antagonized colonial minds that were fearful of what African welfare might mean for their fragile domination, built as it was on paternal control and racial exclusion. In the immediate aftermath of war, an older generation of white Kenyans felt spent and anxious about the future. Many clung to a view of government and state expenditure that had been forged during the years of the Depression (Mitchell, 1954: 219). They scoffed at the state-sponsored mollycoddling at home, peddled by what had become to many a distinctly un-English Parliament. After the Second World War, welfare quickly became a controversial and contested concept. It acted as a catalyst to white frustration and

[64] Tatton Brown to Capon, Limuru, 10 May 1946, KNA MAA7/859. This answer was supplied by Dr Philip.

[65] Dr Philip to CNC, 9 May 1946, ibid.

[66] Extracts from the *East African Standard*, KNA MAA7/859.

stimulated many racially motivated statements about African capabilites. Yet it ensured that settlers had to work harder to convince a wider public at home and abroad that their self-determination was not incompatible with, but in fact vital to, the economic and social advance of the African population. This did not commit them to adjusting political relationships. On the contrary. It was used to argue that white rule would have to be in place 'for a very long time' and was a line of argument which Europeans would constantly endeavour to assert with decreasing success throughout what remained of the late colonial period.[67]

As this series of public denunciations illustrates, many groups had a stake in opposing a vision of social welfare that challenged their paternalism as a system capable of providing the standard of living now expected for Africans. In the view of most white Kenyans, the Philip and Ross strategy of energizing African capabilities was inappropriate for Kenya: it simply meant throwing scarce resources at African mendacity or encouraging beer drinking. And – horror of horrors for European settler farmers – African villages and amenities in the Highlands signified the presence of permanently settled African labour living outside European paternalism, with rights to land outside their Reserves not directly tied to a labour contract. The Welfare Organization's plans had been subject to a short, sharp discrediting process by an influential set of lobbyists. Its modest goals had unwittingly acted as a conduit to the full range of free-floating European anxiety rooted in the wider political economy of the colony following the war. It seemed increasingly unlikely that the organization could survive beyond 1947.

Men behaving badly

Dogged by a shortage of resources, an absence of local intelligence, a far from coherent relationship with the Colonial Office and now hostile settler opinion, frustration among the welfare fraternity naturally mounted. This branch of the late colonial state appeared to be withering. Behind the scenes, the social welfare duo had managed to keep up a minimalist operation. Dr Philip had made an extensive tour of the major districts in early 1947 and was keen to establish a local focus for social welfare activities. He set out plans for the distribution of information rooms, European staff, African social welfare workers, wireless sets and film projectors. At the heart of this vision of social welfare were Africans as energizers of community development. This was what the men on the Jeanes School courses had been trained for: 'we were training men very much for Adult Education', Ross reflected much later.[68]

[67] Ibid. For an account of settler attempts to maintain this position in the 1950s, see Lewis, 2000.

[68] Written correspondence from Fortie Ross, 9 January 1995; 'Detailed Plan for African Welfare for Kenya for 1947' by C.R. Philip, forwarded to CNC, 17 March 1947, KNA MAA7/588.

The new syllabus for African social welfare workers at Jeanes – the second component of the plans for 1947 – illustrated this. Instruction in how to teach literacy, organize sports and games and maintain information rooms were core course components. These were supplemented with lessons on how to give talks using play-acting; how to liaise with departments; and how to run youth and homecraft groups. An impressive range of government officials had agreed to give lectures. Norman Humphrey was booked to speak on official agricultural policy, Harry Lambert on land tenure and Colonel Brooke Anderson on African settlement. Charles Mortimer had agreed to talk on race relations, Hope-Jones on Economics. The Chief Native Commissioner was to give an address on the relation of social workers with European officers and chiefs, concluding with a pep-talk on loyalty to the government. Representatives from the Information Office and *Pamoja* were also participating. They would talk on special campaigns, Chaundy from Education on Young Farmers' Clubs, and Dr Philip would bring up the rear with nutrition. Trainees were also expected to learn how to function as a safety-net for those who had fallen outside family care and discipline in an urban setting, indicating the dual social welfare role they were being ascribed. So, Mary Kenny, Nairobi's social welfare officer, was to talk on remedial social welfare; Cameron on the after-care of prisoners; and Owen on probation. A series of talks on municipal social welfare work would be given by Nicolina Deverell, Thomas Askwith and Dedan Githegi.

Dr Philip was trying to get off the ground a project that could engineer the much sought-after informed public opinion through adult education. It was a modest attempt and not the only one being made by the colonial state to manufacture a civil society. The range of participants in the course illustrates that it was an initiative that had secured more than a modicum of official support in Nairobi. However, beneath these projections and the list of celebrity drop-ins there lurked many unresolved issues and one very disillusioned social welfare adviser.

A week after submitting his plans, Dr Philip stormed the office of the Deputy Chief Secretary, Colin Thornley, brandishing a list of complaints.[69] He was unequivocal. Taking the post of social welfare adviser had been a terrible mistake and he threatened to resign. He had two main grouses: the government did not possess a clear mind as to what was meant by social welfare and he was never consulted about things going on that were 'right up his street'. He presented a litany of examples. The government had excluded him from discussions about a sociological survey of Mombasa at the time of the recent strike; he had only learned of Professor Isaac Shapera's visit to make a survey of anthropological study needs at a drinks party. Helping to prioritize sociological research projects

[69] Notes from a meeting between the ag. Deputy Chief Secretary and C.R. Philip, 25 March 1947, KNA MAA7/528.

in the colony was, he claimed, a legitimate part of his job. Secondly, no one had told him about Dr Northcote's efficiency survey of railway employees in Nairobi: he had only been introduced to one government sociologist. Thirdly, it was only through a chance reading of *Sauti a Bomani* that he had discovered that Aidan Southall, from Makerere College, was undertaking a sociological investigation in Nyanza Province. In addition, two personal bones of contention also aggrieved him: his personal allowance had been overlooked nor had he been considered for current Medical Department vacancies.

Thornley tried to placate him. He assured him that there was no deliberate intention to keep him in the dark. Part of the problem, he insisted, was that social welfare covered such a large range of subjects. Also, as he admitted privately, he was himself unaware of a couple of social surveys that were going on. Thornley offered an olive branch: a memorandum instructing the Secretariat to do their best to keep Dr Philip in close touch with all social welfare developments.[70] A mild circular in Nairobi would do little to reverse Philip's experience of being marginalized and unsupported. He had come up against a huge rock: the civil establishment's opposition to adjusting their local set-up.

A key battleground during the second colonial occupation was the generation and control of local intelligence. Generally, the district administration was not predisposed to share out its near monopoly over a commodity that was precious and often gleaned from investments in social relations. As a result, it was also a measure of prestige. New arrivals, with little in the form of recognized local expertise or similar local attachments, were not naturally embraced as collaborators. Dr Philip came up against this tendency in at least two instances when he tried to put his intentions into practice. First, he needed to draw up a map of the districts in order to plot where the new social welfare centres would be placed. He had asked DCs to send him copies of their district maps showing locational boundaries, roads etc. Likewise, government departments were asked to supply details of local social service activities listed as hospitals, dispensaries, clinics, schools, agricultural stations and veterinary centres, whether government, LNC or Mission-controlled.[71] This information would enable him to construct a unique colony-wide profile that reflected a different emphasis on government. Previous mapping exercises were about setting boundaries and demarcating Reserves, denoting the racial and tribal basis for government to follow. Philip's quest for a new definition of administrative space using social services and infrastructure represented an attempt to create new entry points into rural society, inspired by an increasingly variegated concept of what government was now required to provide. Unfortunately, by October 1946 he had received no replies. All

[70] Ibid., p.2; note in margin for Chief Secretary. Ibid.

[71] C.R. Philip to CNC 18 September 1946, KNA MAA7/588.

he could do was to ask the CNC to make another request on his behalf. Local officers evidently felt they had better things to do with their time.

Secondly, Dr Philip was unable to get social welfare officers accepted as information gatherers in their own right. Both African and European welfare workers were in a position to collect district news and views, both highly prized commodities. The Information Office in Nairobi put pressure on Dr Philip to supply them with local material. This was urgently needed to spice up government output, considered by their African staff to have become very dull by comparison with African newspapers.[72] Dr. Philip happily agreed and issued a reminder that news gathering formed part of his welfare workers' training. Reports of traditional and locational council meetings concerning community social welfare work, of talks given at the community centres by departmental officers and lists of those attending classes, organizing plays or employing modern farming techniques were in future to be sent to him and the Information Office where appropriate. He asked that district monthly intelligence reports – the basic form of collating information about events and issues in each district – should be included 'whether or not they contain accounts of social welfare activities'.[73]

Central Province's new PC, Aubrey 'Mug' Mullins, would have none of this. No DC of his was going to forward Intelligence Reports to the Social Welfare Adviser. It would involve additional work and paper; the individual concerned could get the information from the Director of Manpower or the Information Office.[74] However, Mullins' major objection was that the Information Officer and Dr Philip 'may very likely put a different interpretation or emphasis on an item of local news and this may do more harm than good'. In a gesture that typified the recourse to petty insult, Mullins added that he would not be sending a copy of the letter to Dr Philip since he understood him to be working under the CNC. Not all administrators were quite so negative. Discussing the future of Civil Reabsorption Officers, Nyanza's DCs, who faced less district tension than their counterparts in Central Province, were more flexible. They wanted these officers to become permanent, merging into social welfare officers providing they were 'part of the administration staff and ... directly responsible to the District Commissioner'.[75] They suggested the Information Officer be used to supply materials, whilst the social welfare adviser would be approached on matters of policy. Perhaps they were persuaded partly because the CROs had better trucks than they did, for they also insisted that the CRO vehicles should be handed over to the administration and

[72] J.L. Reiss (Information Office) to C.R. Philip, 17 April 1947, KNA DC/KSM/1/1/196.

[73] Circular letter to all DCs, CROs, DOs (Social Welfare), Settlement Officers and Municipal Social Welfare Officers, 19 April 1947; ibid.

[74] Mullins to CNC 14 May 1947, KNA MAA7/494.

[75] Minutes of DCs' Conference 13–15 January, 1947 forwarded to Secretariat by Hunter, KNA MAA7/588.

made available for general use. As Philip had learnt the hard way, whilst on paper most people accepted his existence, few in practice wanted to share their local intelligence with him or indeed allow him to gather his own.

Another weakness in the system which the Thornley circular had failed to address, or possibly could not, was ineffective lines of communication. Continued confusion over an agreed definition of social welfare by London, by the Welfare Organization and by the administration soon had important practical repercussions when the wrong sort of social welfare officer was recruited in London. Mary Kenny, the government's social welfare worker in Nairobi, needed help. In 1946 Philip had successfully fought to have her and her remedial work placed under his jurisdiction. Mrs Kenny soon forged strong links with voluntary organizations. She undertook much individual casework, registering and relocating Nairobi's chronically poor and vulnerable and those deemed socially delinquent.[76] However, her workload soon became unacceptable; she had to cover twice the number of cases recommended for one person. Philip asked the Social Welfare Advisory Committee for help. The Colonial Office recruited Nancy Shepherd who arrived in early 1947 and stepped straight into an administrative fiasco.

What caused a young unmarried woman to apply for such a post in the colonial service after the Second World War? Nancy Shepherd already had a connection with Kenya. She was born in Mombasa where her father was working as a CMS missionary doctor (she had a younger sister who was still living in the colony). At the age of three, her parents sent her to boarding school in England; missionary compassion abroad sometimes came with a brutal price at home. Seven years later they collected her and went to live on the outskirts of Cardiff, the home of her paternal grandparents, where her father set up a new practice. Her schooling was often disrupted through illnesses such as scarlet fever, diphtheria and measles. She failed to matriculate in mathematics which ruled out going to university. She wanted to go to the Slade School to study art, but her father forbade her. However, in line with the family ethos and her own needs, she had to find a way to make a living. Eventually 'poor old Nance' was sent to learn how to be a domestic science teacher at a college in Cardiff. Here she received instruction in the latest nutritional theories, babycare, dietetics and how to launder clothes; part of the training included working as a housekeeper and a maid. She found she possessed a flair for teaching thanks to her natural ability in art. After a number of unsatisfying teaching jobs she applied to the CMS to become a missionary. Her interview went badly; she was considered too worldly and not dedicated enough.

[76] See previous discussion in Chapter 4. She described her work and that of the organization to the EAWL in January 1947; Notes of a meeting in Nairobi, 22 January 1947, KNA CD5/301.

Then came a job that was to shape the direction of her life dramatically. Helped by a patient of her father's, she secured employment as an assistant to the head of a new social welfare department for the town of Abergavenny. Unemployment and poverty were endemic with the effects of the Depression hitting already poor communities. The majority of men were on the dole and a strike by miners worsened the situation. Unlike many women of her time, Nancy could drive. She had learnt so that she could help her father on his medical rounds, sometimes going with him to visit the very poor 'panel patients', whom he sometimes did not even bill for his services. She was given a Morris Minor and had a much prized mileage allowance. Although used to seeing extreme poverty, what she witnessed driving around the Welsh Valleys during this time was 'heartbreaking'. Fraying rope ladders led to squalid attic bedrooms. Many houses had no furniture. Large dogs roamed the rooms. The squalor and poverty contrasted so vividly with the standard of living of the 'fat cats in Cardiff' during the 1930s that she decided to join the Labour Party. Particularly shocking to her was the lot of many of the women. One household might be made up of twelve men and one woman who would have to do all the domestic chores. Their daily lives were dreary and drab. The women often had little access to money, the men drinking or gambling much of it away as soon as they received their allowances. Their children wore rags and some went without shoes. She would offer instruction in laundering and how to make cheap but nutritious food with seasonal and locally grown ingredients.

It was not a job that many women did at the time and it was physically very demanding. Shepherd eventually caught bronchitis and reluctantly had to resign. She was sent to Madeira, where her uncle was an anglican Archbishop, to recover. As the threat of war mounted, she returned and enrolled in the WRNS. A stint as driver for an admiral was rewarded with promotion to London, followed by postings to Windsor and various sea port barracks. She fell in love. But the war was a harsh as well as a liberating experience. Her new love as well as her own brother were killed. Likewise, her duties revolved around dispatching men across the Channel knowing that many of them were destined never to return. In 1945 she was granted compassionate leave as her father had cancer. She nursed him through his defiant struggle to continue working until he finally died of uraemia. By the end of 1946, she had a reason to leave, a familiarity with Empire and a wealth of experience in ministering social welfare to poor working-class women.[77]

Yet her appointment provoked great despair. On her arrival in Kenya, Dr Philip was aghast to learn that she had no experience of individual casework, nor did she consider herself competent to undertake it; the Colonial Office had told her that her duties would be teaching domestic science and training African women in homecrafts.[78] This placed him in

[77] Interview with Nancy Shepherd, 25 May 1996.

[78] Philip to Chief Secretary, 18 April 1947, KNA MAA7/528.

what he confessed was an 'embarrassing situation'. Although one other woman was undergoing training in England prior to becoming a social welfare officer in Nairobi, the situation had become critical and in addition, extra clerical staff were desperately needed. Dr Philip wrote to the Chief Secretary in April 1947 explaining the situation in candid terms. Mary Kenny was making herself ill, he warned, by 'working continuously overtime and facing problems most of which are difficult to solve and for many of which present conditions in Kenya allow of no solution'. Despondency was setting in amidst the confusion and lack of means to tackle Nairobi's increasing poverty. Also other areas remained neglected. Dr Philip had a list of urgent wants. Kenny needed to get out into the Reserves and do 'much needed work amongst African women, for whom at present nothing is being done'.[79] Education for children of mixed racial parentage, plus homes for the aged and the destitute, were desperately needed. Remedial social welfare was also in a chaotic state. The district administration continually by-passed the Welfare Organization, preferring to deal directly with organizations like the YWCA or EAWL. However, all cases ultimately made their way back to Mary Kenny.

Hampered by obstacles to sharing information and effective assistance to meet local needs, the work of the organization was clearly being undermined. Certainly from Dr Philip's vantage point, Kenya's welfare structure did not look too healthy. Beleaguered and possibly embittered, his enthusiasm showed understandable signs of waning. Kenya seemed to be slipping behind other East African territories, and Philip saw little merit in co-operating with them. The Colonial Office suggested an East African welfare conference be held at the end of 1947. Philip wanted to wait another year on the grounds of needing to collect more information, although Mary Kenny clearly had made progress in Nairobi. When he was pressed again less than a year later, the government agreed that social welfare and mass education had not advanced enough for the colony to benefit from such a conference.[80]

Philip was reluctant to establish firm links with the social science training offered to Africans at Makerere. Aidan Southall had asked for clarification of the employment possibilities for Africans who had specialised in social studies. Philip argued – somewhat sagaciously perhaps – that commitment and maturity were not necessarily found in post-graduates; Kenyans, who had attended the nine-month Jeanes course and proved themselves after two years practical work in community centres, could go to Makerere.[81] Southall was mortified by attitudes in Kenya and aghast that Kenya's

79 Philip discussion with ag. DCS, 25 March 1947, KNA MAA7/528.

80 Philip to CS, 22 November 1947, discussing agenda prepared by Miss Darlow at the CO, August 1947; KNA MAA7/504. Blaxter to CS, 16 September 1948 and ag CS to the Administrator, East Africa High Commission, Nairobi, 22 October 1948, ibid.

81 Philip to CNC 26 August 1947, KNA MAA7/495; Philip to Southall, 16 January 1948; ibid.

CNC should reply by asking his advice as to what social science-trained Makerere graduates could do in the colony. Surely Dr Philip could direct them to whatever jobs needed doing in Kenya within the wide field of social welfare, Southall asked. Uganda's own social welfare department, he pointed out, was taking a few students every year.[82]

Turning down closer co-operation with Uganda might well have been a mistake. The Uganda authorities, it seemed, had agreed upon a simpler view of the scope and function of social welfare and how to implement it, creating a department of Public Relations and Social Welfare in 1946.[83] In a straightforward manner that Kenya could not match, this department had set out its remit in 1947. Public relations was to have a threefold function: to stimulate production; to help social development, defined as efforts made by the government and the people to raise the general standard of living; and to build up a 'two-way channel of information'. Social welfare was defined as 'the social advance of the peoples of Uganda by all means available, but especially by encouraging individual and group initiative, self-help and community spirit'. Uganda already had in place fifty-two ex-servicemen trained in demonstration techniques that were geared to stimulating African interest in improvement by putting into practice 'current ideas on agriculture, veterinary and health matters'. There was little sign of attention to remedial work but women seemed to have a higher profile .Official policy did allege that classes in homecraft and general welfare had been arranged for women. On paper at least, Uganda had apparently quietly found consensus and clarity while Kenya continued to muddy the waters. Kenyan officials did occasionally complain that their administration was 'makeshift and dilapidated' by 1939 because of the Depression and the way so much money was siphoned off to make the machinery of white settlement work. Uganda was routinely envied because it lacked these constraints and had a larger administrative budget.[84]

However, at a number of other sites within Kenya's administration, the spirit and impact of social welfare were being carried forward with vigour and optimism. The second colonial occupation was kept afloat as much by individuals' energetic commitment to their own particular self-styled projects, as by external directives. At the level of social welfare, three categories of civil servants were pouring their own learnt experience into the new post-war administrative spaces. First, there were the professional women given new posts in local government. Mary Kenny, for example, was employed as a metropolitan trained social welfare worker, thanks to

[82] Southall to Philip. 7 February 1948, ibid.

[83] Various documents received from the Ugandan Public Relations and Social Welfare Department, Kampala, 19 March 1947 and 4 January 1947, KNA MAA7/588.

[84] Ugandan Public Relations and Social Welfare Department, 'Statement of policy', 4 January 1947. p.1, KNA MAA7/588. For an overview of Uganda's welfare provisions see also Iliffe, 1984: 204; Askwith, 1995: 5; RH Mss.Afr.s.1770.

the imperial consensus of the late 1930s that more women were needed in the colonies to work among women and children. Despite the confusion that existed in Nairobi over remedial welfare, Kenny was able to make progress in clarifying the colony's provision for those unable to look after themselves. She persistently worked to build up a detailed profile of the colony's remedial social welfare needs. She sacrificed her bank-holidays, week-ends and health to produce two papers, 'Remedial Social Welfare' and 'The Training of African Women for Community Service'.[85]

Mary Kenny was an important new publicist for her particular brand of welfare amongst organizations like the EAWL. She spoke to them on the need for comprehensive legislation on remedial and welfare provision in the colony, inspiring the earnest wives of many administrators.[86] Kenny recommended that a non-governmental child welfare council be set up in the colony; she also called for the training of African women as part of a systematic social development programme. What the colony urgently needed, she argued, was a full-time social welfare officer experienced in teaching simple dietetics and homecrafts to instruct African women at the Jeanes School and to work on a pilot scheme which would investigate their future activities at community centres.[87]

Meticulous in her approach, Mary Kenny had undertaken the unglamorous dirty work, producing a shopping list, for the first time, of all that the colony lacked with regard to provision for those who could not rely on family or clan systems to care for them in their moment of vulnerability, and the type of care needed for those who appeared to have become immune to traditional forms of social discipline, such as juvenile vagrants and prostitutes. She was able to talk with authority and calm about issues like the apparent increase in prostitution in Nairobi. Rather than blame African immorality, she offered a list of social factors: housing conditions precluded the possibility of men bringing their wives or families to Nairobi; bride-price was high; and social change had produced a decrease in polygamy, increased the pressure on suitable paid employment for women and brought improvements in transport. She recommended training programmes in constructive work-room employment, rather than in domestic work, since that might discourage respectable girls from entering this field. Thus women and the growing vulnerability of sectors of an urban population were given much needed expert coverage and a range of solutions put forward. At the very least, the Welfare Organization had allowed individuals like Kenny to gain a foothold in the colonial structure and document the incoherence. Thus, the Welfare Organization's existence since 1946 had enabled new bearers of power to administer and suggest solutions.

[85] Philip to CS, 18 April 1947, KNA MAA7/528.

[86] 3rd Meeting of the EAWL Standing Health Committee, 8 May 1946, KNA CD5/301.

[87] Summary of recommendations contained in a letter from C.R. Philip, 18 April 1947, KNA MAA7/528.

New players like Dr Philip and Mary Kenny were aided by a second group, those who had come into the administration during the war and had experience of the army. Patrick Williams's work as Director of Training reinforced his view that government could take action to shore up the family, African women and co-operation amongst technical administrators. He took great pride in the work of the Jeanes School which he promoted at all times: the retraining of ex-*askari* which commanded respect throughout the colony, particularly for its promotion of civic virtues and citizenship; the vocational training in commerce, trading, agriculture and social welfare; the wives' course; and the flourishing religious groups, student societies, sports and co-operative shop.[88] Williams's twofold explanation of the school's value attests to his vision of it which he would work to secure when he eventually took over from Dr Philip to become Commissioner for Welfare in 1948. First, it was unique, as a 'community training centre where men, women and children' were all trained together. Secondly, it was 'a composite training centre where the future Social Welfare Worker, teacher or Agricultural Instructor are taught together and can build up personal relationships which should encourage their working together in the reserves after their training'. However, his keenness to publicize the school did not blind him to the practical obstacles in the way of fulfilment of these aims. The esprit de corps might not last long after so brief a training; nor would there be enough follow-up support to prevent inertia creeping in, he warned, echoing the fate of the first generation of Jeanes School teachers of the 1930s. Williams would have known this scenario was a likely one.

The third category of administrators who clung to a vision of energized African families as the basis for welfare and development were a small corps of established members of the administration. They included Nyanza's Provincial Commissioner, Eric Davies, who had worked as the colony's Information Officer during the Second World War. A pioneer of social welfare in Nairobi was Thomas Askwith, Municipal Native Affairs Officer, who had backed the idea of supporting family life – patriarchal-style – in Nairobi back in 1940.[89] Considered by some to be a maverick , he had, unlike Philip and Ross, cut his teeth as a District Officer. A Quaker and a founder member of the United Kenya Club, he insisted that African staff should be appointed to assist him with his work in Nairobi. He was clear about his role, that of social engineer for the relief of the city's poor and vulnerable.

From private reading, he had discovered that sociologists and industrialists in areas like the Belgian Congo were endeavouring to stabilize labour through the provision of housing, social services and social security, and he

[88] *Annual Report from the Director of Training for 1947*, KNA DC/KSM/1/1/196.

[89] See discussion in Chapter 3. He became the third Commissioner and his contribution is assessed in Chapter 6. For further details of his career, see Joanna Lewis, 'Introduction' to Askwith, 1995: 1–28.

applied the same principle to Nairobi. His post-war plan contained three basic components: housing the whole African population of Nairobi in village settlements, each of 3,000 inhabitants with suitable family accommodation for men wishing to live with their wives and children; building up social amenities at each settlement; and fostering a community spirit amongst the tenants. Crucial was the community centre containing a meeting hall, a recreation room, a lending library and a reading room.[90] An example of the way in which tribal identities were reinforced by urban experience, Africans were positively encouraged by Askwith to group themselves into associations that were tribal, in order to preserve their best traditions. He also suggested that they be allowed to form commercial and even political associations to enable them to express their aspirations as well as their grievances. Settlement or village communities were vital, he argued, for a community spirit: Africans had to be given responsibility if they were to support their own welfare. The Municipal Council's African Advisory Council would function as a central African parliament, he boldly told the government, and he planned to increase co-operation with the appointment of African municipal councillors.[91]

Askwith was able to bring greater coherence to the range of obstacles that stood in the way of improved urban social welfare. He predicted that full stabilization of the African population in Nairobi required 40,000 houses and single rooms in 1946. He could also see the push of rural poverty playing an important part. Despite advances in provision, 'many additional women and children, came in from the Reserves when an opportunity occurred'; the population would increase to 60,000 adults and 60,000 children without any increase in the working population of 40,000.[92] And a cost of living survey in 1946 had given further proof that the minimum wage was inadequate for a family to look after itself in Nairobi. In a chilling forewarning of the processes which would begin to move Africans towards Mau Mau, Askwith cautioned in 1947 that the general situation had deteriorated further . A vast influx of men from the Reserves had produced a new threat. These men were given the tag of 'spivs' – a term imported from Britain to describe an urban underclass of sharply dressed men who lived off others or from the proceeds of crime and avoided the discipline of regular work. In Kenya at this time they included young male school-leavers and unemployed ex-*askari*. When not attending mass meetings they could be found in an area known locally as

[90] *Annual Report on African Affairs in Nairobi*, 1946. p.12, PRO CO533/588/7; 'African Social Welfare Work – Nairobi', Summary for Secretariat prepared by T.G. Askwith, 6 September 1945, Conclusion p. 3., KNA MAA7/494; 1946 Municipal African Affairs Report, pp. 12-14., PRO CO533/588/7 and *Annual Report on African Affairs in Nairobi, 1947*, PRO CO533/588/7.

[91] 'African Social Welfare Work – Nairobi', Askwith, 6 September 1945 p.3., KNA MAA7/494.

[92] *Annual Report on African Affairs in Nairobi*, 1946, p. 5, PRO CO533/588/7.

Mikora, meaning 'those uncivilized people who recognize no authority, either of parents, elders or government'.[93] With more leisure time than other men, they were a particular menace.

Despite these bleak forecasts, Askwith kept a cool head. He was of the Beveridge generation which sharply distinguished him from old district hands. He believed strongly that it was part of normal social development for the state to intervene to prevent the exploitation of the weakest members of society, not by establishing monopolies but by introducing an element of competition to safeguard standards and to keep basic costs in check as far as food and housing were concerned. He recognized that there were other barriers to his efforts to associate Africans with their own welfare and he did not shy away from criticizing African leadership, for he was keen to highlight what he described as a psychological barrier. Leaving social welfare in the hands of leading members of the African community, in addition to a loss of efficiency, did not always engender keenness. Organizations often collapsed and there was a tendency to turn to the Council for help.

The second obstacle he identified was 'an over-critical and destructive attitude on the part of the better educated African to all Municipal schemes for his betterment'. An example was the resentment of dairy producers towards the Council's attempt to provide cheap clean milk. 'The African', he lamented, did not appreciate that 'not only does he have to be protected from members of other races but also his own'. There were some successes to which he could draw attention, such as a village committee at Starehe which had managed to transform its residents from 'a disorderly crowd of degenerates to a self-respecting community'.[94]

Working with Askwith in Nairobi was Nicolina Deverell, recently appointed as welfare assistant to work among African women. In November 1946 she began a pioneering scheme to train two African women welfare assistants. There was much that was waiting to be done. Sewing classes were held back because of a shortage of funds, and liaison with the EAWL had resulted only in one mainly Agikuyu Women's Organization, that had been disproved of for its 'political bias'.[95] Two government nursery schools under her jurisdiction gave her the opportunity to make a survey of the living conditions of fifty households. She meticulously investigated the daily food intake for a single family, its expenditure on furniture, haircuts and sundries, and made a clothing census standing at a road junction in down-town Nairobi. Her conclusion, accepted by Askwith, was that only a tiny group earned enough in wages to keep their families in Nairobi. Her results were used after the Mombasa docks strike to adjust minimum wage levels, and her work raised the profile of family welfare,

[93] Appendix to 1946 *Annual Report on African Affairs in Nairobi*, 'Cost of living survey by Miss Deverell', ibid.

[94] *Annual Report*, 1946, p. 15, ibid.

[95] 'Annual report of the social welfare worker for 1946'. Appendix to main report, ibid.

providing vital ammunition in the battle to increase African welfare provision.

Ultimately, however, time was not to be on their side. Conditions in Nairobi were worsening. Some halls were already the site of frequent disorder blamed on 'the cupidity of private clubs'. Yet of greater short-term significance was the fact that her reports and those produced by others were now being read with interest at the Colonial Office. Although during Dr Philip's reign the work of the Welfare Organization was severely undermined by widespread disagreement and local opposition – in particular the problem of accessing information and intelligence had left Dr Philip bruised and professionally frustrated – at the margins there were signs of resistance and revival. Urban administrators, women welfare officers and formed soldiers working in adult education rallied round and ensured that the post-war administrative landscape would never be quite the same. And, by mid-1947 Kenya also had its first African social welfare workers in situ. Would they fare any better than their white counterparts?

'We are the chosen ones'

The Africanization of technical branches of the late colonial state, as recommended by Lord Hailey, was inching forward; social welfare offers an interesting case-study as to how this first generation fared. By early 1947 the first African social welfare workers had finished their training course at the Jeanes School, and were ready to take up their new posts. However, soon after their arrival in the districts, confusion and dissent muddied the waters. The Welfare Organization had not come up with a formula that found universal approval. Opinions were still divided as to what African social welfare workers were expected to do. Despite all the previous discussion, in March 1947 Eric Davies, Nyanza's PC, complained that 'no one is quite sure what they should do; that during their training an undue emphasis had been placed on sport; and there was totally insufficient material in the form of pictures, posters, pamphlets for the Information Rooms'.[96] He appears not to have addressed Dr Philip directly on this matter and clearly did not share his vision.

From Eric Davies's vantage point, the promotion of African families was not being as well-served as it might have been. The focus of social welfare training was influenced by the wartime propaganda and the glamour of *askari* masculinity. He wanted a less adventurous but more technically orientated African welfare worker, like those in Uganda, who would work with his wife as a living example of betterment. At their house and plot, he suggested, the husband (rather than the wife) would show what could be

[96] PC (Coast Province) to E.R.St A. Davies, Information Officer, 17 March 1947, KNA MAA7/495.

done with local materials, home-made furniture, a vegetable and flower garden, tree planting, manure and crop rotation. Davies also prescribed activities for his wife. She would teach simple dressmaking, cookery, child care and domestic cleanliness. He thought the key was to introduce men and women who could advise on the simpler problems arising in the lives of Africans around their centre. African welfare workers should receive six months agricultural training and two months veterinary training at provincial training centres.[97]

The universally acceptable jack-of-all-trades who could dish out the magic pill of betterment remained as elusive as ever. Whilst sympathetic to Nyanza's particular needs, Dr Philip did not think them worthy of instigating a reorientation in African welfare training. There were no government funds available for such an exercise in any case. There was, he explained, 'no intention of Social Welfare Workers (ASWWs) regarding themselves as experts on any of those subjects for which trained Africans already exist'.[98] Philip stuck to his war-time model of propaganda and information-messenger who would concentrate on mass education. The role of ASWWs, he continued to Nyanza's PC, did not embrace expert instruction in any of the activities of the various government departments. Rather, he insisted, their job, as approved and recommended by the Secretary of State, was to encourage team work at the community centre, and to help African and European specialist staff make use of the communication facilities available at the community centres, both technical ones like film-strips, and social ones, such as the locations' welfare committee meetings.

The Colonial Office memorandum on Social Welfare circulated in 1945 had stated that an important task of welfare workers would be to take responsibility for promoting activities not covered by technical departments, such as poultry and bee keeping, although such officers were also to create 'opportunities for the experts to disseminate their wisdoms'. The African social welfare worker as he had been trained in Kenya was clearly canalized towards adult education. The problem was that local needs as well as opinions varied and there was much they could do. What no one could foresee was that the time assumed to be available for trial and error was not going to materialize. By November 1947 a rumour was circulating that the course would not be running in 1948, which necessitated a disclaimer.[99] The beginning of the next course was postponed until March 1948; candidates were to apply only if they had a guarantee of salary from their LNCs.

Nevertheless, a handful of rural welfare centres were stirring into life. It

[97] PC (Nyanza) to Senior Veterinary Officer, 20 May 1947, KNA DC/KSM/1/1/196; also to Information Officer, 17 March 1947 and to CS, 12 June 1947 KNA MAA7/495.

[98] C.R. Philip to CNC, 26 June 1947, KNA MAA7/495.

[99] Circular letter from Philip to the administration, 3 November 1947, KNA DC/KSM/1/1/196.

seemed that social welfare was succeeding. For some, it offered something of a handle on colonial power in an increasingly precarious and competitive rural setting, while for others it simply provided a venue for a bit of fun and a get-together. Upwardly mobile former soldiers sought to extend their social networks and dwindling savings; small-time chiefs wanted to shore up their generational power base; younger women too wanted to see if they could take advantage of whatever might be on offer. And in any case its message was hardly novel. So, in October 1947 Dr Philip was able to produce a ten-page review of community centre activities compiled from monthly reports.[100] Despite the heavy rains, fourteen community centres had regularly held adult education classes attended by men and women, nine held basic English classes, whilst six ran a mixture of homecraft and general welfare classes for African women. There were two in Central Province, three in Nyanza and one in Coast Province where a Mothers' Union had been formed by the wife of the African social welfare worker, which, impressively, ran keep-fit classes twice a week.

Dr Philip conveyed the sense of a small but nevertheless buoyant community centre movement. He was able to list a variety of educational projects apparently being run at the centres, new social welfare committees, sporting events, competitions, exhibitions, and shows, in addition to examples of co-operation between committees, LNCs and voluntary organizations. In the white farming areas there were also signs of progress. Financial negotiations for a social centre in Trans Nzoia District had lasted nearly two years. From a government loan of £1,500 and a grant of £250 from the Native Trust Fund, the District Council planned to build a headman's house, marketplace, dressing station, dispensary, brewery and beer shop, tea shop and a church. The loan came from the DARA Fund at a rate of 3 per cent per annum to be paid over twenty years; thus it represented something of a serious investment in welfare provision. The hope was that rents from the shops would cover the sinking fund charges on the loan and running expenses.[101] Meanwhile Dundori was steaming ahead. By 1948 a cocktail of grants from the Native Trust Fund, the government and the Forest Department, plus donations from farmers, had secured a dispensary, brewery, dispenser's house, tea shop, headman's house, shop and part of a market. The Council then made a request for a £300 DARA loan for water supplies, sanitation, a butcher's shop, staff quarters and the rest of the market.[102] Beneath the official statistics, however, the reality was less healthy.

The fortunes of the first ex-*askari* ASWWs reflect the fortunes of the second colonial occupation in general. Where local interest and politics

[100] 'Notes on Community Centre Activities'. 8 October 1947, KNA DC/KSM/1/1/196 and MAA7/494.

[101] 'Native Social Welfare Centres', Notes from the Secretariat, 24 February 1948, KNA MAA7/859.

[102] 'Social centres in the Settled Areas', 9 March 1948, ibid.

could be served by partnership with the government, then, without recourse to force, the colonial state showed powers of reinvigoration; mutual self-interest was within the realm of colonial welfare and development despite the chronic shortage of funding, staff and equipment. The former soldiers began to apply their training with mixed results. Eric Davies, Nyanza's enthusiastic PC, was impressed enough to write to the Chief Secretary praising the activities at Maseno Welfare Centre, Central Kavirondo District.[103] Aggrey Willis Ahomo, known previously as a black sheep when on the Jeanes course, was now showing what Davies described as 'remarkable powers of organization and most laudable initiative'. He had set up a local social welfare committee which had agreed to contribute funds towards the centre and to try to pay the salary of an assistant at 60 shillings per month. He had arranged spinning and weaving classes, held literacy groups and had plans for classes in child welfare. At the end of March 1947 he dispatched 26 teachers into the field after giving them three and a half weeks training in mass education which included talks by fifteen outside experts and visits to Maseno and Kisumu departmental offices. Aggrey Willis was confident that 'these men are knowledgeable in almost everything'.[104] Davies was thrilled. Repeatedly referring to Maseno as a 'community', he recommended that they should be left to learn from experience, providing they were visited regularly by a European Officer and nothing was purchased on credit. Such communities, he insisted, 'should be given as much latitude as possible' on the grounds that they were 'a concrete example of at least professed "self-help". I would advise', he ended, 'that this and similar manifestations should not be discouraged by too rigid an attitude.'

Here, in the relatively calm atmosphere of Nyanza, were all the ingredients of a successful story of local animation as dreamed of by the welfare experts – a self-organizing civil society. This was partly because local African elites backed the welfare worker. A welfare committee made up of influential local men and women began talking the right language. Contributions from each district were soon agreed, and each meeting ended with a prayer and cups of tea.[105] Motivated by the slogan of mass education for all, the committee made plans to bring their disabled to the centre to learn a trade and to send their blind to the colony's special training centre at Thika. Chief Zakayo Ochieng used the forum to ask for instruction in tile-making. They agreed to hold folk dances, greatly welcomed as a means both of bringing together local children who

[103] PC (Nyanza) to CS 20 May 1947, KNA DC/KSM/1/1/196.

[104] Minutes of 2nd Social Welfare Committee Meeting, Maseno Dept. 28 March 1947, ibid.

[105] Ibid. From Gem had come Revd Simon Nyende (President), Chief Zakayo Ochieng, Asst Chief Daniel Owiti, Paulo Opiche, Mariko Okalo, Miss Nerea Awuor (Vice Treasurer) Miss Lea Odiembo. From Seme, Chief Ibrahim Noi, Barnaba Okuku (Vice President), Sila Adera, Andrea Aila (Treasurer), Ibrahim Ogila, Petro Aila, Miss Rosa Atieno and Revd Festo Olang, the future Anglican Archbishop of Kenya.

attended different schools and of carrying on their traditions. The women also volunteered for a training course at the centre in order to 'prepare the way for other women'. There was also a sense of divine mission in the air. 'As God had given freely', Aggrey Willis told them, so they must give since 'We are the chosen ones to serve our country'.

However, it was not all plain sailing and attitudes were showing signs of the rigidity Eric Davies had warned against. Dr Philip rather grumpily insisted that the appointment of unofficial assistants as requested required 'very careful consideration'. Maseno's commitment to try to pay for an assistant was too vague, he insisted. Part of the brake on local initiative came from the fact that there was no extra money available elsewhere in support.[106] More worryingly for others, Aggrey Willis Ahomo then began to show signs of using his position to advance other ambitions. It appeared that the cement that held the group together was membership of the same church. Charles Atkins, Kisumu's DC, became concerned that the welfare work at the centre was becoming 'too much of a C.M.S. affair'.[107] Whilst Atkins was pleased that Ahomo was bringing a Christian influence to bear, he confessed that he had been 'rather shaken' to learn that part of the buildings being used for social welfare activities, on temporary loan from the council showground, had been dedicated as a chapel. He would be forced to intervene, he warned, unless Aggrey recognized that his work was non-denominational and had 'to benefit Roman Catholics and pagans every bit as much as Protestants'. The fear was that a civil society structured around a non-secular force might well start to behave in an uncivil way.

Although by 1948 some welfare workers quickly showed themselves to be far below the standard required, others made a positive start against tremendous odds.[108] Fortie Ross was heartened when he received a letter from one of his first students working in the field. 'The old men are bending their sinews to learn', he wrote. Another had marked out a sports ground and run athletic meetings which had earned the affectionate title of the Field Marshall.[109] Cosmas John M.B. Owade of Bondo Division was another rising star in his district. Despite falling an early victim to a burst bicycle tyre which condemned him to months without transport, he made Herculean efforts to fulfil a plethora of local welfare functions.[110] The desperateness of the situation comes through the pages of his meticulously hand-written reports on lined A4 paper. No transport meant that to

[106] Philip to CNC 9 May 1947 in response to a request from the CRO passed to the Director of Training, KNA MAA7/495.

[107] Atkins to Revd D.G. Givan, Maseno with a copy sent to Aggrey Willis Ahomo, 30 May 1947, KNA DC/KSM/1/1/196.

[108] Social Welfare Monthly Report for March 1948, Central Kavirondo, from CRO to Philip, 1 April 1948, ibid.

[109] Written correspondence with Fortie Ross, 9 January 1995.

[110] Social Welfare Reports for January and March 1947 by Cosmas John M.B. Owade, KNA DC/KSM/1/1/196.

referee a football match at Kambare in Gem, he had to make a round trip of 10 miles on foot. His written reports show good evidence of co-operation developing between himself, the district administration, Hutchinson, the mobile cinema officer, and on one occasion an Agricultural Officer. But, ominously perhaps, he noted that at Alego he met 'people not ready to be shown cinema'.

On a visit to Ngiya on 2 February 1947, Owade described how they joined forces to give a talk at a girls' school and another at the dispensary on hygiene, followed by a cinema show to a thousand people the next day. He had drawn great comfort from the interest shown in his commentary on manure. His dedication and compassion seemed boundless. So, despite the distance and effort involved, with committed individuals and a sympathetic administration, a message seemed to be getting across. However, these two ingredients were fast disappearing.

In less tranquil districts, such copy-book progress proved more elusive. African welfare workers became embroiled in local disputes where tensions between state and society were rising. Gibson Mwangi took up his appointment in Olenguruone at the end of February 1947. Olenguruone was a settlement recently designed to meet Colonial Office insistence that land be set aside for African squatters who had been sent there during the war. It became a pilot scheme in government-directed smallholder husbandry. The farmers already settled on the land objected to this interference which produced a conflict of authority. This Kikuyu refusal to submit to government interference precipitated the threat of eviction and was one important element feeding the mass adoption of the Kikuyu Oath of Unity.[111] No welfare hall had yet been built and Mwangi found himself working from a district office where eviction orders against recalcitrant Kikuyu settlers were being drafted. Due to the considerable increase in this work, Mwangi was drafted in to help with the orders, to spread information about the facilities offered by the government to those prepared to move and to deal with cases of hardship.[112]

Mwangi's welfare role had been usurped by the local administration. He found himself in the front line of a battle between Kikuyu farmers and the district administration. When called to make a statement for the prosecution in an obstruction charge brought against a number of Kikuyu settlers at Molo Police Court, he had refused to attend and was reprimanded by the magistrate. The irate District Officer was certain of his disloyalty to the government and of his complete sympathy with the recalcitrant. While admitting that Mwangi's task was difficult owing to the prevailing atmosphere and the lack of facilities made worse by his lack of organizing ability, by August the government officer for Olenguruone described him as 'self-opinionated, lacking in initiative and energy, deceitful,

[111] For background details on Olenguruone see Lonsdale, 1992: ch.12 and also Throup, 1987: ch. 6.

[112] DO (Olenguruone Settlement) to DC Nakuru. 29 August 1947, KNA MAA7/495.

resentful of correction. Almost every action that he takes, is influenced by the predominant desire to cut a figure before his fellows.' Dr Philip was more sympathetic. He was disturbed that Mwangi had been engaged with eviction orders, for this would naturally place him in rather a difficult position as a social welfare worker.[113]

Illustrating the climate of suspicion and intrigue that African officials had to face, Mwangi claimed that the Kikuyu who had declared him to be in sympathy with the African settlers were making *fitina* (malicious trouble-making) against him. Without the relative rural tranquillity of Nyanza, in situations of direct conflict between Africans and the state, African welfare workers, paid by the LNCs and working largely unsupervised on their own initiative but living in close proximity with those whose grievances they felt at one with, would find good reason to opt out of the role of state messenger. The democratic energizing welfare ideal turned to dust when faced with such local realities. By the end of 1947 it seemed that the fate of the Welfare Organization was at almost every level subject to forces it could not control. Yet it would survive, and as such it symbolizes the fall and rise of the late colonial state.

Conclusion

As the previous chapter illustrated, the colonial set-up could not prevent the creation of a Welfare Organization in Kenya. However, it did stunt the growth of this new institution. The obstacles to action identified during the period of wartime debate were bound to make the post-war reality problematic. The lack of resources and commitment at the Secretariat; opposition from the district administration; the barriers to combining technical expertise with the techniques in mass communication; and European racial paternalism, had to be continually fielded. Meanwhile, communication between the Social Welfare Committee at the Colonial Office and Nairobi's beleaguered welfare disciples proved elusive. The Welfare Organization's first years illustrate how, in the absence of internal crisis or external pressure, the colonial state found it difficult to learn the lessons of its administrative history and to restructure itself. It was also unable to deliver an officer – European or African – who was universally welcomed as a valuable asset in reducing levels of poverty among rural people.

As Social Welfare Adviser, Dr Philip tried in vain to improve this deteriorating situation. But confusion continued over the purpose of social welfare. Some saw it as the means by which African communities could be animated to organize their development; others concentrated on the state's provision of individual care for those unable to look after themselves. Both views represented reactions to the popular detribalization thesis, in which

[113] Philip to CNC, 3 September 1947, confidential report on Gibson J. Mwangi, ibid.

traditional structures could no longer be relied upon either to support bettered communities, or to care for the incapacitated and socially delinquent. In the meantime, the administration had successfully incorporated the so-called specialist social welfare functions into their district officer's jurisdiction, helped by the lack of budget available to the Welfare Organization.[114] The fundamental self-financing nature of African welfare meant that welfare workers were placed in a precarious position, with their salaries and materials coming from the LNCs. Developments were patchy, since districts varied in wealth. Northern Province's PC complained bitterly that down-country districts were spending government contributions on sports equipment and football when his province was so poorly off and self-help methods were largely out of the question.[115]

Thus this orphan child of the second colonial occupation had limped through its first two years. Dr Philip was caught at almost every turn by the weakness of his administrative position. He may also have lacked sufficient grasp of the obstacles as well as the opportunities to push the organization forward.[116] Nevertheless, he did secure some purchase for his rural energizing model of adult African self-help; African social welfare workers could fulfil their superiors' and their own needs and expectations; and a new administrative generation was poised to look again at the gendered model of African betterment and its implications for a restructured state. Although still largely obscured by the Organization's bias under Dr Philip, the profile of African women was raised by new players. And progressive men in the administration, such as Eric Davies, destined to be the next CNC, talked about gendered community development, using husband and wife teams who could lead the district by example in simple household-orientated improvements. 'From these small individualistic beginnings', Davies argued, 'a good pair might have some chance of building up some corporate sense in their local community.'[117] In these local stirrings, we find the seeds of survival. But it is to London that we must return first to understand why exactly the fortunes of the empire state-building project of social welfare were soon to be dramatically reversed.

[114] Circular from Wyn Harris (CNC) 12 November 1947, KNA MAA6/6, announcing that a second short course in social welfare (the first was held in 1946) for administrative and civil reabsorption officers was to be held at the Jeanes School. Places were available for 14 officers whom the PCs were 'prepared to spare'.

[115] Philip in reply to PC (Northern Province), Isiolo, 18 November 1947, ibid. DARA might be approached for extra funds, he told him, but stressed that 'it was very important that self-help should as far as possible be adopted in "social welfare"'.

[116] In addition to Fortie Ross, Mary Kenny and the six civil reabsorption officers fell under his jurisdiction, plus all ASWWs.

[117] PC (Nyanza) to Senior Vet. Officer, 12 June 1947, KNA DC/KSM/3/1/196.

Six

The Imperial Politics of Inclusion

Community Development & Social Engineering

1948–53

The Welfare Organization did not wither away and die. Quite the reverse. This chapter examines the events which transformed its fortunes. The new post-war attitude at the very apex of the empire began to make a difference. A belligerent Colonial Office pressed the Kenyan Government to bring its provisions for Africans more into line with metropolitan standards of government. Nairobi was also coming under pressure at home from an increasingly frustrated workforce and made a last minute attempt to embrace African welfare through a new committee. Consequently the supporters of social welfare at last found themselves standing on a secure ledge. This firm footing opened up a space in which officials could reorientate social welfare towards the more popular concept of community development. Bureaucratic rationalization and improved communication played their part. By the end of the decade, the cumulative effects of these changes enabled staff to raise the profile of the Organization further. One remarkable outcome was a return to the principle of putting women at the heart of plans for community development. However, the basic structural constraints which had dogged the Organization since its inception were never far away. This reality, plus the growing violence in the colony, ensured that the blossoming institutional coherence was no match for the long-term dynamics of African history. Indeed, just as the second colonial occupation was finding its feet it was running out of track. A human tragedy was about to unfold and it ruptured state-society relations beyond easy repair. The collapse of local community and an African struggle to recast civic virtue provoked not only the arbitrary violence of colonial rule – the use of force was always only just below the surface of government – but also further intervention designed to socially engineer a stable and productive peace. Community development was given a central task in this campaign. The Second World War, army camp life and the post-war imperial politics of inclusion provided a solution to Mau Mau. But it was now within a context of imperial defeat that would yield to decolonization sooner rather than later.

Politicians, pressure groups and mandarins

The Second World War killed off the British Empire. This outcome was twenty years in the making and by no means apparent in 1945, but the war had caused three historical movements to converge and the consequences would be colossal. One process was bureaucratic. Previous trends in colonial policy were applied more vigorously because of the demands of war. Pragmatism was the dominant characteristic of anglo-metropolitan imperial practice. It had gradually evolved out of the combined effects of three processes: first, the self-confidence bequeathed by the experience of the Victorian era and a double victory in Europe; secondly, the inability of one interest group ever to dominate colonial policy; and thirdly, the way in which the empire was only important to the identity of two national institutions, monarchy and church (Marshall, 1996). These layers of historical experience enabled officials to read the lesson of the imperial past as the cost-effectiveness of the strategic political concession. In 1945, this class regarded Britain as a world power despite its weakened economic position. The Empire-Commonwealth was viewed as an important mainstay of that power. All this was underpinned by an unflinching sense of Christian humanitarian obligation towards so-called backward peoples. A self-conscious reputation for trail-blazing enlightenment abroad – it was understood the British had led a reluctant world towards the abolition of slavery – could not be carelessly lost.

The bureaucratic practice of international organizations after the war reinforced the institutional pragmatism developing towards Empire. By the late 1940s, international organizations were again showing interest in the internal affairs of colonies. The United Nations system included a General Assembly and Security Council but also an Economic and Social Council (ECOSOC), a Trusteeship Council and Specialized Agencies. Once the United Nations was up and running and the reconstruction of war-ravaged Europe set in motion, attention to social and economic issues in other areas of the world increased. UNESCO, for example, began to take more of an active role in the area of mass education in Africa by the end of the 1940s, although it was not until 1958 that a UN Economic Commission for Africa (ECA) was created as more colonies began to gain independence – one for Europe had been set up in 1947. Unlike the League's technical committees, however, the members of ECOSOC's functional commissions were government representatives rather than independent experts. This made them comparatively less effective and progressive. However, trusteeship and the dispatch of questionnaires remained an important battleground between the free and the non-free world. The establishment of a Committee of Information from Non-Self-Governing Territories in 1947 ensured that attempts were constantly made to impose UN authority over administration and the determination of whether a territory was ready for self-government. Although Article 68 of the UN Charter provided for a Commission on the Status of Women to report to ECOSOC, it was not until the late 1950s that African women and development issues began to be tackled seriously. International organizations like the ILO and trade union federations were far more interested in colonial issues than the UN before the 1960s (Nicholas, 1975; Snyder and Tadesse, 1995).

The second trend ushered in by the Second World War, and impacting upon Empire, was the ascent of the working class into middle-class calculations of rule: a social category that now had to be respected more than ever before. From the early 1940s, social and economic policy paid more attention than ever before to ensuring a safety net for their well-being. The 1945 Labour Government was particularly keen to widen participation in a particular version of citizenship. Central to this policy was attention to the environment in which people lived. State intervention in areas such as housing, transport and municipal services was believed to be the route towards a more socialist-based citizenship, but only if accompanied by democratic participation (McKibbin, 1998; Tiratsoo, 1998; Fielding et al., 1995). As we have already seen, this influenced attitudes towards colonial peoples during the war. It continued throughout the remainder of the 1940s as the Colonial Office sought ways to practise the politics of inclusion. The strategy of teaching others to have the same material and cultural aspirations as one's own was applied at home and overseas. Since after 1945 British institutions were not made inclusive, merely their ideology, the middle classes remained able to reproduce themselves as the group holding power and setting cultural norms, especially towards the family, home and women. The continuity of power-holders and the collective sense of security and self-belief which oozed naturally from this, ultimately, and paradoxically, enabled the relatively painless relinquishing of empire at the end of the 1950s.

The changes in Africa stimulated by the war were the third and the most dynamic trend that would speed up the formal dismantling of Empire. After 1945, British imperial policy had to react increasingly to circumstances beyond its capacity to control. This was the most important dynamic linking the Second World War to the end of Empire. Colonial peoples were no longer part of communities that could accommodate local politics within imperial systems. Local grievances and tensions would increasingly find expression in anti-colonial sentiment and opposition to racial rule. The white dominions had felt the attraction of greater autonomy during the war; similarly, the call for national self-determination in India grew ever more powerful and the British Raj finally gave way in 1948. Also, the financial cost of the war ensured that Europe's fortunes were now increasingly at the mercy of the economic and political self-interest of the United States, one of the two new superpowers. America was to prove more anti-colonial on paper and less anti-imperial in practice, an inconsistency that the British establishment had to swallow if the special relationship was to develop.[1] And develop it must, despite the tensions spawned as one power rose and the other was being run out of town. American anti-colonial rhetoric was made all the more unpalatable not because of US racial rule at home, but because colonial officials had to field criticism from those who had no comparable experience of imperial responsibilities, indeed a former colony.

Immediately after the war, then, the Colonial Office squared up to these sea-changes as they manifested themselves after 1945. Officials found themselves hedged in by fears of Russian communism, growing nationalism and a more involved Foreign Office. Perhaps because of these pressures, consensus between Colonial Office staff and new ministers was remarkably strong. The views of the new Labour Government were given a coherent form by Arthur Creech Jones. In August 1945 he had become a junior minister as Parliamentary Under Secretary of State and was made Secretary of State for the Colonies in October 1946, a position he held until February 1950. He was ably supported by key civil servants such as Andrew Cohen, responsible for East Africa, also a keen Labour Party supporter and already an admirer of Creech Jones's style and principles. Creech Jones was born in 1891 and had been educated in Whitehall Boys' School, and his first job was as a civil servant. He had once been a member of the Non-Conscription Fellowship and spent nearly three years in prison during the First World War.

By 1945 Creech Jones was in a position to carry forward the policies of Ramsay MacDonald and to bring further consensual progressive thought to the immediate post-war policy towards African colonies. He stood at the centre of a number of groups with a heavy investment in progressive thought towards Empire and he came with an established involvement in colonial issues. He served on the Colonial Office Advisory Committee on Education until 1945 and on the Labour Party's Imperial Advisory Committee. He was known and liked by key figures in the Colonial Office, including Malcolm Macdonald whom he baited when Macdonald was in the job (Macdonald later insisted that he learnt more from Creech Jones's criticism than he ever did from the praise from his own side). And he was in close contact with a range of outside opinions. These included the Fabian Colonial Bureau, put together by Rita Hinden with the idea of encouraging research into colonial problems. Its leading lights included Julian Huxley, Margery Perham and Professor W. A Lewis, and Creech Jones became its first chairman in 1940. He also had long-standing connections with international trade union groups. He was on friendly terms with G. D H. Cole, then Master of Nuffield College, Oxford. Education and social policy were among his specialist concerns; he became Vice-President of the Workers' Educational Association and had links with

[1] Hyam, 1993; Darwin, 1988; Louis and Robinson, 1994 and Hemming, ch.5 in R. Aldous and S. Lee (eds), *Harold Macmillan and Britain's World Role*; (Basingstoke, 1995).

Ruskin College, Oxford. Most crucially at this time perhaps, his intimate and close confidante was Margery Perham, also at Nuffield College (their relationship is discussed in detail in Chapter 2).[2]

Senior officials quickly moved to regard Africa as 'the core of our colonial position; the only continental space from which we can still hope to draw reserves of economic and military strength'.[3] This was due to its wartime contributions, the comparative absence of belligerent demands for self-government and the absence of obvious alternatives on either side. This view was articulated in relation to the problem of the dollar shortage and later became redundant when Africa was perceived as making a minor contribution to economic and military needs in comparison with the growing importance of Europe. Officials in 1945 also spoke with one voice of 'a new policy' that would incorporate gradual self-government with strengthened links with Britain in order that Africans would ultimately prefer to remain in the Commonwealth. Although seeming to contradict the first position, the aim of self-government was initially built on a long-term view. Government intervention in order to support economic and social advancement would underpin the very gradual political maturity of 'African peoples'. A sense of moral obligation, political rhetoric for American consumption and loyalty to national interest blended together, ensuring a commitment to making preparations for self-government but according to a timetable that extended up to and beyond the end of the century.

Naturally, the Colonial Office was keen to roll up its sleeves and get on with trying to put this policy into practice. Constitutionally it was forbidden to do anything, so it could only persuade. Yet the general climate was one of more needing to be done. With the expectations and achievements of modern government having increased at home during the war, the knock-on effect on Empire was a more inclusive approach to the administration of colonial peoples. This desire for government to be brought more into line with metropolitan standards quickly found two needy causes in relation to Kenya: the condition of the colony's labour and finding ways to raise productivity. During the war, colonies like Kenya had got used to ushering through legislation and evading scrutiny under the cloak of insisting that the war had created abnormal conditions. Whereas Kenya was happy to continue this where possible, London proved less sympathetic in the immediate post-war period. Legislation proposed by the Kenyan Government to deal with African labour was subject to analysis in London that was more thorough than ever before. The Colonial Office found few redeeming features in the 1946 Removal of Undesirable Natives Ordinance and even fewer in the Unemployed Persons (Labour Direction)

[2] Various correspondence, Creech Jones Papers, Rhodes House especially ACJ 7/1 -ACJ 7/3.

[3] See F.J. Pedler, 1 November 1946, commenting on a memorandum written by Andrew Cohen on 'Native Administration Policy', PRO CO847/35/6, reprinted in Hyam, 1992: Part I, ch. 2: 117; more generally see Hyam 1992; 'Introduction', xxiii–lxxviii.

Directive of 1948. Andrew Cohen found the first discriminatory; he judged the second to be justifiable only in an emergency. Junior officials also came up with objections: other colonies might want to introduce similar legislation if Kenya succeeded; such legislation would make Britain vulnerable to international criticism especially from the Soviet Union, since the proposal violated international legislation on forced labour.[4] The use of force in colonies like Kenya – its threat, if not use, fairly widespread in day-to-day interactions with labour – was always shadowing official practices.

Likewise, Arthur Creech Jones could see little constructive provision for unemployed Africans. Kenya was going against the policy of settling Africans in towns, he argued; when combined with training centres, this was the correct way to create a steady element in the community and he conveyed his views to Sir Philip Mitchell, Kenya's Governor. He insisted that he would only accept legislation that differentiated between 'genuine unemployed persons' and 'spivs and drones'.[5] Gathering up the blind, sick and infirm as well as those with no work was 'an infringement of personal liberty', he warned. Rather, they should set up labour exchanges and training centres since Kenya's unemployment problem fell under larger economic and social headings and, as such, required a vigorous policy of rural betterment. He called for rural rehabilitation at special centres with improved amenities, attention to social security and plans for economic and social development. Clearly metropolitan solutions and standards were being applied to colonies like Kenya. This was problematic since national insurance for Africans hardly existed in the colonial context; wage-labour was not extensive enough nor usually paid at a rate to allow for much saving. Ironically, Creech Jones's suggestions regarding centres and social welfare chimed with the efforts of the Welfare Organization in Kenya set out in the previous chapter. It was unlikely that its beleaguered staff could have known this at the time.

The tenacity which the Colonial Office now showed towards issues like labour was aided and abetted by improved access to information. Official enquiries threw up sticks that could be used to prod slothful colonial governments, the most the Colonial Office could do, for it had no power to command. One illustration of this was the work of the Colonial Labour Advisory Committee. Sir Granville Orde-Browne had examined the demarcation of responsibility between employers and governments in the provision of services for Africans. His 1946 Report on Labour Conditions in East Africa revealed glaring deficiencies in Kenya's policies.[6] Concerned

[4] Comments by Andrew Cohen, 30 May 1946 and 4 October 1948; E. Parry, Assistant Labour Adviser, 12 August 1948; and Grossmith 26 August 1948. PRO CO533/556/8. Cohen was Assistant Secretary, responsible for East Africa, 1943–47 and Assistant Under Secretary for Africa (the 'King of Africa') 1947–51.

[5] Creech Jones, 5 June 1946; Creech Jones to Governor, 1 January 1949 pp. 3–5, PRO CO533/556/8.

[6] *Labour Conditions in East Africa*, Colonial Report 193, 1946, PRO CO822/130/2. For a thorough exploration of this shift see Cooper, 1996: esp. Parts II and III.

that the young native was degenerating rapidly, he urged that government be expanded especially through the appointment of more labour and medical officers. He found urban housing to be inadequate. The vague tenancy agreements between squatter labour and settlers on white farms would, he prophesied, become a problem in the future (the enquiry he suggested did not materialize, the problem, however, did). He heaped praise on local efforts in social welfare. A social centre at Nakuru was singled out as a model for future welfare policy, and he wanted the various welfare committees, clubs and sports he had found encouraged.

Creech Jones seized on the report as a way of grilling Kenya. The Governor calmly assured him that its recommendations were established policy. He agreed that the government had ultimate responsibility for providing social services such as housing, health and education but – he continued – as with all countries in the early stage of development, employers would naturally have to help.[7] He insisted that once workers acquired a higher standard of living, housing would correspondingly improve. Most workers lived as bachelors, he explained, and once they became stabilized they would 'wish to have their families with them'. This local laissez-faire edifice that put the onus on African choice was blown apart only by serious labour unrest in the colony and the conclusions of the subsequent Mombasa Social and Economic Survey. Nicolina Deverell had carried out a snappy but detailed investigation early in 1947 after Andrew Cohen had demanded assurance that the survey would not be a lengthy one and that action on raising wages would be taken first. Patience was wearing thin. Cohen believed that a local report made after disturbances in 1946 had set out the necessary recommendations.[8] From London's perspective, colonial government was proving to be tiresome and a source of potential embarrassment in its unwillingness to react to disorder. Reports seemed to achieve little. In the deteriorating conditions of post-war Nairobi, the local administrative tradition of ignoring London's directives now ran up against Whitehall's commitment to a more interventionist and professionalized rule from above.

This restrictive view, crafted as it was out of the belief in the inadequacy of the peasant farmer, continued to shape the whole imperial vision. Although agrarian schemes of production had been encouraged – coffee, for example, being introduced in Meru District in the 1930s – the prevailing fashion, as Sir Philip had illustrated in his public statements, was not to put the resources of the government at the disposal of African agrarian development (see, for example, Heyer et al., 1971). Far more pressing was the support of African chiefs and elders as bearers of power, for they were

[7] Governor to Creech Jones, 5 December 1947 in reply to despatch No.183, 24 July 1947, pp.1–3, PRO CO822/130/2.

[8] Comment by Cohen, 25 January 1947, PRO CO533/545/4. see Cooper, 1987. Cooper argues that the strikes and agitation that took place between 1934 and 1947 forced the colonial state to make a distinction between 'the working classes and the dangerous classes'.

needed at least to hold the show together and at most to force through unpopular policies, something the colonial state was not strong enough to do. There was little sensitivity to the hurt created by racial discrimination. Also, two important groups were left out of official prompts, women and the youth. When women were discussed it was usually through the prism of male anxiety. Sir Gerald Clauson cynically remarked that since it was 'the fashion paper and the like which cause many wives and daughters ... to drive their menfolk to the treadmill', then perhaps local experts in Africa could suggest methods which would stimulate 'feminine cupidity and vanity'.[9] Yet by 1948, a few senior officials were keen to promote the value of catering to these two groups according to the local context. White public opinion in Kenya, as we have seen, had ridiculed the idea but old hands at the Colonial Office, such as Sir Frank Stockdale, talked seriously of the effects of boredom and the need to create outlets for the productive energies of Africa's youth. The destruction of the old Africa, he lamented, had eradicated the exciting aspects of being a warrior. Young men were left with only the drabness of tribal life.[10] And in 1948, after an extensive tour of Africa, Marquand, the Paymaster General, told the Cabinet Economic Policy Committee that the productivity problem of African labour was best tackled, not through mechanization, but first by developing standards of health with attention to water supplies, hospitals and diet and all combined with better education. He wanted women to be freed from heavy manual work so that they could play a greater role in improving domestic standards of living.[11]

Yet, whatever the prevailing view at the Colonial Office, it remained difficult to convert thought into action throughout the 1940s. The pace of the centre-periphery dialogue could still be painfully slow, especially if one party decided to drag its heels. It was not until 1950, for example, that Kenya replied to the productivity circular. Mitchell gave the Colonial Office a package of reassurances that belied the increasing tensions in the Reserves. His reply generally impressed London, for he agreed with them that improved African welfare required a combined social, political and economic strategy. He also acknowledged the importance of African administrators. And he cheerfully reported that the African Affairs Committee, which Cohen had singled out for praise in 1946, was busy looking into ways of adapting local systems.[12] He boasted about his refusal to be rattled by the political situation in the colony which referred to the growing unrest in the Kikuyu areas and in Nairobi. As a counter-measure

[9] Clauson (AUSS) quoted in Hyam, 1992: Part II, ch. 3; PRO CO852/1003/3 [African agricultural policy], pp.237–8.

[10] Ibid., minute by Stockdale, pp.238–40.

[11] Report by Marquand on his visit to Africa (extract) 2 April 1948, CAB 124/1089 EPC(48) 35, ibid., pp. 210–17.

[12] Cohen, 3 April 1946, memo on 'Native Administration Policy; notes for further discussion', CO 847/35/6, no.2, ibid., p.107.

he was trying to associate the young with agricultural improvement.

Yet Mitchell's response was mainly a vehicle for him to reiterate the obstacles to improving cash-crop yields which were once again set out before his peers. He enunciated a list of psychological barriers such as peasant conservatism, social customs such as cattle-hoarding, and an absence of African public opinion – what he described as social conscience. He also added to this the predomination of women in agriculture and the political agitation of a minority.[13] The physical and technical barriers were a lack of funds, an absence of capital among Africans and a surplus population. As evidence that these alleged obstacles were being tackled by direct propaganda, Mitchell gave credit to the work of the Jeanes School as the training ground of African civil servants and district welfare officers. Both were linked with the development of LNCs and local democracy. Thus by 1950, on paper at least, the work and vision of the wartime coalition surrounding the *askari* and rural development were being praised by the highest authority in the colonial government. London would not forget.

Despite the resistance coming from the field that was as tough as the proverbial rhino's backside, the Colonial Office was neither willing nor able to lie down quietly. After the war, a coalition of political activists and humanitarians kept up pressure for change. Creech Jones was himself chairman of the Fabian Colonial Bureau, the think tank which was part of the respected and earnest left-wing Fabian Society. A favourite activity for the Fabians was tackling the Colonial Office about its policies towards Africans in Kenya, considered to be the epitome of the failure of trusteeship blamed on the despised 'gin and tonic' set and their oversized estates.[14] In April 1947, Rita Hinden, the Bureau's leading activist, sent Creech Jones, with whom she was in regular correspondence since the early 1940s, a typical list of queries. These included Kenya's report into the Mombasa strike and the resignations of Eliud Mathu and Shirley Cooke from the African Land Utilization Settlement Board. This body had been given the task of organizing settlement schemes for Africans on vacant tracts of land, mainly of poor quality. Both men were on the Board to meet criticism that African interests were not being represented, since they shared a reputation for being pro-African members of the LegCo. Jomo Kenyatta was also brought in later, but then resigned. Rita Hinden had also learned of a petition from the Rift Valley Squatters' Association about their plight, and questioned the Colonial Office about the huge discrepancy according to race in the allocation of money for education.[15]

[13] Mitchell's reply to Creech Jones' circular, 2 June 1950, pp.6–7, PRO CO533/567/4.

[14] See M. P. Cowen and R. W. Shenton, *Doctrines of Development* (London, 1996) for a useful discussion of Kenya in chapter 6, in an otherwise obscurantist account; on the Fabian Colonial Bureau see Porter, 1984.

[15] Hinden to Creech Jones, 24 April 1947; Wallace to Thornley who had previously discussed the matter with Cohen, 11 December 1947. PRO CO533/558/6.

Kenya and particularly racial issues took up increasing amounts of time in Fabian meetings. Although paternalistic in outlook and committed to the gradual unfolding of self-government when social and economic conditions allowed, the Fabians were genuinely outraged by evidence of white privilege at the expense of the African population.

The provision of education in Kenya was an obvious and favourite target for indignant socialists. It could completely dominate a single meeting of the Bureau. Raising teachers' salaries, applying the experience of village education in Nigeria, allocating government grants where they were most needed, in African schools, and an end to racial exclusion in government schools, were all topics the Colonial Office was urged to take up. At the very least, this reminded the CO of what it already knew. In a review of African Secondary Education in East Africa published in 1946, experts had identified an air of social tension in Kenya that was in some parts found to be painful.[16] Indicative of the shift in attitudes, Africans were sympathetically described as parents who unreservedly invested in their children's education in an furious effort to 'make one's pile'. Their racial difference now no longer prevented them from being seen as ordinary people. The report found it disturbing that African education had the lowest support from public funds, only 3 per cent of public revenue, despite the tremendous social need for education. With £150,000 allocated to African education out of public funds, officials could now see at a glance just how unfavourably Kenya compared with other East African territories, Tanganyika allocating £250,000 and Uganda £291,000. The report warned against condescending paternalism. It praised the work of the Jeanes School, recommending that more provision be made for adults and girls so that domestic conditions would improve. It was now part of official thought to suggest that the practice of long and casual weaning be ended.

However, these warnings and the gendered aspect of adult education fell on waste ground. All the Colonial Office could do was to glean some satisfaction from signs that Kenya was taking steps in this direction when final proposals for training African women teachers at Vihiga and Embu, first discussed at the end of the war, were received in 1947 along with plans for agricultural schools and teacher training centres.[17] Rita Hinden and the Fabians had identified a crucial source of African anxiety and frustration. Gradual steps were no longer enough. Access to education for Africans was soon to provide a stimulus to growing dissatisfaction that turned into the fury of Mau Mau. The 1949 Beecher Report on Education fuelled anxiety and disappointment. A ten-year plan for African education only provided, over time, for four years of schooling for all Africans and only sixteen secondary schools. Beecher recommended restrictions on

[16] 'A Review of African Secondary Education in East Africa', p.28., PRO CO533/555/1.

[17] See generally PRO CO533/555/1 and PRO CO533/553/8.

Kikuyu 'independent schools' which often accepted over-age children from poorer families. The hopes of ordinary Kikuyu were dealt a fatal blow. With an increasingly arbitrary state power showing indifference, the question of whether a local leadership could articulate grievances at the highest level now assumed critical importance.[18]

The Colonial Office was not just fielding socialist criticism from home. After the war, Africans continued to track down officials. On the trail of the Secretary of State was the African Women's League of Nairobi, founded in 1946 with the declared aim of improving the status of African women. It quickly set about sending out a petition, now a standard and the only form in which Africans could initiate political dialogue. This was the first organization of its type and reflected the degree of social change that had taken place during the war. Inadequate wages and housing for women – particularly for ayahs working in Nairobi – were among its main complaints.[19] While discrediting this 'exaggerated, possibly bogus document', the Kenya Government took care nevertheless to defend its record as part of an official reply. When Creech Jones finally read the petition in 1948, two years after he had received it during a visit to Kenya, he was furious about the delay. Almost too ashamed to dispatch the usual grateful acknowledgment, he told his juniors 'if we plead for African co-operation, in turn we ought to listen and answer their grievances'.[20] Properly chastised, officials agreed that a European settler petition would not have been delayed so long. A greater sensitivity to issues of race began to surface; it now mattered to officials that they were exhibiting a discriminatory response rather than the civil service ideal, perhaps the conceit of impartiality. Undoubtedly the kind of campaigning being undertaken by the Fabians, of whom Creech Jones was a disciple, did make a difference.

Other African petitioners received a less slow response when they were African men organized around a recognizable political agenda. The Kenya Africa Union, the leading coalition of moderate members of Kenya's growing elite, also petitioned the Colonial Office on the 'Economic, Political, Educational and Social Aspects of the African in Kenya Colony'. Complaints abounded, ranging from land loss, low wages, and lack of schooling to the plight of farm squatters in the White Highlands, health, education and the sexual exploitation of African women.[21] Although

[18] *1949, African Education in Kenya: Report of a Committee Appointed to Enquire into the Scope, Content, and Methods of African Education, its Administration and Finance, and to Make Recommendations* (Beecher Report). For an account of the importance of this report, see Lonsdale, 1992: 424.

[19] Memorandum (undated) received in November; minute by Cohen, 22 November 1947, PRO CO533/544/2.

[20] Ibid., Creech Jones, 7 April 1948.

[21] KAU Memorandum, undated but which reached the CO in early 1947, PRO CO533/557/1. For a discussion of the KAU in the drift towards Mau Mau see Lonsdale, 1992: 409–10. He argues that the KCA failed to deliver a sense of security and representation to those outside the middle class. As potential partners in multiracial politics, the KAU was rejected by officials in favour of their old alliance with the chiefs and it failed to secure

agreeing with the official Kenyan view, that the document was in places immature and untruthful and not representative of African opinion, the Colonial Office did recognize a genuine attempt to understand the colony's problems and to offer solutions. Officials were particularly encouraged by the KAU's apparent acceptance of the role of the white community in the development of the colony.[22] Also, there were noticeable areas of shared thought. The KAU's suggestion that the number of African health inspectors be increased was found to be sound, as was their interest in mobile teams in the rural areas. Senior officials also privately shared the KAU's doubts as to 'whether the European will ever get near enough to the rural African'. This suggests the beginnings of a slow realization that their ideas about development could cross the racial divide but their application was impeded by the residual resentment of racial rule. From 1945 onwards, the official mind in London was gradually learning that issues like productivity and labour had gone beyond the capacity of colonial rule to manage efficiently. The apparent speed of decolonization becomes less sudden in the light of this slow gestation period. However, in 1947 hopes still ran high that reorganized white teams would make the second colonial occupation transformative. White district staff were encouraged to liberate themselves from routine office work. The theory was that technology and office managers – possibly Africans able to handle accounts, issue licences and prepare returns – would enable officers to spend more time developing local government. All the KAU could show its supporters was a letter praising their constructive approach.[23] Reassurances from a conservative elite among the Kikuyu, that they were working to ensure that all would be in a position to learn self-mastery, were beginning to wear thin.

If African politicians were feeling impotent, so too were officials at the Colonial Office. When London acted upon its intelligence or chased answers to complaints, the visible results were less than impressive. Kenya always managed to reassure London with rays of hope and paths of progress when pressed on controversial issues. For example, when answering questions raised by the KAU, the Governor assured Creech Jones that agricultural betterment was going ahead but could only be slow.[24] He had recently opened the first welfare centre for squatters in Nakuru where, he assured the Secretary of State, a spirit of cheerfulness prevailed. He gave the Colonial Office an alternative explanation to that of the KAU. Most squatters preferred to live as dependants of rich and powerful men, clinging

[21] (cont.) more African representation in the LegCo. Simultaneously the Beecher Report tarnished the reputation of Eliud Mathu and showed that those who were not teachers or civil servants had best defend their own interests rather than rely on strangers.

[22] Comments, 9 April 1947, PRO CO533/557/1.

[23] See despatch from Creech Jones to the African Governors, 25 April 1947, CO 847/35/6 nos 15-24, reprinted in Hyam, 1992: Part I, ch. 2; official comments on the African memo (undated) contained in PRO CO533/557/1.

[24] Mitchell to Creech Jones, 14 April 1947, PRO CO533/558/6.

to a type of ancient feudalism. Using the technique of insisting upon possessing untrammelled and specialist knowledge cultivated through personal contact, he went on to explain that their nature was to blame. 'Even if you pitch it out of the window with a fork', he somewhat ludicrously explained, 'it will come running back again.' Moreover, the average agricultural labourer in Kenya was, he claimed, as well-off as his British counterpart of thirty years ago. He thus appealed to a notion of the universal poor condition of the lower orders and to the tradition of trusting the man on the spot.

The tendency for local stalling was greatest over the issue of political concessions. In 1946, 1949 and 1950, repeated Colonial Office hectoring in an effort to make Kenya give serious consideration to unbanning the Kikuyu Central Association came to a fulsome naught.[25] The war had made such action defensible by the colonial government, but there was little will to restore liberty when hostilities abated. Mitchell believed the KCA to be a subversive movement which had communist connections. By 1949 it was more personal. Unbanning would be 'triumph for Kenyatta', he insisted, at a time when the Kikuyu were beginning to see him as 'the venal rogue' that he was. Mitchell could believe this with little compunction. From his perspective the KCA was implicated in fermenting trouble in the Rift Valley; and in any case, Africans could register their views through their LNCs. The file was finally put away at the Colonial Office in 1951 on the grounds that there was no point in reviewing the situation, at a time tragically close to the final loss of hope amongst the Kikuyu. Mitchell had cut himself off from African opinion, ignoring warnings and retreating into stock racial prejudice in order to cling on to the status quo.[26] The best opportunity for giving Africans the means to participate in political debate was turned down. As the Kenyan Government showed how little it had changed, Africans learned there was little point in looking to outsiders for help. Senior officials in London, it seemed, could barely hear their calls for help.

Doubly frustrating for the Colonial Office was the way in which government intransigence in colonies like Kenya was increasing at a time when its specialist advisory committees were finding clearer solutions to local problems. Keen to take action, senior officials at the apex of Empire naturally looked to their advisory bodies to translate wartime pledges into peacetime directives. Some had been set up during the war and stuffed

[25] Memorandum from Bates, official on temporary secondment, after receiving a reply from the Governor, 29 November 1946, PRO CO533/543/2; Cohen's comments and replies, after meeting Mitchell in Nairobi, 18 December 1949, PRO CO533/543/7. The Governor was approached on the subject by Cohen and Rogers at the CO in 1950. The file was put away in 1951; Rogers to Cohen, 27 November 1951, ibid. For a discussion of the KCA as one of the three constituencies of hope for ordinary Kikuyu see Lonsdale, 1992.

[26] Reply from Mitchell, 28 February 1949, PRO CO533/543/7.

with a higher proportion of younger members and outside experts. The Social Welfare Advisory Committee fell into this latter category. Its greatest contribution to the second colonial occupation was to reshape London's concept of social welfare after the end of the war. Since its creation in 1942, members had flung themselves across the Empire gathering data on colonial welfare. They were being encouraged by officials worried about the direction which some social welfare organizations were taking.[27] They also wanted the Committee to examine how expert British staff could be recruited. This was a product of the universalistic thinking which was now being applied to social engineering, for – as the Committee agreed – the underlying problems of youth work and methods of dealing with juvenile delinquency were the same everywhere.

Their wartime enquiries had revealed some worrying features. It was surely a cruel irony that just as Miss Darlow told a sympathetic Committee of Kenya's pressing need for more European staff, closer co-operation with the administration, a concerted effort to promote model projects and a plan, so Dr Philip was battling alone to the point of resignation in the colony.[28] According to the wartime plans issued by the Committee, each colony was supposed to have a least one trained social welfare officer; their audit revealed this to be the exception rather than the norm. And, as was the case in Kenya, social welfare was being confused with mass education. This latter concern prompted a relatively swift response. Since the chairman of the SWAC was a senior official, Sir Charles Jeffries, he ensured that the Education Adviser, Christopher Cox, addressed them on the subject, which he did in July 1947. Also helping to move things along was the personal interest of Creech Jones. The Secretary of State had requested advice on the matter: it was he who urged that they read each other's reports. Cox summarized the recent work of the sub-committee on mass education, which was re-examining its own definitions and exploring 'education for citizenship'. Mass education was now viewed as a strategy that would help colonies to develop politically and, as Cox explained, it was part of the state's educative role to teach them what was euphemistically described as straight thinking. This much favoured notion alluded to a cocktail of behaviour considered to be desirable which came from the same winning cultural stable that bred the oft praised disposition toward cheerfulness. Both straight thinking and cheerfulness were considered indomitable and distinctive features of Englishness.

Adult education had a particular appeal to left-wing politicians at the time. It offered the chance of circumventing the consequences of poor schooling during childhood and adolescence or the curtailment of education through having to work, experiences often closer to their own backgrounds. Colonial officials could see similar merit in a similar scenario

[27] Minutes of 27th SWAC Meeting, 3 December 1946, PRO CO859/158/1.

[28] Miss Darlow, for example, toured East Africa and reported back to the Committee in 1947; 29th SWAC Meeting, 3 June 1947, PRO CO859/158/1.

overseas. The need for mass education had already been mulled over by the sub-committee for Africa as an antidote to the maladjustment believed to have taken place between local and European culture. It was now being exacerbated by nationalism, African politicians, the absence of literacy and the presence of deeply felt local grievances.[29] An ideal of straight thinking was built around notions of democratic and unselfish public spirit, confidence in one's fellow citizens, a belief in the value of the individual and a disdain for pedantic tidy-minded bureaucracy. Clearly, this was the business of reproducing others in one's own image, possibly a useful definition of what precisely was meant by educating the masses. Of significance for Kenya was the opinion expressed by Cox that social welfare officers in Africa were welcome to take part in some of these more informal educational activities especially in relation to youth clubs and community centres. There seemed to have been little discussion as to what the fraught experience of Kenya might tell them.

Nevertheless, the social welfare committee set to work to adjust its own position, buoyed up by evidence of high-level interest in its work, especially since – as we shall see below – it tied into general moves towards preparations for eventual self-government. Thus, the components of social engineering shifted in favour of three principles. First, the social welfare worker must make a contribution to 'tackling poverty and in creating better economic conditions in their communities'. Miss Digby was certain that too much emphasis had gone on social and cultural activities.[30] Added to this was the principle of self-help, as this connected with an individual democratizing element according to Sir Frank Stockdale, Labour Adviser. The objectives of a social welfare worker were, first, economic prosperity, second, social contentment and third, creative empowerment, he insisted, so it was up to officers to stimulate local people 'to do something to help themselves'. Their committee had not stressed this element enough, he lamented, and social welfare in the colonies was only going to be effective if it was dynamic. Finally, another woman – it was rare to have such a preponderance of female members – redirected their attention. Audrey Richards added the task of creating a civic-minded society. She had come to believe that the primary function of such officers was to create village groups or societies. 'Such simple organizations', she stressed, were of great value to communities, citing the example of women headmen in Fiji who were appointed to deal with women's affairs.

Although the list of social welfare functions was now more honed down, this was partly achieved because other activities were simply dispensed with. Social welfare was now less about bridging the gap between the

[29] 29th SWAC Meeting, 1947, 3 June 1947; 30th SWAC Meeting, 14 July 1947, ibid. See also 'Education for Citizenship', skeleton draft interim report of the sub-committee for Africa; W.E.F. Ward (Chairman), 18 July 1946, PRO CO859/89/8 reprinted in Hyam 1992: Part IV, ch.7: 52–3.

[30] Item 5, Minutes of the 30th SWAC Meeting, 14 July 1947, ibid.

specialist departments. Members had initially thought that building up the home ought to be the first priority. They now dropped this in favour of promoting economic prosperity through arousing the interest of the people 'as a community and not as family units'.[31] There were other more serious losers. Although poverty remained an issue the more remedial aspect of social welfare was shed. Previously, Audrey Richards observed, social welfare workers had concentrated on the needs of the incapacitated minority in communities, such as lepers and the blind; now 'the needs of the majority should come first'. Other categories were also lost sight of. Calls to place 'activities for the adolescent' high on the social welfare workers' agenda were set aside. Despite its constant worries about youth, the colonial state equally constantly evaded responsibility for educating the rising generation of young Africans. As Cox elaborated for Kenya, universal primary education would not be achieved for another twenty-five years, and in any case this relatively short time-period spent in school would, for the majority, not be consolidated with any further character or literacy training. Most serious of all, the link between women, low-level economic activity and community development, once so avidly supported by Cox during the 1939 investigations into the education of African women, was not carried forward into the post-war arena of debate. War and the beginnings of preparation for self-government produced a notion of citizenship that naturally gravitated towards men.

Fortunately, all this discussion did produce a new amended memorandum on social welfare for the colonies sent out in 1948.[32] Its guidelines were more straightforward. Social welfare was explicitly linked to achieving economic prosperity, defined by a set of fundamental features: good health, good housing, good food and good water. Secondly, the complex relationship of the social welfare officer with other specialist officers was cleared up. It would be up to him to get their instructions carried out in the homes of the people. Although the memo stressed the need for a high degree of co-operation between the administration, the specialist departments and the social welfare worker, it gave no guidance as to how this could be achieved. Finally, the colonies were told in no uncertain terms that social welfare could not be planned from the top; rather it must grow from the bottom up. The official line was that through associations, clubs and committees people could do this for themselves in their own way, receiving 'maximum of inspiration' and 'minimum of oversight'.

This memorandum represented a watershed, signifying the shift in official thought in favour of community development and away from social welfare. The principle as well as the language of social engineering had

[31] The dilemma over whether the very poor are best helped via intervention to support the family or general community services remains unresolved; see for example, Teka, 1993.

[32] 'Social Welfare in the Colonies', revised memo, January 1948, sent with a covering letter from Creech Jones, 14 April 1948, KNA MAA7/585. See discussion below for how this was used by Kenya's Welfare Organization.

found greater precision. The changes reflected the prioritizing of the needs of an identified majority, later criticized by Wilfred Chinn who became Social Welfare Adviser to the Colonial Office in 1950. For it was charged with bringing about the neglect of the very poor, already neglected by the colonial state and African society.[33] It also represented a synthesis of long-term political development with immediate social and economic amelioration. It testified to the hope that African civil society would do what could not be done by the colonial state. And it supplemented the incorporation into a modern moral economy of selective and selecting Africans, who approved of its opportunities to supplement their local patronage and widen their political arena. It was better than paying taxes and easier to canalize the labour of their women. As such it favoured the strong over the weak.

The promotion of community development as the most appropriate form of social engineering was a product of two converging dynamics at work after the Second World War. One lay within the evolving thought of senior officials at the Colonial Office. Signs of preparation for self-government had to be shown, if American and Soviet criticism of imperial rule was to be neutralized. In terms of policy this was soon reflected in enthusiasm for developing local government structures as well as more enthusiasm for tackling poverty. Influential civil servants were prepared to argue that social welfare could concentrate on encouraging political organizations geared towards self-improvement and the nurturing of public opinion. This appealed to the very ethos of what it was to be a civil servant, the war tugging professional duty towards compassionate action. Civil servants believed in the principle of public opinion; after all they were supposed to be removed from highly partisan politics and to mediate sectional interests. Local organizations, clubs and committees on African soil were designed to do this: to distract from politics, to represent a wider section of society and to be the training ground of home-grown civil servants. If civil servants were reproducing themselves through this form of social engineering, so too were Labour Party politicians.

The second dynamic backing a shift to community development came from the presence of Labour politicians within the Colonial Office. Mass education for citizenship appealed to the collective memory of the origins of the Labour Party. It signified their empowerment, the spread of trade unions, friendly societies and the struggle for a universal male franchise. This is illustrated in the way Arthur Creech Jones took care to insist upon the wide distribution of memoranda such as the 1948 revised text on social welfare. He wanted them to go beyond government and to reach voluntary organizations and the public. This was followed by a discussion on

[33] See PRO CO822/674 for various correspondence and Report of Wilfred Chinn's visit to Kenya, February 1951. 'Community development also offered influential Africans opportunities for self-advancement and patronage, whereas social welfare offered them little but taxes ... '; Iliffe, 1987: 201.

how to promote co-operation with established voluntary organizations such as missions and trade unions and yet another circular entitled 'Social Welfare: Co-operation with Voluntary Organizations'. Proud Labourites were reaching back to the origins of the party at the end of the nineteenth century, war again having pulled at the heart strings of socialists' compassion. Such actions appealed to their belief that something called public opinion could be activated and primed to function for the greater good.

The Second World War had help draw out such a consensus. The Wartime Research Committee and Social Reconstruction Survey, under the chairmanship of G. D. H. Cole, of Nuffield College, Oxford, had considered local government in 1943. Margery Perham had read with interest the result of two days of deliberation to find a way forward that would keep the right balance between central government – bound to increase with the policy of social reconstruction – and local government. Delegates including William Beveridge, Paul S. Cadbury and Sir Ernest Simon listened to the invocation of John Stuart Mill's theory that the public education of the citizen was the key to free institutions and the chief instrument of this was local government: only small-scale institutions could keep in touch with the community and be a focus for patriotism.[34] What this points to, therefore, is the popular mantra – building up among civil servants and ministers alike after the Second World War – of the social utility inherent in free political association, the point at which partnership between state and society was created and cross-fertilized, thus creating a public opinion. Thus politics was civilized. Mindful of their roots and in a majority government, the Left in Britain was less disposed than ever towards arguments for restricting political expression and more enthusiastic about encouraging versions of their own political traditions.

This confident will to reproduce marked out a precarious path for African politics and government throughout the rest of the century. Two potential weak spots became millstones in the resource-scarce and regionally disparate independent African nation states. Political parties in Britain, especially the Labour Party itself, always represented highly sectional interests whilst claiming to speak for public opinion. The civil service was drawn mainly from the middle classes and English public school alumni. However, it could mediate between class and regional divisions in a situation of resource abundance, in the absence of a threat from any comparatively similar sectional or ethnic political grouping, and because Britain was an exceptionally class-conscious society. In the African context, increased competition for scarce resources and labour, which was then compounded by the absence of a national identity, ensured at formal independence that, in many territories, the tendency for sectional interests

[34] 'Nuffield College: Wartime Research Committee and Social Reconstruction Survey: 10th Private Conference – 25–26 September 1943. Local Government Area'. Perham Papers RH 732 27.

to dominate the state structure remained a dominant feature of government beyond the end of colonial rule.[35]

What all this suggests is that a hitherto neglected component central to the new African policy in London was the social engineering of good citizens. This trend in thinking would trickle down and begin to affect local structures. It also gave senior officials a renewed sense of the viability and necessity of British colonial rule, although paradoxically it seems that white rule was already being wound down in 1945. Creech Jones backed the principle that Africans had to be brought into local administration. Officials had agreed that they could no longer rely on 'the white man's prestige to govern Africa', arguing that education, political awareness and returning soldiers demanded something more than the 'obsolescent nostrums of "indirect rule"', and a new CO journal designed for its African administrators set out the new thinking.[36] Central to this revitalization was the principle that African progress depended upon the development of 'a sense of community obligation and social responsibility and service' – how Creech Jones would have defined his own socialism.

However, it was also a conservative form of advance. Gradual experience in civic responsibility was held to be the only preparation for participation in a political system that could eventually support a universal franchise. Of course, self-interest was not absent either. Empire loyalism in Africa would, it was hoped, counter the appeal of communism and bolster the chances of future independent African states wanting to remain in the Commonwealth. Eager for a public relations coup, the government was always keen to suggest that it was advancing African control of local affairs. The 1950 African District Council legislation was described by the government as being of 'far greater importance to Africans than any addition to the number of African members on the LegCo',[37] wishful thinking perhaps. Likewise, local government was presented as an exciting training ground in the acceptance of responsibility and the development of integrity; the place where 'one got down to the fundamentals of common life, to the things with which the average person was really concerned', and much capital was made of the way in which the British system was being applied in Kenya. It was a claim which could easily be used to the advantage of supporters of white racial rule in colonies like Kenya.[38]

Yet it was also quite a revolutionary departure from established patterns of rule building on the lessons learnt in India. Creech Jones warned that

[35] Creech Jones, 1 October 1947 KNA CD5/63.

[36] See Hyam, 1992: Part I, ch. 2, especially memo by Cohen `Native Administration Policy: notes for further discussion', 3 April 1946, CO 847/35/6 no.2, pp.103–9 and 'Introduction', pp. xxx–xxxi, also Creech Jones, 1948. This was preceded by a circular dispatch to the African Governors, 25 February 1947, CO 847/35/6 nos 15–24, reprinted in Hyam, 1992: Part I: 119–29.

[37] Extract from *East African Standard*, 20 January 1950. PRO CO533/566/18.

[38] For a criticism of this thinking see Berman, 1990: 310–14; Pearce, 1984.

this type of reformed government would in turn demand more of colonial officers. Indirect rule had been carried out by men sympathetic to and knowledgeable about traditional African society, the object being its preservation. Now officers had to have the new skills of understanding change, the new classes, urban problems, the impact of education, trade unions, money and cash crops. They had also to be willing to apply new techniques of government developed outside Africa, 'in particular ... the great fund of knowledge in the history and practice of local government and social administration which is available in the United Kingdom' (Creech-Jones, 1948). The Colonial Office took to reorganizing itself again in quite spectacular ways. Of course, a special organizing committee was established. However, despite this, there were fairly swift results. In 1947 the Africa Division was expanded and an African Studies Branch set up. More outside experts were brought in. As part of the morale-boosting policy and to find practical solutions, Cohen made plans for annual summer schools for administrators, a conference of African Governors in November 1947 and a gathering of official and unofficial members of LegCos (see Hyam, 1992: Part I, xxx–xxxiv).

As a result, increasing coherence at the Colonial Office, instigated as part of the new Africa policy, appeared to produce a clearer train of thought: that good government could not succeed unless mass education brought Africans round to the British way of thinking and, for this, new state structures were needed. It also reinforced worries that there was insufficient provision for mass education in African development plans; for the plan was that the surplus population would leave agriculture and work for wages and in crafts and trades. This anxiety had surfaced earlier in the deliberations of a sub-committee of the Economic and Development Committee, chaired by Andrew Cohen.[39] The new training conferences were designed to enable the centre to tackle perceived gaps in administration in the field. This was an important step towards transforming the Colonial Office into an agency that enabled administrators to read their own bureaucratic history. At the 1947 Colonial Office Summer School one group tried to tackle race relations, now felt by officers to be an important issue in administration, and its conclusions were later publicized by the CO.[40] It found, as had the SWAC, that co-operation with Africans through voluntary work was crucial to 'the creation of an active democracy'. Participation in local affairs, councils, church organizations, clubs and youth groups might be the key to 'securing the active co-operation of the educated classes in government policy and in programmes for social and economic betterment'. Admiring glances were awarded to Russia;

[39] A. Creech Jones, Despatch to Kenya, No.417, 10 November 1948, p.1, KNA PC/NZA/3/1/574.

[40] Ibid., Group VI, Appendix I, paras 12–15 of the preliminary paper considered by Group VI (Race Relations) of the 1947 Colonial Office Summer School on African Administration, p.1.

Siberia, it seemed, offered a blueprint, since it had apparently been able to enlist the support of educated people by associating them with the local Communist Party. Likewise, the 1948 Cambridge summer school then examined mass education. In the opening address Creech Jones spoke of 'a new phase in African development', of helping 'the colonial people ... move to better social living and to responsibility. We are here to discuss how initiative can be encouraged ... '.[41] Collaboration between technical officers in rural areas, youth movements, scouting, community self-help in the villages especially in sanitation and public health schemes, anti-soil erosion projects, the extension of ex-*askari* training, plus the need to promote the role of women in and around the home were all mentioned as playing a part.

Seventy officers from the Empire attended to hear this, including Kenya's new Social Welfare Adviser, Patrick Williams. Panels then investigated 'education for citizenship, incentives to progress and the part to be played by women'. All this attention raised the profile of the work Dr Philip had been struggling to carry out in Kenya. A Colonial Office dispatch in November 1948 on mass education and local government elevated the work of social welfare, or, as Creech Jones now called it, community development to the very centre of plans for reconstruction.[42] The official definition of community development was now put forward as a movement designed to promote better living for the whole community, embracing all forms of betterment – both official and unofficial – in agriculture, health and sanitation, infant and maternal welfare, and in the spread of literacy. Its value was perceived to be its capacity to affect community initiative; Creech Jones was confident that officers could apply the new techniques to tease it out. The despatch also stressed the role of co-operation with local government, co-operative movements and voluntary organizations in this process. Thus the new Africa policy had firmly placed the principle of community development and a correspondingly reformed bureaucratic structure at the centre of colonial administration. It might have been a demanding agenda calling for considerable re-organization of government machinery and the provision of substantial finance, but in theory it was good news for the Welfare Organization in Kenya.

However, Creech Jones' neat theory that community development could be slipped in to the districts by provincial teams failed to pay attention to the basic structural constraints that had strangled welfare initiatives from the beginning. Racial paternalism, the lack of political will to make finance available, competition for local turf between administration and departments were the hard rocks of colonial practice that local efforts in

[41] Opening address, Creech Jones, 19 August 1948, CJ(CSC(48)13) CO 852/1053/1 no.18, reprinted in Hyam, 1992: Part I: 162–72.

[42] Despatch to Kenya, No.417 on mass education and local government, 10 November 1948. p.1, KNA PC NZA/3/1/571.

adult education, publicity and technical co-operation were dashed against, as Colonial Office officials debated in Whitehall. Had the imperial structure been less incoherent for longer, then a high-level examination of the first two years of Kenya's Welfare Organization might have produced valuable information about what was taking place on the ground. There was also a serious discrepancy running through these high-level discussions about agrarian containment and local government. Regarding the first, Mitchell sought to persuade Creech Jones that the peasant was useless, which reinforced the local official line that Africans had to be compelled to do what was best for them. The combined liberal civil servant cum Labour line preferred to believe that Africans could be encouraged to do this for themselves, as the British labouring classes had once been. It rejected compulsion, turning instead to a belief in the dynamics of self-help and public opinion.

The Creech Jones and Mitchell arguments highlight the incompatible elements within the imperial high politics of inclusion. Throughout the 1940s, as we shall see, those officials on the ground who picked up the Creech Jones model of local government ran straight into the Mitchell line of defence. The picture was to change in the 1950s. These two schools of thought existed side by side for the last time during Mau Mau when Africans were paradoxically compelled to enact voluntary self-help. The moral and financial cost to the colonial state would draw many into the fast exit lane of imperial policy.

Kenya's new African Affairs

The Colonial Office was not the only layer of imperial administration which adapted to accommodate the changes that came in the wake of the end of war. At the level of the government in Nairobi, a similar, if less precise, shift towards a more inclusive approach to Africans gathered pace as the 1940s drew to an uneasy close. The second constituency of change during this period, the Kenya Government, debated African social welfare in new forums and, remarkably, now took to supporting the work of its Welfare Organization. Although showered with circulars from above, it was mostly the growing signs of social change and African agitation that produced new responses. High-profile disturbances came in the form of the labour unrest in Mombasa and Nairobi in early 1947. It was growing more apparent that these were strange times. In Fort Hall, women refused to work on communal soil conservation projects. Their spirited revolt flummoxed local chiefs and forced an embarrassed administration to abandon its district communal terracing programme (Cooper, 1987; Throup, 1987: 172–202; Kannan, 1998). Kikuyu workers in particular were increasingly unhappy and resistant. But who had eyes to see? Although the government was better able to read the signs of profound tensions within colonial society by the end of the 1940s, it was not so able to respond to what disparate constituent parts now understood to be a gathering storm.

One impact of the Colonial Office spurt to push colonial government towards metropolitan patterns of government was the replacement of the Welfare Committee – a war baby – with a new African Affairs Committee. The label of native had been dropped in favour of African but not from the title of its chairman, who bizarrely carried on as Chief Native Commissioner. The CNC was not equal in status or power to the other heads of department that made up central government, such as local government or finance. However, the CNC did become Member for African Affairs in 1948, although his functions were not defined until 1950 (Berman, 1990: 282–91). This new committee had the attraction of being a tool of appeasement vis-à-vis the Labour-Fabianist alliance which, as we have seen, closely monitored how the government catered for the needs of the African population. It did not, however, have legislative powers. It was a think-tank that brought together for the first time members of the African elite with government officials to discuss issues relating to Africans.[43] The Commissioner for Social Welfare suddenly found himself rubbing shoulders with the five PCs and Officer in Charge (Masai), the Native Courts Officer, the Secretary to the Member for Health and Local Government and to the Member for Agriculture and Natural Resources, the Information Officer, the Chairman of the African Settlement and Land Utilization Board, and the Registrar of Co-operative Societies plus all the directors of the technical departments. (The Governor and the Chief Secretary were not members, nor did they ever ask to attend any meetings.)

Unofficial members were also plentiful. They included H.E. Lambert, Eliud Mathu, J.Jeremiah, B. Ohanga, John Chemallan, Simeon Kioko and Henry Kerre. Some were members of the LegCo. Mathu became a member in 1944 as a result of missionary and political pressure in Kenya and Britain. Ohanga, a Luo civil servant, followed in 1947. When the missionary representative of African interests retired, more African members were added in 1948. From the government's point of view, Africans who had proved their worth in local government or who were the educated voice of a Christian elite, were being brought in to share the responsibility of government, in the belief that they would provide accurate information on African opinion. However, this slow yielding arrangement hardly offered them adequate representation or access to central government. Although African members were periodically encouraged to submit items for the agenda, meetings were often called just for the white official members of the African Affairs Committee alone.

The potential of this new apparatus to make the colonial state more

[43] Minutes of various meetings of the African Affairs Committee, formerly the Native Affairs Committee KNA MAA6/38 and KNA CD5/18.

responsive to African needs was limited by three factors. The CNC was not a very powerful figure and the committee lacked much clout. Secondly, there were wider structural constraints that prevented the kind of reform and restructuring which the Colonial Office had showed itself capable of engineering. Despite all the planning discussions of the early 1940s, very little had changed in terms of evaluating colonial policy, collecting intelligence and then imposing reform. Whilst the provincial administration did not take the Development Committee and the Development and Reconstruction Authority seriously, they found themselves – along with the CNC – being distanced from central executive power, subordinated to ministers and their opinions ignored. Added to all this was an absence of a sense of urgency. Thirdly, relations between Africans and government representatives were deteriorating. Racial prejudice and ignorance continued to make the state incapable of understanding the pain of African social change. Meanwhile, Africans themselves were more and more divided. African politicians were increasingly at odds with chiefs, their political rivals. The destructive effect of social change upon internal moral economies was leading the Kikuyu closer to civil war (Berman, 1990: 282–90 and 314–22; Lonsdale, 1992: 284).

Nevertheless, the African Affairs Committee was the nearest the colonial state could come to comprehending the problems of African welfare. For example, Harry Lambert, an old-hand administrator with a reputation for being an amateur anthropologist, submitted a paper on bride price. The spiralling rate of exchange of young women for material assets was identified as being an anti-social problem acting to the detriment of the community. Lambert's memorandum explained that stock transferred in bride-price were a mutual bond to protect against future insecurity. It was the foundation of the social ethic, a symbol of mutual obligation between families that made cash profoundly anti-social.[44] Subsequent discussion acknowledged the economic hardship and social problems facing Africans in the Reserves, the precariousness of squatter life and the rising hardship experienced by poorer families. 'What worries the aging African', Lambert pronounced, 'is the problem of security.'

Officials could now more easily understand why parents demanded more livestock in exchange for their daughters. Here was a shaft of light to illuminate the rents in the fabric of African society. Producing a response was more difficult. Direct government intervention to reduce bride price was not an option. Lambert's own view was that the Committee ought not

[44] Memorandum by H.E. Lambert, 'Bride Price', p.4, 4 August 1948, submitted to the African Affairs Committee, along with 'The Limitation of Bride Price' by D.O'Hagan, Native Courts Officer, 24 August 1948. KNA MAA6/38. Known always as H.E., Lambert was 'a quiet, staid man, somewhat hypochondriacal ... the last of a series of gifted amateur anthropologists in the administration ... [with] a rare understanding of Africans'; by the late 1940s he was 'the most dangerous kind of adviser, the expert whose knowledge is a trifle out of date', Chevenix Trench, 1993: 81, 207.

to blunder into matters they scarcely understood, giving the impression that 'we are out to smash a native system for some economic or political purpose of our own'. They took refuge in the potential of careful propaganda and the co-operation of elders and LNCs to invoke their own 'sensible modifications', reassuring themselves that 'the African is not a fool and provided we are careful in our presentation of it, propaganda will eventually prevail'. By 1950, comments from LNCs convinced the Committee that the issue was not as serious as had first appeared; bride-price custom was changing no more than other African customs.[45]

What the Committee could not see, because they lacked the means and perhaps the will to interpret the signs, was how the bride-price increases were a symptom of a spiralling social crisis. The structures they had for communicating with African society could not discern the true parameters of change. This exposed two problems. First, past images of African society made it difficult for white and black men to talk about changing gender relations and generational conflict. Secondly, it appears from the Committee discussions that white officials were increasingly tentative in their views of what was best for African society: this lack of confidence and a flexible discourse of change were part of the crisis of paternalism. Those less constrained by administrative prestige and racial prejudice tackled these problems by suggesting that Africans should be left to talk about what needed to be done for their welfare, with the offer of professional help and guidance from the state.

The African Affairs Committee functioned better as one of the few forums where metropolitan solutions were applied to African society. The CNC looked to his committee for advice on how the problem of a surplus African population should be tackled. The congestion in the Reserves was thought to be getting out of hand. Nyanza alone was thought to have a surplus population of 91,000.[46] Thomas Askwith – Nairobi's Municipal Native Affairs Officer – was one of a number of Committee members with clear ideas about how to socially engineer a solution. A number of memoranda on the subject were circulated to official members of the Committee only. Askwith's solution, rooted in the 1941 conference on urban welfare, centred on the urbanization of African men with their families. This could not be achieved, he argued, without an increase in wages, government housing, and educational facilities including trade and craft training. Likewise, Lewis, at the African Land Utilization and Settlement Board, recommended that a committee be set up to carry out such a policy.

[45] Minutes of the 10th Meeting of the African Affairs Committee, 5 October 1950, Minute 12/50, KNA MAA6/38. Law panels in individual districts would be left to investigate demands for alterations, ADCs having no mandate to legislate on such a matter.

[46] Urbanization in Kenya', by T.G. Askwith, 23 June 1948 (circulated 3 August 1948); 'Surplus population and the need for housing African Workers outside Native Reserves'. Memorandum by J.H. Lewis, Office of the Commissioner for African Land Utilization and Settlement, 14 July 1948.) KNA MAA6/38.

Municipalities and townships would have to develop hamlets with family housing, whilst villages were built in the settled areas and Reserves. The problem could not be considered in isolation from social insurance. As he pointed out, a worker and his family would only remain off the land permanently if an alternative safety net existed.[47]

However, as the subsequent enquiry into setting up an African health insurance scheme showed, their options were limited. Officials conceded that a contributory scheme whereby the poll-tax-paying population contributed one shilling per head 'might not be worth the political trouble and discontent'.[48] Even if fees were charged for treatment, there was the problem of introducing a new structure to collect them and worries about securing payment for maternity and child health services. Again, the Committee threw the problem back to the LNCs to deal with, in the hope that metropolitan standards could be applied by someone else, somewhere else. All agreed that Africans should contribute, but the basic services would have to be free for those unable to pay; each LNC should decide local rates for services under their control; and those who paid a fee for entry to hospital could expect not to have another patient put in the same bed.[49] As disorder increased, so the solutions offered to the challenges of administering Africans became less idealistic and more restricted to old patterns of government. In 1949 the deteriorating situation in the Reserves and the problem of uncontrollable African youths vexed the Committee. Discussion of constructive long-term solutions to African welfare was replaced by plans for short-term corrective measures to maintain order. Nyanza Province was experiencing social breakdown as never before. Growing numbers of young men were falling foul of the law, being sent to prison and evading employment. The best the Committee could suggest was an appeal to teachers in the Province, reminding them that they had a duty to be good citizens and to promote loyalty to government, chiefs and leaders. It seemed more a plea than a command to insist that 'no country, district or town, village, school or even home' could function unless 'all are willing to obey orders'.[50]

Warnings that clearly suggested that a crisis was looming also reached the committee. A discussion paper on African vagrancy submitted by Askwith in 1950 spelt out the signs of growing unrest. He warned that

[47] Lewis, 'Surplus population', ibid.

[48] D.S. Mackay, Medical Officer, Msambweni to Director of Medical Services, 15 April 1948, KNA CD5/18; 'Memorandum on the Financing of Medical Services', D.W. Hall, Secretary, African Affairs Committee, 21 March 1949, Minutes of 7th Meeting of Full Committee, 4 August 1949, KNA MAA6/38.

[49] Min.10a/49, Minutes of a meeting of the Official Members of the African Affairs Committee, 13 April 1949, p.3, KNA MAA6/38.

[50] Appeal to all teachers in Nyanza Province from the Senior Education Officer, A.F. Bull, circulated to members of the committee, 10 March 1949. Agreed at meeting of Official Members of the African Affairs Committee, 13 April 1949, Min.8a/49 of Minutes, KNA MAA6/38.

some – mainly Kikuyu – were attempting to create a state of anarchy and he put forward a social profile of the kind of person they ought to be helping, a man who

> ... has probably received little if any education or training, owing to his parents' poverty; he cannot pay proper bride price for proper marriage by native law and custom for the same reason; if he is married, or cohabits, he cannot support his wife unless one or other of them carries on some legal or illegal trade; he cannot feed and bring up children, let alone educate them.[51]

Reminiscent of socialist arguments in inter-war Britain, he argued again that the normal working man's wage was totally insufficient to support a family. Given that there was recurrent lawlessness on the outskirts of Nairobi, put down by widespread police action, Askwith urged an investigation into the social status of habitual criminals, with particular reference to the extent of the problem of the landless or semi-landless class. If a survey proved him right, and the bands of spivs were the younger members of the landless class, then too great a reliance on police tactics would only make matters worse, he warned, and he drew a comparison with the growth of the poor in England in the Middle Ages who were landless and without means of support after the dissolution of the monasteries. He lacked authority and his solutions required financial and political revolution which were beyond any one person's capacity to pull out of the colonial goat bag. However, Askwith's paper did promote discussion and some action. The African Affairs department put it to Horne, Chairman of the Central Minimum Wages Advisory Board, and the Executive Council decided to carry out a cost of living survey in Nairobi and Mombasa although no other research was felt necessary.[52]

Could the anthropologists save the situation? Subsequent pressure from the CNC ensured that an anthropologist would investigate Kikuyu households to establish some 'sound idea of the relative poverty which exists in the native land unit and at the same time information about the activities of landless members'. Dr Audrey Richards – now Director of the East Africa Institute of Social Research at Makerere – was confidentially asked by Cowley, the Native Courts Officer, to find a trained sociologist who could investigate the social and economic background of the habitual criminal; the government apparently had no funds for such research.[53] This research would, Cowley felt, tie up conveniently with Jean Fisher's work on the Kikuyu family. She was a doctoral student from Cambridge University in receipt of financial support from the Colonial Office's funds for research in anthropology. Unfortunately, information was being sought

[51] Askwith to CNC 'African Vagrancy' 12 January 1950, p. 2. KNA MAA7/591.

[52] Note written by CNC, 20 July 1950, KNA MAA7/591.

[53] Draft letter from CNC, 24 July 1950; K.M. Cowley (ag. Native Courts Officer) to Dr Richards, 6 October 1950, ibid.

too late and too slowly. Although, back in London, the Colonial Office Social Science Research Council had established a special anthropological and sociological sub-committee in 1949 such investigative research as that proposed by Askwith had been neither popular nor effective in the past.

Officials and academics alike had served the urban African badly. Senior anthropologists usually preferred fieldwork amongst tribesmen rather than their bastardized brothers, rarely tailoring their studies to administrative issues.[54] Now the backlog was almost overwhelming. Back in London in 1949 senior academics Firth, Stanner and Schapera made a list of projects considered urgent. These included a number of key problems facing African administration in Kenya. Unsurprisingly, research led by academics took years to complete and even longer to produce practical solutions, if it ever did. Likewise, officials involved in research committee decisions also deferred to colonial governments' unwillingness to allow outside academics to poke around at contentious and difficult problems, to avoid possible embarrassment. All too recently the work of one academic had been hushed up. Mary Parker had investigated municipal government in Kenya, under the supervision of Dr Audrey Richards. She found urban conditions to be shocking, but what was recognized by the Colonial Office as political dynamite was her analysis of racial tax contributions and her recommendations on race relations. 'The balance between academic freedom of speech and administrative control over the content of our research workers had to be strictly enforced to avoid a scandal', wrote a Colonial Office official in 1949.[55] There was more than a scandal around the corner and time was running out. The African Affairs Committee could do no more.

In the meantime, senior officials in Kenya resorted to blaming the unrest on the unemployed. Widespread disobedience was the fault of lazy malcontents who contaminated otherwise willing labour. The government even toyed with the idea of becoming an autocratic social engineer and dividing Africans into categories, the deserving and the undeserving poor so that they could take out the latter.[56] When Margery Perham quizzed Kenya's CNC about his strategy for the unemployed, he placed his hopes in legislation planned to remove 'the "three card tricksters", the rogues and the vagabonds who are at present infesting Nairobi'.[57] Wyn Harris – a

[54] Minutes of first meeting of anthropological and sociological sub-committee, 9 August 1949, PRO CO927/63/3. Minutes of Colonial Social Science Research Council (CSSRC), PRO CO901/1-23 1944–51, Meetings and Reports 1944–48 CO927/63/1–4 and CO927/63/3; CSSRC 5th Annual Report for a list of schemes sponsored by CSSRC 1944–49, CO927/63/5. revised, 25 September 1949, CSSRC(49)45, CO927/63/9; see also Lee, 1967: 79–80.

[55] Canham; 11 March 1949, PRO CO927/78/3.

[56] See Cooper, 1987: 7 for the argument that the state tried to subvert the unity of urban Africans by creating manageable categories of the idle, the criminal and the workers.

[57] Wyn Harris to Perham, 17 April 1948, KNA MAA8/70; Chevenix Trench, 1993: 121; and John Lonsdale's infinite mental record of such glorious details.

short powerful Welshman full of energy who had scaled the heights of Everest and was known among the Kikuyu as the headless chicken – believed they could be separated from the honest African citizen without inconveniencing him.[58] As he conceded, the great point in legislation of this type was to retain the co-operation of 'the decent African in order to work it'. He evidently believed they could. But if Askwith was right, few among working Africans would welcome such government intervention. As their sense of insecurity mounted, they would interpret it as giving an increasingly arbitrary state the capacity to return to treating the unemployed at best as lazy, at worst as criminal.

Central government appeared to be running out of ideas and even the most astute officials were losing confidence in their capacity to generate solutions. Much as Mau Mau was the manifestation of Kikuyu social collapse, it was surely also the product of a crisis in government. Reviewing the year 1948 in a letter to Margery Perham, Wyn Harris gloomily noted that Africans were making larger and larger demands for political advancement; a growing number of Europeans were convinced that harmonious race relations were vital to progress, but many were disillusioned by the intelligentsia who were castigated for lacking the character and courage of the older men; and overall, politically things were moving too fast. Yet this was, as he admitted, a good year all in all.[59] Options were simply running out for the government. Wyn Harris took refuge in the solution that decent Africans could still separate racial issues from government policy. Events surely now showed the naiveté of this position. There was an air of hopelessness for, as he confessed, 'we still remain completely stumped as to how to prevent this ever-increasing population pressure on the land'. And whilst many agreed that raising wages to a reasonable level was the only way to get efficient workers, the kind of loyalist African employees which Arthur Creech Jones envisaged were proving very difficult to conjure up. For example, LNCs were finding it extremely difficult to raise primary school teachers' salaries in line with the improved rates for African civil servants. The money just was not there. Meanwhile, white activists like Carey Francis argued that it was a mistake to increase the gap between the peasant and the educated further. So much for the chances of an appeal to a teacher's sense of duty. In the absence of clear alternatives, money and hope, the Voluntarily Unemployed Persons law seemed a feasible measure of control as needs must. Unfortunately, it would only serve to further unsteady African nerves and provoke an urban underclass into growing increasingly reckless.

Yet for others this was a time of hope and optimism. From the Welfare Organization's perspective events were taking a decisive turn for the

[58] Minutes of the 7th Meeting of the Full Committee of the African Affairs Committee, 4 August 1949. Min.14/49. 'Voluntarily Unemployed Persons (Labour Direction Bill)', KNA MAA6/38.

[59] Wyn Harris to Perham with a review of 1948, 8 November 1948, KNA MAA8/70.

better. In the late 1940s some influential members of the government warmed towards the welfare structure, in marked contrast to the immediate post-war period. Pressure emanating from London's consensus on African policy had played an important part in this thawing of attitudes. In line with the post-1945 interest in Africanization, Governor Mitchell found himself having to answer questions posed in parliament about Kenya's efforts to train Africans in local government. In his reply Mitchell focused on the work of the Jeanes School including its courses in civics and local government which were attended by African executive officers and nominated councillors, plus community development assistants. He also described how the Jeanes School had been host to a three-day course on local government, attended by 80 officers.[60] How times had changed.

In addition, the home audience was also subject to a different line. Suddenly the government was publicly defending social centres in the settled areas. By 1950 the African social welfare centre at Dundori was drawing increased criticism from local farmers. The Dundori Welfare Association passed a motion declaring the Centre to be a growing menace to law and order, and demanding swift government action. According to settler eyewitnesses, many Africans were afraid to go near the centre for fear of having their throats cut as everyone was rolling drunk. This sort of complaint tapped into a popular racial stereotype that could spread panic – that the effect of alcohol upon Africans was different from that on Europeans and once Africans were drunk they would become violent and menacing.[61] Officials knew that supervision in centres was a problem. Dundori was run by Hector Munro and his Committee, but it was a one-man show. When Munro went away, the centre deteriorated. The new Social Welfare Commissioner, Patrick Williams, justifiably used this situation to promote the role of his officers. He argued that the problem might be eased when a District Welfare Officer for the Rift Valley was eventually appointed under the Five-Year Plan.[62] Happily for him, the local DC publicly defended the centre, insisting it was unfairly blamed for everything that happened within a ten-mile radius.[63] Nakuru District Council Chairman, R. D. Ryland, went on the record to insist that hundreds of Africans could be found innocently enjoying themselves at the centre on a Sunday.

Even the mighty now spoke out. Hyde-Clarke, the Labour Commissioner, intervened to redress the damning settler report on Dundori, again illustrating how government opinion had turned. He was influenced – as

[60] Mitchell's response to Secretary of State, 21 June 1951 in answer to a parliamentary question from W.M.F. Vane, PRO CO822/565/9.

[61] Extract from *East African Standard*, 22 March 1950, KNA MAA7/859. On racial stereotyyping around arguments that Africans were incapable of moderation and were more menacing and dangerous when intoxicated, see Maughan-Brown, 1985:82.

[62] Memorandum on Social Welfare in Townships and Trading Centres, circulated to all PCs, 18 October 1949, KNA PC/NZA/3/1/574.

[63] Letter to *East African Standard*, 22 March 1950; KNA MAA7/859.

he himself acknowledged – by the 'considerable interest' being shown in the colony's social centre scheme in England.[64] And he made an unequivocal case for Dundori social centre as an important element in Labour Department policy; it was, he insisted, 'one of the ways of producing a contented and therefore more stable and efficient agricultural labour force, upon which the economy of the Colony so much depends'. Officials seemed willing to confront the European anti-welfare lobby. Africans too noticed some changes. In 1949, the CNC tackled the issue of the price paid by European farmers for good quality squatter maize. He ensured that Africans received a higher sum and won the case for a portion also going to the Native Trust Fund 'to be expended on social services in the area' instead of being creamed off on the pretext of marketing and conservation costs.[65] But as protest and crime grew the government would find out just how little and late this gesture was.

Meanwhile the Boy Scout and Girl Guide movements were also enjoying degrees of new support from within the government. On a visit to the colony in 1947 representing the Colonial Office's Social Welfare Advisory Committee, Miss Darlow stressed the link between social welfare and the scout movement.[66] It was only a matter of time before the open-minded CNC of the time became a born-again scouting enthusiast and he urged the administration to do all it could to encourage the movement. He believed there was a good case for having scout troops present at local functions 'for the sake of publicity and heshima'.[67] Kenya now had an organizing commissioner paid for by a government grant but he had little money for travelling, so the onus fell on DCs to become local commissioners and to badger LNCs for money. The reason for the new enthusiasm was twofold. First, an increased concern about Kikuyu youth and the lack of discipline among young Africans. Scouting was the obvious answer. It was seen as a cheap and cheerful way to provide 'some form of character training for young, semi-educated Africans, and to direct their energies into such channels as will help them to become useful citizens'. And it was believed that Africans were particularly susceptible to uniforms. Secondly, the scouting fraternity, notably, Sir Godfrey Rhodes – Chief Commissioner for Kenya – was promoting the movement as a way of increasing racial co-operation.

In the deteriorating atmosphere of the late 1940s officials were more susceptible to thoughts of uniformed young Africans. As the Scouts' Chief

64 Hyde-Clarke, Labour Commissioner to the Clerk Supervisor, Nakuru District Council, 6 April 1950, KNA MAA7/859.

65 Minutes of the 7th Meeting of the full African Affairs Committee, 4 August 1949, Min.15/49, KNA MAA6/38. The fund was renamed the African Trust Fund.

66 Philip to Arthur Brown, Chief Commissioner, Lagos, Nigeria, KNA CD5/269.

67 Circular from CNC, 29 June 1948, ibid. This was followed by a meeting to discuss support for the Boys Scouts Association between the CNC, Social Welfare Commissioner, Sir Godfrey Rhodes, the Chief Commissioner for Scouts, and F.M.J. Dahl, Boy Scouts Travelling Commissioner to the East African Territories.

Commissioner argued in his review for 1950, people were coming to see scouting not just as an antidote to communism but also the route in a country of many races to unity in 'happy harmonious communities'. Scouting offered a cheap and easy formula, for he confidently told his audiences that a cheat and liar would be exposed and reformed by a united patrol. Officials became more open to suggestions of its psychotherapeutic value – an alternative method of achieving sociability outside of the home.[68] Similarly, a request for extra money for Guiding in 1949 was treated with more sympathetic courtesy than had been shown after the war. Betty Brooke Anderson argued that many African women and girls in the colony now felt a strong the need for self-expression. With few trained guiders to meet this demand, companies became open to subversive influence. The Director of Education backed her request for a grant increase from £500 to £1200 to pay for a full-time organizer-trainer and transport. Although the Chief Secretary was happy to agree that one of the principal reasons for African conditions was 'the backwardness of the women', he could give no assurance that money could be found for a full-time organizer such as Uganda already had.[69]

However, how much more seriously the Secretariat now supported the Welfare Organization in theory and in public but how little it did so in practice, was made all too clear in its slow response to the Creech Jones 1948 circular on mass education and local government.[70] Copies were dispatched to all administrative and technical officers after a summary of its recommendations were circulated to all PCs for discussion, so that a reply could be given in the designated time. Able to claim that Kenya was well within London's guidelines, with a Welfare Organization, specialist officers and an African Affairs Committee now designated as 'the Central Council for mass education referred to in the dispatch', and with no mention of Dr Philip's previous complaints, the Secretariat talked itself out of supporting the other recommendations. These were, first, that the administrative and financial control of heads of departments and PCs be devolved to facilitate an intensification and co-ordination of existing work. Such detailed district budgeting covering expenditure on education, agriculture and sanitation would not be welcome by the administration, would probably require extra staff and affected the position of departmental heads. The Secretariat also rebuffed the Colonial Office's suggestion that district committees be created with a variety of non-governmental and official members. London's attempt to promote racial co-operation in the field of betterment according to the politics of inclusion was rebuffed on the grounds of its becoming a second tier of local government, large and

[68] G.D. Rhodes, 26 April 1950; 'Lecture on Boy Scout Movement', p.5, KNA CD5/269.

[69] Betty Brooke Anderson, Colony Commissioner for Guides, to Director of Education, 23 June 1949, DE to CS 4 July 1949; Note, 9 July 1949. KNA CD5/283.

[70] Discussed in an earlier section. 'Community Development in Kenya', circulated to all PCs, 1 January 1949, PC/NZA/3/1/574.

unwieldy. Thirdly, the Secretariat deprecated the proposal for a separate budget for community development, arguing that as the government did not have unlimited funds at its disposal, money for community development could only come if additional revenue was raised. PCs were left to make up their own minds as to how village committees such as the Muhiriga in Kikuyu and Utui in Machakos should be encouraged, and whether community development officers ought to have the same status as DCs. These kinds of initiatives were considered well within the province of local administrators to sort out. If Nairobi was unwilling to enforce what London wanted, then there was little prospect of reform on the ground.

The consolidation of welfare, 1948–50

Nevertheless, these were much better times for Kenya's Welfare Organization, illustrating the restorative potential of the second colonial occupation at certain points. The Africa policy at the Colonial Office and the government's changing attitude both played their part in breathing new life into the battered body of welfare. Consequently, four important self-strengthening activities were able to take effect. The first was in relation to leadership. Patrick Williams, previously Director of Training in the colony, replaced the exhausted Dr Philip, with a new keenness born of an old enthusiasm from his wartime experience with African soldiers. In February 1948 Williams became the colony's first Commissioner for Social Welfare. This was an up-grading of the post of social welfare adviser which reflected the Secretariat's new commitment to the Organization. The job came with a salary of £1,200 per annum and fell within the African Affairs branch of the central government, making the Commissioner subordinate to the direction of the CNC. Williams remained in charge of the three adult training centres in the colony which included Centre C or the Jeanes School, now referred to as the official training centre for African civil servants. Williams was keen to co-operate with others. He moved quickly to repair relations with Aidan Southall at Makerere. He organized a meeting with representatives of voluntary organizations including the Red Cross and the Harrolds, leading figures among the colony's Quakers. He took time to explain the structure and the aims of his organization and to encourage voluntary work at community centres.[71]

Now there was a chance that the welfare profession might be less diminutive as compared with the district administration, for Williams had the good fortune to enlist the support of Percy Wyn Harris, the CNC. He

[71] Wyn Harris to Williams, 14 February 1948, KNA MAA8/6. various correspondence, KNA CD5/147. Williams to Southall, 3 March 1948, KNA MAA7/585; Notes of a meeting attended by Dr Gregory of the Red Cross and Major and Mrs Eyleen Harrold, 2 April 1948, KNA CD5/303. Eyleen Harrold went on to organize the colony's Federation of Social Services in the early 1950s.

was willing to take on less than enthusiastic members of the administration such as Charles Atkins, Central Nyanza's PC. The latter had allocated the sum of £25 for spinning and weaving for the whole of 1949 and for the entire province. This was the final straw for Williams who had watched helplessly as his welfare officer, Hunt, had his duties 'syphoned off'. The usual battle over the control of information was being fought. Atkins – 'a BNC [Brasenose College, Oxford] rowing tough' – had insisted that, since Hunt was part of the administration, all correspondence with him should first go through the PC. Although he reminded Williams that Atkins had a good many other problems to deal with, Wyn Harris took time to have a long talk with Atkins. 'We really mean business over Welfare' he told him and he tried to convince him that women were worth their attention.[72]

Atkins had cut the amount of money given to spinning and weaving on the grounds that most of the girls did not apply their training back home. Wyn Harris argued that the general education the girls had at the centre through doing corporate work was worth a great deal to the district. His reputation for being the outstanding administrative officer of his generation is exemplified by the way he managed to start drawing together various outposts working with women. The Education Department had organized a conference on the education of women and girls. Wyn Harris found out that its Director knew little of the work of the Jeanes School in this area. He told him how the Welfare Organization aimed to encourage 'womenfolk' to make full use of the new community centres, especially women who possessed a certain amount of knowledge which they could share with other women. He suggested that women who had taken the special course for teachers' wives now run by the Education Department be given a part to play in their local social welfare centres.[73]

Patrick Williams might have had cause for concern when Wyn Harris was then promoted to be Governor of Gambia. However, his replacement was the equally sympathetic Eric Davies, who like Williams had wartime experience of working out ways to mould African men. Although less tenacious than his predecessor – it was said about him that 'no nicer man ever ran a district', a highly damning remark – Eric Davies maintained a close and supportive working relationship with the Commissioner for Welfare (Chenevix Trench, 1993: 216). Together they brought more coherence to policy on African welfare in two important ways. First the message of community development was disseminated within the colony. New opportunities for administrators to visit London were bearing fruit. Williams had participated in the 1948 Cambridge Summer School Conference for administrators, and had chaired a panel that had tried to work out what type of structure was best required for mass education. He

[72] Williams to Wyn Harris, 18 September 1948, KNA MAA8/6; Chenevix Trench, 1993: 96. (My thanks to John Lonsdale for correcting my naive translation of BNC as bloody nice chap); Wyn Harris to Williams, 30 September 1948, KNA MAA8/6

[73] Wyn Harris to R. Patrick, DE, 6 March 1949, KNA MAA8/6.

applied their conclusions when he returned to Kenya. In a paper entitled 'Mass Education or Rural Community Development?', he proposed

> ... an organization whereby the African people of the Colony can be led to appreciate the part they play in these district, provincial and departmental development plans ... The organization must be designed to win their interest and co-operation by instruction, discussion and adult teaching techniques generally and thus arouse their initiative and enthusiasm.[74]

The wartime flirtation with mass education had begun to wane at the Colonial Office and, instead, metropolitan ideas about building up a responsible community – particularly in vogue among Labour Party officials and civil servants committed to the wartime plans for resuscitating local government – were once again put forward for Africa.[75] The new line taken was that, for a full-scale rural community development programme to function properly, the Jeanes School would have to become a permanent training centre for African civil servants and be the headquarters for a Commissioner for Community Development, the Registrar of Co-operative Societies and an Information Office. Each district was to have a community development officer, and each location an African assistant, with government providing financial help for each location to have a community hall.[76] Secondly, Williams and Davies built African women into their vision. Following his various district tours in 1948, Williams had noted how spinning and weaving was catching on among African women. With his *askari* re-absorption background, Williams had backed the theory that, to raise the standard of living of soldiers in the East African Command, training courses for their wives were essential. The ensuing courses had brought together representatives of the EAWL and the Red Cross at the Jeanes School. Williams also publicised the role of European wives working voluntarily with African women, as township welfare and order showed increasing signs of deterioration. This relationship was now anchored to official definitions of community development. Williams suggested that, since there was 'a fund of goodwill' amongst European women in the area, 'the problem might best be attacked in the first instance by trying to establish home crafts, hygiene and child welfare

[74] 'Mass Education or Rural Community Development?', 30 November 1948, P. Williams, p.1. Nairobi University Library, Afr.J.750.78.c.6W5.

[75] [Mass education]; minutes by C.J. Jeffries, Sir A Dawe, G.F. Steel and O.G.R. Williams, 7 December 1942–22 November 1943 reproduced in Ashton and Stockwell (eds), *Imperial Policy and Colonial Practice, 1925-1945*, Part II, pp. 330–33; Minutes of conference on local government, 25–26 September 1943, at Nuffield College: Wartime Research Committee and Social Reconstruction Survey. RH.Mss.Perham 732; Fielding et al., 1995: esp ch. 5; Weight and Beach, 1998.

[76] Though the Rural Industries Officer did move to Welfare, the Information Office was sadly never relocated, but titles did change in 1950; KNA PC/NZA/1/1/574.

instruction amongst the African women, and in this way improve the general morale and combat vice and subversion'. Thus – albeit with a very patronizing and narrow definition of female capabilities and needs – they hoped to restrain and canalize African men which partly explains their limited plans regarding women.[77]

With a sense of mission, a clearer line and a wider network of support, the Welfare Organization built up its administrative muscle. Obvious beneficiaries were the organization's field workers who were able to carry forward the mission. The changed mood at the Secretariat ensured that, as demobilization money and duties waned, Williams's wish that civil reabsorption officers be given new posts as development officers was granted.[78] They were to be paid for by the general staff section of the administration's budget, and in the financial estimates for 1948 eight district assistants were listed as Temporary Administrative Staff.[79] It was not exactly a safe career. Their temporary status was not removed until the 1951 Estimates were published, when ten district officers (community development) were listed again under the general staff of the administration, at a cost of £7,460.[80] The officers would be funded by the administration but their job was 'not one which entails the normal duties of an Administrative Officer'.[81]

Nor was it going to be an easy posting. Williams wanted men prepared to live pretty close alongside the African and to learn the local language. They were to work largely from the welfare centres 'suggesting and encouraging, rather than directing; somehow he has got to make the people help themselves and better themselves by their own efforts – led by his example'. In short, he wanted men with 'a bit of a "mission" for the job' who were prepared for a lot of frustration. He briefed them about the hardships which they and their wives would have to accept: no normal round of social life and sports in the evenings; and no automatic stepping-stone to an administrative officer's job. It was a lot to expect of men with no fixed contract and with little local back-up.

These eight officers highlight some of the intractable elements of the

[77] Various reports of tours made in Nyanza, 1948, KNA CD5/38; discussions of East African Command Welfare Committee, 5 July 1949, KNA CD5/52; S.H.La Fontaine for Williams to CNC, 5 December 1949, KNA CD5/111

[78] Williams to all CROs 5 March 1948, approved in April 1949, CS to Commissioner for Welfare, 25 April 1949. KNA CD5/63.

[79] *Estimates of Revenue and Expenditure of the Colony and Protectorate of Kenya and of the Development and Reconstruction Authority for the Year 1948*, p. 40.

[80] 'Annual Report of the Welfare Organization, Kenya Colony, 1949', (1950, Government Printer, Nairobi), p.2; KNA CD5/38. *Estimates of Revenue and Expenditure of the Colony and Protectorate of Kenya*, 1949, 1950 and 1951. Under a separate heading was the Social Welfare Organization headquarters, with a total budget of £12,610 for 1951, Social Welfare Organization Jeanes School, with a budget of £26,412 and the mobile cinema units, with £5,220 for 1951, ibid., pp.58–60.

[81] Williams to all CROs, 5 March 1948, KNA CD5/63.

second colonial occupation that get to the heart of the gradual official acceptance that only decolonization could achieve the goals they had set themselves. They worked at the coalface of Creech Jones's policy to induce a respectable African public opinion. Williams had initially hoped each DWO would make a survey of fifty families in each location.[82] The plan was that they would sample representatives of the educated, uneducated, farmers, traders and government employees, noting the physical condition of heads of households, their wives and children, details of diet, clothing and so on, and would collect information about existing and lapsed rural industries and young farmers' clubs and compile an inventory of what small-scale improvements were most needed in a particular location. Had they been able to carry out these plans they would have provided a unique profile of rural Africa.

Nevertheless, they did compile district reports and carried out Williams's bidding that they get to know Africans. As a result, they stumbled upon the underlying principles of the second colonial occupation that bewildered officers and Africans alike. Already by the end of the 1940s, propaganda efforts were failing to overcome the African desire to hear for the first time about 'self-government' and officers felt they were hampered in their 'flag-wagging' efforts by 'a lack of direction from above as if we ourselves are not sure'.[83] It was difficult to make capital out of the gains being made by African administrative officers, the DWOs argued, when their appointments seemed so obviously politically motivated. And how, they asked, in the future would they fit in with the chiefs who were hereditary, or the plan to build local government out of LNCs to replace the administration? The other problem was the lack of authority vested in technical officers. They complained that headmen, regarding them as departmental officers, always referred back to the DO when they gave instructions.

The shortage of resources was another obvious constraint that shackled the second colonial occupation to half-baked projects. Since he had no budget whatsoever of his own, Willoughby Thompson in Fort Hall could legitimately claim that he and his assistants were the ultimate personification of self-help; locals could hardly view them as 'another Government Father Christmas'. Yet his team consisted of two welfare assistants, trained at the Jeanes School, Paul Gathii and Mburu Ndungu, two untrained welfare workers and a part-time women's teacher, Ruth Njeri. Grants from DARA paid for the building, maintenance and furniture of two community centres, at Kangema and Kandara, which were supplemented with LNC building votes and British Legion donations. They looked to the LNC for contingencies, African staff wages, and the upkeep of equipment. A government grant paid for a newspaper. Money from the British Legion

[82] Ibid.

[83] 'Points that District Welfare Officers would like to discuss with the C.N.C.', undated but file position suggests late 1948, KNA MAA8/6.

and 120 books donated by the British Council were their salvation.[84] Evidently adult mass education remained neglected and under-funded.

The colonial state had not, to its peril, learnt the lesson of wartime propaganda. Fort Hall had one cinema tour for the year and Thompson appealed for more and better mass education equipment. Nor were the cinematic offerings from the Central Office of Information always inspiring or appropriate. Documentaries like London's Water Supply and British Table Glass had unsurprisingly not captured the imagination of the Kikuyu. Vincent St Giffard, Deputy Welfare Officer for Mombasa township, recorded extreme difficulty in finding films he considered suitable for African audiences. Film strip projectors proving to be far the most powerful teaching aid, he dolefully recorded that radio broadcasts were not popular; few Africans went out of their way to listen and, if they did, seldom stayed for more than fifteen minutes. When he stopped showing cowboy films – he considered them not entirely harmless – audiences evaporated and he was forced to return to them to avoid financial disaster.[85]

Similarly Hunt, Central Nyanza's DWO, complained that there were no films on manure or sleeping sickness. He found Africans indifferent to the wireless and, because of the paucity of information, organized debates at his welfare centres made a mockery of his efforts. The motion that boundary furrows do no harm to *shambas* won, whilst the motion that the LNC rate was helping the country lost, despite a heavy presence of LNC members.[86] In desperation he had resorted to experimenting with hand-outs; 10,000 were distributed out of the back of vehicles in Dhuluo about the dangers of boundary furrows. This was an expensive method, time-consuming and difficult to evaluate. This tragi-comic state of affairs contrasted sharply with the prevailing attitude to propaganda at the other end of the colonial structure. A top CO economic adviser, Rees Williams, gave a list of policy recommendations to Creech Jones in 1948. He warned him about the dire need for public relations and mass education. There was an appalling ignorance about government policy which would, he believed, be highly dangerous when 'people are called upon to undertake some task they hate'. Governments should realize that people wanted 'circuses as well as bread' and give a new sparkle to dull administration with bands, parks and fairs. All officers should embrace public relations: 'theirs not to reason why went out with Tennyson', or so he claimed.[87]

[84] 'Report on social welfare activities in the district of Fort Hall for the year 1948', KNA CD5/255; Appendix B 'Finances', ibid.

[85] Welfare Report for Mombasa, 1949, p.13, ibid.

[86] Central Nyanza, Annual Report 1949, pp.2–6, ibid. Attendance at literacy classes was poor. Libraries were used mainly by teachers, the most popular books included *Essential Knowledge For All*, *The Secret of Life* and *The Miracle of Man*. He was only able to find one centre where a book on carpentry and joinery was popular.

[87] 'West African Tour – 1948': report by Rees Williams to Creech Jones, 27 October 1948, CO537/3561, no.1, reprinted in Hyam, 1992: Part II, 219–27.

Had resources been forthcoming and propaganda been more effective, would it have made much difference? From the evidence of Fort Hall it seems not. DWOs did manage to get some activities started, particularly if sport or women were involved. In 1948 Thompson got welfare started in five of the fifteen locations under his jurisdiction in Fort Hall. Sports clubs, self-help committees, women's clubs, a football team, a spinning and weaving school and one youth committee were amongst the successes, but in one area he reported that politics had stopped progress.[88] However, he was optimistic. Fort Hall people understood self-help, he explained; it formed a great part of their tribal background and Africans had been building their own schools for many years. He invested much time in spreading the Boy Scout movement, viewing it, like so many, as an institution well-suited to African needs. It appears that this was an uphill struggle. Thompson became a member of the district Scouting council. He did bring a new strategy to district efforts by suggesting that troops ought to be established at the new welfare centres so that African youths would not dismiss them as mere schoolboy associations. Guiding was not doing so well. Here he came up against the status quo of racial prejudice, European and African. Africans were not permitted to be Guiders and European women with a knowledge of Kikuyu were not in abundance, whilst elders did not approve of too many Europeans leading their women. Also, Thompson had successfully liaised with only one technical officer, a Health Inspector, John Byrne. This was as a result of Byrne's interest in football, a sport which locals took to in great numbers, to the extent that some officials later credited the game with giving Africans a much clearer sense of their identity in relation to other Africans and Europeans.[89]

Generally however, Thompson found that officers 'still do not seriously attempt to use my Community Centres and propaganda schemes as advertising agencies for the schemes they advocate'. He felt he occupied the moral high ground on this point since, when finally given his own Gestetner cyclostyling machine, he had distributed a number of articles written by other departments to community centres, chiefs, headmen, missions and schools. Making alliances with non-governmental organizations was not straightforward either. Smaller European voluntary welfare organizations like the British Legion, the St John's Ambulance and the Salvation Army were more amenable to co-operation. The missions had less interest in doing so. In Fort Hall there were three main religious groups: the African Inland Mission, the Roman Catholic Mission and the

88 Thompson, 1948 Report, Appendix A 'Positive Results in Locations', KNA CD5/255.

89 Interview with Thomas Colchester, (ex Kenya DO, MNAO, Member for Local Government and Secretary of the War Council during Mau Mau), 5 June 1989. Richard Turnbull, 'one of the best read administrators' to have served in Kenya and who rose to become a Governor, when later asked what were the most lasting features bequeathed to Africa by British rule, replied 'association football and the expression F**k off!'; Chenevix Trench, 1993: 144.

CMS. Since Thompson regarded the first – a conservative American church that had been strongly opposed to female circumcision particularly in the Murang'a area – as in a peculiar political position, he judged the lack of contact between them to be no bad thing. The Catholic Fathers had entered their football teams in the district cup, which was perhaps as much as he could hope for. The CMS was potentially his most powerful ally and Thompson had courted them throughout 1948, repeatedly discussing joint action. However, his efforts had produced 'kind words and no action'.[90] It seems, therefore, that the absence of resources and suitable propaganda was only one banana-skin among many others that lay in the path of even the most energized football-playing, Boy scout-supporting officer.

Since an important element of community development was to build up as well as make contact with African civil society, DWOs worked hard at outreach. This was not always successful but co-operation between black and white was more likely when the mutual quest to control the youth was on the agenda. In Mombasa, St Giffard wrote to 39 tribal associations and heard nothing. Trying again in Swahili, he received five replies and met with Yala Old Boys Association and the Luo Union.[91] In Machakos the welfare team tried to enlist the help of clan associations. The fervour of a revivalist meeting greeted the suggestion, according to observers, that a permanent clan council be set up to advise on the larger problems of 'drunkenness, tribal honour etc.'.[92] Officials were often quick to blame African youth for problems in their districts. Thompson in Fort Hall blamed juvenile vagrancy for the district's crime problem. In 1948 he toured the whole district in search of a solution. He had talked with locational councils and met two representatives of the KAU to discuss co-ordination of their separate campaigns. In the face of what he described as the 'creeping distrust' undermining his efforts by 1949, one of the few areas where co-operation blossomed was over youth problems. Ignatio and Erastus were Kikuyu chiefs who enforced a vigorous revival of *muhirig'a* and *ngwatio* labour to carry out the administration's obsession with low bench terracing. These were rather wishful terms for communal labour: the Kikuyu called it simply *mitaro*, meaning ridges. Over-zealous in their efforts, believing that their offices were dependent upon progress in this area, their use of force and compulsion alienated local people who began to show increasing signs of discontent and disobedience by 1948. Three loyal local chiefs, Erastus, Ignatio and Pharis, set up organizations in their locations for the large number of standard IV and VI youths who were believed to form the core of potential thieves and malcontents (Throup 1987: 154–7). Very soon it seemed that 'bad dancing and drunken affrays'

[90] Thompson, Annual Report Fort Hall, 1948, p.5, KNA CD5/255.
[91] Vincent St Giffard, Welfare Report for Mombasa, 1949, p.12, ibid.
[92] Report on Social Welfare Activities, Machakos, 1949, p.11, ibid.

were less common and every Wednesday was set aside for voluntary work on road-building, bush-clearing and soil conservation, with parties averaging 150 in number.

This seemed to testify to the mutually rewarding relationship that could still be gleaned from enlisting the co-operation of the so-called progressive chiefs. It was perhaps no coincidence that the Jeanes School held its first course for chiefs in April 1948. They all seemed to want the same things: Thompson cheerfully reported how 'the idea of a little practical help from the idle male is beginning to spread'.[93] Spurred on, he made a survey of one hundred Kikuyu youth in 1950. He was not unsympathetic and, like many white observers, understood the problem to be a knock-on effect of British rule. The problem, he felt, lay in the shift of circumcision from twenty years of age to twelve, denying adolescents the chance to play out their high spirits and learn respect for elders in battle-schools. His strategy looked back to the appeal to manliness that was believed to have had such success in the Second World War. If you could challenge their manhood, you could cajole 'the most horrible and spivish characters wearing the standard cowboy hat and red shirt open to the waist' into getting involved in the despised bench-terracing work. However, such large gatherings might also have reminded young men of another kind of power capability unleashed by co-operation.

Unfortunately, by 1950, such co-operation was proving more and more elusive. In Fort Hall Thompson admitted to having been watched very closely by the general populace, who were unsure that 'welfare business' was not a catch, and 'a Governmenti [sic] catch at that'. Rather ominously he recorded how, for the first time, 'we were under constant political fire'. There was no more co-operation from the Kenya African Union. Welfare work was subject to a litany of charges. One was that welfare halls were built to steal land, a reflection of the insecurity over land. Another was that the Welfare Officer will 'steal our money'. One which Thompson particularly liked was the accusation that 'there was no sin in Kikuyu until welfare came'.[94] A new criticism, which he was at a loss to explain, was that 'by encouraging youth, I encourage crime'. This illustrates the insensitivity of Europeans to African insecurities. As the activities of the state became increasingly arbitrary and its power less knowable, so their general ignorance about the complexity of the local moral economies widened the growing impasse. Through these criticisms, Kikuyu elites were asserting their traditional view of poverty as delinquency, youth as the absence of self-mastery. It was the discipline of labour that yielded reward – official welfare, therefore, appeared to be an arbitrary gift to the undisciplined and as such was seen as a highly dangerous move in what were now highly insecure times (see Lonsdale, 1992).

93 Annual Report on Welfare, Fort Hall 1950, pp.2–3, KNA CD5/255.

94 Thompson, Annual Report, 1949. p.1, ibid.

Elsewhere, enthusiasms were also waning. Community centres in Central Nyanza were proving unable to keep up their membership. Annual subscriptions set at 2 shillings so as to enable even the poorest to enrol were not being renewed.[95] At Ahero, for example, there were 165 paid up members in 1949. Only 14 had renewed their subscription in 1950, in addition to 24 new members. As well as the massive reduction in members, the whole principle and point of a centre was being destroyed. Subscriptions were designed to relieve the LNCs, to be a first step towards self-sufficiency, and to make the people identify with the centre. Out of a total income of 440.27 shillings for 1949, 279.75 shillings came from membership fees, 87.32 from the tea canteen, 28.80 from the postal agency and 44.40 from dances. Thus subscription formed the largest portion of the centre's income and their reduction was a serious blow to hopes for a clear move towards the goal of self-sufficiency; LNC votes paid for welfare assistants, caretakers, sports, running costs, exhibitions and newspapers. Hunt, the DWO, gloomily concluded what Harden Smith had warned about before the war, that 'Africans will show interest in something new which is for their benefit, but are quite incapable of sustaining their interest'. Attendance was irregular at literacy classes, and advisory committee members were losing interest because it was not a paid job. Newspaper sales had dropped. As for rural industries there was only one basket-chair maker in Asembo worth mentioning.

By the end of the 1940s, the energy and wartime vision of a new Commissioner, a supportive CNC, a clear line on community development, more external links and devoted officers slogging away in the districts were not enough. The underlying features of the second colonial occupation were making little impact on the African landscape. Rural class formation was speeding up the process of social breakdown by the end of the decade. Those under most threat from the increasingly arbitrary nature of colonial power, whether wielded by officials or chiefs, were traumatized by fresh proof of the dangers, whilst Africans learned that there was little point in looking outside for help. With the adoption of the Beecher Report, the abandonment of plans for a non-racial identity card and increased African LegCo representation plus the dismissal of a KAU petition on land, hope seemed to be fading for a peaceful solution.[96]

[95] Report on Community Development and Social Welfare Activities – Central Nyanza, KNA CD5/255.

[96] Lonsdale, 1992: 436. He describes how, divided and discredited, the KCA failed to attain 'the cleanliness of wealth' as leaders in a new moral community. Three events provided further proof that those Africans who had done well from the colonial state now possessed immoral wealth: 'derived from the state rather than sweat' it lacked any obligation to others' labour; p.441. The state was also seen as operating within the realm of immoral action. After the defeat of Olenguruone, the increased isolation of Nairobi townsmen from rural elite structures and their resort to strike action after the spivs and drones legislation, and the events in Nyeri where government and chiefs conspired in an intrusive cattle-dipping campaign, the idea took hold among many Kikuyu that, in 'the terrifying aspect of

Interestingly, some administrators had already resorted to increasingly extreme and dangerous forms of rule. Hunter in Nyanza Province had used the *mbira* oath in African Tribunal Courts. According to custom, a symbolic grave was dug and funeral pieces were placed inside such as a clay pot and a small broom. Anyone testifying would, according to tradition, die if they did not speak the truth. He would also resort to ridicule as a punishment, on one occasion making the culprit kneel down in front of a group of strangers to beg forgiveness.[97] All these trends, and the heightening of racial suspicion they generated, would make the efforts of an even more coherent and stronger Welfare Organization much more flimsy than they already were. Colonial Office solutions were not working and fewer people were prepared to give them a try. Africans, now found to be sullen and unco-operative, were merely retreating into their own internal battlefield and waiting and wondering when they would be called on to act.

Community development to counter insurgency, 1950–52

Yet there was another twist in the tale. The three constituencies of change discussed above – a committed Colonial Office, a more sympathetic government, and a more coherent Welfare Organization with a field staff – were vigorously exploited by Patrick Williams's successor, Thomas Askwith. Williams had resigned to take up a senior post in the Tanganyika groundnut scheme and the future of the Jeanes School was in some doubt as training for ex-servicemen petered out. Yet the CNC – Eric Davies – decided that he wanted to run with Williams' proposals for community development in Kenya. Having no idea how it would work, he approached Askwith, then acting Principal of the school, offering him the task of working out how to apply the principles in Kenya. Askwith had replaced Horace Mason at the Jeanes School; Mason was an ex-army type who had been keen to encourage students to become active in running their own council. This had brought Askwith into conflict with an up and coming pupil in the school, Tom Mboya, who was working for a sanitary inspector qualification. Askwith and Mboya repeatedly clashed, Askwith objecting to the growing executive rather than advisory functions of the student council. Mboya as its President resigned, later insisting that Askwith held views 'similar to local white settlers'.[98] Askwith himself soon left to become Commissioner in 1950 which he later described as being 'rather like the

[96] (cont.) an arbitrary state', the recourse to violence was made legitimate. Militants took over the moribund KCA and began oathing. This reflected the terror felt in confronting power that was increasingly anti-social and unknown; 'immoral wealth' was producing 'personal evil' that could only be defeated by the healing power of anti-sorcery. The need for counter-terror to cleanse moral virtue produced the violence of Mau Mau; pp.401–61.

[97] Memoirs of K L. Hunter. RH Mss.Afr.s.1942.

[98] Goldsworthy, 1982, ch. 2 'Rise to Labour Leadership',

blind, leading the blind'.[99] Nevertheless, he achieved a great deal in a short time and took the organization to a new dimension. However, it was hugely ironic that, just as the second colonial occupation showed signs of adapting Colonial Office solutions to local structures, the whole edifice of colonial rule in Kenya was blown apart in 1952. As welfare and community development found a new coherence and line into rural society, so it lost its foothold and the Organization faced its biggest challenge.

Askwith's appointment heralded another phase in the history of the Organization, since he fitted into a tradition of wartime dissent as well as being somewhat different from his predecessors. He was an Oxbridge product, but fell into the post-First World War cohort of lower middle-class stock who had benefited from an assisted place at a respectable English public school. A former Olympic oarsman, he arrived in Kenya in 1936 to take up a post as district officer, happy to have escaped the tedium of the 'nine to five troglodyte existence'. Both he and his wife Pat – a council member of the Kenya Girl Guides Association – were Quakers. Like many of his generation, the Second World War was a defining moment in his life, when private and public theatres of living could no longer be so artificially separated. He had had the difficult task of looking after African Nairobi during the war. His time as MNAO made a deep impression. He saw extreme levels of poverty and urban squalor that offended his sensibilities: 'Men sleeping ten to a hundred square foot room, men wearing shirts and shorts that were fifty per cent patches, the nauseating smell of choked-up sewers, beer halls over-flowing with men drowning their sorrows at weekends' (Askwith, 1995: 35). Askwith admitted to the absence of administrative control in Nairobi during the war and consequently pushed an urban form of rural government based on the various tribal associations.

Like other white officials, he got used to working with members of the African educated male elite, like his assistant Dedan Githegi, who kept him 'in touch with feelings on the ground', and he deferred to the view that African women ought not to live and work in Nairobi if unmarried.[100] During the war, his racial thought showed some elastic properties. Living in Nairobi, his sense of the awkwardness of racial laws in the public domain had been sharpened by liberal criticisms from Britain. Thus, he helped lay the foundation of the United Kenya Club at the end of the war, the first meeting place for all races, and became its first Chairman. As a final product of this experience, Askwith was convinced that African urban welfare required state support for family life especially since African women, as wives, had an important stabilizing effect on husbands.[101]

[99] RH Mss.Afr.s.1770. Askwith, 1995: 2.

[100] Askwith to Trench, 16 October 1988, RH, Mss.Afr.s.2100; Throup, 1987: 175–8; Askwith, 1995: 25–7.

[101] See discussion in Chapter 3 of Nairobi meeting on welfare where Dr Martin put forward the idea of the urban family and was supported by Askwith.

Askwith was also different from his predecessors working in welfare and propaganda. He had come up through the respected route of district officer, rather than being brought in through demobilization, information or social welfare. He was also used to working on his own and was not afraid of being unpopular. He had a reputation for being stubborn and difficult. He was keen to pursue the path of amateur sociologist, reviving an older administrative tradition. He used the African Affairs Committee to argue again and again in various submissions in the late 1940s that urban and rural problems were linked. He was not afraid to make the unwelcome point that African unemployment was creating increasing unrest. This combination of old and new, of insider and outsider, ensured that he went beyond the boundaries of his structural category in ways that bothered some of his contemporaries (see Cooper, 1991).

Askwith and his co-workers tell us much about the late colonial state. The post-war theme of government, that of centralization both in terms of money and ideas, focused local rivalries as well as revealing local weaknesses. Possibly, the men defending the thin white line got on with each other less and less. Professional relations between officials had always been vulnerable to feelings of competition, aggression and envy. But as problems grew, so did personal dislikes, and professional frustration found expression in squabbles and backbiting. Likewise, the ideology of colonial paternalism was now less fixed than ever before and more fragmented. Askwith testifies to the growing factionalism within paternal rule. More officers were able to sustain contact with liberal opinion inside and outside the colony. A growing number of officials challenged the ruling ideology of paternalism. They agreed with Creech Jones's theory of local government, that through adult education in citizenship and civics Africans would learn how to improve standards of living, and would then do it willingly: they would instinctively organize their own welfare as they had always done. Askwith had told the EAWL in 1950 that, through the gradual extension of the franchise, Africans would learn economic truths and the need to understand the point of view of others.[102] Yet even this gradualism challenged the administration's established paternalism. DCs had happily seen social welfare as the 'exercise of authoritarian paternalism without requiring any rethinking of established administrative methods' (Berman, 1990: 280). Another generation of officers, due to their maverick and unconventional experiences during the Second World War, had come to believe that, if paternal control was relaxed in recognition of the maturity and responsibility of those under its authority, then Africans would experience the liberation of community self-help rather than the oppression of communal compulsory labour.

This conclusion was reached at a time when African social relations were becoming ever more strained from the effects of rural class

[102] Askwith's talk to EAWL Nairobi, 7 June 1950, KNA DC/KSM/1/199.

formation. Most DCs were sceptical. They pointed out that there was nothing particularly novel in the proposals; for years chiefs had been building roads and dams, etc. with the use of communal labour. As insecurities mounted, racial suspicions mounted further. Many administrators grappling with the agrarian crisis found the liberals' message, that voluntary self-help could work where compulsion had failed, more naive, ludicrous or dangerous than ever (Askwith, 1995: 28).

Almost immediately on taking up his new post, Askwith realized what was most needed – a conference for welfare officers. This took place in February 1950.[103] It was a supportive CNC who helped make the event a success. Eric Davies rallied DWOs at the opening session, bringing a clear sense of mission to this small band of foot soldiers. They were a bridge between the state and Africans, he told them; they must get to know Africans, especially the young men, listening to their needs and problems and encouraging them to find their own solutions. He emotively described their job as helping 'the loneliest African on earth': the rising generation who were held back by their fathers. In retrospect, it was a pity that with such a task on the books, he was talking to only eight men.

Nevertheless, the meeting gave further coherence to their work in a number of crucial areas. First, they finally dispensed with the term and concept of social welfare. Clearly their daily duties had moved naturally away from ameliorative intervention that dealt only with the very vulnerable. Community development was also more attractive since it seemed to hold out the possibility of breaking down local prejudice and ending the experience of being treated as social lepers. Many recounted the same story. Welfare usually conjured up 'a frightful picture of tea, buns and clammy handshakes', Thompson lamented, recounting how, when introduced to a man at a district party, the man had replied, 'Good God! What a ghastly appointment! Whatever will they do next?' and then walked off.[104] St Giffard (Mombasa) was more concerned about the negative image it had among Africans. He was unhopeful that their new language would make much difference, illustrating the apathy which existed. Nor could he see any 'positive indication of any genuine desire or capability for community development by creative effort, initiative and character among the African population of Mombasa'. Gloomily, he blamed history and the inescapable consequence of ethnology and his organization's inadequate resources in the unending battle against the terrible hold of blatant materialism and malignant apathy.[105]

Others too found casting off the mantle of social welfare sensible but problematic. Hayes, DWO (Machakos), had already switched his efforts to

[103] District Welfare Officers' Conference, Jeanes School, 27 February–10 March 1950, KNA DC/KSM/1/1/199. Six officers attended from N. Nyanza, C. Nyanza, Machakos, Kitui, Fort Hall, Kiambu and a Forest Welfare Officer from Londiani.

[104] Annual Report, Fort Hall, 1949, p.1. KNA CD5/255.

[105] Mombasa Welfare Report, 1949, p.16, ibid.

building up the local economy. The Machakos social welfare services maintained by the LNC consisted of six Jeanes' School-trained teachers, plus one caretaker-helper. Of the locations in which a worker was maintained, Iveti, Kilungu, Matungulu and Masii had a community hall built from joint DARA-LNC and British Legion funds.[106] This had meant getting welfare out of the locational community halls and out and about as reconstruction teams. Hayes acknowledged that self-help already played an important part in Akamba life but 'the agricultural malpractice of any man is still held to be his own affair'. Undeterred, they had begun village rural campaigns. A full-scale development team had worked in Kamala and Kilungu, whilst a village improvement scheme in Matungulu had built six latrines. Efforts were concentrated on establishing village crafts and cottage industries. Local carvings were marketed and a chicken and egg co-operative set up in Kamala. Carpentry and blacksmith classes and demonstrations in hide preparation were begun, and at women's clubs weaving, rug-making and fibre mat-work were being supervised by the welfare teams.

The conference was an example of the greater bureaucratic possibilities through better communication as well as iniative from the centre achievable by the late 1940s. It yielded a number of positive developments. Titles were changed to 'District Officer – Rural Development'.[107] Officers would continue to help departments in existing work in relation to African welfare; to assume responsibility for new types of services; to encourage community life, voluntary associations and religious associations. Using the revised Colonial Office Memorandum, officers accepted that social welfare and economic prosperity could not be separated. Remedial work was abandoned. DWOs felt that it would not matter if they paid less attention to the care of the destitute and those deemed in need of special care since families provided such care; 'the problem of destitute children does not exist'.[108] An imposed system of social insurance – lacking in Kenya at the time, unlike Britain – such as was being discussed at the Secretariat at the time, was not necessary because of Akamba clan and family ties. Although in 1949 the Machakos DWO recorded a rise in the number of unemployed who were drawing heavily on their capital or family assistance, officers did not want responsibility for this group of new structural poor, those without access to land as well as labour. Officers assumed that the pre-colonial pattern would continue, with Africans caring for most of their poor most of the time (see Iliffe, 1987: 1–8). The problem, DWOs felt, required secondary industries and higher wages which would also halt the sub-division of land, and other qualified experts. Secondly, participants listened to a number of talks from professional specialists such as McKilliam,

[106] Annual Report of Social Welfare Activities, 1949, Machakos, p.1, KNA CD5/255.
[107] Report of DWO Conference, 1950, p.2–3, KNA DC/KSM/1/1/199.
[108] Ibid., p.6.

sports master at the Jeanes School, who gave the now standard reiteration of the value of scouting and youth movements. This time it was explicitly tied in to 'the alarming social disintegration' among the Kikuyu youth and to the practice of democratic government, since it could produce 'sound men among the people who could lead by example'.[109]

Women also received some attention at the conference. Nancy Shepherd, recently transferred to the Jeanes School as welfare and handicrafts teacher, urged that a welfare officer be made responsible for homecrafts in the settled areas and that a course be set up to train European women. The conference provided a space to articulate the growing realization that one of the most successful activities at the community centres was work with women. In Machakos, welfare workers had targeted 'the Akamba baby' on the basis that 'through appeal to the mother, problems pressing urgently in the District might be easier solved'. Women's organizations were also developing at the welfare halls and showed signs of being 'strong and progressive'; although according to the Report women were strong guardians of tradition, the enthusiasm shown for learning and the high club attendance revealed 'a move towards greater personal liberty equal to that of the Nyanza tribes'. Shepherd found her work veering towards combined lessons in needlework and hygiene, when travelling with the DWO in Central Province. Everyone agreed that they must find suitable African women welfare officers, principally on the grounds that European women would train them for free which could improve race relations.

There was no wholescale attention to incorporating women into other aspects of the betterment campaigns. In retrospect Willoughby Thompson concluded that up to 1947 'no real thought had been given to getting the agricultural message across to the women'. No female agricultural instructors or assistants existed; nor were funds provided to train any. The assumption that women were needed to teach women may have held back a growing interest in the contribution of women to food production. However, a feeling that their subordination to men made any efforts superfluous may have thrown cold water on any spark of enthusiasm. Thompson and a few fellow officers regularly composed and put on operettas as part of the weekend entertainment. After the women's revolt in Muranga in 1947, they included a verse to the tune of Old Man River:

> Oh! You women. You damn fool women.
> In every country the same.
> You must say something, but you don't say nothing.
> But it's your menfolk, your lazy menfolk to blame.[110]

Yet, as some missionary evidence suggests, the effect of the war in interupting provisions for female education, and in commandeering more

[109] Ibid., p.10.

[110] Willoughby Thompson, p. 49. RH Mss.s.1519(1).

female labour, was being overturned by the late 1940s. By 1949 in Meru District, more girls were passing through village schools and going on to the girls' boarding schools. At Kagga, more enthusiasm was recorded among the girl pupils than ever before. Efforts were increased to link 'the practical aspects of life to the school lessons'. Visits to seed farms were supplemented with talks from the local forestry officer who demonstrated how to plant trees. The older girls had gone on to plant an unbelievable 1500 trees by nightfall. With that kind of energy it was perhaps not surprising that by 1951 a Women's Teacher Training Centre had been opened at the local Methodist Mission. Protestant women at least now had this outlet, but Catholics were not included.[111]

The battle for turf between professional specialists and the district administration now swung in favour of the former. Complaints over the confusion as to what social welfare meant could now be dealt with more firmly. Nyanza's PC had complained to the CNC that his DCs were unable to form a clear picture of the work of the Social Welfare Department.[112] The Secretary of State's Despatch of November 1948 had not made the position any clearer, so the PC wanted a circular on the subject. Davies agreed and Askwith obliged.[113] He produced a clear mission statement that addressed a number of key problems which had surfaced during the 1940s. He explained the philosophy behind community development as that better health, houses, food and water were the basis of a sound economic system and that social welfare and economic prosperity could not be separated.[114] Whilst he acknowledged that DCs were already involved in breaking down the conservatism and prejudice of the people, larger districts needed the help of specialist staff. The CO blueprint for DWOs, 'accepted by the Provincial Administration in principle', had not worked out in practice, he explained, owing to insufficient preparation of 'the human ground'. Part of the problem in the past had lain in the way DWOs had been engaged with reabsorption work which took up 50 per cent of their time. Similarly, departmental officers had often been reluctant to invite their help in preparing the ground for new policies. And DCs treated DWOs as junior members of staff, assigning them only elementary duties.

This initiative also stirred up established turf wars between the agricultural departments and the administration. In Nyanza, for example, one Agricultural Officer seized on the moment to push for agrarian development first, and social welfare second.[115] His own PC thought that

[111] E. Mary Holding, 'The Education of the Bantu Tribe' (1958) pp. 51–7. RH Mss.Afr. 117.A580.

[112] PC (Nyanza) to CNC 20 February 1950, KNA PC/NZA/3/1/574.

[113] CNC to PCs (Nyanza, Central and Coast Province), 27 March 1950, ibid. Davies was aware that the whole question had already been discussed at the recent conference for District Welfare Officers held at Jeanes School.

[114] Askwith to all DCs, 15 March 1950, KNA PC/N2A/3/1/574..

[115] Provincial Ag.O., Nyanza to PC (Nyanza) 25 June 1950, ibid.

community development could be advanced only if departmental officers became general purpose Officers.[116] Meanwhile, Stokes, Nyanza's Provincial Education Officer, wanted his teachers to spearhead rural betterment, since this was what he understood mass education to be. Only teachers could get real co-operation between the school, chief, headman, agricultural, veterinary and health assistants.[117] He proposed that new locational teams be assembled at the planned intermediary schools to be placed next to the large primary schools. These would consist of eight teachers, one male and one female health assistant, one agricultural assistant, one veterinary and one social welfare worker, not forgetting a policeman.

This was not the only initiative being sponsored by agricultural staff. So profound was the sense of impending crisis by the late 1940s that one senior member of the agricultural department in Machakos had organized a youth conference, held at the LNC hall and showground in Nyeri between 1 and 2 September 1949. Rice described it as a conference of all people of goodwill in order to 'put to them the perilous decline in their social integrity and unity and to try to enlist their support in social uplift'.[118] Two hundred delegates attended; forty of these were women. Speakers included the PC, Carey Francis, and Ben Ngumbu, Headmaster of Kabete Secondary School. What was particularly striking about this initiative was the inclusion of the missionaries, now less willing to remain separated off. As Rice reiterated, the whole *leitmotif* of the conference was that the Christian way of life was the best way to build up a sound economy and society. And tacked on to this was his own professional wisdom: it could achieve the central goal of fertile land. Terracing, manure, grass and trees could perform an agrarian miracle if people believed in these elementary truths. Just before the conference ended with a tea party, delegates were encouraged to make pledges by signing their names in a book that was to be a roll call of 'true men and women of Goodwill in the District'. This mixed customary oathing with Boy Scout initiation; the first pledge was that 'I shall always do my best at all times to help and lead my fellow men to a better way of life'. And as a follow-up scheme, Rice asked that they be given a welfare officer who could coordinate all their efforts.

In the new climate the administration had to take all these suggestions seriously. At a subsequent meeting held between Stokes, Askwith and Nyanza officials, Stokes's idea was accepted in principle but the administration argued that it was not practicable to make the schools the centre of district development, so policy did not change.[119] However, the knee-jerk

[116] PC (Nyanza) to CS, 3 August 1950, ibid.

[117] Stokes to PC, 31 August 1951, KNA PC/NZA/3/6/69.

[118] 'Some notes on a Youth Conference held at LNC Hall and Showground Nyeri, 1–2 September 1949'. Written by T. H. Rice (Senior Assistant Agricultural Officer, Machakos). RH Mss.Afr.s.531.

[119] Minute 70/51 'Mass Education' from DCs Meeting, 1–4 October 1951, KNA PC/NZA/3/6/12.

reaction to project-established turf and the sanctity of the district officers' patch surfaced once again. Privately Nyanza's new PC, C.H. Williams, had called for the Commissioner's position to be clarified.[120] Williams was irritated by his efforts at inclusion. He was sending out material addressed not only to all DOs (CD) – DWOs were now called District Officers (Community Development) – but also to PCs and DCs. What had particularly enraged him was the earlier DWO conference at the Jeanes School. This, he fumed, was quite without precedent. If district views were required, he insisted, the DC should give them and not one of his subordinates. In any case, DOs (CD) were DOs. Williams's bureaucratic ethos revered chains of command and control and it was in his interest that they should remain intact.

Keeping a grip on policy was not so easy for the administration in the early 1950s because the nature and arena of bureaucratic practice were moving at a much more dramatic pace. The example of community development illustrates this well. Helped by the example of his predecessors and propelled by his own misanthropic tendencies, Askwith was well-placed to mount a campaign of self-promotion. When he found a success story he immediately spread the gospel. After his safaris – having been a DC, this was work he was used to – he would send the relevant PC a summary of community development work in each area together with his recommendations. His jewel was the Manyasi Valley project, part of the Alego Betterment Scheme in Central Nyanza. Askwith was able to boast that 7 per cent of farmers in the location had begun to make significant alterations in their farming and domestic practices. The enthusiasm of his man on the spot had been crucial. Hunt had carried out a social survey, held *barazas*, demonstrated how *ogaka* planting worked as a wash-stop, given film shows, developed a new cattle *boma* design that incorporated traditional ideas, spread the good news about manure, raved about compost heaps and warned everyone against the evil of boundary furrows.[121] As Askwith acknowledged, the presence of the DWO and his assistant, who had become well-liked and trusted by the people, had not allowed enthusiasm to wane.

Despite the obvious concentration of effort required for a modest positive result, Askwith had a result he could use to show that literacy campaigns were not a necessary prerequisite for community development programmes. He also used other organizations to sell the work of the Organization. He distributed a paper on rural welfare written by the EAWL which flatteringly described the work of his organization. He maintained a close relationship with the Colonial Office's SWAC which had sent him details of schemes operating in Uganda and Tanganyika. Collaboration with the Press Liaison Officer produced four articles which

[120] C. H. Williams to CNC 20 September 1950, KNA PC/NZA/3/1/574.
[121] Askwith to DC (Nyanza), 19 October 1951, KNA CD7/112.

he circulated right across the administration and sent to the press in Kenya and Britain. 'Self-help amongst the Wakamba' publicized the communal terracing project started in Machakos under the supervision of the DWO. Hunt had undertaken tours with young Wakamba actors supported by an African instructor from each of the departments, encouraging a revival of traditional digging parties complete with dancers and acrobats.[122] Askwith had the audacity to suggest to all DCs, PCs and Senior Education Officers that they read two articles in the *East African Teachers Journal*, which argued that community development was inextricably bound up with the school, and he suggested that the Education Department and the administration work more closely together on this. He suggested teachers attend a civics course at the Jeanes School planned for next year so that they could be given 'a wider responsibility in the general enlightenment of their area, and ... help to lead the inhabitants to a better way of life through co-operation with Government'. The original Jeanes School teachers had been given a makeover.[123]

It was not only that the volume of written material was increasing. Paper and printing presses were much more in abundance. As the constraints of the Depression and the shortages of war were left behind, technology was quietly advancing. Equally important was the way in which the context of colonial policy-making was also changing. The growth of international organizations concerned with development now had more to say about strategies for economic growth. The concept of underdevelopment began to take hold and to unleash global remedies. Publications from organizations like UNESCO now reached the desks of colonial administrators such as Askwith. UNESCO had produced a paper on Fundamental Education which it described as a strategy being designed for underdeveloped regions of the world: a community education for adults and adolescents that would produce services and agencies for social and economic progress.[124] Askwith could use this to argue that specialist officers using new techniques were needed, since DCs could not take on such extra functions. And he urged PCs to apply for DOs (CD) so that every device could be used to make 'conservative and suspicious Africans' realize the benefits to be gained from co-operating with the government. He sent all PCs an extract from Uganda's Public Relations and Social Welfare Department Report for 1949 on the success of their village and rural improvement schemes, which he used to launch his suggestion that

[122] Circular 'Rural Welfare in Kenya', 29 June 1950; circular 5 October 1950 with 'Self-help amongst the Wakamba'; 'Samburu Land Kenya'; 'A Devastated Valley is Watered' and 'The Agricultural Betterment Funds'. Information Services Handout No.138, KNA DC/KSM/1/1/199. For an account of these activities described as achievements see Silberfein, 1989: 156–7.

[123] Circular on 'Community Development', 17 November 1950, KNA DC/KSM/1/1/199.

[124] 'Community Development' circular to all PCs 21 November 1950; UNESCO publication, 'Fundamental Education', PC NZA/3/1/574.

he and the African Information Services be invited to discuss preparations for particular rural betterment projects.[125]

Even the Colonial Office joined in and came up with what they hoped was a new catchphrase. CBA, or Community Betterment in Africa, was an attempt to sell the idea of self-help as a return to traditional communal pulling together. African men and women were called to learn the other side of ABC: 'ABC means learning how to better yourself so that you can better your family and the community you live in. CBA means learning how to better your community so that your community can better your family and yourself.' British grants, they were told, were being used for long-term, large betterment projects; such money could not stretch to every village and in any case it would be wrong to spend this money on things people could do for themselves.[126] Askwith's ability to synthesize external ideas with internal structures clearly impressed the Colonial Office. They requested a copy of a talk he gave at a training course in Crowhurst, England.[127] His presentation of community development as noble adult enlightenment – 'the development of citizens, men and women with a wider sense of appreciation and knowledge of the problems and needs of their bewildering age ... ' – was sure to be well received. It also contained a theme of confusion and insecurity through the absence of total modernization, which liberal thinkers would return to when violence and destruction ravaged Kikuyu communities a year later.[128]

This new language and style of campaigning did provoke some interest from among the administration. Goodbody, a DC in Central Nyanza, decided to recommend a community development-type approach to tree-planting, one of the three principal campaigns planned for 1951, the other two being castration (of animals presumably) which was proving extremely successful and soil conservation terracing which remained very unpopular. It appealed to him since it required individual effort within the limited period of the rains, that would be tailored to each location. And, if any other schemes came to mind, Goodbody pledged that he would apply to the Community Development Commissioner for 'his particular brand of assistance'.[129] But this was no great conversion on the matter of principle throughout the interior. From Goodbody's perspective, no amount of 'Community Development medicine' could make soil conservation terracing popular. The people already recognized the need, he observed, but that did not produce results: only continual pressure week after week in the whole district for the next fifteen weeks would. As Goodbody told his PC,

[125] 'Community Betterment', 24 November 1950, ibid.

[126] *CBA in Africa*, CO publication, undated, KNA DC/KSM/1/1/199.

[127] L.G. Heptinstall (CO) to Askwith, 26 July 1951, Askwith to R. May, Mass Education, CO, 24 July 1951, KNA CD5/40; and various correspondence between Askwith and Chinn in 1951; PRO CO822/652.

[128] Copy of talk given at Crowhurst, KNA CD5/40.

[129] Goodbody to District Agricultural Officer, Kisumu, 29 November 1950, KNA DC/KSM/1/1/199.

it was time some of the false claims being made to 'sell' community development were put into proper perspective.[130] Despite all that had been written about the subject from the CO and UNESCO down, community development was only concentrated propaganda and nothing new: 'it has been employed in varying degrees by administrative and departmental officers for the past sixty years', plausible criticism from someone well-versed in Luo intransigence. What this suggests is that, even when faced with the most progressive development thought of the time, which itself was still in keeping with long-standing colonial negativity towards African agriculture, the use of force and sanction was accepted as the only likely way of achieving the desired results among officers working in the field. It was disheartening, nevertheless, for those at the time who believed differently. Askwith did not give up. He looked at the colony through a lens shaped by the new techniques of social propaganda and he continued to speak the gospel from the Colonial Office and international organizations. He began to popularize the view that economic development in Africa was beset by three main problems: overpopulation; an African youth turning to vice and idleness as tribal law became obsolete; and bewilderment at the rapidity of change. It was hardly surprising that ten years later, after a state of emergency, mass arrest and forced labour, neither group would stand in the way of the transfer of colonial rule. It had not enabled modernizing government to behave in a modern way.

In the meantime, however, the new coherence evolving out of the community development camp did make this corner of the late colonial state more able to read the lessons of its own initiatives. The spate of intelligence-gathering had incontrovertibly shown that the post-war plan for army-type information rooms to function as centres for adult education was largely a failed enterprise. By 1949, four years after they first appeared, many departments did not realize that halls existed in their areas. Neither were they popular among Africans themselves. Annual Reports from welfare officers acknowledged the lack of interest in the centres. and Askwith accepted that as an educative mechanism they had failed. The reading rooms were not used; only a minority read anything more than a news-sheet; the response to literacy classes was disappointing; apart from being the meeting place for LNCs, there was little sign of social activities. Fort Hall's DWO, Willoughby Thompson, reported gloomily the 'usual struggle against superstition, apathy and moral degeneration' in 1950.[131] Athletics and scouting flourished at a few centres but newspaper sales had dropped steadily.

Similarly, African social welfare workers were now acknowledged to have failed to become the hoped-for mentors of the people. Faced with the 'apathy and conservatism' of a peasant community and sometimes open hostility, only a few, through sheer force of personality, had come through.

[130] Goodbody to Acting PC (Nyanza) 29 November 1950. ibid.

[131] 'Community Halls Policy', Askwith, 31 July 1950, KNA PC/NZA/3/1/574; Annual Report for Fort Hall, 1950, KNA DC/KSM/1/1/199.

Others fell into apathy or turned to alcohol. Thompson had complained that his welfare workers had shown that they rated their social position first, and their service to their communities a poor second, throughout 1948, although their performance improved during 1949.[132] Hunt in Central Nyanza was less harsh. He blamed the heavy expectations placed on their shoulders and problems outside their immediate control. His assistants had shown enthusiasm despite working from temporary community centres; his welfare worker at Maseno had organized three traders' courses, but they lacked a sense of profit-making. One problem was that 'as examples, the embodiment of improved standards pay increased dividends', many left 'much to be desired'. Often workers had not set their own house in order in respect of culling stock, dietary improvements or giving attention to 'the women's place in family life'.[133] Also the Jeanes School had emphasized that their first task was to establish local welfare committees, but Hunt had not found them useful since they tended to lack genuinely committed members. Welfare assistants tried too hard to collect revenue and used compulsion in some cases which put people off. Many people lived too far from the location centres to make regular use of their facilities, whilst others were ignorant of their uses and saw the fee as another tax.[134]

Yet it now became clear to the fraternity that 'the desire of the women to learn spinning and weaving and the domestic crafts appears to have been great, in some places ... overwhelming'. Thompson in Fort Hall found that, for some odd reason, women in Chief Peterson's Location 'are very well organized and there are several bodies who run what are almost Women's Institutes. They appear to have been going for some years', one being run by the wife of a health worker, Bedan Karanja.[135] And Hunt in Central Nyanza concluded generally that the women were more interested than the men in improving their knowledge. The only sign of self-help he had come across was in spinning and weaving; women showed 'unwavering enthusiasm', even working on verandahs and in information rooms when there was insufficient room at the welfare halls. If we had trained African instructresses and an enthusiastic European lady supervisor, he advised, much could be achieved, whilst a visit from his counterpart in Busoga, Uganda, a Miss Hastie, who ran fifty women's groups, had left him convinced that a 'mere man cannot expect to cope with the training of African women'.[136]

These and other revelations prompted a change in policy that amounted in effect to a return to the conclusions sketched out in the Colonial Office in 1925, over a quarter of a century before. Community halls were now to

[132] Thompson, 1948 Report, p.8 and 1949 Report, p.6, ibid.

[133] Machakos, Annual Report on welfare activities, 1949, p.2, ibid.

[134] Annual Report, Central Nyanza District, 1948, p.2, KNA CD5/255.

[135] Thompson's Report on Community Development and Social Welfare for Fort Hall, 1950, p.3., KNA DC/KSM/1/1/199. The women's classes were moderately successful overall.

[136] Central Nyanza, Report on Community Development and Social Welfare, 1950, p.3, KNA CD5/255.

be used as training centres for African women in what was called 'the domestic virtues', so that 'the standard of living of the community should be raised largely through their agency'.[137] Hunt suggested that male welfare workers should work in teams on community development projects, which had been tried out successfully in Machakos. Able to concentrate their efforts, each could then specialize in a particular aspect of the work; sports, film commentary or whatever. Such a scheme had already been suggested by Pat Williams but had been dropped for lack of finance. Askwith decided that the term homecrafts would be used in place of domestic science training, and sent circulars to all PCs on how to select the most suitable women candidates for training and how to encourage and run women's societies. Co-operation with the EAWL was inevitable and shaped the developing programme.[138] With a distinct EAWL flavour to the virtues of womanhood, sewing, mending, knitting, washing, ironing, simple cookery, hygiene, agriculture and child-care were on the agenda.

This gave the green light for individual pet projects to get under way. In North Nyanza, for example, the wives of two district officials began teaching Abaluhya women spinning and weaving. They quickly came to the conclusion that nearly all were 'ignorant of any elementary knowledge of sewing', and that they lacked absolutely basic knowledge on how to bring up their children, especially in relation to diet and treating common illness.[139] A Mrs Aylward was a classic example. Shocked by her initial investigation, she visited chiefs' locational headquarters and with their co-operation started teaching elementary hygiene, treatment of common ailments, sewing, etc. In September 1950 the government appointed her as a Woman Homecrafts Officer. With transport and an interpreter, she started twenty classes which were a mixture of sewing, spinning and instruction in child-care, cleanliness in the home, boiling water, fly prevention, maternity care and diet. Sometimes she liaised with health workers and distributed seeds. Women showed a keenness to make clothes for sale but she was unable to help them with this. Other developments included a new course in domestic science at the Jeanes School, and European women who wanted to help, or who were already undertaking such work voluntarily, would be given the opportunity to attend a two-week course planned for the end of 1950. Motives were mixed. One aim was to raise the general standard of living and behaviour of Africans through the women. Another was linked to the search for obedient clients. As Askwith patronizingly commented, reflecting general attitudes of the time, 'the African mother must be taught how to discipline her children'.

[137] Community Halls Policy, 31 July 1950, KNA PC/NZA/3/1/574; Circular, 13 November 1950, KNA PC/NZA/3/1/275.

[138] Hunt to Mrs Millar, EAWL Deputy Vice President, 22 May 1950, KNA DC/KSM/1/1/197; talk given by Askwith, 7 June 1950, KNA CD5/301.

[139] Notes about the life and work of Mrs E. Aylward, Women's Homecraft Officer, RH MSS Afr.s.1857.

Not everyone agreed. Concerned to promote the policy, Askwith gave a short presentation to the Colonial Office's Social Welfare Adviser, Wilfred Chinn, and to the CO Mass Education Committee in July 1951. He argued that in the past general community development had been neglected in favour of training leaders, but now it was realized that the most effective method of improving general standards of living was through women. Indeed, he was prepared to argue that the reason for a lack of progress in many programmes was because 'endeavours were made to work only through the men', exactly what experts had said to each other in the Colonial Office back in 1939, 1936 and even as early as 1925. Chinn's view was different, however, and he seemed to be not so enthusiastic about women. He argued that economic development was often confused with community development, and the 1948 despatch on social welfare needed reconsidering.[140]

Nevertheless, the policy of encouraging homecrafts was applied more vigorously in 1951. Initial results were patchy. Chiefs were indifferent. African husbands were often suspicious and sometimes did not let their wives attend meetings. The women themselves did not always want to be there and could be unenthusiastic.[141] Askwith was not afraid to apply the pattern of local government he had seen in Nairobi to his new department. He had instigated a new committee made up of the CNC, the directors of technical departments, plus the African member of the LegCo, B. Apollo Ohanga, and Reiss from the Information Office. At its first meeting in November 1951 Askwith brought up the issue of concentrating on women. The CNC was in agreement, but not Ohanga; he insisted that men really had the initiative and women would follow.

Since, from the point of view of white administrators, this initiative represented a fundamentally conservative view of African women, there were supporters for the scheme. Tom Watts, DC (Central Nyanza), was hopeful. He thought that African women welfare teams could now be assembled. He had in mind a pilot scheme for Nyahera incorporating the midwife, health visitor and homecrafts instructress.[142] He had realized that he had a potential female team to hand: five women were training in Kisumu Home Crafts Centre; Mary Oloo Ominde was already working at Nyahera; he had trained midwives at other maternity centres and one health visitor had trained at the new Vihiga Women's Training Centre. His Medical Officer hoped that funding would be available for more women to train at Vihiga in 1952. His plans put great emphasis on lessons in hygiene, the construction of a model hut and a small plot. The three women would work as a team, lecturing also in the villages, and ideally

140 Askwith addressing Mass Education Committee, 17 July 1951, PRO CO822/652.

141 Nancy Shepherd, Report for 1951; North Nyanza: WI Report June to December 1951, KNA CD5/237.

142 Watts to Askwith, 16 August 1951 in reply to Askwith's letter, 25 July 1951, KNA DC/KSM/1/1/199.

operating from areas where community development assistants were working. He felt sure the pilot scheme would be a success and would be extended to the whole district, although they were limited by staff, housing and potential centres where classes could be held. The women targeted, he suggested, should be carefully selected and should pay a small fee. His plan was to aim at selected women in selected areas in the first place, so that these women might become 'leaders of their communities around whom, small groups of "progressive" families may be created'.[143]

This again was exactly what Nyanza's Chief Medical Officer had proposed nearly ten years before, but his suggestions had not then found any supporters. A plan to use women to reach women looked like seeing the light of day and by 1952 the colonial administration was beginning to see how women's clubs could work as vital centres of social engineering through the successes of Africans such as Salonia Opiche, a trained Health Worker from the Medical Department, who went out on every medical safari in his district, lecturing about hygiene and running a clinic in conjunction with women's meetings.[144] The movement was given a new title in March 1952, the Maendeleo ya Wanawake organization. Although African men seemed less than enthusiastic, women not completely in support, and support lukewarm at the Colonial Office, the small-scale experiments gave their supporters enough hope and evidence to ensure that Watts's vision would be at the centre of a counter-insurgency plan less than two years away.

As tension mounted in the colony, and in particular in areas where Kikuyu lived and worked as best they could, the community development organization endeavoured to help take the issue of inadequate township provisions for African welfare to the colonial government, before the fragile peace was shattered. Askwith played a crucial role in bringing a sharper focus to township welfare. In 1949 Nyanza's DCs warned their superiors of the 'large numbers of unemployed Africans living on their wits in townships and trading centres ... who are perhaps in greater need of welfare services than Africans in the reserves, and are potentially a greater source of trouble'.[145] Lumbwa township in Nyanza was a case in point. Kericho's DC revealed an appalling state of affairs. As the result of being 'nobody's baby', there was no water supply, no proper sanitation and no medical services and only one first aid kit at the police station for over a thousand people. Without a welfare centre, a football pitch or a canteen, he estimated that nearly five hundred African men had nothing to do in their

[143] Ibid, p. 4.

[144] See discussion in Chapter 3; Women's Homecrafts, Central Nyanza, Annual Report, 1952, KNA CD5/237; for a history of Maendeleo see Wipper, 1975a,b. An unofficial Federation of Social Services also came into existence in 1952, to co-ordinate the work of voluntary agencies in the colony.

[145] 'Social Welfare in Townships and Trading Centres' from DCS, circulated to all PCs, 18 October 1949, KNA PC/NZA/3/1/574.

spare time, in addition to company employees and the usual crowd of *duka* boys. He recommended that a dispensary be built, then a social welfare hall with a tea canteen, a football pitch, a beer hall provided it was watched over by a reputable person, and, finally, a native tribunal hall. A European police officer and labour officer would have to be placed *in situ* to keep a watchful eye on the population.

There was a new urgency in calls such as these for better social amenities to keep the peace. Strategically Lumbwa was important, controlling telegraphic and rail communication between Nairobi and Kisumu. Secondly, there were more Kikuyu in Lumbwa itself and on the adjoining farms than in any other area of the province. A strike would be dangerous since 'we cannot afford to allow Lumbwa to feel neglected and forgotten or we will be extremely sorry in the future', the DC warned, adding that Kikuyu agitators were already known to have been in the area. The 30,000 African employees in the district now required far more 'watching' than those in the Reserves, because it was recognized that they could be mobilized quickly and could cause much more disruption to economic life.

Greater bureaucratic capability at the central nodes of the administration produced a stricter account of local welfare, and township welfare was no exception. So far, the settlers had managed to keep the control of Africans living in their farming areas very much their responsibility. As a result, social service provision was abysmal, a reflection of the wider racial political economy of the colony. Askwith produced a comprehensive summary of established policy which showed unequivocally that no directive existed about funding community centres in townships, municipalities or in Nairobi.[146] He proposed to introduce a uniform system for the settled areas as a whole since social service provisions were lagging behind. First, as the Native Trust Fund rate was going to be raised, although no funds existed for the provision of capital grants, loans from the government for approved community centres should now be forthcoming. Beer profits, he suggested, could form trust funds for individual centres to help meet recurrent charges; the list of Class A townships would now have to be enlarged to allow a greater number to have township accounts. Secondly, he recommended that townships such as Lumbwa – a comparatively small town in Class B and as such with no township account – be allowed to open such trust funds.

In practice such a move represented the acceptance of the permanence of Africans in the settled areas. Europeans were vehemently opposed to this. However, additional pressure soon came from Wilfred Chinn, who made a detailed tour of the colony in February 1951.[147] Askwith had planned an extensive itinerary to ensure that he saw what was happening outside of Nairobi and met a wide range of people. He spent one week in Nairobi, then met district officers (CD) and DCs in rural and township

[146] 'Social Services in Settled Areas and Townships', Askwith to CNC, 6 September 1950, KNA PC/NZA/3/1/574.

[147] PRO CO822/674.

areas. He visited community centres, attended tea-parties, football matches and dances, addressed the EAWL and met members of the government. What became glaringly obvious was the way in which racial divisions were causing serious neglect of African welfare in the townships, and the Colonial Office was informed of this. Since the Member for Health and Local Government was responsible for European and Asian welfare only, Chinn recommended the creation of a new department, as no one was responsible for township welfare in the settled areas.[148] Eight months later the Governor replied, asserting that there was no need for a separate department to be created under a single director of social welfare and community development, as the two were fundamentally different and could be handled much more effectively by separate agencies.[149] Throughout the 1950s the Kenyan Government stubbornly opposed continued CO pressure to establish a separate department to deal with social welfare for all races. This was a disaster. As more and more Africans lived in townships within the settled areas, there continued to be no safety net of any kind. Once again racial division made welfare impossible.

There was worse to come. Just when a new coherence and direction seemed to be bearing fruit and securing a modicum of support the organization's field staff – so vital to the developing structure of community development – were deleted from the 1952 Estimates after a lengthy debate in the LegCo.[150] Three groups united in their opposition to the officers, despite an impassioned speech from the CNC arguing that they could not 'do without these people if we are going to administer this country in a twentieth century properly [sic]'. First, there were those who argued that the work was best carried out by district officials. Then there were African members of the LegCo like Eliud Mathu, who believed that departmental officers would suffice, with additional African administrators trained for development activities. What had particularly irked Mathu was a section in the Community Development Annual Report of 1950 which had described the Kikuyu *anake* as 'an organized gang of healthy spivs with their spears to lean on'. This insensitivity had harmed race relations and clearly upset members of the Kikuyu elite. Finally, also happy to cut community development staff were, not surprisingly, settler representatives in the LegCo. 'God preserve us', exclaimed Lady Shaw, 'from having Kenya as a welfare state ... a great number of the activities of the Community Development [Department] ... tend to produce that atmosphere in this country'. The Member for the Aberdares in defiant nationalist spirit

[148] P. Rogers to H.S. Potter (CS) 3 January 1953; Copy of report from CO sent to Governor with request for comments, 7 November 1951, ibid.

[149] Governor to Secretary of State, 19 June 1952, ibid.

[150] Item 1, no.8, Administration-General Staff, deleted from the 1952 Estimates, saving £7460, *Estimates of Revenue and Expenditure of the Colony and Protectorate of Kenya for the year 1952*, (Colony and Protectorate, Kenya), p. 146; Legislative Council Debates. Vol. XLV (Colony and Protectorate Kenya, 1951) pp.302–29, Cambridge University Library. OP.33710. 328.02(68).

summed up the unbending scepticism of settler society, constantly fighting any attempt to extract taxes, land and exclusive rights over labour. Welfare provision touched upon these three central pillars of the settler political economy. It could not be tolerated.

European and African representatives now combined to ensure that welfare field staff were removed to cut expenditure.[151] They were also made more vulnerable to attack by being listed in the budget Estimates under Administration – General Staff, a legacy of the pressure not to create a separate cadre of officers but to treat them as part of the administration. The Community Development Organization itself was unaffected, including the homecrafts supervisors, listed under a separate heading. Most of the work with African women was able to continue, as it was supported by voluntary women workers and ran on a small budget.[152] However, gone were the pilot schemes and the supervision of self-help projects; the new local relationships being built would be lost. It was a tremendous blow, Askwith later admitted. Eric Davies offered him the post of DC in Kakamega but he made the decision to stay on, a head without a body since 'by that time I had got quite attracted to the idea of community development and decided I would prefer to soldier on' (Askwith, 1995: 20). Yet the story was by no means over. Indeed, it had only just begun.

Conclusion

The Second World War was the single most dynamic event in twentieth-century imperial history. It brought in new policies and new players within colonial government as well as silencing others. It fundamentally altered people's experience and perception of colonial rule, both African and European, in Kenya and in Britain. According to bureaucratic thought, natives became Africans, and thus no longer self-sufficient tribesmen but objects of government. In London, colonial societies became 'extensions of our society' and thus had to be given the basics of modern living, a concession which the working classes in Britain had just won from the state. Margery Perham's post-Singapore colonial reckoning marked the rhetorical breach of a British colonial model of labour from the South African kaffir model. War focused attention on men, and away from women, opening up new opportunities for an alliance between Europeans and African male elites. Nevertheless, new structures of colonial rule emerged from this new will to intervene and socially engineer like-minded chaps. One such innovation in Kenya was social welfare and the use of the African *askari*, which gave greater shape and form to the long-standing ethos of development. Partial and faltering nevertheless, from 1948 onwards the Welfare

[151] Meeting of the Community Development Advisory Committee held in the offices of the African Information Services, 3 March 1952, KNA DC/KSM/1/1/195.

[152] See generally KNA PC/NZA/3/1/255.

Organization found greater coherence and a pathway into rural society. The new Africa policy at the Colonial Office and the socialist leanings of senior officials finally created a supportive arch, forcing the colonial government to make some modifications. The attempts to combine the politics of inclusion within racial rule did bring Europeans closer to the problems of African society, but they were too little and too late.

The empire state-building project which included welfare had failed to reorientate the colonial administration towards the realization of the transformatory project it had been set during the war. Welfare remained idiosyncratic and racialistic for too long in the 1940s, because of a range of local opposition not just from the settler community. The war had further obscured the contributions of women and refocused attention on how to incorporate detribalized African men into a rural programme of 'betterment and control'. The health and agricultural needs of women remained neglected. The technical departments remained subordinate to the administration and as such found it difficult to co-operate and to reconstruct their roles according to their perception of local needs. A technical jack-of-all-trades remained beyond the capacity of the colonial state to engineer. Community development instead applied notions of citizenship and community imported from Britain to older ideas of self-help, and threw the responsibility of social welfare back on to society. Few believed it would work.

Social welfare survived as community development. Community development survived in turn as international development practice. By the late 1940s a new coalition had emerged in Kenya. First, a more critical and intrusive Colonial Office was increasingly applying metropolitan standards and solutions to the colony. Senior officials ducked and dived, but the government in Nairobi made concessions and tried to begin to talk to Africans to find ways of repairing the torn fabric of social stability. It was too little, too late. With the barriers of race still intact and unrest growing, many officials balked at dramatic solutions and once again dreamed of compulsion, discipline and, if need be, the use of force to achieve their vision of a more productive Africa. Meanwhile, technology and information-gathering were improving to the benefit of smaller governmental departments. The Welfare Organization communicated better with London and with the new international organizations now interested in development. With a clearer head, they processed information coming from the districts, namely, that the community centre initiative was being sustained by the interest and energy of women. Also, rural betterment schemes were, in some areas, showing signs of taking off. Success stories were publicized widely and the future suddenly looked rosy for an organization that had narrowly escaped extermination. But not for long. Settlers, Africans and the administration ganged up to delete its finances from the next budget. Symbolic of the internationalization of colonial affairs and the prominence of the United States in this trend, staff were reprieved by American money. But their greatest triumph was yet to come.

Conclusion

This book has been about the colonial project of social transformation. It has charted the way in which metropolitan Britain encouraged state-sponsored social welfare initiatives within the Empire and how this took a particular turn in the racially restricted colony of Kenya. The recurring theme has been the paradoxical effect of war upon the attempts to modernize trusteeship according to the task colonial government had set itself. The template for this study has incorporated the Colonial Office during the 1930s and the Second World War, an imperial arena of war-time debate, the different interest groups in Kenya which then responded, the soldiering fraternity in and outside the colony, the immediate post-war period in Kenya, and last-minute reforms made on the eve of Mau Mau.

First and foremost, the Second World War enabled Colonial Office thought and practice on welfare in Africa to be morally and financially rearmed. The most famous example of this was the Colonial Development and Welfare Act of 1940, a culmination of cumulative thought in the 1930s. Indirect rule was seen not to be working; unrest was building up and culminating in urban riots. The more visible social effects of the Depression at home had increased support for state intervention to alleviate poverty which was supported by a growing coalition of philanthropists, liberals, Labour MPs, trade unionists, and religious figures. Improved technological capabilities were improving information gathering by the centre from the periphery. Inquiries into nutrition, for example, produced worrying evidence of the consequences of inadequate food intake for labour output. A raft of suggestions were also put forward on how to apply techniques of mass communication to this challenge. The onset of war increased the tempo of new initiatives on social welfare at the Colonial Office. One manifestation of this phenomenon was the 1939 inquiry into the relationship between educated women and welfare. The work of the League of Nations in relation to the welfare of women and girls, and the evidence of neglect in state provisions for women produced by professional women working in the colonial service, spurred on officials to devise ways in which living standards might be raised through initiatives geared towards African women. Another product of the war in the field was the creation of an Advisory Committee on Social Welfare in 1943.

Yet war also had a negative impact on welfare policy at this level. It distracted officials from the growing consensus about the role of women in society. The report of the enquiry into women and welfare sank without trace. The fashion for treating women as a separate problem also ensured that key discussions about how the colonial state might be reformed to reorient society away from dearth remained obscured. One was the issue of community centres – the key post-war vehicle for rural social welfare plans – and how they would relate to established local institutions such as missions and Local Native Councils. Another was the relationship between technical staff and the administration. A few officials realized that the contribution health, sanitary and agricultural staff could make to welfare and development outstripped the contribution of the district officers who traditionally had more authority. This imbalance was destined never to be reworked.

Another negative impact of war at this level was the way in which policy-makers lost sight of the particularity of the African context. The social welfare advisory committee treated African poverty as an extension of the social problems of urban Britain. Wartime anxiety about male delinquency ensured that models of men as bearers of social welfare replaced the growing inter-war recognition of the role of women. Macro-strategies were equally skewed away from the African reality. State-centric solutions modelled on William Beveridge's plan for social insurance could not easily transfer to colonies like Kenya. The absence of a basic and extensive state system, a much lower tax base and per capita levels of government revenue, and the lack of an agreed crusade backed up by a single moral community, were some of the local conditions that scuppered universalizing state-building plans. War thus ensured that the transformatory tools and theory which the Colonial Office gave to the late colonial state were ill-matched for the task in hand. Long-standing features of colonial rule – weak local control, opposition from settlers and slow centre-periphery dialogue – combined with the rush to apply metropolitan solutions to African problems.

The long-term results of this were destined to continue into and through the post-colonial period: namely, the neglect of women by the state and the continued diminution of the technical expert (embodying development as health, education and agricultural services) in relation to the administrative officer, for whom development was more directed towards submission to his authority and extension of political control. In 1962 just before Independence, local government specialists were still searching, after two decades of debate and opportunity, for an administrative category which as a Jack-of-all-trades could deliver welfare to rural Africa. Poverty eradication had failed to make it into the mainstream of colonial administration:

> Although the basic need for good administration is that staff should be well trained in the normal functions of local government, there is also a need for wider training, such as will enable officers to give a lead in activities outside the functions of ordinary governing – the kind of lead that has in the past been given by DOs. For this a knowledge of various arts and crafts is desirable – how to plan and construct a simple building, how to lay out the track of a new road, how to replan a congested land of houses, how to lay out a new market, how to advise on agricultural improvement (Hicks, 1961: 538).

However, the war probably helped guarantee that the end of the British Empire was less bloody and protracted than it otherwise would have been. In addition to depleting resources including those available for the repression of nationalists, it reinforced a sense of national prestige and established the pattern of extending metropolitan-style state paternalism to the empire. A legitimate space was thus created for colonial nationalisms. National self-confidence combined with the lesson that incorporation of the lower classes did not mean emasculation for the middle classes; the official response to the 'winds of change' was destined to be a positive one. Overall, then, war ensured that the Colonial Office's attempt to modernize an empire state remained as incomplete as it was incoherent and inappropriate.

The effect of war on welfare and development discussions went beyond the Colonial Office. Action and dialogue moved out, across and downward. An imperial arena of debate about how trusteeship was to be conducted after the war was stimulated by the war. The Colonial Office sent out its prized troubleshooter, Lord Hailey, to make recommendations about the direction native administration ought to take in Africa after the war. He produced a universalizing overview of present and future policy, in which he gave much weight to the need to improve the material condition of people's lives. The events of the war threw up a rival. In the aftermath of the fall of Singapore, in 1942, university aunt to the colonial service Margery Perham – with her experience of journalism as a means of supplementing her semi-permanent academic work in Oxford in the 1930s – was used by *The Times* newspaper to produce a colonial reading of the event which Winston Churchill regarded as a bitter blow. She too drew attention to the impoverished state of colonial peoples, and the way their economic life-chances swung perilously up and down; she damned racially constricted communities as embarrassing anomalies; and she called for a modernization of colonial government on lines similar to those of communist countries. Echoing her call for a modern type of government overseas, were the complaints coming from the nationalist community in Kenya. Many activists had been imprisoned by the colonial government during the war on the spurious grounds of espionage. They drew attention to the social crisis enveloping their people, and asked that they be allowed to contribute to solutions as free men. Unsurprisingly the Kenya Government had to respond to all this debate. It turned to a soldier trained in public relations, and the result was a series of policy statements which pledged the government to improving the welfare of 'Africans' – the term now used by London.

Thus the war had stimulated the inclusion of welfare and material advance in imperial visions of the future. Yet at the time when a more consistent line was sought by the Colonial Office, a more variegated and incompatible set of answers came back. At this level of imperial debate, war might have opened up new spaces for new players to contribute, but the effect was to increase the contradictions and anomalies in any empire state-building project. Hailey's prescriptions were flawed. He wanted more attention to social advance, but he acknowledged that technical expertise would have to be subordinate to other administrative issues. Perham wanted a state-centric solution but acknowledged that the money to pay for such a solution was not present: poverty was simply pushed back on to the tribe in the absence of a large and adequately paid workforce. Kenya's nationalists believed the route to welfare was their freedom, whilst the Kenya Government made it clear that that was not its solution. Whilst it used the language of the African, implying a citizenry with a claim on government, it settled for a solution that was total and a racial one, namely that 'the native' would have to work harder and learn more thrifty ways first. It was caught between two versions of colonial paternalism and opted for the more racially restrictive one. It was cheaper.

Moving downwards and deeper into colonial Kenya, again we find the dynamic effect of war to be a mixed bag. Undeniably the war unleashed a plethora of suggestions and planning for African welfare in Kenya. As in metropolitan Britain, it was expected and seen as desirable that the state would have a greater role in planning and providing for a transformation in African society. Much was written, often in unwitting consensus, but with scant realization of how much the tensions within the colonial state and society would impinge upon their vision. A stream of ideas emerged, often focused on further detribalization, riding high upon the new expectation of modern administrative capabilities. There was little understanding of the obstacles to achieving such a programme. At least four sets of contributors rallied round the idea of engineering model African families. Urban administrators in Nairobi and towns like Kisumu recognized that African welfare was not being looked after. Medical staff, in particular, wanted recognition that the urban African existed and that he must be paid wages sufficient to support a family in the town. The government in turn, had a responsibility to provide housing and social services. Meanwhile, technical staff also talked excitedly about using their expertise to target families and to build up model villages. Likewise, the district administration made plans for reorganized villages that would fit into district development plans. White settlers also suggested ways in which disciplined and orderly labourers could live in clean villages, working hard and willing to contribute to the kinds of amenities found in the shires of 1930s England.

But the more one examines the African family ideal, the more it reveals itself to be a struggling orphan. The urban administrators faced a legacy of neglect and did not have access to sufficient resources to put their plans into action. Technical staff were also divided. Profound differences existed about the capabilities of Africans within the same departments. Some medical staff believed that training Africans, particularly African women, was the best strategy; others that it was only the authority of the DC that could make a difference. The district administration was also at sea. It seemed to many that social change was producing more selfish, profit-orientated African families. Better, then, to re-orientate them along clan lines, going back to the authority of the elders and the chiefs, rather than pinning their hopes on new patterns of state-society relations. Likewise, settler dreams of sleepy African villages were also settler nightmares: of Africans living permanently in the reserves. Arguments for paying more attention to African women had racial aims: first, to make them have fewer children, and secondly, to take them off the land and make them domesticated mothers who would not wean their children so late, thus making the African character allegedly backward and unstable.

Inevitably, debates became less about the issue of poverty eradication and more about buttressing control. In the end, the African family ideal was lost sight of. At this level, the inequalities of racial rule were obvious barriers. European plans never addressed these problems. Resources for betterment were fundamentally constrained. The legacy of neglect, particularly in urban areas, was already quite overwhelming. Attempts to conjure up a European development and welfare jack-of-all trades failed to materialize because of entrenched bureaucratic compartmentalization, lack of resources and general cynicism that such a new type of officer could make a difference. Likewise, endeavours to train an African equivalent fell by the wayside. When the issues of training women came up occasionally, only a few could see any point in such a project.

The late colonial state was ill-equipped to tackle poverty meaningfully. Ultimately all European welfare antidotes in favour of betterment and control, however well-meaning, were hamstrung because they were constructed in the absence of a single moral community, a universality which the experience of the Second World War had help manufacture in Britain, tagged on to a maturing universal franchise, which had been conceded after centuries of forging national unity and wealth creation, each reinforcing the other. Such a condition was absent in colonial Kenya, and has remained so.

Another major obstacle was the fact that the kind of state social engineering projects deemed to be necessary for transformation were beyond the capacity of the colonial state to enforce on African society. The state system in place was so flimsy in terms of numbers that attempts at direct rule always required more indirect rule to get them translated into action. Likewise, there was a growing divide in administrative practice. A clear divergence was opening up within the paternalism of the colonial administration. There were those who applied the humanizing and universalizing trends with regard to native administration coming from London. They believed in African capabilities and believed that Africans could be coaxed into being community-minded modern economic individuals. Then there were those who remained convinced that the chief/tribe model was the best Africa could hope for, and any improvements came by means of force or compulsion. This split was omnipresent in Kenya and found its most extreme incarnation in the efforts to socially engineer a solution to the Mau Mau uprising in the 1950s. Here the use of force was applied by conservative elements of the administration and colonial society – prison staff and part time soldiers, for example – within a framework of rehabilitation designed by liberal pacifists.

Of course, the failure to produce a generalist welfare officer to deal with poverty contributed less in itself to the failure to tackle poverty effectively than did the wider racially-skewed political economy. This framework kept Kenya behind in the post-war attempt to reform state–society relations in comparison with other East African colonies such as Uganda. Reprivileging old forms of power over new, controlling production for sectional interest, rejecting the right to freedom of speech and association for Africans, and marginalizing women from public power, were the major obstacles to improving welfare. And as the post-colonial government struggled to run a country without a sense of nationhood, inheriting a state system without the money to pay for it, they took refuge in these established colonial strategies, ensuring that a single moral community became less rather than more obtainable a process of social formation.

However, the soldier saved the day. Just as more European soldiers were helping to run Kenya during the war (and continued to do so in new government posts after the war), so more African soldiers were being trained and put into the war effort. The sight of uniformed, disciplined and muscular young African men stimulated the imaginations of a range of onlookers. Military commanders boasted about what such men could achieve thanks to the loving care of army life. Social commentators in Britain began to see the potential of a peacetime army of detribalized Africans who could help lift Africans out of the torpor of rural life. Army educationalists and propagandists publicized how, with a little help from the new techniques of mass communication applied in the war, retrained soldiers could be sent back into the reserves to improve living standards by working on specific projects and spreading good habits through personal example. Although the district administrators were not so convinced, they were keen to make plans for post-war development schemes and the prospect of respectable ex-soldiers returning to the reserves might well help them achieve these plans. Meanwhile, the colonial administration in Kenya was coming under pressure from social welfare specialists in London, including anthropologists, to get into line with other colonies plans and establish a social welfare organization. Fearing that returning *askari* might well cause trouble if they were not gainfully employed, the government reluctantly agreed that the European soldiers working as remittance officers ought to be engaged as social welfare workers. In addition, a scheme was set up for 40 ex-*askari* to be retrained each year to go and work in the reserves as social welfare workers, running community centres and educating the adult population in betterment and self-help schemes.

Yet, although the soldier-citizen social welfare model saved the day in terms of the creation of a new welfare organization, it was a fatally flawed exercise. The Second World War prevented the late colonial state from reading the lessons of its own bureaucratic history. It forgot the lessons of the Jeanes School teachers and reintroduced a profoundly masculine concept of social transformation. Indeed, the wartime plans for *askari* and social welfare reflect some of the ways in which the Second World War had changed the meaning and practice of government by 1945. War was a giant watershed; end of Empire was a far less momentous event in this sense, and this dynamic of change far outweighed the effects of independence. The ensuing continuity was a product of African collaboration as well as European force, shaped by an inexorable logic of events as much as deliberate strategy on either side.

War encouraged a view that solutions for Africa were best if they were solutions that had been applied in Britain. The same questions and answers were applied because of a belief in the universal nature of welfare and development. Government became much more interventionist, working from the centre and regulating many more aspects of economic and social relations. The potential of technology and the mass media was elevated to new levels. Soldiering reinforced the perception that a little roughing up could do more good than harm – an approach that would later be applied to Mau Mau's miscreants. Social engineering naturally settled on supporting character and men of the right type who could control and discipline others. The war largely bypassed women. By 1945, the worsening terms of trade and of legal status and the diminished access to land, education and the state which women had experienced from the onset of colonial rule were now complete.[1] The post-colonial state would continue to travel along these tramlines.

The *askari* and social welfare formula in post-war Kenya encapsulates

[1]For an argument that by 1945 a primarily male agrarian bourgeosie had emerged in the countryside, see Coquery-Vidrovitch, 1997: esp. p. 61; also Roberston, 1997: esp. 1–145.

two profound legacies of the Second World War for government. First, its interventionism; extending state interference at the point of production were the regulations, constraints, and controls on both labour and produce which the needs of war demanded. As the experience of the many Africans in Nairobi testified, the war also entrenched heavy-handed civilian surveillance practices plus restrictions on the media and freedom of expression and association. The belief in state-sponsored social engineering had been fortified, and was sustained by the support of metropolitan expertise, in particular anthropology. The energy underpinning the subsequent 'second colonial occupation' came from many quarters. The post-war goals of African betterment and welfare could be underpinned by a sense of mission to reduce poverty, as an end in itself. Or they could be upheld by those keen to increase government exchequers. Technophiles could offer enthusiastic projections based on the application of their own particular mechanical obsessions. European soldier-administrators, many fired by excessive optimism and an outpouring of emotion which followed in the wake of conflict, believed that the men who had sung 'Kingi Georgi' were not enfeebled by race. They would try to put into practice what they had learnt during the war. Those more racially minded could see the intervention as a way of crafting less indolent 'natives'. Likewise, there was an increasingly influential corps of Africans who had digested the civilian propaganda, or who had seen and read much of the 'ways of the whiteman' during army service, who believed they had earned a stake in a system of rule which had much to recommend itself.

Secondly, we have the capacity to privilege along established fault-lines. As the *askari* and social welfare model illustrates, another feature of government that reached new heights during the Second World War was the gendering of power in favour of men. The most famous liberal settler-paternalist Michael Blundell (1994: 82) later reflected with pride that, as a result of the changes wrought by the Second World War, 'the adolescence of colonial rule grew into the manhood of African nationalism'. This is suggestive of another phenomenon. The *askari* dealt the final wartime body-blow to women and a gendered concept of adult education and betterment. A revised agenda of African welfare was anchored to wartime adult education that was administered by men, largely for men. A more rigidly homo-social concept and structure smothered older ideas coming from the Medical Department and suggestions coming from educational experts (see Chapter 1). Notions of improving African welfare in line with the pattern of wartime adult education that emphasized citizenship, leadership and self-help became the preferred path that could lead to prosperous communities. Also, the idea that women were involved in agriculture seemed to disappear from view.

The first years in the new Welfare Organization's history were painful, if not torturous. The new head of social welfare in Nairobi and his assistant immediately had their activities limited by the district administration, which felt they were welfare officers already and so preferred to see welfare officers encouraging saving and overseeing community centres but not getting involved in setting up betterment schemes or holding meetings with local figures. Dr Philip and Fortie Ross thought differently. They wanted a more active, collaborative role and saw mass adult education as their domain. Unfortunately the Colonial Office's new advisory committee on social welfare gave them little help, for it did not believe that adult education was part of the remit. Also, there was little in the form of resources to fund a basic mass education programme. Officials were reduced to handing out leaflets from the back of vehicles to any passer-by. Africans were proving less and less receptive, as they struggled against the restrictions of race in the colony. The final straw came when individuals in the district administration began actively to block the work of the organization by withholding information. Yet all was not lost. A minority of officials continued to believe in the potential of adult education by sending trained African men and also women into the field. And, where rural conditions were fairly tranquil, African social welfare workers were administering to their flock, especially when inspired by religious fervour.

The history of the first years of the Welfare Organization highlight the contradictory positions sustained under the opportunities brought in by the Second Colonial Occupation. The aims of the Second Colonial Occupation were not always the same for everyone involved. The metropolitan commitment to state-building in the empire was partly a product of viewing the colonies as an extension of British society. Particularly for those within the colonial service who supported the Labour Party, the wartime ascendancy of development and welfare became a morally energizing principle that led away from indirect rule and toward the new politicians, educated Africans and entrepreneurs. Rather than cynically seeing welfare as a device to mop up the inequalities exacerbated by capitalism, the extension of state activity in regulating the lives of poor people was viewed as a positive step towards establishing the principle of a more egalitarian, modern and community-based society. This was the thinking in the minds of some of the footsoldiers of the Second Colonial Occupation, often those who worked in social welfare, for example. Yet senior officials like Sir Philip Mitchell fought a more modern approach to governing Africans which social welfare epitomized for many white settlers. Sir Philip, like many others in the administration, opposed a more tentacular type of state operation, unless it reorientated African societies back to the days of indirect rule when chiefs and elders appeared to be able to do one's bidding. They did not share the socialist vision of building communities by means of breaking down separation and investing in social services and infrastructure. The story of social welfare in post-war Kenya highlights the swings and roundabouts that befell the Second Colonial Occupation in general.

The history of welfare in colonial Kenya was profoundly shaped by the racial restrictions in the colony, as well as the weak nature of the colonial state and the imported metropolitan prescriptions. After the war, subversive elements tried to break free from this restriction of race. By the end of the 1940s some administrators looked to replace social welfare with community development. Community development demanded less white orchestration from above and allowed space for the release of African energies from below, the idea being that Africans could learn to build community welfare with their own efforts and materials. This fledgling organization grew out of the way in which the experiences of colonial administrators had become increasingly differentiated by 1945. Some of these maverick officials were converts because of contact with the wartime techniques of adult mass education. A few felt it to be in their interest to break with the local autonomy of administration and to collaborate with other marginals such as technical officers. Others were affected by administering the new urban spaces where they were taken closer to the reality of African poverty by male elites who shared their worries: both wanted to reverse the 'denunciation of fatherly rights'. Community development tried to redefine paternal tolerance in the colonial context. Its supporters tried to link into the general principle of training in local government. This was contested and often treated with contempt. The district administration had their own ideas and constituencies to appease. Many believed that compulsion was the only way to bring about a change in social and economic practice, or that it was best to acknowledge that little could be done.

By the late 1940s, however, the fortunes of the welfare organization had dramatically changed. This was a product of four mutually reinforcing processes.

Although failure and frustration mounted in some quarters, the colonial state which emerged from the second colonial occupation turned out to be much more enduring than its immediate impact on the ground would suggest. Its practical features and underlying principles were carried forward beyond the end of Empire and by non-Europeans. Thus the end of formal colonial rule made much less of a difference to the actual exercise of power and the Second World War stood to be a much greater watershed for East Africa in the twentieth century than independence would ever be.

However weak and partial was the state-building of the second colonial occupation, it survived. Since another effect of war had also speeded up social change and political awareness among Africans, this second process scuppered the prospects of the first. Yet, whilst the growing political incompatibilities of black and white prevented the effective realization of the pledges of metropolitan imperialism within Kenya's racial setting, a growing consensus between black and white also ensured that its rhetoric, framework and principles lasted beyond the formal end of Empire. This underlies the process of an increasing internal disaffection with the colonial state as a functioning form of power. A mounting number of frustrated, marginal and less racially inclined officials were learning the limitations of restructuring state-society relations through colonial relationships as well as of their personal effectiveness as bearers of power. However, they were not learning that their version of state-society relations or modernization was wrong or went unsupported by local African men.

Just as the Welfare Organization transformed itself into Community Development and its field officers produced new local intelligence that brought the role of women and the dangers of township neglect to the fore, so scepticism and financial shortages guillotined their efforts. However, colonial rule in Kenya was becoming less of a British enterprise. What the government would not or could not fund, outsiders might well be sympathetic towards. Highly symbolic of the wider changes in the balance of world power that had swung so decisively in favour of the United States, was the way in which the Community Development Organization received funding from America to keep its show on the road in 1952.

Despite a less than auspicious start, by the early 1950s Kenya was closer to catching up with neighbouring colonies such as Uganda in its social development provisions. However, all this was too little too late, if not irrelevant to the day-to-day welfare for Africans living in crowded reserves, unhealthy towns or facing eviction from squatter land. The overall framework for these changes was one of belated response to growing African disaffection and distress. Despite the improvements made, Wilfred Chinn, who became Social Welfare Adviser to the Colonial Office in 1950, found the provision flawed and wholly inadequate. It was not simply charged with being racialist but also with neglecting the very poor, already ignored by the colonial state and African society.[2] Then funding for community development officers was deleted from the colony's budget by the Legislative Council in 1951. Mau Mau reversed its fortunes. Askwith became the head of community development and rehabilitation, with a budget and remit beyond anything that had gone before. The policy of using force ended after the murder of eleven detainees at the Hola Camp in 1959. Subsequently the British Government made up its mind to disengage rapidly from administering an empire.

Yet the partial reconstructive capacity of the late colonial state proved durable, especially when development theory coincided with high imperial policy and the needs of African men. It proved to be so, even when facing a much greater dynamic that was gathering momentum. This came from African society as a result of the growing impact of long-term changes to the distribution of wealth, population growth and access to white power. By 1952, the acute stresses and strains placed on established social systems

[2]See PRO CO822/674 for various correspondence and Report of Wilfred Chinn's visit to Kenya, February 1951. 'Community development also offered influential Africans opportunities for self-advancement and patronage, whereas social welfare offered them little but taxes...' Iliffe, 1987: 201.

were generating an intensified violence among Kikuyu and against Europeans which could no longer be contained by established state-society relations. Newspapers contained more and more accounts of arson, evidence of the destructive effect of the panga knife and, most horrible of all, descriptions of hamstrung cattle left to bleed to death. The violence became identified with a movement among the Kikuyu that had the name of Mau Mau (Maw Maw), thought to be meaningless which added to its menacing reputation. By the early 1950s over 90 per cent of the Kikuyu were believed to have become bound to the movement by an oath of unity.

Oathing ceremonies were established rituals whereby elders used trees, branches and the remains of animals on consecrated spaces to bind communities and generations together – a practice which as an observer at the time later remarked was no less silly than the behaviour of Freemasons (Best, 1979: 164; see also Frost, 1992: ch. 6). The novelty of the Mau Mau oaths as compared with normal Kikuyu oaths was twofold. First – and this was not universally appreciated at the time – they increasingly flouted custom by being held in the forests, often at night, and were administered by less respected and much younger members of the community. Secondly – and this was a widespread belief at the time – they turned what were considered to be friendly if secretive servants into deadly creatures bound by superstition, now anti-white and capable of murder.

As the attacks continued, murders increased and ordinary life was abandoned, so settlers agitated for drastic action. Sir Philip Mitchell was reluctant to respond; he was close to retirement and hoped the situation would go away. He was pinning his hopes on a successful royal visit in early 1952. Princess Elizabeth and her husband were on safari at Treetops when the news of her father's sudden death was broken to her following a night-time animal watch deep in the Aberdare Forest. Kenya was propelled into the headlines of the world's press with the story of how she climbed into a tree a princess and came down a queen. As her plane took off to London, five grass fires allegedly burnt out of control within sight of Nairobi airport. The government could no longer ignore the situation and in October 1952 it declared a state of emergency. Those thought to be the leaders were arrested and exiled before an attempt was made to round up all Kikuyu and imprison them so that their involvement in Mau Mau could be measured and their punishment tailored accordingly. The liberal conscience-keepers nearly lost their nerve. Elspeth Huxley recorded how her mother had exchanged views with Tom Askwith who

> ... saw all this coming and reported it two years ago. He painted an appallingly gloomy picture of the Kikuyu young men, who of course, are the murderers, not the older ones. He says they are desperadoes with nothing else to live for and nothing to care about except murder and theft. They must be exterminated or controlled before anything can be

done. They have grown up like this as a result of frustration after the War. (Huxley, 1973: 182)

However, the principles of the second colonial occupation – the modernization of Africans and the politics of inclusion – did eventually emerge as the dominant solution to Mau Mau, amidst the callous retribution of white society and the arbitrary violence of a state structure built on the foundations of white racism. For, as in Malaya, counter-insurgency operations included attention to hearts and minds. Social engineering became part of the solution to Mau Mau. It was applied to Kikuyu men and women through a varied combination of quick-fix secular teaching, religious doctrine, confession, hard labour, forced villagization and concentrated bouts of exposure to the old discipline of the elders. There was little that was new in this theory of adaptation and the department of community development found itself at centre-stage. A budget of £31,000 in 1953 had grown to £38,000 by 1957, by which time Askwith had become Permanent Secretary of a Ministry of Community Development and Rehabilitation under the first African Minister, Beniah Ohanga. Mau Mau had made the difference. The talk of habilitating detribalized Africans and battle-hardened soldiers during the Second World War had been easily transformed into the rehabilitation of all lost souls that had fallen by the wayside when walking the path towards modern living. This time an enthusiastic Colonial Office, a compliant government and a buoyant administrative structure worked together, having the threat of force and the prospect of material reward at their disposal. Askwith was the right man in the right place at the right time.

The key ingredient was past evidence that Africans would work within the system being set up for them. Even radicals like Tom Mboya testifed to this. He had travelled the long distance to Yala Mission school in 1942, clinging on for dear life in the back of a wartime goods van. He had seen advantage in taking a sanitary inspector's certificate that came with a training allowance, making him one of Creech Jones's new post-war African foot-soldiers. He had co-operated with the colony's Scottish trade union adviser, James Patrick, and formed a workers council in 1951. The alternatives were limited, the competition amongst peers fierce and the sense of personal achievement great. He had also heard Kenyatta speak in Nairobi and, after his arrest, was asked to step into the breach and join the KAU in 1952 (Goldsworthy, 1982: ch. 6). His was not an isolated experience nor an unnoticed one. As the experience of extending middle-class values and institutions to the metropolitan working class had recently shown, Africans too were capable of coming on board. Community development had some degree of appeal to sections of the rural elite and those with ambition, because it seemed to offer the chance of redressing their sense of losing out to townsmen and city life. Counter-insurgency was wrapped up from the beginning in efforts to reallocate land, to offer more Western education and to subordinate settler plans for racial domination of the political system, all in order to shore up the peasant farmer within a wartime notion of what it was to achieve habilitation. Thus the paradox of war was set to repeat itself: out of the application of rule by force and organized violence, the more professional and humane element within government found a stronger voice and a more compelling argument. So it was throughout British colonial occupation that the abuse of rule and the will to be professional fed off each other. The use of force, the belief in compulsion as the only surefire way of instilling social engineering, was omnipresent in colonial Kenya. It increasingly had to compete with a belief in self-help through free will. Mau Mau merely allowed for its rationalized application through a framework set up by the liberals. It was fitting but tragic that the violent death of eleven African men held in British custody in 1959 shocked ministers and mandarins enough to sanction the peaceful dismantling of the most far-reaching Empire in the world's history.

This book has narrated a localized series of events relating to the low politics of the post-war history of welfare and development in Kenya. Yet it has much to say about the passing of the late colonial state. First, its demise was destined to be mercifully brief partly because of a decade of disillusionment. As the accusations against social welfare officers suggest, perceptions and debates about the effects and capabilities of colonial rule were fairly sophisticated. Both sides, Europeans and Africans, were sceptical about what could be achieved in the circumstances. This had significance for the end of Empire. By the late 1940s, disillusionment amongst officials and a desire for self-government among Africans, were fairly ordinary positions to hold. How much more so would they be after the disruption of Mau Mau. Resistance to colonial capitulation thus has a long history of diminution. Social welfare and development illustrates the basic conundrum that the late colonial state could not solve: to deliver its social transformation project through direct rule required more indirect rule which in turn undermined the social transformation project.

Secondly, the use of force to achieve social transformation was omnipresent within the late colonial state: the subsequent use of force against Mau Mau in the 1950s was therefore not exceptional but merely a triumph of those who always believed it to be a justifiable option. True, it had to compete increasingly with the ethos of the exercise of free will as an essential component of development. In this way, two mechanisms of social transformation that fell under the pattern of racial paternalism fractured the late colonial state. The South African *kaffir* model of labour control from which Margery Perham turned the British imperial mind away from after the fall of Singapore, was not so easily abandoned at the local level. Yet its expectation that natives were self-sufficient, and that government intervened only to segregate, to discipline and to force labour, increasingly ran up against a view of Africans as being capable of self-help, whilst the state had a duty to help them to help themselves: these two variants of racial paternalism ran side by side. However, the use of force was always a tacit, and often dreamed of, official sanction.

Thirdly, its legacy was to be particularly enduring with regard to international development practice. Despite being exposed to similar exported imperial solutions, Kenya's experience was markedly different, pushed and pulled by settler obdurance, maverick officials and rural migrant labour issues. Yet sooner rather than later convergence won the day. Indeed, all colonial attempts to move from indirect rule to that of providers of the kind of social services increasingly expected from modern states, were ultimately doomed in the absence of a single moral community. Independence was achieved in 1963. But the development lore colonial governments bequeathed to their successors has been strikingly enduring. Community development became entrenched in the 1950s and was carried on after independence. Its colonial flavourings – authoritarian intervention which was selective and arbitrary; the neglect of the very poor; a bias against women; the submission of technical expertise to the interests of control; and the difficulty that bureaucrats have in accepting multi-task workers and female authority – have all endured. Ruling compassions through empire state-building was perhaps the most ambiguous element of British colonial government.

Bibliography

Archival Sources

KENYA NATIONAL ARCHIVES, NAIROBI

KNA/CS/1	Chief Secretary Deposit One
KNA/CS/2	Chief Secretary Deposit Two
KNA/CS/3	Chief Secretary Deposit Three
KNA/CD/1	Community Development Deposit One
KNA/CD/4	Community Development Deposit Four
KNA/CD/5	Community Development Deposit Five
KNA/CD/9	Community Development Deposit Nine
KNA/DEF/2	Defence Deposit Two
KNA/DEF/10	Defence Deposit Ten
KNA/DEF/14	Defence Deposit Fourteen
KNA/DC/KSM/1	District Commissioner Kisumu Deposit One
KNA/DC/KSM/6	District Commissioner Kiambu Deposit Six
KNA/MAA/1	Member for African Affairs Deposit One
KNA/MAA/2	Member for African Affairs Deposit Two
KNA/MAA/6	Member for African Affairs Deposit Six
KNA/MAA/7	Member for African Affairs Deposit Seven
KNA/MAA/8	Member for African Affairs Deposit Eight
KNA/PC/NZA/1	Provincial Commissioner Nyanza Deposit One
KNA/PC/NZA/3	Provincial Commissioner Nyanza Deposit Three
KNA/PC/NZA/4	Provincial Commissioner Nyanza Deposit Four
KNA/JZ/26	Prison Department

PUBLIC RECORD OFFICE, LONDON

CO 533 Kenya Original Correspondence
CO 822 East Africa Original Correspondence
CO 847 Africa Original Correspondence
CO 859 Social Service Original Correspondence
CO 875 Public Relations and Information
CO 901 Colonial Social Science Research Council Papers
CO 927 Research Department
CO 936 International Relations
CO 987 Advisory Committee on Education in the Colonies
CO 994 Colonial Advisory Medical Committee Minutes
CO 997 Colonial Social Welfare Advisory Committee Minutes and Papers

RHODES HOUSE LIBRARY OXFORD

Papers of Dame Margery Perham
Papers of Arthur Creech Jones

T. G. Askwith. RH Mss.Afr.s.1770, 2100.
Mrs E. Aylward. RH Mss.Afr.s.1857.
Sydney T. Kelson. RH Mss.Afr.s.735.
Willoughby Thompson. RH Mss.Afr.s.1534; Mss.Afr.s.839; Mss Afr.s.519(1).
T.R.L. Neston. RH Mss.Afr.s.1086.
Aubrey Mullins. RH Mss.Afr.s.760(1 & 2)
M.W. Dobbs. RH Mss.Afr.s.504.A162
Colin Maher. RH Mss.Afr.s.740
Paul Kelly. RH. Mss. Afr.s.2229(1).
K.L. Hunter. RH Mss.Afr.s.1942.
E. Powys Cobb – daughter's reminisces. RH. Mss.Afr.s.2058.
E. Mary Holding. RH Mss.Afr.s.A580.
J. E. Moore. RH Mss.Afr.s.1715(191).
Thomas Leahy. RH Mss.Afr.s.1715(163).
Donald Bowie. RH Mss.Afr.s.(241A).
A. Selwood Walford, RH Mss Afr.s.1702

INTERVIEWS/PERSONAL CORRESPONDENCE

Sir Roger Swynnerton to Tim Parsons, (undated letter)
Tom and Nancy Colchester, 5 June 1989.
Cloda Alison, 21–22 May 1996.
Nancy Shepherd, 25 June 1996.
George Hampson, Tunbridge Wells, 20 June, 1996.
George Shepperson to Tim Parsons, 23 July 1996.
Brigadier M. W. Biggs to Tim Parsons, 10 Oct. 1996.
Sir Derk Oulton, Magdalene College, Cambridge, 18 Nov. 1997.
John Cowan, 4 Feb., 1998 and 'Random Recollections' (unpublished paper).
John Nottingham, 12 April 1998.
Tom Askwith, June 18 1989.

Official Publications

UNITED KINGDOM GOVERNMENT: PARLIAMENTARY PAPERS AND COLONIAL REPORTS

1923 Cmd 1922, Memorandum relating to Indians in Kenya.
1925 Cmd. 2374, Memorandum submitted to the Secretary of State for the Colonies by the Advisory Committee on Native Education in the British Tropical African Dependencies.
1932 Cmd. 4093, Report by Financial Commissioner on Certain Questions in Kenya, 1931–32.
1935 Colonial No. 103, Memorandum submitted by the Advisory Committee on Education in the Colonies on the Education of African Communities.
1938 Cmd. 5784, Correspondence relating to the Welfare of Women in Tropical Africa 1933–37.
1938, Home Office Report, *Young Offenders*.
1939 Cmd. 6050, Nutrition in the Colonial Empire. Economic Advisory Council. Committee on Nutrition in the Colonial Empire. First Report – Part 1.
1942 Cmd. 6404, Report on the Social Insurance and Allied Services (The Beveridge Report).
1946 Col. 193, Labour Conditions in East Africa (G. St J. Orde-Browne).

KENYA GOVERNMENT PUBLICATIONS

Estimates of Revenue and Expenditure of the Colony and Protectorate of Kenya and of the

Development and Reconstruction Authority for the year 1947.
Estimates of Revenue and Expenditure of the Colony and Protectorate of Kenya and of the Development and Reconstruction Authority for the year 1948.
Estimates of Revenue and Expenditure of the Colony and Protectorate of Kenya and of the Development and Reconstruction Authority for the year 1949.
Estimates of Revenue and Expenditure of the Colony and Protectorate of Kenya and of the Development and Reconstruction Authority for the year 1950.
Estimates of Revenue and Expenditure of the Colony and Protectorate of Kenya for the year 1951.
Legislative Council Debates, Vol. XLV, 1951
1932 Native Affairs Annual Report
1933 Native Affairs Annual Report
1936 Native Affairs Annual Report
1937 Native Affairs Annual Report
1943 Report of the Sub-Committee on the Post-War Employment of Africans
1945 Youth Camps – A proposal by P. E. Williams
1949 Annual Report of the Welfare Organisation Kenya
1949 African Education in Kenya: Report of a Committee Appointed to Enquire into the Scope, Content, and Methods of African Education, its Administration and Finance, and to Make Recommendations. (Chairman Rev. L. J. Beecher)
1954 The Psychology of Mau Mau. (J. C. Carrothers).

MISCELLANEOUS

The Treaty of Versailles. Part I. The Covenant of the League of Nations. 1919.

Articles, Books and Unpublished Theses and Papers

Abel-Smith, B., 1992, 'The Benefit of Beveridge', *New Statesman and Society*, 5, 230, 27 November.
Addison, Paul, 1982, *The Road to 1945*. London.
Aldrich, Robert, 1996, 'Colonialism and Homosexuality', *Thamyris*, 3, 1: 175–191.
Allen, L. W., 1984, *Burma: The Longest War*. London.
Allman, J., 1996, 'Rounding up spinsters: gender chaos and married women in colonial Asante', *JAH*, 37, 2: 195–21.
Amin,. S., 1988, 'Agrarian Bases of Nationalist Agitations' in D. A. Low (ed.) *Indian National Congress: Centenary Hindsights*. Oxford.
Anderson, D. M., 1982, 'Herder, Settler, and Colonial Rule. A History of the peoples of the Baringo Plains, Kenya c.1890–1940', unpublished thesis, Cambridge University.
Anderson, D. M., 1992, 'Maidens, Missions and Morality: The Kikuyu Female Circumcision Crisis', unpublished paper, East African Seminar Series, February 1992, African Studies Centre, Cambridge University.
Anderson, D.M. and Throup, D.W., 1985, 'Africans and Agricultural Production in Colonial Kenya: The Myth of the War as a Watershed', *JAH*, 26: 327–44.
Anderson, D.M., 1984, 'Depression, Dust Bowl, Demography and Drought: The Colonial State and Soil Conservation in East Africa during the 1930s', *African Affairs*, 83, 332: 321–43.
Asher, Michael, *Lawrence: The Uncrowned King of Arabia*, London.
Ashton, S. R. and Stockwell, S. E (eds), 1996, *Imperial Policy and Colonial Practice 1925–1945. Part 1. Metropolitan Reorganisation, Defence and International Relations, Political Change and Constitutional Reform*. British Documents on the End of Empire. Series A, Volume 1, Part I and Part II, London, HMSO.
Askwith, Tom, 1995, *From Mau Mau to Harambee: Memoirs and Memoranda of Colonial Kenya*, Cambridge.

Bibliography

Baden Powell, R. S. S., Lord, 1940, *More Sketches of Kenya*. London.

Bagot, J. H., 1940, *Juvenile Delinquency*. Cape.

Bagot, J. H., 1944, *Juvenile Delinquency: a comparative study of the position in Liverpool and England and Wales*. London.

Bayly, C.A., 1996, *Empire and Information: Intelligence gathering and social communication in India, 1780–1870,* Cambridge.

Beach, Abigail, 1998), 'Forging a "nation of participants": Political and Economic Planning in Labour's Britain' in R. Weight and A. Beach (eds), *The Right to Belong: Citizenship and National Identity in Britain, 1930–1960*, London: 89–115.

Bennett, George, 1963, *Kenya, a Political History. The Colonial Period*, London.

Berman, B. and Lonsdale, J. (eds), 1992, *Unhappy Valley: Conflict and Kenya. Book Two: Violence and Ethnicity*, London.

Berman, Bruce and Lonsdale, John, *The House of Custom*, (forthcoming).

Berman, Bruce, 1990, *Control and Crisis in Colonial Kenya: The Dialectic of Domination*, London.

Best, Nicholas, 1979, *Happy Valley: The Story of the English in Kenya*, London.

Blacklock, M.P., 1936, 'Welfare of Women and Children in the Colonies', *Annals of Tropical Medicine and Parasitology*, 2: 221–63.

Blake, Lord and Nicholls, C. S., (eds), 1990, *The Dictionary of National Biography 1981-1985*, Oxford.

Blumer, Martin, Lewis, Jane and Piachaud, David (eds),1989.*The Goals of Social Policy*, London.

Blundell, Michael, 1994, *A Love Affair with the Sun: A Memoir of Seventy Years in Kenya,* Nairobi.

Boserup, E., 1970, *Women's Role in Economic Development,* New York.

Bourdillon, A. F. C. (ed.), 1945, *The Voluntary Social Services; Their Place in the Modern State*, London.

Bowlby, J.B., 1945, 'Childhood Origins of Recidivism', *The Howard Journal*, 6: 1: 30–3.

Bradlow, Edna, 1972, 'The Evolution of Trusteeship in Kenya', *South African Historical J.*, 4: 64-80.

Bristow, Joseph, 1991, *Empire Boys: Adventures in a Man's World*, London.

Brooks, Chris and Faulkner, Peter (eds), 1996. *The White Man's Burdens: An Anthology of British Poetry of the Empire*, Exeter.

Brouwer, Ruth Compton, 1995, 'Margaret Wrong's Literacy Work and the 'Remaking of Woman' in Africa, 1929–48', *Journal of Imperial and Commonwealth History*, 23, 3: 427–52.

Brown, Judith and Louis, Wm. Roger (eds), 1999, *Oxford History of the British Empire, Volume IV.* Oxford.

Burroughs, Edgar Rice, 1916, *Tarzan*, New York.

Bush, Barbara, 1997, '"Britain's Conscience on Africa": white women, race and imperial politics in inter-war Britain', in Clare Midgley (ed.), *Gender and Imperialism*, Manchester: 200–23.

Cain, P. J., and Hopkins, A. G., 1993, *British Imperialism: Innovation and Expansion 1688–1914*, London.

Calloway, H., 1993, 'Purity and Exotica in Legitimating the Empire: Cultural Constructions of Gender, Sexuality and Race', in T. R. O. Ranger and O. Vaughan (eds), *Legitimacy and the State in Twentieth-Century Africa,* Oxford.

Calloway, Helen, 1987, *Gender, Culture and Empire*, London.

Carman, J. A., 1976, *A Medical History of Kenya: A Personal Memoir.* London.

Cell, J. W., 1989, 'Lord Hailey and the Making of the Africa Survey', *African Affairs*, 88, 353: 481–505.

Cell, J.W., 1992, *Hailey: A Study in British Imperialism, 1872–1969*, Cambridge.

Chenevix Trench, C.,1993, *The Men Who Ruled Kenya. The Kenya Administration, 1892–1963,* London.

Clark, Peter, 1997, *Hope and Glory: Britain, 1900–1990*, Cambridge.

Clayton, Anthony and Killingray, David, 1989, *Khaki and Blue: Military and Police in British Colonial Africa,* Athens, OH.

Clayton, Anthony, 1978, *Communication for New Loyalties: African Soldier's Songs,* Athens, OH.

Clayton, Anthony, 1988, *France, Soldiers and Africa*, London.

Cooper F., 1987, *On the African Waterfront: urban disorder and the transformation of work in colonial Mombasa*. New Haven, CT.

Cooper, F., 1991, review of B. Berman, 'Control and Crisis in Colonial Kenya', *African Affairs*, 90, 36: 629–30.

Cooper, F., 1996, *Decolonization and African Society: The Labour Question in French and British Africa*, Cambridge.

Coquery-Vidrovitch, Catherine, 1997, *African Women: A Modern History*. Translated by Gillian Raps, Oxford.

Costello, John, 1985, *Love, Sex and War, 1939–45*, London.

Coward, R., 1992, *Our Treacherous Hearts: Why Women Let Men Get Their Way*, London.

Creech Jones, Arthur, 1948, 'The Place of African Local Administration in Colonial Policy', *J. of African Administration*, 1, 1: 3–6.

Crew, F. A. E., Brigadier, 1944, 'Pre-habilitation, Re-Habilitaiton and Revocation', *The Army Quarterly*, 49, 1: 84–92.

Crowder, M., 1987, 'Tshekedi Khama, Smuts and South West Africa', *Journal of Modern Afrcian Studies*, 25, 1: 25–42.

Darwin, J., 1988, *Britain and Decolonisation*, London.

Davin, Anna, 1978, 'Imperialism and Motherhood', *History Workshop Journal*, 5: 9–65.

Dawson, Graham, 1994, *Soldier Heroes: British Adventure, Empire and the Imaginary of Masculinities*, London.

Dickson, A. G. Capt., 1944, 'Studies in War-Time Organization: (3) The Mobile Propaganda Unit, East African Command', *African Affairs*, 43, 174: 9–18.

Dubow, S., 1995, *Scientific Racism in Modern South Africa*, Cambridge.

Duncan, D., 1992, 'The Origins of the "Welfare State" in Pre-Apartheid South Africa'. The Societies of Southern Africa in the 19th and 20th centuries Seminar Series, Institute of Commonwealth Studies, University of London.

Easterbrook D. L., 1975, 'Kenyan Askari in World War II and their Demobilization with special reference to Machakos District', in J.M. Lonsdale (ed.), *Three Aspects of Crisis in Colonial Kenya*, Foreign and Comparative Studies, Eastern African Series, 21, Syracuse, NY: 27–58.

Editorial Review, 1944, 'African Intelligence by S. Biesheuvel', *African Affairs*, 43, 173: 174–7.

Editorial, 1945, 'Africa and the British Political Parties', *African Affairs*, 44, 176: 107–19.

Editorial, 1945, 'Army Education in and for Africa', *Oversea Education*, 17, 1: 230.

Englander, David and Mason, Tony, 1944, 'The British Soldier in World War II', Warwick Working Paper in Social History.

Fage, J. D. and Oliver, R. (eds), 1985, *Cambridge History of Africa c1870–c.1905, Vol. 6*, Cambridge.

Fane, Mrs R., 1944, 'The Return of the Soldier: East Africa', *African Affairs*, 43, 171: 56–60.

Fieldhouse, D. K., 1986, *Black Africa 1945–80. Economic Decolonization and Arrested Development*, London.

Fieldhouse, D. K., 1981, *Colonialism 1870–1945: An Introdcution*, London.

Fielding, Steven, Thompson, Peter and Tiratsoo, Nick, 1995, *'England Arise!': The Labour Party and Popular Politics in 1940s Britain*, Manchester.

Foucault, M., 1969, *Discipline and Punish*, London.

Fox, James, 1982, *White Mischief*, London.

Fraser, Derek, 1990, *The Evolution of the British Welfare State*, 2nd edn. London.

Frederiksen, B. F., 1991, 'Making Popular Culture from Above: Leisure in Nairobi, 1945–60', Roskilde University, Denmark.

Frost, Richard, 1992, *Enigmatic Proconsul: Sir Philip Mitchell and the Twilight of Empire*, London.

Furedi, Frank, 1989, *The Mau Mau War in Perspective*, London.

Furnivall, J. S., 1948, *Colonial Policy and Practice*, Cambridge,

Gadsden, Fay, 1980, 'The African Press in Kenya, 1945–1952', *Journal of African History*, 21: 497–514.

Gallagher, J. et al., 1973, *Locality, Province and Nation*, Cambridge.

Geisler, G., 1996, 'Troubled Sisterhood: Women and Politics in Southern Africa', *African Affairs*, 95, 377: 545–78.

Gicaru, Muga, 1958, *Land of Sunshine: Scenes of Life in Kenya before Mau Mau*, London.

Giddens, A., 1990, 'Modernity and Utopia', *New Statesman and Society*, 3, 129: 20–22.

Goldsworthy, D. 1982, *Tom Mboya: The Man Kenya Wanted to Forget*, London.

Gough, Ian, 1979, *The Political Economy of the Welfare State*, London.

Grant, Mariel, *1994, Propaganda and the Role of the State in Inter-War Britain*, Oxford.

Green, S. J. D. 1995, '"Christian Manliness" and the Nonconformist Tradition in West Yorkshire, c 1800–920', *Northern History*, 31: 273–80.

Green, T. H., 1941 edn, *Lectures on the Principles of Political Obligation*, London.

Greenstein, R., 1995, 'History, Historiography and the Production of Knowledge', *South African Historical Journal*, 32: 217–232

Gregory, Robert G., 1993, *South Asians in East Africa: an Economic and Social History, 1890–1960*, Boulder, CO.

Grewa, Inderpal, 1996, *Home and Harem: Nation, Gender, Empire and the Cultures of Travel*, London.

Haggith, Toby, 1998, 'Citizenship, nationhood and empire in British official film and propaganda 1939–45', in R. Weight and A. Beach, (eds), *The Right to Belong: Citizenship and National Identity in Britain, 1930–1960*, London: 59–88.

Hailey, Lord, 1945, *An African Survey*. 2nd edn, London.

Hailey, Lord, 1943, *Britain and her Dependencies*, London,

Hailey, Lord, 1940–42, *Native Administration and Political Development in British Tropical Africa...* , 1979 edn. Compiled and with an introduction by A. H. M. Kirk-Greene, Liechtenstein.

Hake, Andrew, 1977, *African Metropolis*, London.

Hanley, Gerald, 1955, *Drinkers of Darkness* , London.

Hanley, Gerald, 1946, *Monsoon Victory*, London.

Hansen, Holger Bernt, 1991, 'Pre-Colonial Immigrants and Colonial Servants: The Nubians of Uganda Revisited' *African Affairs* , 90: 559–80.

Harper, T. N., 1991, 'The Colonial Inheritance: State and Society in Malaya 1945–57', unpublished thesis, Cambridge University.

Harper, T.N., 1990, 'The Politics of Disease and Disorder in Post-War Malaya', *Journal of South-east Asian Studies*, 21: 88–111.

Harris, J., 1975, 'Social planning in wartime – some aspects of the Beveridge Report' in J. Winter (ed.), *War and Economic Development* , Cambridge.

Harris, Jose, 1992, 'War and Social History: Britain and the Home Front during the Second World War', *Contemporary European History*, 1, 3: 17–36.

Harrison, B., 1984, *Separate Spheres: The Opposition to Women's Suffrage in Britain*, London.

Hastings, Adrian, 1994, *The Church in Africa*, Oxford.

Hawkins T. H., and Brimble, J. F., 1947, *Adult Education: the Record of the 'British Army*, London.

Headrick, Rita, 1978, 'African Soldiers in World War II', *Armed Forces and Society*, 4, 3: 510–26.

Hennessy, Peter, 1992, *Never Again: Britain, 1945–51*, London.

Hennings, R., 1951, *African Morning*, London.

Heussler, R. 1963, *Yesterday's Rulers: The Making of the British Colonial Service*, London.

Heyer, J., Ireri, D. and Morris, D., 1971, *Rural Development in Kenya*, Nairobi.

Hicks, Ursula K., 1961, *Development From Below: Local Government and Finance in Developing Countries of the Commonwealth*, Oxford.

Hill, Martin J. D., 1991, *The Harambee Movement in Kenya: Self-Help, Development and Education among the Kamba of Kitui District*, London.

Hitchens, Erin, 1998, 'Mau Mau and the settler press in Kenya, 1950–54', unpublished BA dissertation, Cambridge University.

Hobsbawm, E. and Ranger, T. (eds), 1993 edn, *The Invention of Tradition*, Cambridge.

Hoch, P., 1979, *White Hero Black Beast: Racism, Sexism and the Mask of Masculinity*, London.

Holland, R.F., 1985, *European Decolonization, 1918–1981: An Introductory Survey*, London.

Holtby, Winifred, 1934, *Women and a Changing Civilization*, London.

Hopkins, A.G., 1973, *Economic History of West Africa.*, London.

Howe, Stephen, 1993, *Anti-Colonialism in British Politics: The Left and the End of Empire 1918–1964*, Oxford.

Hunt, Nancy Rose, 1996, 'Introduction', *Gender and History*, 8, 3: 323–37.

Hunter, G., 1944, 'East Africa – Its Difficulties and Possibilities', *African Affairs*, 43, 172: 128–33.

Hurst, Ida, 1937, *A Vagabond Typist: In Africa, Abyssinia and the Gulf*, London.

Huxley, Elspeth, 1945, 'A review of African as Suckling and as Adult', by J. F. Ritchie, *African Affairs*, 44, 175: 87–8.

Huxley, Elspeth, 1945, 'A review of "African Conversation Piece", by Sylvia Leith-Ross', *African Affairs*, 44, 172: 142–3.

Huxley, Elspeth, 1941, *East Africa*, London.

Huxley, Elspeth, 1973, *Nellie*, London.

Huxley, E. and Perham, M., 1943, *Race and Politics in Kenya*, London.

Hyam, Ronald (ed.), 1992, *The Labour Government and the End of Empire, 1945–51*. Part I, High Policy and Administration; Part II, Economics and International Relations; Part III, Strategy, Politics and Constitutional Change; Part IV, Race Relations and the Commonwealth. British Documents on the End of Empire, Series A, Vol. 2, London.

Hyam, Ronald, 1991, 'The End of Empire'. Commonwealth and Overseas Seminar Series, Cambridge University.

Hyam, Ronald, 1993, 2nd edn, *Britain's Imperial Century, 1815–1914: A Study of Empire and Expansion*, London.

Hyam, Ronald, 1986, 'Empire and Sexual Opportunity', *J. of Imperial and Commonwealth History*, 14, 2: 34–90.

Hyam, Ronald, 1990, *Empire and Sexuality: the British Experience*, Manchester.

Hyam, Ronald, 1979, 'The Colonial Office Mind 1900–1914', *J. of Imperial and Commonwealth History*, 8, 1: 30–55.

Hygiene Committee of the Women's Group on Public Welfare, 1943 edn, *Our Towns*, Oxford.

Iliffe, John, 1979, *A Modern History of Tanganyika* , Cambridge.

Iliffe, John, 1996, *Africans: The History of a Continent*, Cambridge.

Iliffe, John, 1987, *The African Poor: A History*, Cambridge.

Iliffe, John. 1998, *East African Doctors: A History of the Modern Profession*, Cambridge.

Isaacman, A., 1996, *Cotton is the Mother of Poverty: Peasants, Work and Rural Struggle in Colonial Mozambique, 1938–1961*, London.

Isichei, Elizabeth, 1995, *A History of Christianity in Africa* , London.

Jackson, Ashley, 1997, 'Motivation and Mobilization for War: Recruitment for the British Army in the Bechuanaland Protectorate, 1941–42', *African Affairs*, 96, 399–417.

Jeffreys, Kevin, 1987, 'British Politics and Social Policy during the Second World War', *Historical Journal*, 30 1: 123–44.

Jessop, Bob, 1990, *State Theory: Putting Capitalist States in their Place*, Oxford.

Johnson, Douglas H., 1989, 'The Structure of a Legacy: Military Slavery in Northeast Africa', *Ethnohistory*, 36: 72–88.

Jones, Dorothy V., 1994, 'The League of Nations Experiment in International Protection', *Ethics and International Affairs*, 8: 77–96.

Jones, Howard, 1990, *Social Welfare in Third World Development*, London.

Kale, S. I., 1941, 'Must Education Lead to Detribalisation?' *Oversea Education*, 12, 2: 60–4.

Kannan, Joyce, 1998, 'The revolt of the women, Muranga' District 1947, soil conservation and the question of labour'. African Studies Centre, Cambridge University.

Kanogo, Tabitha, 1989, *Squatters and the Roots of Mau Mau*, London.

Keating, Peter, (ed.), 1993, *Rudyard Kipling: Selected Poems*, London.

Kennedy, Dane, 1996, 'Imperial History and Post-Colonial Theory', *J. of Imperial and Commonwealth History*, 24,3: 354–63.

Kennedy, Dane, 1987, *Islands of White: settler society and culture in Kenya and Southern Rhodsia, 1890–1939*, Durham.

Kent, John, 1988, 'William Temple, the Church of England and British national identity', in

R. Weight and A. Beach (eds), *The Right to Belong: Citizenship and National Identity in Britain, 1930–1960*, London, 30–1.

Kenyatta, Jomo, 1938, *Facing Mount Kenya*, London.

Kenyatta, Jomo, 1945, *Kenya. Land of Conflict*, Manchester.

Keylor, W. R., 1992 edn, *The Twentieth Century World*, Oxford.

Keynes, M, Coleman, D. A, and Dimsdale, N. H., (eds), 1988, *The politcal economy of health and welfare*, London.

Killingray, David, 1994, '"The Rod of Empire": The Debate Over Corporal Punishment in the British African Colonial Forces. 1888–1946', *JAH*, 35: 201–16.

Killingray, D., 1983, 'Soldiers, Ex-Servicemen and Politics in the Gold Coast, 1939–50', *J. of Modern African Studies*, 21, 3: 523–34.

Killingray, David, 1989, 'Labour Exploitation for Military Campaigns in British Colonial Africa, 1870–1945', *J. of Contemporary History*, 24, 483–501.

Killingray, David, 1979, 'The Idea of a British Imperial African Army', *Journal of African History*, 20, 3: 421–36.

King, K. J., 1971, *Pan-Africanism and Education: A Study of Race, Philanthropy and Education in the Southern States of America and East Africa*, Oxford.

Kipkorir, B. E., 1969, 'The Alliance High School and the Making of the Kenya African Elite 1926–62', unpublished thesis, Cambridge University.

Kirk-Greene, A. H. M., 1991, 'Forging a Relationship with the Administrative Service 1921–39' in A. Smith and M. Bull (eds), *Margery Perham and British Rule in Africa*, London: 62–82.

Kirk-Greene, A. H. M. 1982, 'Margery Perham and Colonial Administration: A Direct Influence on Indirect Rule', in F. Madden and D. K. Fieldhouse, (eds), *Oxford and the Idea of Commonwealth*, London: 122–43.

Kirk-Greene, A. H. M., 1980, 'The Thin White Line: the Size of the British Colonial Service in Africa', *African Affairs*, 79, 314: 25–44.

Kirk-Greene, A. H. M., 1991, *A Biographical Dictionary of the British Colonial Service, 1939–66*, London.

Kirk-Greene, Antony, 1999, *On Crown Service: A History of HM Colonial and Overseas Civil Services, 1837–1997*, London.

Kitching, Gavin, 1980, *Class and Economic Change in Kenya: The Making of an African Petite Bourgeoisie, 1905–1970*. New Haven.

Knott, A. J., 1947, 'East Africa and the Returning Askari'. *Quarterly Review*, 28, 571: 98–111.

Lane, Christopher, 1995, *The Ruling Passion: British Colonial Allegory and the Paradox of Homosexual Desire*, Durham, NC.

Latham, A. J. H., 1981, *The Depression and the Developing World, 1914–1939*, London.

Leakey, L. S. B., 1974, *By the Evidence: Memoirs, 1932–1951*, New York.

Lee, J. M., 1977, '"Forward Thinking" and War: The Colonial Office during the 1940s', *J. of Imperial and Commonwealth History*, 61: 64–79.

Lee, J. M., 1967, *Colonial Development and Good Government*, Oxford.

Leith-Ross, Sylvia, 1944, *African Conversation Piece*, London.

Lemielle, Sidney J. and Kelley, Robin D. G. (eds), 1994, *Imagining Home: Class, Culture and Nationalism in the African Diaspora*, London.

Lewis, Joanna, 2000, 'Mau Mau's War of Words: the Battle of the Pamphlets' in James Raven (ed.), *Free Print and Non-Commerical Publishing since 1700*, London.

Lipscomb, J. F., 1956, *We Built a Country*, London.

Loch, C. S., 1942, Revised edn, *The Prevention of Relief and Distress: The Life of T. H. Nunn*, London.

Lofthouse, W. F., 1944, *The Family and the State*, London.

Lonsdale, J. (ed.), 1975, *Three Aspects of Crisis in Colonial Kenya*. Syracuse, NY.

Lonsdale, J. M., 1963, 'Archdeacon Owen and the Kavirondo taxpayers welfare association', in 'Proceedings of the East African Institute of Social Research Conference held at Kivukoni College, Dar es Salaam, January 1963'.

Lonsdale, J. M., 1975, 'Introduction On the Periodization of Kenya's Colonial History,' in J.M. Lonsdale (ed.), *Three Aspects of Crisis in Colonial Kenya*, v–xxiii.

Lonsdale, John, 1999, 'East Africa' in Judith Brown and Wm. Roger Louis (eds), *Oxford History of the British Empire, Part IV*, Oxford: 530–44.

Lonsdale, John, 1968, 'European Attitudes and African Pressures: Missions and Government in Kenya between the Wars', *Race*, 10, 1: 143–51.

Lonsdale, John, 1989, 'The Conquest State 1895–1904' in W. R. Ochieng (ed.), *A Modern History of Kenya*, London, 6–34.

Lonsdale, John, 1986, 'The Depression and the Second World War in the Transformation of Kenya', in R. Rathbone and D. Killingray (eds), *Africa and the Second World War*. Basingstoke.

Lonsdale, John, 1985, 'The European Scramble and Conquest in African History', ch.12 in J. D. Fage and R. Oliver, (eds), *Cambridge History of Africa c1870–c.1905, Vol. 6*, Cambridge: 680–766.

Lonsdale, John, 1992, 'The Moral Economy of Mau Mau: Wealth, Poverty and Civic Virtue in Kikuyu Political Thought', in B. Berman and J. Lonsdale (eds), *Unhappy Valley. Conflict in Kenya and Africa. Book Two: Violence and Ethnicity*, London: 315–467.

Louis, Wm. Roger 1986, 'India, Africa, and the Second World War', *Ethnic and Racial Studies*, 9, 3: 306–20.

Louis, W. R and Robinson, W. R. 1994, 'Imperialism of decolonisation', *JICH*, 22, 462–511.

Low, D. A. and Lonsdale, J. M., 1976, 'Introduction: Towards the New Order, 1945–1963', in D. A. Low and A. Smith (eds), *History of East Africa*, Vol. 3, Oxford: 1–63.

Low, D. A. and Smith, A. (eds), 1976, *History of East Africa*. Vol. III. Oxford.

Low, D. A., (ed.), 1988, *Indian National Congress: Centenary Hindsights*. Oxford.

Lugard, F. J. D. Baron, 1965, 5th edn, *The Dual Mandate in British Tropical Africa*, London.

Maberly, Alan, 1948, 'Family Relationships', *Journal of Social Work*, 5, 2: 163–5.

MacKenzie, John M., 1988, *The Empire of Nature: Hunting, Conservation and British Imperialism*, Manchester.

Mamdani, Mahmood, 1996, *Citizen and Subject: Contemporary Africa and the Legacy of Late Colonialism*, London.

Mangan, J. A. (ed.), 1990, *Making Imperial Mentalities*. Manchester.

Mangan, J.A., 1986, *Games Ethics and Imperialism: Aspects of the Diffusion of an Ideal*, London.

Marshall, P. J., (ed.), 1996, *The Cambridge Illustrated History of the British Empire*, Cambridge.

Marshall, P. J., 1996, 'Imperial Britain', ch. 12 in P. J. Marshall (ed.), *The Cambridge Illustrated History of the British Empire*, Cambridge: 318–37.

Maughan-Brown, David, 1985, *Land, Freedom and Fiction: History and Ideology in Kenya*, London.

McKibbin, Ross, 1998, *Classes and Culture: England 1918–1951*. Oxford.

McKibbin, Ross, 1990, *The Ideologies of Class: Social Relations in Britain 1880–1950*. Oxford.

McLaine, Ian, 1979, *Ministry of Morale: Home Front Morale and the Ministry of Information in World War II*, London.

Mellor, W. F., 1972, *Casualties and Medical Statistics: Official Medical History of World War Two*, London.

Merfield, F. G., 1956, *Gorillas Were My Neighbours*, London.

Midgley, Claire, (ed.), 1998, *Gender and Imperialism*, Manchester.

Miles Taylor, 1991, 'Imperium et Libertas? Rethinking the Radical Critique of Imperialism during the Nineteenth Century', *J. of Imperial and Commonwealth History*, 19, 1: 1–23.

Miller, Carol, 1992, 'Lobbying the League: Women's International Organizations and the League of Nations'. Unpublished D.Phil thesis, University of Oxford.

Milward, A. S., 1972, *The Economic Effects of the Two World Wars on Britain*, London.

Mishra, R., 1989, 'The academic tradition in social policy: The Titmuss years', in M. Blumer, J. Lewis, D. Piachaud, (eds), *The Goals of Social Policy*, London: 64–83.

Mitchell, Sir Philip, 1954, *African Afterthoughts*, London.

Mitzman, A., 1985, 'The Civilizing Offensive', *Journal of Social History*,: 663–87.

Moore, H. and Vaughan, M., 1994, *Cutting Down Trees: Gender, Nutrition and Agricultural Change in the Northern Province of Zambia*, London and Lusaka.

Morgan, D. J., 1980, *The Official History of Colonial Development: Changes in British Aid Policy, 1951–1970*, Vol. IV, London.

Mosley, Paul, 1983, *The Settler Economies: Kenya and Southern Rhodesia*, Cambridge.

Moyse-Bartlett, Hubert, 1956, *The King's African Rifles*. Aldershot.

Mullins, C., 1943, *Crime and Psychology, with an introduction by E. Glover*, London.

Mumford, L., 1943, *The Social Foundations of Post-war Building*, London.

Mutiso, R. M., 1974, 'The Evolution of Social Welfare and Community Development in Kenya, 1940–1973', unpublished thesis, Department of Sociology, Nairobi University.

Nandy, Ashis, 1983, *The Intimate Enemy: Loss and Recovery of Self under Colonialism*. Delhi.

Nicholas, H.G., 1975 edn, *The United Nations as a Political Institution*. Oxford.

Nicholas, Sian, 1996, *The Echo of War: Home Front Propaganda and the Wartime BBC, 1939–45*. Manchester.

Notes, 1945, 'The Higher Education of Women in the Colonies', *Oversea Education*, 17, 1: 216.

Obbo, Christine, 1980, *African Women: their Struggle for Economic Independence, London*, 1980.

Ochieng', W. R. (ed.), 1989, *A Modern History of Kenya 1895–1980: in Honour of B. A. Ogot*, London.

Oliver, Roland, 1991, 'Prologue: The Two Miss Perhams', in A. Smith and M. Bull, *Margery Perham and British Rule in Africa*, London: 21–6.

Orwell, George, 1950 edn, *Burmese Days*. New York.

Parsons, T., 2000, *The African Rank-and-File: Social Implications of Colonial Service in the King's African Rifles, 1902–1964*, Oxford.

Parsons, Timothy H., 1996, 'East African Soldiers in Britain's Colonial Army: A Social History, 1902–1964', unpublished thesis, Johns Hopkins University, Baltimore.

Pearce, R., 1984, 'The Colonial Office and planned decolonization in Africa', *African Affairs*, 83, 330, 77–93.

Perham, Margery, 1967, *Colonial Sequence, 1930 to 1949, London.*

Perham, Margery, 1976, *East African Journey*, London.

Perham, Margery, 1960, *Lugard, The Years of Authority 1890–1945*, Vol. III, London.

Philips, Richard, 1997, *Mapping, Men and Empire: a geography of adventure*, London.

Pimlott, Ben (ed.), 1984, *Fabian Essays in Socialist Thought*, London.

Pinker, R., 1989, 'Social work and social policy in the twentieth century: retrospect and prospect', in M. Blumer, J. Lewis and D. Piachaud, (eds), *The Goals of Social Policy*, London: 84–107.

Pinker, Robert, 1979, *The Idea of Welfare*, London.

Platt, General Sir William, G.O.C., 1941–1944, 1946, 'Studies in War-time Organisation: (b) The East African Command, *African Affairs*, 45, 178: 27–35.

Porter, A. N. and Stockwell, A. J. 1987, *British Imperial Policy and Decolonization 1938–64. Vol. I, 1938–51*. Basingstoke.

Porter, A., 1991, 'Margery Perham, Christian Missions and Indirect Rule', in A. Smith and M. Bull (eds) *Margery Perham and British Rule in Africa*, London: 83–99.

Porter, Bernard, 1984, 'Fabians, Imperialists and the International Order', in Ben Pimlott (ed.), *Fabian Essays in Socialist Thought*, London: 54–67.

Quarterly Notes, 1945, 'Community Centres', *African Affairs*, 44, 176: 95–6.

Quarterly Notes, 1945, 'Reorganisation in Kenya', *African Affairs*, 44, 177: 141–42.

Ranger, T. R. O., 1975, *Dance and Society in Eastern Africa*, London.

Ranger, T. R. O. and Vaughan, O., 1993, *Legitimacy and the State in Twentieth-Century Africa: Essays in Honour of A.H.M. Kirk-Greene*, Oxford.

Ranger, Terence, 1993, 'The Invention of Tradition in Colonial Africa', in E. Hobsbawm and T. Ranger (eds), *The Invention of Tradition*, Cambridge.

Ranger, Terence, 1993, 'The Invention of Tradition Revisited: The Case of Colonial Africa', ch 2 in Terence Ranger and Olufemi Vaughan (eds), *Legitimacy and the State in Twentieth Century Africa*, London.

Rathbone, R. and Killingray, D. (eds), 1986, *Africa and the Second World War*. New York and Basingstoke.

Raven, James (ed.), 2000, *Free Print and Non-Commercial Publishing since 1700*, London.

Reynolds, D. J. 1991, *Britannia Overruled: British Policy and World Power in the Twentieth Century*, London.

Ricciardi, Mirella, 1981, *African Saga*, London.
Richter, M., 1964, *The Politics of Conscience: T.H. Green and his Age*, London.
Riddell, Neil, 1995, 'The Age of Cole?: G.D.H. Cole and the British Labour Movement, 1929–1933', *Historical Journal*, 30, 4: 933–57.
Ritchie, J. F., 1945, *The African as Suckling and as Adult.* Rhodes-Livingstone Paper No.9.
Roberston, Claire C., 1997, *Trouble Showed the Way: Women, Men and Trade in the Nairobi Area, 1890–1990*, Bloomington, IN.
Robertson, Claire. C., 1986, *Sharing the Same Bowl: a Socioeconomic History of Women and Class in Accra, Ghana.* Bloomington, IN.
Robinson, K., 1991, 'Margery Perham and the Colonial Office' in A. Smith and M. Bull (eds), *Margery Perham and British Rule in Africa*, London: 185–96.
Robinson, Ronald, 1979, 'The Moral Disarmament of African Empire, 1919–1947' *J. of Imperial and Commonwealth History*, 8: 86–104.
Roelker, Jack R., 1976, *Mathu of Kenya: A Political Study*. Stanford.
Roper, M. and Tosh, J. (eds), 1991, *Manful Assertions: Masculinities in Britain since 1800*, London.
Ross, F. E. V., 1961, *How to Mark Out Fields, Grounds, Courts and Tracks*, Oxford.
Ruark, Robert, 1954, *Horn of the Hunter; the Story of an African Safari*, London.
Sandison, A. 1967, *The Wheel of Empire: a Study of the Imperial Idea in Some Late Nineteenth and Early Twentieth Century Fiction*, London.
Sanger, Clive, 1995, *Malcolm MacDonald: Bringing an End to Empire*, Liverpool.
Saul, J., 1991, 'South Africa: Between "Barbarism" and "Structural Reform"', *New Left Review*, 188: 3–44.
Seeley, J. A., 1985, 'Praise, Prestige and Power: The Organisation of Social Welfare in a Developing Kenyan Town', unpublished thesis, Cambridge University.
Sen, A., 1981, *Poverty and Famines*, Oxford.
Shilling, Ton, 1957, *Tigermen of Anai* , London.
Shiroya, O. J. E., 1992, *African Politics in Colonial Kenya: Contribution of World War II Veterans 1945–1960*, Nairobi.
Shyllon, F., 1977, *Black People in Britain, 1555–1833*, Oxford.
Silberfein, Marilyn, 1989, *Rural Change in Machakos, Kenya: A Historical Geographic Perspective.* Lanham, MD.
Simnett, W. E., 1942, *The British Colonial Empire*, London.
Sinnoven, Seppo, 1995, *White Collar or Hoe Handle?: African Education under British Colonial Policy, 1920–1945*, Helsinki.
Smallwood, R.E.R., Capt., 1945, 'Developing the KAR', *The Army Quarterly*, 49, 2: 214–18.
Smith A. and Bull, M., 1991, 'Introduction' in A. Smith and M. Bull (eds), *Margery Perham and British Rule in Africa*, London 1991: 1–20.
Smith, Alison and Bull, Mary (eds), 1991, *Margery Perham and British Rule in Africa*, London.
Smith, Joan, 1987, *Misogynies*, London.
Smyth, R., 1985, 'Britain's African Colonies and British Propaganda during the Second World War', *JICH*, 14, 1: 65–82.
Snyder, Margaret C. and Tadesse, Mary, 1995, *African Women and Development: A History*, London.
Sommer, Francois, 1953, *Man and Beast in Africa.* Foreword by Ernest Hemingway. Translated from French by Edward Fitzgerald, London.
Spencer, Ian, 1984, 'Settler Dominance, Agricultural Production and the Second World War in Kenya', *JAH*, 21: 497–514.
Spencer, John, 1985, *The Kenya African Union*, London.
Stapleton, James W., 1956, *The Gate Hangs Well*, London.
Stevenson, John, 1984, 'From Philanthropy to Fabianism', in B. Pimlott (ed.), *Fabian Essays in Socialist Thought*, London: 15–26.
Stoneham, C. T., 1954, *Big Stuff*, London.
Summerfield, Penny, 1981, 'Education and politics in the armed forces in the Second World War', *International Review of Social History*, 26, 2: 133–58.
Teka, Tegegne, 1993, 'A Norwegian International NGO in Rural Development in Ethiopia:

some evidence from grassroots'. East African Seminar Series, African Studies Centre, Cambridge University.

Temple, William, 1942, *Christianity and The Social Order*, London.

Thomas, L., 1996, 'Ngaitana (I will circumcise myself)': the Gender and Generational Politics of the 1956 Ban on Clitoridectomy in Meru, Kenya', *Gender and History*, 8, 3: 338–63.

Thomas, Lynn, 1998, 'Imperial Concerns and "Women's Affairs": State Efforts to Regulate Clitoridectomy and Eradicate Abortion in Meru, Kenya, c. 1910–1950' *J. of African History*, 121–46.

Thomas, N., 1994, *Colonialism's Culture: Anthropology, Travel and Government*, Princeton, NJ.

Thornton, A. P., 1966, *The Habit of Authority. Paternalism and British History*, London.

Throup, David W., 1987, *The Social and Economic Origins of Mau Mau*, London.

Tidrick, Kathryn, 1992, *Empire and the English Character*, London.

Tiratsoo, Nick, 1998, 'New vistas': the Labour Party, Citzenship and the Built Environment in the 1940s', in R. Weight and A. Beach (eds), *The Right to Belong: Citizenship and National Identity in Britain, 1930–1960*, London: 136–56.

Trenman, J. and Emmett, B. P., 1949, 'Crime – A Mass Problem?', *The Howard Journal*, 8, 1: 49.

Valentine, C. W., 1942, *The Psychology of Early Childhood*, London.

van Onselen, C., 1991, 'The Social and Economic Underpinnings of Paternalism and Violence on the Maize Farms of the South Western Transvaal, 1900–50'. unpublished paper, University of Witwaterstrand, South Africa.

van Zwanenberg, R. M. A., 1975, *Colonial Capitalism and Labour in Kenya, 1919–1933*. Nairobi

Vance, Norman, 1985, *The Sinews of the Spirit: the Ideal of Christian Manliness in Victorian Literature and Religious Thought*, Cambridge.

Vaughan, Megan, 1991, *Curing Their Ills: Colonial Power and African Illness*, Oxford.

Ware, V., 1992, *Beyond the Pale: White Women, Racism and History*, London.

Waruhiu, Iote, 1975, *'Mau Mau' General*. Nairobi.

Watkins, E., 1995, *Oscar from Africa: the Biography of Oscar Watkins*, Oxford.

Webster, Wendy, 1997, '"Heroes don't snivel"': Elspeth Huxley and Narratives of Imperial Adventure', Institute of Commonweatlh Studies Seminar, November.

Weight, Richard and Beach, Abigail (eds), 1998, *The Right to Belong: Citizenship and National Identity in Britain, 1930–1960*, London.

White, L., 1990, 'Separating the Men from the Boys: Constructions of Gender, Sexuality and Terrorism in Central Kenya, 1939–1959', *International Journal of African Historical Studies* 23,1: 1–23.

White, Luise, 1991, *The Comforts of Home: Prostitution in Colonial Nairobi*. Chicago.

Wilson, Elizabeth, 1977, *Women and the Welfare State*, London.

Winter, J (ed.), 1975, *War and Economic Development*, Cambridge.

Winter, J.M., 1988, 'Public Health and the Extension of Life 1901–60' in M. Keynes, D.A. Coleman and N.H. Dimsdale (eds), *The Politcal Economy of Health and Welfare*, London: 184–206.

Wipper, Audrey, 1975, 'The Maendeleo ya Wanawake Movement in the Colonial Period: The Canadian Connection, Mau Mau Embroidery, and Agriculture', *Rural Africana*, 29: 195–214.

Wipper, Audrey, 1975, 'The Maendeleo ya Wanawake Organization: the Co-optation of Leadership', *The African Studies Review*, 18, 3: 99–120.

Wright, A., 1984, 'Tawneyism Revisited: Equality, Welfare and Socialism', in B. Pimlott (ed.), *Fabian Essays in Socialist Thought*, London, 81–100.

Wrong, Margaret, 1944, 'Mass Education in Africa' *African Affairs*, 43, 172: 105–10.

Yellowby, M. A., 1980, *Social Theory and Psychoanalysis*, London.

Yiman, Arega, 1990, *Social Development in Africa 1950–1985*. Aldershot.

Index